Mass Media and
American Politics
Eleventh Edition

To Tom, Susan, Lee, Jim, and Jack—my very special students.

—D. A. G.

To the memory of Doris A. Graber - scholar, pioneer, exemplar and mentor –
Professor Graber will continue to shape the field of media and politics for many years to come.

—J. L. D.

Mass Media and American Politics

Eleventh Edition

Johanna L. Dunaway

Texas A&M University

Doris A. Graber

University of Illinois at Chicago

FOR INFORMATION:

SAGE Publications, Inc.
2455 Teller Road
Thousand Oaks, California 91320
E-mail: order@sagepub.com

SAGE Publications Ltd.
1 Oliver's Yard
55 City Road
London EC1Y 1SP
United Kingdom

SAGE Publications India Pvt. Ltd.
B 1/I 1 Mohan Cooperative Industrial Area
Mathura Road, New Delhi 110 044
India

SAGE Publications Asia-Pacific Pte. Ltd.
18 Cross Street #10-10/11/12
China Square Central
Singapore 048423

Printed in Canada

Library of Congress Cataloging-in-Publication Data

Names: Graber, Doris A. (Doris Appel), 1923- author. | Dunaway, Johanna, author.

Title: Mass media and American politics / Doris A. Graber, University of Illinois at Chicago, Johanna L. Dunaway, Texas A&M University.

Description: Eleventh edition. | London ; Washington, DC : Sage/CQ Press, [2023] | Includes bibliographical references and index.

Identifiers: LCCN 2021043506 | ISBN 9781544390932 (paperback) | ISBN 9781544391007 (epub) | ISBN 9781544391014 (epub) | ISBN 9781544390994 (pdf)

Subjects: LCSH: Mass media—Social aspects—United States. | Mass media—Political aspects—United States.

Classification: LCC HN90.M3 G7 2023 | DDC 302.23—dc23
LC record available at https://lccn.loc.gov/2021043506

This book is printed on acid-free paper.

MIX
Paper from
responsible sources
FSC® C103567

Acquisitions Editor: Anna Villarruel
Product Associate: Tiara Beatty
Production Editor: Megha Negi
Copy Editor: Erin Livingston
Typesetter: C&M Digitals (P) Ltd.
Cover Designer: Scott Van Atta
Marketing Manager: Erica DeLuca

22 23 24 25 26 10 9 8 7 6 5 4 3 2 1

Brief Table of Contents

Detailed Table of Contents

Tables, Figures, and Boxes

Tables

Boxes

Acknowledgments

I n my third opportunity to work on a revision of this text, I could not help but be reminded of Doris Graber's enormous contributions to the field of political science and the subfield of political communication, including her years of work on the many editions of this book, which has significantly shaped our understanding of mass media and politics. As many readers may know, we lost Doris shortly after the publication of the last edition. She passed away on February 27, 2018, dealing a significant blow to the field of media and politics.

Doris Graber's contributions to the field were not merely enormous in terms of their significant scholarly value, they were also pioneering. Despite that Doris's graduate education and early academic career occurred during a time in which women were a rarity in academia, she flourished. As a graduate student at Columbia University in the early 1940s, Doris persevered to complete her doctorate despite sex-based discrimination from faculty. Such discriminatory practices were not limited to Columbia at the time; they were academy-wide. Doris was undeterred by such obstacles. Early in her career, Doris published only as D.A. Graber, using her initials instead of her first name because she was savvy enough to realize that she would be unlikely as a woman to have her work published. Her strategy paid off. Though initially hired as a lecturer at University of Illinois–Chicago (UIC) in 1963, Doris quickly moved up the academic ranks. She was promoted to assistant professor in 1964, advanced to associate professor in 1967, and promoted to the rank of full professor in 1970. By the time professor Graber retired from UIC in 2012, she was one of the most prolific and highly cited scholars in the field of political science.

In addition to **Mass Media and American Politics**, Doris published 18 books and hundreds of peer-reviewed journal articles, book chapters, and book reviews over the course of her career. It is little wonder that in addition to receiving numerous awards for her original research—including the prestigious Goldsmith Book Prize from the Joan Shorenstein Center on the Media and Public Policy at Harvard University's Kennedy School of government—her legacy, service, and leadership were also honored by the American Political Science Association's (APSA) Goodnow Distinguished Service Award and the Doris Graber Book Award. The APSA political communication division's Graber Best Book Award is bestowed annually to the author of the best book in political communication published within the last ten years. It is fitting that the APSA political communication section's top honor bears Doris Graber's name.

It is amazing that even with such an accomplished research agenda, Professor Graber dedicated the time and energy to author a best-selling textbook. *Mass Media and American Politics* is so popular largely due to its comprehensive coverage and unique multidisciplinary perspective, both of which were afforded by the breadth and quality of Doris's research and depth of knowledge about media politics. *Mass Media and American Politics* informed our understanding of media and politics for decades and remains influential today. It was first published in 1980 as a single-author endeavor and remained so through the first eight editions; it did not become a co-authored project until after Professor Graber's retirement, at which time I was brought on board for the ninth edition, published in 2014. I was honored to be asked, and I remain thankful for the opportunity to contribute to a project pioneered by Doris Graber.

Charisse Kiino and Jennifer Jerit also deserve my gratitude for their roles in bringing me onto *Mass Media and American Politics* and for the confidence they expressed in my ability to add to the project in a positive way. Several other friends, colleagues, co-authors, and mentors deserve mention for encouragement or listening regarding this book: Vin Arceneaux, Amber Boydstun, Bill Clark, Josh Darr, Belinda Davis, Richard Davis, Kirby Goidel, Eric Juenke, Paul Kellstedt, Regina Lawrence, Shannon McGregor, Erik Peterson, Markus Prior, Travis Ridout, Brandon Rottinghaus, Kathleen Searles, Jaime Settle, Paru Shah, Stuart Soroka, Jason Turcotte, Stacy Ulbig, and Guy Whitten. Finally, I must thank my most important cadre of supporters: my family. My mom, my sisters, and Gene and Cindy Pipes are always a source of encouragement and support. I could not accomplish much without them. I remain especially grateful to my amazing daughter Pace and co-parent Toby Pipes; they are patient with me when I am stretched too thin and they keep me laughing all the time.

—Johanna L. Dunaway

I am delighted to pass the baton to such a well-qualified and talented young scholar as Johanna Dunaway. I hope she feels as much joy as I have every time a new edition is published and makes its way into the classroom. As always, I am grateful to my family for cheering me on. Memories of my husband's loving support during all prior editions continue to inspire me; he was and is a source of strength in all I do.

—Doris A. Graber

Preface

The expansion of media choice continues to create challenges for established media institutions. Questions remain about the manner and extent to which changes in the contemporary media landscape foster or inhibit healthy democratic function and political life. What are the implications for citizens as newsroom budgets are slashed in response to increasing competition and declining revenues? How does the increased choice of content, devices, and platforms influence the media selections of the average citizen? How will news-gathering organizations respond to changes in audience behaviors? These questions are still unanswered, and our understanding of what these changes mean for mass media and politics is still limited.

Established media are surviving in familiar formats or in hybrid shapes, such as digital versions of traditional offerings, organizational Twitter feeds, and applications for mobile devices. However, legacy media are hampered by radically reduced resources, and their control over news content is sharply diminished. Most "new media" upstarts are not living up to the initial expectations that they would fill some of the information gaps left from closing news outlets and lower newsroom investment. Truly "digitally native" outfits attract very little traffic and still largely rely on legacy media professionals for deciding what becomes news and then for gathering and reporting it. When digital media do engage in the gathering and dissemination of news, their credibility is variable. Much discussion on the Web is interactive, and news is often presented in an opinion and news mix. Social media sites now regularly serve as news transmission channels for a vast proportion of the public, affording the opportunity for ordinary citizens and media elites to engage in genuine conversations. The democratic value of two-way communications between media elites and audiences is not yet clear, but social media are increasingly becoming a staple of the processes of news gathering and disseminating. A popular take on the expansion of choice and platforms in the current media environment is positive and based on the idea that a more diverse and accessible media playing field is more democratic. Existing evidence raises questions about the effectiveness of this interactivity and the promise of a digital democracy.

Other concerns threaten the promise of new technology as well. Expanded media choice, stiffening competition for news organizations, the rapid development of niche news media, and worries about digital media as venues for mis- and disinformation raise concerns about whether media technology will foster political polarization, increase partisan acrimony, and stifle democratic deliberation. Are news organizations more negative and sensational in their effort to retain audiences? Have we abandoned nonpartisan media? Perhaps more importantly, has the expansion of choice introduced so many options that citizens always find something available that is more appealing than the news?

Worse than concerns about low- or no-information citizens today are those about misinformed citizens: Are audiences susceptible to the mis- and disinformation to which they are regularly exposed on digital and social media? If so, who is most likely to be exposed, where is it originating, and who is most likely to be vulnerable to its persuasive effects?

The most urgent problem still looming over the media industry is uncertainty about the means to pay for news creation and distribution. Clearly, advertising can no longer be the financial mainstay of established media, nor can it sustain the many new channels mushrooming on the internet. What should take its place? What will take its place? There are continuing discussions about new models for news but no sure answers about the viability of any of these. It also remains unclear what choices various publics will make to assemble their individual news packages from the overabundance of available news sources on digital and social media. Nor is it clear what the implications of these consumer decisions are for political learning and behavior. The explosion of mobile devices as a means by which people access the news raises questions about attention to and learning from mobile news and how journalists should present the news on mobile formats. In this era of advancing technology, who will gather and disseminate the majority of political news? Who will learn from and pay attention to the news? How will news be consumed in the coming years?

To make sense of what is currently happening, one must understand the characteristics of the U.S. mass media system as well as the political, economic, and technological forces that are propelling the current transformations. The eleventh edition of *Mass Media and American Politics* serves as a guide and interpreter, featuring several new chapters aimed at better describing and explaining the changes to the modern media landscape and the implications of those changes for the business of media and for democratic life.

This new edition also includes important updates and examples from the 2020 presidential election campaign and the evolving influence of social media and partisan and polarizing rhetoric in political campaigns. Social networking platforms allow for interactivity between political elites and ordinary voters, but to what extent do campaigns engage in truly interactive digital dialogues? In addition, these platforms are increasingly and adeptly being used by political elites as direct communication channels with potential voters, which allows for the circumventing of traditional media and the spread of misinformation.

The eleventh edition draws on the rich array of current political communication studies, including some of our own research on changes in the news environment and citizens' understanding of politics. The book's perspective is multidisciplinary and objective, offering a variety of viewpoints about controversial issues. Readers can form their own opinions and evaluations from this evidence and from other studies of the news media reported in the ample, up-to-date citations. The text is written simply and clearly to serve the needs of novices in this area of knowledge without sacrificing the scholarly depth, documentation, and precision that more advanced readers require.

This new edition of *Mass Media and American Politics*, like prior editions, takes a broad approach to mass-mediated political communication. It covers the impact of media on all spheres and phases of political life at all levels of government as well as the political and social context of the times. It does not limit itself to studying the relationships between media and politics during elections, which have been the prime focus of many news media studies.

The eleventh edition is divided into four sections. Part I focuses on media purpose and structure. Chapters 1 and 2 set the stage with descriptions of the mass media as institutions within the U.S. political system. The chapters explain how governmental structures and functions affect journalists and media institutions and how the media, in turn, influence politicians and the work of all branches of government. The discussion highlights the consequences of the proliferation of news outlets and the continuing debate about appropriate regulatory policies. Chapter 3 examines the routines of news making and reporting and deals with the many factors that affect the daily selection of news topics and the creation of stories about people and events. The chapter highlights reporters' backgrounds and orientations and details how they go about their work and the major challenges they face. It also appraises the quality of current news compared to that of the past. Chapter 4 describes ongoing changes to the media landscape and explores their implications for mass media and politics in the United States.

Part II of this edition examines the people, institutions, and events that shape the news. Chapter 5 examines the interplay between the press and the presidency. The media's coverage of Congress and the judicial system is set forth in Chapter 6. The discussion covers news about Congress and the courts at the national level. Chapter 7 examines how news media cover politics and governance at state and local levels. The chapter describes and explains the inadequacies of news about subnational political issues. Chapter 8 details the dwindling impact of American news media on global politics and even on the conduct of American foreign policy. We compare several theories about how the American press selects events abroad for coverage. Chapter 9 is new to the eleventh edition. It examines the world of media and politics through the lenses of diversity and inclusion. We examine trends in newsroom diversity and media representation.

Part III covers media effects. In Chapter 10, we explore the wealth of new information that political communication scholars have accumulated to understand political socialization and learning. We also discuss the role of news in fostering prosocial and asocial behaviors, along with conflicting theories about the circumstances that increase or decrease media influence on political action. In Chapter 11, we explore how modern elections are influenced by mass media and the various reasons campaigns are covered by the news media in unique ways. We focus specifically on effects from campaigns and political advertising. Chapter 12 tackles media effects associated with some of the potentially harmful trends in media depictions of politics—incivility, negativity, and bias. This chapter is timely as more citizens and scholars are paying intense attention to these trends. Chapter 13 is another new chapter developed for the eleventh edition. It provides an overview of the history and theories of media effects, namely with the purpose of providing an understanding of how media effects occur and how what we know about them has changed over the years, through periods of disruption in media and communication technology. We pay special attention to the question of whether media effects are still powerful in the contemporary world of digital and social media.

Mass Media and American Politics concludes with a final section on current trends and future directions. Chapter 14 contains a revised and updated discussion of key recent developments and emerging challenges in media and politics and examines the merit of policy options for dealing with them. In this chapter in the eleventh edition, we pay particular attention to the emerging trends of rising affective and social polarization, declining local news, the spread and possible effects of mis- and disinformation, and lingering digital information inequalities. We conclude with a section evaluating the associated regulatory challenges.

The changes in this new edition reflect the political events and the continuing technological development events that have transpired since the publication of the previous edition. We have also introduced many new mass media studies and much-appreciated suggestions from colleagues, reviewers, and students who have adopted the book for their classes. In particular, we would like to thank those reviewers who took a look at the current edition and provided helpful feedback: Anthony "Jack" Gierzynski, University of Vermont, Geoffrey Peterson, University of Wisconsin-Eau Claire, Jason Zenor, SUNY-Oswego . We are indebted to our friends and colleagues, especially Marisa Abrajano, Joshua Darr, Erika Franklin Fowler, Kirby Goidel, Matthew Hitt, Joanna Jolly, Dan Kennedy, Yanna Krupnikov, Travis Ridout, Kathleen Searles, Stuart Soroka, Mingxiao Sui, and Jason Turcotte, who provided synopses of their work for chapter boxes and/or shared or created useful or new data sets, tables, and figures; their help and contributions have been invaluable. Jason Turcotte provided helpful feedback on this addition. Similar to the last one, this edition benefits from numerous important insights from Jennifer Stromer-Galley and Daniel Kreiss, who were kind enough to deliver research talks at the A&M Aggie Agora Conference in 2016. Insights from each of their cutting-edge research projects were enormously useful for revisions to several chapters. We are grateful to Jennifer Mercieca, director of Aggie Agora, who made their visit possible. The editorial team at CQ Press and its freelance staff provided valuable assistance that greatly eased the many chores that are part of writing books.

About the Authors

Johanna L. Dunaway is associate professor of political science at Texas A&M University. She has written extensively in the areas of media and politics and political communication, with an emphasis on how the changing media environment is shaping political knowledge, attitudes, and behavior. Her research appears in journals such as the *American Journal of Political Science*, *Journal of Politics*, *Journal of Communication*, *Journal of Computer-Mediated Communication*, and *Political Communication*. Two of her recent articles earned top paper awards: the Walter Lippmann Best Article Award from the American Political Science Association political communication division and the Lynda Lee Kaid Best Article Award from the political communication division of the Association of Educators in Journalism and Mass Communication. Her recent book, *Home Style Opinion: How Local Newspapers Can Slow Polarization*, co-authored with Joshua Darr and Matthew Hitt, was published in March 2021 with Cambridge University Press. *News Attention in a Mobile Era*, co-authored with Kathleen Searles, is forthcoming with Oxford University Press. She is also currently working on a book manuscript still in-progress: *The House That Fox Built? Representation, Political Accountability, and the Rise of Cable News*, co-authored with Kevin (Vin) Arceneaux, Martin Johnson, and Ryan J. Vander Wielen. Dunaway currently serves as an associate editor for *Political Communication* and on three additional editorial boards. From 2016 to 2018, she chaired the American Political Science Association's political communication division. In 2015, she was a Joan Shorenstein Fellow at Harvard's Shorenstein Center for Media, Politics, and Public Policy.

Doris A. Graber was professor emeritus of political science and communication at the University of Illinois at Chicago. She wrote and edited numerous articles and books on the news media, public opinion, and information processing. They include *Media Power in Politics, Sixth Edition* (2010), *The Power of Communication: Managing Information in Public Organizations* (2003), the prize-winning book *Processing Politics: Learning from Television in the Internet Age* (2001), and *On Media and Making Sense of Politics* (2012), a comparative study of learning about politics from entertainment broadcasts.

Media Purpose and Structure

CHAPTER

1

Media Power and Government Control

Learning Objectives

1. Summarize the political importance of the mass media in the United States (U.S.).

2. Describe the major functions mass media serve and why they are important in a democratic society.

3. Examine why ownership and control of the media are uniquely important in democratic systems for shaping the news content we see.

4. Explain the various models of news making, the theories underlying them, and how they shape our news coverage.

Perhaps more than any other contemporary example, Donald Trump's presidency highlights both the power and failures of mass media in American politics. From the earliest days of the 2016 primary season—when he earned more air time than all other Republican contenders, time worth millions in paid ad dollars—all the way through the aftermath of his electoral defeat in 2020, Trump thoroughly dominated American press coverage.

During the 2016 primaries, candidate Trump captured press attention at levels normally reserved for candidates leading in the polls, and media fascination is widely blamed/credited for Trump's eventual primary win. Even with very little money raised and no political base, Trump effectively worked the media as a free platform for his message and a chance to build a following. According to Thomas E. Patterson, "Trump is arguably the first bona fide media-created presidential nominee. Although he subsequently tapped a political nerve, journalists fueled his launch."[1] Even as the Trump phenomenon illustrates the importance of the press in presidential primaries, his dominance in press coverage and the tumult of the press–presidential relationship during his presidency highlights the limitations of our press system. Press fascination with Trump reflects the market-driven nature of the U.S. press, which prioritizes news values over political values. Coverage of politics is determined by what is timely, novel, and sensational—focusing on the aspects of politics that capture and hold the attention of mass audiences.

Press coverage of Trump reflects the news values of many journalists and news organizations. From the outset of the pre-primary season in 2016, the press intuited that his outspoken and unconventional style would draw audiences of unprecedented proportions, and they were not wrong. The 2016 primaries were a ratings boom for the cable news networks, one that persisted through Trump's term in office.[2] In September 2016, CNN reported its best ratings quarter in eight years,[3] and it charged forty times its normal rate for advertising spots during the Republican primary debates. The wealth was spread across cable news networks—the average cost of ad spots during the ten primary debates between August and January was exponentially higher than the historical average of a CNN prime-time ad spot.[4]

In 2016, general election coverage of both candidates was decidedly negative, but Trump leveraged the press's penchant for novelty and sensationalism to command three times the coverage earned by former Secretary of State Hillary Clinton—much of which was comprised of excerpts from speeches delivered in his own words. Meanwhile, over the course of the entire campaign, negative coverage of Hillary Clinton nearly doubled that of her positive coverage. An additional press problem for Hillary Clinton was that the focus of coverage did not play to her strengths as a candidate. Only 3% of campaign stories focused on leadership or experience, and only 10% of stories examined the policy stances of the candidates. A majority of coverage focused on the horserace (42%) and controversies (17%).[5]

Press fascination with Trump remained in place during his entire term and through the 2020 election and its aftermath. Trump's press dominance was clear in coverage of the general election campaign, and this pattern was not limited to coverage from conservative news outlets. Though the Fox News ratio of aired Trump-to-Biden statements approached 60:40; CBS's Trump-to-Biden ratio was closer to 70:30. These figures reflect the peak of Biden's election coverage; during earlier phases of the campaign, he received hardly any press attention. In coverage spanning the entire general election campaign, Trump earned four times the coverage of Biden on CBS and three times as much on Fox.[6]

The failures of the press during the Trump era are not about advantaging one candidate over the other; the problems stem from the fact that the choices journalists make about what to cover are driven by ratings and audiences, often with little regard for broader societal ramifications. Trump often boasted about his ability to dominate the headlines by sending a single tweet, regardless of whatever reporting is interrupted in response. News values stressing the entertaining and sensational breed superficial and negative campaign news coverage that does not speak to issues of governance. Given the importance of the press for democratic governance, media watchers are increasingly concerned that these trends encourage a brand of politics based on personality, negativity, and style over civility and policy substance.

Political Importance of Mass Media

Tales from recent presidential elections illustrate how mass media reports, in combination with other political factors, shape the views of citizens about public policies and public officials.[7] News stories take millions of Americans, in all walks of life, to the political and military battlefields of the world. They give them ringside seats for presidential inaugurations and basketball championships. They allow the public to share political experiences, such as watching political debates and congressional investigations. These experiences then undergird public opinions and political actions.[8]

Mass media often serve as attitude and behavior models. The images that media create suggest which views and behaviors are acceptable and even praiseworthy and which are outside the mainstream. Audiences can learn how to conduct themselves at home and at work, how to cope with crises, and how to evaluate social institutions such as the medical profession and grocery chains. The mass media also are powerful guardians of proper political behavior because Americans believe that the press should inform them about government wrongdoing. Media stories indicate what different groups deem important or unimportant, what conforms to prevailing standards of justice and morality, and how events are related to each other. In the process, the media set forth cultural values that their audiences are likely to accept in whole or in part as typical of U.S. society. The media thus help to integrate and homogenize our society.

Media images are especially potent when they involve aspects of life that people experience only through the media. The personal and professional conduct of politicians, political events beyond hometown boundaries, frenzied trading at stock exchanges, medical breakthroughs, and corrupt corporate dealings are not generally experienced firsthand. Rather, popular perceptions of these aspects of life take shape largely in response to news and fictional stories in media. Like caricatures, media stories often create skewed impressions because the media cannot report most stories in detail or within a full context.[9] For example, thanks to a heavy focus on crime news and police dramas, television exaggerates the likelihood of an individual becoming a victim of crime. Viewers therefore fear crime excessively, especially if they watch a lot of television.[10]

Attention to the mass media is pervasive among 21st-century Americans. Even in school, media are the basis for much learning about current events. An average adult in the United States spends nearly half of their leisure time consuming media. Averaged over an entire week, this amounts to more than seven hours of exposure per day to some form of mass media news or entertainment. The ability to attract such vast audiences of ordinary people, as well as political elites, is a major ingredient in the power of the mass media and makes them extraordinarily important for the individuals and groups whose stories and causes are publicized. Although their percentages have been shrinking, as Table 1-1 shows, some traditional media retain their dominance, even while the audiences for political news on digital and social media are growing. Recent years saw a gradual decline in local news consumption in particular. In 2018, local news programs' morning timeslots saw a 10% drop in viewership, and audiences for midday and prime-time news both declined by 19%. Advertising revenue from the newspaper industry dropped by 13% from 2017. Cable television news viewership for prime-time programming (on CNN, Fox News, and MSNBC) increased by about 8% in 2018, viewership for daytime programming increased by about 5%. Viewership for nightly network television news increased by 11% in 2018. During the 2020 election cycle, cable TV was the most relied-on platform for election night returns. Although nearly a quarter of Americans reported relying mainly on news websites or apps, 22% followed national network television news (ABC, CBS, or NBC), and only 9% turned mainly to social media.[11]

Politically relevant information is often conveyed through stories that are not concerned explicitly with politics. In fact, because most people are exposed far more to nonpolitical information, fictional media (such as movies and entertainment television) are major suppliers of political images. For example, the 2020 season premiere of NBC's *Saturday Night Live* (*SNL*) had its highest ratings since 2016—the 46th season opener, hosted by Chris Rock, attracted 8.24 million viewers from the coveted 18–49 age group, revealing a return to its usual election-year ratings bump.[12] Young viewers in particular regularly cite shows such as *SNL* or John Oliver's *Last Week Tonight* as a primary source of news.[13] During the 2016 cycle, *SNL* provided ample coverage of the presidential election campaign in its comedy skits with Kate McKinnon as Hillary Clinton and Alec Baldwin as Donald Trump.[14] During the 2020 cycle, Baldwin continued as Trump, while Jim Carrey joined the cast to portray Joe Biden.

Entertainment shows portray social institutions, such as the police or the schools, in ways that either convey esteem or heap scorn upon them. These shows also express social judgments about various types of people. For instance, in its infancy, television sometimes depicted African Americans and women as politically naive and having limited abilities. This type of coverage conveys messages that audiences, including the misrepresented groups, may accept at face value, even when the portrayals distort real-world conditions. Audience members may also think that social conditions and judgments shown on television are widely accepted and therefore socially sanctioned.[15]

Not only are the media the chief source of most Americans' views of the world, but they also provide the fastest way to disperse information throughout society. Major political news broadcasts by 24-hour services such as CNN or Fox News spread breaking stories throughout the country in minutes. People hear the stories directly from radio, television, or digital or social media or from other people.

All forms and types of mass media are politically important because of their potential to reach large audiences. However, the influence of each medium varies depending on its characteristics, the nature and quantity of the political messages it carries, and the size of the audience reached (see Box 1-1 for more on the various types of media and their audiences). Print media, including websites that feature text, generally supply the largest quantity of factual political information and analysis. They need readers who are literate at appropriate levels. Electronic media, especially audiovisual stories, provide a greater sense of reality, which explains why some audiences find audiovisual media more credible than print media. Moreover, large segments of the U.S. population have limited reading skills and find it far easier to capture meanings from pictures and spoken language. Audiovisual media also convey physical images, including body language and facial expressions, making them especially well-suited to attract viewers' attention and arouse their emotions.[16]

Table 1-1 Election Night News Consumption Patterns, 2020 (Percentage)

Medium	2020
Cable TV news	30
News website or app	24
National network TV news	22
Social media feed	9
Presidential candidate/campaign	2
Something else	6

Source: Americans paid close attention as election returns came in. (2020, November 23). *Pew Research Center.* https://www.journalism.org/2020/11/23/americans-paid-close-attention-as-election-returns-came-in/.

Note: Table shows the percentage of U.S. adults who used the listed medium the most to follow the results of the presidential election after polls closed on Election Day. Respondents who did not give an answer or who tuned out the election results are not shown.

Box 1-1
Media Is a Plural Noun

It has become fashionable to talk about news media behavior and effects using the singular, as if the media were one giant, undifferentiated institution. Researchers strengthen that impression because they commonly generalize about media behavior and effects based on data drawn from a single news source—most often *The New York Times*. The resulting caricature hides the immense richness of the news media in topics and framing, in presentation forms and styles, and in the unique social and political environments that they reflect. Yes, indeed, *media* should be treated as a plural noun.

How does one medium differ from the next? Communications scholar Michael Schudson answers that question in the opening essay of a volume about the role of the news media in the contemporary United States. Schudson warns,

It is a mistake to identify American journalism exclusively with the dominant mainstream-television network news and high circulation metropolitan daily newspapers. This error is compounded . . . if attention is paid exclusively to leading hard-news reporting, and features, editorials, news analysis, opinion columns, and other elements of the journalistic mix are ignored.[1]

Schudson identifies four distinct types of journalism, which are often combined to please various audiences. There is traditional mainstream journalism, often called "hard" news, and there is "soft" news tabloid journalism. Both differ from advocacy journalism, which is devoted to pleading particular causes, and from entertainment journalism, which may offer news but only as a by-product. The stories produced in these styles also bear the imprint of the various types of venues that present them: newspapers and magazines of all shapes and sizes, radio and television broadcast stations, and internet news sites and blogs. These diverse venues brim with a veritable smorgasbord of news stories, told from different perspectives and framed to carry unique shades of meanings effectively.

Their impact varies, depending on audience characteristics. U.S. scholars tend to think that "hard" print news is and should be king, but those claims are debatable. Compared to print news, audiovisual news captures much bigger audiences, and evidence is growing that it may also be the public's most effective teacher. Some messages are primarily important because they reach huge audiences; others attract comparatively tiny audiences but are enormously influential nonetheless because some audience members have access to the country's networks of power.

Finally, in the global world in which news now circulates, it is unduly parochial to think of U.S. media performing inside a national cocoon. *Media* is a plural noun in the truest sense because news media now have a global reach. Like the biblical tower of Babel, they carry a multiplicity of voices, each reflecting different environments and perspectives. Fortunately, unlike in biblical times, the discordant voices today, besides being heard, can be translated and considered. How they will be construed then becomes the paramount question.

---

1. Schudson, M. (2005). Orientations: The press and democracy in time and space. In G. Overholser & K. Hall Jamieson (Eds.), *The press* (pp. 1–3). Oxford University Press.

Functions of Mass Media

What major societal functions do the mass media perform? Political scientist Harold Lasswell, a pioneer in media studies, mentions three things: surveillance of the world to report ongoing events, interpretation of the meaning of events, and socialization of individuals into their cultural settings.[17] To these three, a fourth function must be added: manipulation of politics. The manner in which these four functions are performed affects the political fate of individuals, groups, and social organizations as well as the course of domestic and international politics.

Surveillance

Surveillance involves two major tasks. When it serves the collective needs of the public, it constitutes *public surveillance*, and when it serves the needs of individual citizens, we call it *private surveillance*. Although private surveillance may lead to political activities, its primary functions are gratifying personal needs and quieting personal anxieties.

Public Surveillance

Newspeople determine what is news—that is, which political happenings will be reported and which will be ignored. Their choices are politically significant because they affect who and what will have a good chance to become the focus for political discussion and action.[18] News stories may force politicians to respond to situations on which their views would not have been aired otherwise. Without media attention, the people and events covered by the news might have less influence on decision makers—or none at all. Conditions that might be tolerated in obscurity can become intolerable in the glare of publicity. Take the example of the disastrous statement made by 2020 presidential election candidate Joe Biden during an interview on the radio program *The Breakfast Club*. In an attempt to emphasize the strength of his connection with the Black community, Biden said, "I tell you, if you have a problem figuring out whether you're for me or for Trump, then you ain't Black." Though it was just one of several Biden gaffes from the 2020 election, it was particularly embarrassing. The ill-considered, awkward comment earned Biden and the campaign an enormous amount of not-very-flattering social (and mainstream) media attention.[19] Many also undoubtedly recall a now infamous example from the 2016 cycle: Donald Trump's sexually explicit off-camera comments about kissing and groping women on an *Access Hollywood* bus.[20] The public airings of such remarks can lead to the political downfall of major political candidates and officeholders. Politicians are keenly aware of the media's agenda-setting power. That is why they try mightily to time and structure events to yield as much favorable publicity as possible and to forestall damaging coverage.

The consequences of media surveillance can be good as well as bad. Misperceptions and scares created by media stories have undermined confidence in good policies and practices, good people, and good products on many occasions. The human and economic costs are often vast. For example, if media stories overemphasize crime and corruption in the city, scared residents may move to the suburbs, leaving the city deserted and even less safe and deprived of tax revenues. Speculation that international conflicts or economic downturns are in the offing may scare investors and produce fluctuations in domestic and international stock markets and commodity exchanges. Serious economic (and hence political) consequences may ensue.

Fear of publicity can be as powerful a force in shaping action as actual exposure. Politicians and business leaders know what damage an unfavorable story can do and act accordingly, either to avoid or conceal objectionable behaviors or to atone for them by public confessions. President Bill Clinton, whose eight-year term was pockmarked with scandals, tried valiantly to hide some of them by forceful denials of allegations. But whenever proof made the charges undeniable, he escaped much public wrath by publicly apologizing for his misbehavior.[21] In the past, presidents with the skill or good fortune to ensure that negative news stories did not "stick to them" in career-ending ways were referred to as "Teflon" presidents. (Teflon is a type of nonstick cooking pan.) Donald Trump earned the Teflon label during his presidential candidacy and his term in office. His 2016 candidacy survived the aforementioned *Access Hollywood* scandal as well as other scandals related to inappropriate sexual behavior, many of which were brought on by lawsuits and public allegations of sexual assault and harassment from several women. His term in office was similarly characterized by a steady stream of scandals. Even in the last months and weeks of his presidency, Trump was reported to have referred to American veterans who lost their lives in war as "losers," and this account was confirmed by multiple news outlets. Mere weeks later, he was caught on tape—by one of America's most famous investigative reporters—admitting that he lied to the American public about risks and threats associated with COVID-19. Despite all this (and numerous other scandals unnamed here), President Trump's approval numbers barely shifted throughout his time in office, certainly little enough to earn Teflon status. However, unfortunately for Trump, his Teflon coating also prevented benefits from coverage of his administration's accomplishments from sticking. There was very little movement among his approval ratings in either direction over the course of his term, indicating that the numbers for those who disapproved did not move much either.[22]

The media can doom people and events to obscurity by inattention as well. When the media have more information than they can transmit, many important stories remain untold. That happens most dramatically when the news becomes focused on a single upheaval, such as a major natural or human-made disaster, an election outcome, or a scandal. The time and space used for the single event usurp the time and space of happenings that otherwise would be reported. The size of "news holes"—the time and space available for reporting the news—is fairly inelastic. Newspeople also ignore important events that do not seem "newsworthy" by accepted journalistic criteria or that fail to catch their attention. Conscious attempts to suppress information for ideological or political reasons are another, but far less frequent, reason for lack of coverage.

For many years, left-wing social critics often faulted mainstream U.S. journalists for using their news selection power to strengthen white middle-class values and disparage liberal viewpoints. These critics claim that the media deliberately perpetuate capitalist exploitation of the masses, in line with the ideological preferences of media owners. Critics also claim that the media have intentionally suppressed the facts about dangerous products, such as alcohol and tobacco, and about the socially harmful activities of large corporations, which may be responsible for water and air pollution or unsafe consumer goods.[23] By the same token, right-wing critics complain that the media give undue attention to enemies of the established social and political order in hopes of undermining it. Each camp cites a long list of stories to support its contentions.[24] Of course, largely in response to both rising polarization and the re-emergence and popularity of partisan news, claims of bias from both the left and right have only increased in recent years.

Journalists reject these charges. Most journalists deny political motives in news selection and defend their choices on the basis of the general criteria of newsworthiness (see Chapters 3 and 14 for more extensive treatments of this subject). They, too, can muster evidence from news stories to support their claims. Yet, as the media environment grows in complexity with so many content choices available on an array of platforms and devices, it is increasingly difficult for citizen-audiences to differentiate between mainstream news (which ostensibly attempts to produce objective reporting), partisan news, political opinion or commentary, and so-called fake news. This difficulty is reflected in news consumers' growing dissatisfaction with, and distrust of, journalists and news organizations.

Besides calling attention to matters of potential public concern, the media also provide cues about the importance of an issue. Important stories are covered prominently on websites and front pages with big headlines and pictures or as major television or radio features. Less important matters are more likely to be buried in the back pages, be listed at the bottom of a web page, or have brief exposure on television or radio. However, nearly all coverage, even when it is brief and comparatively inconspicuous, lends an aura of significance to publicized topics. Through the sheer fact of coverage, the media can confer status on individuals and organizations. The media "function essentially as agencies of social legitimation—as forces, that is, which reaffirm those ultimate value standards and beliefs, which in turn uphold the social and political status quo."[25]

Television helped to make African American civil rights leaders and their causes household names. Martin Luther King Jr. and Jesse Jackson became national figures in part because television showed them giving speeches and leading marches and protests. In King's case, television captured the riots following his assassination. An individual who gains a hearing on radio or television often becomes an instant celebrity, whether they are an emerging political candidate on the national scene, such as 2020 presidential primary contender "Mayor Pete" Buttigieg, later nominated as President Joe Biden's pick for transportation secretary; a teenage climate activist and crusader such as Greta Thunberg, whose goals and activism are so newsworthy that she is now the subject of the highly acclaimed documentary film *I Am Greta*; or a young poet such as Amanda Gorman, who was widely acknowledged as having stolen the show at Joe Biden's presidential inauguration (see Photo 1-1). Their unpublicized counterparts remain obscure. Because publicity is crucial for political success, actors on the political scene often deliberately create situations likely to receive media coverage. Daniel Boorstin labeled events arranged primarily to stimulate media coverage as "pseudo-events."[26] Such events range from news conferences called by public figures (even when there is no news to announce) to physical assaults on people and property by members of protest groups who want to dramatize grievances. Newspeople who must cover such events may feel manipulated and resentful, but they are loath to allow competing media to scoop these events.

Photo 1-1 WASHINGTON, DC; JANUARY 20: American poet Amanda Gorman recites one of her poems during the 59th inaugural ceremony on the West Front of the U.S. Capitol on January 20, 2021, in Washington, DC. During the inauguration ceremony, Joe Biden became the 46th president of the United States.

Source: Photo by Patrick Semansky-Pool/Getty Images

When events are exceptionally significant or widely known already, or when the story is reported by competing media, the journalism community loses control over the news flow. For example, journalistic standards demand the reporting of news about prominent political leaders and major domestic and international events.[27] Aside from such unavoidable situations, coverage is discretionary for a wide range of people and happenings.

The power of the media to set the agenda for politics is not subject to a system of formal checks and balances as is the power of the U.S. government. Media power does not undergo periodic review through the electoral process. If media emphases or claims are incorrect, remedies are few. Truth-in-advertising laws protect citizens from false advertising of consumer goods but not from false political claims or improper news selection or biases by media personnel. The courts have interpreted restrictions on the news media's power to choose freely what to report and how to frame it as impeding the constitutional right to free speech and a free press. Media critic Jay Blumler expresses the dilemma well:

Media power is not supposed to be shared: That's an infringement of editorial autonomy. It is not supposed to be controlled: That's censorship. It's not even supposed to be influenced: That's news management! But why should media personnel be exempt from Lord Acton's dictum that all power corrupts and absolute power corrupts absolutely? And if they are not exempt, who exactly is best fitted to guard the press guardians, as it were?[28]

Private Surveillance

Average citizens may not think much about the broader political impact of the news they read, hear, and watch. They use the media primarily to keep in touch with what they deem personally important. The media are their eyes and ears to the world, their means of surveillance. The media, as Marshall McLuhan (another pioneering media scholar) observed, are "sense extensions" for individuals who cannot directly witness most of the events of interest to them and their communities.[29] The media tell their audiences about weather, sports, jobs, fashions, economic conditions, social and cultural events, health and science, and the public and private lives of famous people.

The ability to stay informed makes people feel secure, whether or not they remember what they read or hear or see. Even though the news may be bad, people feel that at least there will be no startling surprises. News reassures us that the political system continues to operate despite constant crises and frequent mistakes. Reassurance is important for peace of mind, but it also tends to encourage political quiescence because there is no need to act if political leaders seem to be doing their jobs. For good or ill, the public's quiescence helps maintain the political and economic status quo.[30]

Other significant private functions that the mass media fulfill for many people are entertainment, companionship, tension relief, and a way to pass the time with minimal physical or mental exertion. The mass media can satisfy these important personal needs conveniently and cheaply. People who otherwise might be frustrated and dissatisfied can participate vicariously in current political happenings, in sports and musical events, in the lives of famous people, and in the lives of families and communities featured in the news.[31]

Interpretation

Media not only survey the events of the day and bring them to public and private attention, but they also interpret the events' meanings, put them into context, and speculate about their consequences. Most incidents lend themselves to a variety of interpretations, depending on the values and experiences of the interpreter. The kind of interpretation affects the political consequences of media reports. For example, research shows that low-income communities and communities of color are disproportionately harmed by climate change and environmental problems. Policies aimed at improving the environment do not help these communities as much.[32] In response, a growing number of political elites are framing discussions about climate change and environmental policy as inseparable from issues of social justice. The same is true of the economy and national security, both of which face threats from climate change. In late January of 2021, during the first weeks of his presidency, Joe Biden signed a new executive order creating a White House Council on Environmental Justice. He described the executive order as part of a broad effort to "place environmental justice at the center of all we do, addressing the disproportionate health and environmental and economic impacts on communities of color, so-called fenceline communities, especially those communities—Brown, Black, Native American, poor whites."

Political leaders know that in addition to potentially broadening the constituency of people concerned about climate change, introducing these new policy considerations into climate change debates may allow journalists to use a new vocabulary, which may help them steer clear of the negative connotations some party members associate with this policy domain. For example, on January 27, 2021, Biden signed an executive order to discontinue the practice of oil and gas leasing on federal lands and waters.[33] Tellingly, in the effort to court bipartisan support for these actions in the wake of criticisms on the grounds that ending this practice will hurt jobs, he opened his public remarks on the order with this statement: "Today is Climate Day at the White House, which means it's Jobs Day at the White House." Referring to the health and national security impact of climate change, he called it a "maximum threat." National climate advisor Gina McCarthy also reiterated the administration's strategy: "to address climate change as one of four major interrelated crises that include COVID-19, the economic downturn, and racial inequality."[34]

As the difficulty in untangling environmental policy efforts from these domains becomes more apparent in the political debates among elites, social justice, the economy, and national security it will be increasingly reflected in the words and phrases journalists use in their reporting on climate change. This may change journalists' interpretation of the issue in ways that shape opinion or the contours of the constituency interested in the implications of climate change, possibly making it wider. Such thinking was undoubtedly part of the Biden administration's strategy for their framing of the issue in those early days of the Biden presidency.

Regardless of which frame they end up favoring, news media reporting will likely continue to influence the type of interpretation that climate change and environmental policy stories receive. In the end, interpretations will largely hinge on journalists' decisions, made independently or in response to pressures, to frame the story in a specific way and to choose informants accordingly. Journalists' inclinations help determine how the news is framed, which in turn affects its likely impact.

By suggesting the causes and relationships of events, the media may shape opinions without explicitly telling audiences which views seem right or wrong. This is one reason many people were critical about coverage of police responses to Black Lives Matter protests relative to coverage of the police response to the violent mob that attacked the U.S. Capitol on January 6, 2021. Press portrayals of such events can determine whether American audiences view violent protests and a lack of adequate police response (or violent police responses to peaceful protests) with considerable alarm.[35]

News presentations can shape people's conclusions in countless ways.

> We [journalists] can attribute any social problem to official policies, the machinations of those who benefit from it, or the pathology of those who suffer from it. We can trace it back to class or racial inequalities, to ideologies such as nationalism or patriotism, or to resistance to the regime. We can root the problem in God, in its historic genesis, in the accidental or systematic conjuncture of events, in rationality, in irrationality, or in a combination of these or other origins. In choosing any such ultimate cause we are also depicting a setting, an appropriate course of action, and sets of virtuous and evil characters, and doing so in a way that will appeal to some part of the public that sees its own sentiments or interests reflected in that choice of a social scene.[36]

The items that media personnel select to illustrate a point or to characterize a political actor need not be intrinsically important to be influential in shaping opinions and evaluations. They do not even need exposure in respected media outlets; the mere threat of widespread publicity through traditional or social media is often enough. That is why in the weeks and months of protests and social justice activism following George Floyd's killing by police, teenagers around the country started strategically leveraging social media to call out their peers for racist behavior, hoping to attract publicity to force apologies, curb behavior, or lead to other repercussions such as the revoking of college admissions, job offers, scholarships, or other important privileges.[37]

Socialization

The third function of major mass media that Lasswell mentions is political socialization (Chapter 10). It involves learning basic values and orientations that prepare individuals to fit into their cultural milieu. Before the 1970s, studies largely ignored the mass media because parents and the schools were deemed the primary agents of socialization. Research in the 1970s finally established that the media play a crucial role in political socialization.[38] Most information that young people acquire about their political world comes directly or indirectly from the mass media either through news offerings or entertainment shows or through social media sites such as Facebook or Twitter. The media present specific facts as well as general values, teaching young people which elements produce desirable outcomes. Media also provide people with behavior models. Because young people generally have attitudes and behaviors that are less firmly established, they are receptive to using such information to develop their opinions.

Many of the new orientations and opinions that adults acquire during their lifetime also are based on information from the mass media. People do not necessarily adopt the precise attitudes and opinions that earn the media's praise; rather, mass media information provides the ingredients that people use to adjust their existing attitudes and opinions to keep pace with a changing world. The mass media deserve credit, therefore, for a sizable share of adult political socialization and resocialization. Examples of resocialization—the restructuring of established basic attitudes—include the shifts in sexual morality and racial attitudes that the American public has undergone since the middle of the last century and the changing views about relations with mainland China and with Russia.[39]

Manipulation

The work journalists do has political implications. Intentionally or not, journalists sometimes become major players in the game of politics; they do not always play their traditional role as chroniclers of information provided by others. The most common way for a journalist to break out of the role of political bystander is through an investigation. Many major media enterprises contain investigative units because investigative stories are both important and popular. They are also expensive to produce and tend to become scarce when media organizations are forced to economize.

In democratic societies, the purpose of many journalistic investigations is to *muckrake,* serving as an adversarial watchdog. Journalists who investigate corruption and wrongdoing to stimulate the government to clean up the "dirt" they have exposed are called *muckrakers.* The term comes from a rake designed to collect manure. President Theodore Roosevelt was the first to apply the term to journalism. Muckraking may have several goals.[40] The primary purpose may be to expose misconduct in government and produce reforms, or the chief purpose may be to present sensational information that attracts large media audiences and enhances profits. Other investigative stories (or story interpretations) may be designed to affect politics in line with a media outlet's political brand (Chapter 12).

Who Should Control News Making?

Attempts by governments to control and manipulate the media are universal because public officials everywhere believe that media are important political forces. This belief is based on the assumption that institutions that control the public's information supply can shape public knowledge and behavior and thereby determine support for government or opposition to it. Although media control occurs in all societies, its extent, nature, and purposes vary for several reasons. Political ideology is an important one. In countries in which free expression of opinion is highly valued and in which dissent is respected, the media tend to be comparatively unrestrained. The right of the press to criticize governments also flourishes when the prevailing ideology grants that governments are fallible and often corrupt and that average citizens are capable of forming valuable opinions about the conduct of government. Finally, freedom of the press, even when it becomes a thorn in the side of the government, is more easily tolerated when governments are well established and politically and economically secure. In nations where governments are unstable and resources are insufficient to meet the country's needs, it may be difficult to put up with press behavior that is apt to topple the government or slow its plans for economic development.

Nowhere are the media totally free from formal and informal government and social controls, even in times of peace. On the whole, authoritarian governments control more extensively and more rigidly than nonauthoritarian ones, but all control systems represent points on a continuum. There are also gradations of control within nations, depending on the current regime and political setting, regional and local variations, and the nature of news. The specifics of control systems vary from country to country, but the overall patterns are similar.[41]

Authoritarian Control Systems

Authoritarian control systems may be based on a totalitarian ideology and designed to control and use the media to support ideological goals, or they may be nonideological and simply represent the desire of the ruling elites to control media output tightly so that it does not interfere with their conduct of government. Examples of nonideological authoritarian control exist in states ruled by military governments or where constitutional guarantees have been suspended. Cuba and China are examples of control based on communist ideology.

In today's world, fully or partially authoritarian systems of media control prevail in the majority of countries, although many governments profess to want a less-controlled system and are struggling to move in that direction. Nonetheless, governmental attempts to control internal and external news flows are omnipresent because governments fear that unrestrained media will create serious political instability, whether through accurate messages or through unintentionally or deliberately false ones. The arrival of the digital era has presented challenges for government efforts to control the spread of information. Digital and social media, especially when coupled with mobile access to the internet, are viewed by authoritarian governments as tools for collective action, on-the-ground mobilization, and regime instability. Some have developed aggressive strategies for coping with these challenges. China, for example, is credited with developing the most sophisticated system for controlling internet content in the world as well as the most broadly reaching effort to suppress social media. Authoritarian systems operate on the assumption that government must control the media because news stories are essential for engendering support for the government's mission (see Table 1-2). The media may point out minor deficiencies or corruption of low-level officials and suggest adjustments in line with prevailing policies, but criticism of the basic system or its rulers is considered destructive. Chinese internet censorship is an example: Criticism of the state, leaders, and policies is published while posts that facilitate collective action are censored.[42]

Beyond that, the media are free to choose the stories they wish to publish, so long as government officials agree that the stories do not interfere with public policies. In totalitarian societies, the likely political and social effects of a story—rather than its general significance, novelty, or audience appeal—determine what will be published and what will be buried in silence. For instance, news about accidents, disasters, and crimes is often suppressed because of fears that it may weaken the image of an all-powerful political system. Even entertainment programs, such as music and drama performances and cartoon shorts in movie theaters, must carry appropriate social messages or have historical significance. The government supports such entertainment financially because it serves the important public purpose of shaping people's minds in support of the political system.

Democratic Systems

In democracies, the public sees journalists as its eyes and ears. Journalists are expected to scrutinize government performance and report their findings. If media surveillance causes governments to fall and public officials to be ousted, democracy is well served.

Although this is the theory behind the role of media in democratic societies, the practice is less clear-cut. In the United States, for example, neither newspeople nor government officials are completely at ease with the media's watchdog role. This is especially true in the contemporary era, where press criticism abounds, trust in media is extremely low, and charges of media bias are rampant. The media limit their criticism to what they perceive as perversions of the public's basic social and political values or noteworthy examples of corruption and waste. They rarely question the widely accepted fundamentals of the political system, such as its orientation toward majority rule or private capitalism or individualism.

Because American journalists tend to choose established elites as their primary sources of news, their links to the existing power structures are strong.[43] They may even share information with government agencies, including law enforcement bodies such as the Federal Bureau of Investigation (FBI) and the Central Intelligence Agency (CIA). When disclosure might cause harm, reporters in a democratic society occasionally withhold important news at the request of the government. This has happened repeatedly when the lives of hostages were at stake or when military interventions were imminent. In an effort to keep their images untarnished by media attacks, government officials may try to control the media through regulatory legislation or through rewards and punishments.

The chief responsibility of the news media in democratic societies is to provide the general public with information and entertainment. According to the U.S. version of the libertarian philosophy, anything that happens that seems interesting or important for media audiences may become news. It should be reported quickly, accurately, and without any attempt to convey a particular point of view. Topics with the widest audience appeal should be pervasive, which explains the ample doses of sex and violence. Audience appeal is then expected to translate into good profits for media owners either through fees paid by audience members or through advertising revenues. Although audiences may learn important things from the media, libertarians believe that teaching is not the media's chief task. Nor is it their responsibility to question the truth, accuracy, or merits of the information supplied to them by their sources. Rather, it is left to the news audience to decide what to believe and what to doubt.

By contrast, adherents to the tenets of social responsibility believe that news and entertainment presented by the mass media should reflect societal concerns. Media personnel should be participants in the political process, not merely reporters of the passing scene. As guardians of the public welfare, they should foster political action when necessary by publicizing social evils such as rampant industrial pollution of air and water. In a similar vein, undesirable viewpoints and questionable accusations should be denied exposure, however sensational they may be. If reporters believe that the government is hiding information that the public needs to know, they should try to discover the facts and publicize them.

Social responsibility journalism and totalitarian journalism share some important features. Both approaches advocate using the media to support the basic ideals of their societies and to shape people into better beings. Proponents of both kinds of journalism are convinced that their goals are good and would not be achieved in a media system dominated by the whims of media owners, advertisers, or audiences. But the similarities should not be exaggerated. Social advocacy in democratic systems lacks the fervor, clout, and single-mindedness it has in its totalitarian counterpart. Social responsibility journalism rarely speaks with a single uncontested voice throughout society. Nevertheless, it frightens and antagonizes many news professionals and news audiences. If one agrees that the media should be used to influence social thought and behavior for "good" purposes, who should decide which purposes deserve to be included in that category? Critics of social responsibility journalism point out that journalists do not have a public mandate to act as arbiters of social values and policies in a society that has many disparate visions of truth and goodness. Newspeople lack the legitimacy that comes only from being elected by the public or appointed by duly elected officials.

Irrespective of the merits or faults of these arguments, today, social responsibility journalism is popular with a sizable portion of the news

Table 1-2 Media Roles Under Different Regime Types

Authoritarian Regime Assumptions	Democratic Regime Assumptions
• Governments know and serve people's best interests.	• Governments often fail to serve people's best interests.
• Media should stress the government's virtues.	• Media should confront the government when officials and policies seem flawed.
• News should engender support for major policies.	• News should stimulate critical thinking about major policies.
• News and entertainment programs should be selected for their social values.	• News and entertainment programs should be selected for audience appeal.

Source: Composed by Doris A. Graber.

profession.[44] Pulitzer Prizes and other honors go to journalists who have successfully exposed questionable practices in the interest of social improvement. The most prominent "villains" targeted for exposure are usually big government and big business.[45]

Models of News Making

Beyond the basic concerns reflected in the philosophies of libertarians and social responsibility advocates, there are many other guiding principles for reporting events. For example, news making can be described in terms of five distinct models: the mirror model, the professional model, the organizational model, the political model, and the civic journalism model. Each represents judgments about the major forces behind news making that shape the nature of news and its political impact.

Underlying Theories

Proponents of the mirror model contend that news is and should be a reflection of reality. "We don't make the news, we just report it" is their slogan. The implication is that newspeople impartially report all significant happenings that come to their attention. Critics of the mirror model point out that this conception of news making is unrealistic. Countless significant events take place daily, forcing journalists to determine their relative newsworthiness and decide which to report. Events that are publicized inevitably loom disproportionately large compared with unpublicized events. The way the story is framed in words and pictures further distorts reality.

In the professional model, news making is viewed as an endeavor of highly skilled professionals who put together a balanced and interesting collage of events selected for importance and attractiveness to specific media audiences. There is no pretense that the end product mirrors the world. For economic reasons, anticipated audience reaction is especially influential in determining which stories pass scrutiny and which are ignored. This is also sometimes referred to as the *economic model* of news.

The organizational model, sometimes called the *bargaining model*, is based on organizational theory. Its proponents contend that the pressures inherent in organizational processes and goals determine which items will be published. Pressures spring from interpersonal relations among journalists and between them and their information sources, from professional norms within the news organization and from constraints arising from technical news production processes, cost–benefit considerations, and legal regulations.

The political model rests on the assumption that news everywhere reflects the ideological biases of individual newspeople as well as the pressures of the political environment in which the news organization operates. The media cover high-status people and approved institutions; people and events outside the dominant system or remote from the centers of power are generally ignored. Supporters of the prevailing system are pictured as good guys and opponents as bad guys.

In the 1990s, public journalism or *civic journalism* became popular, spurred by widespread concern that average citizens shun participation in public affairs and distrust government and the news media. Proponents of the civic journalism model believe that the press can discover citizens' concerns and then write stories that help audiences play an active and successful role in public life.[46] Journalists must articulate and explain public policy choices in understandable language. They must facilitate a public dialogue that encourages and respects diverse views. After consensus has been reached among the clients of a particular news venue, the venue and its clients must vigorously champion appropriate public policies.

None of these models fully explains news making; rather, the process reflects all of them in varying degrees. Because the influences that shape news making fluctuate, one needs to examine individual news making situations carefully to account for the factors at work. Organizational pressures, for instance, depend on the interactions of people within the organization, and these can also be linked to professional or economic considerations.

Audience tastes change or are interpreted differently. Perceptions of "facts" differ, depending on reporters' dispositions. Moreover, the precise mix of factors that explains news making in any particular instance depends largely on chance and on the needs of a particular news medium.

Control Methods

Societies use legal, normative, structural, and economic means to control news media within their countries. All countries have laws to prevent common press misbehavior. For instance, laws may forbid publication of deliberate falsehoods. All societies also have social norms that the press generally heeds because it craves public approval or fears government or private sector retaliation. Hence, media are unlikely to ridicule sacred concepts or widely accepted values. The way media organizations are structured, operated, and financed also shapes their product. The Russian government closely regulates, controls, and finances media enterprises. In December 2020, Russian President Vladimir Putin signed a set of controversial new laws to expand his government's ability to label organizations as foreign agents and introduce several harsh new restrictions on media organizations.[47] Russian media are constrained under these kinds of conditions, and they will usually not dare to criticize the government's decision making and tactics. Journalists' behavior largely reflects the nature of their environments.[48] They are often docile and obey rules strictly in countries where media control is heavy-handed, and they become far more daring and unconventional in liberal, individualistically oriented countries such as the United States and England.

The combination of methods by which governments control the media varies, and so do the major objectives of control. Governments can control media content by limiting entry into the media business. For example, the government may require licenses for entry and grant them only to people it deems desirable, as is common in authoritarian societies. By contrast, democratic regimes rarely make formal attempts to deny foes of the regime access to the media. However, because the capacity of the broadcast spectrum is limited, control through franchise is quite common for television and radio media. Franchises often bestow monopoly control. In most democracies, newspapers rarely need licenses, and access to the internet has remained equally unrestricted. In the United States, for instance, anyone with sufficient money can start a newspaper or newsletter or create a website or blog.

Media also may be controlled through the manipulation of access to news. Information may be put beyond the reach of media by declaring it to be confidential and by barring reporters from government archives. In addition to such formal control of potentially damaging news, informal restraints curb the actual flow of news. All government units, and often many of their subdivisions, have information control systems by which they determine which news to conceal or release and how to frame it (Chapter 5). In 1993, President Clinton, who was annoyed with reporting about his presidency, took the unusual step of limiting reporters' easy access to the White House communication office by closing off a connecting hallway to the press room.[49]

In the time since Clinton's administration, White House efforts to control information are increasingly aggressive. The Obama administration was notorious for its press dealings, and the immediate future looks no better.[50] From the earliest days of Hillary Clinton's 2016 campaign for the presidency, the press complained about access and her refusal to hold press conferences.[51] In fact, both 2016 contenders exhibited troubling signs for press–White House relations during the campaign. Trump held regular press conferences and granted many interviews, but by October 2016, the White House Correspondents' Association was publicly complaining that both candidates were violating public trust by restricting access and failing to abide by the norm of keeping a regular "protective press pool."[52] As president-elect, Trump was soundly criticized by the press for a lack of access and the failure to provide the American public with transparency about the administration's plans and transition into power.[53] Press struggles for access to the White House persisted throughout President Trump's term in office. In 2019, the Trump administration rolled out a new set of criteria that journalists must meet in order to qualify for a "hard pass," which granted the highest level of press access. The criteria set an extremely high bar for earning this level of access, mandating that journalists be present in the White House for at least 90 days out of a 180-day period. When dozens of prominent journalists, including all six of The Washington Post's White House correspondents, were determined to have failed to meet those criteria in May, their press passes were promptly revoked.[54]

On January 20, 2021, President Joe Biden's press secretary, Jen Psaki, held her first press briefing with the White House press corps (Photo 1-2). In it, Psaki pledged to bring transparency back to the briefing room and to rebuild trust with the American people. She also announced the Biden communication team's plan to restore daily press briefings as part of that effort. The tradition of White House daily press briefings all but disappeared during the Trump administration.[55]

Authoritarian governments often use censorship laws or regulations to control the flow of news. In some countries, nothing may be printed or broadcast until the government censor has approved it. At times,

Photo 1-2 White House Press Secretary Jen Psaki Holds News Briefing on President Biden's Inauguration Day.

Source: Photo by Chip Somodevilla/Getty Images

governments will direct papers or magazines to make deletions after their product has been prepared for printing or is already printed. This leaves tantalizing white spaces or missing pages. Government officials often write or edit television and radio scripts, and media outlets must broadcast these without editorial changes. In the past, totalitarian countries could frequently block all unapproved communications from abroad by jamming foreign broadcasts and prohibiting the import of foreign printed materials. In the internet age, such controls have become well-nigh impossible. Democratic governments also often use legal and normative pressures to avert potentially damaging political news or news that violates widely cherished social norms. They commonly claim that concerns about press freedoms have motivated the restrictions on news. Publication controls increase markedly in periods of crisis and war.

All governments use treason and sedition laws to control media output. "Treason" and "sedition" can be defined broadly or narrowly. Anything that is critical of the government can be called treasonable or seditious, especially in times of war. In democratic societies, media and the government are in perennial disagreement about the tipping point. Governments lean toward protection; the media lean toward disclosure. People judged guilty of treason or sedition may be sentenced to prison or even executed. Given the social pressures to act patriotically and the severity of the penalty, treason is rare. Most journalists avoid difficulties with official censors and with treason and sedition laws by refraining from using material that is likely to be objectionable. Formal government censorship then becomes replaced largely by social pressures and self-censorship—which are the most potent forms of constraint on human behaviors.

The First Amendment to the U.S. Constitution, which provides that "Congress shall make no law . . . abridging the freedom of speech, or of the press," has given the media an exceptionally strong basis for resisting government controls in the United States. The courts have ruled, however, that the protection is not absolute. On occasion, it must give way to social rights that the courts consider to be superior. For example, media are forbidden from publicizing the names of CIA secret agents because that would endanger them and destroy their usefulness.

A limited number of controls, such as regulatory laws, court decisions, and informal social pressures, guard against excesses by the media. In the United States, the courts have been loath to impose restraints prior to publication, such as granting injunctions that would stop publication of information, on the grounds that it would cause irreparable harm. But informal social and political pressures and the fear of indictments after publication have restrained presentation of potentially disturbing stories. Besides guarding state survival through treason and sedition laws, government controls commonly shield sensitive governmental proceedings, protect individual reputations and privacy, and safeguard the prevailing moral standards of the community. Curbs on publication of government secrets—so-called classified information—often engender controversy because governments tend to be overzealous in controlling material that they deem potentially harmful to themselves. Finally, most governments also have laws protecting the reputations of individuals or groups and laws against obscenity.

Defining the limits of government control over information dissemination raises difficult questions for democratic societies. Does official censorship, however minimal, open the way for excessive curbs on free expression? What guidelines are available to determine how far censorship should go? What types of material, if any, can harm children? Or adults? Should ethnic and racial slurs be prohibited on the ground that they damage minorities' self-image? The answers are controversial and problematic.

The limitations on the freedom of publication in democratic societies raise questions about the actual differences in press freedom in democratic and authoritarian societies. Is there really a difference, for example, in the independence of government-operated television networks in France and in North Korea? The answer is a resounding yes. The degree of restraint varies so sharply that the systems are fundamentally different. In authoritarian societies, the main objective of controls is to support the regime in power. In democratic societies, the media are usually free to oppose the regime, to weaken it, and even to topple it. Although the media rarely carry their power to the latter extreme, the potential is there. It is this potential that makes the media in democratic societies a genuine restraint on governmental abuses of power and a potent shaper of government action.

SUMMARY

The mass media are an important influence on politics because they regularly and rapidly present politically crucial information to huge audiences. These audiences include political elites and decision makers as well as large numbers of average citizens whose political activities, however sporadic, are shaped by information from the mass media.

Decisions made by media personnel about what and whom to cover determine what information becomes available to media audiences and what remains unavailable. By putting stories into perspective and interpreting them, reporters assign meaning to the information and indicate the standards by which it ought to be judged. At times, reporters even generate political action directly through their own investigations or indirectly through their capacity to stimulate pseudo-events.

Although social scientists still find it difficult to pinpoint the scope of media impact on particular political events, politicians and their governments everywhere are keenly aware of the political importance of the media. Therefore, these governments have policies to shape the media's political role in their societies. Those policies have been buttressed by constitutional and legal rules as well as by a host of informal arrangements. In this chapter, we have briefly described how the basic policies, constitutional arrangements, and legal provisions differ in authoritarian and democratic regimes.

DISCUSSION QUESTIONS ────────────

1. Why is the mass media in the U.S. important for politics and for democratic society? What is it about democratic governance in particular that makes the media so important?

2. What are the major functions mass media serve in the U.S.? Why are these the key functions? Do you think all of these functions are being served as well as possible by the U.S. media today? If not, why not? Are some outlets doing better than others?

3. Why does it matter who owns and controls the media? How does ownership and control (at least potentially) change the nature of the coverage we might see? Why does it matter within the context of a democratic system in particular?

4. What are the various models of news making? Which model do you think is the one behind most of the news you encounter? Which of the models do you think is most common? Which model or combination of models do you think would be best for serving society's needs today?

READINGS ────────────────────────

Boczkowski, P. J., & Papacharissi, Z. (Eds.). (2018). *Trump and the media*. MIT Press.

Forgette, R. (2018). *News grazers: Media, politics, and trust in an information age*. CQ Press.

Graber, D. A. (Ed.). (2011). *Media power in politics* (6th ed.). CQ Press.

Hemmer, N. (2018). *Messengers of the right: Conservative media and the transformation of American politics*. University of Pennsylvania Press.

Hibbing, J. R. (2020). *The securitarian personality: What really motivates Trump's base and why it matters for the post-Trump era*. Oxford University Press.

Johnson, J. (2020). *Political rhetoric, social media, and American presidential campaigns: Candidates' use of new media*. Lexington Books.

Karl, J. (2020). *Front row at the Trump show*. Dutton.

Patterson, T. E. (2019). *How American lost its mind*. Oklahoma University Press.

Patterson, T. E. (2020). *Is the Republican Party destroying itself?* KDP Publishing.

Pollard, M. S., & Kavanagh, J. (2019). *Profiles of news consumption: Platform choices, perceptions of reliability, and partisanship*. Rand Corporation.

Repnikova, M. (2017). *Media politics in China: Improvising power under authoritarianism.* Cambridge University Press.

Ridout, T. N. (Ed.). (2018). *New directions in media and politics.* Routledge.

Sides, J., Tesler, M., & Vavreck, L. (2018). *Identity crisis: The 2016 presidential election campaign and the battle for the meaning of America.* Princeton University Press.

Wahl-Jorgensen, K. (2019). *Emotions, media and politics.* John Wiley & Sons.

Wahl-Jorgensen, K. (Ed.). (2020). *Journalism, citizenship and surveillance society.* Routledge.

Williams, B. A., & Delli Carpini, M. X. (2011). *After broadcast news: Media regimes, democracy, and the new information environment.* Cambridge University Press.

NOTES

1. Patterson, T. E. (2016, June 13). Pre-primary news coverage of the 2016 presidential race: Trump's rise, Sanders' emergence, Clinton's struggle. Shorenstein Center on the Media, Politics and Public Policy, Kennedy School of Government, Harvard University. http://shorensteincenter.org/pre-primary-news-coverage-2016-trump-clinton-sanders.

2. Battaglio, S. (2020, November 23). Trump has been a ratings driver for cable TV news. How will the networks adapt? *Chicago Tribune.* https://www.chicago tribune.com/entertainment/tv/ct-ent-trump-cable-tv-ratings-1124-20201123-wxre3kvj5bdyfepxtgodvfyyee-story.html

3. CNN Pressroom. (2016, September 26). Q3: CNN has best quarter in eight years. *CNN.* http://cnnpressroom.blogs.cnn.com/2016/09/26/q3-cnn-has-best-quarter-in-eight-years.

4. Risen, T. (2016, March 18). Who's winning the election? Networks. *U.S. News & World Report.* http://www.usnews.com/news/the-report/articles/2016-03-18/forget-trump-and-clinton-cable-news-networks-are-winning-the-2016-election

5. Patterson, T. E. (2016, December 7). News coverage of the 2016 general election: How the press failed the voters. *Shorenstein Center on the Media, Politics and Public Policy, Kennedy School of Government, Harvard University.* http://shorensteincenter.org/news-coverage-2016-general-election.

6. Patterson, T. E. (2020, December 17). A tale of two elections: CBS and Fox News' portrayal of the 2020 presidential campaign. *Shorenstein Center on the Media, Politics and Public Policy, Kennedy School of Government, Harvard University.* https://shorensteincenter.org/patterson-2020-election-coverage.

7. For an overview of the effects of mass media, see Bennett, W. L. (2016). *News: The politics of illusion* (10th ed.). Longman, Chapter 11; Iyengar, S. (2016).

Media politics: A citizen's guide (3rd ed.). Norton; Jeffres, L. W. (1997). *Mass media effects* (2nd ed.). Waveland Press.

8. Gans, H. J. (2004). *Deciding what's news: A study of CBS evening news, NBC nightly news, Newsweek, and Time.* Northwestern University Press; Campbell, R., Martin, C. R., & Fabos, B. (2009). *Media and culture* (7th ed.). Bedford/St. Martin's; Shoemaker, P. J., & Reese, S. D. (2014). *Mediating the message in the 21st century* (3rd ed.). Routledge.

9. Soroka, S. (2012). The gatekeeping function: Distributions of information in media and the real world. *Journal of Politics, 74*(2), 514–528; Althaus, S. L., Swigger, N., Chernykh, S., Hendry, D. J., Wals, S. C., & Tiwald, C. (2011). Assumed transmission in political science: A call for bringing description back in. *Journal of Politics, 73*(4), 1065–1080. https://10.1017/S00223816 11000788.

10. Romer, D., Jamieson, K. H., Aday, S. (2003). Television news and the cultivation of fear of crime. *Journal of Communication, 53*(1), 88–104.

11. State of the news media (project). (2021). *Pew Research Center.* https://www.pewresearch.org/topics/state-of-the-news-media/.

12. O'Connell, M. (2016, November 6). TV ratings: "Saturday Night Live" holds strong on election eve. http://www.hollywoodreporter.com/live-feed/tv-ratings-saturday-night-live-holds-strong-election-eve-944516.

13. Baumgartner, J. C., & Morris, J. S. (Eds.). (2008). *Laughing matters: Humor and American politics in the media age.* Routledge; see also Williams, B. A., & Delli Carpini, M. X. (2011). *After broadcast news.* Cambridge University Press; Jones, J. P. (2004). *Entertaining politics: New political television and civic culture.* Rowman and Littlefield; Baym, G. (2010). *From Cronkite to Colbert: The evolution of broadcast news.* Paradigm; van Zoonen, L. (2004). *Entertaining the citizen: When politics and popular culture converge.* Rowman and Littlefield; Watercutter, A. (2016, November 14). John Oliver sums up election 2016 in one devastating *Last Week Tonight* episode. *Wired.* https://www.wired.com/2016/11/john-oliver-summed-election-2016-one-last-week-tonight-episode

14. Porter, R. (2020, October 6). TV ratings: "Saturday Night Live" gets election year bump. *The Hollywood Reporter.* https://www.hollywoodreporter.com/live-feed/tv-ratings-saturday-sunday-oct-3-4-2020; Porter, R. (2020, December 8). TV ratings: "Saturday Night Live" suffers post-election slide. *The Hollywood Reporter.* https://www.hollywoodreporter.com/live-feed/tv-ratings-saturday-sunday-dec-5-6-2020.

15. Entman, R. M., & Rojecki, A. (2000). *The Black image in the White mind: Media and race in America.* University of Chicago Press.

16. For a discussion of many aspects of visual presentations, see Stanczak, G. (2004). Visual research: Method and representation. *American Behavioral*

Scientist, 47(12), 1471–1642; also see Grabe, M. E., & Bucy, E. P. (2009). *Image bite politics: News and the visual framing of elections.* Oxford University Press.

17. Lasswell, H. D. (1969). The structure and function of communication in society. In W. Schramm (Ed.), *Mass Communications.* University of Illinois Press, p. 103.

18. Chapter 4 gives a more detailed definition of *news.* Evidence that the media set the agenda for national issues is presented in Protess, D. L., & McCombs, M. (Eds.). (1991). *Agenda setting: Readings on media, public opinion, and policy making.* Erlbaum. For a more recent discussion of agenda setting for news consumers, see McCombs, M. (2004). *Setting the agenda: The mass media and public opinion.* Polity.

19. Blitzer, R. (2020, December 21). The most memorable political gaffes of 2020. *Fox News.* https://www.foxnews.com/politics/most-memorable-political-gaffes-2020

20. Fahrenthold, D. (2016, October 8). Trump recorded having extremely lewd conversation about women in 2005. *The Washington Post.* https://www.washingtonpost.com/politics/trump-recorded-having-extremely-lewd-conversation-about-women-in-2005/2016/10/07/3b9ce776-8cb4-11e6-bf8a-3d26847eeed4_story.html?utm_term=.e6cf4c32852b.

21. Sabato, L. J., Stencel, M., & Robert Lichter, S. R. (2000). *Peep show: Media and politics in an age of scandal.* Rowman and Littlefield. The authors discuss the appropriate ways to deal with scandal stories.

22. Hunt, A. (2020, September 27). Trump's Teflon problem: Nothing sticks, including the "wins." *The Hill.* https://thehill.com/opinion/campaign/518460-trumps-teflon-problem-nothing-sticks-including-the-wins

23. Examples of such criticism can be found in Bennett (2016); McChesney, R. W. (2008). *The political economy of media: Enduring issues, emerging dilemmas.* Monthly Review Press; Parenti, M. (1993). *Inventing reality: The politics of the news media* (3rd ed.). St. Martin's Press.

24. An example of a conservative Washington, DC–based media analysis group is Accuracy in Media, which publishes periodic reports of its media investigations. For claims that journalists in the elite media are ultraliberal, see Lichter, S. R., Rothman, S., & Lichter, L. S. (1986). *The Media Elite.* Adler and Adler. Also see Schmitt, K. M., Gunther, A. C., & Liebhart, J. L. (2004). Why partisans see mass media as biased. *Communication Research, 31,* 623–641.

25. Blumler, J. G. (1978). Purposes of mass communications research: A transatlantic perspective. *Journalism Quarterly, 55*(Summer), 226.

26. Boorstin, D. (1971). *The image: A guide to pseudo-events.* Athenaeum.

27. Criteria of what constitutes "news" are discussed fully in a historical context in Barnhurst, K. G., & Nerone, J. (2001). *The form of news.* Guilford Press.

Also see Winch, S. P. (1997). *Mapping the cultural space of journalism*. Praeger; Gans, H. (2003). *Democracy and the news*. Oxford University Press.

28. Blumler (1978), p. 228.

29. McLuhan, M. (1964). *Understanding media: The extensions of man*. McGraw-Hill.

30. The numbing effects of reassuring publicity are discussed by Edelman, M. (1985). *The symbolic uses of politics*. University of Illinois Press, pp. 38–43. Originally published in 1964.

31. Kubey, R., & Csikszentmihalyi, M. (1990). *Television and the quality of life: How viewing shapes everyday experience*. Erlbaum, Chapters 5, 7.

32. O'Neil, S. G. (2007, July 1). Superfund: Evaluating the Impact of Executive Order 12898. Environmental Health Perspectives. https://ehp.niehs.nih.gov/doi/10.1289/ehp.9903

33. Rott, N., Detrow, S., & Wise, A. (2021, January 27). Biden hits "pause" on oil and gas leasing on public lands and waters. *NPR*. https://www.npr.org/sections/president-biden-takes-office/2021/01/27/960941799/biden-to-pause-oil-and-gas-leasing-on-public-lands-and-waters

34. Calma, J. (2021, January 27). Joe Biden made climate change a national security priority—what's next? *The Verge*. https://www.theverge.com/2021/1/27/22251298/joe-biden-executive-order-climate-change-national-security; Biden signs "existential" executive orders on climate and environment. (2021, January 27). *BBC*. https://www.bbc.com/news/world-us-canada-55829189; Brave NoiseCat, J. (2019, June 11). No, climate action can't be separated from social justice. *The Guardian*. https://www.theguardian.com/commentisfree/2019/jun/10/no-climate-action-cant-be-separated-from-social-justice

35. Kilgo, D. K. (2021, January 7). The insurrection at the Capitol challenged how US media frames unrest and shapes public opinion. *The Conversation*. https://theconversation.com/the-insurrection-at-the-capitol-challenged-how-us-media-frames-unrest-and-shapes-public-opinion-152805; Harlow, S. (2021, January 13). There's a double standard in how news media cover liberal and conservative protests, but the Capitol riot might change that. *The Washington Post*. https://www.washingtonpost.com/politics/2021/01/13/theres-double-standard-how-news-media-cover-liberal-conservative-protests/; Pierre-Louis, K. (2020, June 24). It's time to change the way the media reports on protests. Here are some ideas. *Nieman Lab*. https://www.niemanlab.org/2020/06/its-time-to-change-the-way-the-media-reports-on-protests-here-are-some-ideas/

36. Bennett, W. L., & Edelman, M. (1985). Toward a new political narrative. *Journal of Communication, 35*, 156–171.

37. Levin, D. (2020, December 26). A racial slur, a viral video, and a reckoning. *The New York Times*. https://www.nytimes.com/2020/12/26/us/mimi-groves-jimmy-galligan-racial-slurs.html

38. The early writings include Easton, D., & Dennis, J. (1969). *Children in the political system: Origins of political legitimacy.* McGraw-Hill; Greenstein, F. I. (1965). *Children and politics.* Yale University Press; Dawson, R., & Prewitt, K. (1969). *Political socialization.* Little, Brown; Hess, R. D., & Torney, J. (1967). *The development of political attitudes in children.* Aldine; Kraus, S., & Davis, D. (1976). *The effects of mass communication on political behavior.* Pennsylvania State University Press; Chaffee, S. H. (1977). Mass communication in political socialization. In S. Renshon (Ed.), *Handbook of political socialization.* Free Press.

39. For example, see Page, B. I., & Shapiro, R. Y. (1992). *The rational public: Fifty years of trends in Americans' policy preferences.* University of Chicago Press; Page, B. I. (1996). *Who deliberates?* University of Chicago Press; Iyengar, S., & Kinder, D. (1987). *News that matters: Television and American opinion.* University of Chicago Press; Zaller, J. (2001). Monica Lewinsky and the mainspring of American politics. In W. L. Bennett & R. M. Entman (Eds.), *Mediated politics: Communication in the future of democracy.* Cambridge University Press.

40. Protess, D. L., Doppelt, J. C., Ettema, J. S., Gordon, M. T., & Cook, F. L. (1991). *The journalism of outrage: Investigative reporting and agenda building in America.* Guilford Press, pp. 8–12. Also see Sabato, Stencel, and Lichter (2000).

41. The discussion is modeled on Fred Siebert, Theodore Peterson, and Wilbur Schramm's foundational book, *Four Theories of the Press* (University of Illinois Press, 1963). For a critique of the model, see Hallin, D. C., & Mancini, P. (2004). *Comparing media systems: Three models of media and politics.* Cambridge University Press; for an updated discussion, see Hallin, D. C., & Mancini, P. (2016). Ten years after *Comparing Media Systems:* What have we learned? *Political Communication.* https://10.1080/10584609.2016.1233158.

42. King, G., Pan, J., & Roberts, M. E. (2014). Reverse-engineering censorship in China: Randomized experimentation and participant observation. *Science, 6199*(345), 1–10.

43. See Hayes, D., & Guardino, M. (2013). *Influence from abroad: Foreign voices, the media, and U.S. public opinion.* Cambridge University Press.

44. Weaver, D. H., & Wilhoit, G. C. (2005). *The American journalist in the 21st century.* Erlbaum. Public journalism embodies most of the principles of social responsibility journalism. See Lambeth, E. D., Meyers, P. E., & Thorson, E. (Eds.). (1998). *Assessing public journalism.* University of Missouri Press; Glasser, T. L. (Ed.). (1999). *The idea of public journalism.* Guilford Press.

45. See, for example, Alger, D. (1998). *Megamedia: How giant corporations dominate mass media, distort competition, and endanger democracy.* Rowman and Littlefield. Also see the annual reports of The Goldsmith Prize Investigative Reporting Finalists, issued by the Joan Shorenstein Center on the Press, Politics and Public Policy, Harvard University.

46. Lambeth, Meyers, and Thorson (1998).

47. Odynova, A. (2020, December 31). Putin ends 2020 by tightening the legal news on press and individual freedoms. *CBS NEWS*. https://www.cbsnews.com/news/russia-vladimir-putin-ends-2020-laws-foreign-agents-limits-press-individual-freedoms/

48. Hallin and Mancini (2004).

49. Maltese, J. A. (1994). *Spin control: The White House Office of Communication and the management of presidential news* (2nd ed.). University of North Carolina Press, pp. 232–233.

50. Milligan, S. (2015). The president and the press. *Columbia Journalism Review* (March/April). https://www.cjr.org/analysis/the_president_and_the_press.php

51. Gold, H. (2016, August 12). Clinton's press problem. *Politico*. http://www.politico.com/story/2016/08/hillary-clinton-media-press-problem-226944; Byers, D. (2016, September 1). Clinton campaign unmoved by press squawks over lack of press conferences. *CNN*. http://money.cnn.com/2016/09/01/media/hillary-clinton-press-conference; Folkenflick, D. (2016, August 26). Has Hillary Clinton actually been dodging the press? *NPR*. http://www.npr.org/2016/08/25/491311747/tallying-hillary-clintons-appearances-with-the-news-media.

52. Gold, H. (2016, October 24). WCHA appeals to Clinton and Trump campaigns. *Politico*. http://www.politico.com/blogs/on-media/2016/10/whca-appeals-to-clinton-and-trump-campaigns-on-press-access-230246

53. Weprin, A. (2016, November 16). WHCH says lack of media access to president-elect is "unacceptable." *Politico*. http://www.politico.com/blogs/on-media/2016/11/whca-to-trump-transition-team-it-is-unacceptable-for-president-elect-to-not-have-a-press-pool-231471; Burr, T. (2016, November 16). An open letter to president-elect Donald Trump. *The National Press Club*. http://www.press.org/news-multimedia/president/2016/11/open-letter-president-elect-donald-trump; Hennessey, K. (2016, November 11). Trump bucks protocol on press access. *Associated Press*. https://apnews.com/22b62277e34b47008a760c660084968a.

54. Ingram, M. (2019, May 9). White House revokes press passes for dozens of journalists. *Columbia Journalism Review*. https://www.cjr.org/the_media_today/white-house-press-passes.php

55. Joyella, M. (2021, January 20). Biden's White House press secretary promises "trust and transparency." *Forbes*. https://www.forbes.com/sites/markjoyella/2021/01/20/bidens-white-house-press-secretary-promises-trust-and-transparency/?sh=77a492574616

2

Ownership, Regulation, and Guidance of Media

Learning Objectives

1. Identify the difference between public/semipublic and private media.

2. Classify the different forms of ownership among private media, including patterns of media consolidation.

3. Describe the consequences of these different media ownership types and media economics for news coverage.

4. Analyze the debates over media regulation and regulation in the United States (U.S.), including stakes and regulatory policy.

5. Explain the various forces, beyond regulation and economics, that attempt to control media.

Media play a central role in democratic governance. They perform a critical watchdog function, informing the public of government waste, overreach, and corruption so that leaders are held accountable at the voting booth. Recent studies of declines in local news, for example, find the ongoing reductions in local newsrooms and local coverage to be associated with numerous troubling consequences for political accountability at state and local levels. Less local coverage is associated with less-competitive local elections and more of incumbency advantage.[1] At the state level, government corruption is more frequent in the absence of robust local coverage. When state capitals are remote—further from the local press in other state localities—corruption is higher amongst state officials.[2] When members of the U.S. House of Representatives are not monitored closely by the local press in their home districts, they do not work as hard for their constituencies, are less active in congressional hearings, are less likely to vote against their party, are less likely to serve on district-relevant committees, and bring less money and fewer benefits to the districts they serve.[3] As citizens move away from quality sources of geographically tied local news and move to other venues such as cable news networks and online news, House members have less incentive to provide services to the district in order to earn praise from the local press. Citizens are also more attentive to and more knowledgeable about state and local politics and participate at higher rates when local media cover local politics.[4] Ongoing cuts to local newsrooms and disappearing news venues substantially weaken the links through which local citizens learn about what local leaders and representatives are doing, making citizens less able to hold them accountable.[5]

Concern about who will wield media power has been a central issue in U.S. politics since colonial days. In this chapter, we will weigh the pros and cons of various forms of ownership and control of the mass media as well as the implications of changing patterns. We will also assess the impact of various pressures on the mass media industry, such as economic constraints and lobbies. The policy issues involved in media ownership and control are complex and tightly intertwined with political preferences. It is no wonder that attempts in the United States to legislate media ownership and control have produced little agreement on what the laws should be.

Control and Ownership: Public and Semipublic

Who controls and owns the media affect not only media behavior but also the substance of media output, in line with the old adage, "He who pays the piper calls the tune." People concerned about self-serving politicians are likely to oppose government ownership and operation of the media. They also are apt to be leery about extensive government regulation of privately owned and operated media. By contrast, people who believe that for-profit media enterprises cater to low-level mass tastes or who distrust the business ethics of corporations, especially huge ones, do not want a media system in which private ownership and control dominate.

The Crux of the Debate

Opponents of *public media ownership*—referring to media owned wholly or in part by the government—fear that it leads to programming that uncritically supports government policies, even in democratic countries. The fear is well founded. However, evidence from long-standing public media such as the British government's nonpartisan British Broadcasting

Corporation shows that public media can produce programming without direct political interference from governments.[6]

Private control of media—referring to media owned by individuals or businesses and operating for profit—if divided among many owners, is likely to bring more conflicting interests into play than government control does. Even within large corporations, business interests are apt to be diverse and often incompatible, so company leaders support diverse policies. Overall, when business enterprises control broadcasting, the prevailing political values reflected in the choice of programs are likely to be mainstream and middle class. The pressures springing from profit considerations lead to offerings with mass appeal rather than controversial social or cultural crusades. Advertisers generate the largest share of the media's income. They pay for the privilege of reaching large numbers of potential customers, particularly 18- to 49-year-olds who are the most active shoppers. Government-owned and government-controlled media are free from commercial pressures because they can use tax money to finance whatever programs they believe to be in the public interest. They must consider intragovernmental power struggles, but they do not need to consider the economic consequences of the size of their audience.

When most Americans distrust government more than business, private ownership and control of the mass media are the preferred option. Consequently, the bulk of American news media fare, especially on television, is geared toward simple, emotion-laden programming that attracts large, diverse audiences. Controversial or troublesome issues that may antagonize or deplete media audiences and diminish advertising revenues are largely shunned.

Popular, "lightweight" programming draws the wrath of many people, particularly intellectual elites who scorn the mass public's tastes even when they themselves flock to fluff programs. Some critics argue that people would choose highbrow, intellectual programs over lightweight entertainment if they had the chance, even though proof is plentiful that the public prefers shallow entertainment to more serious programs.[7] In print news, magazines featuring sex or violence far outsell journals that treat political and social issues seriously. Huge crowds are willing to pay heavily in time and money to see movies featuring heinous crimes and explicit sex. The most popular pay television channels show what is euphemistically called "adult entertainment," whereas channels devoted to highbrow culture languish and often perish. On the internet, one-fourth of daily search engine requests and one-third of all downloads involve sexually explicit content.[8]

During recent White House administrations, however, politics often gave entertainment programming a run for its money. In 2018, for example, President Trump's State of the Union address drew an audience of 45.6 million. Though his audience was smaller than that of Obama's first State of the Union address in 2010 (48 million), it beat ratings for the Grammys, which attracted 26 million viewers. Though the Obama and Trump presidencies seem unique thus far in their ability to capture the attention of the mass public, it's typically been the case that politics rarely trumps entertainment in the modern media era. It remains to be seen whether high levels of interest in presidential politics will continue.[9]

Related to concerns about news media domination by powerful government or private interests is the fear of undue influence if only a small number of organizations share media control. Diversity of media ownership presumably encourages the expression of diverse views, which to many Americans is the essence of democracy. The marketplace where ideas and opinions are debated must be wide open. But there is no agreement on exactly how many owners are required for sufficient diversity.[10] Americans appear to be more concerned about the concentration of media ownership in comparatively few hands than about control of the media by business. Social reformers, however, are more concerned about business control, claiming that it fosters tabloid journalism and suppresses discussion of pressing social problems.

How the Public and Semipublic System Works

In the United States, outright government ownership and control over media is limited. However, it is growing as more local governments own cable television systems or operate channels on privately owned systems. Government ownership raises serious unresolved questions about the limitations, if any, to be placed on the government's right to use these outlets to further partisan political purposes.

The federal government is most heavily involved in broadcasting, with local governments in second place. The federal government controls broadcasts to U.S. military posts throughout the world through the United States Armed Forces Radio and Television Service in the Department of Defense. It also owns foreign media outlets, which often relay U.S. government policy, though not exclusively. The Voice of America (VOA) is a fully government-funded multimedia news source. It serves as the official external broadcasting institution of the United States, providing English and foreign-language news, information, and cultural programming for radio, television, and the internet outside the U.S. The VOA serves an estimated weekly audience of more than 280 million. It broadcasts more than 1,500 hours of programs weekly to a foreign audience through radio, television, and the internet. VOA has more than 2,500 affiliate stations and communicates in more than forty languages.[11]

Broadcasting by semipublic institutions is another control option. The American public broadcasting system, created through the Public Broadcasting Act of 1967, represents a mixture of public and private financing and programming and public and private operation of radio and television stations. The public broadcasting system supports educational and public service television stations whose programs generally do not attract large audiences. Those stations need subsidies because they usually cannot find enough commercial sponsors to pay for their shows.

Members of the public broadcasting system include more than 1,500 noncommercial public radio and television stations, primarily owned and operated by community organizations and colleges and universities. In recent years, National Public Radio (NPR) increased its broadcasting reach across all three affiliate types, and more than 1,000 noncommercial radio stations linked together as the independently financed NPR (see Table 2-1). Approximately 98.5% of the U.S. population is within a listening area of an NPR-carrying station.

The administrative arrangements for the public broadcasting system are complex. The Corporation for Public Broadcasting (CPB), staffed by political appointees, handles the general administration, but it has been kept separate from the programming side of the operation to insulate public broadcasting from political pressures. A separate Public Broadcasting Service (PBS) produces programming. Largely through the awarding of grants, the CPB tries to encourage the development of programming aimed at addressing the needs of previously underserved audiences—minority

Table 2-1	Weekly Broadcast Audience for Top 20 NPR-Affiliated Radio Stations, 2015–2018
Year	**Listenership**
2015	8,724,100
2016	10,212,600
2017	11,210,500
2018	11,047,900

Source: Based on data from Nielsen Audio Nationwide for persons 12+. Public broadcasting: Fact sheet. (2019, July 23). *Pew Research Center on Journalism & Media.* https://www.journalism.org/fact-sheet/public-broadcasting/.

populations and children in particular.[12] More than 70% of CPB's federal funding goes directly to local stations.

The attempt to keep the CPB from influencing programming has failed. The corporation does not tell public television stations what programs they should feature; instead, it has guided programming by paying for some types of programs and refusing to pay for others. This has constituted purse-string control of programming by the government. The results have earned praise along with scorn. In radio, NPR was created to both produce and distribute programs. Because cost considerations made it impossible to include all noncommercial radio stations, only the largest, best organized ones were included and are eligible for CPB funding grants and participation in NPR programs.

Private foundations and big business enterprises have subsidized a significant portion of the public broadcasting system income (Table 2-2). The Reagan administration authorized PBS to engage in some commercial broadcasting of economic news and to accept a limited amount of advertising. These changes have enhanced corporate influence over programming. The general public also has influenced public broadcasting through donations—individual giving—which constitutes its other primary source of income. Nevertheless, securing adequate financing is an enduring problem. Dependence on federal funds, even when those funds constitute a fraction of total funding, entails some subservience to federal control, despite barriers to direct government influence.

An emphasis on experimental programs—cultural offerings such as plays, classical music, and ballet—and a stress on high-quality news and public affairs programs distinguish public television broadcasts from commercial television.[13] The nature and quality of programming vary widely because public television represents a decentralized bevy of local stations. The audience for public television, except for its children's programs, has been relatively small, rarely more than 2% of television viewers. Even minority groups, to whom a number of public broadcast programs are targeted, prefer commercial entertainment. Still, PBS reaches 63.7 million primetime television viewers and 14 million visitors to pbs.org monthly, and 146 million episodes of PBS programs are streamed per year.[14] During the 2020 election, NPR's website drew its largest audience ever—34.7 million unique users, generating 158.9 million page views during the week of the election. Election Day audiences were up 65% from 2016, and on the day after the election, there were 41 million story views across NPR platforms.[15] The typical monthly NPR cross-platform audience is 163 million.[16] Still, because of the relatively limited appeal of public broadcasting and the need to reduce public expenditures, there has been some pressure to disband the system completely and reallocate its frequencies to commercial channels. In 2016, the Obama administration requested $445 million for the CPB for 2019. The Departments of Labor, Health and Human Services, and Education bill would be the funding vehicle, approved by the Senate and Appropriations Committees in June and July 2016. However, in the wake of the 2016 election, public broadcasting advocates began speculating about CPB funding prospects during the Trump administration. Their concerns were not unwarranted. In each of the four consecutive years of his term, President Trump proposed eliminating funding for the CPB.[17] With continuing pressure to reduce deficits, the CPB will likely remain a target of budget cuts—and not only from Republicans; even President Obama's bipartisan deficit reduction committee proposed to eliminate funding for the CPB. If the CPB does eventually lose federal funding, the impact will be variable across affiliates, and some of its programs then might be shown on commercial cable stations, possibly with federal subsidies.[18]

Supporters of the system contend that it provides special services that commercial television neglects because they lack mass appeal. Innovations pioneered by public broadcasting have spread to commercial broadcasting, these supporters say. For example, public broadcasting played a leading role in developing captions for individuals with hearing impairments. At the turn of the century, it led in pioneering digital television, including interactive news and feature programs. Public radio and public television were among the first to move to satellite distribution, which made it possible to deliver multiple national programs to communities. Nonetheless, the future of public broadcasting seems precarious.

Patterns of Private Ownership

The overarching feature of media ownership in the United States is that it is predominantly in private hands; media companies and outlets operate primarily as for-profit businesses. Arrangements vary from individual ownership, where one person owns a newspaper or radio or television station, to ownership by corporate conglomerates. Owners include small and large business enterprises, labor groups, religious and ethnic organizations, and many other types of interest groups in society. Explaining private media control patterns is relatively simple; agreeing on their consequences is not.

Table 2-2   Public Broadcasting Revenue by Source, 2008–2017

Year	Individual Giving	Underwriting
2008	$252,188,412	$191,368,970
2009	$266,879,214	$169,783,646
2010	$273,641,191	$169,662,827
2011	$297,404,887	$170,980,687
2012	$301,896,974	$183,138,683
2013	$316,851,081	$183,378,779
2014	$329,574,209	$195,853,661
2015	$352,159,144	$204,335,864
2016	$362,070,403	$209,451,245
2017	$383,819,720	$211,637,752

Source: Individual giving and underwriting revenue for local public radio news stations. (2021, June 29). *Pew Research Center.* https://www.journalism.org/fact-sheet/public-broadcasting/

Note: Figures are based on revenue for the 123 largest news-oriented public radio licensees (in U.S. dollars).

Business Configurations

Independents is the term used to describe individuals, families, or corporations that own a single media venture and little else. They are increasingly rare in the media business. Various forms of multiple ownership or *media chains* have become the norm. In media chains, individuals or corporations own several media outlets—mostly radio or television stations or cable channels or newspapers. The Gannett Company is a good example. Gannett owns more than 100 local media properties in the United States, including the giant *USA Today* and hundreds of nondaily publications. It was recently acquired by New Media Investment Group, Inc., now its parent company. The deal brought 263 media outlets across 47 states together under the same ownership umbrella, the properties of which reach over 145 million unique visitors a month.[19] The predictable consequence of chain ownership has been a large degree of homogeneity in news offerings.[20]

National and regional chains control a majority of daily papers in the United States.[21] Like the Gannett Company, most of these newspaper groups also own nondaily papers. The proportion of circulation controlled by chain-owned papers has been on the rise in recent years. Although individual papers within chains generally enjoy editorial page autonomy, they tend to be more uniform in making political endorsements than is true for independently owned papers.[22]

Many of the major media companies own several chains of media outlets across platforms. When media enterprises own different types of media, it is called *cross-media ownership*. Although the arrangement carries the usual advantages of giant enterprises—ample resources for good performance and economies of scale—it is worrisome when one company controls all (or most) of the news media in a single local market. It diminishes the chance for democratic dialogue. Efforts to use the government's regulatory powers to curb cross-media ownership in the United States have been applied at both the national and local level. Rules exist to limit cross-ownership within local media markets; other rules limit the national reach of any one media company. Despite their existence, these regulations and further regulatory efforts have been continually stymied by powerful lobbying by large media enterprises.[23]

Because its leadership is appointed by partisan presidents, the Federal Communications Commission (FCC) has intermittently favored loosening constraints on cross-media ownership. The FCC position on ownership restrictions typically depends on party control of the White House. Following the 2016 presidential election, looking forward to the return of a friendlier Republican administration, big media redoubled their efforts to persuade the FCC to further loosen restrictions. In November 2016, the News Media Alliance, a consortium of big media groups, moved quickly to urge president-elect Trump to drop remaining ownership restrictions, arguing that the regulations are no longer appropriate in the fragmented and increasingly competitive news business. The group contended that while news organizations are struggling to innovate and adapt to the digital media environment, outdated policies are dampening investment and growth.[24]

A *market* is the geographic area served by a media outlet and where it typically attracts a substantial audience. For instance, each television station has a signal that can be received clearly by people living within a certain radius of the station. All of the people within that radius who can receive the signal are considered to be within the market. Television media markets are classified as designated market areas (DMAs). Residents in a given media market are generally exposed to much of the same programming, allowing for some variation across cable providers and packages. Newspapers also serve geographic markets, which often roughly map to the town, city, or county level. Program sponsors and those advertising in newspapers pay for advertising based on how well the demographics of the media market audiences match the ideal consumer for their products or services. By owning many local television stations or newspapers, large media companies may supply news for more than a hundred markets and therefore reach a broad consumer base for advertisers.

A fourth type of ownership is the *conglomerate*—individuals or corporations that own media enterprises along with other types of businesses. CBS Corporation, General Electric, and the Walt Disney Company are examples. They own the CBS, NBC, and ABC networks. Along with Fox, these four major television networks supply most of the content broadcast by U.S. television stations. Conglomerate ownership raises fears that the companies' nonmedia business interests may color their news policies. If, for instance, there is a need to reduce the size of the military or to oppose construction of a missile system, the management of a conglomerate such as General Electric, which holds many defense contracts, may examine these questions from a biased perspective in the media outlets that it controls. A significant amount of early research on the effects of media ownership examined these kinds of conflicts of interest. In a recent study, Catie Snow Bailard found that newspapers owned by parent companies who stood to benefit economically from campaign finance changes resulting from the *Citizens United v. Federal Elections Commission* (2010) decision covered it more favorably.[25]

In major urban centers, most media fall into the media chain, cross-media, and conglomerate classifications. For instance, the two major media companies that used to be the Tribune Company—Tribune Publishing and Tribune Media—reach enormous proportions of audiences in major markets around the country. Tribune Publishing owns 10 daily newspapers and 60 digital properties in major markets such as Los Angeles, Chicago, and Orlando. Tribune Media's holdings include 42 owned or operated broadcast stations, one radio station, and one national cable outlet, along with the websites associated with these enterprises.[26] Despite early intentions to avoid cross-ownership and market dominance, most of the major outlets in several of the top media markets are owned by the national television networks and conglomerates or members of conglomerates. Two prominent examples are the Chicago market, ranked third among the top 100 media markets, and Dallas–Fort Worth, ranked fifth.[27]

Radio and television stations that remain under single ownership are, for the most part, small with comparatively weak signals. The number of media outlets controlled by various entrepreneurs ranges widely and fluctuates considerably, especially in an era of widespread consolidation. Since the turn of the century, many news media companies have added multiple websites to their holdings as well as online versions of their newspapers and television programs.

Recent research suggests a different classification of media ownership if the goal is to understand how ownership influences content. This work argues that it is the governance structure and profit orientation of media outlets' parent companies that influence the nature and quality of news coverage. Specifically, the content produced by many news outlets is influenced by the structure and nature of its ownership, both of which shape profit-making considerations in conjunction with the outlet's financial health and competitive standing in the market. For example, parent companies fully owned and controlled by public shareholders have a fiduciary responsibility to provide a profitable return on investments for stockholders. Under this model, profit maximization is the overarching goal of the organization, which means that content is driven by the preferences of audiences and advertisers. These outlets are most vulnerable to demand-side bias in which the makeup of the market can produce biases by suggesting certain compilations of audience tastes. Typically, this translates into news coverage that is less substantive, more sensational, and more negative in tone. When news organizations are concerned about profit at the expense of all else, they are more likely to offer political news content that is appealing to mass audiences—who tend to prefer more sensational, more negative, and less substantive news.[28] At times, these pressures can also produce coverage that is slanted or biased, particularly when outlets operate in markets with a clear preference for one side or another.[29]

Recent years have witnessed the rapid emergence of a new media ownership type—one born from acquisitions of media companies by hedge funds, private equity firms, and owners with investment backgrounds. For these hedge fund owners, the primary purpose of media acquisitions is to turn a profit, much to the dismay of critics already weary of corporate media consolidation. Hedge fund owners are known for purchasing distressed media outlets for a bargain price, then slashing the staff and reporting profits. Several notable examples link hedge fund purchases to major newsroom layoffs.[30] A major concern is that this new class of owners is likely to accelerate the already ongoing declines in the nation's news-reporting capacity.[31]

Under more concentrated parent company ownership structures, content may be less subject to audience preferences but is more vulnerable to owner influence over content.[32] One owner or family has a limited set of ideological or issue preferences that are easily handed down or inferred by editors and journalists, making control over content much easier than for a large group of diverse shareholders. When shareholders have competing or varied ideas, this somewhat frees editors and journalists from top-down pressure.

The ten largest media owners as ranked in 2019 reflect a mix of conglomerates, publicly and privately owned media companies, and hedge fund owners (see Table 2-3).

The Costs and Benefits of Big Business Control

Strong trends toward consolidation in the media industry have given a few very large organizations a great deal of control over the news that reaches the American public.[33] Is it sound public policy to allow such consolidation? Does it bring undesirable uniformity and lead to neglect of local needs? Does it prevent diverse viewpoints from reaching the public? In short, what are the advantages and disadvantages of big business control over substantial portions of the public's news supply?

On the plus side of the ledger, producing television programs and gathering news worldwide are expensive tasks. Only large, well-financed organizations capable of spreading their costs are able to spread their costs over many customers can provide the lavish media fare that attracts ample audiences. Compared to small, individually owned enterprises, large enterprises can more readily absorb the losses that are often incurred in producing expensive documentaries and public service programs. Large enterprises also can spend more money on talented people, research, investigations, and costly entertainment shows. Nonetheless, these advantages are bought at a high price. The brilliant, full spectrum of viewpoints that could be available has been contracted and grayed, and fresh new talents have far fewer opportunities to come to the fore.

Until more recently, many of the worst fears about the consequences of big business dominance have proved largely groundless. For years, media mergers generated little systematic change in the uniformity of news; the simultaneous multiplication of cable, satellite, and internet television diversified the media marketplace in some respects, even if not to the extent once anticipated.[34] Nor was there solid evidence that media giants squelch antibusiness news or uniformly and routinely favor conservative political orientations.[35] For example, there has been ample antibusiness news that has tarnished such business giants as Microsoft, Nike, Wal-Mart, Merck, and the major tobacco companies.[36] However, while we know what was covered, outside the newsroom, it is difficult to know much about what stories were squelched.

More evident is that serious news has been increasingly replaced by "infotainment" in the wake of mergers of news enterprises with entertainment giants, especially when the public prefers such shows to hard news

Table 2-3 Ten Largest Owners in 2019, Ranked by Number of Papers Owned

Rank	Owner Name	Owner Type	Total Papers	Daily Papers	Total Circulation
1.	Gannett/ Gatehouse	Public/ Investment	613	262	8,596,000
2.	Digital First/ Tribune	Public/ Investment	207	70	5,163,000
3.	Lee/BH Media	Public/ Investment	170	84	2,464,000
4.	Adams Publishing Group	Private	158	40	1,233,000
5.	CNHI	Investment	112	71	993,000
6.	Ogden Newspapers	Private	84	49	851,000
7.	Paxton Media Group	Private	75	42	575,000
8.	Boone Newspapers	Private	65	29	458,000
9.	Community Media Group	Private	57	14	331,000
10.	Landmark Media Enterprises	Private	55	3	443,000

Source: Abernathy, P. M. (2020). The new media giants. *Hussman School of Journalism and Media, University of North Carolina.* https://www.usnewsdeserts.com/reports/news-deserts-and-ghost-newspapers-will-local-news-survive/the-news-landscape-in-2020-transformed-and-diminished/the-new-media-giants/.

offerings. Further, studies suggest that the various business configurations of for-profit media outlets do shape their profit orientations, the degree to which they focus on local issues, and the amount of hard news they offer. The jury is still out on whether an ample supply of hard news or an adequate diversity of viewpoints remains available when also taking into account the news available on cable stations, news radio, and the internet, but the subject is hotly debated.[37]

Despite that many of the original fears about consolidation proved groundless, two recent trends have raised or revived concerns among critics of consolidation. Research from Penelope Muse Abernathy at the UNC Hussman School of Journalism and Media shows that despite numerous closures and steeply declining circulation among local newspapers, newspaper-owning chains are larger than ever (Figure 2-2). A report from early 2020 predicted continued growth and consolidation, including the formation of "highly leveraged mega-chains formed by the union of large publicly traded newspaper companies with large hedge funds and private equity chains."[38] The report also documents continued growth among privately held regional newspaper chains. Media watchers find these trends troubling for several reasons. First, this kind of substantial consolidation in the news industry shifts many editorial decisions to a handful of people running a few very large corporations. Second, these large, centralized corporations are removed from (and lack strong ties with) the local communities in which their papers are located. This reduces their ability to understand and meet the information needs of local communities and their citizens. Third, continued consolidation with large, publicly traded chains and hedge fund owners means more ownership and control by those ownership types most associated with massive newsroom layoffs and prioritizing profits over gathering and reporting the news.

For the most part, concerns about consolidation revolve around its possible detrimental effects on localism and diversity of perspectives. However, one growing media chain, Sinclair Broadcasting (Photo 2-1), has been controversial due to more than its efforts to rapidly acquire media properties across numerous markets. Sinclair has also drawn sharp criticism for its lack of localism in coverage and its ideologically tinged editorial practices in which the owners require their affiliates to insert right-leaning editorial content—now called *must-run* segments—into the local news program without acknowledging on air that the material is mandated from the top-down. A now infamous video clip from 2018 shows anchors from thirty of 294 Sinclair affiliate stations simultaneously parroting identically worded complaints about liberal media bias. These must-run segments were also the subject of a scathing commentary on HBO's *John Oliver, Last Week Tonight*.[39] While Americans and the professional norms of journalism have grown more accommodating to partisan news programming since the arrival of cable, many would prefer local television news to remain focused

Photo 2-1 Sinclair Broadcasting in Spotlight After Viral Video Shows Local TV Anchors Reading Identical Script Lambasting Fake News

Source: Photo by Win McNamee/Getty Images.

on what's relevant to the local community and less steeped in national partisan politics. The fact that Sinclair already owns 186 stations in 87 markets makes any surreptitious insertions of ideological content troubling.[40]

Obviously, current policies designed to reduce media concentration and encourage local programming have failed to meet their objectives. The merits of these policies must be reconsidered, keeping in mind the media's mandate to serve the public interests of a democratic society. It has also become clear over many decades that most efforts to put broadcast media into a regulatory harness are doomed to fail because owners with major stakes in this business sector maintain close ties with high-level politicians who need their support for winning public office and promoting policies.

The Impact of New Media on the Media Marketplace

Digital media continues to have a marked impact on the structure and behavior of news media enterprises, providing alternative avenues for both news consumers and political elites. These avenues not only provide emerging sources of news for the public but outlets for public officials or other parties to circumvent mainstream media. Newsmakers and ordinary citizens alike are increasingly adept at using digital and social media to get their message directly out to the public without any filtering from the mainstream media[41] and at successfully highjacking or controlling the media narrative. The Trump presidency showcased these trends well. During the 2016 election, Donald Trump was highly effective on social media in two ways: first by racking up a huge following on social media and second by earning constant coverage of his tweets on traditional media. Trump earned 12 million Facebook likes compared to Clinton's 7.8 million, had 12.9 million Twitter followers to Clinton's 10.2 million, and issued 33,000 tweets to Clinton's 9,500.[42] The 2016 election also showcased a more sinister use of digital and social media—the purposive dissemination of fake news. Throughout the Trump administration and the 2020 presidential campaign, social media remained central to presidential and candidate communications. Early contenders for the Democratic nomination used social media platforms to announce candidacies and campaign appearances and to work toward the general goal of seeming relatable and authentic, albeit with mixed success.[43]

The term *digital media* refers to the growing number of electronic forms of communication made possible through computer technologies. These include microblogging (or blogging), content sharing, and social networking websites such as Twitter, YouTube, Facebook, Instagram, TikTok, Likee, and Snapchat, most of which dabble in news and politics while primarily functioning as social networking.[44] Use of social media for news among adults remains high but is no longer growing. In 2016, roughly 60% of U.S. adults reported getting news on social media and nearly 20% reported doing so often. Recently, this trend has reversed, possibly due to declining trust in information on the platforms, with more Americans getting digital news on websites or apps (68%) or search engines (65%) than social media (53%). One source of continued growth is mobile news use. A large majority of Americans—at 86%—report getting their news on a digital device sometimes (26%) or often (60%), while only 68% say the same of television.[45] (See Figure 2-1.)

The most profound effect of the new media on the news media business springs from the multiplication of outlets that distribute news and other forms of content. This trend of media fragmentation or expanding media choice means that, in combination, there are nearly as many providers of digital news as potential consumers of their services. Now, thanks to mobile technology, these channels and platforms are available to most people all the time. This imbalance between supply and demand has created a chaotic marketplace in which news suppliers compete for audiences and advertisers in novel ways. Many traditional media institutions have been

Figure 2.1   Modes for News Consumption Among
                    U.S. Adults, 2020

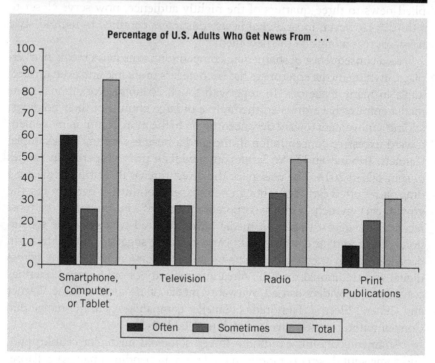

Percentage of U.S. Adults Who Get News From . . .

Often   Sometimes   Total

Smartphone, Computer, or Tablet — Television — Radio — Print Publications

Source: Adapted from Shearer, E. (2021, January 12). More than eight-in-ten Americans get news from digital devices. *Pew Research Center.* https://www.pewresearch.org/fact-tank/2021/01/12/more-than-eight-in-ten-americans-get-news-from-digital-devices/. Report is based on data from a survey of U.S. adults conducted August 31–Sept 7, 2020.

weakened by the struggle—local newspapers in particular—and some have succumbed as we have discussed.[46] But there are many survivors, and some of them, such as local and network television news, remain popular.[47] The coronavirus outbreak and associated downturn had variable effects on media industries, hitting newspapers hard while providing a much-needed shot in the arm for television news (See Figure 2-2).[48]

The vast majority of digital media news providers produce very few, if any, original stories. They largely feed off news collected by the traditional media, who use their shrinking corps of journalists to report ongoing events. This is yet another reason why the declining ranks in the American newspaper reporting capacity is troubling. New media news distributors elaborate stories gathered by old media, often interpreting them from distinct perspectives. They have captured fragments of old media audiences. The three original networks—ABC, CBS, and NBC—which once supplied news to three-quarters of the nightly audience, now serve closer to a third.[49] However, most digital news consumers continue to use old-style news sources alongside the new media.

As a consequence of sharpening competition in the news media marketplace, owning media enterprises has become less profitable and even unprofitable in many instances. To cope with tough economic conditions, some media empires have divested themselves of large chunks of their holdings, adding a movement toward deconcentration to the more common movement toward excessive concentration in the media business sector. For example, Gannett, Tribune, and E. W. Scripts dumped their print properties in a series of spin-offs in 2014. The reason for the divestitures is that print media are a drag on reported earnings. Though newspapers continue to earn profits, the growth isn't enough to satisfy corporate investors.[50] Unfortunately, the most recent data suggest that print media have not fared well since the separation relative to their counterparts.[51] And evidence suggests that the trend in deconcentration was a short one—more consolidation is occurring across digital and traditional media.[52] Already, a majority of online news offerings come from providers owned by twenty media titans such as Time Warner and General Electric. Hundreds of smaller companies share the remainder. Concentration remains alive and well (see Table 2-3).

Strained economic conditions forced some old media into bankruptcy, and some shut down operations in the face of impending financial collapse. Still others sharply cut costs by sharing resources, trimming staffs and the scope of news gathering, and shutting down bureaus, especially abroad. The upshot is a reduction in the scope and quality of coverage of serious news and an increase in human-interest stories that are inexpensive to produce.[53]

The growth of digital media has thinned out traditional media, but many survive and continue to innovate. As in previous communications revolutions, newcomers—such as the telephone, radio, or television in earlier ages—have forced the industry to adjust; they have not wiped them out.[54] Traditional media eventually learned many ways to adapt new technologies to their own needs. For example, newspapers, along with television and cable stations, have created websites and mobile apps and have cultivated a sustained presence on social media. The news collected for the traditional enterprise now does double duty by serving the needs of the digital platforms as well. In fact, much of the information collected by reporters that the traditional media could not publish in the past because

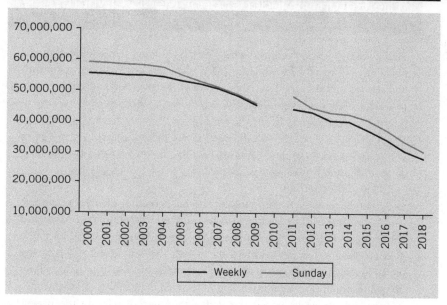

Figure 2.2   Total Estimated Circulation of U.S. Daily Newspapers, 2000–2018

Source: Adapted from Newspapers fact sheet. (2021, June 29). *Pew Research Center.* https://www.journalism.org/fact-sheet/newspapers/.

Notes: Data for 2000–2014 were obtained from Editor & Publisher; data for 2015–2018 are based on estimates from Pew Research Center analysis of Alliance for Audited Media (AAM) data. Data are missing for 2010. For 2015 onward, researchers analyzed the year-over-year change in total weekday and Sunday circulation using AAM data and applied these percentage changes to the previous year's total. Only those daily U.S. newspapers that report to AAM are included; affiliated publications are not included in the analysis. Weekday circulation only includes those publications reporting a Monday–Friday average. For each year, the comparison is for all newspapers meeting these criteria for the three-month period ending Dec. 31 of the given year. Comparisons are between the three-month averages for the period ending Dec. 31 of the given year and the same period of the previous year.

of space and time constraints is now available on the Web and is often distributed via links through the organizations' or journalists' Twitter feeds. It enriches the old-style media because they can refer audience members to the expanded offerings. In addition, digital platforms allow dissemination of breaking news when it happens, rather than waiting for scheduled editions and broadcasts, which restores the traditional media's scooping ability. They can once again be the first to break a story.

Box 2-1
The Return of Independent Media Owners?

Media observers were intrigued when Amazon founder Jeff Bezos announced in August 2013 that he would buy *The Washington Post*. With his vast wealth and technological know-how, the hope was that Bezos could chart a path forward for the newspaper business, which was in steep decline because of internet-driven changes in advertising and readership patterns.

Three years later, the *Post* emerged as a notable success story, reporting that it had achieved profitability even as it had increased its costs by adding some 140 journalists to its newsroom.[1]

How did Bezos do it?

First, he resolved a long-standing internal debate about whether the *Post* should be a regional or a national newspaper by repositioning the *Post* as a national digital news source. Online traffic grew exponentially, and for much of 2016, the *Post* competed head-to-head with *The New York Times* in having the largest digital audience of any American newspaper—about 100 million unique visitors per month, according to the web metrics firm comScore.[2]

Second, Bezos leveraged the *Post* with Amazon, offering the paper's national digital edition—an inexpensive magazine-like app for tablets and mobile devices—at reduced rates through Amazon Prime and on the Kindle Fire. This was no doubt a key to what the *Post* claimed was a rapid increase in paid digital subscribers (it does not report subscriber data).

At a public forum in October 2016, Bezos explained his strategy for the *Post* in terms reminiscent of the "get big fast" philosophy he had embraced in building Amazon into a retail behemoth:

> We need to move from making a relatively large amount of money
> per reader on a relatively small number of readers . . . to a model
> where we make a very small amount of money per reader on a
> much much larger number of readers.[3]

But perhaps Bezos's most important step was that he chose to run the *Post* as a privately owned institution. Over the course of several decades, hundreds of daily newspapers had been acquired by publicly traded corporations, many of which eliminated jobs in their newsrooms in order to boost earnings for the benefit of their shareholders. The legendary Graham family, from whom Bezos purchased the *Post*, had taken the *Post* public in the 1970s and thus had to answer to Wall Street and its demands for quarterly profits. Although the Grahams were dedicated to the view that journalism was a public trust, they lacked the freedom that Bezos had to take the long view and build the *Post* as he saw fit.

Under executive editor Martin Baron, a Graham holdover retained by Bezos, the *Post* was fearless in covering the 2016 presidential campaign, breaking big stories about dubious practices at the Clinton and Trump foundations and revealing the existence of a tape on which Donald Trump was heard bragging about sexually assaulting women. Trump banned the *Post* and several other news organizations from his campaign events and threatened to investigate Amazon's tax status.

A wealthy, independent newspaper owner can afford to stand up to power—provided they are willing to do so. Referring to a crude threat against then-publisher Katharine Graham delivered by one of Richard Nixon's henchmen, John Mitchell, during the Watergate scandal, Bezos once said, "I have a lot of very sensitive and vulnerable body parts. If need be, they can all go through the wringer rather than do the wrong thing."[4]

During an era when the role and credibility of the news media have come under increasing attack, news organizations such as the *Post*, and tough-minded owners such as Bezos, will prove to be essential in standing up to political pressure so they can meet the information needs of the public in a democratic society.

---

1. For an in-depth discussion of *The Washington Post* under Jeff Bezos, see Kennedy, D. (2016, June 8). The Bezos effect: How Amazon's founder is reinventing *The Washington Post*—and what lessons it might hold for the beleaguered newspaper business. *Shorenstein Center on Media, Politics, and Public Policy.* https://shorensteincenter.org/bezos-effect-washington-post. The *Post*'s claim that it had achieved profitability came in the form of a message to the staff from publisher Frederick Ryan; Beaujon, A. (2016, December 13). *The Washington Post* says it was profitable in 2016. *Washingtonian.* https://www.washingtonian.com/2016/12/13/washington-post-profitable-2016.

2. *The Washington Post* records nearly 100 million visitors in October, greatly exceeding previous traffic records. (2016, November 14). *The Washington Post.* https://www.washingtonpost.com/pr/wp/2016/11/14/the-washington-post-records-nearly-100-million-visitors-in-october-greatly-exceeding-previous-traffic-records/?utm_term=.abcb0 1f14513

(Continued)

Privatization is another major consequence of new media proliferation. When media properties are owned by publicly traded corporations, bottom-line concerns are paramount. If their published reports show that the media segments of the business are not as profitable as expected, management feels pressured to change the situation, often at the expense of the quality of media offerings. Such unwelcome pressures have produced a trend to privatize major media. Jeff Bezos's purchase of *The Washington Post* is a noteworthy example (see Box 2-1). While privatized media ultimately need to be economically viable so they can pay their operating costs, they are not forced to show the large profit margins to which media owners have been accustomed in the past. They also are less subject to public scrutiny, making media operations less transparent.

Further loosening of the economic constraints that currently hobble news media operations may be in the offing. Wealthy philanthropists such as Bezos have indicated their willingness to operate high-quality media on a break-even basis or to subsidize their operations. One subsidy example is ProPublica, a nonprofit investigative service that develops news stories and then offers them free to existing news organizations or assists news organizations in developing their own stories.[55] That is an exciting development because it points to a move away from news media as profit-making businesses to a system of media focused on public service that deserves support from private philanthropies. Yet we must remember that any major change in the system of media financing will not change the age-old fact that whoever pays the piper controls the tune. We can only guess what the new tune would be.

Media Influence Variables: Prestige, Market Size, and Competition

One cannot judge the sweep of control exercised by any group of news media owners merely by looking at the number of outlets. Three additional factors need to be considered: prestige of each media institution, market size, and competition within the market. The prestige a media enterprise enjoys is an important component of its political influence. Journalism has widely accepted standards of professionalism, as do law, medicine, and engineering. As part of this system of norms, certain members and products are accepted widely as models for the profession. Other news professionals watch what information the high-prestige news organizations present, how they present it, and what interpretations they give to it; they then adjust their own presentations accordingly. Critics derisively call this the "jackal syndrome" or "pack journalism." For political news, *The New York Times* is the lion whom the jackals follow. In television, major networks are models for the profession, strengthening the trend toward news uniformity. The many voices in the media marketplace sing in unison much of the time. Newcomers quickly join the chorus and hum the tunes orchestrated by the prestige leadership.

Media enterprises also gain influence based on the size of their market rather than the total number of markets accessible. The hundreds of newspaper and broadcast markets in the United States vary widely in audience size. In such major metropolitan areas as New York, Chicago, or Los Angeles, a market with a fifty-mile radius may have a population of several million. The same radius for a station in Wyoming might cover more cows than people. In the digital era, metrics of audience size and influence are based on unique visitors to websites, minutes per site visit, minutes per site visitor, audience reach, and click-through rates.

Competition within most media markets used to be quite limited. A single newspaper and a handful of radio and television stations were the rule. That picture changed dramatically in the wake of technology advances. Nonetheless, most Americans still get the bulk of their political news from mainstream television, although digital news consumption has surpassed newspapers and radio as sources of public affairs news, and news websites continue to see the most audience growth.[56] It still means something to have extensive reach in local media markets through traditional media outlets. The extent to which market-level media concentration will remain an issue of concern will depend on future patterns of consolidation across digital media companies and traditional media companies.

Another factor to consider in gauging the influence of various media enterprises is the composition of their audiences in terms of age, education, and income (see Box 2-2 for an examination of news audience demographics). However, numbers may be deceptive because the fragmentation of news channels and the multiplication of news content on entertainment programs make it hard to judge people's news sources. Evidence shows that most Americans who consume news on social media also get news from a variety of other sources. It is important to recall that much of the internet consumption is done via website or app-based versions of mainstream newspapers and television.

Box 2-2
Audiences Under the Microscope

Demographic differences matter hugely when it comes to audiences for various types of media. This is especially true in the digital era. Not only are there large age differences across users of digital and traditional media, but there are also vast differences across social media and manner of access. For example, 41% of social media users ages 30 to 49 get news on Facebook, compared to 22% of 18- to 29-year-olds. On Instagram, that pattern is reversed: 47% of the 18–29 bracket get news on Instagram compared to only 37% of those ages 30–49.[1] The maturing young—mid-20s to mid-30s—are most prized by news organizations. That age group is likely to have reasonably good income in various job categories and to spend a good portion of it on big-ticket purchases such as furniture, appliances, electronics, and cars. Garnering young families as audience members equates to attracting advertisers who are willing to pay high rates for the chance to reach as many young eyeballs and readily opened, full wallets as possible.

Of course, not all media venues cater to the young. There are venues that cater to older audiences, to partisan audiences, to the prosperous, to the politically sophisticated, and to many others. Given that preferences for news varies to some degree along demographic lines, targeted offerings that cater to specific needs and likes are a good thing. It also makes it essential to be knowledgeable about the range of tastes for news among Americans.

Figure 2-3 is instructive. In 2018, digital advertising surpassed non-digital advertising for the first time. It reflects, among other things, the great migration of audiences to mobile devices, especially among young people. Ad dollars follow the habits of audiences.

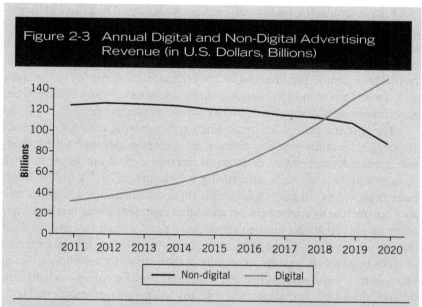

Figure 2-3 Annual Digital and Non-Digital Advertising Revenue (in U.S. Dollars, Billions)

Source: Adapted from Digital news fact sheet. (2021, July 27). *Pew Research Center.* https://www.journalism.org/fact-sheet/digital-news/. Data obtained by Pew Research Center from eMarketer, U.S. Ad Spending Estimates.

1. Shearer, E., & Mitchell, A. (2021, January 12). News use across social media platforms in 2020. *Pew Research Center.* https://www.journalism.org/2021/01/12/news-use-across-social-media-platforms-in-2020/.

New Ways to Pay for News

The decline in readers, viewers, and listeners brought about by audience defections to the internet plunged the legacy media into serious financial difficulties. This is particularly the case for the print media, where bankruptcies became common during the recession that started in 2007. Many newspapers went out of business entirely; others cut back on the number of publication days, and still others abandoned their hard copy operations and published Web versions only. Nearly all companies, including flagship enterprises, cut staff, reduced the scope of news gathering, and replaced hard news with cheaper, softer news in hopes of retaining their dwindling audiences. Still, profits continued to plunge. The financial shocks led to reconsideration of the main financial underpinnings of the private sector press in the United States, based on the firm belief that the news values of old-style journalism must survive.

First, a look at the traditional financial structures: The pillars of financing for a profit-reliant press are advertiser support, audience payments, and government subsidies. Each has different policy consequences, which become blurred when they are used in combination, as is common. Print media, for example, are financed by the price audiences pay for newspapers and, more importantly, by revenue from advertisers. They also received government subsidies in the form of below-cost mailing rates.

The revenue system fell apart when earnings from advertising, which are pegged to audience size, plunged as audiences defected to the internet. Some advertisers also defected to internet outlets but never in large enough numbers to make advertising a financial pillar for online information providers. In fact, outlets with small audiences, or audiences that are unattractive to advertisers because they represent small markets, may never be able to attract enough sponsors to pay for their operations. That then raises questions about who, in the long run, will pay for the expenses of website news operations, especially if they strive for excellence. Good journalism is expensive. What will happen if the alternative—reliance on unpaid, unskilled, and unaccountable amateurs—proves unacceptable in the long run? More recently, several prominent news organizations began charging for access to their digital content. Configurations of the pricing and delivery methods vary widely, and there is little evidence as yet about which of these new business models will prove successful.

To cope with reduced revenues, traditional media tried to cut costs in various ways. These include news-sharing arrangements, drastic staffing cuts, and combining multiplatform operations.[57] As mentioned, the legacy networks also expanded into their own Web enterprises, so the same news production operation can serve traditional and new media platforms. Journalism training has changed accordingly, forcing new graduates to become adept in handling traditional and emerging formats.

Most new media broadcast facilities, along with cable television, rely heavily on audience payments. These generally take the form of monthly service charges for programs, plus installation or equipment charges. Additional programming may be available for a flat monthly rate or on a per-program basis. Service-charge financing for broadcasting is accepted abroad. In the United States, however, it initially met with resistance because good broadcast services were available everywhere free of charge. By the mid-1980s, much of the initial resistance to paying for broadcasts vanished. Many U.S. households were paying for special programs in addition to their standard monthly fees. Today, cable reaches most American households; the average number of channels per household is around 160.

A major social drawback of service charges for broadcasts is that poor families who need many of the specialized programs are unable to pay for them. Middle-income families, who already enjoy many social advantages, benefit most from the information resources available through new media platforms; low-income people who lack access fall further behind.[58] The problem can be reduced through government subsidies paid to cable and internet companies or directly to the poor. Direct payment to citizens seems preferable in that it avoids making media enterprises financially dependent on the government and thereby hampering their freedom of action.

The need for a new business model is clear when the I-beam of media financing—advertising money—no longer bears the load of expenses for news production and distribution and when people below middle-class economic status cannot afford service charges for news and entertainment. Newspapers are trying to stop the hemorrhaging in novel ways because website readers are not yet the financial equivalent of hard copy readers.[59] Other models for financing old and new media operations are government financing or financing by privately controlled foundations such as the Knight Foundation, help in news production from university centers such as those at Columbia University or Northwestern University, and grants from individual philanthropists such as billionaire George Soros. Another experimental model for investigative journalism involves the creation of freestanding research centers that employ professional reporters to cover particular types of news. Examples are the Center for Public Integrity in Washington, DC, and New York–based ProPublica. Such centers can operate in a way similar to their predecessor, the Associated Press (AP), which functions as a membership association. Payment of a membership fee entitles the member organization to use AP news reports. Instead of using membership fees, news-gathering associations, which usually are nonprofits, are operated by private entrepreneurs or by foundations. Their products can be available for a fee or they can be distributed free of charge. Such organizations can also produce particular stories on demand for news organizations that lack the resources to do the necessary work on their own. Regardless of the source of financial support, the financial supporters are likely to influence the thrust of the news product to some degree. That is an important consideration in deciding which model for financing high-quality news is best for preserving the independence of the press—be it the control methods of the past, the internet free-for-all model of citizen journalism, a government or nonprofit subsidized model, some form of subscription for access to news websites or payment for individual articles, or a mixture of several of these.

The Regulation/Deregulation Debate

When the FCC compared the number of broadcast news outlets available to Americans living in communities of various sizes at the dawn of the 21st century, it found that, on average, the number of outlets had more than tripled since 1960. Congress had ordered the research to ascertain whether it was time to scrap rules restricting companies from owning multiple news enterprises in the same market. The rules were designed to ensure that the limited number of broadcast frequencies would represent a wide spectrum of interests. The conclusion of majorities in Congress, hotly disputed by the minority, was that a substantial loosening of restrictions was in order because advancing technology has multiplied available channels. Besides, companies eager to increase their holdings claimed that economies of scale would allow them to improve their offerings. They would also be better able to compete with unregulated cable and satellite television and the internet.

Opponents of deregulation have pointed out that large conglomerates, such as Viacom and News Corporation, already control the most popular stations and often share programs and content across media holdings within the larger media parent company, contrary to the government's communication diversity goals. They also claim that loosening the existing restrictions encourages replacing local programming with bland, generic coverage suitable for large, diverse markets. The competition between giant corporations and smaller enterprises, similar to the fight between supermarkets and mom-and-pop grocery shops, invariably ends with the giants garnering most of the rights to exclusive stories and most of the advertising revenues while the smaller economic base crumbles.

Opponents of deregulation point out that deregulation of radio in 1996 led to a frenzy of mergers that ended with a handful of giant corporations, led by Clear Channel and Infiniti Broadcasting Corporation, dominating the industry. Clear Channel grew from 43 to more than 1,200 stations nationwide. Altogether, 21 companies had each acquired more than 40 stations.[60] Some observers hailed this development as beneficial to consumers because larger companies have more resources to produce sophisticated programming. Others condemned it as a major disaster that shrank the diversity of offerings and reduced experimentation and creativity.

Despite the strong pressures for deregulation in the United States at the dawn of the 21st century, the federal government continues to regulate private electronic media to ensure that they "serve the public interest, convenience, and necessity," as mandated by the Communications Act of 1934 and its 1996 counterpart. The FCC, a bipartisan body appointed by the president and confirmed by the Senate, handles most regulation.[61] The FCC was a seven-member body until the summer of 1984, when, for financial reasons, Congress downsized it to five commissioners. In 1986, the appointment term was shortened from seven to five years, ensuring faster turnover of commission personnel and greater control by the government. In theory, the commission is an independent regulatory body. In practice, congressional purse strings, public and industry pressures, and presidential control over appointment of new members, including naming the chair, have greatly curtailed the FCC's freedom of operation. The commission's independence is weakened also because its rulings can be appealed to the courts, which frequently overturn them. Conflicting political pressures from outside the agency as well as internal political pressures further limit FCC policy making, so it tends to be "a reactive rather than an innovative system sluggish to respond to change in its environment, particularly to technological change. . . . Clearly there are problems with this kind of policy making system."[62] On balance, the FCC's record of setting goals and enforcing its rules has earned it the reputation of being at best an ineffective watchdog over the public interest and at worst an industry-kept, pressure group–dominated lapdog.

The FCC controls only over-the-air television. Cable television and the internet have been excluded because they are considered *common carriers*—channels that carry information compiled by others rather than originating their own information. U.S. print media are also beyond the FCC's reach thanks to the press clause of the First Amendment. However, similar to cable and the internet, print media are subject to general laws such as those limiting monopolies and trusts. These regulations become operative when the eight largest firms in a particular type of business control more than half of the market and the twenty largest firms control three-quarters or more. Concentration in the news media business has remained substantially below these levels. The Justice Department does permit economically weak newspapers to combine their business and production facilities free from antitrust and monopoly restraints, as long as their news and editorial operations are kept separate.

FCC control takes four forms: rules limiting the number of stations owned or controlled by a single organization, examination of the goals and performance of stations as part of periodic licensing, rules mandating public service and local interest programs, and rules to protect individuals from damage caused by unfair media coverage. Although none of these rules prescribes specific content, all of them were designed to increase the chances that content would be diverse and of civic importance.

In practice, none of the rules have been effective enough to overcome the pull of political and market forces, including the dawning of the internet age. Despite the mushrooming of broadcast enterprises, the news diet that most Americans consume is surprisingly uniform, politically lightweight, and dominated by oligopolies. Licensing has become almost automatic with minimal quality controls. When processing licenses, the FCC usually looks at the mix of programs, the proportion of public service offerings, and the inclusion of programs geared to selected minorities and interests. It does not scrutinize the subject matter of broadcasts in detail.

Compared with regulatory agencies in other countries, even in western Europe, Canada, and Australia, the FCC controls the electronic media with a very light hand. The members of the FCC could, if they wished, rigorously define what constitutes "programming in the public interest." They could enforce FCC rulings more strictly and verify that stations are meeting their public service and local programming obligations before renewing their licenses. The threat of license withdrawal for rule violations could be used as a powerful deterrent to misbehavior and a strong guide to programming. That does not happen because political cross-pressures are strong, including the fear that FCC enforcement could impair press freedom. Besides, the FCC staff is much too small to cope with all their assigned duties. The FCC's performance in protecting individuals from unfair publicity has been somewhat stronger.

Other Media Controls

Given the FCC's relatively light touch, what are the other means of controlling mass media policies? Various special interest groups—typically associated groups from the media or advertising industry—have substantial political or financial interest in mass media policy. These lobbying groups represent one set of pressures on media policy; citizen lobbying groups provide another source.

Pressures by Media Associations and Advertisers

Media lobbies are another means of controlling mass media policies. Radio and television interests, especially the networks and their affiliated stations, are active lobbyists. Most belong to the National Association of Broadcasters (NAB), a Washington, DC, lobby that is powerful despite the diversity and often clashing interests of its members. A number of trade associations and publications also lobby, often at cross-purposes. For newspapers, the American Newspaper Publishers Association, now merged with several other press associations, has been one of the most prominent groups. These organizations try to influence appointments to the FCC and to guide public policies affecting new technologies that may threaten established systems or practices. For instance, the network lobbies for many years tried to stifle cable television and to acquire control over domestic satellites. The National Cable Television Association and the NAB have used members' stations to urge support for their policy recommendations. On other occasions, such as the passage of the Telecommunications Act of 1996, they have tried to downplay coverage that might arouse unwanted opposition. Presently, conditions are uncertain for anti-regulation advocates. The White House is no longer in the hands of a pro-business Republican. At the same time, revenues continue to decline in some sectors of traditional media, exemplifying the case for mechanisms to free up capital for innovation and investment. Media groups may be able to capitalize on these circumstances to win the day for further deregulation.

To forestall regulation on content by outside bodies, the media industry has developed mechanisms for self-control. The NAB has had a radio code since 1929 and a television code since 1952 that set rules on program content and form. The NAB modernizes both codes periodically. Individual codes in major broadcast enterprises and codes adopted by the Council of Better Business Bureaus have supplemented or superseded industrywide codes. Print press self-policing has developed along similar lines. Scholars, too, have set forth codes of journalism ethics.

Most codes are quite vague, mandating honesty, fairness, independence, and concern for the public interest. Media outlets then decide what these principles mean in practice. Overall, the impact of industrywide codes has been limited. They typically apply only to organization members that explicitly subscribe to them. Penalties for code violations have been minimal. The codes have been useful in blunting demands by pressure groups for government intervention to set and enforce standards. For instance, congressional leaders lifted a threat to pass laws limiting excessively violent and sexually explicit shows on programs available to children in return for industry promises to develop a rating system to guide parents.

In the 1970s, advertisers began to influence program content by withdrawing their commercials from programs they considered obscene or excessively violent. Sears Roebuck was one of the earliest and largest advertisers to do so. McDonald's, American Express, and AT&T refused to place commercials on such shows. Other large advertisers, such as Procter & Gamble, retained consultants to seek out acceptable programs for their advertisements and avoid unacceptable ones. With advertisements on such top-rated shows as the Super Bowl yielding millions per thirty-second spot, threats of withdrawal have had some impact on programming.[63]

While reductions in programs featuring sex and violence have been welcome, other changes have been problematic. There is deep concern that advertisers, spurred by pressure groups, may become unofficial censors. For instance, General Motors canceled its sponsorship of an Easter program on the life of Jesus because evangelical groups objected to the content. A CBS documentary on gun control, opposed by the gun control lobby, suffered crippling withdrawals of advertising. Fearing similar punishments from fundamentalist religious groups, the networks have refused advertising designed to instruct viewers about the use of condoms for protection against unwanted pregnancies and AIDS. Such unofficial censorship at the behest of advertisers impairs press freedom.

Citizen Lobby Control

Citizens' efforts to affect the quality of broadcasting began in earnest in 1966, when the Office of Communication of the United Church of Christ, a public interest lobby, challenged the license renewal of WLBT-TV in Jackson, Mississippi, accusing the station of discriminating against African American viewers.[64] At the time, 45% of Jackson's population was African American. The challenge failed, but it was the beginning of efforts by many other citizens groups to challenge license renewals.

Citizen groups won a major victory in 1975 when the FCC refused to renew the licenses of eight educational television stations in Alabama and denied a construction permit for a ninth because citizen lobbies had charged racial discrimination in employment at the stations. There also had been complaints that the stations unduly excluded programs dealing with affairs of the African American community.[65] Since then, numerous stations have yielded to pressure for increased minority employment and programming rather than face legal action. It is one of many examples that demonstrate that the threat of legal action is a powerful stimulant of social behavior.

During the 1980s, many citizens groups formed to lobby for better programming and tighter government controls. They represented a broad array of ideological viewpoints and a variety of demographic groups. Despite the substantial impact of such groups on FCC rule-making and licensing procedures, citizen lobbying efforts at the national level have declined somewhat since the 1980s and have never regained their original vigor. One reason has been the difficulty of sustaining citizen interest over time; others were lack of financial support and loss of leadership. The broadcast lobby defeated efforts to obtain public funding for citizens' lobby groups, and foundation support has dried up. Many groups also were discouraged when an appeals court reversed substantial victories won in the lower courts and when the U.S. Supreme Court voided the 1996 Communications Decency Act.[66] Some citizens' groups have redirected their energy into local lobbying to ensure that cable systems in their locality serve the interests of various publics at reasonable prices to consumers.

In addition to the more than sixty organizations concerned exclusively with media reform, other organizations, such as the Parent–Teacher Association (PTA), the National Organization for Women, and the American Medical Association, have lobbied intermittently on a variety of media issues. They have shown concern about stereotyping, access to media coverage and to media employment and ownership, advertising on children's programs, and enforcement of FCC program regulations. The groups' tactics include monitoring media content, publicizing their findings, and pressuring broadcasters, advertisers, media audiences, and government control agencies. PTA members have pressured advertisers, who in turn have succeeded in reducing the number of violent programs shown in the early evening. Legal maneuvers have ranged from challenges of license renewals to damage suits for the harmful effects of media content.

Assessing the precise influence of these organizations is difficult because many of their goals overlap with other forces that affect media policy. Some of the causes for which they have worked, such as measures fostering good programming for children, have prospered over the years, however, and part of the credit undoubtedly belongs to them. Yet these groups have a long road to travel before they can match the influence enjoyed by the broadcast lobby in protecting its interests even when they run counter to the concerns of many citizens.

SUMMARY

We have examined the most common types of ownership and control of the news media in this chapter. While most of the media establishment is in private sector hands, the federal government plays an important role as well. It owns and operates vast overseas radio and television enterprises and partially controls a far-flung system of domestic public television and radio broadcasting that provides an alternative to commercial programming. For the average American, the government-controlled systems are peripheral, and privately owned print and electronic media enterprises are the focus of concern.

The major political problems in the private sector are concentration of ownership of media in the hands of large business conglomerates and concentrated control over the production of news and entertainment programs. Scrutiny of the impact of the existing system on the quality of the news showed that business ownership has enhanced the focus on soft news and entertainment at the expense of serious political news that citizens need to perform their political roles. But it has not led to programming dominated by business perspectives, as many observers feared, nor has coverage of local news withered in the wake of media mergers. Large enterprises, rather than small ones, have excelled in providing news and entertainment.

In this chapter, we have also outlined the major changes in the news media system spawned by the mushrooming of novice news providers that populate and crowd the internet. We found that as yet, the newcomers have remained a limited influence. The traditional media, thanks to creating their own digital content and strategically acquiring some of the more popular newcomers, are retaining their market dominance. In addition, we examined the regulatory structures created by the federal government to ensure a diverse supply of information. We found that enforcement of regulations has been weak, primarily because it is a political football kept in play by multiple powerful stakeholders.

The multiplicity of influences at work in making news and entertainment programs makes it impossible to assess the precise impact of those influences on media content in general or even on a particular story. In the next chapter, we will focus on major aspects of news production for additional clues to the mystery of what shapes the news.

DISCUSSION QUESTIONS ─────────────

1. How are public, semipublic, and private media different? Which form dominates the U.S. media system? What are the potential drawbacks and benefits for the nature of our media system?

2. What are the different forms of private media ownership? Which of these forms are most common, on the rise, or in decline in the U.S.? Are there any trends about which we should be concerned? Why or why not?

3. What are the various factors that have influence over the content of news? Which factors do you think matter most? Are there any factors or resulting patterns in coverage to be particularly concerned about?

4. Why has media regulation and deregulation been such as source of debate in the U.S.? Who are the stakeholders, and which side seems to be winning or losing?

5. What are some of the other forces, beyond regulation and economics, that attempt to control media? Have they reached any level of success over the years? Do you expect the influence of these sources (or any others) to continue in the years to come? Why or why not?

READINGS

Ali, C. (2017). *Media localism: The policies of place*. University of Illinois Press.

Berry, M. (2019). *The media, the public and the great financial crisis*. Springer.

Birkinbine, B., Gómez, R., & Wasko, J. (Eds.). (2016). *Global media giants*. Routledge.

Campbell, R., Martin, C. R., & Fabos, B. (2015). *Media and culture: An introduction to mass communication* (10th ed.). Bedford/St. Martin's.

Hamilton, J. T. (2004). *All the news that's fit to sell: How the market transforms information into news*. Princeton University Press.

Hill, F. B., & Broening, S. (2016). *The life of kings: The Baltimore Sun and the golden age of the American newspaper*. Rowman & Littlefield.

Kennedy, D. (2013). *The wired city: Reimagining journalism and civic life in the post-newspaper age*. University of Massachusetts Press.

Kohl, U. (2017). *The net and the nation state: Multidisciplinary perspectives on Internet governance*. University of Chicago Press.

Napoli, P. M. (2007). *Media diversity and localism: Meaning and metrics*. Lawrence Erlbaum.

Napoli, P. M. (2011). *Audience evolution: New technologies and the transformation of media audiences*. Columbia University Press.

Napoli, P. M. (2019). *Social media and the public interest: Media regulation in the disinformation age*. Columbia University Press.

Pickard, V. (2015). *America's battle for media democracy: The triumph of corporate libertarianism and the future of media reform*. Cambridge University Press.

Ponce de Leon, C. L. (2015). *That's the way it is: A history of television news in America*. University of Chicago Press.

Schlosberg, J. (2016). *Media ownership and agenda control: The hidden limits of the information age*. Routledge.

Webster, J. (2016). *The marketplace of attention: How audiences take shape in a digital age*. MIT Press.

Wu, I. S. (2015). *Forging trust communities: How technology changes politics*. Johns Hopkins University Press.

NOTES

1. Schulhofer-Wohl, S., & Garrido, M. (2013). Do newspapers matter? Short-run and long-run evidence from the closure of *The Cincinnati Post*. *Journal of Media Economics*, 26(2), 60–81; Rubado, M. E., & Jennings, J. T. (2019). Political consequences of the endangered local watchdog: Newspaper decline and mayoral elections in the United States. *Urban Affairs Review*. https://doi .org/10.1177%2F1078087419838058; Gentzkow, M., Shapiro, J. M., & Sinkinson, M. (2011). The effect of newspaper entry and exit on electoral politics. *American Economic Review*, 101(7), 2980–3018.

2. Campante, F., & Do, Q.-A. (2014). Isolated capital cities, accountability and corruption: Evidence from U.S. States. *American Economic Review*, 104, 2456–2481.

3. Snyder, J., & Stromberg, D. (2010). Press coverage and political accountability. *Journal of Political Economy*, 118, 355–408. https://www.journals.uchicago .edu/doi/10.1086/652903

4. Hayes, D., & Lawless, J. (2015). As local news goes, so goes citizen engagement: Media, knowledge, and participation in U.S. House elections. *Journal of Politics*, 77, 447–462. https://www.journals.uchicago.edu/doi/10.1086/679749; Hopkins, D. J. (2018). *The increasingly United States: How and why American political behavior nationalized*. University of Chicago Press.

5. Trussler, M. (2020). Get information or get in formation: The effects of high-information environments on legislative elections. *British Journal of Political Science*, 1–21; Peterson, E. (2019). Paper cuts: How reporting resources affect political news coverage. *American Journal of Political Science*. https://doi .org/10.1111/ajps.12560; Hayes, D., & Lawless, J. L. (2018). The decline of local news and its effects: New evidence from longitudinal data. *Journal of Politics*, 80(1), 332–336.

6. Hallin, D. C., & Mancini, P. (2004). *Comparing media systems: Three models of media and politics*. Cambridge University Press. This book describes different government control styles in selected Western democracies.

7. See the Top 10 lists maintained by Nielsen at http://www.nielsen.com/us/en/top-ten/. Examples of shows from the Top 10 (February 2021) are *Firefly Lane* (Netflix), *Bridgerton* (Netflix), *Wandavision* (Disney+), *The Crown* (Netflix), and *Longmire* (Netflix). Also see Hamilton, J. T. (2004). *All the news that's fit to sell: How the market transforms information into news*. Princeton University Press.

8. See Kleinman, A. (2017, December 6). Porn sites get more visitors each month than Netflix, Amazon and Twitter combined. *HuffPost*. https://www.huffpost .com/entry/internet-porn-stats_n_3187682.

9. Koblin, J. (2018, January 31). Trump's State of the Union ratings don't match Obama's (but beat the Grammys). *The New York Times*. https://www.nytimes

.com/2018/01/31/business/media/trumps-state-of-the-union-ratings-dont-match-obamas-but-beat-the-grammys.html

10. Bagdikian, B. H. (2004). *The new media monopoly*. Beacon Press; Picard, R. (2008). The challenges of public functions and commercialized media. In D. Graber, D. McQuail, & P. Norris (Eds.), *The politics of news, the news of politics* (2nd ed.). CQ Press. For a negative view of the "marketplace of ideas" concept, see Ginsberg, B. (1986). *The captive public: How mass opinion promotes state power*. Basic Books, pp. 98–148.

11. See VOA. (n. d.). *VOA history*. https://www.insidevoa.com/p/5829.html; VAOA. (n. d.). *About VOA*. https://www.insidevoa.com/p/5831.html.

12. See Corporation for Public Broadcasting. (n. d.). *About CPB*. https://www.cpb.org/aboutcpb

13. A content analysis of political discourse on PBS led to the conclusion that its stories focused primarily on the strategic aspects of domestic politics and the economy and featured the views of political elites, especially insiders drawn from the government and the business world. Hoynes, W. (2002). Political discourse and the "new PBS." *Press/Politics*, 7(4), 34–56.

14. See PBS National Sales. (2021). *Reach a quality audience*. https://www.pbs.org/sponsorship/audience/

15. See NPR Press Releases and Statements. (2020, November 11). NPR digital platforms see largest audience ever. *NPR*. https://www.npr.org/about-npr/933918860/npr-digital-see-largest-audience-ever

16. See National Public Media. (n. d.). *NPR audience*. https://www.nationalpublicmedia.com/Audience/#audiences

17. Wylie, J. (2020, February 10). Trump budge attain proposes zeroing out public broadcasting funds. *Current*. https://current.org/2020/02/trump-again-seeks-cpb-funding-cuts-in-proposed-budget/

18. Burlij, T. (2011, March 17). U.S. House votes to cut NPR funding. *PBS*. http://www.pbs.org/newshour/rundown/2011/03/us-house-votes-to-cut-npr-funding.html; Erb, K. P. (2012, October 4). Romney promises to cut taxpayer funding for PBS (but says he still loves Big Bird). *Forbes*, http://www.forbes.com/sites/kellyphillipserb/2012/10/04/romney-promises-to-cut-taxpayer-funding-for-pbs-but-says-he-still-loves-big-bird; Farhi, P. (2011, April 12). NPR, public television won't get budget ax. *The Washington Post*. http://www.washingtonpost.com/lifestyle/style/npr-public-television-wont-get-budget-ax/2011/04/12/AF5CtwSD_story.html. For an impassioned analysis of the trials and tribulations of U.S. public television, see Ledbetter, J. (1997). *Made possible by . . . the death of public broadcasting in the United States*. Verso.

19. Hansen, D. (2019, November 20). Gannett shareholders sign off on GateHouse deal. *Washington Business Journal.* https://www.bizjournals.com/washington/news/2019/11/14/gannett-shareholders-sign-off-on-gatehouse-deal.html

20. Mitchell, A., Holcomb, J., & Weisel, R. (2016, June). State of the news media 2016. *Pew Research Center.*

21. Mitchell, A., Holcomb, J., & Weisel, R. (2016, June). State of the news media 2016. *Pew Research Center.*

22. Media critic Dean Alger claims that quality deteriorates when papers are acquired by a chain; Alger, D. (1998). *Megamedia: How giant corporations dominate mass media, distort competition, and endanger democracy.* Rowman and Littlefield, pp. 180–182. Other research suggests that concentration of ownership and control influences editorial independence in the newsroom; Hanretty, C. (2014). Media outlets and their moguls: Why concentrated individual or family ownership is bad for editorial independence. *European Journal of Communication, 29*(3), 335–350. For a more recent example, see Martin, G. J., & McCrain, J. (2019). Local news and national politics. *American Political Science Review, 113*(2), 372–384.

23. Federal Communications Commission. (n. d.). [Website]. http://www.fcc.gov; see also Chester, J. (2002). Strict scrutiny: Why journalists should be concerned about new federal and industry deregulation proposals. *Press/Politics, 7*(2), 105–115.

24. Eggerton, J. (2016, November 30). Media alliance to Trump: Dump cross-ownership rules. *Broadcasting and Cable.* http://www.broadcastingcable.com/news/washington/media-alliance-trump-dump-cross-ownership-rules/161481

25. Bailard, C. S. (2016). Corporate ownership and news bias revisited: Newspaper coverage of the Supreme Court's *Citizens United* ruling. *Political Communication, 33*(4), 583–604.

26. Tribune Media. (2016, August 14). *Tribune Media company completes spin-off of its publishing business.* http://www.tribunemedia.com/tribune-media-company-completes-spin-off-of-its-publishing-business.

27. Foote, K. (2012, July 12). Brief history of DFW's crowded media market. *CBS DFW.* http://dfw.cbslocal.com/2012/07/12/ a-brief-history-of-a-crowded-dallasfort-worth-media-market. See also News Generation. (2016, April). *Top 100 media markets.* http://www.newsgeneration.com/broadcast-resources/top-100-radio-markets.

28. Hamilton, J. T. (2004). *All the news that's fit to sell: How the market transforms information into news.* Princeton University Press; Dunaway, J. (2013). Media ownership and story tone in campaign news coverage. *American Politics*

Research, 41, 24–53; Dunaway, J. (2008). Markets, ownership, and the quality of campaign news coverage. *Journal of Politics, 70*(4), 1193–1202.

29. Mullainathan, S., & Shleifer, A. (2005). the market for news. *American Economic Review, 95*(4), 1031–1053; Baron, D. P. (2006). Persistent media bias. *Journal of Public Economics, 90,* 1–36; Gentzkow, M., & Shapiro, J. (2010). What drives media slant? Evidence from U.S. daily newspapers. *Econometrica, 78*(1), 35–71.

30. Pompeo, J. (2020, February 5). The hedge fund vampire that bleeds newspapers dry now has *The Chicago Tribune* by the throat. *Vanity Fair.* https://www.vanityfair.com/news/2020/02/hedge-fund-vampire-alden-global-capital-that-bleeds-newspapers-dry-has-chicago-tribune-by-the-throat

31. Abernathy, P. M. (2020). *News deserts and ghost newspapers: Will local news survive?* University of North Carolina Press; Peterson, E., & Dunaway, J. (2020). *The new news barons: Investment ownership reduces newspaper reporting capacity.* Paper presented at the Annual Meeting of the American Political Science Association.

32. Hanretty, C. (2014). Media outlets and their moguls: Why concentrated individual or family ownership is bad for editorial independence. *European Journal of Communication, 29*(3), 335–350.

33. McAlone, N. (2016, November 11). Insiders say the 2017 "frenzy" of media consolidation predicted by vice's CEO is about to arrive: Here's why. *Business Insider.* http://www.businessinsider.com/2017-media-consolidation-frenzy-is-coming-2016-11

34. Benson, R. (2016). Institutional forms of media ownership and their modes of power. In M. Eide, L. O. Larsen, H. Sjøvaag (Eds.), *The journalistic institution reexamined.* Intellect; Hamilton, J. T. (2004). *All the news that's fit to sell: How the market transforms information into news.* Princeton University Press. For contrary views, see Alger, D. (1998). *Megamedia: How giant corporations dominate mass media, distort competition, and endanger democracy.* Rowman and Littlefield, pp. 153–194; McChesney, R. W. (1999). *Rich media, poor democracy.* New Press. See also McAllister, M. P., & Proffitt, J. M. (2020). Media ownership, autonomy, and democracy in a corporate age. In L. Wilkins & C. G. Christians (Eds.), *The Routledge handbook of mass media ethics,* p. 465; Humprecht, E., & Esser, F. Diversity in online news: On the importance of ownership types and media system types. *Journalism Studies, 19*(12), 1825–1847.

35. Bennett, L., & Cook, T. E. (1996). Journalism Norms and News Construction: Rules for Representing Politics. *Political Communication, 13*(4).

36. Manheim, J. B. (2001). *The death of a thousand cuts: Corporate campaigns and the attack on the corporation.* Erlbaum.

37. Dunaway, J. (2013). Media ownership and story tone in campaign news coverage. *American Politics Research*, *41*; Hindman, M. (2009). *The myth of digital democracy*. Princeton University Press.

38. Abernathy, P. M. (2020). *News deserts and ghost newspapers: Will local news survive?* University of North Carolina Press.

39. Last Week Tonight. (2017, July 3). *Sinclair Broadcast Group: Last Week Tonight with John Oliver (HBO)* [Video]. YouTube. https://www.youtube.com/watch?v=GvtNyOzGogc

40. Chang, A. (2018, April 6). Sinclair's takeover of local news, in one striking map. *Vox*. https://www.vox.com/2018/4/6/17202824/sinclair-tribune-map

41. Rosentiel, T. (2012, March 19). The state of the news media 2012. *Pew Research Center*. http://www.pewresearch.org/2012/03/19/state-of-the-news-media-2012.

42. Goidel, K., & Gaddie, K. (2016, November 3). The wildcatters: The twitter candidate, social media campaigns, and democracy. *The Huffington Post*. http://www.huffingtonpost.com/entry/the-wildcatters-the-twitter-candidate-social-media_us_581b5211e4b0f1c7d77c968d

43. Verhovek, J. (2019, January 11). In the 2020 campaign, candidate social media posts of visits to the dentist, enjoying a beer and more pull back the curtain: Some 2020 hopefuls are embracing a more personal social media style. *ABC News*. https://abcnews.go.com/Politics/2020-campaign-candidate-social-media-posts-visits-dentist/story?id=60311500

44. Facebook reached 69% of U.S. adults by 2019 while Twitter reached 22%; for both sites, most users access the site via mobile devices. YouTube reaches the highest percent of U.S. adults at 73%; Social media fact sheet. (2019, June 12). *Pew Research Center*. https://www.pewresearch.org/internet/fact-sheet/social-media/#which-social-media-platforms-are-most-popular.

45. Gottfried, J., & Shearer, E. (2016, May 26). News use across social media platforms 2016. *Pew Research Center*. http://www.journalism.org/2016/05/26/news-use-across-social-media-platforms-2016.

46. For example, 2015 saw newsroom employment and investment continue to fall, and more newspaper companies saw losses in 2015 relative to 2014; Barthel, M. (2016, June 15). Newspapers: Fact sheet. *Pew Research Center* http://www.journalism.org/2016/06/15/newspapers-fact-sheet.

47. Barthel, M. (2016, June 15). 5 key takeaways about the state of the news media in 2016. *Pew Research Center*. http://www.pewresearch.org/fact-tank/2016/06/15/state-of-the-news-media-2016-key-takeaways.

48. Barthel, M., Matsa, K. E., & Worden, K. (2020, October 9). Coronavirus-driven downturn hits newspapers hard as TV news thrives: The financial state

of the U.S. news media in the second quarter of 2020. *Pew Research Center.* https://www.journalism.org/2020/10/29/coronavirus-driven-downturn-hits-newspapers-hard-as-tv-news-thrives/

49. Webster, J. (2016). *The marketplace of attention: How audiences take shape in a digital age.* MIT Press.

50. Carr, D. (2014, August 10). Print is down, and now out: media companies spin off newspapers, to uncertain futures. *The New York Times.* https://www.nytimes.com/2014/08/11/business/media/media-companies-spin-off-newspapers-to-uncertain-futures.html?_r=0.

51. Williams, A. T. (2016, August 9). Newspaper companies lag behind their broadcast siblings after spinoffs. *Pew Research Center.* http://www.pewresearch.org/fact-tank/2016/08/09/newspaper-companies-lag-behind-their-broadcast-siblings-after-spinoffs.

52. Abernathy, P. M. (2020). The news landscape in 2020 transformed and diminished: The new media giants. *Hussman School of Journalism and Media, University of North Carolina.* https://www.usnewsdeserts.com/reports/news-deserts-and-ghost-newspapers-will-local-news-survive/the-news-landscape-in-2020-transformed-and-diminished/the-new-media-giants/

53. Peterson, E. (2019). Paper cuts: How reporting resources affect political news coverage. *American Journal of Political Science.* https://doi.org/10.1111/ajps.12560

54. Bimber, B. (2003). *Information and American democracy: Technology and the evolution of political power.* Cambridge University Press.

55. About us. (2021). *ProPublica.* https://www.propublica.org/about/

56. Gottfried, J., & Shearer, E. (2016, May 26). News use across social media platforms 2016. *Pew Research Center.* http://www.journalism.org/2016/05/26/news-use-across-social-media-platforms-2016.

57. Martin, G. J., & McCrain, J. (2019). Local news and national politics. *American Political Science Review, 113*(2), 372–384; Peterson, E. (2019). Paper cuts: How reporting resources affect political news coverage. *American Journal of Political Science.* https://doi.org/10.1111/ajps.12560

58. DiMaggio, P., & Hargittai, E. (2001). From the "digital divide" to "digital inequality": Studying internet use as penetration increases. *Princeton: Center for Arts and Cultural Policy Studies, Woodrow Wilson School, Princeton University,* 4(1), 4–2.

59. Patterson, T. E. (2007, August). *Creative destruction: An exploratory look at news on the internet.* Joan Shorenstein Center on the Press, Politics and Public Policy. https://shorensteincenter.org/wp-content/uploads/2012/03/creative_destruction_2007.pdf.

60. Patterson, T. E. (2007, August). *Creative destruction: An exploratory look at news on the internet*. Joan Shorenstein Center on the Press, Politics and Public Policy. https://shorensteincenter.org/wp-content/uploads/2012/03/creative_destruction_2007.pdf.

61. 47 U.S.C.A. §307(a), 1934.

62. Krasnow, E. G., Longley, L. D., & Terry, H. A. (1982). *The politics of broadcast regulation* (3rd ed.). St. Martin's Press, p. 284.

63. The Associated Press. (2008, September 22). GM won't advertise during Super Bowl. *NBC*. http://www.nbcnews.com/id/26842347/ns/business-us_business/t/gm-wont-advertise-during-super-bowl/#.WMngGfkrLic.

64. *Office of Communication of the United Church of Christ v. FCC*, 359 F.2d 994 (D.C. Cir. 1966).

65. Krasnow, E. G., Longley, L. D., & Terry, H. A. (1982). *The politics of broadcast regulation* (3rd ed.). St. Martin's Press, pp. 54–62.

66. *Reno v. American Civil Liberties Union*, 521 U.S. 844 (1997).

CHAPTER

3

News Making and Reporting Routines

Learning Objectives

1. Discuss the profiles of American journalists and how their characteristics might influence coverage.

2. Explain gatekeeping and how it affects which stories are covered, how they are covered, and selection bias.

3. Summarize the effects of gatekeeping on patterns of coverage found in news content.

4. Identify reasonable ways to appraise news making in the United States (U.S.).

The United Kingdom's Brexit and Donald J. Trump's upset victory in the 2016 U.S. presidential election served as a wake-up call for journalists. Commentary on why journalists and political experts failed to anticipate two major political upsets in their backyards was frequent during the months following both events. Journalists from both countries marveled at their failure to anticipate the depth of discontent felt among broad swaths of the public. In the American case, ongoing economic challenges facing news organizations no doubt contributed. The press serves a vital function as an intermediary institution by facilitating the representative relationship between democratic citizens and their governments. The press monitoring required to fulfill this role is only possible in a diffuse democratic republic when there are numerous installations of news outlets capable of accurately and consistently keeping a finger on the pulse of local communities and reporting on violations of the public trust by those in office. Historically, the mechanism for this kind of monitoring was the local newspaper. Though their structural forms vary, local newspapers have traditionally been the outlets most likely to retain an adequately deep bench of news workers who are experts on the local people, government, and community at large. There are countless examples of what this kind of journalism can produce and the injustices it can prevent when allowed to flourish. An excellent example is *The Boston Globe* Spotlight team whose reporting put an end to years of child abuse cover-ups by the Catholic Church. Yet the ongoing depletion of U.S. local news ranks is now storied—in the time between 2004 and 2018, 2,100 local newspapers died. And between 2000 and 2018, weekday newspaper circulation dropped by 12%, declining from a reach of 56 million American homes to just over 28 million. Across the newspaper industry, employment fell over 40% between 2007 and 2015. Each newspaper death leaves a local community without a paper. Surviving local newspapers are struggling to maintain the reporting staff they need.[1] When they cannot, the scope and quality of their reporting declines.[2] As newspapers decline and disappear, we are losing our best mechanism for informing leaders about what the public wants and for informing the public when they are not getting it. Declining local newspapers might explain why journalists and elites are out of touch.

When local newspapers disappear, hyperlocal digital media outlets don't typically emerge in their place. Instead, their displaced audiences migrate to national news outlets for public affairs information, where they are left without coverage of local issues. They are fed news diets dominated by national party politics instead, which is rancorous and filled with partisan cues. Such coverage often bears little relevance to the daily lives of many Americans. It is no wonder so much of the public feels that neither political party represents their views and that the media are not to be trusted.[3] Nor is it a surprise that—without the help of their journalist colleagues stationed in local communities across the country—elite national journalists failed to pick up on public discontent prior to the 2016 presidential elections.

Many journalists realize the profound effect that the economic constraints on their profession are having on their ability to do their jobs well. Most also realize the need to embrace the very technologies that helped facilitate the economic challenges facing journalism and are recalibrating their quality measurement scales accordingly. They are willing, even eager, to work in the digital media environment. However, the nagging question is whether and how digital journalism can become profitable enough to sustain broad-gauge journalistic enterprises in ways that allow them to perform their intermediary functions well. When asked, journalists say that the biggest challenges they face are adapting their content for mobile platforms, building trust with diverse audiences, adapting to constantly changing revenue models, and finding new formats for good stories as technology shapes content.[4] In this chapter, we provide insights on these issues by focusing on reporters and their work under normal circumstances.

Profile Sketch of U.S. Journalists

How do journalists decide which information to report as news and how to shape it into news stories? The answers can be approached from three theoretical perspectives: personality theory, organization theory, and role theory.

Personality and Social Background Factors

What are some of the personality and background factors that influence the substance and shape of news? Newspeople's demographic profile resembles that of other professionals in the United States. At the start of the 21st century, four out of five American journalists were white, two-thirds were male, and nearly all were college graduates, though many did not major in journalism. Education appears to be the single most important background characteristic that shapes newspeople's general philosophy of reporting. Like most people with a social science or humanities degree, journalists tend to be socially more liberal than the general population and to have a keener sense of social responsibility.[5]

In 2007, 8% of national journalists (14% at the local level) professed to conservative leanings compared to 36% of the general public. Roughly one-third claimed to be liberal, and more than half called themselves moderate. Other studies reflect similar patterns,[6] though existing research fails to show evidence of systematic liberal bias in mainstream news content.[7] Nevertheless, journalists working for mainstream news outlets are still thought to be left-leaning and to have preferences for economic and social liberalism and internationalist foreign policy, caution about military intervention, and some suspicion about the ethics of established large institutions, particularly big business and big government.[8] However, despite perennial complaints about partisan media bias in political coverage, most studies show that mainstream media personnel—and all but a handful of news outlets that lean heavily to the right or left—attempt to treat both of the major political parties fairly. Anticipation of scrutiny and criticism encourages evenhandedness. The extent to which biased reporting from ostensibly neutral outlets based on party preference is a problem in U.S. media is not fully known, and the evidence is muddled by the re-emergence of partisan news outlets and the blending of opinion and news content. Nevertheless, there is more evidence against systematic media bias among mainstream outlets than otherwise.[9] Perhaps more important in a democratic system, however, is what citizens *think* about media bias. In 2017, a full 64% of nationally representative Gallup Poll respondents reported believing that the mainstream media favors the Democratic Party. Only 22% said the media favor the Republican party. We will return to the issue of media bias and its effects in Chapter 12.[10]

Organizational Factors

Colleagues and settings strongly influence newspeople. Every news organization has its own internal power structure that develops from the interaction of owners, journalists, news sources, audiences, advertisers, and government authorities. By and large, print and broadcast journalists believe that many of the structural changes in the news business in the 21st century have harmed the quality of news. This includes the incorporation of media enterprises within large corporate entities (discussed in Chapter 2), which has increased the emphasis on high profits and led to damaging cutbacks in staff and other resources for gathering news. The pressure to produce news around the clock with diminished resources accounts for bouts of sloppy, error-prone reporting. Not all organizational changes have been harmful, however. For example, most journalists say that the internet has made journalism better because it is an excellent source of information that is easily available to anybody with a computer.

Organizational pressures begin to operate even before the job starts. To win advancement, professional recognition, and approval from their colleagues, reporters learn quickly which types of stories are acceptable to their editors and colleagues. Relationships with colleagues are particularly important within large, prominent news enterprises in which newspeople receive their main social and professional support from coworkers rather than from the community at large.[11] The opposite holds true in small towns, where newspeople often interact freely with community leaders and receive their support.

Role Models

Although editors and reporters throughout the country take cues about stories from the eastern media elite—*The New York Times, The Wall Street Journal*, and *The Washington Post*—they shape their basic news policies according to their own views about the role that media should play in society. The effects of favoring a social responsibility role over other stances were discussed in Chapter 1. News stories also vary depending on whether newspeople see themselves largely as objective observers who must present facts and diverse views voiced by others or as interpreters who must supply meanings and evaluations.

Divisions are especially sharp among proponents of traditional journalism and advocates for civic or public journalism.[12] Civic journalism fans believe that reporters must tailor the news so that it not only informs citizens about important happenings but also helps them take collective action to resolve problems.[13] Public journalism has been primarily a print news movement, but the digital era has brought with it a revival of public journalism formats and a robust discussion of journalistic roles.[14] Beyond turning reporters into interpreters of what the news means, this approach also makes them deliberate participants in the political process. That may be laudable in many instances, but it sacrifices journalists' role as neutral observers, which is a central tenet of traditional journalism. When journalists are asked about the core values of their calling, most acknowledge neutrality as a core value that serves their audience's interests.[15]

What do journalists identify as *news*?[16] U.S. journalists see it as their role to cover exceptional events rather than ordinary ones. What seems exceptional depends on the conditions within a particular society at a particular point in time. It also depends on journalists' perception of which of the many extraordinary events that surround them is likely to interest their audiences and deserves and needs coverage. The fact that the decision of what is news hinges on multiple subjective judgments explains why there is much disagreement about what ought to be news on a given day. But it also explains the widespread uniformity of story types in U.S. print and electronic media.

Gatekeeping

A small number of journalists have final control over story choices. These *gatekeepers* include wire service reporters, Web editors, and other reporters who initially select stories; the editors who assign the reporters and accept or reject what they submit; disc jockeys at radio stations who present five-minute news breaks; and television program executives. Even many citizen journalism websites have developed gatekeeping practices and editorial staffs.[17]

These few gatekeepers, particularly those who make news choices for nationwide audiences, wield an awesome amount of political power because their choices determine what will be widely available as news. This is why rankings of the political influence of U.S. institutions routinely place the news media among the top ten. As we will discuss in Chapter 12, news stories influence the issues that ordinary people, as well as political elites, think about. Of course, media gatekeepers are not entirely free in their story choices. Coverage of major events, such as wars, assassinations, and airline hijackings, is compelling. Other events can be included or omitted at will within the limits set by news conventions.

Gatekeepers also select the sources for news. Government officials are the chief source of most political stories reported by the wire services, which are the main information source for the nation's news venues. This gives public officials an excellent chance to influence the slant of the news. However, when highly controversial issues are at stake, gatekeepers usually turn to unofficial sources as well.[18] Basing the news on a narrow spectrum of sources can lead to biased reporting. Reporters may give the widest publicity to the views of celebrity authorities and ignore important specialists whose names are unfamiliar to the public. Sources who have gained recognition as experts through media publicity tend to be used over and over again while other, less publicized sources are neglected.

When multiple media cover the same story, as happens routinely, they often use sources representing different elites. When that happens, the thrust of the story may vary widely even though the underlying facts are the same. For example, news outlets' coverage and analysis of the January 6, 2021, insurrection at the U.S. Capitol varied widely, especially across left- and right-leaning cable news outlets. The causes and effects were assessed in quite a diverse fashion by CNN, MSNBC, Fox News, and Newsmax. CNN's Jake Tapper described the extremists who stormed the capitol in the following terms, "We have a name for people who commit violence in the name of various political ideology. We call them terrorists."[19] Fox News's Pete Hegseth's account was quite different,

These are not conspiracy theorists motivated just by lies. That's a bunch of nonsense that people want to tell us. These are people that understand first principles. They love freedom, and they love free markets. And they see exactly what the anti-American left has done to America.

At the same time, Van Jones of CNN and Joy Reid of MSNBC were reflecting on differences between how the protesters at the capitol on

January 6 were treated compared to Black Lives Matter protestors, speculating about why January 6 protesters were not treated more harshly. Accounts of the capitol insurrection were so different across these major sources, it prompted some to question the nation's ability to come away with a shared understanding of the events from that day.

In the age of fragmented media, people worry a great deal about how source selection influences bias in news reporting, especially the ideologically branded cable news outlets such as Fox News and MSNBC, as the example above suggests. A 2019 analysis of how the major news and cable networks use congressional elites as sources reveals some troubling trends. As critics of partisan media might expect, Fox News and MSNBC disproportionately source the most ideologically extreme House members, providing them with far more opportunities to explain, address, or justify their policies, issues, or actions (see Figure 3-1). The analyses reveal information biases as well—the members of Congress least likely to be sourced are those with the most legislative success, and other major predictors of coverage are party leadership status and involvement in scandal. Rather than sourcing those members working hard for policy change, the partisan extremists, party leaders, and those involved in scandals earn the most coverage. What's more is that partisan media are only the worst offenders, CNN also sourced extreme members more regularly (but not to the extent of the other cable networks). In patterns like these, we see evidence again that news values—the desire to cover the negative, sensational, and entertaining—rather than political values drive the news selection process.[20]

In the past, highly respected national newscasters were also extraordinarily influential in putting their versions of news events on the political agenda. By singling out news events for positive or negative commentary, these media figures could sway public and official opinions. A 60-second verbal barrage on the evening news or a few embarrassing questions can still destroy programs, politicians, and the reputations of major organizations.

Americans today are much less likely to view their media as effective guardians of the public interest, and they often question news story choices and their consequences. For example, when it became clear in 2004 that reports about Iraq's possession of weapons of mass destruction were false, *The New York Times* and *The Washington Post* assumed some of the blame for the consequences. Better reporting, they argued, could have aborted the costly war against Iraq.[21]

Figure 3-1 How Ideological Extremism Influences Congressional Members' Speaking Opportunities on Cable and Network News

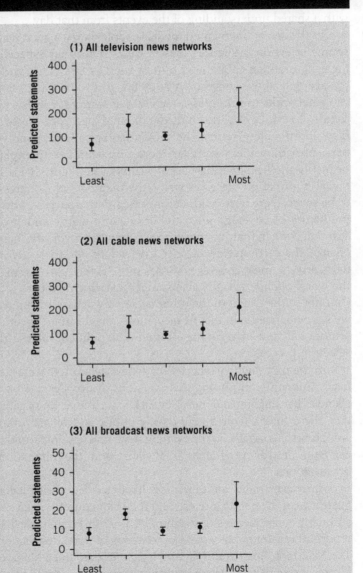

(1) All television news networks

(2) All cable news networks

(3) All broadcast news networks

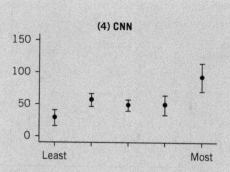

(4) CNN

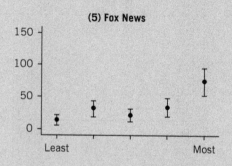

(5) Fox News

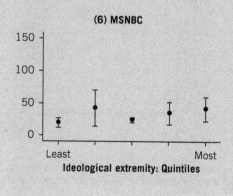

(6) MSNBC

Ideological extremity: Quintiles

(Continued)

(Continued)

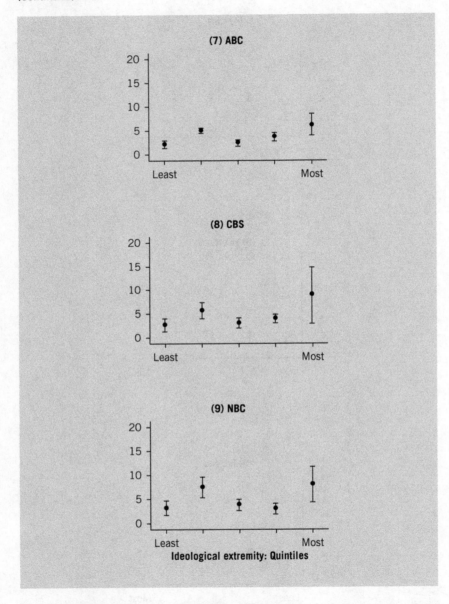

(7) ABC

(8) CBS

(9) NBC

Ideological extremity: Quintiles

Source: Padgett, J. S., Dunaway, J. L., & Darr, J. P. (2019). As seen on TV? How gatekeeping makes the U.S. House seem more extreme. *Journal of Communication, 69*(6), 696–719.

Note: Calculated using -marginsplot- in Stata, using a poisson regression; Standard errors clustered by Congress.

General Factors in News Selection

As mentioned earlier, what becomes news depends in part on the demographics, training, personality, and professional socialization of news personnel. News selection also hinges on norms within a news organization and how newspeople conceptualize their professional roles, plus pressure from internal and external competition. Within each news organization, reporters and editors compete for time, space, and prominence of position for their stories. News organizations also compete with each other for audience attention, for advertisers, and (in the case of the networks) for affiliates. In other words, media outlets may feel compelled to carry stories simply because another medium in the same market has carried them.

News personnel operate within the broad political context of their societies in general and their circulation communities in particular. Most have internalized these contexts so they become the frame of reference for personnel. As media scholar George Gerbner observed long ago, there is "no fundamentally nonideological, apolitical, nonpartisan news gathering and reporting system."[22] For example, if a reporter's political context demands favorable images of religious leaders, news and entertainment will reflect this outlook. That used to be the case in the United States until the 21st century, when multiple stories unveiled sexual misconduct by priests.[23]

As the example above suggests, political pressures also leave their mark. Media personnel depend on political leaders for information and are therefore vulnerable to manipulation by them. Powerful elites flood the media with self-serving stories that are often hard to resist. Intensive, frequent contacts between journalists and leaders and the desire to keep associations cordial may lead to cozy relationships that hamper critical detachment. Wooing reporters to elicit favorable media coverage is the mark of the astute politician. Reporters often succumb to the blandishments of politicians for fear of alienating powerful and important news sources.

Economic pressures are even more potent than political pressures in molding news and entertainment. Newspapers and magazines need to earn profits. That means that news organizations must direct their programs and stories either to general audiences in the prime consumption years of life (roughly ages 25–45) or to selected special audiences that are key targets for particular advertiser appeals. The desire to keep audiences watching a particular station affects the format of news and public service programs. Stations select newscasters for their physical attractiveness. The stations encourage informal banter, and nearly every newscast contains some fascinating bits of trivia or a touching yet inconsequential human-interest story.[24] The news becomes "infotainment"—a marriage of information and entertainment values. Networks avoid complicated stories for fear of confusing audiences, just as they slightly dull economic news irrespective of importance. However, journalists often underestimate the public's tastes for serious presentations.

Criteria for Choosing Specific Stories

In addition to deciding what is publishable news, gatekeepers must choose particular news items to include in their mix of offerings. The motto of *The New York Times*, "All the News That's Fit to Print," is an impossible myth; there is far more publishable news available than any daily news medium can possibly use. Gatekeepers also must decide how they want to frame each item so that it carries a particular message. For instance, when journalists cast stories about controversial policies, such as health care reform, as games of strategy—as they are wont to do—the policy issues blur and lose importance.[25] In 1993 and 1994, for example, when President Bill Clinton mounted a major campaign for health care reform, 67% of the health news coverage was framed as political gaming. Stories focused on who was winning and losing supporters for their favorite policy. Only 25% of the stories addressed substantive issues in health care reform. When political scientist Regina Lawrence studied use of the game frame in welfare reform debates, she discovered that frame choice hinged on the context. When the story was linked to elections or political battles in Washington, DC, the game frame was prevalent. That was not the case when the story was linked to state policies or issues concerning implementation of reforms.[26]

The criteria newspeople use in story selection relate primarily to audience appeal rather than to the political significance of stories, their educational value, their broad social purposes, or the reporter's own political views. The emphasis on audience appeal and the economic pressures that mandate it must be kept in mind when evaluating the totality of media output. These factors explain why the amounts and kinds of coverage of important issues often are not commensurate with their true significance at the time of publication. For instance, stories about politicians' sex scandals, Meghan and Harry's struggles as British royals, or the ups and downs of the careers of entertainers Zendaya, Ariana Grande, or Harry Styles receive inordinate amounts of coverage at the expense of more significant events.

Newspeople use five criteria for choosing news stories. First, stories must picture conditions that could have *a strong impact* on readers or listeners. Stories about health hazards, consumer fraud, or pensions for the elderly influence American audiences more than do unfamiliar happenings such as student riots in Greece or bank failures in China, with which they cannot identify. To make stories attractive, newspeople commonly present them as events that happened to ordinary people. Inflation news becomes the story of the housewife at the supermarket; foreign competition becomes the story of laid-off workers in a local textile plant. This tendency is called the *personalization bias*. In the process of personalization, the broader political significance of the story is often lost, and the news is trivialized.[27]

Violence, conflict, disaster, or scandal is the second criterion of newsworthiness. Wars, murders, strikes, earthquakes, accidents, and sex scandals involving prominent people are the sorts of happenings that excite audiences. In fact, inexpensive mass newspapers became viable business ventures in the United States only after the publishers of *The New York Sun* discovered in 1833 that papers filled with breezy crime and sex stories far outsold their more staid competitors. Mass sales permitted sharp price reductions and led to the birth of the "penny press." A substantial body of research demonstrates a clear link between the human negativity bias—our tendency to pay more attention to negative information over positive or neutral information—and the journalistic tendency to focus on violence, conflict, disaster, scandal, and bad news more generally.[28]

A third element of newsworthiness is *familiarity*. News is attractive if it pertains to well-known people or involves familiar situations of concern to many. Newspeople try to cast unfamiliar situations, such as mass famines in Africa, into more familiar stories of individual babies dying from malnutrition. The amount of detail that people can retain about the powerful and famous demonstrates that the public is keenly interested in celebrities. More than five decades after the assassination of President John F. Kennedy in 1963, many Americans still remember details of the funeral ceremony as well as where they were when they heard about the murder. People value the feeling of personal intimacy that comes from knowing details of another person's life, especially if that person is beloved. They avidly follow the trials and tribulations of these people and may try to model themselves after them.

Proximity is the fourth element of newsworthiness. Strong preference for local news signifies that people are most interested in what happens near them. Next to news about crime and health, people pay most attention to local news, far ahead of news about national and international affairs.[29] Local media flourish because they concentrate on events close to home; typically, these outlets allocate roughly 75% of their space for local stories, though recent evidence suggests that gains in large chain acquisitions of local media will have a nationalizing effect on local news content. Proximity as a news value is still clearly displayed in the limited coverage of foreign affairs provided by U.S. news outlets.[30]

The fifth element is that news should be *timely and novel*. It must be something that has recently occurred and is out of the ordinary, either in the sense that it does not happen all the time or in the sense that it is not part of people's everyday lives. Stories about space exploration or the puzzling death of honeybee colonies or reports about the latest weather conditions fall into this category.

Gathering the News

News organizations establish regular listening posts, or *beats*, in places where events of interest to the public are most likely to occur. In the United States, government beats cover political executives, legislative bodies, court systems, and international organizations. Locations that record deviant behaviors, such as police stations or hospitals, are routinely monitored and publicized. So are fluctuations in economic trends, which can be checked easily at stock and commodity markets and at institutions designed to measure the pulse of the nation's business. Some beats, such as health or education, are functionally defined. Stories emanating from the traditional national beats, such as the White House, Capitol, or Pentagon, have an excellent chance of publication because of their intrinsic significance or the prominence of their sources.

In the past, all major traditional media monitored similar beats. Consequently, overall news patterns—the types of stories that were covered—were relatively uniform throughout the country and changed in tandem. In recent years, newsroom cutbacks have meant a shift from the beat structure to a pattern of general assignment, which minimizes source development and reporter expertise. Many credit the loss of newsbeats and reporter expertise as one factor contributing to a shift away from hard news, if one defines *hard news* as "breaking events involving top leaders, major issues, or significant disruptions in the routines of daily life, such as an earthquake or airline disasters."[31] The trend has been toward softer news and features. In electoral politics, fewer reporters on political newsbeats translates into less substantive issue coverage and more coverage on the basic horserace.[32] Figures vary depending on researchers' definition of *soft news*, but there seems to be widespread agreement that more than half of print and broadcast news falls into the "soft" category today.

Table 3-1 shows examples of major news topics covered by month in 2020, as described by a major television news network, CBS. Typically, there are significant uniformities across the major national broadcast networks—ABC, CBS, and NBC. All venues allocated substantial time and space to President Trump's impeachment, COVID-19, and the U.S. presidential campaign, but the amount of coverage dedicated to other issues varied across outlets. PBS devoted proportionately more attention to events happening beyond U.S. borders and to foreign affairs, a consistent tendency among U.S. public media outlets. Overall, coverage shows more homogeneity than diversity in news topics and agendas, if not tone or angle of story, and these agendas are not always reflective of public information needs.

Walter Lippmann famously criticized the press for its sporadic coverage, noting that governance is not possible when society is only seen as "episodes, incidents, and eruptions."[33] The extremely uneven, often sparse network coverage of news about the American states is an example. About 20% of American states are covered by fewer than twenty-five stories annually, and another 20% are covered by no more than fifty. Such sparse coverage by network television denies these states a national audience. At the other end of the spectrum, a handful of states are featured in hundreds of stories. As is typical for presidential election years, states with special political significance—such as New Hampshire and Iowa, where the campaign starts in earnest, as well as the most populous states, such as California and New York—receive the lion's share of coverage. Overall, the states can be grouped by those who suffer from neglect, those that are vastly overcovered, and those who receive an appropriate share of attention.[34] An example of an important story the major national media often miss is a labor strike that occurred in 2016 in prisons across twenty-four states. The strike lasted several weeks, and estimates are that roughly 20,000 prisoners were on strike. The unreported story is important because it spoke to the challenges in funding state prisons, which is a widespread issue. It also highlighted the deplorable conditions prisoners face daily as well as specific and sometimes brutal punishments prisoners endured for striking.[35]

The distribution of visual images in news media is also askew. Most pictures are from East Coast cities, such as Washington, DC, and New York, with a sprinkling of pictures from Chicago and Los Angeles. Of course, reporters will cover special events anywhere in the country. Every network reports presidential election debates, wherever they are held, and routinely follows presidential travels, whether the destination is a secluded beach in Hawaii—Barack Obama's home state—or the Great Wall of China. States receive exceptional coverage when major news happens there. Newsworthy events in remote sites are most likely to be covered if they involve prominent people and are scheduled in advance so that news venues can plan to have media crews available.

Prior planning is even important for more accessible events. News organizations need time to allocate reporters and camera crews and edit pictures and stories. The need to plan ahead leads to an emphasis on predictable events, such as formal visits by dignitaries, legislative hearings, or executive press conferences. Technology advances have eased this problem, providing one of hundreds of examples of the profound impact of technology on the content of news. "Spot news" can now be filmed and broadcast rapidly, using equipment that has been redesigned for mobility while growing exponentially in capability. One enduring challenge is that addressing the reporter coverage problem is costly. For many of the reasons described in this chapter as well as in Chapters 1 and 2, fewer reporters are deployed for both international and domestic coverage. Between newsroom cutbacks and the number of dailies that have collapsed, there are not enough reporters to cover state and local communities. National papers and the broadcast networks are not equipped to provide coverage of all fifty states and the thousands of local communities within them.[36]

Table 3-1   CBS Coverage of Major Topics by Month, 2020

January	The first COVID case arrived in the U.S.
February	The House impeachment of President Trump and his acquittal by the Senate
March	The World Health Organization declared COVID a global pandemic.
April	Tensions over COVID erupted and armed demonstrators took to the Michigan State Capitol.
May	The death of George Floyd sparked protests all around the country.
June	A peaceful protest near the White House was broken up to allow President Trump to pose outside a church holding a Bible.
July	Major League Baseball returned in front of cardboard cut-outs.
August	Hurricane Laura—one of 12 named storms for 2020 season— slammed into the Louisiana Gulf Coast.
September	The death of Justice Ruth Bader Ginsburg; Trump nomination and Senate confirmation of Judge Amy Coney Barrett.
October	President Trump was diagnosed with COVID-19, hospitalized, and released.
November	Joe Biden won the 2020 election. President Trump disagreed and tried to overturn the result both in the courts and in certain state legislatures.
December	COVID vaccines were finally here.

Source: The year in review: Top news stories of 2020 month-by-month. (2020, December 27). *CBS News.* https://www.cbsnews.com/news/2020-the-year-in-review-top-news-stories-month-by-month/.

New Tools for News Gathering

In addition to serving as platforms for sharing news, digital and social media provide new tools for news gathering. Though some worry about the consequences of this practice, social media feeds are a rich source for stories. Journalists report that Twitter is a social media platform especially useful for news, especially for help with finding and keeping up with breaking news stories, crowdsourcing, and tracking political elites.[37] A recent study of journalists on Twitter finds there is also potential for influence. The ideological lean of journalists' Twitter networks is significantly correlated with the content they produce, even after accounting for the news outlet in which they work.[38]

Tweets and other social media posts also influence content when they operate similarly to pseudo-events. This is one reason why images from Twitter feeds make up an increasing proportion of news stories. Social media feeds provide quick and easy ways to get fresh story material as well as reactions from the public and other elites. The sheer volume of data publicly available through various social media sites provides nearly endless sources of news stories for journalists equipped to navigate and analyze data.

News Production Constraints

Many news selection criteria reflect the pressure to edit and publish news rapidly. That is why pseudo-events—events created to generate press coverage—constitute more than half of all television news stories. Reporters attend events such as bridge dedications or county fairs because these are quick and easy ways to get fresh story material. When access to a newsworthy event is difficult, reporters resort to interviews with on-scene observers or ever-available "experts" anywhere in the country eager to discuss the situation. Since interviews are a comparatively cheap way to collect story material, they have become increasingly common in an era of strained resources. Tight resources contribute to the official source bias we see in the news.

Once stories reach media news offices, editors must make selections quickly. Ben Bagdikian, a former *Washington Post* editor, in a classic study of gatekeeping at eight newspapers, found that editors usually sift through and choose stories on the spot.[39] They do not assemble and carefully balance them with an eye to the overall effects of a particular issue of the paper. The typical newspaper editor is able to scan and discard individual stories in seconds. At such speeds, there is no time to reflect or to weigh the merits or intrinsic importance of one story over another. If the editor has ideological preferences, they are served instinctively (if at all) rather than deliberately. Papers ordinarily will not save stories left over at the end of the day for the next day's news because newer stories will supersede them. A late-breaking story, therefore, unless it is very unusual or significant, has little chance for publication in the print edition of a newspaper—although it may make it onto the paper's website. Digital media face different timing constraints. Though hard deadlines are not as firm relative to print, the fluidity and pressure for constantly fresh material impose different constraints. The relative ease of updating and correcting a news story only partially offsets the constant pressure for new spin and breaking news.

Public relations experts and campaign managers know the deadlines of important publications, such as *The New York Times* and *The Wall Street Journal,* and of the network television news. They schedule events and news releases to arrive in editors' offices precisely when needed and in easy-to-use formats. Public relations firms and political strategists distribute thousands of releases annually. If these releases are attractively presented and meet newsworthiness criteria, journalists find it hard to resist using them. This is especially true for smaller news organizations that lack adequate resources to produce their own stories. They relish receiving such information subsidies.[40] Powerful elites in the public and private sectors make ample use of these opportunities. Even though news organizations discard the bulk of public relations releases, they do use them in a substantial portion of news stories, usually without identifying the source. Television news staffs, especially those working for stations that broadcast around the clock, have even less time than newspaper staffs to investigate most stories (see Photo 3-1). That is why background or investigative stories that appear on television frequently originate in the print media. The problem of insufficient time pertains not only to preparing stories but also to presenting them. The average news story on television and radio takes about a minute to deliver, just enough time to announce an event and present a fact or two. Newscasters may have to ignore complex stories if they cannot drastically condense them or broadcast them live, blow by blow as they are happening. Print media have space problems as well, but these are less severe than the time constraints that broadcast media face. Some papers reserve a fixed amount of space for news; others expand or contract the news space depending on the flow of news and advertising. But whether the paper is a slim, eight-page version or five to ten times that size, there is rarely enough space to cover stories as fully as reporters and editors would like.[41] The fact that many newspapers now publish online versions eases that situation, except in the case of mobile platforms. Today, tweets and other means of posting to social media are comparable to press releases. Decades ago, media critics complained that news outlets were only slightly modifying press releases before publication. Now, seeing television, newspaper, and digital news stories highlighting a stream of tweets or a Twitter exchange is more than commonplace.

Besides the need to capsule news stories, reporters working with audiovisual media also seek stories with visual appeal. Events that lack good video footage may not make the cut. This is one reason recent election cycles have seen more coverage of political advertising. Stories about political ads are easy to write, are cheap to produce, and come with already-produced audiovisuals.[42] Unfortunately, the most visually appealing aspects of a story may not be as important as the political ad example suggests. Except in the case of fact-checking, ad coverage is more likely to focus on the strategic maneuvering of candidates than substantive policy issues.

Effects of Gatekeeping

The gatekeeping influences discussed in this chapter give a distinctive character to U.S. news. There are many exceptions, of course, among individual programs or stories. There are also noticeable differences in emphases across different media outlets and platforms. For example, the unique conditions of digital journalism have an even more profound impact on news presentation.[43] Unlike journalists in traditional media, who must be highly selective when choosing among incoming news stories because time or space is scarce, some types of digital media outlets have abundant time and space because the structure of websites allows voluminous content. For a time, traditional media operations used their internet sites to expand stories covered in their traditional media rather than enhancing the pool of news stories. The news organizations update these stories throughout the day and night, often scooping the printed and broadcast stories that they will later feature in their traditional venues. A more recent challenge facing journalism on digital platforms is the major shift to news consumption on mobile devices. Recent data show that nearly 80% of time spent on social media sites occurs on mobile devices, and the fact that mobile advertising has surpassed desktop ads illustrates the point. For journalists, the challenge lies in how to craft informative news content for the short attention span of the average mobile news user. While traditional computing and websites allow an unprecedented depth of information for those who want it, the mobile setting is not optimal for clicking, searching, or other means of in-depth information seeking. What this means is that when news outlets optimize their content for mobile use, we are more likely to see cutting and trimming rather than expansion.[44] Most news websites also provide links to information that broadens and deepens the story by adding new data or refreshing previously published details. While mobile constrains attention to links, there are also thousands of unaffiliated websites that graze on the news crop provided by traditional media and report it from fresh perspectives. The digital news environment is not short on choice. Despite variations in the news story environment, four features of U.S. news are noteworthy: people in the news, action in the news, infotainment news, and support for the establishment.[45]

People in the News

Gatekeeping winnows the group of newsworthy people to a small cadre of familiar and unfamiliar figures. Most stories in newsmagazines and network television news feature familiar people, predominantly entertainers, athletes, and political figures. Fewer than fifty politicians are in the news regularly, and the most popular is the incumbent president; incumbent presidents receive coverage regardless of what they do. News about leading presidential candidates ranks next; in presidential election years, stories about the leading presidential candidates often outnumber stories about second-term incumbent presidents, such as during the 2016 election.[46]

Another well-covered group consists of major federal government officials, such as the leaders of the House and Senate, the heads of major congressional committees, and cabinet members in active departments. Major White House staff members are part of the circle. So are former officials such as secretaries of state and secretaries of defense when asked to comment on the current scene. Ample coverage also goes to targets of congressional investigations and politicians indicted for wrongdoing in office. The Supreme Court is in the news only intermittently, generally when it announces important decisions or during confirmation hearings for Supreme Court justices. Agency heads rarely make the news. Below the federal level, the activities of governors and mayors of large states and cities are newsworthy if they involve important public policy issues or if the incumbent is unusual because of race, gender, or prior newsworthy activities.

Among the many powerful people rarely covered in the news, except when they commit crimes, are economic leaders (such as the heads of large corporations), financiers, and leaders of organized business (such as the U.S. Chamber of Commerce). Political party leaders surface during elections but remain in the shadows at other times. Political activists, such as civil rights leaders or the heads of minority parties, come and go from the news scene, depending on the amount of controversy they are able to produce. Most people never make the news because their activities are not unusual enough to command media attention. Ordinary people have their best chance for publicity if they protest, riot, or strike (particularly against the government) or if they are victims of disasters, personal tragedy, or crime.

Action in the News

The range of activities reported in the news is largely limited to conflicts and disagreements among government officials (particularly friction between the president and Congress), violent and nonviolent protests, crime, scandals and investigations, and impending or actual disasters. When the nation is at war, the media report a large number of war stories but cut back on criticism of the government lest they seem disloyal.

Government policies involving health care reform, energy, or changes in tax rates also provide frequent story material. These stories often highlight the political maneuvers leading to policy decisions rather than the substance of the policy and its likely impact. Government personnel changes, including details about campaigns for office, are another news focus. Finally, two aspects of the ever-changing societal scene periodically receive substantial coverage: national events, such as inaugurations or space adventures, and important technological, social, or cultural developments, such as overhauls of the public school system or advances in the fight against cancer.

Infotainment News

Newsworthiness criteria and news production constraints shape U.S. news and its impact, regardless of the particular subject under discussion.

Among the constraints, economic pressures to generate large audiences are often paramount. Economist James T. Hamilton amassed evidence that evening news broadcasts are pitched largely to fickle younger viewers who are likely to quit watching if the program does not please them. The result is a program mix that is short on hard news and long on infotainment.[47] Comparisons of news story topics show that the shift toward soft news has been dramatic. For example, between 1977 and 1997, soft news increased by an average of 25% in all news venues at the expense of hard news.[48] Many critics inside and outside journalism deplore this turn, claiming that it diminishes citizens' concern about politics and weakens democracy.

Novelty and Excitement

When the goal is to attract young viewers, sensational and novel occurrences often drown out news of more significance that lacks excitement. For instance, a fairly typical newspaper such as the *Chicago Sun-Times* devotes nearly twenty times more space to sports than to news about the state's government. Dramatic events, such as airline hijackings or serial murders, preempt more far-reaching consequential happenings. Preoccupation with a single striking event, such as the 2020 impeachment of President Trump, can shortchange coverage of other news.

The emphasis on excitement also leads to a stress on the more trivial aspects of serious stories. Inflation becomes a human-interest drama about John and Jane Doe, working-class homeowners who are struggling to pay their mortgage. Journalists are apt to ignore the larger issues involved in inflation unless they can be combined with human-interest aspects. In such cases, dramatization helps because personalized, dramatic stories are far more likely to catch audience attention than dry, learned discussions by economic experts. However, audiences are more likely to remember the drama than the underlying serious problem.

The orientation toward novelty and entertainment produces fragmented, discontinuous news that focuses on the present and ignores the past. Fragmentation makes it difficult for audiences to piece together a coherent narrative of events. Snippets of news may drive home an easily understandable theme, such as "Washington is a mess" or "The inner city is decaying," thereby blurring individual news items. A few papers, such as the *Christian Science Monitor* in its heyday, and a few news programs, such as *The PBS NewsHour,* have covered fewer stories, allowing them to present more detail.[49]

Familiarity and Similarity

Young audiences enjoy stories about familiar people and events close to home. That preference has circular effects. When familiar people and situations are covered in minute detail, they become even more familiar and therefore even more worthy of publicity. The reverse is also true. Journalists ignore unfamiliar people and events. Celebrities may become objects of prying curiosity. The details of their private lives may take up an inordinately large amount of time and space in the mass media. The sudden and unexpected death of a beloved entertainer may command news and special feature coverage for days or weeks. Tabloids and serious media alike cover such stories at length.

Conflict and Violence

The heavy news emphasis on conflict and bad news, which is most prevalent in big-city media, has three major consequences.[30] The first and perhaps most far-reaching is the dangerous distortion of reality. Crime coverage provides examples. Media stories rarely mention that many inner-city neighborhoods are relatively free of crime. Instead, they convey the impression that entire cities are dangerous jungles. Studies of people's perceptions of the incidence of crime and the actual chances that they will be victimized indicate that their fears are geared to media realities. In the world of television drama, the average character has a 30% to 64% chance of being involved in violence; in the real world, the average person's chance of becoming a crime victim is a small fraction of that.[51] In the same way, heavy media emphasis on airplane crashes and scant coverage of automobile accidents leave the public with distorted notions of the relative dangers of these modes of transportation.

A second consequence is that average people have the disquieting sense that conflict and turmoil reign nearly everywhere. This impression is likely to affect people's feelings toward society in general. They may contract *videomalaise*, characterized by distrust, cynicism, and fear.[52] Such feelings undermine support for government, destroy faith in leaders, produce political apathy, and generally sap the vigor of the democratic process. The media usually dramatize and oversimplify conflict, picturing it as a confrontation between two clearly defined sides. The reality is murkier. Issues are rarely clear-cut, and viewpoints divide in multiple ways, rather than only two.[53]

A taste for conflict is not the same as a taste for controversy, however. Fear of offending members of the mass audience or annoying prominent critics and business associates may keep some topics—such as misconduct by clergy or high-level educators—out of the news, especially on network television. When news outlets do report such stories, the treatment is ordinarily bland, carefully hedged, and rarely provocative. In fact, the world that television presents to the viewer often lags behind the real world in its recognition of controversial social changes. The civil rights struggle, women's fight for equality, and changing sexual mores were widespread long before they received serious attention in the media.

Neglect of Major Societal Problems

The constraints of news production force the media to slight serious and persistent societal problems such as poverty, alcoholism, truancy, environmental pollution, and the care of preschool children, the elderly, and the disabled. The turn toward softer, human interest–oriented news that began in the 1970s has brought greater attention to such stories, but they rarely remain in the media limelight long enough to generate widespread public debate and political action. When trivial, sensational happenings dominate the news, matters of long-range significance become "old" news, which dooms them to oblivion.

Inadequate training of media staff is another reason for unsatisfactory coverage of major stories. Proper appraisal of the merits of health care plans, prison systems, or pollution control programs requires technical knowledge. Only large news organizations have specialized reporters with expertise in such areas as urban affairs, science, or finance. Because most news organizations throughout the country lack the trained staffs needed to discuss major social and political problems constructively, politicians and all kinds of "experts" can easily challenge the merits of unpalatable media stories.

Support for the Establishment

Gatekeeping also yields news that supports political and social institutions in the United States. Although the media regularly expose the misbehavior and inefficiencies of government officials and routinely disparage politicians, they show respect and support for the political system and its high offices in general. Misconduct and poor policies are treated as deviations that implicitly reaffirm the merit of prevailing norms. News stories routinely embed assumptions that underscore the legitimacy of the current political system. The media treat U.S. political symbols and rituals, such as the presidency, the courts, elections, and patriotic celebrations, with respect, enhancing their legitimacy. By contrast, news stories cast a negative light on antiestablishment behavior, such as protest demonstrations that disrupt normal activities, inflammatory speeches by militants, or looting during a riot.[54]

Generalized support for the establishment and the status quo is not unique to the media, of course.[55] Most institutions within any particular political system go along with it if they wish to prosper. People on government staffs have been socialized to believe in the merits of their political structures. People are socialized throughout their lives to support their country and its policies. They often resent exposés that undermine this comfortable sense of security. Media support for the establishment thus helps to maintain and perpetuate existing respect for it.[56] The media's heavy reliance on government sources and press releases further strengthens establishment support. Official viewpoints tend to dominate the news when story production requires government assistance for data collection or when reporters must preserve access to government beats.[57]

Appraising News Making

Do newspeople do a good job in selecting the types of news and entertainment they cover? Do they allot appropriate time and space to each of these categories? Do they fill them with good individual stories? The answers depend on the standards that the analyst applies. If one contends that news can and should be a mirror of society, then news making leaves much to be desired. By emphasizing the exceptional rather than the ordinary, a few regular beats rather than a wide range of news sources, and conflict and bad news rather than the ups and downs of daily life, the media picture a world that is far from reality. Reality is further distorted because the process of shaping news events into interesting, coherent stories often gives those events new meanings and significance. That is why critics claim that the news creates reality rather than reports it.[58]

If one shares the belief of many journalists and other elites that the media should serve as the eyes and ears of intelligent citizens who are hungry for news of major social and political significance, one will again find fault with news making. The media devote much space and time to trivia and ignore many interesting developments or report them so briefly that their meaning is lost. Often, the human interest appeal of a story or its sensational aspects distract the audience from the story's real significance.[59]

Appraisal scores are far from perfect when one measures the media by their professed story formulas. An analysis of 352 average-length television news reports, selected from November 24 to December 23, 2008, yielded 271 routine stories and showed that only one of seven key story elements (who, what, where, when, why, how, and context) was nearly always covered. Most stories included major factual elements—what actually took place. Slightly fewer stories told who was involved and where and when it happened. Coverage stating why the reported event took place, how it occurred, and in what context was less common. The audience received the facts of what had happened but not the information that would help it grasp the meaning and implications of the facts. News values predict what stories make the news and how they are covered.

To find fault is easy; to suggest realistic remedies is far more difficult. Few critics agree on what is noteworthy enough to deserve publication. Gradations and ranks in significance depend on the observer's worldview and political orientation. One person's intellectual meat is another's poison. Conservatives would like to see more stories about the misdeeds of the country's enemies and about waste and abuse in social service programs. Liberals complain that the media legitimize big business and the military and neglect social reforms and radical perspectives.

When the media feature controversial public policy issues, such as the dangers of nuclear energy generation or the merits of a new health care system, or when they cover political campaigns or demonstrations, each side often charges that political bias dictated the choices about inclusion and exclusion of content and about the story's focus and tone. A number of content analyses of such stories definitively refute the charges of pervasive political bias, if *bias* is defined as deliberately lopsided coverage or intentional slanting of news. These analyses show instead that most newspeople try to cover a balanced array of issues in a neutral manner. They do so by including at least a few contrasting viewpoints. But given the constraints on the number of sources that can be used and the desire to produce exciting stories that top the competition, the end product is rarely a balanced reflection of all elite viewpoints and all shades of public opinion.[60] Moreover, as mentioned, the prevailing political culture colors everything because it provides the standards by which events are judged and interpreted.

When coverage is unbalanced, as happens often, the reasons generally spring from the news-making process rather than from politically or ideologically motivated slanting. For instance, the media covered famine conditions in Somalia because that country was fairly accessible. They ignored similar conditions in Sudan because travel was too difficult there. Journalists report events happening in major cities more fully nationwide than similar events in smaller communities because the cities are better equipped for news collection and transmission. The New Hampshire presidential primary receives disproportionately heavy coverage because it happens to be the first one in a presidential election year. (As the first caucus in the election cycle, Iowa also receives enormous attention from candidates and the press.) These imbalances are common across many media systems. In India, the norms of the for-profit English-language press prioritize victim status and sensationalism when deciding when and how to cover rape (see Box 3-1).

Box 3-1
Norms of Rape Reporting in India

When details of the December 2012 gang rape first began to filter into India's newsrooms, editors were faced with the decision of whether to run the story on the front page. Three facts stood out: The victim was a student, she had been to an upmarket shopping mall before she was attacked, and she had also recently watched an English-language movie. These factors marked her as a middle- or upper-class Indian woman, which in turn made her story more compelling for the wealthy, urban readership of India's English-language press. There is this term we use called PLU—it means 'people like us,'" says former *Times of India* reporter Smriti Singh. "Whenever there is a murder or rape case involving a female, in your head you have a checklist as to whether the story qualifies to be reported or not."

(Continued)

(Continued)

Being a PLU, or of the right socioeconomic class, means your story is far more likely to be covered by the English-language press. On the surface, the Delhi student appeared to be the ultimate PLU victim. However, as details emerged of her family background, it became clear she was not from the established middle class but was aspiring to transcend her working-class roots as the daughter of a laborer. But by the time this was known, the case was unstoppable. Every newspaper wanted as much detail as it could get about the case.

"There is a vast country beyond Delhi and Mumbai, and there is a lot of crime happening there, and those people are in need of exposure and a platform," says Priyanka Dubey, a reporter who describes herself as a lower-middle-class Hindu who has struggled to have stories on sexual violence published in the English-language media.

Two other factors led to the Delhi gang rape dominating the English-language press: The victim was seen as blameless for her crime, and the crime was especially violent. The Indian media often report rape as a crime of lust and passion, in which sexually precocious women can provoke men to attack. There is a lack of analysis of the complex patriarchal, societal, and economic factors that underlie much sexual violence. In the case of the Delhi rape, the victim was brutally raped after the innocent action of boarding a bus to go home. The dispute over victim and perpetrator accounts that often accompanies rape was absent in this case. The victim was heralded as "Nirbhaya"—the braveheart or fearless one. There was no ambiguity in her status as a heroine who could be celebrated.

Similarly, the extreme nature of the violence against the victim meant that her story could be championed by the press, which highlighted the visceral details of how she had been repeatedly raped and sodomized. "The story was inherently sensational and the coverage was driven by the conviction that people were very curious to know about it and there was competition with other newspapers," says former *Times of India* editor Manoj Mitta. This extreme violence has now become a benchmark for reporting new rape cases in India.

It is now more than five years since the Delhi gang rape, and although other recent incidents have gained press attention, no other case has caught the public imagination in the same way as Nirbhaya. In fact, there are signs that India's English-language press may be reflecting a less sympathetic view toward rape victims. A data analysis of the term *false rape* (wherein a victim withdraws their claim before or during prosecution) shows a small but significant rise in reports on this issue since 2012.

Journalists have attributed this rise to the persistent Indian narrative that women are prone to file false cases when they have been caught having a sexual relationship outside marriage, have been let down after a promise of marriage, are pursuing a personal vendetta, or are trying to extort money.

Although the coverage of the Delhi gang rape showed that Indian English-language newspapers were prepared to report on and highlight the issue of sexual violence, much could be done to improve how publications tackle this issue. There could be better press regulation to prevent salacious and sensationalized coverage, greater sensitivity in reporting, the inclusion of non-PLU cases, the appointment of specially focused gender reporters, and the reframing of rape from a lust crime to a political, economic, and social phenomenon. Although rape is now news in the Indian press, it may take many years before this issue is given the sustained and enlightened attention it deserves.

Source: Adapted from Jolly, J. (2016, July). *Rape culture in India: The role of the English-language press*. Shorenstein Center on Media, Politics and Public Policy, Harvard Kennedy School. https://shorensteincenter.org/rape-culture-india-english-language-press/ CC BY 3.0. https://creativecommons.org/licenses/by/3.0/.

Press output inevitably represents a small, unsystematic, and unrepresentative sample of the news of the day. In that sense, every issue of a newspaper and every television newscast is biased. Published stories often generate follow-up coverage, heightening the bias effect. Attempts to be evenhanded may lead to similar coverage for events of dissimilar importance, thereby introducing bias. For example, environmentalists complain that the quest for balanced news skews the coverage of information about global warming.

By giving equal time to opposing views, these newspapers [*The New York Times, The Washington Post, Los Angeles Times, The Wall Street Journal*] significantly downplayed scientific understanding of the role humans play in global warming. . . . When generally agreed-upon scientific findings are presented side-by-side with the viewpoints of a handful of skeptics, readers are poorly served.[61]

When news is evaluated from the standpoint of the audience's preference, rather than as a mirror image of society or as a reflection of socially and politically significant events, media gatekeepers appear to be doing well. People like the products of the mass media industry well enough to devote huge chunks of their leisure time to broadcasts and the internet. Millions of viewers, by their own free choice, watch shows condemned as "trash" by social critics and often even by the viewers themselves. These same people ignore shows and newspaper stories with the critics' seal of approval. Most claim to enjoy broadcast news and to gain important information from it.[62]

Putting Criticism Into Perspective

Most of the concerns voiced by critics of the news media are echoed in the pages of this book. Nonetheless, the evidence does not support a blanket indictment of the media for failure to serve the public well and give audiences what they want—as well as what they need—as citizens.[63] First and foremost, the collective noun *news media* covers a broad range of institutions. It does not refer only to newspapers, newsmagazines, television, radio, and the internet as news media types; it also refers to individual news suppliers within these broad categories. There is a wide gulf between the broad sweep of global news offered by *The New York Times,* on one hand, and the scores of tabloids and small-town newspapers that highlight local society news, on the other. U.S. media contain much journalistic wheat along with generous portions of chaff, and the proportions vary widely in individual media. In fact, any citizen willing to make the effort can find essential current information more readily in the internet age than ever before, especially in the legacy media's internet versions.[64] Those versions even include the views of citizen pundits along with the commentary of professionals.

Any fair indictment of the news media must consider mitigating circumstances. This does not mean that the charges are invalid; it means that they must be put into context to assess the degree of guilt. Critics should consider the pressures under which journalists do their work under both normal and crisis conditions. Among them, the necessity to produce profits for the parent organization is paramount. It accounts for excesses of negativism and voyeur journalism. Other stresses arise from journalistic values and the conventions of news production. For example, the zeal to rush to publication with breaking news fosters mistakes and misinterpretations; the beat system privileges newsworthy events occurring on regular beats over important happenings that occur beyond these beats; and pack journalism homogenizes criteria for news selection, leading most media to become rivals in conformity.

Economic developments continue to heighten pressures. The multiplication of readily accessible news channels in the United States and elsewhere forced electronic as well as print media to compete more fiercely for audiences and advertisers. Shrinking profit margins in individual enterprises forced cutbacks in staff that put additional workloads on the remaining employees. Rich databases grew exponentially. They are now regularly mined to enrich the context for stories. Sadly, the time available to individual reporters to search them is shrinking. However, some news organizations are dedicating more resources to database searching for important news stories. The traditional media find their news turf eroded by the new media's ability to publish breaking stories instantly. Accordingly, print media must abandon the lure of featuring freshly breaking news and attract audiences in other ways. But when they turn to more analytical and interpretive reporting, they are accused of improperly straying into the terrain of editorial commentary. The upshot is that the public increasingly perceives newspaper reporting as unduly biased.

Finally, judging complaints about the media requires a historical perspective. We are living in a period when regard for most major institutions in the United States is at a low ebb. The 2016 election cycle prompted many Americans to profess being exhausted and overwhelmed by the amount of campaign news while not feeling very informed by it. Media trust is at historic lows, and politicians are more aggressively campaigning against the press. History also shows that politicians and the general public are fickle in their condemnations as well as in their praise. The founders of our nation were the first to carp, on the one hand, about its venal, lying press and the first to agree, on the other, that warts and all, it was the bedrock on which democratic freedoms rest.

SUMMARY

What is news depends on what a particular society deems socially significant or personally satisfying. The prevailing political and social ideology therefore determines what type of information journalists will gather and the range of meanings they will give it.

Beyond the larger framework, which is rooted in the country's current political ideology, overt political considerations rarely play a major part in news selection. Instead, the profit motive and the technical constraints of news production are paramount selection criteria. These criteria impose more stringent constraints on television than on print media because television deals with more competition and larger, more heterogeneous audiences and requires pictures to match story texts. News making remains almost exclusively in the hands of the traditional news media. The majority of news consumers who rely on the internet visit the news sites offered by major mainstream media, which mirror offline news. The stories offered there mostly reflect the news gathered by traditional media, though they are often told from different, more critical perspectives.

The end products of the various constraints on news making are stories that generally support the U.S. political system but emphasize its shortcomings and conflicts because conflict is exciting and journalists see themselves as watchdogs of public honesty. News is geared primarily to attract and entertain rather than to educate the audience about politically significant events. The pressures to report news rapidly while it is happening often lead to disjointed fragments and disparate commentary. Judged in terms of the information needs of the model citizen in an ideal democracy, news is plentiful but inadequate. This is especially true of broadcast news, which generally provides little more than a headline service for news and which mirrors the world about as much as the curved mirrors at the county fair. The news does reflect reality, but the picture is badly out of shape and proportion. Most Americans only faintly resemble the ideal citizen, and most look to the media for entertainment rather than enlightenment. As a result, news outlets intersperse entertainment with a smattering of serious information. They prefer breadth of coverage over narrow depth. In times of acute crisis, serious news displaces entertainment, and the broad sweep of events turns into a narrow, in-depth focus on the crisis. But short of acute crisis, kaleidoscopic, shallow storytelling prevails most of the time.

DISCUSSION QUESTIONS

1. What does the typical American journalist look like? Are journalists generally reflective of the American citizenry in terms of ideological beliefs; levels of education and income; or gender, race, and ethnicity? How might journalists' traits and characteristics shape coverage? What does that mean for how we should evaluate news content?

2. What is gatekeeping and why is it a part of the news-making process? What are the various considerations that shape gatekeeping decisions?

3. What are the effects of gatekeeping? What patterns do we typically see in coverage that are attributable to journalistic gatekeeping? Thinking back to Question 1, might we see different patterns in coverage if the profiles of journalists were somehow different?

4. Given all that we have learned about news making and reporting routines as well as what influences them, how should we appraise news making? Do news media play their democratic role and serve their functions well or badly?

READINGS

Alexander, J. C., Breese, E. B., & Luengo, M. (2016). *The crisis of journalism reconsidered: Democratic culture, professional codes, digital future.* Cambridge University Press.

Anderson, C. W. (2018). *Apostles of certainty: Data journalism and the politics of doubt.* Oxford University Press.

Atkeson, L. R., & Maestas, C. D. (2014). *Catastrophic politics: How extraordinary events redefine perceptions of government.* Cambridge University Press.

Batsell, J. (2015). *Engaged journalism: Connecting with digitally empowered news audiences.* Columbia University Press.

Bennett, W. L., Lawrence, R. G., & Livingston, S. (2007). *When the press fails.* University of Chicago Press.

Clark, L. S., & Marchi, R. (2017). *Young people and the future of news: Social media and the rise of connective journalism.* Cambridge University Press.

Cushion, S. (2012). *The democratic value of news: Why public service media matter.* Palgrave Macmillan.

Ellinas, A. A. (2018). *Media and the radical right.* Oxford University Press.

Gutsche, R. E., Jr. (Ed.). (2018). *The Trump presidency, journalism, and democracy.* Routledge.

Kennedy, D. (2013). *The wired city: Reimagining journalism and civic life in the post-newspaper age.* University of Massachusetts Press.

Kovach, B., & Rosenstiel, T. (2014). *The elements of journalism: What newspeople should know and the public should expect.* Three Rivers Press.

Lawrence, R. G. (2000). *The politics of force: Media and the construction of police brutality.* University of California Press.

Peters, C., & Broersma, M. (Eds.). (2016). *Rethinking journalism again: Societal role and public relevance in a digital age.* Routledge.

Robinson, S. (Ed). (2016). *Community journalism midst media revolution.* Routledge.

Schudson, M. (2003). *Sociology of news.* Norton.

Tolchin, M. (2019). *Politics, journalism, and the way things were: My life at The Times, The Hill, and Politico.* Routledge.

Wahl-Jorgensen, K. (2019). *Emotions, media and politics.* John Wiley & Sons.

Weaver, D. H., & Willnat, L. (Eds.). (2020). *The global journalist in the 21st century.* Routledge.

Zelizer, B. (2017). *What journalism could be.* John Wiley & Sons.

NOTES

1. Darr, J. P., Hitt, M. P., & Dunaway, J. (2018). Newspaper closures polarize voting behavior. *Journal of Communication, 68*(6), 1007–1028; Abernathy, P. M. (2018). The expanding news desert. *Center for Innovation and Sustainability in Local Media, School of Media and Journalism, University of North Carolina at Chapel Hill*; Newspapers Fact Sheet. (2021, June 29). *Pew Research Center.* https://www.journalism.org/fact-sheet/newspapers/

2. Peterson, E. (2019). Paper cuts: How reporting resources affect political news coverage. *American Journal of Political Science.* https://doi.org/10.1111/ajps.12560

3. Peterson, E. (2019). Paper cuts: How reporting resources affect political news coverage. *American Journal of Political Science.* https://doi.org/10.1111/ajps.12560; Darr, J. P., Hitt, M. P., & Dunaway, J. L. (2021). *Home style opinion: How local newspapers can slow polarization.* Cambridge University Press. https://doi.org/10.1017/9781108950930

4. Parrish, C. (2016, January 4). The biggest challenges facing the news industry in 2016. *Fast Company.* https://www.fastcompany.com/3054408/elasticity/the-biggest-challenges-facing-the-news-industry-in-2016.

5. The Web: Alarming, appealing and a challenge to journalistic values: Financial woes now overshadow all other concerns for journalists. (2008). *Pew Research Center for the People and the Press.* http://assets.pewresearch.org/wp-content/uploads/sites/4/2011/01/Journalist-report-2008.pdf

6. Dautrich, K., & Hartley, T. H. (1999). *How the news media fail American voters: Causes, consequences, and remedies.* Columbia University Press.

7. For recent examples, see Hassell, H. J. G., Holbein, J. B., & Miles, M. R. (2020). There is no liberal media bias in which news stories political journalists choose to cover. *Science Advances, 6*(14). https://www.science.org/doi/10.1126/sciadv.aay9344; Budak, C., Goel, S., & Rao, J. M. (2016). Fair and balanced? Quantifying media bias through crowdsourced content analysis. *Public Opinion Quarterly, 80*(S1), 250–271.

8. Weaver, D. H., Beam, R. A., Brownlee, B. J., Voakes, P. S., & Wilhoit, G. C. (2007). *The American journalist in the twenty-first century.* Erlbaum.

9. Kallen, S. (Ed.). (2004). *Media bias.* Greenhaven Press; Ecarma, R. E. (2003). *Beyond ideology: A case of egalitarian bias in the news.* University Press of America; Sheppard, S. (2008). *The partisan press: A history of media bias in the United States.* McFarland.

10. Minority journalists and women present a slightly different demographic profile, which may reflect different political preferences and leanings. However, they have historically made up a smaller proportion of the ranks of U.S. journalists. We discuss changing newsroom demographics and how they affect representation and coverage in Chapter 9.

11. Coverage patterns for prominent stories may set the mold for subsequent reporting, although this did not happen in the O. J. Simpson murder case; Maxwell, K. A., Huxford, J., Borum, C., & Hornik, R. (2000). Covering domestic violence: How the O. J. Simpson case shaped reporting of domestic violence in the news media. *Journalism and Mass Communication Quarterly, 77*(Summer), 258–272.

12. Patterson, T. E. (2007). Political roles of the journalist. In D. Graber, D. McQuail, & P. Norris (Eds.), *The politics of news, the news of politics* (2nd ed.). CQ Press. For comparisons of roles across international borders, see Hallin, D. C., & Mancini, P. (2004). *Comparing media systems: Three models of media and politics.* Cambridge University Press.

13. Glasser, T. L. (Ed.). (1999). *The idea of public journalism.* Guilford; Haas, T. (2007). *The pursuit of public journalism: Theory, practice, and criticism.* Routledge.

14. Boyles, J. L., & Meyer, E. (2016). Letting the data speak: Role perceptions of data journalists in fostering democratic conversation. *Digital Journalism, 4*(7), 944–954; Batsell, J. (2015). *Engaged journalism: Connecting with digitally empowered news audiences.* Columbia University Press; De Maeyer, J., & Trudel, D. (2016). Rebirth of popular journalism. *NiemanLab.* http://www.niemanlab.org/2016/12/a-rebirth-of-populist-journalism/; O'Leary, A. (2016). Not just covering communities, reaching them. *NiemanLab.* http://www.niemanlab.org/2016/12/not-just-covering-communities-reaching-them/

15. Other highly rated values are acting as the public's watchdog over government, supplying news needed for citizenship duties, and analyzing complex

problems to help the public understand them. See Weaver, D. H., Beam, R. A., Brownlee, B. J., Voakes, P. S., & Wilhoit, G. C. (2007). *The American journalist in the twenty-first century.* Erlbaum.

16. The question is explored briefly, but poignantly, by Oreskes, M., The Harvard International Journal of Press/Politics, The MIT Press. (2000). What's news? News: A bit hard to define. *Harvard International Journal of Press/Politics*, 5(Summer), 102–113.

17. Linder, A. M. (2016). Editorial gatekeeping in citizen journalism. *New Media & Society.* https://doi.org/10.1177%2F1461444816631506

18. Cabosky, J., & Gibson, R. (2021). A longitudinal content analysis of the use of radical and mainstream, pro-and anti-LGBT organizations as sources in *The New York Times & The Washington Post. Journal of Homosexuality, 68*(3), 365–388; For complaints about news selection processes, see Bennett, W. L. (2009). *News: The politics of illusion* (8th ed.). Pearson/Longman; Bennett, W. L., Lawrence, R. G., & Livingston, S. (2007). *When the press fails.* University of Chicago Press.

19. Deggans, E., & Folkenflik, D. (2021, January 7). A look at how different U.S. media outlets covered the Pro-Trump riot on Capitol Hill, January 7, 2021. *NPR.* https://www.npr.org/2021/01/07/954562181/a-look-at-how-different-u-s-media-outlets-covered-the-pro-trump-riot-on-capitol-

20. Padgett, J. S., Dunaway, J. L., & Darr, J. P. (2019). As seen on TV? How gatekeeping makes the US House seem more extreme. *Journal of Communication*, 69(6), 696–719.

21. Steinberg, J. (2004, August 13). *Washington Post* rethinks its coverage of war debate. *The New York Times.* Also see Bennett, W. L., Lawrence, R. G., & Livingston, S. (2007). *When the press fails.* University of Chicago Press, Chapter 1.

22. Gerbner, G. (1964). Ideological perspective and political tendencies in news reporting. *Journalism Quarterly, 41*(August), 495–508.

23. For a discussion of the social systems framework for mass communications analysis, see Ettema, J. S. (1982). The organizational context of creativity. In J. S. Ettema & D. C. Whitney (Eds.), *Individuals in mass media organizations: Creativity and constraint* (pp. 91–106). SAGE.

24. Hamilton, J. T. (2004). *All the news that's fit to sell: How the market transforms information into news.* Princeton University Press.

25. Cappella, J. N., & Jamieson, K. H. (1997). *Spiral of cynicism: The press and the public good.* Oxford University Press.

26. Lawrence, R. (2000). Game-framing the issues: Tracking the strategy frame in public policy news. *Political Communication, 17,* 93–114; also see Kuypers, J. A. (2002). *Press bias and politics: How the media frame controversial issues.* Praeger.

27. Iyengar, S., & Kinder, D. (1987). *News that matters*. University of Chicago Press; Iyengar, S. (1991). *Is anyone responsible? How television frames political issues*. University of Chicago Press.

28. Soroka, S., Fournier, P., & Nir, L. (2019). Cross-national evidence of a negativity bias in psychophysiological reactions to news. *Proceedings of the National Academy of Sciences, 116*(38), 18888–18892; Soroka, S., Daku, M., Hiaeshutter-Rice, D., Guggenheim, L., & Pasek, J. (2018). Negativity and positivity biases in economic news coverage: Traditional versus social media. *Communication Research, 45*(7), 1078–1098; Soroka, S., & McAdams, S. (2015). News, politics, and negativity. *Political Communication, 32*(1), 1–22; Soroka, S. (2014). *Negativity in democratic politics: Causes and consequences*. Cambridge University Press; Trussler, M., & Soroka, S. (2014). Consumer demand for cynical and negative news frames. *The International Journal of Press/Politics, 19*(3), 360–379.

29. Graber, D. (2001). *Processing politics*. University of Chicago Press; see also Bennett, S. E., Rhine, S. L., & Flickinger, R. S. (2004). The things they cared about: Americans' attention to different news stories, 1989–2002. *Press/Politics, 9*(1), 75–99.

30. Sui, M., Dunaway, J., Sobek, D., Abad, A., Goodman, L., & Saha, P. (2017). US news coverage of global terrorist incidents. *Mass Communication and Society, 20*(6), 895–908.

31. Patterson, T. E. (2000, December). *Doing well and doing good: How soft news and critical journalism are shrinking the news audience and weakening democracy—and what news outlets can do about it* [Working Papers Series RWP01-001]. John F. Kennedy School of Government.

32. Dunaway, J. (2008). Media outlets, ownership, and campaign news coverage. *Journal of Politics, 70*(4), 1193–1202.

33. Lippmann, W. (1965). *Public opinion*. Free Press, p. 229.

34. Data compiled from the Vanderbilt Television News Archive. Electoral vote percentage based on allocation for the 2008 presidential election. $N = 4,629$ mentions in stories.

35. King, S. (2016, September 30). The largest prison strike in history is being largely ignored by major media outlets. *Paste*. https://www.pastemagazine.com/articles/2016/09/the-largest-prison-strike-in-history-is-being-larg.html

36. For an extensive discussion, see Arnold, R. D. (2004). *Congress, the press, and political accountability*. Russell Sage Foundation.

37. Parmelee, J. H. (2013). Political journalists and Twitter: Influences on norms and practices. *Journal of Media Practice, 14*(4), 291–305.

38. Wihbey, J., Joseph, K., & Lazer, D. (2019). The social silos of journalism? Twitter, news media and partisan segregation. *New Media & Society, 21*(4), 815–835.

39. Bagdikian, B. (1971). *The information machines*. Harper and Row.

40. Pavlik, J. V. (2006). Disguised as news. *Television Quarterly, 36*(3–4), 17–25; Lordan, E. J., & Saint John, B., III. (2009). Video news release policies and usage at US television news stations: Deontological implications for the newsroom. *Journalism Practice, 3*(1), 46–58; Ketelaars, P., & Sevenans, J. (2020). It's a matter of timing. How the timing of politicians' information subsidies affects what becomes news. *Political Communication, 38*(3), 1–21.

41. See Lordan, E. J., & Saint John, B., III. (2009). Video news release policies and usage at US television news stations: Deontological implications for the newsroom. *Journalism Practice, 3*(1), 46–58; Campbell, R., Martin, C. R., & Fabos, B. (2009). *Media and culture* (7th ed.). Bedford/St. Martin's. Also see Kovach, B., & Rosenstiel, T. (2007). *The elements of journalism: What newspeople should know and the public should expect* (1st rev. ed.). Three Rivers Press.

42. Fowler, E. F., & Ridout, T. N. (2009). Local television and newspaper coverage of political advertising. *Political Communication, 26*(2), 119–136; Ridout, T., & Smith, G. R. (2008). Free advertising: How the media amplify campaign messages. *Political Research Quarterly, 61*(4), 598–608.

43. The content of websites sponsored by print and broadcast media mostly parallels their mainstream versions but covers the stories more extensively. Hindman, M. (2011). *Less of the same*. FCC.

44. Dunaway, J. (2016, August). *Mobile vs. computers: Implications for audiences and outlets* [Discussion Paper Series #D-103]. Harvard University, Shorenstein Center.

45. The first two headings have been adapted from Herbert Gans's study of newsmagazines and network television news. See Gans, H. (1979). *Deciding what's news*. Pantheon; see also Tuchman, G. (1978). *Making news: A study in the construction of reality*. Free Press; Bennett, W. L. (2009). *News: The politics of illusion* (8th ed.). Pearson/Longman.

46. Patterson, T. E. (2016, June 13). *Pre-primary news coverage of the 2016 presidential race: Trump's rise, Sanders' emergence, Clinton's struggle*. Shorenstein Center on Media, Politics and Public Policy, Harvard Kennedy School; for a broad discussion of the coverage mix at the federal government level, see Hess, S. (1981). *The Washington reporters*. Brookings Institution Press.

47. Hamilton, J. T. (2004). *All the news that's fit to sell: How the market transforms information into news*. Princeton University Press.

48. Graber, D. (2001). *Processing politics*. University of Chicago Press.

49. After a century of printing on weekdays, the *Christian Science Monitor* moved its operations online in the spring of 2009, printing only once a week.

50. Kerbel, M. R. (2018). *If it bleeds, it leads: An anatomy of television news*. Westview Press.

51. Gerbner, G., Gross, L., Morgan, M., & Signorielli, N. (1982, June). Charting the mainstream: Television's contributions to political orientations. *Journal of Communication, 32*(Spring), 106–107. Small-town newspapers are more apt to highlight the positive, telling what is good rather than what is bad, because conflict is less tolerable in social systems in which most of the leaders constantly rub elbows.

52. *Videomalaise* is Michael J. Robinson's term. See Robinson, M. J. (1975). American political legitimacy in an era of electronic journalism: Reflections on the evening news. In R. Adler (Ed.), *Television as a social force: New approaches to TV criticism* (pp. 97–139). Praeger.

53. See Brüggemann, M., & Engesser, S. (2017). Beyond false balance: How interpretive journalism shapes media coverage of climate change. *Global Environmental Change, 42*, 58–67.

54. See Kilgo, D. K., Mourão, R. R., & Sylvie, G. (2019). Martin to Brown: How time and platform impact coverage of the Black Lives Matter movement. *Journalism Practice, 13*(4), 413–430.

55. For a strong attack on status quo support, see Herman, E. S., & Chomsky, N. (2002). *Manufacturing consent: The political economy of the mass media.* Pantheon.

56. There is resistance to change, even in entertainment program formats. See Blumler, J. G., & Spicer, C. M. (1990). Prospects for creativity in the new television marketplace: Evidence from program-makers. *Journal of Communication, 40*(Autumn), 78–101.

57. A comparison of war movies made with and without Pentagon aid showed that aided movies depicted the military in a more favorable light; Shain, R. E. (1972). Effects of Pentagon influence on war movies, 1948–70. *Public Opinion Quarterly, 38*(Fall), 641–647.

58. For a fuller exploration of this issue, see Altheide, D. L. (1976). *Creating reality: How TV news distorts events.* SAGE; Tuchman, G. (1978). *Making news: A study in the construction of reality.* Free Press; Fishman, M. (1980). *Manufacturing the news.* University of Texas Press; Bennett, W. L. (2016). *News: The politics of illusion* (10th ed.). University of Chicago Press.

59. But sensational news often contains a great deal of information; see Baum, M. A. (2003). *Soft news goes to war: Public opinion and American foreign policy in the new media age.* Princeton University Press.

60. Fico, F., & Soffin, S. (1995). Fairness and balance of selected newspaper coverage of controversial national, state, and local issues. *Journalism and Mass Communication Quarterly, 72*(Autumn), 621–633; Kressel, N. J. (1987). Biased judgments of media bias: A case study of the Arab-Israeli dispute. *Political Psychology, 8*(June), 211–226; Lichter, S. R., Rothman, S., & Lichter, L. S. (1986). *The media elite.* Adler and Adler, pp. 293–301. The difficulties of

defining *bias* are explained in Lacy, S., Fico, F., & Simon, T. F. (1991). Fairness and balance in the prestige press. *Journalism Quarterly, 68*(Fall), 363–370; Simon, T. F., Fico, F., & Lacy, S. (1989). Covering conflict and controversy: Measuring balance, fairness, defamation. *Journalism Quarterly, 62*(Summer), 427–434.

61. McNulty, J. (2004, September 6). Top U.S. newspapers' focus on balance skewed coverage of global warming, analysis reveals. *UC Santa Cruz Currents Online.* http://currents.ucsc.edu/04-05/09-06/coverage.html; also see Brüggemann, M., & Engesser, S. (2017). Beyond false balance: How interpretive journalism shapes media coverage of climate change. *Global Environmental Change, 42*(2017), 58–67.

62. Americans paid close attention as elections returns came in. (2020, November 23). *Pew Research Center.* https://www.journalism.org/2020/11/23/americans-paid-close-attention-as-election-returns-came-in/

63. For an excellent comparative analysis of these issues, see Norris, P. (2000). *A virtuous circle: Political communications in postindustrial societies.* Cambridge University Press.

64. Entman, R. M. (2005). The nature and sources of news. In G. Overholser & K. H. Jamieson (Eds.), *Institutions of American democracy: The press* (pp. 48–65). Oxford University Press. Entman identifies four types of journalism: traditional, advocacy, tabloid, and entertainment, each characterized by distinctive organizational values and missions.

4

News and Politics in the Changing Media Landscape

Early research following the arrival of the internet anticipated the dramatic changes new communication technologies could bring. Bruce Bimber predicted in 2003 that technological evolution since the 1990s would bring in an era of "information abundance." Bimber described technological developments as political because they could "affect social and economic structures as well as values" and "alter the identity and organization of political actors and interests."[1] W. Russell Neuman anticipated an age of personalized media and a network that would "blur the distinction between mass and interpersonal communications." His vision included a single electronic network that would "combine computing, telephony, broadcasting, motion pictures and publishing."[2] But Neuman also warned that many of the provocative predictions that are apt to follow new technologies—often characterized as *technological determinism*—are generally off the mark because they ignore the human context that determines if, how, and when new technologies will be used. According to Neuman, "Technology does not determine, but it can make a difference."[3]

Several changes prompted by the arrival of digital information technologies have potential for political influence:

1. Nonprofessional citizen journalism

2. The digitally enabled interactivity tools

3. The leveling of barriers to communication (time, space, politics, and economics)

4. The multiplication of communication channels and hypercompetitive media world

5. The modernization of legacy journalism

6. The growth of new approaches for financing the creation and distribution of news

Some of these changes generated more political effects than others. This chapter explores their political impact and describes and explains how the changes in mass media and communication technology have influenced politics by changing the market for news, news making, and news consumption in the United States. This includes the dramatic expansion of media choice brought about by cable television, the explosion of political and news websites, the proliferation and popularity of social media platforms, and the expanding number of devices through which media content is made available. In particular, this chapter describes how changes in our modern media landscape have influenced citizen news habits and the practice and profession of journalism.

The Expansion of Media Choice and the Market for News

The most significant change in the modern media environment is the dramatic expansion of content choice—the wide array of entertainment and public affairs content available to us at any given time or place. Seemingly endless content is available on mobile devices, online, and through our television and computer screens, made available through media companies scrambling to make their content ready for consumption across a host of distribution mechanisms. This expansion has important consequences for citizens' news consumption habits, the news profession, news content, politicians, and governance. More and more people are seeking political information online and through social media. These trends are only accelerating as mobile access to the internet continues to proliferate and improve.

The media market and the expansion of choices it provides raises many questions about the implications of the changing media environment. The expanding number of outlets and distribution mechanisms created economic incentives for media organizations to isolate markets and provide special interest or niche programming, a phenomenon also referred to as *media fragmentation*. This is true of cable entertainment venues such as HGTV, Lifetime, and Nickelodeon and extends to content offerings online and to the political arena. For example, most cable television packages have at least three major 24-hour news networks, which together reflect a political continuum from MSNBC on the left to CNN in the middle to Fox News on the right. Online there are countless partisan and ideologically oriented news sites and blogs. This re-emergence of partisan media is why scholars of media and politics are investigating several research questions related to the fragmenting media environment: (1) Is today's media environment more polarized than in the past? (2) Do audiences purposely seek out news that agrees with their partisanship? (3) What are the implications when citizens seek out only the news that fits their viewpoints?

Niche News and Selective Exposure

Several content-based studies examined whether outlets in the new media environment are more polarized than traditional broadcast or print media outlets; evidence clearly suggests they are. For example, in a content analytic study of the 2020 election, Thomas E. Patterson found that Fox News's reporting about the candidates was far more supportive of Trump than CBS's coverage, supporting the view that Fox News is oriented toward the political right. A host of other studies also demonstrate the polarized partisan orientations of the three major cable news networks.[4]

A potentially more important question is whether citizens take advantage of the diversity of content available in today's media environment. When people choose news or public affairs information, how do they choose? Researchers are thoroughly investigating the degree to which people engage in *partisan selective exposure*—the behavior of allowing political beliefs to dictate media choices. Partisan selective exposure predicts that citizens purposefully select pro-attitudinal messages and deliberately ignore counter-attitudinal messages. Though evidence clearly suggests that partisan selective exposure does occur, recent research documents a more nuanced relationship, showing that attraction to agreeable information and the avoidance of disagreeable information are two different things, and that the extent to which they occur varies across individuals and by partisanship. People of both parties are, on average, more receptive of agreeable content or content with a mix of perspectives over information with which they clearly disagree, but Republicans are more prone toward active avoidance of disagreeable information. Non-Republicans are more likely to select stories with agreeable information, even if they also contain disagreeable information. In other words, for most people, selective exposure behaviors seem to be more about preferences for like-minded information than about avoiding disagreeable information.[5] As this study and other research demonstrates, partisan selective exposure is not absolute; its occurrence depends on the individual, the information being considered, and the context.[6]

The evidence about how much selective exposure occurs in digital media environments—whether the internet and social media enhance or repress exposure diversity—is mixed. The internet is clearly a contributor to the vast expansion of media choices available, including partisan sources of information; it provides countless opportunities to explore viewpoints of all kinds. Further, there is evidence of cross-party sampling of content. Matthew Hindman, for example, finds website traffic that crosses ideological lines, where twelve of the top fifty political websites receive or send traffic from the other ideological side. However, his research still provides more evidence of online political factions or echo chambers than cross-ideology traffic; web traffic is most common between websites of the same ideological viewpoint.[7] Several studies also document that online users seek out like-minded information, while others show that a large proportion of the public still samples heavily from mainstream outlets; and some studies show evidence for both.[8] Some differences in findings are explained by different research methodologies.

Evidence of exposure diversity on social media is still emerging but is increasingly important to understand since people often utilize these platforms for consuming information on news and public affairs. Researchers find some amount of like-mindedness among individuals in the same social networks, but there is not much evidence of complete ideological or partisan uniformity in social media networks. In addition, an important factor determining exposure diversity on social media is individual user behaviors on social networking sites. Many people report avoiding political information on social networking sites by blocking, unfriending, or hiding those who post counter-attitudinal information,[9] but exposure to cross-ideological (and oppositional party) content still occurs with some regularity, though less often than like-minded content. In a 2015 study of more than 10 million Facebook users in the United States (U.S.), Eytan Bakshy, Solomon Messing, and Lada Adamic report that "friends" are much less likely to share news content when it comes from news sources they disagree with. Friend networks were exposed to about 15% less counter-attitudinal content relative to content they agreed with, and they engaged with (as defined by clicking) 70% less disagreeable content than agreeable content. This selectivity limited exposure to counter-attitudinal news more than Facebook's algorithm for ranking stories in the news feed.[10]

The research suggests clear patterns of citizen gravitation toward like-minded information online, even if these behaviors do not produce complete isolation into silos of agreeable viewpoints and information. Though selective exposure is variable across individuals, messages, and contexts, these behaviors are documented in cable television selections, internet use, and social networking behaviors. It is no surprise that the next questions scholars asked were about the impact of partisan media and selective exposure. Early concern around the topic of selective exposure focused on the potential for a spiral of selective attention in which partisans seek out information only from sources supportive of their view while never getting exposed to opposing perspectives. As noted above, other research suggests that selection of pro-attitudinal content does not necessarily mean partisans are rarely exposed to information from opposing viewpoints or sources.[11] Several experimental studies demonstrate negative effects from exposure to one-sided information, such as increasing dislike or hostility between the partisans on the other side and the strengthening of partisan identities.[12]

Individuals also use motivated reasoning to guide their selections and interpretations of media messages. Jennifer Jerit and Jason Barabas demonstrate the relationship between the characteristics of the new information environment and the problem of *partisan perceptual bias*, which is the different interpretation of facts that members of opposing parties sometimes hold. They find that partisan perceptual bias is rooted in the news environment and the way we learn information when it does not fit with our predispositions. These scholars conclude that "even though aggregate levels of knowledge increase as information in the mass media becomes more plentiful, both Democrats and Republicans learn at different rates depending on whether the information they encounter squares with their partisan predilections."[13] Emerging evidence suggests additional and perhaps less anticipated consequences from changes to the media environment, too, such as direct effects on the political behavior of elites in Congress and growing levels of partisan sorting and negative political affect in the mass public.[14]

Even though citizens prefer like-minded information and opportunities for selective exposure are common, some evidence suggests concerns about online echo chambers or spirals of complete selectivity and avoidance may be overstated. Attempts to actively avoid counter-attitudinal information are not as strong as once thought, and once people are confronted with counter information, they often spend time consuming that information. Moreover, the enormous volume of entertainment content available means that the negative impact of partisan media is tempered by the high proportion of users and audiences that opt out of political content altogether.[15] We will revisit questions about the impact of selective exposure on learning, attitudes, and behavior in Chapters 9, 11, and 13.

Platform Multiplication and Changing News Habits

Changes to the modern media landscape dramatically altered news audience behaviors and the practice and profession of journalism. These changes are also influencing news content in many ways, but of particular importance is how new platforms and distribution mechanisms for news influence the provision of information to citizens.

Platform Multiplication

Today, most people can receive internet messages and broadcast their own at relatively low cost. This was not always the case. The Web, with its wide open, relatively inexpensive, and minimally regulated access features, encouraged the creation of a multiplicity of different types of channels and services. The vast number of available channels expanded the range of news that can be covered and instantaneously transmitted. For this reason, the internet is the largest competitive threat to newspapers and traditional over-the-air and cable television. It duplicates many of their news and entertainment offerings and guides people to other information sources by listing links to other relevant websites that are only one click away. Popular streaming services such as Netflix, Amazon Prime, and Hulu compound the competitive troubles brought by digital media, especially as younger cohorts engage in cord-cutting behaviors, opting to rely on streaming services alone.

Contrary to earlier forecasts, the multiplication of news providers did not immediately split off large chunks of the traditional media's audience. The reason is twofold. Most important, the traditional media have become a major presence on the Web, using an assortment of internet channels to transmit their news products. In the newspaper field, many major papers have more readers for their Web version than for their traditional "hard"—that is, paper—copies. Second, in the earlier battle for audiences, the traditional media had the advantage of being known and trusted, though this trust is eroding as audiences increasingly perceive bias in the news. Recent years have witnessed a gradual eroding of network news audiences as well as significant numbers of local newspaper deaths. Despite the fact that the majority of internet offerings initially failed to establish trust, some Web-native arrivals to the media scene have overcome the trust hurdle and are heavily used sources for news. High audience numbers have been their reward. Examples include Yahoo, Google, and HuffPost.

The political consequences of the multiplication of news providers were substantial, although observers measure them with various scales and therefore disagree about their magnitude and significance. Most importantly, the store of information provided by news radio, television, cable, and digital channels by communication satellites and by round-the-clock news programs offers an unrivaled diversity of news.[16] Small communities with limited information sources can now readily escape from their communication ghettoes by turning to the internet. Although they are unlikely to find news outlets with information about their local community,[17] digital communication technologies can supply an assortment of major newspapers to the citizens who seek them. Similarly, cable television systems offer programs across hundreds of separate channels. That increases choice for consumers, which means many will choose one of countless entertainment options over news.

However, the impression of a widely used, rich menu of choices is often more a mirage than reality because there is an informal concentration of control over the news supply. It springs from American news consumers' preference for news from brand-name media. When audiences turn to brand-name media for most of their news and internet news organizations do the same, the pool from which the thousands of news channels feed is small indeed. What all of this means for individuals and organizations and political life in specific situations is still unclear. Besides, technology remains in flux and offers new products at an amazing pace. Some, such as Facebook and Twitter, become popular and stay awhile; others die on the vine or after a brief life. The changing mix of news providers, channels, programs, and platforms therefore makes it difficult to assess the full impact of digital communication technologies.[18]

New Versus Old and Media Hybridity

How is the availability of news affected by platform multiplication? How is the depth and focus of news coverage affected? These are particularly important questions because a parallel consequence of changes to the media environment is competitive stress and economic hardship for traditional news media—print media in particular. For example, in 2009, the Hearst-owned *Seattle Post-Intelligencer* was the first major metropolitan daily to cease publication of its print version, shifting all resources to its digital platform. Many other papers followed suit. *Newsweek* magazine published its final print edition in December 2012 before channeling resources to its online news offerings. Daily newspaper circulation continues its steep decline, and between 2004 and 2018, 2,100 local newspapers across the country closed, succumbing to untenable economics.[19] As news becomes more readily available from more sources—and from a diverse array of sources—many traditional venues of news gathering are losing resources.[20]

There are mixed opinions about whether conflicting pressures from the emergence of digital and social media offset one another. One view is that the diversity of content available in the digital news environment eases past concerns about consolidation among traditional media outlets restricting diversity in viewpoints. This perspective views the "open source" nature of journalism in the contemporary information setting as a democratizing force. Others suggest that the emergence of so many new distribution mechanisms for news has not increased or sustained diversity of content because most news content is still produced and gathered by the same traditional outlets. They regard it as the same old content, simply aggregated, shared, and distributed through a variety of news brands and platforms.[21] At the same time, news gathering by those key traditional outlets is being hampered by more competition for attention and audiences, and many aspects of peer-produced content fall short of democratic ideals.[22]

Though this debate is vigorous, empirical evidence is not yet sufficient to settle the argument. Research on content differences between online and traditional news shows that local newspaper and television outlets' digital content does not differ substantially from traditional content, suggesting the addition of online versions of newspapers and news stations does not expand news diversity. The entry of digital-native news outlets into markets could have an effect if enough emerge and attract audiences. Matthew Hindman's research finds very little evidence that digital-native local media outlets emerged online to offset local newspaper losses. Rather, most online local outlets are simply the digital versions of local newspapers and television stations. Among those he finds, the audience metrics are dismal. The online audience for local news spends only a tiny fraction of time consuming local news online.[23] In their 2017 study on the health of local information ecosystems, Philip Napoli and colleagues find high variability in the degree to which traditional and digital forms of local media combine to sufficiently address the critical information needs of local communities. Depending on a host of factors, including the socioeconomic status of the market, some communities' critical information needs are met while others are often left lacking.[24]

Comparisons of print and online media outlets also find much similarity across traditional and online news, at least in terms of campaign coverage. Analyses of coverage of the 2016 presidential primaries show content patterns reflective of traditional broadcast media—revealing the same old audience preference for game frame–style campaign reporting. When political strategy is featured in campaign stories, news websites earn more page views.[25] Digital media has more source diversity than traditional outlets and less reliance on White House sources, but this positive finding is tempered somewhat by the fact that some of the additional sourcing was attributed to analysis provided by their own journalists. This research underscores an apparent paradox of the current media environment: Increasing media abundance seems to do little to diversify news content.[26]

Changing News Habits

While it makes some sense to compare old and newer forms of news, what the research consistently shows is that digital forms of news are here to stay and that traditional media are not rendered obsolete or irrelevant as a result. Online news includes both digital versions of traditional legacy media outlets and those originally founded on the Web (digital-native outlets).

As Table 4.1 shows, legacy media attract a significant about of the digital market share, and although some of the top digital-native outlets have impressive audience reach (see Figure 4-1), only 37 of these attracted at least 10 million unique visitors per month in 2018. Not only are the high-traffic digital-native outlets relatively few in number, growth in their audience reach was rather slow and the average duration of site visits declined between 2014 and 2018.

Table 4-1 Top 10 USA News Websites, 2021

News Website	Facebook Fans	Twitter Followers	Instagram Followers
CNN	33.2 M	53.1 M	10 M
The New York Times	17.4 M	44.7 M	12.6 M
HuffPost	10.2 M	11.4 M	2.4 M
Fox News	17.7 M	18.5 M	4.3 M
USA Today	8.2 M	4.3 M	1.6 M
Reuters	4.2 M	21 M	2.8 M
Politico	1.9 M	4 M	951 K
Yahoo News	7.9 M	1.1 M	159.8 K
NPR News	6.6 M	8.7 M	2.7 M
Los Angeles Times	2.9 M	3.5 M	369.5 K

Source: Adapted from *Top 100 USA news websites, blogs, & influences in 2021.* (2021, October 8). Feedspot. http://blog.feedspot.com/usa_news_websites/; ranking by Feedspot team is based on relevancy, post frequency, social media follower counts and engagements, domain authority, Alexa Web Traffic Rank, and other criteria. Twitter follower data for *HuffPost* and Instagram follower data for *The New York Times* was compiled by Dunaway.

According to media scholar Andrew Chadwick, media systems such as that of the United States—which reflect both the emergence of digital media and a continuing strong presence among traditional media—can now be described as *hybrid*, where both old and new media exert substantial influence on the interplay between the public and public officials. This hybrid view argues that both old and new media logics are still in play. It stresses the importance of understanding how they fit together and interact to influence elite and mass behavior. The lens of media hybridity facilitates a more nuanced understanding of the implications of the changing media environment and avoids simplistic conclusions.[27] For example, though Donald Trump was dubbed "the first Twitter candidate" during the 2016 presidential election, his successful use of Twitter was largely predicated on the manipulation of old media logics. Trump knows the traditional media and their incentives well, and he is a master of using well-timed newsworthy tweets to disrupt the news cycle of mainstream media. He effectively used a social media platform to change the narrative of traditional media during the campaign by serving up material he knew they could not help but cover.

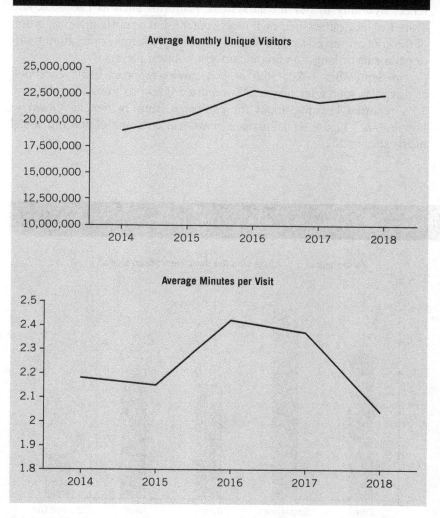

Figure 4-1 Audience Reach and Engagement of Digital-Native News Outlets, 2014–2018

Source: Digital news fact sheet. (2021, July 27). *Pew Research Center.* https://www.journalism.org/fact-sheet/digital-news/.

Note: Data are based on Comscore Media Metrix® Multi-Platform, United States, Unique Visitors, October–December 2014–2018. Figures reflect average monthly unique visitors to the digital-native news outlets with the highest traffic and the average minutes per visit spent by site visitors. The digital-native news outlets with the highest traffic are defined as those that had a monthly average of at least 10 million unique visitors from October–December of the year being analyzed, according to Comscore data.

Social Media and News Use

Upticks in public reliance on social media platforms for news also reflect hybridity in our media system. Platforms such as Facebook and Twitter do not gather their own news content, but a substantial proportion of the content served up and shared on these platforms comes from traditional media or long-standing incumbent political players.[28]

In September 2020, 36% of U.S. adults reported using Facebook as a regular source for news, 23% reported doing so from YouTube, and 15% reported learning about the campaign from Twitter, as shown in Figure 4-2.[29] Figure 4-3 illustrates news use on some of the top social media sites in 2020.

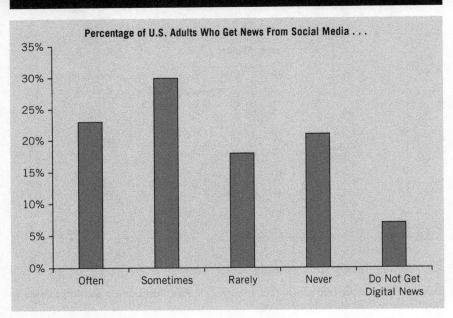

Figure 4-2 News Use on Social Media, 2020

Percentage of U.S. Adults Who Get News From Social Media . . .

Source: Adapted from News use across social media platforms in 2020. (2021, January 11). *Pew Research Center.* https://www.journalism.org/2021/01/12/news-use-across-social-media -platforms-in-2020/pj_2021-01-12_news-social-media_0-01/

Note: Data are based on a Pew Research Center survey of U.S. adults conducted August 31–September 7, 2020.

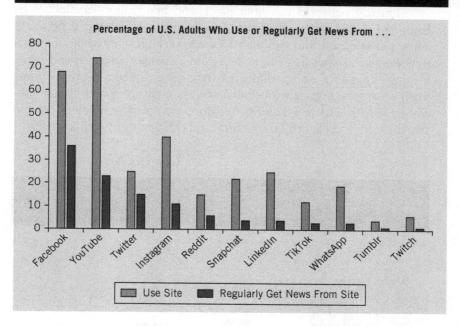

Figure 4-3 News Use Across Various Popular Social Media Platforms, 2020

Percentage of U.S. Adults Who Use or Regularly Get News From . . .

Use Site   Regularly Get News From Site

Source: Adapted from Shearer, E., & Mitchell, A. (2021, January 12). News use across social media platforms in 2020. *Pew Research Center*. https://www.journalism.org/2021/01/12/news-use-across-social-media-platforms-in-2020/.

Note: Figures reflect the percentage of U.S. adults who report using platform as a regular source of news.

Though much of the news and political information served and shared on social media is gathered and disseminated by traditional media, several features of social media make political learning opportunities distinct from those provided by traditional media. First, social media are network centered, which means that individuals can construct social networks in ways that either limit or maximize their potential for learning from or engaging with political news. Networks can be composed of people generally uninterested in politics or people interested in politics. This means that social media users' degree of interest in political news determines their rates of exposure because news exposure is largely determined by the news interest and sharing behaviors of one's social network. Research also suggests that exposure on the sites might not equate to attention or result in learning.

One study found that even when Facebook feeds produce incidental exposure to more political news than individuals typically encounter, there was no correlated increase in their overall levels of political knowledge.[30]

Similarly, networks can limit or expand information capabilities by being either diverse in perspective or one-sided. Like-minded networks allow self-selection into exposure to a silo of largely agreeable information. Research shows that although there is ideological diversity and cross-ideology content sharing within networks, social media users are more likely to see and engage with shared news content from outlets they usually agree with. Figure 4-4 shows the proportion of cross-ideology content shared, seen, and clicked on by liberal and conservative Facebook users.

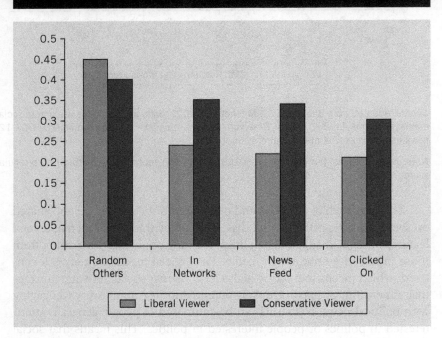

Figure 4-4   Exposure to Cross-Ideology News and Opinion on Facebook

Source: Adapted from Bakshy, E., Messing, S., & Adamic, L. A. (2015). Exposure to ideologically diverse news and opinion on Facebook. *Science, 348*(6239), 1130–1132.

Notes: Figure shows the proportion of content that is ideologically cross-cutting for shares by random others (i.e., not in network), shares from within individuals' social networks, shares that appeared in the News Feed, and shares that individuals clicked on.

Another distinguishing feature of social media is that they allow direct one- and two-way communications between political elites such as candidates, politicians, and party leaders and the public.[31] This means that elites can share their messages in completely unfiltered forms.[32] Researchers Jason Gainous and Kevin M. Wagner argue that this combination of like-minded networks and unfiltered communication from elites keeps messages intact, allowing opinion leaders to have unprecedented message control and persuasive impact.[33] Political elites are among those most followed on social networking sites such as Twitter, and people who follow politicians and other political elites are often opinion leaders in their own right and actively exert influence in online and offline networks.[34] Though traditional institutions of journalism have a heavy presence on social media sites, political elites now have their own competing channels for messages without being interfered with by journalist watchdogs. In some cases, those unfiltered messages are shared and re-shared by networks of followers. Some social media platforms provide significant opportunities to disrupt mainstream media's independent hold on public attention.

Evidence suggests that candidates and campaigns are well aware of this and seek to maximize these strategic advantages. Though some accounts tout the interactive potential among citizens, voters, officials, and political candidates, campaigns are focused on the win and only participate in strategies of "controlled interactivity" wherein the engagement opportunities afforded by these platforms are used only in ways that benefit the campaign. Most often they are used to make citizen-supporters work in concert to achieve strategic campaign goals or to attract earned coverage from the mainstream media.[35] The size, attentiveness, and political engagement of the networks politicians accrue on platforms such as Facebook and Twitter show their strategic potential. Politicians' networks are large, and so are those of opinion leaders within networks. And social networks pay quite a bit of attention to politicians' content. Table 4-2 shows the March 2021 Twitter following among prominent political leaders and candidates.

As Table 4-2 shows, several of these prominent political figures have enormous reach through social media. Twitter is only one example. Other opinion leaders, movements, and groups can earn similarly large followings, and they are not always legitimate. Political events such as the attack on the U.S. Capitol in January 2021, and the rise of the domestic terrorist threat in the U.S. more generally, have many observers worried about the potential these sites have for mobilizing people for illegal and/or violent activities. Yet having a large following is not necessarily equivalent to having an impact on the attitudes and behavior of that following. In Chapter 11, we will examine how much political elites and other actors

Table 4-2 Twitter Following Among Prominent Political Leaders and Candidates, 2021

Candidate/Officeholder	Twitter Handle	Following
Elizabeth Warren	@SenWarren	5.7 M
Alexandria Ocasio-Cortez	@AOC	12.6 M
Bernie Sanders	@BernieSanders	15.2 M
Donald J. Trump	@realDonaldTrump/ @POTUS45	33.2 M
Joe Biden/President Biden	@JoeBiden/@POTUS	29.5 M
Nancy Pelosi	@SpeakerPelosi	7 M
Mitch McConnell	@LeaderMcConnell	2.1 M
Kevin McCarthy	@GOPLeader	1.2 M
Kamala Harris	@VP	9.5 M

Source: Twitter.com; follower data compiled by Dunaway on March 19, 2021. Follower numbers change regularly and reflect counts as reported by Twitter for that date only.

Note: @POTUS45 is an archive of a Trump Administration Twitter account, which is maintained by National Archives and Records Administration. As of March 19, 2021, @realDonaldTrump was still suspended from Twitter following the events at the U.S. Capitol on January 6, 2021. @POTUS became President Biden's official account when he took office in January 2021.

and groups can persuade and mobilize members of the public through social media platforms.

Mobile News Consumption

The public gets a significant amount of news through social media, and the means by which most people access social media is changing.[36] Nearly 80% of time spent on social media platforms happens on mobile devices,[37] and the recent growth rate of mobile news consumption is dramatic. Figure 4-5 shows growth between 2013 and 2019.

The explosion of mobile news consumption is reflected in politicians' behavior as well as news industry practices. During the 2020 presidential election contest, every detail of the race was accessible to mobile news

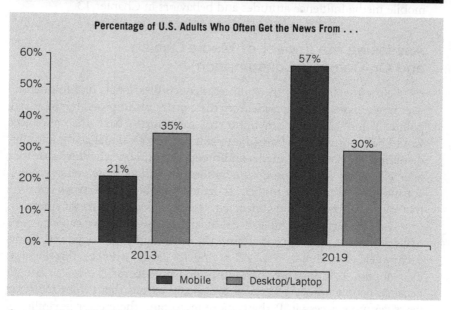

Figure 4-5 Percentage of U.S. Adults Using Mobile Devices for News, 2013 Versus 2019

Percentage of U.S. Adults Who Often Get the News From . . .

2013: Mobile 21%, Desktop/Laptop 35%
2019: Mobile 57%, Desktop/Laptop 30%

■ Mobile ▨ Desktop/Laptop

Source: Adapted from Walker, M. (2019, November 19). Americans favor mobile devices over desktops and laptops for getting news. *Pew Research Center.* https://www.pewresearch .org/fact-tank/2019/11/19/americans-favor-mobile-devices-over-desktops-and-laptops -for-getting-news/

Note: Figure represents the percentage of adults who report that they get their news on mobile devices, desktops, or laptops "often."

audiences no matter their location. News outlets are formulating best practices for mobile programming as they compete for audience attention in the saturated media environment. Well-resourced and savvy news outlets are adopting "mobile first" strategies to meet audiences on their smartphones and tablets, and we do not yet know what this means for the information available in news content.

Systematic and detailed content analyses of differences in news content across platforms is difficult to obtain, but anecdotal accounts of campaign communication strategies and empirical data on audience behaviors provide telling evidence. The potential that social media and mobile devices have for reaching younger audiences means that political practitioners and news media package their messaging in ways that allow for easy sharing on mobile devices. In electoral politics, these strategies are particularly important; campaign messages conveyed through social media have some of the strongest mobilizing effects.[38] We will revisit the topic of how social and mobile media influence attitudes and behaviors in Chapter 13.

Assessing the Impact of Media Choice and On-Demand Consumption

Before the advent of the internet, news professionals had full control over news dissemination, aside from the constraints imposed by the social, political, and economic environment. Journalists chose the news that would be reported, they framed it to suit their professional goals, and they disseminated it via print media and broadcasts run on schedules that they selected, albeit with some considerations of audience preferences. News consumers had to adjust to these schedules and accept the news offerings that various providers had concocted. It was a take-it-or-leave-it situation.

That scenario has changed drastically, so people now can consume news whenever they want it around the clock and seven days and nights each week. Researchers are still trying to gauge whether this flexibility amounts to little more than a nice convenience or is a major benefit because people whose schedules previously barred them from receiving news can now access it. Perhaps more important, the greater flexibility of access to the news allows citizens to graze among a variety of news outlets, picking and choosing entire programs or specific stories as they wish; they can even assemble their own news packages manually or arrange to have them assembled electronically. They can use one of the numerous available services that deliver regularly changing digital information to keep up with the latest developments in just about any field and covering any topic. They can also use news-ranking sites such as Reddit or Digg to check what news their peers are watching and join them, becoming a shared-news community.

Mobile devices, which are an essential piece of equipment for most Americans, further reduce the barriers of space and time. No longer must anyone be physically present at a place with computer access to get the news. It is available on their smartphone at any time or any place they wish (provided there is decent wireless internet coverage). Again, the scope of opportunities to stay in touch with people boggles the imagination. Mobile access, for example, provides internet access to many people who would not otherwise have it. However, research also shows that the mobile platform is not ideal for news seeking and engagement.[39] The reality is that only a small portion of the public actually uses these new opportunities to become more informed about public life and contribute to it.[40]

The proliferation of news venues and the ability to customize news packages to suit news consumers' individual tastes have important downsides along with their benefits. Among them, the fragmentation issue looms large. Will the lack of a shared-news supply fragment the nation's political consensus? When people rely primarily on specialized broadcasts, will their attention to politics diminish?[41] As we will discuss in Chapter 11, in the past, nationwide dissemination of similar news fostered shared political socialization. When news becomes fragmented, people are more likely to be socialized in disparate ways. What will be the consequences? Researchers are still debating whether this means the country may be carved up into mutually exclusive, often hostile political enclaves.[42] We will revisit those debates in later chapters.

Changes to Political Journalism

Studies conducted over the last several decades show the many ways political news content of the broadcast era was significantly influenced by the constraints of journalism and the news making process.[43] Now researchers must confront the impact of the contemporary media landscape, some aspects of which are constantly changing and dramatically altering news reporting routines and the dissemination of news content.

Changing Reporting Routines

One finds further evidence of the impact of changing media technology in traditional journalists' use of digital and social media in their reporting and sharing of news. Though digital and social media compete with traditional news organizations and journalists, they also serve as a tool to supplement coverage and maximize the influence of their work. Journalists use social media sites to cover stories in real time and from any location. Social networking sites allow a different manner of news sourcing and news sharing, providing another venue of communication to audiences outside the constraints of the normal media platforms. Depending on what media company they work for, social media can allow journalists to work outside of traditional market demands, allowing more flexibility in their posting of information. To be sure, use of social media such as Twitter has its own set of prohibitive constraints (i.e., 140/280 character limit), but tweets create another avenue for sharing content—and to a different type of audience. In fact, in her study of national journalists, Ashley Kirzinger finds that this supplemental venue tends to produce a high-quality political news product—addressing more substantive topics than what we find in traditionally distributed political news content.[44] It is no surprise that traditional journalists and news organizations are dedicating more and more resources to looking to digital and social media for sources and story ideas as a routine part of their news gathering.[45] The complex interdependence between traditional and digital media lend credence to the concept of a hybrid media system. Digital media are supplementing traditional news content in ways that can, at times, enhance the substance populating the political information environment, at least when considering national journalists and national political news. Digital and social media transformed the manner in which political reporters produce and share information; the communication avenues made available to journalists via social media such as Twitter are shaping and adding complexity to the political information environment.[46]

Citizen Journalism and User-Generated Content

If citizens had their choice, how would they reshape the news media? Answering that question is no longer a counterfactual exercise because news-ranking sites such as Digg and Reddit keep track of the stories their members favor. Countless people have become amateur reporters, whose work has been published on their own websites or on host websites, including the sites of professional news providers. Systematic studies of the content of citizen-generated news offerings are scarce. In one example, a Pew Research Center study of YouTube conducted January 2011–March 2012 found that 39% of the most watched videos came from citizens. Citizen journalists are producing a great deal of popular content; much of it is footage or images about breaking news events, both emergencies or disasters. Citizen journalists are also developing skills and expertise—the same YouTube study found that many citizen-posted videos were edited.[47] As further testament to their skills, traditional news organizations now frequently partner with citizen journalists by airing their content. One problem with this model, however, is that amateur and citizen journalists do not consistently get credit for their contributions.[48]

People will disagree about the respective merits of professional and nonprofessional reporting, and expectations about the impact of citizen journalism have been mixed. Some observers bemoan the fact that the role of professional journalists as selectors and framers of news is undercut by lay news consumers' ability to perform these tasks themselves, albeit inexpertly. Others hail the weakening of the traditional media. News consumers, they say, are relieved of the tyranny of the press, in which unelected journalists determined what became news and framed it in ways that suited their own purposes better than the audience's goals. These critics claim that citizen-generated news is likely to yield a better fit between audience needs and the messages that reach them. Jay Rosen, scholar and staunch advocate of citizen journalism, defines *citizen journalism* as "when the people formerly known as the audience employ the press tools they have in their possession to inform one another."[49] Citizen journalism has great potential for expanding the diversity of viewpoints and sources and for providing access where journalists' reach is limited or during major breaking crises and events. Yet, some enthusiasm for the benefits of citizen journalism is dampened by concerns about nontraditional journalists' lack of ethical and professional training and the lack of a systematic means by which to classify content as professional journalism content versus citizen-generated content.[50]

Research on citizen journalism provides support for both views. Studies comparing citizen journalism websites with websites of traditional news organizations reveal that citizen journalism sites are more likely to offer a plurality of views and more diversified content, use more diverse sources, and offer more interactivity and multimedia features than traditional news sites.[51] Research also shows an increasingly important role for editorial gatekeeping on citizen journalism websites.[52]

Many fears about citizen journalists' lack of news norms and routines and professional training relate to bias and misinformation. A lack of professional journalistic training or oversight may result in biased or unverified and inaccurate information. An example of potential problems that can emerge from citizen journalism behaviors occurred after the April 15, 2013, bombings at the Boston Marathon, when erroneous information from crowdsourcing was posted to the user-generated news website Reddit.[53] The false leads linked a missing, innocent student to the bombings; his family subsequently received death threats and was forced to deactivate their son's missing persons Facebook page. The missing student was later found dead, and Reddit made a public apology. The posting and instant dissemination of false information can harm individuals and hinder investigations.

Research also provides support for concerns about citizen journalism; a survey-based study comparing the effects of user-generated news and news from traditional and professional media finds that consuming citizen journalism content negatively correlates with political knowledge while consumption of traditional/professional media positively correlates with political knowledge. However, the same study finds that consuming citizen journalism holds a positive relationship with both off- and online engagement; this suggests that citizen journalism may have negative implications for knowledge but positive influences on citizen engagement with news.[54]

Social Media

Video streaming and social networking sites are also platforms for alternative news sources dominated by nonprofessionals. The most prominent of these sites attract huge audiences each month. According to the digital analytics firm Comscore, in January 2016, Facebook's U.S. audience topped 207 million users, LinkedIn's topped 119 million, Twitter's topped 118 million, and Google Sites had a combined audience of more than 245 million unique U.S. visitors.[55] Along with YouTube, these sites offer citizen-generated news to their audiences. However, they also rely heavily on news content from popular legacy media, posting or providing links to traditional media content.

Millions of Americans whose identities are unknown now post their views on sites where other people can read them, comment about them, and pass them on to others. Anyone, at little cost and with no training in news collection and verification, can produce content and post any message, true or false. Ordinary people as content producers are not bound by journalistic criteria such as accuracy, objectivity, fairness, and balance. There is practically no form of censorship, governmental or private, on the internet nor are there requirements for ensuring transparency or accountability.

The upshot is a flourishing marketplace of disparate views—far richer than ever before. Thanks to links, citizen news sites often provide more background information and more access to diverse points of view than other venues. However, a small fraction of their stories are originals; the remainder come from the pool of stories available from traditional news sources.[56]

Some user-generated content has contributed to the public dialogue and even spawned significant political action. Examples are the vivid, firsthand accounts in which bloggers and citizen journalists described the horrors of Hurricane Katrina in 2005 and inspired audiences to help the victims. Many of their stories received wide attention because traditional media used them as part of their own reporting. Nonprofessionals unearth important stories that the media increasingly miss because the ranks of professional journalists are thinner than ever. Other sites have become megaphones for spreading dangerous falsehoods, often without the antidote of counterarguments that are common in mainstream media.

Many online messages, of course, fall by the wayside. For example, though a lot of websites attract millions of unique visitors, many have high "bounce rates," meaning that users remain on the page only for a second or two. Given the growth of social networking sites and YouTube's continued success, more members of the public than ever are exposed to various forms of user-generated content through these venues. Obviously, the right and opportunity to share one's views with the world are limited by the right and opportunity of potential audiences to ignore most messages. When Americans turn to the Web for news, 80% of their visits are to brand-name newspaper, television, and search engine sites because they are deemed more trustworthy than other websites. Table 4-1 makes that clear; it shows the audience numbers for the top news websites, where sites such as CNN and *The New York Times* lead the pack. Alternatively, audience reach for many, if not most, digital-native news sites is tiny. Citizens characterize digital media as the most up-to-date, the easiest to use, and the most enjoyable. Despite such high praise, television remains their first choice for news. As election returns came in for the 2020 presidential campaign, which aroused tremendous public interest, 30% of the audience relied primarily on cable television news, 22% relied on national network TV news, 24% relied on news websites or apps, and only 9% named social media as their primary election-night news source. Despite popularity of digital, social, and mobile news, on election night, over half (52%) of U.S. adults reported that they relied most on either cable or network television news. [57]

Blogs

Blogs are another source of online political information operating outside the confines of traditional professional journalism. Many are produced by professional or semiprofessional journalists or commentators; many others are not. As a result, the nature and quality of blog content and the size of their audiences vary dramatically. Blogs emerged in the late 1990s, primarily as an outlet for sharing information and commentary. In the political sphere, blogs are characterized by commentary peppered with links to news items or other supporting materials. The initial popularity of blogs captured the attention of researchers interested in their democratic consequences. By 2008, the number of blogs skyrocketed, with thousands more started each day. The number of active bloggers in the United States grew to 31.7 million between 2015 and 2020, up by 12%. In such a crowded field, most bloggers' voices go largely unheard, but there is little doubt that the blogosphere as a whole has some political impact—even if that impact is exerted by a prominent few.

Traditional journalism has a periodically uneasy relationship with the blogosphere. At least initially, the arrival of blogs meant yet another variant of competition for mainstream news outlets because they represented one more type of venue with which newspapers and broadcast journalism were competing for audiences. More recently, many journalistic outfits have worked to incorporate bloggers and their style of content (along with other forms of user-generated content) into their reporting practices and organizations.[58] Some prominent examples are ESPN's FiveThirtyEight, *The Washington Post*'s Monkey Cage, *The New York Times*'s The Upshot, and Vox's Mischiefs of Faction.[59]

At the same time, many unaffiliated blogs remain popular, and some have wide reach. Journalists worry that bloggers unaffiliated with news organizations do not employ the same cautionary procedures for verifying and presenting information as journalists and that news audiences are losing the ability to distinguish between online news and online commentary. Richard Davis describes bloggers as participatory journalists, less detached than mainstream media. They may view themselves as journalists, commentators, activists, or all three. Blogs alter the gatekeeping role of media and can cover things the mainstream press does not. Most blogs, however, are personal rather than news oriented, which opens the door for advocacy journalism and critical analysis. While some traditional journalists may be uncomfortable with this, there can be a symbiotic relationship between bloggers and journalists as they feed off each other for resources and leads. As do most journalists, bloggers have more in common with the political elite with than the general public, and many have backgrounds in journalism. Bloggers do often bypass mainstream media to leak stories, which challenges the mainstream media's ability to control the agenda.[60]

Assessing the Impact of Citizen Journalism and User Content

Is citizen journalism and user-generated content, then, a dream or a nightmare? The answer is that for the public, for news media professionals, and for American democracy, it is a bit of both. Fortunately or unfortunately, effects that run simultaneously in opposite directions are common in the evolving media scene and account for widely divergent appraisals by experts and publics. When it comes to the digital media environment, the public benefits from a richer marketplace of ideas, but it is harmed when messages are based on misinformation or deliberate deception, sometimes fueled by hate. News professionals benefit from user-contributed content when the pool of ideas from which they can select their stories is enriched, particularly when the new voices cover unique slices of reality from fresh, previously unheard sources. But journalists and citizens suffer when stories of questionable newsworthiness dominate the news agenda and force journalists to focus on them at the expense of covering more important news.

Journalists typically express mixed feelings about the impact of the internet on traditional news values. Back in 2007, roughly half thought the internet would strengthen these values, while half thought the opposite. The strengths mentioned included more transparency because more eyes are scrutinizing the political scene and the lengthier, more detailed coverage of specific events. The weaknesses mentioned were insufficient quality control, use of sources with unproven reliability records, and increased time pressures in the 24/7 cycle, leading to sloppy reporting.[61] Journalists attribute current shortcomings in their work to the need to constantly worry about the bottom line, which, unfortunately, is tied tightly to economic competition exacerbated by the arrival and proliferation of the internet.

Without a doubt, the internet reduced the power and influence of traditional media, which no longer enjoy a near-monopoly over news production and distribution. They share the control of news with nonprofessional providers. Their power to control the flow of news to and from various world regions also eroded because the internet empowers American news consumers to access news from all parts of the world. Moreover, the multiplication of news sources is a global phenomenon.

The mainstream traditional media's diminished control over the audience pool is partly compensated by news improvements. Thanks to the new technologies, traditional news media made noteworthy advances on three fronts: news gathering, news processing, and news dissemination. Access to computer databases and satellites put an enormous store of usable information within reach of journalists wherever they may be. Even foreign countries kept off-limits by hostile rulers can be explored by satellite, as can remote areas of the globe and even the private retreats of powerful elites. The ability to search databases electronically for specific bits of information and to combine those data in a variety of ways opens up countless new possibilities for creating news stories and providing valuable contextual information for fast-moving current developments.

When it comes to the distribution of news gathered in far-flung locations, the array of channels for immediate or delayed transmission multiplied far beyond the range deemed possible in the late 20th century. Local stations can now import video footage from satellites and thereby eliminate their dependence on national network programming and vastly expand their programming options. Broadband technology made internet use far more attractive because it allows nearly instant, constant access without the delays and hassles of a modem. Information available on the Web reaches journalists faster, from more diverse sources, and in modes that allow reporters to question sources quickly with the expectation of a prompt response. The potential for producing excellent news therefore grew by leaps and bounds, which is a welcome benefit for news consumers everywhere.

New broadcasting and narrowcasting technologies generate problems along with their benefits. Even as these technologies improved news production capabilities, the cost-cutting measures that newsrooms endured may offset the news improvements. Newsroom staffs are shrinking all over the country, and ranks of foreign bureaus are now the exception rather than the rule for major news organizations. And there is, as of yet, no widely available solution to the problem of finding one's way through the internet's lush jungles of information, where search engines such as Google and Yahoo provide only limited guidance.[62] Moreover, the stock of information that requires searching doubles every few months. For most news consumers, journalists therefore remain essential because they are trained to ferret out what seems most important within a particular cultural milieu and present it in language that average people can understand. As mentioned before, news aggregating sites that list each day's most popular stories, as well as social networks and other websites that present summaries of the day's most important news, are active competitors in determining what should be on the daily news agenda.

Digital Democracy: Myth or Reality?

People disappointed with the traditional media's democratic performance are optimistic that the choice and interactivity of the modern media environment would help level the playing field in terms of access and voice—citizens anywhere can access any outlet, and diversity of media is therefore at anyone's fingertips, regardless of the media market in which they reside.

However, much of the burgeoning research on the subject shows us why this optimism may be premature. Researchers asked questions about whether the lower costs of the production and distribution of information afforded by digital media better enables less well-funded groups or individuals to compete with the better-funded and more institutionalized groups that traditionally dominated the political process. The answer they found is mixed. In highly structured traditional venues such as presidential elections, more traditional entities with better funding can still retain an advantage. Scholars also argue that these technological changes will not alter the power structure such that media dominance of campaigns erodes and parties regain power or that new political parties might emerge more easily.[63] Still others point to a hybrid media environment, wherein the changing media environment is fluid and variable in the communication advantages it provides individuals, groups, and incumbent political players.[64]

Matthew Hindman argues that the Web has limited ability to democratize because democracy is not solely about voicing opinion but about being heard. His research shows that the Web does a poor job of promoting egalitarian democracy or leveling the playing field. Search algorithms are based on popularity and lack diversity, blogs are overwhelmingly run by educational and political elites, and the distracting chaos of the Web has not raised opinions of marginalized groups. Political blog readership is also concentrated among elites.[65] Moreover, not everything is as it seems on the Web. Powerful lobbyists, big business, and dominant political parties are frequently accused of "astroturfing," a deceptive campaign strategy that spreads information virally in an effort to disguise well-funded special interests as grassroots organizing.[66] Research also consistently shows how differences in access to high-quality digital media technologies tend to heighten sociopolitical inequalities.[67]

Comparative studies show that the impact of digital communication technologies on raising the voices of the politically disadvantaged is conditional on the political and institutional contexts already in place. Internet proliferation, for example, has the effect of increasing vote shares for small and fringe political parties, but only in more permissive party systems in which the number of competitive parties is already quite high. In more restrictive party systems, where most power rests in the hands of a few parties, digital technology has no effect on the electoral performance of small and fringe parties. The conditional nature of the findings may explain why several U.S.–based studies find little evidence of digital communication technologies' ability to democratize and point to the need for research beyond the U.S.[68]

Interactivity and Democratization

Interactivity is an extremely important feature for the democratizing potential of the digital era. The stream of information about ongoing events is no longer one-directional, with news media voices doing all the talking and the audience, like dutiful children, listening silently. The new technologies permit audiences to use internet channels to talk back to message senders, asking questions and providing new information and fresh comments. Many news providers, including traditional media, encourage feedback. Millions of people voice their ideas, and a few of those ideas arouse public attention and dialogue. But many more millions of citizens—the "silent majorities" of the Nixon era—remain mute.

The internet, as an open-access megaphone, diminished the traditional news media's tight control over access to mass audiences. Individuals and groups who were regularly barred from access to traditional media platforms—minor or nascent electoral parties, underfunded candidates, or candidates for lesser-known political offices, and groups advocating for those experiencing homelessness or people identifying as LGBTQ+ (lesbian, gay, bisexual, transgender, and queer/questioning) are examples. They now have viable channels to target receptive audiences. Modest resources are no longer a barrier to individuals and groups who want to reach audiences widely dispersed throughout the United States and most other parts of the world. Moreover, they can shape the messages freely, deciding what is acceptable and credible and what is not, because the internet, unlike most other news transmission venues, is largely free from censorship.

The digital media ecology provides excellent tools to rally supporters for specific causes and raise money. Students use these tools to mobilize death penalty opponents when an execution is imminent; political and citizen groups use them to gather support for recall elections. Politicians who felt victimized by journalists boiling their comments down to meaningless nuggets now customize their messages and send them quickly, easily, and cheaply to specific populations. Additionally, emails and websites are used to raise staggering amounts of money. During the 2020 presidential contest, then-candidate Joe Biden raised nearly $35 million from individual donors in small donations of $200 or less, presumably through the Web.[69] Liberal websites such as MoveOn.org helped to recruit campaign workers, organize campaign rallies, and mobilize Democratic voters. Conservative websites energized citizens on the other side of the political fence.

Digital technologies make it possible for audiences tuning in to talk shows on radio and television to interact instantaneously with others who are listening to or watching the same programs. Dual-screening, for example, is a trending use of digital media for news consumption and a perfect example of the hybrid nature of our media system.[70] The boom in interactive communication over long distances offers the promise that every American, regardless of expertise, can have a voice in the nation's political life. Undoubtedly the opportunity is there, but the reality remains far from the ideal. The people whose voices are heard in technology-enabled interactions predominantly are members of the upper crust: well educated, successful, confident, and economically secure. Most people who fall below these socioeconomic levels have not publicly voiced to their views and may or may not in the future. Still, interactivity is a good thing because it expanded the number of voices in the public sphere.

SUMMARY

The changing media environment precipitated by digital and social media holds numerous implications for the intersection of media and politics. The changing media environment influences citizens, journalists, and political elites as well as everyday behaviors and routines including news consumption, news-gathering, political mobilization, and electoral campaigns. While research in this area is still emerging, scholars point to a number of trends and effects worth noting. Expanding media choice is changing news consumption habits while increasing competitive pressures for media organizations. This expansion of choice also increases the ease with which people engage in selective exposure by seeking out news sources in line with their political predispositions and the ease with which they can avoid news altogether by seeking entertainment programming over news. Upticks in social media as sources for news mean that content selectivity is network dependent; the compilation of ideologies and political interest in online social networks will shape news exposure. Growing use of mobile devices for news may have implications for attention to news, engagement, and learning from news content. On the other hand, digital and social media hold promise for engendering new forms of civic engagement.

The new media environment also offers an abundance of opportunities impossible to imagine pre-internet and pre–digital media. The blogosphere and social media provide avenues for journalists and politicians to circumvent traditional media in disseminating information. What is more, those without a professional background in journalism also have a voice through citizen journalism websites, blogs, and social networking platforms. News consumers can quickly become news creators in the interactive digital environment. Politicians can use social media to communicate directly with supporters, who can, in turn, re-share the information with their networks.

While the changing media landscape threatens print media and network television, alternative avenues of information most often work in tandem with traditional media rather than altogether displacing them. Much of the content circulated in the digital media ecology derives from mainstream news organizations, and those penning popular political blogs often have a journalism background. These new tools also enable a symbiotic relationship between news professionals and citizen journalists/bloggers, which may offset, somewhat, growing competitive pressures in an era of media abundance. Additionally, citizens and groups can mobilize with greater ease and speed through the Web, as it offers an accessible platform for the hierarchies of various social and political movements. Social media sites have also become a hotbed of public discourse and made accidental exposure to political news and opposing and diverse views possible. Even elected officials are seizing digital and social media for strategic use. The digital news environment has transformed the nature of campaigning for public office; no longer can candidates be timid about embracing digital technology as sites such as Facebook and Twitter have become election necessities and effective tools for both fundraising and mobilization. While the changing media landscape offers promise, it also poses problems—problems our society and democracy will continue grappling with for years to come.

The new media environment encompasses a mixed bag of effects— some arguably beneficial to democracy; some arguably harmful. Media choice not only creates an expanding knowledge gap between people preferring public affairs news and those preferring entertainment content but also provides more opportunity for partisan selective exposure. This trend could prove troubling if selective exposure habits coincide with a more sorted, hostile, or polarized electorate. While digital and social media offer convenient forms of engagement, there is also reason to suspect such online participation is more superficial—and a number of scholars caution that the Web has achieved little in fostering greater diversity in the news. Furthermore, trends such as the rise of citizen journalism and increasing use of social media for news raise new questions about information accuracy and misinformation in the changing media environment. What lasting effects does this digital world hold for democracy? While scholarship in this area is emerging, research to date raises more questions than it answers.

DISCUSSION QUESTIONS

1. Why does it matter that the market for media and news has expanded so dramatically? Do you think the expansion of news and entertainment options afforded through cable and the internet makes more people see more news than they would have otherwise? How is news content different now, relative to how it used to be, and how are people's news choices different as a result? Do you think these changes have any important effects on political learning, attitudes, or behavior?

2. How has the arrival of so many new platforms and devices influenced the nature of the political information people see, the context in which they see it, and the frequency with which they encounter it? Do you think that news habits are different because of this array of platforms and devices? What about the effects from news exposure from social media platforms and mobile devices? Do you think learning or persuasive effects might be different? Why or why not?

3. What are the various ways these technological developments are introducing changes to the way political journalism is conducted? Does the availability of social media sites such as Facebook and Twitter make reporting better, worse, or does it have any effect at all? What about the proliferation of citizen journalists and user-generated content? Is the introduction of these less-professionalized news products helpful or not so helpful from a democratic point of view?

4. Have all of these various changes in communication technology helped to democratize the political information environment, as many people initially anticipated with the arrival of the internet? Depending on your answer, please explain how so or why not.

READINGS

Anderson, C. W. (2018). *Apostles of certainty: Data journalism and the politics of doubt*. Oxford University Press.

Arceneaux, K., & Johnson, M. (2013). *Changing minds or changing channels? Partisan news in an age of choice*. University of Chicago Press.

Baldwin-Philippi, J. (2015). *Using technology, building democracy*. Oxford University Press.

Batsell, J. (2015). *Engaged journalism: Connecting with digitally empowered news audiences.* Columbia University Press.

Boczkowski, P. J., & Papacharissi, Z. (Eds.). (2018). *Trump and the media.* MIT Press.

Chadwick, A. (2013). *The hybrid media system: Politics and power.* Oxford University Press.

Clark, L. S., & Marchi, R. (2017). *Young people and the future of news: Social media and the rise of connective journalism.* Cambridge University Press.

Darr, J. P., Hitt, M. P., & Dunaway, J. L. (2021). *Home style: How local newspapers can slow polarization.* Cambridge University Press.

Dunaway, J. L., & Searles, K. (forthcoming). *News attention in a mobile era.* Oxford University Press.

Forgette, R. (2018). *News grazers: Media, politics, and trust in an information age.* CQ Press.

Hindman, M. (2009). *The myth of digital democracy.* Princeton University Press.

Hindman, M. (2018). *The internet trap.* Princeton University Press.

Jamieson, K. H. (2018). *Cyberwar: How Russian hackers and trolls helped elect a president.* Oxford University Press.

Margetts, H., John, P., Hale, S., & Yasseri, T. (2016). *Political turbulence: How social media shape collective action.* Princeton University Press.

Mossberger, K., Tolbert, C., & Franko, W. W. (2013). *Digital cities: The internet and the geography of opportunity.* Oxford University Press.

Napoli, P. M. (2019). *Social media and the public interest: Media regulation in the disinformation age.* Columbia University Press.

Nielsen, R. K. (2015). *Local journalism: The decline of newspapers and the rise of digital media.* IB Tauris.

Peters, C., & Broersma, M. (Eds.). (2016). *Rethinking journalism again: Societal role and public relevance in a digital age.* Routledge.

Robinson, S. (Ed.). (2016). *Community journalism midst media revolution.* Routledge.

Settle, J. (2018). *Frenemies: How social media is polarizing America.* Cambridge University Press.

Sinclair, B. (2012). *The social citizen: Peer networks and political behavior.* University of Chicago Press.

Stromer-Galley, J. (2014). *Presidential campaigning in the internet age.* Oxford University Press.

Stroud, N. J. (2011). *Niche news: The politics of news choice.* Oxford University Press.

Webster, J. (2016). *The marketplace of attention: How audiences take shape in a digital age.* MIT Press.

Wu, I. S. (2015). *Forging trust communities: How technology changes politics.* Johns Hopkins University Press.

NOTES

1. Bimber, B. (2003). *Information and American democracy: Technology in the evolution of political power*. Cambridge University Press, p. 23.

2. Neuman, W. R. (1991). *The future of the mass audience*. Cambridge University Press, pp. ix–x.

3. Neuman, W. R. (2008). Globalization and the new media. In D. A. Graber (Ed.), *The politics of news, the news of politics* (2nd ed.). CQ Press, p. 230.

4. Martin, G. J., & Yurukoglu, A. (2017). Bias in cable news: Persuasion and polarization. *American Economic Review, 107*(9), 2565–2599.

5. Garrett, R. K., & Stroud, N. J. (2014). Partisan paths to exposure diversity: Differences in pro-and counter attitudinal news consumption. *Journal of Communication, 64*(4), 680–701.

6. Stroud, N. J., & Muddiman, A. (2013). The American media system today: Is the public fragmenting? In T. Ridout (Ed.), *New directions in media and politics*. Routledge; Iyengar, S., & Hahn, K. S. (2009). Red media, blue media: Evidence of ideological selectivity in media use. *Journal of Communication, 59*, 19–39; Song, H. (2017). Why do people (sometimes) become selective about news? The role of emotions and partisan differences in selective approach and avoidance. *Mass Communication and Society, 20*(1), 47–67; Stroud, N. J. (2017). Selective exposure theories. In K. Kenski & K. H. Jamieson (Eds.), *The Oxford handbook of political communication*.

7. Hindman, M. (2009). *The myth of digital democracy*. Princeton University Press.

8. Iyengar, S., & Hahn, K. S. (2009). Red media, blue media: Evidence of ideological selectivity in media use. *Journal of Communication, 59*, 19–39; Stroud, N. J. (2011). *Niche news: The politics of news choice*. Oxford University Press; Gentzkow, M., & Shapiro, J. M. (2011). Ideological segregation online and offline. *Quarterly Journal of Economics, 126*, 1799–1839; Flaxman, S., Goel, S., & Rao, J. M. (2016). Filter bubbles, echo chambers, and online news consumption. *Public Opinion Quarterly, 80*(S1), 298–320; Guess, A. (2018). (Almost) everything in moderation: New evidence on Americans' online media diets. *American Journal of Political Science*.

9. Rainie, L., & Smith, A. (2012). Social networking sites and politics. *Pew Research Center*. https://www.pewresearch.org/internet/2012/03/12/social-networking-sites-and-politics/; Stroud, N. J., & Muddiman, A. (2013). The American media system today: Is the public fragmenting? In T. Ridout (Ed.), *New directions in media and politics*. Routledge.

10. Bakshy, E., Messing, S., & Adamic, L. A. (2015). Exposure to ideologically diverse news and opinion on Facebook. *Science, 348*(6239), 1130–1132.

11. Garrett, R. K. (2009). Echo chambers online? Politically motivated selective exposure among internet news users. *Journal of Computer-Mediated Communication, 14*, 265–285; Webster, J. G. (2014). *The marketplace of attention*. MIT Press.

12. Levendusky, M. (2013). Why do partisan media polarize viewers? *American Journal of Political Science, 57*(3), 611–623; Levendusky, M. (2013). *How partisan media polarize America*. University of Chicago Press.

13. Jerit, J., & Barabas, J. (2012). Partisan perceptual bias and the information environment. *Journal of Politics, 74*(3), 672.

14. Arceneaux, K. Johnson, M., Lindstadt, R., & Vander Wielen, R. J. (2015). The influence of news media on political elites: Investigating strategic responsiveness in Congress. *American Journal of Political Science, 60*(1), 5–29; Lelkes, Y., Sood, G., & Iyengar, S. (2017). The hostile audience: The effect of access to broadband internet on partisan affect. *American Journal of Political Science, 61*(1), 5–20.

15. Garrett, R. K. (2009). Echo chambers online? Politically motivated selective exposure among internet news users. *Journal of Computer-Mediated Communication, 14*, 265–285; Arceneaux, K., & Johnson, M. (2013). *Changing minds or changing channels? Partisan news in an age of choice*. University of Chicago Press; Hindman, M. (2009). *The myth of digital democracy*. Princeton University Press.

16. Neuman, W. R., McKnight, L., & Solomon, R. J. (1996). *The Gordian knot: Political gridlock on the information highway*. MIT Press; Nissenbaum, H., & Price, M. (Eds.). (2004). *Academy and the internet*. Peter Lang; Dahlberg, L. (2004). Democracy via cyberspace: Mapping the rhetorics and practices of three prominent camps. *New Media and Society, 3*(2), 157–177.

17. Hindman, M. (2011). *Less of the same: The lack of local news on the internet*. FCC. http://www.fcc.gov/document/media-ownership-study-6-submitted-study; Napoli, P. M., Stonbely, S., McCollough, K., & Renninger, B. (2015, June). *Assessing the health of local news ecosystems*. Rutgers. http://mpii.rutgers.edu/assessing-the-health-of-local-journalism-ecosystems/.

18. Graber, D. A., Bimber, B., Bennett, W. L., Davis, R., & Norris, P. (2004). The internet and politics: Emerging perspectives. In H. Nissenbaum & M. E. Price (Eds.), *Academy and the Internet* (pp. 90–119). Peter Lang.

19. Darr, J. P., Hitt, M. P., & Dunaway, J. (2021). *Home style opinion: How local newspapers can slow polarization*. Cambridge University Press; Abernathy, P. M. (2020). *News deserts and ghost newspapers: Will local news survive?* A report published by the Center for Innovation and Sustainability in Local Media, Chapel Hill, NC, University of North Carolina Press. https://www.usnewsdeserts.com/wp-content/uploads/2020/06/2020_News_Deserts_and_Ghost_Newspapers.pdf

20. Jones, A. S. (2009). *Losing the news: The future of the news that feeds democracy.* Oxford University Press; Hayes, D., & Lawless, J. L. (2015). As local news goes, so goes citizen engagement: Media, knowledge, and participation in US House elections. *The Journal of Politics, 77*(2), 447–462; Peterson, E. (2019). Paper cuts: How reporting resources affect political news coverage. *American Journal of Political Science.*

21. Baker, C. E. (2007). *Media concentration and democracy: Why ownership matters.* Cambridge University Press; Rosenstiel, T. (2005). Political polling and the new media culture: A case of more being less. *Public Opinion Quarterly, 69,* 698–715.

22. Kreiss, D., Finn, M., & Turner, F. (2011). The limits of peer production: Some reminders from Max Weber for the network society. *New Media & Society, 13*(2), 243–259.

23. Hindman, M. (2018). *The internet trap.* Princeton University Press.

24. Napoli, P. M., Stonbely, S., McCollough, K., & Renninger, B. (2017). Local journalism and the information needs of local communities: Toward a scalable approach. *Journalism Practice, 11*(4), 373–395.

25. Scacco, J., Stroud, N. J., Hearit, L., Potts, L., & Sonderman, J. (2016, October). Primary election coverage: What types of news engage audiences. *Center for Media Engagement.* https://engagingnewsproject.org/research/election-coverage.

26. Horan, T. J. (2011). "Soft" versus "hard" news on microblogging networks. *Information, Communication & Society, 16*(1), 43–60; Boczkowski, P. (2010). *News at work: Imitation in an age of information abundance.* University of Chicago Press.

27. Chadwick, A. (2013). *The hybrid media system.* Oxford University Press.

28. Barthel, M., & Shearer, E. (2015, August 19). How do Americans use Twitter for news? *Pew Research Center.* http://www.pewresearch.org/fact-tank/2015/08/19/how-do-americans-use-twitter-for-news; Gainous, J., & Wagner, K. M. (2014). *Tweeting to power: The social media revolution in American politics.* Oxford University Press; Tenscher, J., Koc-Michalska, K., Lilleker, D. G., Mykkanen, J., Walter, A. S., Findor, A., Jalali, C., & Roka, J. (2016). The professionals speak: Practitioners' perspectives on professional election campaigning. *European Journal of Communication, 31*(2), 95–119.

29. Mitchell, A., Gottfried, J., Barthel, M., & Shearer, E. (2016, July 7). The modern news consumer. *Pew Research Center.* http://www.journalism.org/2016/07/07/the-modern-news-consumer.

30. Feezell, J. T., & Ortiz, B. (2019, December 6). "I saw it on Facebook": An experimental analysis of political learning through social media. *Information, Communication & Society, 24*(9), 1283–1302. https://doi.org/10.1080/1369118X.2019.1697340

31. Stromer-Galley, J. (2014). *Presidential campaigning in the internet age*. Oxford University Press; Kreiss, D. (2012). *Taking our country back*. Oxford University Press; Kreiss, D. (2016). *Prototype politics: Technology-intensive campaigning and the data of democracy*. Oxford University Press.

32. Gainous, J., & Wagner, K. M. (2014). *Tweeting to power: The social media revolution in American politics*. Oxford University Press

33. Gainous, J., & Wagner, K. M. (2014). *Tweeting to power: The social media revolution in American politics*. Oxford University Press

34. Karlsen, R. (2015). Followers are opinion leaders: The role of people in the flow of political communication and beyond social networking sites. *European Journal of Communication, 30*(3), 301–318.

35. Stromer-Galley, J. (2014). *Presidential campaigning in the internet age*. Oxford University Press; Kreiss, D. (2016). *Prototype politics: Technology-intensive campaigning and the data of democracy*. Oxford University Press.

36. This section draws heavily on author research; see Dunaway, J. (2016, August 30). *Mobile vs. computer: Implications for news audiences and outlets*. Shorenstein Center on Media, Politics and Public Policy, Harvard Kennedy School. https://shorensteincenter.org/mobile-vs-computer-news-audiences-and-outlets; Dunaway, J. (2016). *Left to our own devices: Political news attention and engagement in a mobile era* [Working paper].

37. Bakshy, E., Messing, S., & Adamic, L. A. (2015, June 5). Exposure to ideologically diverse news. *Science, 348*(6239), 1130–1132; Sterling, G. (2016, April 4). *Nearly 80 percent of social media time now spent on mobile devices*. MarTech. http://marketingland.com/facebook-usage-accounts-1-5-minutes-spent-mobile-171561

38. Byers, D. (2015, April 1). The mobile election: How smartphones will change the 2016 presidential race. *Politico*. https://www.politico.com/blogs/media/2015/04/the-mobile-election-how-smartphones-will-change-the-2016-presidential-race-204855; Lilleker, D. G., & Koc-Michalska, K. (2017). What drives political participation? Motivations and mobilization in a digital age. *Political Communication, 34*(1), 21–43.

39. Mossberger, K., Tolbert, C., & Franko, W. W. (2013). *Digital cities: The internet and the geography of opportunity*. Oxford University Press; Napoli, P. M., & Obar, J. A. (2014). The emerging mobile internet underclass: A critique of mobile internet access. *The Information Society, 30*(5), 323–334.

40. Prior, M. (2013). Mass media and political polarization. *Annual Review of Political Science, 16*, 101–127; Webster, J. G. (2016). *The marketplace of attention: How audiences take shape in a digital age*. MIT Press.

41. Webster, J. G. (1986). Audience behavior in the new media environment. *Journal of Communication, 36*(Summer), 77–91.

42. Grossman, L. K. (1995). *The electronic republic: Reshaping democracy in the information age*. Viking; Stroud, N. J. (2011). *Niche news: The politics of news choice*. Oxford University Press; Levendusky, M. (2013). *How partisan media polarize America*. University of Chicago Press; Lelkes, Y., Sood, G., & Iyengar, S. (2017). The hostile audience: The effect of access to broadband internet on partisan affect. *American Journal of Political Science, 61*(1), 5–20.

43. Epstein, E. J. (1973). *News from nowhere*. Random House; Gans, H. J. (1979). *Deciding what's news*. Random House; Kaniss, P. (1991). *Making local news*. University of Chicago Press; Cook, T. E. (1998). *Governing with the news: The news media as a political institution*. University of Chicago Press; Sparrow, B. H. (1999). *Uncertain guardians: The news media as a political institution*. Johns Hopkins University Press; Tuchman, G. (1978). *Making news: A study in the construction of reality*. Free Press.

44. Kirzinger, A. (2012). Making news in 140 characters: How the new media environment is changing our examination of audiences, journalists, and content [PhD dissertation]. Louisiana State University. http://digitalcommons.lsu.edu/gradschool_dissertations/622

45. Lasorsa, D. L., Lewis, S. C., & Holton, A. E. (2011, May). *"Normalizing" Twitter: Journalism practice in an emerging communication space* [Paper presentation]. Communication and Technology Division of ICA, Boston, MA, United States; Jacobs, L. R., & Shapiro, R. Y. (2011). Informational interdependence: Public opinion and the media in the new communications era. In G. C. Edwards III, L. R. Jacobs, & R. Y. Shapiro (Eds.), *The Oxford handbook of American public opinion and the media*. Oxford University Press.

46. Jacobs, L. R., & Shapiro, R. Y. (2011). Informational interdependence: Public opinion and the media in the new communications era. In G. C. Edwards III, L. R. Jacobs, & R. Y. Shapiro (Eds.), *The Oxford handbook of American public opinion and the media*. Oxford University Press; Chadwick, A. (2013). *The hybrid media system*. Oxford University Press.

47. Holcombe, J. (2013). NBC makes a bet on getting user-generated content from citizen videographers. *Pew Research Center*. https://www.pewresearch.org/fact-tank/2013/08/20/nbc-makes-a-bet-on-getting-user-generated-content-from-citizen-videographers/

48. Holcombe, J. (2014). On TV, few amateur journalists get credit for their contributions to the news. *Pew Research Center*. https://www.pewresearch.org/fact-tank/2014/06/05/on-tv-few-amateur-journalists-get-credit-for-their-contributions-to-the-news/

49. See Rosen, J. (2008, July 14). A most useful definition of citizen journalism. *PressThink*. http://www.archive.pressthink.org/2008/07/14/a_most_useful_d.html

50. Chung, D. S., Nah, S., & Yamamoto, M. (2017). Conceptualizing citizen journalism: US news editors' views. *Journalism.* https://doi.org/10.1177%2F1464884916686596

51. Carpenter, S. (2010). A study of content diversity in online citizen journalism and online newspaper articles. *New Media & Society, 12*(7), 1064–1084; Chung, D. S., Nah, S., & Yamamoto, M. (2017). Conceptualizing citizen journalism: US news editors' views. *Journalism.* https://doi.org/10.1177%2F1464884916686596

52. Lindner, A. M. (2016). Editorial gatekeeping in citizen journalism. *New Media & Society.* https://doi.org/10.1177/1461444816631506

53. Stanglin, D. (2013, April 25). Student wrongly tied to Boston bombings found dead. *USA Today.* http://www.usatoday.com/story/news/2013/04/25/boston-bombing-social-media-student-brown-university-reddit/2112309; Hollander, C. (2013, April 17). What you need to know about Reddit, the FBI and the Boston marathon suspects. *National Journal.* https://www.nationaljournal.com/s/80779/what-you-need-know-about-reddit-fbi-boston-marathon-suspects

54. Kaufhold, K., Valenzuela, S., & de Zunigam, H. G. (2010). Citizen journalism and democracy: How user-generated news use relates to political knowledge and participation. *Journalism & Mass Communication Quarterly, 87*, 515–529.

55. Comscore ranks the top 50 U.S. digital media properties for January 2016. (2016, February 24). *Comscore.com.* https://www.comscore.com/Insights/Rankings/comScore-Ranks-the-Top-50-US-Digital-Media-Properties-for-January-2016.

56. Fritz, B. (2011, January 10). Most original news reporting comes from traditional sources, study finds. *Los Angeles Times.* https://www.latimes.com/archives/la-xpm-2010-jan-11-la-fi-ct-newspapers11-2010jan11-story.html; The state of the news media 2005. (2005, March 14). *Pew Research Center.* https://www.pewtrusts.org/en/research-and-analysis/reports/2005/03/14/the-state-of-the-news-media-2005; Hindman, M. (2011). *Less of the same: The lack of local news on the internet.* FCC. http://www.fcc.gov/document/media-ownership-study-6-submitted-study

57. Americans paid close attention as election returns came in. (2020, November 3). *Pew Research Center.* https://www.journalism.org/2020/11/23/americans-paid-close-attention-as-election-returns-came-in/.

58. Nah, S., Yamamoto, M., Chung, D. S., & Zuercher, R. (2015). Modeling the adoption and use of citizen journalism by online newspapers. *Journalism & Mass Communication Quarterly, 92*(2), 399–420.

59. ESPN's FiveThirtyEight: http://fivethirtyeight.com; *The Washington Post's* Monkey Cage: https://www.washingtonpost.com/news/monkey-cage; *The*

New York Times's The Upshot: http://www.nytimes.com/upshot; Vox's Mischiefs of Faction: http://www.vox.com/mischiefs-of-faction

60. Davis, R. (2009). *Typing politics: The role of blogs in American politics.* Oxford University Press; Perlmutter, D. D. (2008). *Blogwars.* Oxford University Press, pp. 69–70.

61. The Web: Alarming, appealing and a challenge to journalistic values. (2008, March 17). *The Pew Research Center for the People and the Press.* https://assets.pewresearch.org/wp-content/uploads/sites/4/2011/01/Journalist-report-2008.pdf

62. Campbell, R., Martin, C. R., & Fabos, B. (2008). *Media and culture* (6th ed.). Bedford/St. Martin's. Google, for example, ranks its listings by their popularity, judged by how many other pages are linked to them. That puts small enterprises, featured well below the leaders, at a self-perpetuating disadvantage.

63. Bimber, B. (2003). *Information and American democracy: Technology in the evolution of political power.* Cambridge University Press; Norris, P. (2001). *Digital divide: Civic engagement, information poverty, and the internet in democratic societies.* Cambridge University Press.

64. Chadwick, A. (2013). *The hybrid media system.* Oxford University Press.

65. Hindman, M. (2009). *The myth of digital democracy.* Princeton University Press.

66. See Monbiot, G. (2010, October 25). The Tea Party movement: Deluded and inspired by billionaires. *Guardian.* http://www.guardian.co.uk/commentisfree/cifamerica/2010/oct/25/tea-party-koch-brothers; also see Street, P., & DiMaggio, A. (2011). *Crashing the Tea Party: Mass media and the campaign to remake American politics.* Paradigm.

67. Schlozman, K. L., Verba, S., & Brady, H. E. (2012). *The unheavenly chorus: Unequal political voice and the broken promise of American democracy.* Princeton University Press.

68. Potter, P., & Dunaway, J. (2016). Reinforcing or breaking party systems: Internet communication technologies and party competition in comparative context. *Political Communication, 33,* 392–413; also see Vaccari, C. (2013). *Digital politics in Western democracies.* Johns Hopkins University Press.

69. McMinn, S., Hurt, A., & Talbot, R. (2020, December 4). Money tracker: How much Trump and Biden have raised in the 2020 election. *NPR.* https://www.npr.org/2020/05/20/858347477/money-tracker-how-much-trump-and-biden-have-raised-in-the-2020-election.

70. de Zuniga, H. G., Garcia-Perdomo, V., & McGregor, S. C. (2015). What is second screening? Exploring motivations of second screen use and its effect on online political participation. *Journal of Communication, 65,* 793–815.

Who and What Makes the News?

News From the Presidency

Learning Objectives

1. Describe the adversarial relationship between the media and public officials.

2. Explain the media's impact on the executive branch and public perception.

Though an extreme case, there may not be a better modern exemplar for illustrating the adversarial relationship between presidents and the press than the presidency of Donald J. Trump. Perhaps that is because his term in office was bookended with disputes over electoral interference and legitimacy. President Trump's first hundred days in office were marred by stories covering lingering questions about whether anyone in his campaign or administration colluded with Russia to interfere in the 2016 election.[1] His last days and weeks in office were all but consumed by stories covering his false claims about widespread election fraud, his attempts to intimidate state and local election officials into overturning election results, the role he played in inciting the January 6 attack on the United States (U.S.) Capitol using claims the election was stolen, and stories of his impeachment in the House and his eventual acquittal in the Senate.

While the circumstances surrounding coverage of the Trump presidency were in many ways unique, the struggle for control between the Trump White House and the press over the flow of information to the public was not. Such agenda struggles are par for the course for all presidential administrations. Even though negative press coverage of the young Biden administration has been infrequent relative to Trump's, negative coverage of a looming immigration crisis at the U.S.–Mexico border started to eclipse the many positive stories about Biden's handling of the COVID-19 response barely halfway into his first hundred days in office.[2] Presidents receive vastly more coverage than any other political actor in the

United States, and coverage often strays from presidential policy agendas, with much of it personalized and negative in tone. What may be good news for presidents is that today's news media are not as influential in shaping public opinion about the president as they once were.[3]

Personal attacks on presidents have been the rule more often than the exception since the birth of the nation. For example, the press smeared Andrew Jackson's reputation by calling his mother a prostitute; it routinely referred to President Rutherford B. Hayes as "his fraudulency" following a disputed election. Abraham Lincoln was called a horrid-looking wretch and a fourth-rate speaker who delivered hackneyed and illiterate speeches.[4]

When Katharine Graham was publisher of *The Washington Post*, she told her listeners during a speech that harsh assessments were praiseworthy. The press must be independent, skeptical, and irreverent. Periods of truce between the press and presidents, in her opinion, were contrary to the spirit of the First Amendment, which ordains the press as the watchdog that alerts the public to government sins. The Depression years, World War II, the Korean War, the Cold War, and the time period immediately following 9/11 were exceptions to that hallowed tradition. In times of crisis, much of the Washington, DC, press viewed itself as responsible adjuncts to the government's efforts to cope with the country's problems. There was criticism, of course, but it did not seriously question the veracity of administration statements nor did it attack the motivations for or substance of policies.

The tone of media evaluations of the president changed sharply after Vietnam and Watergate, which journalists saw as ventures based on false premises and involving government propaganda, lies, and cover-ups. From then on, the press again became suspicious and adversarial, assuming flawed policies, sinister motivations, and deceptive spinning of news most of the time, unless proven otherwise. If anyone was concerned about press softening its adversarial stance in the many years since Watergate, the tumultuous and often toxic relationship between President Trump and the press—he once famously referred to the press as the enemy of the people in a tweet—should handily disabuse that notion (see Photo 5-1).

Why do political leaders in democratic nations worldwide put so much energy into their media strategies when in the end the media may be their undoing? Why do they expose themselves to frequently hostile interrogations by journalists who routinely write stories attacking them and their policies? The answer is that politicians desperately need the media to achieve their goals. Conversely, journalists need politicians to get information for important stories. Because the two institutions have conflicting goals and missions and operate under different constraints, they

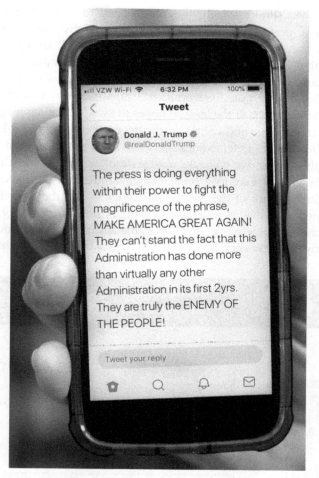

Photo 5-1 SANTA FE, NEW MEXICO; April 7, 2019: A man reads a tweet from U.S. President Donald Trump on his iPhone that is highly critical of the American press, which he calls "the enemy of the people."

Source: Photo by Robert Alexander/Getty Images.

cannot live comfortably with each other. Yet they dare not part company. Interdependence tempers their love–hate relationship.[5]

The Adversarial Relationship

To gain and retain public support and maintain power, executives and legislators strive to influence the information that media pass on to the public and to other officials. They seek to define situations and project images in their own way to further their objectives. Newspeople, however, have different goals. Professionally, they are trained to monitor and appraise government performance, and they feel bound by the economics of the news business to present exciting stories that will attract large audiences in their markets. This often means prying into conflict, controversy, or ordinary wheeling and dealing—matters that government officials would like to keep quiet. Government wants its portrait taken from the most flattering angle; at the least, it hopes to avoid an unflattering picture. The media, eager to find chinks in the government's armor and to maximize audience size, prefer candid shots that show government at its worst.

In this chapter, we will take a closer look at the interrelationship of the media and the executive branch of government at the national level, leaving the interface of the media and Congress and the Supreme Court for Chapter 6. Casual as well as systematic observations readily establish that the media devote much attention to the affairs of national government, particularly the presidency. In the first 100 days of the Trump administration,

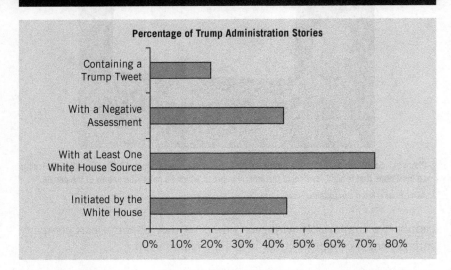

Figure 5-1   White House Influence in News Stories on the Trump Administration's First 100 Days

Source: Adapted from Mitchell, A., Gottfried, J., Stocking, G., Matsa, K., & Grieco, E. M. (2017, October 2). Covering President Trump in a polarized media environment. https://www .journalism.org/2017/10/02/covering-president-trump-in-a-polarized-media-environment/

Data are from a Pew Research Center content analysis of the Trump administration in news stories from national newspaper websites, radio, cable and network broadcasts, and websites and digital-native outlets, January 21–April 20, 2017. N = 3,013 stories.

major news outlets across cable, network news, radio, and digital news published or aired over 3,000 stories that were primarily about Trump, his presidency, or the administration (Figure 5-1). Relative to the other two major branches of government, it was the most common story topic by far. The White House did not merely dominate in terms of topic, either. The Trump administration played a large role in determining which stories ended up getting covered—45% of stories were written or produced in response to something said or done by the president or a White House staffer. In nearly 75% of these stories, at least one source from the White House was included. The White House has influence over both stories covered and perspectives aired in those stories, if not over their tone. Despite their influence in terms of source and topic, the same stories were about four times more likely to contain negative assessments of Trump or the administration relative to positive assessments.[6]

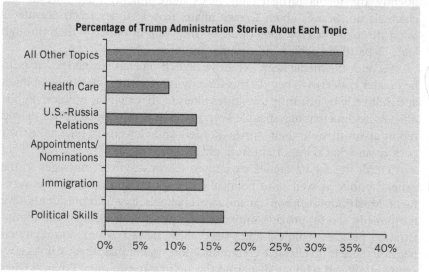

Figure 5-2   Most Frequent Topics in Presidential Coverage, Trump's First 100 Days

Percentage of Trump Administration Stories About Each Topic

Source: Adapted from Mitchell, A., Gottfried, J., Stocking, G., Matsa, K., & Grieco, E. M. (2017, October 2). Covering President Trump in a polarized media environment. https://www.journal ism.org/2017/10/02/five-topics-accounted-for-two-thirds-of-coverage-in-first-100-days/.

Data are from a Pew Research Center content analysis of Trump administration news stories from national newspaper websites, radio, cable and network broadcasts, and websites and digital-native outlets, January 21–April 20, 2017. N = 3,013 stories.

Changes in patterns of presidential news coverage are quite common. Emphasis on political news wanes in times of relative political calm, only to rise again during crises. Patterns depicted in Figure 5-2 reflect the politics of the early days of the Trump administration. Research suggests that both cable and online news outlets cover more presidential news relative to traditional media outlets and that they often use different frames in coverage.[7] During the early days of the Trump administration, story topics also varied by the sources used and the ideological lean of news outlets audiences. Overall, five topics made up two-thirds of all coverage of Trump's first 100 days in office.

The Media and the Executive Branch

The media perform four major functions for government executives.[8] First, they inform them about current events, including developments in other parts of the government. This information sets the scene for policy making. When the media highlight environmental hazards or growing home foreclosure sales, major or minor executive action often follows. Not infrequently, the media furnish daily news more quickly than bureaucratic channels do. Stories about foreign affairs may at times reach presidents faster through *The New York Times*, on the Web, or on CNN than through State Department cables and communications.

Second, the media keep executive branch officials attuned to the public's major concerns. They do this directly by reporting on public opinion and indirectly by featuring the stories likely to shape public opinion. Public officials assume that newspeople keep in touch with popular concerns and report about them in their stories. Readers and viewers, in turn, take their cues about what is important from old and new media.

Third, the media enable executives to convey their messages to the general public as well as to political elites within and outside of government. Mushrooming news transmission channels, to which presidents have fairly ready access, provide unparalleled opportunities to explain administration policies. Political elites need these news transmission channels because there is no effective communication system that directly links government officials who are dispersed throughout the country. Political elites also use media channels to publicly attack opponents' positions.

The second and third functions of the mass media are supplemented with internal polling. Presidents use extensive polling to track public preferences about various issues and to shape their messages according to what framing and language plays best to the public. They also use these internal polls to gather detailed information about which issues are most important to the public, freeing them to act at will on issues that are less salient to the public.[9]

(4) Fourth, the media allow chief executives to remain in full public view on the political stage, keeping their human qualities and professional skills on almost constant display. Newspapers, television, radio, and the internet supply a steady stream of commentary about a president's daily routines. Coverage of personal life may be extensive, even for the vice president. For instance, when President Trump and First Lady Melania Trump contracted COVID-19, daily medical news briefings kept the public apprised of their status. The media reported details of the president's condition, including his energy level, his tolerance of medical procedures, his mood, and his progress toward recovery. Beyond providing human interest tidbits, such coverage reassures the public that it is fully informed about the president's fitness to serve. Human interest stories help to forge close personal ties between people and their leaders. They make it easier for them to trust leaders and therefore support their policies. Political communication scholars Joshua M. Scacco and Kevin Coe argue that these frequent public displays of presidential personality are especially important to governance strategy in an era when fragmented media and professionalized politics may limit presidents' rhetorical powers.[10]

Media, Power, and Presidential Politics

The political significance of the relationship between the media and the executive branch is much greater than the functions just described. Media coverage is the lifeblood of politics because it shapes the perceptions that form the reality on which political action is based. Media do more than depict the political environment; they strongly affect the political environment. Because direct contact with political actors and situations is limited, media images define people and situations for nearly all participants in the political process. The richness of such images is rising thanks to new technologies.

As discussed in previous chapters, the age of live audiovisual politics, which began in the 1950s, vastly enhanced the impact—and hence the power—of news media. In the past, a story might have caused ripples on the political seas when thousands of people in one corner of the country read it in the paper or heard it on the radio. Today, that same story can cause political tidal waves when millions worldwide see and hear it simultaneously on television, computer, and mobile device screens. Politicians feel compelled to react. They now can visit with millions of potential followers in their living rooms, creating the kinds of emotional ties that hitherto came only from personal contact. Electronic contacts may affect the political future of a member of Congress more than service on an important congressional committee. As we will discuss in Chapter 7, digital media play an important role in the legislator–constituent relationship.

Television tipped the political scales of power among the three branches of government in favor of the presidency. Though outside group and candidates' direct contacts with voters through political ads and digital media are increasingly important, the news media still strongly influence who becomes eligible for the presidency and how profoundly they affect the conduct and outcome of elections. In fact, a key way that advertising and social media strategies are successful is through shaping news media narratives about the campaign. For example, Donald Trump's ability to maneuver the mainstream media narrative of the 2016 campaign through social media and is widely credited as one of the factors that gave him an electoral edge over Hillary Clinton. Getting the traditional media to cover his social media antics was key to his strategy. Also demonstrative of the lingering power of television news: Trump experienced a rare bump in approval ratings during the time period in which he gave regular televised press briefings in the early days of the COVID-19 pandemic.

After elections, the length, vigor, and effectiveness of a president's political life and the general level of support for the political system depend heavily on news media images. Making sure that the images are favorable therefore becomes a prime concern. Staffs of various presidents concur that

> the national media play a very significant role in the White House decision-making process. . . . [I]n White House meetings, on the whole, more time is spent discussing the media than any other institution, including Congress. . . . [A]ll policies are developed and presented with media reaction in mind.[11]

The media frequently raise issues that presidents and other public officials prefer to keep out of the limelight. Budget deficits, crumbling highways and bridges, and inefficient veterans' hospitals are only a few examples. Constant media prodding can keep damaging issues at the top of the public agenda. The list of major and minor scandals that the media highlighted to the government's dismay is seemingly endless. The names of scandals, such as "Watergate" in the Nixon years and "Whitewater" during the Clinton era, are examples, as are the Benghazi, IRS [Internal Revenue Service], and NSA [National Security Agency] scandals that plagued the Obama administration. Similarly, President Trump's administration undoubtedly preferred less media attention to Russia's alleged interference in the 2016 election and possible conflicts of interest with the vast Trump business empire, two lingering stories from his first days and weeks as president-elect.[12] Trump was no fan of reading about either of his two impeachment trials in the news nor was the newly elected Biden team pleased in March 2021 when coverage shifted away from the administration's favorably viewed handling of the COVID-19 crisis and the recent passage of the $1.9 trillion COVID-19 relief package to the immigration crisis at the border. In fact, Biden administration officials' displeasure over the shift in focus was clear in their refusal to use the word *crisis* to describe the influx of unaccompanied migrant minors. Their rejection of the term to describe the situation—a clear effort to avoid media framing of the events at the border as a crisis—was not only telling but were also widely reported on.[13]

Media coverage can also increase public support for a president's policies and raise approval ratings. This is particularly important in national emergencies when backing by Congress and the public is vital. Following the 2001 terrorist attacks on the United States, President George W. Bush's positive evaluations in the news jumped from 36% to 63%. Such steep gains may be short-lived because memories fade quickly. By 2002, Bush's positive media scores slumped again to 38%. They rose to 56% during the initial stages of the Iraq War and plunged to 32% afterward.[14] Perhaps that's why, in 2005, President Bush felt the need to take a "Social Security reform tour" to various locations around the country in an effort to earn some positive coverage and public support for his proposed reforms. The public and the press observed similar efforts early in the Biden administration. Shortly following the passage of the COVID-19 relief package, both President Biden and Vice President Kamala Harris held public speaking engagements in an effort to attract and maintain public support for the bill.[15] (See Photo 5-2.) The effort was likely also aimed at claiming credit for the bill's passage in order to keep those high approval ratings and the coveted presidential honeymoon period alive.

Adverse publicity can kill the president's programs and abort new policies. Media publicity can also be crucial in determining whether a presidential appointee will be confirmed by the Senate. Media stories about unpaid taxes forced former Senate majority leader Tom Daschle to withdraw from consideration as secretary of the Department of Health and Human Services in the Obama administration, and fears of adverse publicity about a corruption scandal persuaded New Mexico's governor, Bill Richardson, to withdraw from a nomination as secretary of commerce. The degree to which negative press coverage can adversely affect presidential nominees also depends on whether the president's party controls

Photo 5-2 Vice President Kamala Harris and Treasury Secretary Janet Yellen Hosts Virtual Roundtable With Local Black Chambers of Commerce

Source: Photo by Drew Angerer/Getty Images.

the Senate and the level of party unity or polarization in that chamber. Though all of President Trump's nominees to the U.S. Supreme Court endured press scrutiny and at least some negative press coverage—most notably Justice Brett Kavanaugh's nomination and hearings due to several public allegations of sexual misconduct—they were still all confirmed by the Republican-controlled Senate.

Despite the political significance of the media for American presidents, research suggests that news does not appear to dictate public approval of the president as directly as in the past. Media scholars say this is explained in part by changes in conceptions of the presidency, changes in the media environment, and rising affective and social partisan polarization in the mass public. As we know from Chapter 4, the expansion of media choice means media is fragmented and, to some extent, so are audience content selections. Fewer people pay attention to the major broadcast news outlets, which used to praise or criticize the president with a surprisingly unified voice. When fewer Americans are subject to the same chorus of information about the president and instead have a choice of avoiding news about the president or selecting an ideologically filtered version of events, this weakens the ability of the news media to shape public evaluations of the president.[16] This is even more true when the politically attentive members of the public are increasingly team-minded about their partisanship and party's candidates, making it very difficult to move public sentiment toward the president.[17] This is one reason why, despite the fact that presidential politics was often tumultuous during the Trump administration, his public approval ratings were remarkably stable. His negative ratings rarely went up during periods of intensely negative coverage nor did his approval ratings rise much in response to policy accomplishments or improvements to the economy.

While this may sound like welcome news in some respects, it also reflects that modern presidents have a harder time shaping public opinion with respect to their policy agendas. That challenge may be one reason they developed apparatuses to manipulate media and public opinion. Presidential leadership of public opinion is much more difficult in the current political landscape. Today's media environment is characterized by fragmented media, polarized public audiences, hypercritical and increasingly negative news media, and a smaller proportion of the public interested in paying attention to news about the president. This environment makes it much more difficult for presidents to persuade the public about the benefits of the presidential policy agenda.[18] Internal polling and message testing frees administrations from the need to persuade in the face of strong public opposition. Instead, they target and frame issues in ways that avoid or soften opposition.[19]

Direct and Mediated Transmission

News about the government reaches the public both directly and indirectly. Direct transmission allows government officials to convey their messages with a minimum of media shaping. President Harry S. Truman was the first to use the direct mode of television by broadcasting his entire State of the Union message in 1947 to a nationwide audience. In January 1961, President John F. Kennedy further expanded direct coverage by allowing news conferences to be broadcast live. Because of his preference for using social media as a direct means of communicating with the public, President Trump was quick to earn the moniker of "the first Twitter president." Among public officials, presidents enjoy the greatest opportunities for uncontrolled access to the American people. Other political leaders competing with the president for power and public support have tried for matching privileges with only moderate success.

Of course, even live television, radio, and virtual events held by the president are not devoid of media influence. Camera angles and other photographic techniques that journalists and political communication practitioners use can slant presentations and impressions. When Barack Obama battled Hillary Clinton for nomination as the Democratic standard-bearer, he benefited from favorable camera angles. He was usually photographed from an upward camera angle that conveys deference, whereas the reverse was true for Clinton. During the 2016 election, awkward camera angles during one of the televised debates between candidates Donald Trump and Hillary Clinton created the impression that Trump was "menacingly looming" over Clinton; the images and buzz about them was central in post-debate press coverage the following day. As one NBC News story put it, "Trump's awkward physicality steals headlines."[20] The visuals from the debate were heartily mocked in a skit on the following Saturday's episode of NBC's *Saturday Night Live* as well (see Photo 5-3).

Once the election is over, the presidential image benefits from photographs by the official White House photographer, whose job is to take photos that record the president's activities—and in doing so, generally enhance the president's stature. Naturally, presidents, first ladies, and their communications teams are keenly aware of how visual framing can shape public impressions. In reporting about Trump's requirement that his chief White House photographer, Shealah Craighead, carry around a stool so that he could be photographed from an above angle (as selfie culture has taught us, the above angle makes everyone look slimmer and taller), it was revealed that it was actually First Lady Laura Bush who started the practice. Craighead was formerly a staff photographer for the George W. Bush administration.[21] Though Trump was often depicted as highly image-conscious during his term, concern over such things is practically a requirement in modern presidencies.

Indirect or mediated transmission—the framing of news presentations by media personnel—lies at the heart of the tensions between media and government because it permits journalists to pick and choose among the facts given to them. Lengthy official statements are routinely condensed into brief, one- or two-sentence quotations and then woven into an account constructed by journalists to match their goals. The president's pronouncements are often supplemented by information from hostile sources. Television sound bites

Photo 5-3 Images From Second Presidential Election Debate in 2016

Source: PAUL J. RICHARDS/AFP via Getty Images

featuring a speaking president averaged forty-five seconds in earlier decades; today they average less than nine seconds and rarely exceed twenty seconds. In recent years, much presidential coverage contains reprinted tweets rather than soundbites, and tweets are similarly brief due to the 280-character limit imposed by Twitter. Journalists' comments take up the slack.

By judiciously selecting spokespeople for specific points of view and structuring questions to elicit answers that fit neatly into desired scripts, newspeople can counteract politicians' pro-government spin and shape the public's evaluations of public officials and policies. Their appraisals are frequently negative, especially when the popularity of an administration is low or falling. Newspeople are often accused of using mediated coverage deliberately, or at the least carelessly, to hurt public officials and their policies. They may give equal amounts of coverage to various viewpoints but favor one side with a preponderance of positive emphases. During the 2020 presidential general election campaign, for example, mainstream news gave much more coverage to the incumbent Republican candidate, Donald Trump, relative to Joe Biden. However, the tone of coverage varied across outlets. A comparison between CBS and Fox News coverage of the election revealed that on CBS,

89% of statements about Biden were positive and 11% were negative, while 95% of statements about Trump were negative and only 5% were positive. Yet, on Fox News, the candidates received more even treatment with 59% of statements about Biden being negative compared to 58% of negative statements about Trump.[22] Figure 5-3 displays differences in the volume and tone of coverage of both candidates across the two networks.

Media personnel deny that they deliberately show incumbent administrations in a bad light. They see themselves as guardians of the public interest who help to make government more honest and efficient. The politicians who produced the problematic situation featured in the news—not the newspeople who reported it—should be blamed, they argue. They point out that news focuses on nonroutine aspects of political life and therefore deals with isolated instances of socially undesirable behavior that, unfortunately, reflect badly on government. Journalists periodically generate political upheavals by blowing up minor sins as if they were major transgressions, particularly if politically influential opponents voice attacks. For example, during the 2004 presidential primaries,

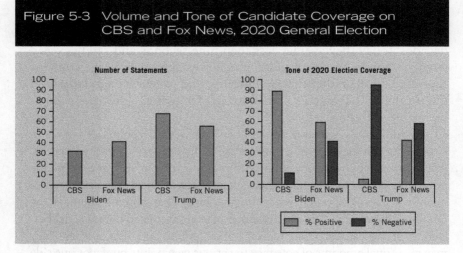

Figure 5-3 Volume and Tone of Candidate Coverage on CBS and Fox News, 2020 General Election

Source: Patterson, T. E. (2020, December 17). A tale of two elections. *Shorenstein Center on Media, Politics and Public Policy, Harvard Kennedy School.* https://shorensteincenter .org/patterson-2020-election-coverage/ Licensed under CC BY 3.0. https://creativecommons .org/licenses/by/3.0/

Note: Data are from Media Tenor and the Shorenstein Center. Copyright belongs to the author(s). Use is governed by the Harvard Kennedy School and Shorenstein Center Open Access Policies.

Howard Dean's campaign was badly hurt by reports that he uttered an unseemly scream when told about his disappointing third-place finish in the Iowa caucus. Such instances bely the explanation that the public interest is what drives coverage. Rather, they underscore that news values are paramount.

Managing a Rocky Relationship

All presidents profess to believe in a free press and to run an open government, but they rapidly develop a distaste for many of the reports about their administrations. When asked about news reporting midway into his term in 1962, President Kennedy told a news conference, "[I am] reading more and enjoying it less."[23]

Presidents' displeasure with media coverage is readily understandable. Media coverage not only embarrasses them regularly and deprives them, to varying degrees, of control over the definition of political situations, but it also forces them to talk in sound bites that reporters find attractive and, in the process, to put themselves on record in ways that may narrow their options for future action. Media disclosures of secret activities, such as an impending military intervention or a planned tax hike, may actually force the president's hand. Bargaining advantages may be lost through premature publication of news.

In the rocky relationship between the press and the president, open battles are comparatively rare, though this was not true during the recent Trump administration. Despite traded accusations that the government manipulates and lies and that the press distorts and entraps, each side is fully aware that it depends on the other. If presidents refuse to talk to hostile reporters, as happened periodically during most administrations, or if they instruct their staff and departments and agencies to refuse interviews, important stories cannot be covered firsthand. Alienating the prime news maker and source of government news is a serious loss for any news organization. Reporters' eagerness to get the news firsthand gives the president a tremendous advantage in influencing the substance and spin of news stories. Despite all this, press–presidency relations have increasingly deteriorated over the last several administrations.

The media, for their part, can withhold publicity that the president needs or damage the president's administration through unwanted publicity. Journalists can stress the positive or accent the negative. They can give instantaneous, live coverage to an event or delay broadcasts until a time of their choosing. In 1993, for example, NBC broadcast only thirty minutes of President Bill Clinton's first evening news conference. ABC and CBS, despite presidential pleading, refused to carry the event. All of the networks refused to broadcast President George H. W. Bush's last prime-time news conference in June 1992.[24] In several recent election years, network news periodically slighted the presidential election debates and the nominating conventions.

In this respect, the press–presidential candidate relationships have been relatively anomalous since the presidential election of 2016. That election started a ratings boom for news media, cable news in particular, and none considered forgoing the record-setting ratings that accompanied the 2016 debates. Public interest in news about the president and presidency persisted throughout Trump's term in office, including the 2020 campaign and its contentious aftermath. Shortly following the Biden inauguration in 2021, however, reports of declining ratings for news media started circulating. As of March 2021, ratings were still plummeting, but it is still too early to tell whether the high levels of public interest in presidential politics during the Trump era was truly an anomaly.[25]

Historically, one consequence of the interdependence of the press and the government is a good deal of fraternizing and cronyism between the two, often to the dismay of those who favor an adversarial relationship. Each side works hard to cultivate the other's friendship, recent examples aside. They often collaborate in examining political issues and problems. Such coziness may sap journalists' zeal to investigate government's misdeeds. Indeed, charges of collusion arise, particularly when media suppress news at the request of government departments or the White House. Many of these instances concerned national security. In 1980, for example, the press delayed publicizing plans for a U.S. invasion of Iran to rescue U.S. hostages. In 1987, it suppressed technical data about eavesdropping devices designed to intercept information from Soviet marine cables. Television executives agreed in 2001 not to broadcast messages from Al Qaeda leader Osama bin Laden.[26] In recent years, too much cooperation and coziness is most commonly suspected between those news outlets with partisan and ideological views and editorial stances consistent with the party of the current president. The Obama administration considered MSNBC a friendly outlet for interviews and appearances, while the Trump administration preferred Fox News. Though that can be troubling, there is an upside. The re-emergence and popularity of partisan media means there is always a handful of "out party" news outlets who will maintain an adversarial relationship with the White House.

The relationship between the media and the chief executive generally goes through three distinct phases.[27] There is an initial honeymoon period, a time of cooperation when the media convey the president's messages about organization of the new administration, appointments of new officials, and plans and proposals for new policies. At this early stage, few policies and proposals have been implemented, minimizing opportunities for harsh criticism. Presidents and their advisers, eager to get their stories across, make themselves readily available to the media and supply them with ample information. Here again, the 2016 election and early phases of the Trump administration were unique. Once the major party nominees were in place for 2016, the prospects for a press–White House honeymoon already looked bleak. For its part, the Obama administration did not set a recent precedent for openness with the press, and during the lead-up to the general election campaign, both Donald Trump and Hillary Clinton (the two major party general election candidates) were criticized for their handling of the press. Trump had overt and public battles with the press, dragged his feet on allowing access to a press pool, and actively ran against the press as vociferously as any candidate in recent memory. Clinton's campaign also bucked tradition by holding few press conferences and for using Trump's stalling as a reason to deny access to her own press pool. President-elect Trump's transition period did not hold promise for a press–presidency honeymoon period either; the White House Correspondents' Association lodged public complaints in November 2016 that the lack of media access during transition violated long-held traditions of press access.[28] Though the Trump administration is now infamous for its volatile and often hostile dealings with the press, it was not consistently an issue of access. President Trump regularly made himself available to the media for comments and interviews.

As of March 2021, mainstream media coverage of the nascent Biden administration seemed to mark a return to the historical honeymoon phase. This was likely both a cause and a consequence of the high public approval ratings Biden earned to that point relative to the historical average of 53% for presidents. However, those numbers were largely driven by very high approval among Democrats and most independents, Biden earned high disapproval ratings among Republicans. Biden's early high approval was also largely based on his response to the COVID-19 crisis and vaccine roll-out.[29] It later dropped in response to emerging challenges such as the migrant surge at the U.S.–Mexico border, COVID-19 surges from its Delta variant, the U.S. withdrawal from Afghanistan, lengthy haggling over a massive infrastructure bill, and rising inflation. By November 2021, the honeymoon was over.

Once an administration embarks on controversial programs, it is vulnerable to criticism of its record and the honeymoon ends. That is happening earlier and more abruptly now than in the past.[30] For example, President George W. Bush received far less favorable attention from newspapers, newsmagazines, and network television news during his early days in office than either Bill Clinton or George H. W. Bush.[31] President Obama's honeymoon was short as well, even though he began his presidency with high approval ratings across party lines. Controversial measures designed to halt and reverse a major economic recession tarnished his image. As noted earlier, the unprecedented wave of unaccompanied migrant children arriving at the border was among the first ongoing stories to tarnish Biden's honeymoon with the press. Related (and mostly negative) coverage started picking up steam about halfway through his first 100 days in office. If Biden did get a honeymoon, it was short, lasting only fifty to sixty days. Generally, studies of presidential news reveal that it is becoming more negative over time, as is coverage of presidential campaigns.[32]

Piqued by adverse publicity, the White House may retaliate by withholding news, restricting presidential contacts with the press, and increasing public relations activities. If the rifts between media and the executive branch become exceptionally wide, there may be a third phase in which both sides retreat from their mutually hostile behavior to take a more moderate stance. This phase frequently coincides with a reelection campaign, when newspeople try harder to provide impartial coverage and presidents are more eager to keep newspeople happy. The president may also arrange trips abroad to switch the focus of coverage to diplomatic ventures, which ordinarily is the area least likely to generate unfavorable coverage. There is political magic in scenes of U.S. presidents meeting with world leaders in foreign capitals.

Digital and social media provide other channels through which the White House can outmaneuver the press or circumvent them all together. In December 2016, President-elect Trump let 140 days pass between news conferences. It was the longest gap in recent years. But during that time, he sent approximately 1,500 tweets. Though the social media platforms are relatively new, the strategy of direct appeals to the public is not. Presidents have often used radio addresses, speeches, press releases, and interviews in lieu of news conferences. The wide reach and instantaneous nature of social media make it a particularly useful tool for direct communication with the public. Because President-elect Trump was so effective at using social media to dominate the news cycle during the campaign, pundits and media watchers speculated about how well it would be used as a bully pulpit during his administration.[33] Trump continued to rely heavily on Twitter as a primary communication platform for his entire time in office. In fact, he did so until he was banned from it and several other social media platforms in January 2021.

The ability of administrations to get along with the media differs considerably. The president's interpersonal skills, as well as the nature of the political problems that an administration faces, account for much of the variation. The Kennedy and Reagan administrations were particularly good at press relations, whereas the Nixon administration was especially bad. Nixon's Watergate problems might never have developed into a major scandal if he charmed the press more effectively. The Clinton years featured a mercurial relationship, fluctuating between affection and distaste on both sides. Crackdowns on leaks and Justice Department investigations of news organizations' sources added tensions to the relationship between the press and the Obama administration and to the perception of many journalists and critics that Obama did not fully respect the importance of a free press in a democratic system.[34] As the examples described above suggest, the Trump administration's relations with the press were volatile at best, toxic at worst.

The relationship between the chief executive and the media varies not only from one administration to the next but also from one part of the country to another. Frictions are greatest between the White House and the Washington, DC, press corps because they are most interdependent. Familiarity breeds a certain amount of contempt, and dependence breeds resentment. The northeastern seaboard press has a reputation of being more caustic than the press in the rest of the country. This is why recent presidents have often scheduled news conferences in other parts of the country and made major policy announcements away from the East Coast. For instance, President George W. Bush undertook a "Social Security reform tour" to friendly locations in 2005. As expected, it yielded a lush crop of favorable publicity for the reforms. Administrations have also made concerted efforts to schedule media interviews for cabinet members and other high-level officials away from the Washington, DC, area.

All recent presidents have visited small communities throughout the country to bask in the adulation of local audiences and local media for the benefit of nationwide television viewers. By taking advantage of advances in communication technology, they can grant interviews to local television and radio stations throughout the country directly from the White House television studio. Presidents can tailor unedited, unfiltered messages for specific demographic groups and transmit them to local anchors in selected locations, pleading for their support. Most presidents broadcast weekly addresses—originally on the radio—hoping to bring their unfiltered messages to the public. The Obama administration added to the weekly radio address, also posting it as a video on the White House website. At the beginning of his term, President Trump continued the tradition, posting his weekly addresses on YouTube. However, by late 2017, they became sporadic and eventually stopped entirely. One explanation was that such scripted addresses did not fit President Trump's communication style. It appears, however, that the weekly presidential address will be revived under the Biden administration. Biden gave his first address, which was called "A Weekly Conversation" and posted across the official @POTUS social media accounts, on February 6, 2021.[35] Heavy reliance on social media platforms for communicating to the public was clearly not specific to the Trump administration, despite his status as the first Twitter president. It is telling that the Biden administration's "revival" of the historical tradition of the weekly presidential radio address was described by Jen Psaki as something that will "take a variety of forms," the first of which was a video posted across the @POTUS official social media accounts (see Photo 5-4).

Presidential Communication Strategies

Presidents use an array of strategies to control the substance and tenor of news. Four approaches are particularly common. First and most important, presidents try to win reporters' favor. This is not difficult because presidents are constantly surrounded by people who must have fresh news to earn their pay. Second, presidents try to shape the flow of news to make good publicity more likely and bad publicity less likely. Third, they pace and arrange their work schedules to produce opportunities for favorable media coverage. Fourth—and this is a recent trend—they try to evade the hurdles of news media gatekeeping by publishing their news on government websites, through video news releases, or through the social network sites on the internet. We will discuss each of these strategies in turn.

Winning Favor

To woo reporters, presidents offer good story material as well as occasional scoops that may bring distinction to individual reporters. They cultivate reporters' friendship by being accessible, treating them with respect, and arranging for their creature comforts. To keep reporters in line, presidents may threaten them directly or obliquely with withdrawal of privileges. Privileges include accommodations on the presidential airplane, special interviews, or answers to their questions during news conferences. Presidents may also publicly condemn individual reporters or their organizations for undesirable reporting.

Orchestrating Coverage

The many tactics available for generating favorable publicity include creating newsworthy events, heightening suspense through news blackouts before major pronouncements, and staging public ceremonies as media spectacles at times when there are few competing events. Political successes may be coupled with political failures in hopes that publicity for the success will draw attention away from the failure.

Shaping the News Flow

Presidents try to guide the flow of news by the thrust of their commentary and by controlling contacts with the press. To avoid questions about embarrassing failures, presidents may even periodically restrict their contacts with the media to picture sessions. Presidents also may space out news releases to create a steady, manageable flow of news. If they want emphasis on a particular story, they may withhold competing news that breaks simultaneously. Sometimes administrations release a barrage of news or even create news to distract attention from sensitive developments. Administrations can avert criticism from the eastern press by withholding advance copies of speeches or by timing them late enough in the evening to preclude adequate coverage in the morning papers.

Shrinking financial resources forced mainstream media to reduce hard news reporting and turn to more soft news and commentary. For the presidency, that meant more "gotcha" negative stories, countered by White House official efforts to broadcast their own messages (including rebuttals) via digital and social media.[36] The relatively new media sites, including blogs, social websites, and various talk and comedy shows, are receptive to covering presidents and their policies, albeit sometimes inaccurately and sensationally. Research suggests that appearances on entertainment talk shows can be beneficial to politicians in office, such as increasing their level of public trust; however, such effects are found mainly among audiences low in political sophistication.[37]

For many types of messages, social networks seem more credible than the legacy media because people trust their peers more than outsiders.[38] The fact that President Obama's social media profile had millions of friends as he began his administration turned out to be a major asset. President Trump relied heavily on his vast social media following as well. As of January 2017, Trump had 18.4 million followers on Twitter and nearly 17.5 million followers on Facebook. In early 2021, after his term ended, his Twitter @POTUS45 archive account had 33.1 million followers. Whatever political influence he will continue to yield over national politics will almost certainly occur through social media, should his privileges ever be reinstated.

Publishing on Government Websites

The White House maintains its own website at http://www.whitehouse .gov. It is an electronic portal to the images and videos of the president, the first family, and the official mansion. It is also a means by which to broadcast messages prepared for public display by the incumbent and the presidential staff. Now quite interactive, the site contains opportunities to communicate with White House personnel and to sign up for regular updates. It also features the White House blog, which contains timely political pronouncements and responses regarding the politics of the day. The site includes links to documents and briefings about a multitude of events and issues related to the ongoing business of the administration. The White House website was redesigned in 2007 to highlight the president's daily activities and his policies and speeches,[39] and the Obama White House continued to improve the site. It was redesigned and updated several times since then. Aside from being unfailingly supportive of the president's policies, the whitehouse.gov site tries to meet citizens' information needs and to be transparent about the president's activities.

On May 13, 2009, the Obama White House sent its first email to people who signed up for alerts at the whitehouse.gov site; the email was about health care reform. It was sent as part of a phased unveiling of the White House's digital and social media presence, which also included profiles on MySpace, Facebook, and Twitter. The White House new media director, Macon Phillips (later at the State Department, in an attempt to better use new media to reach global audiences), lauded his team's efforts at utilizing new media technologies to build a new type of relationship between the president and the public. White House communication teams and staffers' use of digital media strategies is increasingly sophisticated.

Modern messaging technologies provide several advantages for mobilizing and sustaining public support while also circumventing media agenda setting. The White House uses these messages to update the public on what is going on, set the narrative, and provide countless opportunities for the public to be involved by sharing and/or liking messages or taking more traditional political actions such as calling members of Congress. Emails, posts, and tweets from the White House are an orchestrated mixture of official updates and personalized language. Some read as friendly, informal notes from the president, and others read more like a policy brief. This combination artfully leaves recipients with the sense of being part of something important and official while also feeling as if they share a personal link with the president.[40]

A great deal of research is still needed to assess how useful these digital communications are for the president's communication within the executive branch, with Congress, with interest groups, and with the citizenry at large. We do know that the White House website is widely used; millions of people access the website monthly.[41] The executive branch considers digital and social media communications to be important enough to allocate ample resources to them. This translates into attractive, user-friendly websites, online profiles, and messages that present the government's story in words and pictures that reflect the president's—rather than journalists'—preferences.

Photo 5-4 Image of Tweet Containing Biden's First Weekly Presidential Address

Source: The White House/@POTUS/Twitter.

Institutional Settings

Relations between the president and the media are so important and so complex that they require the involvement of established as well as specially created institutions.

On the President's Side

Presidents can shape the news indirectly through appointments to the Federal Communications Commission (FCC) and other public agencies concerned with media regulation and through informal contacts with personnel in those agencies. Presidents can control financial lifelines through the Office of Management and Budget, which screens the budgetary requests of all federal agencies, including those dealing with the mass media. An administration can also wield control through the Justice Department. For instance, the Antitrust Division can challenge the FCC's approval of mergers and can carry appeals through the courts and ultimately to the Supreme Court.

Presidents involve themselves directly in media policy making through White House organizations, study commissions, and task forces. In 1970, President Nixon created the Office of Telecommunications Policy—the first permanent agency within the White House to plan communications policy. Since then, every president has tinkered with institutional arrangements. Changes have generally revolved around four standing offices: the Press Office, the Office of Communications, the Office of Media Affairs, and Speechwriting—to use the post-Clinton nomenclature.[42] The Obama White House also included the Office of Digital Strategy and the Office of Public Engagement and Intergovernmental Affairs. Staffs for these offices usually are not large, but communications experts in other offices in the executive branch perform additional work.

The Press Office supplies Washington, DC–based reporters with news about the White House. By custom, the press secretary meets almost daily with the White House press corps to make announcements and take questions. These briefings supply reporters with the president's interpretation of events. Reporters then cast their stories into perspectives of their own choice.[43] In November 2020, President-elect Biden named veteran Democratic spokesperson Jen Psaki as his chosen White House press secretary. Psaki is one of seven women serving in the upper ranks of Biden's White House communications team. Biden's communication team is being led by Kate Bedingfield, who served as the Biden campaign communications manager.[44]

The Office of Communications is concerned with long-range public relations management of the presidency. In consultation with the president, it determines the images that the administration needs to convey to gain and retain the approval of important constituencies in the public and private sectors and to win support for desired policies. The office also coordinates the public relations activities of executive branch departments and agencies to make sure that the chorus of public voices is harmonious. If the president's approval ratings plunge, the communications director is likely to get the ax. As George Stephanopoulos, a victim of the communications wars during the Clinton administration, explained, "By definition, if the President isn't doing well, it's a communication problem. That's always going to be a natural place to make a change."[45]

The Office of Media Affairs serves the regional and local press and various news organizations in Washington, DC. It also handles publicity during the president's travels. The office lets the president know how well his messages are faring with audiences. It also manages the president's website. Those in the Speechwriting Office keep busy by composing remarks for the huge number of annual public events featuring the president.[46]

Modern public relations activities involve many different techniques:

Focus groups and polling data are used to fashion
presidential messages; sound bites are written into the public
pronouncements of the president and his underlings to articulate
those messages; public appearances are choreographed so that
the messages are reinforced by visual images.[47]

To spread messages throughout the country, the administration sends cabinet officers and others on speaking tours and arranges satellite interviews in local markets.

It is, of course, essential for presidents to sell their policies by soliciting wide support for them and by presenting a united front within their administrations. However, in the process, democracy may be imperiled because

style is substituted for substance. Complicated issues are
transformed into simple slogans and slick sound-bites. . . .
[T]imid, self-interested policy makers . . . shy away from
responsibility for their actions and delude themselves and their
constituents with their own symbolic spectacle.[48]

Ethical issues arise when the president or executive agencies commission propaganda messages from public relations firms and then distribute them as official news releases. In 2005, for example, Congress's Government Accountability Office (GAO) criticized the Office of National Drug Control Policy for distributing what it called "covert propaganda."[49] The GAO had admonished the Department of Education earlier for paying $240,000 to a syndicated columnist for promoting the president's education reforms.[50]

On the Media's Side

Close to 8,000 print and broadcast reporters are accredited to attend White House press operations, though only a small fraction—generally fewer than fifty—actually attend press conferences. Given the small quarters in which presidential news conferences are held (a space even more limited under COVID-19 restrictions), attendees are usually selected to represent a balanced pool of news venues, including wire services. Seats in the White House briefing room are coveted and so is their location with respect to the podium. Journalists and news organizations vie for prominent seats; assignments are given by the White House Correspondents' Association (WHCA). Seat allocations rotate regularly with changes to the media environment, such as shifting patterns of media ownership, disappearing news organizations, and the emergence of new media outlets. The WHCA has struggled with how to fairly integrate prominent new media outlets into the scheme as they emerge as serious contenders. For example, as of 2010, well-known online news sources such as *HuffPost* and *FiveThirtyEight* did not yet have a seat, while *Politico* had a seat in 2009. By 2015, outlets such as Yahoo! News and BuzzFeed had seats or partial seats. In 2020, the press briefing room included spots for new additions to the ranks of partisan cable news, such as Newsmax. Briefing room spots and desk space decisions by the WHCA are based on a number of factors such as reporter tenure, attendance at briefings, and the size of a news outlet's audience.[51] In recent years, political considerations—primarily about the partisan lean of various outlets—have also shaped these prized seat allocations. Photo 5-5 shows a tweet depicting the seating chart in 2020, including adaptations made to accommodate COVID-19 restrictions in place at the time.

Many reporters who serve routinely in the White House press corps have considerable experience and notable reputations. As a group, they are older and better educated and trained than the average U.S. journalist.[52] *The New York Times, The Washington Post, Los Angeles Times,* and other major newspapers have full-time reporters assigned exclusively to the president. So do a number of major newspaper chains such as McClatchy. Smaller papers may send their Washington, DC, bureau chiefs to the White House whenever there is news of special interest to their region.

Each of the major broadcast networks, as well as CNN, has several reporters at the White House on a regular basis; smaller networks have one. C-SPAN provides coverage of White House events open to the public as well as complete coverage of sessions of the House of Representatives.[53] The White House is also covered by several all-news cable services, internet news operations such as the *HuffPost*, weekly newsmagazines, and periodicals as well as photographers and their supporting staffs. Hard economic times have forced cutbacks in personnel and increased pooling of resources among media organizations. Even big events such as presidential trips abroad or the national party conventions are covered by a smaller corps of journalists, and many reporters now work for several news organizations.

Most of the country's dailies and television and radio stations do not have a regular Washington, DC, correspondent or part-time stringer to cover the White House. Inexpensive satellite time, however, lowered news transmission costs and boosted the number of stations that can afford direct coverage of the Washington scene, often through the prism of local interests.

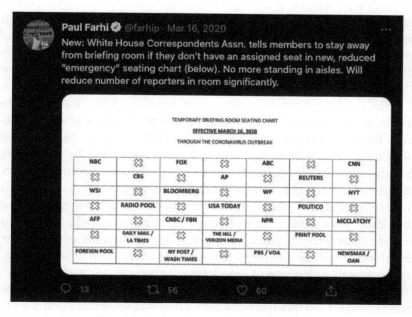

Photo 5-5 Image of Tweet on Changes to White House Briefing Room Seating Chart

Source: Twitter.com, Tweet from Paul Farhi, @farhip, writer for @washingtonpost, March 16, 2020.

Forms of Contact

Press Releases, Posts, and News Briefings

The release of news by chief executives or their aides takes several routine forms. Most of these represent a concerted effort to control the news output. The most common is the press release, a story prepared by government officials and handed to members of the press, usually without an opportunity for questions. These are often posted across the White House official social media accounts and on the website. In a news briefing, reporters have an opportunity to ask the press secretary about the news releases (see Photo 5-6). But because executive officials furnish the news for the briefing, they control the substance and tone of the discussion.

News Conferences

Although a news conference may appear to be a wide-open question period, the official being questioned tries to control it tightly. Seemingly spontaneous answers usually have been carefully prepared by experts on the executive's staff and rehearsed during extensive briefings. Before Kennedy's presidency, press conferences were not covered live, permitting the White House to make corrections before conference records were published. Kennedy, who was a gifted extemporaneous speaker, stripped away this cloak of protection by allowing live filming of conferences. At the time, press critics called it "goofy" and likened it to "making love in Carnegie Hall."[54]

The live format remains controversial because it leads to posturing by the president as well as by members of the press. It also causes embarrassment for presidents who misspeak or suffer memory lapses. Presidents can often control the subject and tone of a news conference by recognizing friendly reporters for questions and avoiding follow-up questions. But no president has been able to squelch embarrassing questions entirely or to deny reporters the chance to use their questions as opportunities to express their own views about controversial issues.[55] By posing leading questions, reporters may force the president or press secretary to comment on matters that these officials may not wish to discuss. As a result, administrations can be stingy with such access to presidents.

According to journalists in the Obama White House press corps, presidents can exert too much control over access and information. In the first year of Obama's second term, White House correspondents complained

Photo 5-6 White House Press Secretary Jen Psaki Holds Briefing in the White House

Source: Photo by Drew Angerer/Getty Images.

about a lack of access to the president or too much administration control over information. An opinion piece by Jim VandeHei and Mike Allen of *Politico* described it this way:

> President Barack Obama is a master at limiting, shaping
> and manipulating media coverage of himself and his White
> House. Not for the reason that conservatives suspect: namely,
> that a liberal press willingly and eagerly allows itself to get
> manipulated. Instead, the mastery mostly flows from a White
> House that has taken old tricks for shaping coverage (staged
> leaks, friendly interviews) and put them on steroids using new
> ones (social media, content creation, precision targeting). And
> it's an equal opportunity strategy: Media across the ideological
> spectrum are left scrambling for access.[56]

The questions listed in Box 5-1 give a taste of the sort of interrogation that presidents face when they hold press conferences.

Backgrounders

Some news conferences are off-the-record "backgrounders." High officials call such events to give newspeople important background information that they are honor bound to keep entirely secret or to publish only without revealing the source. Forms of vague attribution are usually permitted, such as "Government sources say," "It has been reported by reliable sources," or even more specifically, "The White House discloses" or the "Defense Department indicates."

Government officials prefer backgrounders because they are a relatively safe way to test the waters. They permit officials to bring a variety of policy ideas before their colleagues and the public without openly identifying with them. Unlike government officials, reporters are ambivalent about backgrounders. They enjoy having access to news that might otherwise be unavailable, but they dislike being prevented from publishing all aspects of the story or identifying the source of the information so the story can be placed in its proper perspective. In addition to formal encounters, reporters and the president or White House staff meet informally in work or social settings.

Top government officials, and occasionally the president, give interviews on daytime news programs; on nighttime serious, satirical, and humorous shows; and during town hall meetings where the president meets with ordinary citizens in various locations. Questioning on these occasions can resemble a no-holds-barred cross-examination. More likely, they are friendly exchanges. Because they are broadcast by large media enterprises, they provide excellent opportunities to present the administration's position to an interested worldwide audience.

Leaks

An even less formal release of news occurs through *leaks*, the surreptitious release of information by high- and low-level government sources who wish to remain anonymous or who do not want to release the information formally. Many leaks are sanctioned at the highest levels. But some officials may also leak information that they are not authorized to release. Sometimes low-level officials leak information to gain attention from top officials.

Leaks are a mixed blessing. They can destroy the timing of negotiations, alienate the parties whose secrets have been exposed, and cause great harm by disclosing politically sensitive matters. They also allow scrutiny of important suppressed issues, serve as trial runs, and permit government officials to release information anonymously. Although presidents frequently leak confidential stories, they passionately hate news leaked by others. Recent administrations were no different; Obama prosecuted more leaks than any previous president during his time in office.[57] All recent presidents used federal investigative agencies and the Justice Department to find the sources of news leaks.

Leaks were a particular aggravation for the Obama and Trump White Houses. During Obama's first term in October 2011, Army Pfc. Chelsea Manning sent hundreds of thousands of classified diplomatic cables and documents to WikiLeaks. In 2013, defense contractor Edward Snowden leaked information about a vast U.S. government surveillance program involving the collection of communication records of Americans and governments abroad. Even before that, the Obama administration was building a reputation for prosecuting a historic number of leaks. Leaks were even more frequent under the Trump administration, reaching record highs.[58] It remains to be seen whether leaks will be a major problem for the Biden administration. Continuing struggles with leaks and the administrations' crackdown efforts continue to raise questions about appropriate balance between government transparency, privacy, press freedom, and national security.[59] The harm that leaks cause must be weighed against their benefits. In a system in which the executive maintains tight control over the formal channels of news, leaks provide a valuable counterbalance.

Box 5-1
Quizzing the President

On March 25, 2021, President Joe Biden gave his first formal press conference at the White House. It began with the president's progress report on where the country stood with regard to COVID-19 vaccines and several key issues 65 days into his term. Here is a slightly abbreviated version of Biden's opening remarks followed by some of the reporters' questions. The answers have been omitted.

Opening Remarks

Please, please sit down. Thank you. Thank you. Good afternoon. Before I take questions, I want to give you a progress report on where we stand 65 days into office here on vaccinations and a few other top priorities for the American people. First on vaccinations. On December 8th, I indicated that I hoped to get 100 million shots in people's arms in my first 100 days. We met that goal last week by day 58, 42 days ahead of schedule. Now, today I'm setting a

(Continued)

(Continued)

second goal: by my 100th day in office, we will have administered 200 million shots in people's arms. That's right, 200 million shots in 100 days. I know it's ambitious, twice our original goal, but no other country in the world has even come close to what we are doing. And I believe we can do it.

And today, we made a historic investment in reaching the hardest hit communities by investing an additional $10 billion to reach them. I also set a goal before I took office of getting a majority of schools in K–8 fully open in the first 100 days. Now, thanks to the enormous amount of work done by our administration, educators, parents, local, and state education officials, a recent Department of Education survey shows that nearly half of K–8 schools are open full-time, five days a week for in-person learning. Not yet a majority, but we're really close, and I believe in the 35 days left to go, we'll meet that goal as well. As of yesterday, more than 100 million payments of $1,400 have gone into people's bank accounts. That's real money in people's pockets, and millions more will get their money very soon.

One final note, since we passed the American Rescue Plan, we're starting to see new signs of hope in our economy. Since it was passed, a majority of economic forecasters have significantly increased their projections on the economic growth that's going to take place this year. They're now projecting it will exceed 6%, a 6% growth in GDP [gross domestic product]. And just this morning, we learned that the number of people filing for weekly unemployment insurance fell by nearly 100,000 persons. This is the first time in a year the number has fallen below the pre-pandemic high. There are still too many Americans out of work, and too many families hurting, but I can say to you, the American people, help is here. Now, I'll be happy to take your questions.

- Thank you, Mr. President. You mentioned your progress on COVID-19. I'd like to ask you about some of the other issues facing your presidency. One of the defining challenges you face in the coming months is how to deliver on your promise to Americans on issues like immigration reform, gun control, voting rights, climate change. Those are facing stiff united opposition from Republicans on Capitol Hill. How far are you willing to go to achieve those promises?

- A follow-up, Mr. President. Can your presidency be a success if you can't make progress on those four challenges: climate change, immigration reform, gun control, voting rights?

- Thanks so much, Mr. President. You've said over and over again that immigrants shouldn't come to this country right now. This isn't the time to come. That message is not being received. Instead, the perception of you that got you elected as a moral decent man is the reason why a lot of immigrants are coming to this country and entrusting you with unaccompanied minors. How do you resolve that tension, and how are you choosing which families can stay and which can go given the fact that even though with Title 42 there are some families that are staying? And is there a timeline for when we won't be seeing these overcrowded facilities run by CBP [Customs and Border Protection] when it comes to unaccompanied minors?

- My follow-up question is, one, if you could talk a little bit about which families are being allowed to stay [and] why they're being allowed to stay. In addition to that, when it comes to the filibuster, immigration is a big issue, of course, related to the filibuster, but Republicans are also passing bill after bill trying to restrict voting rights. Chuck Schumer is calling it an existential threat to democracy. Why not back a filibuster rule that at least gets around issues, including voting rights or immigration?

- I'd like to circle back to immigration, please. You just listed the reasons that people are coming, talking about in-country problems, saying that it happens every year. You blamed the last administration, sir. I just got back last night from a reporting trip to the border where I met a nine-year-old who walked here from Honduras by himself along with another little boy. He had that phone number on him and we were able to call his family. His mother says that she sent her son to this country because she believes that you are not deporting unaccompanied minors like her son. That's why she sent him alone from Honduras. So, sir, you blamed the last administration, but is your messaging saying that these children are and will be allowed to stay in this country and work their way through this process, encouraging families like his to come?

- A quick follow-up, if I may. Do you want to see these unaccompanied minors staying in this country? Or should they be deported eventually?

(Continued)

(Continued)

- Final follow-up, sir. You mentioned circumstances that must be horrific. The customs and border protection facility in Donna, Texas, is at 1,556% capacity right now with mostly unaccompanied minors. There are kids that are sleeping on floors. They are packed into these pods. I've spoken to lawyers who say that some of these children have not seen the sun in days. What is your reaction to these images that have come out from that particular facility? Is what's happening inside acceptable to you? And when is this going to be fixed?

- Thank you, Mr. President. I wanted to ask you about Afghanistan. You face a May 1st deadline for the withdrawal of U.S. troops from that country. As a candidate in foreign affairs, you wrote that it is past time to end these forever wars. Can you commit to the American people that by May 2nd, the U.S. will no longer have forces in Afghanistan?

- Thank you very much, Mr. President. Given the conditions that were just laid out at the migrant facilities at the U.S. border, will you commit to allowing journalists to have access to the facilities that are overcrowded moving forward?

- How soon will journalists be able to have access to the facilities? We've obviously been allowed to be inside one, but we haven't seen the facilities in which children are packed together to really give the American people a chance to see that. Will you commit to transparency on this issue?

- Did you move too quickly to roll back some of the executive orders of your predecessor?

- I want to ask you about foreign policy, Mr. President. Overnight, we learned that North Korea tested two ballistic missiles. What, if any, actions will you take? And what is your red line on North Korea?

- Thank you very much, Mr. President. I want to go back to voting rights. Republican legislatures across the country are working to pass bills that would restrict voting, particularly, Democrats fear, impacting minority voters and young voters, the very people who helped to get you elected in November. Are you worried that if you don't manage to pass voting rights legislation, that your party is going to lose seats and possibly lose control of the House and the Senate in 2022?

Source: Excerpted from President Joe Biden's First White House Press Conference Transcript March 25. (2021, March 25). *Rev.* https://www.rev.com/blog/transcripts/president-joe-biden-first-white-house-press-conference-transcript-march-25

SUMMARY

In this chapter, we examined the relationship between the media and the presidency—a rocky one because the goals of these institutions differ and often conflict. Officials want favorable stories that mirror their sense of what is important and what is unimportant. Newspeople want stories that please the public. Newspeople believe that their audiences are more interested in exciting events and human-interest tales than in academic discussions of public policies. Newspeople also feel a special mission, like Shakespeare's Mark Antony, "to bury Caesar, not to praise him." And like Brutus, they claim that their criticism is not disloyalty. They do not love the government less; they only love the nation and its people more.

Each side in this tug-of-war uses wiles and ruses as well as clout to have its own way. The outcome is a seesaw contest in which both sides score victories and suffer defeats, but each side is more attuned to its own failures than to its victories. The public interest is served in an equally uneven fashion. If we equate the public interest with a maximum of intelligible information about important issues and events, media presentations fall short. But coverage also is good because it is continuous and often well informed, with sufficient attention to audience appeal to make dry information palatable. Investigative reporting brings to light many shortcomings and scandals that otherwise might remain hidden. Additionally, fear of exposure by the media undoubtedly keeps government officials from straying into many questionable ventures, although this effect is hard to document. On the negative side, fear of media coverage and publicity probably inhibits many desirable actions.

Because the contacts between officials of the national government and the media are so constant, a formal institutional structure was established to handle their interactions. This chapter describes the fairly elaborate setup at the presidential level and the way changes to the modern media environment influence White House communication strategies. It also explores some of the problems that newspeople face in covering a flood of complex news expeditiously, accurately, and with a modicum of critical detachment and analysis.

Problems in communications policy making remain. All three branches of government shape communications policy, but there is little coordination among them. Even within the executive branch, so many different committees and agencies share control that the outcome tends to be a compromise that pleases nobody. The government's weakness in this area may be a blessing in disguise and in the spirit of the First Amendment. Because the Constitution commands that Congress shall make no law abridging the freedom of the press, it may be well to keep all communications policy making to the barest minimum. As Chief Justice John Marshall warned early in the nation's history, the power to regulate is the power to destroy.[60] Policy making and regulation overlap. A uniform, well-articulated communications policy, however beneficial it may seem to many people, still puts the government imprint indelibly on the flow of information.

DISCUSSION QUESTIONS

1. Why is an adversarial relationship between the media and public officials not only appropriate but necessary in a representative democracy?

2. What functions do the media serve for the president, and how does the media's performance of these functions shape public opinion and policy making?

READINGS

Boczkowski, P. J., & Papacharissi, Z. (Eds.). (2018). *Trump and the media*. MIT Press.

Farnsworth, S. J. (2018). *Presidential communication and character: White House news management from Clinton and cable to Twitter and Trump*. Routledge.

Fowler, L. L. (2015). *Watchdogs on the hill: The decline of congressional oversight of US foreign relations*. Princeton University Press.

Gutsche, R. E., Jr. (Ed.). (2018). *The Trump presidency, journalism, and democracy*. Routledge.

Hart, R. P. (2020). *Trump and us: What he says and why people listen*. Cambridge University Press.

Hibbing, J. T. (2020). *The securitarian personality*. Oxford University Press.

Jamieson, K. H. (2018). *Cyberwar: How Russian hackers and trolls helped elect a president*. Oxford University Press.

Karl, J. (2020). *Front row at the Trump show*. Dutton Press.

Kelley, C. E. (2018). *A rhetoric of divisive partisanship: The 2016 American presidential campaign discourse of Bernie Sanders and Donald Trump*. Lexington Books.

Kurtz, H. (2018). *Media madness: Donald Trump, the press, and the war over the truth*. Simon and Schuster.

Lockhart, M. (2018). *President Donald Trump and his political discourse: Ramifications of rhetoric via Twitter*. Routledge.

Mercieca, J. (2020). *Demagogue for president: The rhetorical genius of Donald Trump*. Texas A&M University Press.

Sides, J., Tessler, M., & Vavreck, L. (2018). *Identity crisis: The 2016 presidential campaign and the battle for the meaning of America*. Princeton University Press.

Stromer-Galley, J. (2019). *Presidential campaigning in the internet age* (2nd ed.). Oxford University Press.

NOTES

1. Steinhauser, P. (2013, June 25). Second term blues: Obama not the first to feel the pain. *CNN*. http://politicalticker.blogs.cnn.com/2013/06/25/second-term-blues-obama-not-the-first-to-feel-the-pain/; Dunkley, G. (2013, May 22). Obama second-term curse? A look into presidential scandals after reelection. *Huffington Post*. http://www.huffingtonpost.com/2013/05/22/obama-second-term-curse_n_3313800.html; Pace, J. (2013, May 29). Obama's second term agenda waylaid by controversies. *Huffington Post*; Collinson, S. (2017, March 28). There's a Russian storm over Trump's struggling presidency. *CNN*. http://www.cnn.com/2017/03/28/politics/donald-trump-russia-presidency/.

2. Rose, J. (2021, March 22). Despite ample warning, U.S. as unprepared for latest surge of migrant children. *NPR Morning Edition*. https://www.npr.org/2021/03/22/979886083/white-house-scrambles-to-deal-with-migrant-influx-at-southern-border; Ordonez, F. (2021, March 23). Ex-DHS chief says Biden was warned about dismantling Trump's border policies. https://www.npr.org/2021/03/23/980272165/ex-dhs-chief-says-biden-was-warned-about-dismantling-trumps-border-policies

3. Cohen, J. E. (2008). *The presidency in the era of 24-hour news*. Princeton University Press.

4. Boller, P. F., Jr. (2004). *Presidential campaigns: From George Washington to George W. Bush*. Oxford University Press.

5. Foote, J. S. (1990). *Television access and political power: The networks, the presidency, and the "loyal opposition."* Praeger; for an updated discussion see C. Danielle Vinson, C. D. (2013). Congress and the media: Who has the upper hand?" In T. N. Rideout (Ed.), *New directions in media and politics*. Routledge.

6. Mitchell, A., Gottfried, J., Stocking, G., Matsa, K., & Grieco, E. M. (2017, October 2). Covering President Trump in a polarized media environment. https://www.journalism.org/2017/10/02/covering-president-trump-in-a-polarized-media-environment/

7. Eshbaugh-Soha, M. (2016). Presidential agenda-setting of traditional and non-traditional news media. *Political Communication, 33,* 1–20.

8. Presidential communication in general is discussed by Hinckley, B. (1990). *The symbolic presidency: How presidents portray themselves.* Routledge; also see Kernell, S. (2007). *Going public: New strategies of presidential leadership* (4th ed.). CQ Press; Cohen, J. E. (2008). *The presidency in the era of 24-hour news.* Princeton University Press; "The White House Transition Project," Office Briefs 31–34. (https://whitehousetransitionproject.org/transition-resources-2/office-briefs/) and *Managing the president's message: The White House communications operation.* (Johns Hopkins University Press, 2007) provide excellent observation-based accounts of White House press operations.

9. Druckman, J. N., & Jacobs, L. R. (2015). *Who governs? Presidents, public opinion, and manipulation.* University of Chicago Press.

10. Scacco, J. M., & Coe, K. (2016). The ubiquitous presidency: Toward a new paradigm for studying presidential communication. *International Journal of Communication, 10,* 2014–2037.

11. Quoted in Cook, T. E. (1998). *Governing with the news: The news media as a political institution.* University of Chicago Press, p. 131.

12. Steinhauser, P. (2013, June 25). Second term blues: Obama not the first to feel the pain. *CNN.* http://politicalticker.blogs.cnn.com/2013/06/25/second-term-blues-obama-not-the-first-to-feel-the-pain/; Dunkley, G. (2013, May 22). Obama second-term curse? A look into presidential scandals after reelection. *Huffington Post.* http://www.huffingtonpost.com/2013/05/22/obama-second-term-curse_n_3313800.html; Pace, Pace, J. (2013, May 29). Obama's second term agenda waylaid by controversies. *Huffington Post;* Jackson, D. (2016, December 11). Trump dismisses CIA findings of Russian election tampering. *USA Today,* http://www.usatoday.com/story/news/politics/2016/12/11/trump-dismisses-allegations-russian-election-tampering/95297756/; Venook, J. (2016, December 27). Donald Trump's conflicts of interest: A crib sheet. *Atlantic.* https://www.theatlantic.com/business/archive/2017/01/trumps-appointees-conflicts-of-interest-a-crib-sheet/512711/

13. Luhby, T., & Lobosco, K. (2021, March 20). Here's what's in the Covid relieve package. *CNN.* https://www.cnn.com/2021/03/10/politics/whats-in-the-covid-relief-bill/index.html; Kolinovsky, S. (2021, March 18). White House press secretary slips up, calls border migrant surge a "crisis," Jen Psaki referred to "the crisis in the border" after resisting calls to do so. https://abcnews.go.com/Politics/white-house-press-secretary-slips-calls-border-migrant/story?id=76540202.

14. George Bush's Postwar Blues. (2003). *Media Monitor, 17*(4), p. 5. http://cmpa.gmu.edu/wp-content/uploads/2014/02/2003-1.pdf

15. Collins, E., Restuccia, A., & Lucey, C. (2021, March 14). Biden, Harris plan cross-country tour to tout Covid-19 aid. https://www.wsj.com/articles/biden-harris-plan-cross-country-tour-to-tout-covid-19-aid-11615723200

16. Cohen, J. E. (2008). *The presidency in the era of 24-hour news.* Princeton University Press.

17. Lelkes, Y., Sood, G., & Iyengar, S. (2017). The hostile audience: The effect of access to broadband internet on partisan affect. *American Journal of Political Science, 61*(1), 5–20.

18. Rottinghaus, B., & Lang, M. (2013). To speak is to lead? Conditional modern presidential leadership of public opinion," In T. N. Rideout (Ed.), *New directions in media and politics.* Routledge; Scacco, J. M., & Coe, K. (2016). The ubiquitous presidency: Toward a new paradigm for studying presidential communication. *International Journal of Communication, 10,* 2014–2037.

19. Druckman, J. N., & Jacobs, L. R. (2015). *Who governs? Presidents, public opinion, and manipulation.* University of Chicago Press.

20. Jamieson, A. (2016, October 10). 2016 debate: Trump accused of "stalking" Clinton on stage. *NBC News.* https://www.nbcnews.com/storyline/2016-presidential-debates/presidential-debate-trump-accused-stalking-clinton-stage-n663516

21. Smith, E. (2017, April 2017). Buzz that Trump angles photos to appear taller and thinner. *Page Six.* https://pagesix.com/2017/04/03/buzz-that-trump-angles-photos-to-appear-taller-and-thinner/

22. Patterson, T. E. (2020, December 17). A tale of two elections. *Shorenstein Center on Media, Politics and Public Policy, Harvard Kennedy School.* https://shorensteincenter.org/patterson-2020-election-coverage/

23. Chase, H. W., & Lerman, A. H. (Eds.). (1965). *Kennedy and the press: The news conferences.* Crowell, p. 239.

24. Refusal problems are discussed in Baum, M. A., & Kernell, S. (1999). Has cable ended the golden age of presidential television? *American Political Science Review, 93*(1), 99–114.

25. Bowden, J. (2021, March 22). News ratings, traffic plummet post-Trump. *The Hill.* https://thehill.com/homenews/media/544410-news-ratings-traffic-plummet-post-trump

26. Graber, D. A. (2003). Terrorism, censorship and the First Amendment: In search of policy guidelines. In P. Norris, M. Kern, & M. Just (Eds.), *Framing terrorism: The news media, the government, and the public* (pp. 27–42). Routledge.

27. Grossman, M. B., & Kumar, M. J. (1981). *Portraying the president: The White House and the news media.* Johns Hopkins University Press; Kumar, M. J., &

Jones, A. (2005). Government and the press: Issues and trends. In G. Overholser & K. H. Jamieson (Eds.), *The institutions of American democracy: The press*. Oxford University Press; Kumar, M. J. (2005). The importance and evolution of presidential press conferences. *Presidential Studies Quarterly, 35*(1), 166–192.

28. Gold, H. (2016, August 12). Clinton's press problem: As Trump wars with the media, Clinton moves just as slowly to allow reporters' full access, bucking tradition. *Politico*. http://www.politico.com/story/2016/08/hillary-clinton-media-press-problem-226944; Weprin, A. (2016, November 16). WHCA says lack of media access to president-elect Trump is "unacceptable." *Politico*. http://www.politico.com/blogs/on-media/2016/11/whca-to-trump-transition-team-it-is-unacceptable-for-president-elect-to-not-have-a-press-pool-231471

29. Jones, J. M. (2021, March 18). Biden approval ratings diverge by gender, education, race. *Gallup*. https://news.gallup.com/poll/339977/biden-approval-ratings-diverge-gender-education-race.aspx.

30. Smoller, F. T. (1990). *The six o'clock presidency*. Praeger, pp. 61–77.

31. The disappearing honeymoon: TV news coverage of President George W. Bush's first 100 days. (2001). *Media Monitor, 15*(3), 1–5; The first 100 days. (2001, April 30). *Pew Research Center*. http://www.journalism.org/2001/04/30/the-first-100-days/

32. Cohen, J. E. (2008). *The presidency in the era of 24-hour news*. Princeton University Press; Geer, J. G. (2012). The news media and the rise of negativity in presidential campaigns. *PS: Political Science, 45*(3), 422–427.

33. Morino, I. (2016, December 16). Social media: Politicians bypass press and control their message. *The Denver Post*. http://www.denverpost.com/2016/12/16/social-media-politicians-press-message/; Warren, J. (2016, December 7). Revolutionizing the Bully pulpit: Trump's twitter tirades are redefining presidential communication. *U.S. News & World Report*. http://www.usnews.com/opinion/thomas-jefferson-street/articles/2016-12-07/donald-trumps-twitter-use-is-revolutionizing-the-presidents-bully-pulpit

34. Calderone, M., Stein, S., & Reilly, R. J. (2013, May 14). AP phone records seized by Justice Department as war on leaks continues. *Huffington Post*. http://www.huffingtonpost.com/2013/05/13/ap-phone-records-doj-leaks_n_3268932.html

35. Herman, S. (2017, November 20). President Trump goes radio silent. *VOA*. https://www.voanews.com/a/president-trump-goes-radio-silent/4127869.html; Slotkin, J. (2021, February 6). Biden revives presidential tradition, releasing first weekly address. https://www.npr.org/2021/02/06/964889898/biden-revives-presidential-tradition-releasing-first-weekly-address

36. Cohen, J. E. (2008). *The presidency in the era of 24-hour news*. Princeton University Press.

37. Boukes, M., & Boomgaarden, H. G. (2016). Politician seeking voter: How interviews on entertainment talk shows affect trust in politicians. *International Journal of Communication, 10*, 1145–1166.

38. Graf, J. (2008). New media: The cutting edge of campaign communications. In R. J. Semiatin (Ed.), *Campaigns on the cutting edge* (pp. 48–68). CQ Press.

39. Almacy, D. (2007, March 1). Ask the White House. https://georgewbush-whitehouse.archives.gov/ask/20070301.html

40. Vargas, J. A. (2009, May 13). White House sends its first e-mail, on health care reform. *The Washington Post*. http://voices.washingtonpost.com/44/2009/05/13/white_house_sends_its_first_e-.html

41. Margolis, M., & Resnick, D. (2000). *Politics as usual: The cyberspace "revolution."* SAGE; Kumar, M. J. (2007). *Managing the president's message: The White House communications operation*. Johns Hopkins University Press.

42. Maltese, J. A. (1994). *Spin control: The White House Office of Communications and the management of presidential news* (2nd ed.). University of North Carolina Press; also see Kumar, M. J. (2017). The Office of the Press Secretary. *The White House Transition Project, 1997–2017*. http://whitehousetransitionproject.org/wp-content/uploads/2016/03/WHTP2017-31-Press-Secretary.pdf; Kumar, M. J. (2017). The Office of Communications. *The White House Transition Project, 1997–2017*. http://whitehousetransitionproject.org/wp-content/uploads/2016/03/WHTP2017-33-Communications.pdf

43. Klein, W. (2008). *All the presidents' spokesmen: Spinning the news: White House press secretaries from Franklin D. Roosevelt to George W. Bush*. Praeger.

44. Zoellner, D. (2021, January 21). Jen Psaki: Who is Joe Biden's White House press secretary? *Independent*. https://www.independent.co.uk/news/world/americas/us-politics/jen-psaki-joe-biden-press-secretary-b1763676.html

45. Quoted in Kumar, M. J. (2017). The Office of Communications. *The White House Transition Project, 1997–2017*, p. 5. http://whitehousetransitionproject.org/wp-content/uploads/2016/03/WHTP2017-33-Communications.pdf

46. Kumar, M. J. (2003). Communications operation in the White House of President George W. Bush: Making news on his terms. *Presidential Studies Quarterly, 33*(2), 366–393; Kumar, M. J. (2003). The White House and the press: News organizations as a presidential resource and as a source of pressure. *Presidential Studies Quarterly, 33*(3), 669–683; Kumar, M. J., & Jones, A. (2005). Government and the press: Issues and trends. In G. Overholser & K. H. Jamieson (Eds.), *The institutions of American democracy: The press*. Oxford University Press.

47. Maltese, J. A. (1994). *Spin control: The White House Office of Communications and the management of presidential news* (2nd ed.). University of North Carolina Press, p. 253.

48. Maltese, J. A. (1994). *Spin control: The White House Office of Communications and the management of presidential news* (2nd ed.). University of North Carolina Press, p. 6.

49. Silva, M. (2005, March 14). Is it public relations or propaganda? *Chicago Tribune*.

50. Barstow, D., & Stein, R. (2005, March 13). Under Bush, a new age of prepackaged TV news. *The New York Times*.

51. Quinn, S. (2009, March 8). Who sits where? *FiveThirtyEight*. http://www.fivethirtyeight.com/2009/03/who-sits-where.html; Gold, H. (2015, March 25). In White House press room seating charts. *Politico*. http://www.politico.com/blogs/media/2015/03/the-white-house-press-room-seating-chart-204543

52. Kumar, M. J., & Jones, A. (2005). Government and the press: Issues and trends. In G. Overholser & K. H. Jamieson (Eds.), *The institutions of American democracy: The press*. Oxford University Press; Kumar, M. J. (1992). The importance and evolution of presidential press conferences. *Presidential Studies Quarterly*, 35(1), 166–192; also see Hess, S. (1992). A new survey of the White House press corps. *Presidential Studies Quarterly*, 22(2), 311–321.

53. In addition, C-SPAN 2 provides gavel-to-gavel coverage of the Senate and on weekends offers Book TV. C-SPAN 3 covers public affairs events, congressional hearings, and history programming. When the House and Senate are out of session, C-SPAN and C-SPAN 2 provide live or taped coverage of press briefings, speeches, news conferences, and other events.

54. Smith, C. D. (1990). *Presidential press conferences: A critical approach*. Praeger Pub Text, p. 41.

55. For a thorough analysis of presidential press conferences, see Smith, *Presidential Press Conferences*; Cormier, F., Deakin, J., & Thomas, H. (1983). *The White House press on the presidency: News management and co-option*. University Press of America; Kumar, M. J. (2005). The importance and evolution of presidential press conferences. *Presidential Studies Quarterly*, 35(1), 166–192.

56. VandeHei, J., & Allen, M. (2013, February 18). Obama, the puppet master. *Politico*. http://www.politico.com/story/2013/02/obama-the-puppet-master-87764.html#ixzz2YlTcQpDA

57. Hudson, J. (2011, May 24). Obama's war on whistle-blowers. *Atlantic*. https://www.theatlantic.com/politics/archive/2011/05/obamas-war-whistle-blowers/351051/

58. Dilanian, K. (2019, April 8). Under Trump, more leaks—and more leak investigations. *NBC News*. https://www.nbcnews.com/politics/justice-department/under-trump-more-leaks-more-leak-investigations-n992121

59. Taylor, M., & Landay, J. S. (2013, June 20). Obama's crackdown views leaks as aiding enemies of U.S. *McClatchy*, https://www.mcclatchydc.com/news/special-reports/insider-threats/article24750244.html; Hudson, J. (2011, May 24). Obama's war on whistle-blowers. *Atlantic*. https://www.theatlantic.com/politics/archive/2011/05/obamas-war-whistle-blowers/351051/

60. *McCulloch v. Maryland*, 17 U.S. (4 Wheat.) 316 (1819).

6

Media Coverage of Congress and the Courts

Learning Objectives

1. Identify the conflicts, power struggles, and interdependencies between the media and members of the United States (U.S.) Congress.

2. Summarize how Congressional reporting is done and its impact.

3. Compare the relationship between the press and the Supreme Court with press–presidency and press–Congress relationships.

4. Assess how journalistic coverage of the court is executed and the way coverage differs from other branches of government.

On Monday, January 4, 2017, NPR (National Public Radio) listeners woke up to a news story about House Republicans' secret vote to weaken the Office of Congressional Ethics. The change was significant because it would place the office under the control of the House Ethics Committee, removing its independence and weakening ethics oversight for the House. In a *Morning Edition* interview with NPR's Rachel Martin, Richard Painter, former chief ethics council for President George W. Bush, likened the move to "putting the fox in charge of the chicken coop with the American taxpayers being the chickens." Throughout the early part of the day, public outcry and complaints by government watchdog groups mounted, capped by a disapproving tweet by President-elect Donald Trump. By afternoon drive time, NPR listeners learned that in response to the public backlash, House Republicans dropped the rules change and reversed course.[1]

Examples such as this highlight several features of the press–Congress relationship. First, it shows that the adversarial relationship officials have with the press is not only reserved for the president. Second, coverage of Congress typically portrays the chambers or their members in a negative light. Third, the watchdog function remains intact and effective when news media shed light on questionable behavior in our governing institutions. What this example does not reveal is an unfortunate truth: This kind of coverage of Congress and its dealings is all too infrequent in an era of declining newsroom resources.

This chapter examines the nature of the relationships between the Congress, the Courts, and the press. It also describes how these institutions have developed to manage their interdependent relationships, especially in light of the arrival and continuing evolution of the digital media environment. The chapter also explores the various challenges that news outlets and the journalists working within them face when trying to cover an overwhelming tide of news expeditiously, accurately, and with objective but critical analysis, which is especially difficult amidst rising polarization among political elites and an increasingly sorted and affectively charged citizenry divided along partisan and ideological lines.

The Media and Congress

According to political folklore, the television age has permanently altered the balance of political power. The presidency basks in the limelight of publicity at all times while Congress waits in the shadows, making the president dominant and the legislature inferior. As Senator J. William Fulbright (D–AR) told Congress in 1970, "Television has done as much to expand the powers of the president as would a constitutional amendment formally abolishing the co-equality of the three branches of government."[2]

Image Versus Reality

If one probes beyond the impression that Congress is a media stepchild, the situation appears less clear. When coverage of legislative concerns is added to coverage that mentions Congress explicitly, Congress and the presidency receive roughly the same amount of national news attention. But, historically, the bulk of congressional coverage came through local news stories about individual members that were published in their home states and districts. Figure 6-1 shows the amount of attention members of the House get from national broadcast and cable news networks.

National stories about Congress are generally fewer, shorter, and less prominently placed than news linked to the presidency, feeding claims that "435 members of the House and 100 members of the Senate compete for the crumbs of network time left after the president has got his share."[3] Why does Congress earn so much less national coverage than the presidency? There are several reasons. Some have to do with the features of the institutions; some have to do with characteristics of the news media. Most important, the presidency makes a better media target because it is an institution with a single head, readily personified and filmed in the visible person of the chief executive. This gives media audiences a familiar, easily dramatized focus of attention. A president is like a superstar surrounded by a cast of supporting actors. Even stories originating from congressional sources frequently feature the president as the main actor. As the personification of the nation, the president can usually command national media attention across a growing number of news venues. In the past, the press was more likely to refuse than grant Congress members' requests for coverage. That has changed dramatically, starting with the Clinton presidency. Still, the president retains the lead in coverage, but as media grow more important to Congress, members are becoming more successful in attracting and shaping coverage.[4]

There are many reasons why Congress is unable to attract as much media coverage as the president. Unlike the chief executive, Congress has no single, widely familiar person on whom to focus. It conducts its activities in many locations, including hearing rooms, press rooms, meeting rooms in the Capitol Building, and on the House and Senate sides of Capitol Hill. No individual member can command nationwide media coverage at will because no one is regarded as a spokesperson for the entire Congress. Consequently, most stories about Congress deal with individual members or legislative activity on specific issues rather than with the body as a whole, and national media outlets do not have the news space to cover 535 members of Congress. When members do get national coverage, it is usually the party leadership, who largely serve as the party voice in their respective chambers (see Figure 6-1).[5]

Another reason why stories about Congress escape wide attention lies in the nature of its work. The legislative branch drafts laws, makes compromises among conflicting interests, forges shifting coalitions, and works

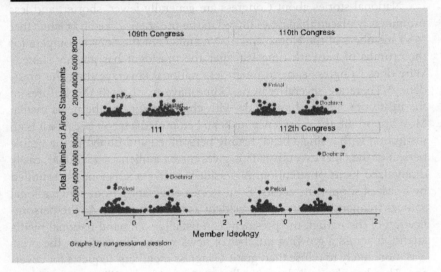

Source: Adapted from Padgett, J. S., Dunaway, J. L., & Darr, J. P. (2019). As seen on TV? How gatekeeping makes the U.S. House seem more extreme. *Journal of Communication*, *69*(6), 696–719.

Note: Data plots count aired speaking opportunities on broadcast and cable networks by member and congressional session. Data points for major party leaders are labeled. Data cover the 109th Congress through the 112th Congress. On cable networks (CNN, Fox News, MSNBC), 24% of the sample had no opportunities to speak and 29% had twenty or fewer opportunities. On broadcast networks (ABC, CBS, NBC), 48% had no opportunities and 41% were granted twenty or fewer opportunities. Congressional sessions are stacked such that members may appear several times across the entire sample.

out legal details. Americans typically do not enjoy the sausage-making process.[6] Stories about the executive branch that describe *what* is actually done are far more memorable than reports about *how* the laborious process of hammering out legislation works. Besides, the most interesting aspect of the legislative process—the shaping of broad guidelines for policy—has become the territory of the president rather than Congress.

Congressional coverage is frequently useless for the public influence over policy making because it tends to be sparse in the early stages of the

Photo 6-1 **WASHINGTON, DC; MARCH 19:** Speaker of the House Nancy Pelosi (D–CA; center) is joined by (left to right) Representative Lauren Underwood (D–IL), Representative Teresa Leger-Fernandez (D–NM), and Representative Angie Craig (D–MN) for a news conference in the U.S. Capitol Visitors Center on March 19, 2021, in Washington, DC. The members of Congress spoke to reporters about the American Rescue Act's enhancements to the Affordable Care Act.

Source: Photo by Chip Somodevilla/Getty Images.

legislative process, when there is still time for citizens to influence a bill. Coverage usually focuses on final action after the shape of the legislation is already firm.[7] Citizens then learn what the new policies are without being exposed to the pros and cons and the political interplay that led to the ultimate compromise. Instead, they get coverage of bills that pass and legislators who claim credit about their role in the policy success.[8] This problem is enhanced by the game framing of policy issues—where policy efforts are discussed in terms of who will "win" rather than the implications of the policy proposals themselves.[9]

Fearing that legislative floor sessions would present an unedifying, boring spectacle, Congress resisted live radio and television coverage of most sessions until the late 1970s. Before 1979, only selected committee hearings were televised, primarily those involving spicy topics such as labor racketeering, communists in government, or high-level corruption. In 1979, the House of Representatives lifted the prohibition on televising its floor sessions. The action was prompted in part by the desire to counterbalance the political advantages the executive branch was reaping from heavy media attention. The rules for coverage by the House-run closed circuit system are strict: Only the member speaking may be filmed, not the listeners, unless the Speaker of the House decrees otherwise. This stipulation bars the public from seeing the typically near-empty House chamber and inattentive members during routine sessions. Commercial, cable, and public television systems have access to House broadcasts but rarely cover them, except for the live coverage by C-SPAN. In 1986, the Senate finally followed suit and permitted live coverage of its proceedings. It was prodded by Senator Robert Byrd (D–WV), who was concerned that the Senate was "fast becoming the invisible half of Congress" compared with the White House and the House of Representatives.[10]

How Congress Uses the Media

Unlike the presidency, Congress is rarely a first-rate show for the U.S. public, although its media coverage is vital for inside-the-beltway Washington politics and serves several functions for members of Congress. Representatives themselves are among the most avid watchers of House coverage because the television cameras permit them to keep up with floor action and issues reported by committees other than their own. Coverage acts as a procedural monitoring service of sorts.

Members of Congress try to use their appearances to create favorable images for themselves and their pet political projects among congressional and executive branch constituencies, the elite media, and the public. Members try to shape the debate around their policy proposals in an effort to pass legislation; if they can attract media attention, they can help frame the debate. More members want to be heard, and they are likely to take more extreme positions because the media tend to focus on such confrontations; this is especially the case as Congress grows more polarized over time.[11] In his recent memoir, *On the House*, former House Speaker John Boehner expresses frustration about members (including those of his own party), who seem to do more to simply attract media attention for themselves than anything else.[12] In an interview with *NPR Morning Edition*'s Steve Inskeep, Boehner named Senator Ted Cruz

(R–TX), House Representative Jim Jordan (R–OH), and House Representative Alexandria Ocasio-Cortez (D–NY) as examples of those engaging in publicity-seeking behaviors. Members often utilized highly publicized speaking engagements to attract national media attention. Increasingly, heated Twitter exchanges can do the same (see Photos 6-2 and 6-3).

Members of Congress also utilize the media to send messages to one another, interest groups, the White House, and other political elites. Messages from the media can be used to signal support, opposition, or avenues for compromise and negotiation, especially across governing institutions. For example, dueling press conferences across parties, branches, or legislative chambers often include suggestions from one side about what they would like to hear from the other. Today, members use social media platforms such as Twitter in much the same way—social media posts can elicit attention and responses from political opponents and the media alike and aid in agenda setting.[13]

Photo 6-2 U.S. House Rep. Jim Jordan (R–OH) Addresses the Conservative Political Action Conference (CPAC)

Source: Joe Raedle/Getty Images.

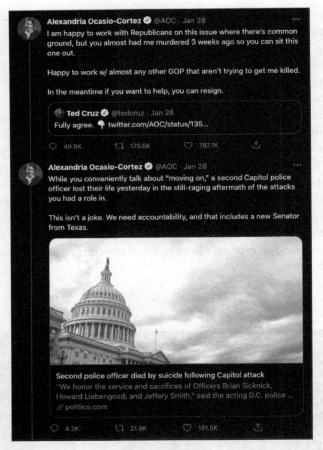

Photo 6-3 Heated Twitter Exchange Between U.S. House Representative Alexandria Ocasio-Cortez and Senator Ted Cruz

Source: Ocasio-Cortez, A. [@AOC]. (2021, January 28). *I am happy to work with Republicans on this issue where there's common ground, but you almost had me murdered.* Twitter.com. https://twitter.com/AOC/status/1354848253729234944?s=20

Nationalizing News Environment and Congressional Accountability

Of course, members of Congress also use the media—historically it was the *local* media—to (1) communicate with their constituencies, (2) as an indicator of public policy preferences, and (3) as a barometer of their own performance in the district, all of which are required for their individual reelection goals. Local news stories can show constituents in the home district that their member is working hard to represent the interests of the district. News can also convey power and policy expertise to home districts, enhancing perceptions of legislator credibility at home.[14]

However, evidence from several recent studies suggests that this local media-enabled accountability mechanism is in jeopardy. This is because as local media are declining and dying out (along with the depth of reporting staffs and local coverage) and people have access to more readily available sources for national news, citizens' political news consumption is nationalizing.[15] According to research by political scientist Dan Hopkins, this change in consumption patterns is occurring because people generally prefer news about national public affairs over local news. As the changing media environment has made more national news sources readily available to everyone at any given time or place, people are increasingly opting out of local news. This is at once contributing to the nationalization of our politics and to further declines in local news.

Research by Marc Trussler identifies two consequences indicative of the relationship between the expanding media environment and nationalization. The first is the erosion of the incumbency advantage. Trussler argues that the cross-party voting once commonly seen in House elections—when citizens would more regularly cast split-ticket ballots to vote for their incumbent House representative based on a record of good service—was made possible by a robust local media. As the information environment expanded, it eroded local news, which people replace with the ample available sources for national news. As a result, voting is increasingly based on national considerations instead of local issues, a consequence of which is higher rates of straight-ticket voting and a corresponding reduction in an advantage for incumbents.[16] This matters for representation because the absence of a locally oriented accountability structure that facilitates legislators' ability to earn a personal vote (i.e., attracting votes from independents and voters of the other party) reduces representatives' incentives to earn reelection on the basis of providing good representation and service to the district. Instead, they are incentivized to enhance the power and reputation of their party. In another study, Trussler identifies a second set of effects that are quite telling on this point: Members representing districts with higher levels of media choice voted more consistently with their party in-chamber, with the in-party president, and with party-aligned interest groups.[17] Clearly the incentives in a more nationalized media environment do not always induce behavior in the best interest of constituents in the home district.

Decades of research on congressional representation shows that news media serve as critical intermediaries between members and their states or districts. In addition to serving as a top-down means by which representative communicate to their constituencies, legislators use information conveyed by local news media to inform their perceptions about policy preferences and partisan composition in the home district. Another possible consequence of the nationalizing news environment is that local media are no longer always the primary conduit through which members try to keep tabs on district policy preferences and partisanship. Instead, they rely on national news sources, including partisan cable news. Research shows several implications from this, ranging from influencing legislative voting to the decision to run for office. In a significant display, Kevin Arceneaux, Martin Johnson, René Lindstädt, and Ryan Vander Wielen investigated the effect of the initial roll-out of Fox News on congressional voting behavior. Fearing negative publicity from the right-leaning Fox News, Republicans and Democrats in Fox News districts increased their support for Republican issues on contentious votes. Underscoring the strategic motivations underlying their behavior, this effect occurred only among members with a sizable portion of Republican voters in their districts and in the final months of their reelection campaigns.[18]

Reliance on cues from the national media environment about the composition of the district also has implications for decisions about whether to run for congressional office. A more recent study by Arceneaux and his colleagues finds that the presence of Fox News in a district influenced potential candidates' decisions about whether to run for office. It did so by shaping their perceptions about the partisan composition of the district and the electoral vulnerability of the incumbent.[19] One unresolved question in research on this topic is whether shifting reliance on national sources for news is affecting the accuracy with which members perceive their constituents' preferences. We know that legislators often have perceptions of constituency opinions that are wildly off the mark,[20] but we do not yet know whether these inaccuracies are linked to the nationalizing media environment. Other recent work shows additional evidence for, and effects from, the erosion of local media and news nationalization, such as rising polarization, but we will return to that subject in Chapter 7.

The Impact of Digital and Social Media

Obviously, the arrival of cable was not the only change to the media landscape to affect congressional behavior. Congress entered the internet scene in earnest in 1995 with a formal House website that features all texts of bills, resolutions, and amendments introduced in the House of Representatives along with brief, nontechnical descriptions of their content.[21] The website also provides a minute-by-minute summary of floor action. The actual debates can be monitored via an online version of the *Congressional Record*. The Senate has a similar website. In addition, members of Congress have their own websites. Besides featuring the member's biographical data and major accomplishments—but not failures—most also link to the websites of committees on which the member serves and describe committee actions and the current status of specific bills. The most comprehensive information about ongoing congressional activities is available at the Library of Congress's legislative website (https://www.congress.gov/). C-SPAN also digitally archives floor debates and other congressional events through the C-SPAN Video Library (https://www.c-span.org/).

Detailed coverage of congressional activities is extremely useful for lobby groups and other Congress watchers. It enhances their ability to make their views known at key junctures in the legislative process. The Library of Congress website and its links are also a gold mine of information for reporters who want to incorporate detailed current information into their stories. In addition, three out of four individual congressional member websites provide online newsrooms to serve the special needs of the press.[22] There also are a few sites—such as the Legislative Information System, which offers research material on legislation, and sites operated by each party and its subdivisions—that are purely for internal use by members of Congress.

The capabilities of digital and social media also created incentives for members of Congress to interact more regularly and personally with constituents. A modern feature of most member websites is a list of buttons that offer multiple ways of contacting the member or their office. Members now regularly interact with constituents through several forms of digital media well beyond websites. Members can connect with constituents via blog posts, virtual town hall meetings, and YouTube channels, not to mention popular social media sites such as Facebook, Twitter, and Instagram. Social media are by definition a social communication tool. Evidence suggests that those who are most effective at communicating with voters and constituents through sites such as Facebook and Twitter do so by maintaining a credible level of authenticity through sincere and somewhat personalized posts and content.[23]

Though social media ostensibly supply legislators with a new venue for shaping their message and courting various constituencies, the use of these tools also brings risks. Social media allow for two-way communication, opening new channels to the public to ask questions or seek casework assistance, and members of Congress can appear unresponsive if they are unable or unwilling to dedicate time or staff to responding to social media queries. In addition, the level of personalization required of social media may not mesh well with a member's desired professional reputation or personality, and there is always the risk that the instantaneous nature of digital media will mean rapid dissemination of a regrettable post or tweet. Still, members of the House and Senate have a social media presence on the most popular platforms.

Advances in communication technology and the expansion of media choice may make it more difficult for congressional leaders to muffle dissident members and reach legislative compromises after representatives have publicly committed themselves to definite positions. Spin inside Congress is a series of communication decisions made by party leaders first (the content of the message), then members' decisions about whether to adopt the spin and journalists' decisions about whether to cover the message.[24] When members do not adopt their party's spin, more communication channels are now afforded to them through other news outlets and digital and social media. These channels may be used to promote a countermessage. However, there is little solid proof thus far that increasing platforms for news and communication has harmed consensus building in the chamber or that the added publicity is making incumbents even more unbeatable at the polls than they are now. Email may still be the most prolific digital resource linking Congress with its various publics. But there are drawbacks; the flood of incoming emails threatens to overwhelm congressional resources. Given their limited staffs, members of Congress find it impossible to cope promptly and adequately with email from constituents, not to mention email from outsiders (including spammers) and from computer hackers who generate email to clog communication arteries. Efficient electronic sorting and automatic response protocols partly address the problem but are far from resolving it.

Members of Congress also utilize social networking sites to communicate with the public and attract media attention. Nearly all members are now on Twitter and have Facebook pages. These venues provide additional and more targeted opportunities to communicate directly with the public, other leaders, and the media. Members and their staffs also report social media as a useful tool for understanding the preferences and positions of their constituents. Research suggests that members use social media in an attempt to reach a wider audience.[25] Scholars also highlight some downsides of using these new communication channels. Messaging across multiple platforms to various constituencies may make it more difficult to maintain a unified message and to get any message to fragmented audiences. Similarly, the speed, multiplicity, and permanency of messages today can make a story very hard to control once released.[26]

Writing Stories About Congress

Journalists assigned to the congressional beat use normal criteria of newsworthiness and gatekeeping to decide who and what to cover and who and what to ignore. They prefer exciting, novel, or controversial topics that can be made personally relevant to the public and be presented simply rather than recurrent, complex, and mundane problems, such as congressional reorganizations or the annual farm bill. Orderly, dispassionate debate usually is passed over in favor of pompous rhetoric and wild accusations that can produce catchy headlines.

Because Congress is a regular beat, the leaders of each chamber conduct daily press briefings (see Photo 6-1). Major media organizations, such as The *Washington Post* and The *New York Times,* the big newspaper chains, and the television networks and wire services have full-time reporters covering Congress. Specialized news services such as *Congressional Quarterly* and two highly competitive newspapers—*Roll Call* and *The Hill*—cover the congressional beat in detail. The Library of Congress provides much information that is sparse on the websites of individual representatives; most congressional websites link to it. For example, the Library of Congress website contains information about bill sponsorship and the texts of otherwise unrecorded speeches. Notably, in the mid-1990s and early 2000s, approximately 7,000 correspondents were accredited to the press galleries in the House and Senate; thus, the ratio of journalists to senators was seventy to one, and for representatives, it was sixteen to one.[27] Today the numbers are much lower, though more than 1,500 correspondents are accredited to the press galleries in the House and Senate.[28]

Congressional press releases and written reports provide news to media sources that lack regular reporters on Capitol Hill. These documents are prepared and distributed via websites and congressional press secretaries because reporters accredited to Congress are unable to attend the many hearings occurring simultaneously. Press releases enable members of Congress to tell their stories in their own words. They often use the opportunity to highlight problem areas, hoping that news media publicity will shame Congress into action.[29] Although all representatives now assign staff to serve the needs of the press, less than 10% of House members receive weekly coverage on national television. Newspaper coverage is somewhat more frequent, especially in nationally circulating papers or local newspapers from members' own states and districts.[30]

Senators generally receive considerably more press coverage than representatives. On network television, stories about senators outnumber those about representatives almost seven to one. The reasons include senators' greater prominence, prestige, and publicity resources. Their larger constituencies hold the promise of larger audiences. In general, high media visibility for senators as well as representatives depends on their seniority and whether they serve in important leadership positions. By contrast, sponsoring legislation or regular committee service matters little. Who one *is* obviously counts for more than what one *does*. In practice, this means that more than half of the congressional membership receives no national television exposure at all. A mere twenty members of the Senate garner the lion's share of attention.[31] Such spotty coverage—especially in light of declines in local news discussed above—deprives the public of a chance to evaluate the contributions of the most representative branch of government. It also may explain why public approval of Congress ranged from a low of 12% to a high of 36% between 2010 and 2021. As of March 2021, Congressional approval was at an unusually high 36%, but historically it is usually quite low, especially relative to the other branches (see Figure 6-2).[32]

The effects of neglect at the national level were, historically, mitigated by local news coverage. Most members of Congress used to receive

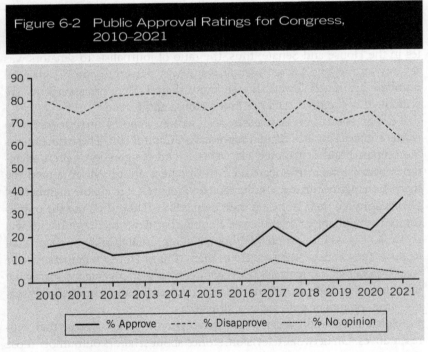

Figure 6-2   Public Approval Ratings for Congress, 2010–2021

Source: Adapted from Congress and the public. (n. d.). *Gallup.* https://news.gallup.com/poll/1600/congress-public.aspx

Note: Each data point is from early March of that year; March was the most recent data point available for 2021 at the writing of this textbook.

regular local coverage through their own news columns or radio or television programs.[33] Some still do, depending on whether local news media have a presence in the district. If available to representatives, they usually find relations with the local media far more congenial than relations with a national press corps, whose members usually have neither the time nor the space (nor the incentive) to cover the problems of particular congressional districts. Local media, on the other hand, depend on senators and representatives for local angles to national stories because local slants make these stories more attractive to the local target market audience. Because Washington, DC–based senators and representatives are ideal sources, local newspeople are often loath to criticize them. The Washington press corps lacks such qualms. In the first year and a half of the 103rd Congress, during the Clinton presidency, 64% of all congressional stories broadcast on national news were negative. Senate scores were a bit worse than House scores, whereas the president's press was a shade better than both chambers during this time.[34] As local news resources and organizations continue to erode, House and Senate members may need to seek alternative means of publicity.

Functions of Media

The functions that the national media perform for Congress and those that Congress perform for the national media parallel press–president relations. However, there are major qualitative differences. The relationship between members of Congress and the media is not as interdependent as the one between the president and the press. The national media can afford to alienate some legislators without losing direct access to congressional news. But many legislators can no longer ignore national publicity and rely instead on publicity in their own districts. This makes news items about national events and national public opinion more important to members of Congress than in the past. Less able to rely on the home district local media (discussed in the next chapter), rather than national news providers, many legislators lack sources of news relevant for their own constituents and as channels for transmitting messages to the home district while they are in Washington, DC.

Publicity is especially important for minority party leaders, who may need the media to pressure an unresponsive majority to consider their concerns. However, most members cannot use "outsider strategies," as publicity efforts by the out-of-power party are called, because Congress members rarely receive enough coverage. Once members achieve visibility, their fame often grows by its own momentum. They become regulars on interview shows, and their opinions are solicited on national issues.[35] For most members, however, national media attention has several drawbacks; for example, elected officials become more visible targets for lobby groups, and their exposure provides ammunition for rival oppositional groups and political candidates. For members of Congress who do not need nationwide attention to achieve their legislative or political goals, favorable coverage by traditional media in their districts is the key objective.

Many members also communicate through newsletters, mailers, and individual correspondence sent to selected constituents. Some prepare cable television programs for their district or transmit carefully chosen video excerpts from committee meetings to their websites and to the media in their home districts. Still others, eager to push their legislative agendas, write op-ed pieces for the local or national media.

A Cautious Relationship

Just as the functions that media perform are similar for the executive and legislative branches, so is the love–hate relationship. But it, too, is less ardent for Congress, even though mutual recriminations are plentiful. Senators and representatives compete with peers for media attention and bemoan the lack of coverage for their pet projects and pronouncements. They complain that reporters treat them like scoundrels conspiring to defraud the public and resent the cross-examinations that reporters love to conduct with an air of infallibility. Legislators charge, and can prove, that the media emphasize trivia, scandals, internal dissent, and official misconduct but generally ignore congressional consensus and the passage of significant legislation. They blame the media for the low approval ratings of Congress.

Journalists, in turn, complain with justification about legislators' efforts to manage the news through their professional publicity staffs, which grew in both size and sophistication over time. They point to members' lack of candor and grumble about being excluded from many congressional meetings and executive sessions. Broadcasters also resent the strict controls placed on their coverage of congressional sessions. They are barred from taping their own stories and are limited in the subjects they can photograph.

The realization of interdependence smooths the ruffled feathers. Senators and representatives realize that they need the media for information and for the publicity that is crucial to pass or defeat legislation and for realizing their political goals. Newspeople, in turn, understand that they need individual legislators for information about congressional activities and as a counterfoil and source of leaks to check the executive branch.

Members are valuable for inside comments that can personalize otherwise dull stories. Congress often creates story topics for the media by investigating dramatic ongoing problems such as auto or aircraft safety. A congressional inquiry may be the catalyst that turns an everyday event into a newsworthy item. The story may then ride the crest of publicity for quite some time, creating its own fresh and reportable events until it recedes into limbo once more. Newspeople do not want to dry up these sources.

C. Danielle Vinson concludes that in the relationship between Congress and the press, the press may have the upper hand. Media messages are now an integral component of the legislative process—the media control the channels through which legislators can communicate with one another and the public in the effort to influence policy outcomes and legislative debates. Though members of Congress are more media savvy relative to years past, as members of a legislative body of 535, individual legislators need the press a bit more than the press needs them.[36]

Congress and Communications Policy

Journalists, particularly those who work in radio and television, appreciate the power that Congress has over regulatory legislation. In the past, Congress used its power to legislate communications policy sparingly, viewing it as a hornet's nest of political conflict that was best left alone. The major exceptions were passage of the Communications Act of 1934 and its 1996 sequel and the supplementary laws dealing with technical innovations and other changes in the mass communication scene. Whenever concerted, unified pressures from industry or consumer groups develop and overcome the strong resistance to change in this controversial policy field, which also has multiple powerful stakeholders, Congress's power to legislate communications policy becomes extremely important. As the 62-year time gap between major communications laws demonstrates, there usually is a vacuum in both policy formulation and oversight that neither the president nor the Federal Communications Commission (FCC) is eager to fill.[37]

The communications subcommittees of the Commerce, Science, and Transportation Committee in the Senate and of the Energy and Commerce Committee in the House also influence communications policy, primarily through the power of investigation. They investigated the FCC more frequently than most regulatory bodies are by their oversight committees. In fact, since 1970, scores of congressional committees and subcommittees reviewed FCC activities, with few dramatic results. Investigations included reviews of specific FCC actions, studies of corruption in television game shows, and examinations of such broad policy issues as the impact of television's portrayal of the aged or of alcohol and drug abuse. The appropriations committees occasionally denied funds for FCC operations or explicitly directed which particular programs should be funded.[38] However, monetary control was stricter once Congress changed the FCC in 1982 from the status of a permanently authorized agency to one requiring biennial renewal.

Although the Senate seldom uses confirmation hearings to impress its views on new FCC commissioners, this does not mean that agency staff ignores the views of powerful senators. Prospective commissioners are likely to study past confirmation hearings carefully and take their cues from them. Most presidential nominees are confirmed. Appointments usually reward the politically faithful. Although congressional control over the FCC is light, there is always the possibility of stricter control. All the parties interested in communications policy, including the White House and the courts, pay deference to that possibility.

Congressional control over the media includes such matters as postal rates and subsidies and legislation on permissible mergers and chain control of papers. Copyright laws, which affect print and electronic media production, are involved, along with policies and regulations about telecommunication satellites, broadcast spectrum allocations, and cable television. The vast, congressionally guided changes in the telephone industry are yet another area of major concern to media interests.

Laws regulating media procedures occasionally have a strong impact on media content and policies. For instance, FCC encouragement of the diversification of radio programs was largely responsible for the development of a sizable number of FM rock music stations that provide alternatives to more conventional programs. Congressional scrutiny of documentaries can chill investigative reporting. Congress has barely regulated cable television since 1996, leaving this medium mostly under control of the courts and state and local governments.

The Media and the Courts

Of the three branches of the national government, only the judiciary is sparsely covered. This is the case even for the highest court in the nation. Over the span of 2020, the Supreme Court was named in the headline or lead paragraph of 1,696 news stories from major broadcast news outlets. While this sounds like a lot, it amounted to only about a quarter of all major national news stories allotted to all three branches of the national government, and this was a year in which Associate Justice Ruth Bader Ginsburg died, and in which her replacement, Justice Amy Coney Barrett, was nominated by the Trump administration and put through Senate confirmation hearings before eventually earning confirmation. That same year, stories with headlines mentioning President Trump comprised 57% of major national news stories about the three main branches of government, and Congress made the headline of a mere 17% of stories (see Figure 6-3). The pattern of sparse coverage is typically worse than for 2020, which saw more coverage of the Court than usual, and the same trend is reflected in coverage from the major newspapers. But generally, this trend is getting worse as newsrooms are losing resources around the country. In an interview in February 2013, Justice Anthony Kennedy highlighted serious concerns about the media's decline and the diminishing number of journalists covering the courts.[39]

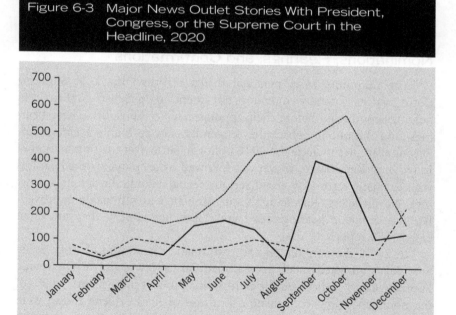

Figure 6-3   Major News Outlet Stories With President, Congress, or the Supreme Court in the Headline, 2020

Source: Data gathered by Dunaway, based on search of news archives using Newsbank, Inc. Searches included content from popular news programs from the major broadcast (ABC, CBS, NBC) and cable news channels (CNN, Fox News, MSNBC), several major digital news providers (e.g., Politico), and major newspaper groups (e.g., McClatchy).

One reason for the Court's usual relatively low levels of coverage is that federal judges are rarely in the limelight. They grant interviews infrequently, except when on book tours, and they almost never hold news conferences. In recent years, Supreme Court justices received more press attention, but historically, they generally do not seek or welcome media attention. They worry it will compromise their impartiality and mystique. Remoteness enhances the impression that judges are a breed apart, doling out justice to lesser mortals. When any deliberative political process is observed, it is almost universally harmful to the public esteem; as a result, the federal judiciary is held in relatively high regard in comparison to Congress and the president.[40] At the state and local levels, where many judges are elected rather than appointed to office, media coverage is relatively more common, especially during judicial elections. The aura of judicial majesty recedes accordingly.[41] In other words, media attention can politicize the courts and threaten public perceptions of judicial legitimacy and authority. Consequently, federal judges and Supreme Court justices tend to avoid media publicity relative to their presidential and congressional counterparts.

Nominations, Hearings, and Confirmations

The immunity from personal media scrutiny that U.S. Supreme Court justices generally enjoy does not extend to the Senate confirmation hearings conducted before their appointment to the Court. These hearings, and the public debate they engender, can be highly acrimonious. Recent examples include the 2018 political battle over the nomination of Judge Brett Kavanaugh, which was followed by soap opera–like hearings with dramatic testimony about serious sexual assault allegations against him. Nevertheless, Kavenaugh's appointment was ultimately approved. Because dramatic hearings have great audience appeal, they are often extensively reported.

In 2009, the nomination and confirmation hearings of Justice Sonia Sotomayor attracted much media attention. She was the first Hispanic Supreme Court justice and the third woman to sit on the Court. In 2010, the nomination and confirmation hearings of Justice Elena Kagan were also heavily covered. Kagan's appointment would place her as only the fourth female justice to serve on the bench and would mark the first time that three women served on the Court at one time. Her nomination was also somewhat controversial amid claims she lacked judicial experience.[42] The 2020 appointment and confirmation of Justice Amy Coney Barrett following the death of Justice Ruth Bader Ginsburg all but guarantees several more years of having at least three women justices on the Court.

Senate confirmation hearings also demonstrate how pressure groups use the media to influence judicial politics. During the confirmation hearings for Justice Amy Coney Barret, 150 civil rights and public interest groups submitted a joint letter urging the Senate to oppose her confirmation. Spokespersons for such groups as the Leadership Conference on Civil and Human Rights, the National Association for the Advancement of Colored People (NAACP), the National Organization for Women, the Center for Transgender Equality, and the Women's Law Project wrote to highlight several areas of Coney Barrett's record they deemed problematic. The areas included access to healthcare; reproductive rights and freedoms; lesbian, gay, bisexual, transgender, and queer/questioning (LGBTQ) rights; employment discrimination; gun safety; and immigrant and criminal justice.[43] Despite heavy opposition from the left and high levels of media attention on Kavenaugh and Coney Barrett, all three of President Trump's Supreme Court nominees—Neil Gorsuch (2018, 54–45 vote), Brett Kavenaugh (2018, 50–48–1 vote), and Amy Coney Barrett (2020, 52–48 vote)—were eventually confirmed by the Senate and appointed to the high Court. However, observers note that confirmations amid such staunch opposition in an evenly divided and polarized Senate was largely possible due to a Senate rules change—the ability to apply the so-called nuclear option to high court nominees, allowing presidential picks to be confirmed by a simple majority in lieu of the 60–vote 2/3 majority, which was pushed through by Senate leader Mitch McConnell in 2017.

The Supreme Court and the Justices as Newsmakers

Though justices interacted with the media more in recent years, the institutional aspects of the federal courts still receive comparatively little coverage. There are exceptions, of course, including debate over the recent aforementioned change to the rules governing Senate confirmation of presidential court appointments. Supreme Court justices' public comments and speeches about the institution are also often telecast and reported nationwide. Though once quite rare, this is becoming increasingly common as elite politics grows increasingly polarized and acrimonious, with the Supreme Court getting caught up in partisan politics. In two recent notable instances, widely reported-on comments about the Court from justices were clearly aimed at keeping the court above the partisan fray in the effort to preserve its institutional legitimacy. The first was when Chief Justice John Roberts spoke out in response to one of several statements President Trump made that were disparaging to the federal court or those occupying its benches. Trump complained about the Ninth Circuit blocking yet another of his policies, saying

> "That's not the law. . . . Every case, no matter where it is . . . they file in in what's called the Ninth Circuit. This was an Obama judge. I'll tell you what, it's not going to happen like this anymore.[44]

In response, Justice Roberts issued a rare public statement:

> "We do not have Obama judges or Trump judges, Bush judges or Clinton judges. What we have is an extraordinary group of dedicated judges doing their level best to do equal right to those appearing before them. That independent judiciary is something we should all be thankful for.

More recently, Justice Stephen Breyer made headlines when, in a speech at Harvard Law School, he spoke out about the Biden administration announcement of a new commission to consider the possibility of expanding the Court. Clearly worried about what such a move would do to public perception of the Court's legitimacy, Breyer argued that trust in the Court relies on the public perception that "the court is guided by legal principle, not politics." Talk of expanding the Court began near the end of Trump's term following confirmation of his third Supreme Court nominee, which left liberal and democratic leaning proponents concerned about the political influence of the now right-leaning bench. Justice Breyer's concern is likely spot-on in the sense that any effort to change the structure of the Court would clearly be political and therefore likely to erode public trust in the Court as a legal, rather than political, institution.[45]

Writing Stories About Court Decisions

The work product of federal judges and court systems—judicial decisions—often makes the news. This is particularly true of U.S. Supreme Court decisions, which frequently have major consequences for the political system. For example, *Brown v. Board of Education* (1954) was widely publicized because it declared the separate schooling of children of different races unconstitutional. *Roe v. Wade* (1973) and *Planned Parenthood v. Casey* (1992) received ample media attention because they involved the emotional issue of a woman's right to have an abortion.[46] *Ledbetter v. Goodyear Tire and Rubber Co.* (2007), an employment discrimination case, led to the passage of the 2009 Lilly Ledbetter Fair Pay Act, which expanded civil rights protections to equal-pay issues. More recently, the case which upheld President Barak Obama's health care overhaul law, the Affordable Care Act, *National Federation of Independent Business (NFIB) v. Sebelius* (2012), earned a substantial amount of coverage, most likely due to the millions of people whose healthcare coverage would have been affected by changes to the law.

Volume and Quality of Decision Coverage

In general, the news media give disproportionately heavy attention to civil rights and First Amendment cases; they slight cases involving economic and business matters. *Citizens United v. Federal Election Commission* (2010) won a significant amount of coverage for its implications regarding the power and role of outside interest groups in electoral campaigns. In 2013, two of the Court's decisions, in *United States v. Windsor* and *Hollingsworth v. Perry*, received substantial coverage for striking down the federal Defense of Marriage Act and declining to hear a challenge to a California ban on same-sex marriage, respectively.[47] Overall, the media cover only a fraction of the Court's decisions. The focus of news stories is typically limited to the formal decision; the Court's decision-making process remains largely shrouded in secrecy.[48]

Publicity about Supreme Court decisions is very important because it informs public officials at all government levels, as well as the general public, about the law of the land governing important, controversial issues. A small corps of reporters is responsible for singling out the decisions that will receive abundant media attention. Some fifty reporters cover the Supreme Court, and of those, only a dozen correspondents for major wire services and newspapers work full-time.[49]

Supreme Court coverage is difficult for reporters. The justices usually announce multiple decisions on a single day, forcing reporters to digest several complex opinions rapidly, including both majority and dissenting opinions—and often more than one of each. This must be done without help from the justices who wrote the opinions. Reporters' deadlines may be only minutes away, and the news may be stale after more than 24 hours elapses. Advice from outside commentators, including legal experts, is usually unavailable initially because experts are not allowed to preview the opinions, and advance leaks are extremely rare. The Supreme Court has a press office, which provides some reference materials and bare-bones records of the Court's activities. But it refuses to interpret the justices' decisions in laypersons' terms, fearing entanglement in legal controversies. However, publications sponsored by the legal profession make short analyses of important pending cases available to the media. In addition, universities and leading newspapers feature archived decisions and even audio files of arguments before the Court.[50]

Because of the shortage of skilled legal reporters, much reporting on the courts—even the Supreme Court—is imprecise and sometimes outright wrong. Justice Felix Frankfurter once complained that editors who would never consider covering a baseball game through a reporter unfamiliar with the sport regularly assigned reporters unfamiliar with the law to cover the Supreme Court. The situation improved considerably in recent years, but it is far from resolved. Many editors do not want to assign reporters with legal expertise, fearing their stories would be too technical and dull.

A relatively recent example from coverage of a landmark decision—*National Federation of Independent Business (NFIB) v. Sebelius* (2012), which upheld President Barak Obama's health care overhaul law, the Affordable Care Act (also known as Obamacare)—illustrates an instance of faulty reporting and the ongoing need for caution and expertise in legal reporting. On June 27, 2012, both CNN and Fox News misinterpreted the Supreme Court's ruling on the Obama health care law. Initial stories about the decision aired with serious errors.[51] Both networks initially reported the Supreme Court struck down the portion of the law known as the "individual mandate," which requires that most citizens and legal residents of the U.S. carry health insurance. In fact, the Court upheld the law, and the mandate as a tax, in a 5 to 4 decision.[52] Aside from inaccuracy, pressures to make coverage of the Court more appealing for audiences often result in the use of common story frames, some of which have negative consequences for public responses to Court decisions (see Box 6-1).

Box 6-1
Game Framing the Court

At the end of June 2020, the U.S. Supreme Court rejected the Trump administration's attempts to add a citizenship question to the 2020 census. Media coverage of the US Supreme Court's major decision emphasized the case's winners and losers. For example, one outlet claimed the Court had "struck a blow" against the Trump administration while another headline described the case as a "battle." Few stories highlighted the legal intricacies of the Court's opinion in the case which, despite the 5–4 final vote, included shifting coalitions of justices joining and rejecting various components of the opinion. In the media's coverage of the decision, discussion of this intense legal debate between the justices is missing.

News coverage commonly focuses on tactics and strategies, what scholars call a *game frame*, but we wanted to know what happens when news media use such a frame in coverage of the Supreme Court, an institution the public perceives to be above politics. We first analyzed prime-time television news coverage of major Supreme Court decisions for 20 years on the three major broadcast networks and three major cable news networks. We found that journalists often rely on the game frame as a vehicle. Figure 6-4 presents the total number of television news stories about the Court's decision in a given quarter, multiplied by the average proportion of game framed words in those stories in the same quarter. We contend that this measure approximates the total volume of game frame coverage of Court decisions in a given time period. Figure 6-4 shows an enormous spike in this kind of media framing in the aftermath of the Court's *Bush v. Gore* decision in late 2000; there may be no better example of a highly politicized and scrutinized decision in the modern era.

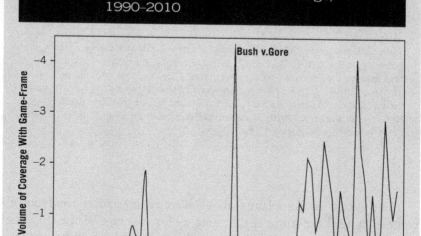

Figure 6-4 Volume of Game Frame Coverage, 1990–2010

(*Continued*)

(Continued)

But how does such coverage affect public approval of the Court? To look at this, we started by conducting an experiment in which we randomly exposed people to different kinds of coverage. When we showed people an actual clip of television news coverage that used the game frame to describe a Supreme Court decision, they reported reduced support for that decision relative to people who saw a clip that talked about the same decision's legal context. Then we looked at 20 years of public opinion data on Supreme Court approval. We found that as game frame coverage on television news increased, public approval of the Court fell, even after we adjusted for whether the Court's decisions in that period were out of step with the public ideologically.

While critics often cast blame on the media, it is hard to deny that the Supreme Court is party to the disapproval of their public image. Without professionals in charge of public communication, the Court issues lengthy, complex judgements without explanation. It is no wonder that members of the media face incentives to simplify decisions. Some high courts around the world prepare short summaries of their judgments in plain English. Our research suggests that such a change could make it easier for reporters to discuss legal and constitutional elements of the Court's decisions.

Source: Adapted by the authors of the piece, Matthew P. Hitt and Kathleen Searles, from Hitt, M. P., & Searles, K. (2019, July 22). Why plain English summaries of judgments could help improve the Supreme Court's public image. *LSE US Centre.* https://blogs.lse.ac.uk/usappblog/2019/07/22/why-plain-english-summaries-of-judgments-could-help-improve-the-supreme-courts-public-image/. The LSE article and box are based on original research: Hitt, M. P., & Searles, K. (2018). Media coverage and public approval of the U.S. Supreme Court. *Political Communication, 35*(4), 566–586.

The thrust of complaints about sketchy, inaccurate, and out-of-context judicial reporting is the same as for coverage of the president and Congress. But complaints about judicial coverage are more justified. Reporting of Court activities is infrequent, superficial, and flawed relative to its presidential and congressional counterparts.[53] The reasons are not difficult to understand. The volume of decisions clusters near the end of the annual term. The subject matter is often highly technical and is hard for reporters to understand and make understandable. With notable exceptions, stories about judicial decisions lack the potential to become exciting, front-page news. They are hard to boil down into catchy phrases and clichés. They rarely lend themselves to exciting visual coverage. The Supreme Court beat tends to be understaffed. All of these factors make it difficult for the assigned reporters to prepare interesting, well-researched accounts. At times, however, decision coverage is high-quality, including commentary on legal issues and the long-range implications of cases.[54] For example, coverage of Court decisions provided by NPR's award-winning legal affairs correspondent, Nina Totenberg, is excellent.[55]

The Impact of Coverage: Is It Politicizing the Supreme Court?

The court-related information supplied to the public, though inadequate for providing important insights into the law and the judicial process, usually sustains respect for the judiciary and compliance with its rulings. That's why the majority of the public holds its work in relatively high esteem, though in July 2016, Gallup reported that approval of the Supreme Court tied its all-time low at 42%.[56] Public support for the Court is crucial because the Court lacks the power and institutional structure to enforce its decisions. So, why might public approval ratings for the Court be dropping? Can anything be done?

Some research indicates that the Court may also be growing more concerned about public opinion. As described above, justices increased their interaction with the media in recent years. Media scholar Richard Davis argues that the justices employ external strategies to influence portrayals of themselves and their institution as a way to protect the integrity of the Court. The recent anecdotal examples about public comments from Chief Justice Roberts and Justice Breyer certainly support that line of argument. Other work also suggests these strategies may be necessary; sensationalist and politically polarizing news frames may influence public support for the Supreme Court as an institution, as Box 6-1 suggests.[57] Public reactions to Supreme Court decisions may affect future decisions of the Court because justices are influenced in their work by what they read and hear from the media. This makes it a serious problem—much of the reporting leaves the public unprepared to make sound assessments of the Court's rulings.

Much of what might be contributing to the politicization of the court may be outside the control of the Supreme Court justices. In recent years, circumstances have placed the Court in the crux of political controversies that were difficult for anyone to anticipate. During its 2020 term, the Supreme Court ruled on politically charged issues such as abortion, religion, immigration, and support for LGBTQ employee rights. Highly charged political cases are certainly par for the course. However, the Court was also in the uncomfortable position of ruling on cases with direct effects on President Trump's personal or personal–political interests. In *Trump vs. Vance*, the Court's 7–2 ruling refuted the president's claims of having "absolute immunity," stating that a New York grand jury could require his accountants and bankers to turn over records of his financial status and dealings. In *Trump vs. Mazars*, the Court produced another 7–2 decision, this time saying three House committees—at least without demonstrating need and relevance to a judge—could not require the president and his accountants to turn over financial and bank records going all the way back to 2010. In *Seila Law vs. CFPB*, the Court sided with the president in a 5–4 ruling stating that Congress violated the separation of powers and executive authority when it created the Consumer Financial Protection Bureau as an independent bureau whose director could not be fired except in cases of "neglect of duty or malfeasance in office." The Court maintained that the president must retain the power to remove top officials. Finally, in what was perhaps one of its most consequential decisions with respect to President Trump's political fortunes, the Court's 9–0 decision on *Chiafalo vs. Washington* overturned a Denver federal appeals court decision permitting state electors to behave as free agents, which would allow them to vote against the candidate that won the state's popular vote.[58]

When circumstances allow it, the justices undoubtedly prefer to avoid ruling on cases that could potentially affect the outcomes of major elections. We saw evidence of this in the cases they refused to hear as President Trump sought to overturn lower court rulings with bearing on the outcome of the 2020 election.[59] As keen observers and students of the law, they know the risks of politicization. When the Supreme Court has been accused of unduly meddling in politics, it loses its luster in the eyes of the public. This is what happened when, in the 2000 presidential election, its decision on the legality of vote counts in Florida decided the outcome.[60]

It remains an open question whether the Court is truly being politicized; if it is, we know little about the extent to which press coverage is contributing. But the recent frequency with which the Court finds itself in the center of major political disputes, the press's tendency to cover judicial politics like a game, and the highly polarized political climate do not seem to bode well for the Court's ability to remain shrouded from political publicity, which may have negative implications for public approval of and support for the Court, and perceptions of its institutional legitimacy.

News About Crime and the Justice System

Publications of decisions by the Supreme Court and lower courts are by no means the only significant news about the judiciary. General news about crime and the work of the justice system is also important in creating images of the quality of public justice.

Recent research provides evidence that news stories can influence the behavior of court personnel more generally. For example, the amount of publicity given to a crime influences prosecutors. When there is little publicity, prosecutors are less likely to press for a trial of the case and more likely to agree to a plea bargain settlement. In federal murder trials, longer sentences tend to follow more pretrial publicity for defendants.[61] The effects of media coverage tend to persist for subsequent similar cases. News stories also have lasting effects on the public's perception of who is likely to be a perpetrator or victim of crime. For instance, television news often shows young Black males as criminal offenders. Viewers then associate that demographic group with reported incidents of violent crime.[62]

Similar to stories about other government activities, crime and justice system stories tend to focus on sensational events, often at the expense of significant trends and problems in the legal system that might benefit from greater public attention.[63] In national media outlets, probably the most graphic aspect of the "tabloidization" of court-related news is the overemphasis on crimes involving prominent politicians, celebrities, or crimes that seem particularly heinous. The total amount of coverage is disproportionate, especially when we consider resources being drawn away from other important stories that need attention. For example, reports about the investigation of President Bill Clinton's relations with intern Monica Lewinsky totaled 25,975 stories in sixty-five papers in one year (1998), including 1,959 front-page stories. In the first several months of 2021, news outlets reported heavily on ongoing criminal investigations into former President Trump, namely covering efforts to flip former Trump associates to provide incriminating evidence against him. April 2021 marked the beginning of extensive coverage of the murder trial of Derek Chauvin, the former police officer charged with killing George Floyd, who died shortly after Chauvin pressed his knee on Floyd's neck for nine minutes during an arrest. Since Floyd's death was credited with sparking protests against police violence around the world, the Chauvin trial was the subject of intense public interest. To give a sense of the intensity of public interest, on April 12, 2021, a Google search for "Derek Chauvin murder trial" returned 35,300,000 results.

Such stories are bonanzas for media enterprises because they sharply increase audience size and, thereby, rates that can be charged for advertising. CNN, for example, more than quadrupled its average ratings during the peak phases of the Lewinsky trial.[64] The same was true of the Chauvin trial.[65] No wonder, then, that a vast majority of the public is familiar with these kinds of cases, compared with 12% who can identify the chief justice of the United States.

Judicial Censorship

There are several significant systematic omissions in media coverage of the U.S. justice system. The Supreme Court bars reporters from all of its deliberations before the announcement of decisions. On the few occasions when forthcoming decisions were leaked ahead of time, justices have reacted with great anger and have curtailed contacts between newspeople and Court personnel. Television cameras are barred most of the time from federal courts, and proceedings may not be broadcast live. Federal district and appellate courts allowed cameras in the courtroom as a three-year experiment starting in 1991. They ended coverage in 1994 on the grounds that the cameras were distracting to the jurors and witnesses, even though appraisals of the experiment found little or no impact on the administration of justice.

For years, many state courts prohibited radio and television reporters from covering trials and other proceedings. They feared that recording devices might produce a carnival-like atmosphere that would intimidate participants, endanger witnesses, and harm the fairness of the proceedings. To allow citizens to watch how their courts operate, all states now allow cameras to record court proceedings subject to rules that protect the parties in the judicial drama from undue invasion of their privacy.[66] The debate about the wisdom of televising court proceedings surged in the wake of the massive media attention to the O. J. Simpson murder trial, which drowned out much other news for nearly a year. Critics of televised sessions claim that the judges' and lawyers' showboating distorted and delayed the verdict and diminished the public's regard for the legal system. Televised trials tend to focus on courtroom drama at the expense of explaining legal issues. Others argue that the public is entitled to monitor the courts' performance via television in a public trial.[67] Restraints on live audio and video coverage are not the only limitations on judicial publicity. In the interest of ensuring fair trials, courts also limit the information that may be printed while court proceedings are in progress.

SUMMARY ————————————————————————————————

The media spotlight falls unevenly on politics. In this chapter, we examined institutions that do not receive sufficient light for the U.S. public to adequately assess them and the roles they play in the nation's political life. At the national level, both the legislative and judicial branches suffer from inadequate news coverage. Congressional coverage is more plentiful than judicial coverage, but it lacks the depth and substance ideal for use in democratic citizens' decision making. Judicial coverage is not only scant; it is often rushed and inaccurately reported. We explained the reasons for neglect and some of the political consequences, given the importance of Congress and the federal courts in shaping U.S. politics.

Just as in the case of the presidency, the relationship between the media and Congress is both interdependent and adversarial. The adversarial elements arise from differing goals of actors within the two institutions. Members of Congress with legislative goals want coverage to provide publicity for their legislative proposals. Members with reelection goals want positive image coverage and on-air opportunities to claim credit for their policy and political successes. Congressional leaders want coverage that communicates the national parties' policy agendas in a way that facilitates party cohesion and enhances their party's brand. Journalists and news organizations, on the other hand, are beholden to the preferences and tastes of audiences, the norms and routines of professionalized journalism, and their public service obligation to provide the public with information they need to hold democratic leaders accountable. Neither the audience nor the journalism and public service roles produce ideal coverage from the perspectives of legislators. Media may report on members' proposed policies, but not without raising questions and concerns raised by the other side, and they certainly won't report on policy except during critical points in the legislative process. Though legislators may sometimes be rewarded with opportunities to claim credit, rank-and-file members are more likely to earn coverage on the basis of scandal or outrageous statements or behavior. Rarely are members' degree of legislative effort accurately reflected with coverage. The ability to manipulate news routines and bad behavior are more consistently correlated with airtime.

Though the courts have a less adversarial role with the press, they suffer from extreme neglect. This is even true of the Supreme Court, the highest decision-making body in the U.S. political system. Various institutional and procedural features of the Court, such as the tendency to release decisions in clusters, complicate the press's ability to gather and report case facts in a timely and accurate fashion. Institutional constraints from the media side, such as declining newsroom resources and personnel, mean that fewer news organizations dedicate reporters to a full-time judicial news beat, leaving coverage of the Court to reporters without the necessary expertise to quickly process and then explain complicated judicial decisions.

The outcome is that the public interest is not well served. Media presentations of both institutions fall short, albeit in different ways. Congressional coverage is there but favors show horses over work horses. Judicial coverage is piecemeal at best, scant at worst. This chapter describes the arrangements that Congress, the courts, and the press have developed to manage their interdependent relationships. It also examines the way these institutions are navigating changes to the modern media environment that have influenced communication strategies of both journalists and officials. It also explores some of the problems that newspeople face in covering a flood of complex news expeditiously, accurately, and with a modicum of critical detachment and analysis.

DISCUSSION QUESTIONS

1. What functions do the media serve for members of the U.S. Congress? Who benefits most in the interdependent relationship between members of Congress and the press?

2. What explains the volume and nature of congressional press coverage? How does coverage of Congress affect public opinion? Does it affect legislative behavior at all? If so, how?

3. How is the relationship between the press and the Supreme Court unique relative to that of the president and the press and Congress and the press?

4. How is journalistic coverage of the court different from reporting on the other major branches of the U.S. government? Does this change how press coverage affects judicial behavior? Do these differences matter for how the public evaluates the judicial branch?

READINGS

Arceneaux, K., & Vander Wielen. R. (2017). *Taming intuition: How reflection minimizes partisan reasoning and promotes democratic accountability*. Cambridge University Press.

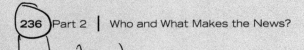

Atkinson, M. L. (2017). *Combative politics: The media and public perceptions of lawmaking.* University of Chicago Press.

Barendt, E. (Ed.). (2017). *Media freedom and contempt of court.* Routledge.

Baum, L. (2017). *Ideology in the Supreme Court.* Princeton University Press.

Black, R. C., Owens, R. J., Wedeking, J., & Wohlfarth, P. C. (2019). *The conscientious justice: How Supreme Court justices' personalities influence the law, the high court, and the Constitution.* Cambridge University Press.

Bonica, A., & Sen, M. (2020). *The judicial tug of war: How lawyers, politicians, and ideological incentives shape the American judiciary.* Cambridge University Press.

Collins, P. M., Jr., & Eshbaugh-Soha, M. (2020). *The president and the Supreme Court: Going public on judicial decisions from Washington to Trump.* Cambridge University Press.

Davis, R. (2016). *Covering the United States Supreme Court in the digital age.* Cambridge University Press.

Davis, R., & Taras, D. (2017). *Justices and journalists: The global perspective.* Cambridge University Press.

Fiorina, M. P. (2017). *Unstable majorities: Polarization, party sorting, and political stalemate.* Hoover Press.

Forgette, R. (2018). *News grazers: Media, politics, and trust in an information age.* CQ Press.

Frantzich, S. E. (2015). *Congress, the media, and the public: Who reveals what, when, and how?* Routledge.

Gerber, A. S., & Schickler, E. (2016). *Governing in a polarized age: Elections, parties, and political representation in America.* Cambridge University Press.

Hall, M. E. K. (2018). *What justices want: Goals and personality on the US Supreme Court.* Cambridge University Press.

Jamil, S. (Ed.). (2019). *Handbook of research on combating threats to media freedom and journalist safety.* IGI Global.

Lee, F. E. (2016). *Insecure majorities: Congress and the perpetual campaign.* University of Chicago Press.

Ramey, A. J., Klinger, J. D., & Hollibaugh, G. E., Jr. (2017). *More than a feeling: Personality, polarization, and the transformation of the U.S. Congress.* University of Chicago Press.

Thomsen, D. M. (2017). *Opting out of Congress: Party polarization and the decline of moderate candidates.* Cambridge University Press.

Vander Wielen, R., Park, H. M., & Smith, S. S. (2017). *Politics over process: Partisan conflict and post-passage processes in the U.S. Congress.* University of Michigan Press.

Vinson, C. D. (2017). *Congress and the media: Beyond institutional power.* Oxford University Press.

NOTES

1. Martin, R. (2017, January 2). House Republicans act in secret to weaken ethics panel. *NPR.* http://www.npr.org/2017/01/03/508008421/house-republicans-act-in-secret-to-weaken-ethics-panel; Davis, S., & Naylor, B. (2017, January 3). after backlash, including from Trump, GOP drops weakening of ethics office. *NPR.* http://www.npr.org/2017/01/03/508043376/after-trump-tweets-criticism-house-gop-drops-weakening-of-house-ethics-office.

2. Blanchard, R. O. (Ed.). (1974). *Congress and the news media.* Hastings House, p. 105.

3. Jamieson, K. H. (1988). *Eloquence in an electronic age: The transformation of political speechmaking.* Oxford University Press, p. 14.

4. Hess, S. (1981). *The Washington reporters.* Brookings Institution Press, p. 99. The figures are based on 921 newspaper and 87 television stories; Vinson, C. D. (2013). Congress and the media: Who has the upper hand? In T. N. Ridout (Ed.), *New directions in media and politics.* Routledge.

5. Arnold, R. D. (2004). *Congress, the press, and political accountability.* Princeton University Press; Vinson, C. D. (2013). Congress and the media: Who has the upper hand? In T. N. Ridout (Ed.), *New directions in media and politics.* Routledge.

6. Hibbing, J. R., & Theiss-Morse, E. (2002). *Stealth democracy: Americans' beliefs about how government should work.* Cambridge University Press.

7. Elving, R. D. (1996). Making news, making law. *Media Studies Journal,* *10*(Winter), 50; Fogarty, B. J. (2008). The strategy of the story: Media monitoring legislative activity. *Legislative Studies Quarterly, 33*(3), 445–469.

8. Hess, S. (1981). *The Washington reporters.* Brookings Institution Press, pp. 104–105; Kedrowski, K. M. (1996). *Media entrepreneurs and the media enterprise in the U.S. Congress.* Hampton Press, p. 5; Grimmer, J., Westwood, S. J., & Messing, S. (2013). *The impression of influence.* Princeton University Press.

9. Lawrence, R. G. (2000). Game framing the issues: Tracking the strategy frame in public policy news. *Political Communication, 17,* 93–114.

10. Quoted in Roberts, S. V. (1986, February 4). Senators squint into a future under TV's gaze. *The New York Times.*

11. Cook, T. E. (1989). *Making laws and making news: Media strategies in the U.S. House of Representatives.* Brookings Institution Press; for detailed analyses of congressional news making, see Kedrowski, K. M. (1996). *Media entrepreneurs and the media enterprise in the U.S. Congress.* Hampton Press; Arnold, R. D. (2004). *Congress, the press, and political accountability.* Princeton University Press; Padgett, J. S. (2014). *Predictors of national broadcast and cable television*

news coverage of the members of the US House of Representatives [Doctoral dissertation]. Louisiana State University, Baton Rouge, LA, 2014.

12. Boehner, J. (2021). *On the house*. St. Martin's Press; Inskeep, S., Doubek, J., Hamby, V., & Advani, R. (2012, April 12). John Boehner on the 'noisemakers' of the republican party. *NPR's Morning Edition*. https://www.npr .org/2021/04/12/985722549/john-boehner-on-the-noisemakers-of-the-republican-party

13. Shapiro, M. A., & Hemphill, L. (2017). Politicians and the policy agenda: Does use of Twitter by the U.S. Congress direct *New York Times* content? *Policy & Internet*, 9(1), 109–132.

14. Vinson, C. D. (2013). Congress and the media: Who has the upper hand? In T. N. Ridout (Ed.), *New directions in media and politics*. Routledge.

15. See Hopkins, D. J. (2018). *The increasingly United States: How and why American political behavior nationalized*. University of Chicago Press; Darr, J. P., Hitt, M. P., & Dunaway, J. L. (2018). Newspaper closures polarize voting behavior. *Journal of Communication*, 68(6), 1007–1028; Martin, G. J., & McCrain, J. (2019). Local news and national politics. *American Political Science Review*, 113(2), 372–384; Trussler, M. (2020). Get information or get in formation: The effects of high-information environments on legislative elections. *British Journal of Political Science*. https://doi.org/10.1017/S0007123419000577; Trussler, M. (2020). The effects of high-information environments on legislative behavior in the U.S. House of Representatives. *Legislative Studies Quarterly*. https://doi .org/10.1111/lsq.12325; Peterson, E. (2019). Paper cuts: How reporting resources affect political news coverage. *American Journal of Political Science*.

16. Trussler, M. (2020). Get information or get in formation: The effects of high-information environments on legislative elections. *British Journal of Political Science*. https://doi.org/10.1017/S0007123419000577

17. Trussler, M. (2020). The effects of high-information environments on legislative behavior in the U.S. House of Representatives. *Legislative Studies Quarterly*. https://doi.org/10.1111/lsq.12325

18. Arceneaux, K., Johnson, M., Lindstädt, R., & Vander Wielen, R. (2015). The influence of news media on political elites: Investigating strategic responsiveness in Congress. *American Journal of Political Science*, 60(1), 5–29.

19. Arceneaux, K., Dunaway, J., Johnson, M., & Vander Wielen, R. J. (2020). Strategic candidate entry and congressional elections in the era of Fox News. *American Journal of Political Science*, 64(2), 398–415.

20. Broockman, D. E., & Skovron, C. (2018). Bias in perceptions of public opinion among political elites. *American Political Science Review*, 112(3), 542–563.

21. Owen, D., Davis, R., & Strickler, V. J. (1999). Congress and the internet. *Press/Politics*, 4(2), 10–29.

22. Lipinski, D., & Neddenriep, G. (2004). Using "new" media to get "old" media coverage: How members of Congress use their web sites. *Press/Politics*, 9(1), 7–21.

23. Gunn, S. E., & Skogerbø, E. (2013). Personalized campaigns in party-centred politics: Twitter and Facebook as arenas for political communication. *Information, Communication & Society*, 16(5), 757–774; Gunn, S. E. (2015). *Mediated authenticity*. Peter Lang.

24. Sellers, P. J. (2010). *Cycles of spin: Strategic communication in the U.S. Congress*. Cambridge University Press.

25. Straus, J. R., Glassman, M. E., & Smelcer, S. N. (2013). Communication in 140 characters or less: Congressional adoption of Twitter in the 111th Congress. *PS: Political Science & Politics*, 46(1), 60–66.

26. Vinson, C. D. (2013). Congress and the media: Who has the upper hand? In T. N. Ridout (Ed.), *New directions in media and politics*. Routledge; Malecha, G. L., & Reagan, D. J. (2012). *The public congress: Congressional deliberation in a new media age*. Routledge; Congressional Management Foundation. (2011). *#SocialCongress: Perceptions and use of social media on Capitol Hill*. Author. http://www.congressfoundation.org/storage/documents/CMF_Pubs/cmf-social-congress.pdf

27. Media and Congress. (1996). *Media Studies Journal*, 10(1); Hess, S. (1991). *Live from Capitol Hill: Studies of Congress and the media*. Brookings Institution Press, p. 117; also see Kedrowski, K. M. (1996). *Media entrepreneurs and the media enterprise in the U.S. Congress*. Hampton Press; Arnold, R. D. (2004). *Congress, the press, and political accountability*. Princeton University Press. For an excellent discussion of congressional press galleries, see Merson, M. (1996). Big picture and local angle. *Media Studies Journal*, 10(1), 55–66.

28. See Who We Are. (n. d.). *U.S. Senate Press Gallery*. http://www.dailypress.senate.gov/?page_id=17.

29. Sellers, P. J. (2000). Congress and the news media: Manipulating the message in the U.S. Congress. *Press/Politics*, 5(1), 22–31.

30. How TV news has covered the 103rd Congress. (1994). *Media Monitor*, 8(5), 2; Padgett, J. S. (2014). *Predictors of national broadcast and cable television news coverage of the members of the US House of Representatives* [Doctoral dissertation]. Louisiana State University, Baton Rouge, LA, United States.

31. How TV news has covered the 103rd Congress. (1994). *Media Monitor*, 8(5), 2; Padgett, J. S. (2014). *Predictors of national broadcast and cable television news coverage of the members of the US House of Representatives* [Doctoral dissertation]. Louisiana State University, Baton Rouge, LA, United States; Cook, T. E. (1986). House members as national newsmakers: The effects of televising Congress. *Legislative Studies Quarterly*, 11(Summer), 203–226; Hess, S. (1986).

The ultimate insiders: U.S. Senators and the national media. Brookings Institution Press; also see Hess, S. (1991). *Live from Capitol Hill: Studies of Congress and the media.* Brookings Institution Press, pp. 55–58; Kedrowski, K. M. (1996). *Media entrepreneurs and the media enterprise in the U.S. Congress.* Hampton Press, Chapters 5 and 8; for a more updated account revealing similar patterns, see Padgett, J. S. (2014). *Predictors of national broadcast and cable television news coverage of the members of the US House of Representatives* [Doctoral dissertation]. Louisiana State University, Baton Rouge, LA, 2014

32. Congress and the public. (2021, April 9). *Gallup.* https://news.gallup.com/poll/1600/congress-public.aspx.

33. Gulati, G. J. (2004). Members of Congress and presentation of self on the World Wide Web. *Press/Politics, 9*(1), 22–40; Fogarty, B. J. (2008). The strategy of the story: Media monitoring legislative activity. *Legislative Studies Quarterly, 33*(3), 445–469.

34. How TV news has covered the 103rd Congress. (1994). *Media Monitor, 8*(5), 2; Arnold, R. D. (2004). *Congress, the press, and political accountability.* Princeton University Press.

35. Padgett, J. S. (2014). *Predictors of national broadcast and cable television news coverage of the members of the US House of Representatives* [Doctoral dissertation]. Louisiana State University, Baton Rouge, LA, 2014.

36. Vinson, C. D. (2013). Congress and the media: Who has the upper hand? In T. N. Ridout (Ed.), *New directions in media and politics.* Routledge.

37. For a history on the politics of communications policy formulation, see Krasnow, E. G., Longley, L. D., & Terry, H. A. (1982). *The politics of broadcast regulation* (3rd ed., pp. 87–132). St. Martin's; Britt, R. (1989). *The irony of regulatory reform: The deregulation of American telecommunications.* Oxford University Press; also Aufderheide, P. (1999). *Communications policy and the public interest.* Guilford Press.

38. Krasnow, E. G., Longley, L. D., & Terry, H. A. (1982). *The politics of broadcast regulation* (3rd ed., pp. 87–132). St. Martin's.

39. Haine-Roberts, L. (2013, April 13). Lack of media court coverage poses a serious problem for the legal system. *University of Miami Law Review.* http://lawreview.law.miami.edu/lack-media-court-coverage-poses-problem-legal-system/.

40. Davis, R. (2011). *Justices and journalists: The U.S. Supreme Court and the media.* Cambridge University Press; Johnson, C., & Bartels, B. (2010). Sensationalism and sobriety: Differential media exposure and attitudes toward American courts. *Public Opinion Quarterly, 74*(2), 260–258.

41. Gibson, J. (2009). New style judicial campaigns and the legitimacy of state high courts. *Journal of Politics, 71*(4), 1285–1304.

42. Christensen, A. (2010, May 11). Special edition round-up: Kagan Nomination V. *Scotus Blog*. http://www.scotusblog.com/2010/05/special-edition-round-up-kagan-nomination-v/.

43. Medina, R. (2020, October 6). 150 civil rights and public interest groups urge Senate to oppose Amy Coney Barrett's Supreme Court confirmation. *The Leadership Conference on Civil and Human Rights*. https://civilrights .org/2020/10/06/150-civil-rights-and-public-interest-groups-urge-senate-to-oppose-amy-coney-barretts-supreme-court-nomination/

44. Cassidy, J. (2018, November 21). Why did Chief Justice John Roberts decide to speak out against Trump?" *New Yorker*. https://www.newyorker.com/news/our-columnists/why-did-chief-justice-john-roberts-decide-to-speak-out-against-trump

45. Howe, A. (2021, April 7). In Harvard speech, Breyer speaks out against "court packing." *Scotus Blog*. https://www.scotusblog.com/2021/04/in-harvard-speech-breyer-speaks-out-against-court-packing/.

46. *Brown v. Board of Education*, 347 U.S. 483 (1954); *Roe v. Wade*, 410 U.S. 113 (1973); *Planned Parenthood v. Casey*, 112 S. Ct. 2791 (1992).

47. *Citizens United v. Federal Elections Commission* (2010); *United States v. Windsor*, No. 12-307 (2013); *Hollingsworth v. Perry* No. 12-144 (2013).

48. Davis, R. (1987). Lifting the shroud: News media portrayal of the U.S. Supreme Court. *Communications and the Law*, 9(October), 46; Woodward, B., & Armstrong, S. (1979). *The brethren*. Simon and Schuster. Both of these sources claim to present an insider's view of Court proceedings.

49. Davis, R. (1994). *Decisions and images: The Supreme Court and the press*. Prentice Hall.

50. Davis, R. (1994). *Decisions and images: The Supreme Court and the press*. Prentice Hall.

51. Newland, C. A. (1964). Press coverage of the United States Supreme Court. *Western Political Quarterly*, 17, 15–36. Also see Devol, K. S. (1990). *Mass media and the Supreme Court* (4th ed.). Hastings House.

52. *National Federation of Independent Business (NFIB) v. Sebelius*, 567 U.S. 519 (2012); see Stelter, B. (2012, June 28). CNN and Fox trip up in rush to get the news on the air. *The New York Times*. https://www.nytimes.com/2012/06/29/us/cnn-and-foxs-supreme-court-mistake.html; Liptak, L. (2012, June 28). Supreme Court upholds health care law, 5-4, in victory for Obama. *The New York Times*. https://www.nytimes.com/2012/06/29/us/supreme-court-lets-health-law-largely-stand.html

53. Davis, R. (1994). *Decisions and images: The Supreme Court and the press*. Prentice Hall, Chapters 4–6; also see Sorauf, F. J. (1987). Campaign money and the press: Three soundings. *Political Science Quarterly*, 102(Spring), 25–42.

54. Larson, S. G. (1985). How *The New York Times* covered discrimination cases. *Journalism Quarterly*, 62(Winter), 894–896; also see Stephanie Greco Larson, S. G. (1989, April). *Supreme Court coverage and consequences*. [Paper presented at the annual meeting of the Midwest Political Science Association, Chicago, Illinois, United States].

55. Nina Totenberg's bio can be found here: https://www.npr.org/people/2101289/nina-totenberg

56. Caldeira, G. (1986). Neither the purse nor the sword: Dynamics of public confidence in the Supreme Court. *American Political Science Review*, 80(December), 1209–1228; Scheb, J. M., II, & Lyons, W. (2005). Public perception of the Supreme Court in the 1990s. In E. E. Slotnick (Ed.), *Judicial Politics* (pp. 496–499). CQ Press; Jeffrey M. Jones, J. M. (2016, July 29). U.S. Supreme Court job approval rating ties record low. *Gallup*. http://www.gallup.com/poll/194057/supreme-court-job-approval-rating-ties-record-low.aspx.

57. Davis, R. (2011). *Justices and journalists: The U.S. Supreme Court and the media*. Cambridge University Press; Johnson, C., & Bartels, B. (2010). Sensationalism and sobriety: Differential media exposure and attitudes toward American courts. *Public Opinion Quarterly*, 74(2), 260–258; Casillas, C. J., Enns, P. K., & Wohlfarth, P. C. (2012). How public opinion constrains the U.S. Supreme Court. *American Journal of Political Science*, 55(1), 74–88; Enns, P. K., & Wohlfarth, P. C. (2013). The swing justice. *Journal of Politics*, 75(4), 1089–1107; Hall, M. E. K. (2014). The semiconstrained court: Public opinion, the separation of powers, and the U.S. Supreme Court's fear of nonimplementation. *American Journal of Political Science*, 58(2), 352–366.

58. Savage, D. G. (2020, June 24). Major rulings from Supreme Court in 2020 term on abortion, religion and Trump taxes. *Los Angeles Times*. https://www.latimes.com/politics/story/2020-06-24/supreme-court-2020-term-major-cases

59. Hurley, L. (2020, December 11). U.S. Supreme Court swiftly ends Trump-backed Texas bid to upend election results. *Reuters*. https://www.reuters.com/article/us-usa-election-trump/u-s-supreme-court-swiftly-ends-trump-backed-texas-bid-to-upend-election-results-idUSKBN28L2YY

60. Kritzer, H. M. (2005). The impact of *Bush v. Gore* on public perceptions and knowledge of the Supreme Court. In E. E. Slotnick (Ed.), *Judicial politics: Readings from judicature* (3rd ed.). CQ Press, pp. 500–506.

61. Pritchard, D. (1986). Homicide and bargained justice: The agenda-setting effect of crime news on prosecutors. *Public Opinion Quarterly*, 50(Spring), 143–159; Bruschke, J., & and Loges, W. E. (1999). Relationship between pretrial publicity and trial outcomes. *Journal of Communication*, 49(4), 104–120; Imrich, D., Mullin, C., & Linz, D. (1995). Measuring the extent of prejudicial pretrial publicity in American newspapers: A content analysis. *Journal of Communication*, 45(3), 94–117.

62. Dixon, T. L., & Azocar, C. L. (2007). Priming crime and activating Blackness: Understanding the psychological impact of the overrepresentation of Blacks as lawbreakers on television news. *Journal of Communication, 57*, 229–253; also see Kellstedt, P. M. (2003). *The mass media and the dynamics of American racial attitudes.* Cambridge University Press.

63. Barber, S. (1987). *News cameras in the courtroom: A free press–fair trial debate.* Ablex; also see Vinson, C. D., & Ertter, J. S. (2002). Entertainment or education: How the media cover the courts. *Press/Politics, 7*(4), 80–89.

64. Fox, R. L., Van Sickel, R. W., Steiger, T. L. (2007). *Tabloid justice: Criminal justice in an age of media frenzy.* Lynne Rienner Publishers; Graham, F. (1998). Doing justice with cameras in the courts. *Media Studies Journal, 12*(1), 32–37.

65. Ellefson, L. (2021, April 21). CNN tops all cable and broadcast networks for Chauvin Verdict ratings. *The Wrap.* https://www.thewrap.com/chauvin-verdict-ratings-cnn-tops-cable-broadcast-networks/

66. Barber, S. (1987). *News cameras in the courtroom: A free press–fair trial debate.* Ablex; also see Vinson, C. D., & Ertter, J. S. (2002). Entertainment or education: How the media cover the courts. *Press/Politics, 7*(4), 80–89.

67. Fox, R. L., Van Sickel, R. W., Steiger, T. L. (2007). *Tabloid justice: Criminal justice in an age of media frenzy.* Lynne Rienner Publishers; Graham, F. (1998). Doing justice with cameras in the courts. *Media Studies Journal, 12*(1), 32–37; also see Plaisance, P. L., & Deppa, J. A. (2009). Perceptions and manifestations of autonomy, transparency and harm among U.S. newspaper journalists. *Journalism Communication Monographs, 10*(4), 327–386.

State and Local News

Learning Objectives

1. Describe how the media environment is changing in ways that affect the provision and consumption of local and state news.

2. Discuss press–government relations at the state and local levels, as well as how those relationships shape news coverage.

3. Explain how local news is gathered and distributed, including decisions about which stories get covered and which do not.

4. Discuss whether the media environment is nationalizing and, if so, the consequences of that trend.

5. Assess the quality of local news provided to most communities to determine whether it is sufficient for meeting the information needs of state and local citizens.

6. Indicate if (and how well) state and local elections are covered by local media.

In a classic study of media and public opinion, the renowned U.S. journalist Walter Lippmann likened the performance of the media to "the beam of a searchlight that moves restlessly about, bringing one episode and then another out of darkness into vision." The media were not a "mirror on the world," as others had claimed. Lippmann concluded, "Men cannot do the work of the world by this light alone. They cannot govern society by episodes, incidents, and eruptions."[1]

What Lippmann observed in 1922 is still true today, and in some ways, the problem is getting worse. The media provide spotty coverage, leaving much of the political landscape obscured. Unfortunately, the institutions covered in this chapter—state and local governments—remain in the shadows of media coverage even though peoples' personal lives are affected more directly by these institutions than by the White House and Congress,

which are media darlings. Citizens' chances for influencing local government and local policies are also much greater than on the national scene.
Civic engagement and political knowledge also correlate with local news
habits. Local newspaper readers are more likely to recall the name of their
House member.[2]

The good news is that, as of 2019, local television news remained one
of the most regularly used political information sources,[3] and citizens still
report that they trust local news more than national news. This is somewhat surprising, given the generally poor quality of news about state and
local matters, but local television news revenues held steady through 2018
nevertheless—even after accounting for election cycle–related fluctuations due to political advertising revenue (see Figure 7-1).[4] The other good
news is that local stations are providing more hours of locally oriented
programming on a daily basis; daily local news hours have been gradually
on the rise since 2003 (see Figure 7-2).

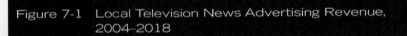

**Figure 7-1   Local Television News Advertising Revenue,
2004–2018**

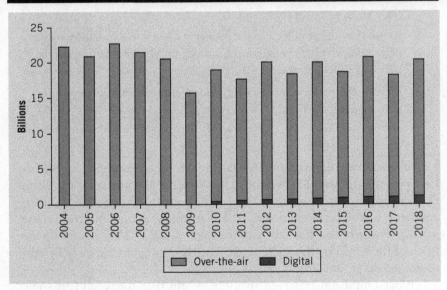

Source: Adapted from Pew Research Center analysis of MEDIA Access Pro & BIA Advisory
Services data. Local TV news fact sheet. (2019, June 25). *Pew Research Center.* https://www
.journalism.org/fact-sheet/local-tv-news/

Note: Local TV advertising revenue figures include over-the-air (OTA) revenue and digital revenue. Digital revenue numbers are not available prior to 2010. Numbers are updated annually.

Figure 7-2   Number of Hours Dedicated to Local Television News

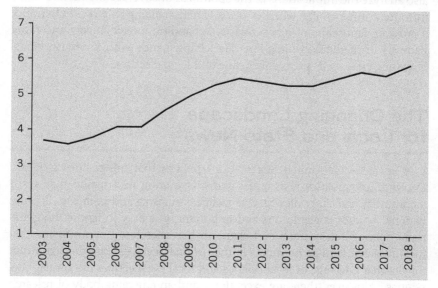

Source: Local TV news fact sheet. (2019, June 25). *Pew Research Center.* https://www.journalism.org/fact-sheet/local-tv-news/

Note: Based on RTDNA/Hofstra University Surveys, survey responses of news directors at all commercial local television stations in the fourth quarter of each year among operating, non-satellite television stations.

But if local television news revenues are holding steady and local television news hours are on the rise, what then is driving the concerns about declining local news and a nationalizing news environment? In this chapter, we will explore this and other questions about the rapidly changing provision and consumption of local, state, and regional news. The chapter will also describe the numerous forms local news can take, and the audiences they serve. As earlier chapters did for presidents, Congress, and the Supreme Court, we will also explore the nature of the relationship between local press and state and local political institutions and actors. In addition, the chapter will describe the characteristics of the content found in various kinds of local news and explain how local news is gathered and distributed. We will also examine the impact of the economics of local news, including patterns of local media ownership and the changing regulations governing these structures. The chapter will assess whether the amount and quality of local news provided to most communities is sufficient for meeting critical information needs and holding local leaders accountable. The chapter will also analyze the implications of the spottiness of coverage mentioned in the introduction—namely, whether news is nationalizing as a consequence of a growing landscape of news deserts, expanding media choice, and rapid patterns of media consolidation. The chapter ends with a description of how (and how well) press cover state and local elections.

The Changing Landscape for Local and State News

It is an axiom of United States (U.S.) politics that "all politics is local." Decentralized politics is essential and invigorating in a nation that spans a continent and embodies diverse political cultures and contexts. Because national politics is glamorous and important, it is easy to ignore the grass-roots politics that nourish and shape it. It is therefore not surprising that most research focuses on media at the national level, despite the significant impact that coverage of local politics and local perspectives has on national politics.[5] However, there are exceptions, and an emerging body of research is beginning to more fully explore the implications of the changing media environment, paying particular attention to what it means for the provision of, and attention to, local, state, and regional news as well as what that means for representation and political accountability at state and local levels.

The Demise and Decline of Local Newspapers

Local newspapers and radio and television stations in the U.S. are designed to serve a multitude of local markets. At the start of the 20th century, every large and medium-size city—and even many small towns—had at least one newspaper (and often more) geared to local politics, interests, and critical information needs. Today, most cities have only a single news-paper at best; many have no paper at all.[6] According to a report from Penny Abernathy of University of North Carolina at Chapel Hill (UNC), there were 2,100 fewer local newspapers in 2018 than in 2004. During that time period, newspaper closures robbed 1,800 former newspaper communities of their daily paper.[7]

Even in places fortunate enough to still have a newspaper, the news-paper is likely to be in peril. Recent declines in local newspaper circulation and advertising revenues are steep. In 2018, U.S. weekday local newspaper circulation was 28.6 million; it was 30.8 million on Sundays. Weekday circulation fell by 8% and Sunday fell by 9%. Those are the numbers for print and digital combined; weekday print circulation decreased by 12% and Sunday print circulation decreased by 13%. Advertising revenues declined steadily since 2008. They declined despite the fact that local news websites are seeing more traffic and rising digital advertising revenue.[8]

What may be less obvious is how these losses in revenues affect state and local news provision. If revenue loss is not severe enough to force closure, local newspapers still may need to cut costs and reduce their reporting investments. This is typically observed in several ways. Most commonly, revenue losses manifest in patterns of declining newsroom employment, instigated with buyouts, and layoffs for newsroom personnel, leading to fewer news workers dedicated to gathering, editing, and disseminating the news. In 2018, 37,900 people worked in the newsroom in the newspaper industry. This number represents a 14% drop relative to 2015 and a 47% drop when compared to 2004. In terms of revenue and news investment, the newspaper industry's decline continues (see Figures 7-3 through 7-5).[9]

Figure 7-3   U.S. Local Newspaper Deaths, 2000–2014

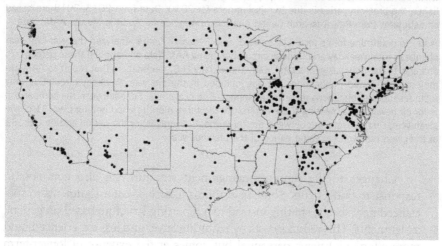

Source: Darr, J. P., Hitt, M. P., & Dunaway, J. (2021). *Home style opinion: How local newspapers can slow polarization.* Cambridge University Press.

Note: Data are drawn from the Chronicling America project, part of the National Digital Newspaper Program, which maintains a searchable database of the founding and folding dates of past and current U.S. newspapers (Library of Congress, 2016).

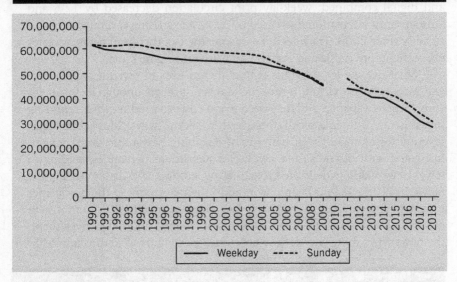

Figure 7-4 Total Estimated Circulation of U.S. Daily Newspapers, 1990–2018

Source: Adapted from Newspapers: Fact sheet. (2019, July 9). *Pew Research Center.* https://www.journalism.org/fact-sheet/newspapers/. Through 2014, the data source was Editor & Publisher; the break in series is due to missing data for 2010. Data from 2015–2018 are based on estimates from Pew Research Center analysis of Alliance for Audited Media (AAM) data.

Note: To determine totals for 2015 onward, Pew Research Center analyzed the year-over-year change in total weekday and Sunday circulation using AAM data and applied these percentage changes to the previous year's total. Only those daily U.S. newspapers that report to AAM are included. Affiliated publications are not included in the analysis. Weekday circulation only includes those publications reporting a Monday–Friday average. For each year, the comparison is for all newspapers meeting these criteria for the three-month period ending Dec. 31 of the given year. Comparisons are between the three-month averages for the period ending Dec. 31 of the given year and the same period of the previous year.

Changes to the reporting assignment structure are also common in response to budget cuts. Some newsrooms reduce or cut assignments to specialized news beats, shifting instead to a reporting structure based on general assignments. This reduces costs by requiring fewer and less experienced (and more affordable) news personnel but comes at the expense of longer-term development of reporter subject matter expertise and cultivation of sources.[10]

Another consequence of newspaper revenue loss is closures of satellite reporting locations or news bureaus that provide a remote location for

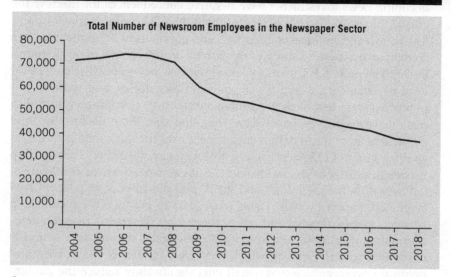

Figure 7-5 Newspaper Newsroom Employment, 2004–2018

Total Number of Newsroom Employees in the Newspaper Sector

Source: Adapted from Newspapers: Fact sheet. (2019, July 9). *Pew Research Center.* https://www.journalism.org/fact-sheet/newspapers/

Note: Data is from Pew Research Center analysis of Bureau of Labor Statistics Occupational Employment Statistics Data.

on-the-ground reporting of news occurring elsewhere. Bureaus can be located in other metropolitan areas, the state capitol, other parts of the region, happenings at the nation's capital, or, for some of the major metro papers, even foreign countries. Alternatively, some papers cut costs by reducing the frequency of publication or shifting away from print to become an entirely digital (or web-based) newspaper.

In the effort to attract new audiences, some local newspapers expanded their offerings to include suburban dailies, weekly newspapers, or free shoppers to target different units within or proximate to their geographic markets.[11] The emphasis on local news varies across these spinoffs. But because of the lack of fit between media markets and political units, most local news lacks detailed discussion and in-depth analysis of local public issues. It does not provide the information citizens need to effectively monitor local politics.

What's most important to understand is that a growing body of research shows that both newspaper closures and the various forms of declining news investments have negative consequences for meeting the critical information needs of local communities. The same is true for political knowledge, political engagement, and government accountability. In a content analysis-based study of more than 10,000 campaign news stories, Danny Hayes and Jennifer Lawless show that between 2010 and 2014, local newspapers covered fewer political news stories, and those stories published were less likely to contain substantive, election-relevant information. Using survey panel data, they find that these declines in local political news reduced citizen engagement over the same time period.[12] In another study of U.S. newspapers, Erik Peterson identifies a relationship between industry-wide declines in U.S. newspapers, where employment fell over 40% between 2007 and 2015, and the amount of political coverage newspapers provide. Using panel data to examine the relationship between newsroom cuts and political coverage, Peterson's research demonstrates how cuts to newsroom reporting staffs amount to a seriously reduced reporting capacity, which negatively influences the provision of political coverage. Newsroom staff cuts significantly reduce the amount of local newspaper coverage of politics. Peterson finds that a standard newsroom reporting staff cut reduces its yearly political coverage by somewhere between 300 and 500 stories.[13]

Changes in Local Television News

One might wonder why the declines in local newspapers are so problematic, especially when the beginning of the chapter described the relative economic health and popularity of local television news. While that's true, the local media grid is also changing market and competitive structures for local television, and it is doing so in ways that are likely to affect the availability, volume, and quality of local news on television. Nearly every city also used to have its own television media outlets to serve local audiences. Urban sprawl is eroding this local focus, so broadcast and print media now serve ever-larger regions. Some television stations and metropolitan dailies serve people in fifty counties, making comprehensive local coverage impossible. Reporting, of necessity, becomes highly selective and superficial. Coverage areas typically include some 1,300 government units, whose policies should be reported because they involve important public issues, including the power to tax. Numerous state legislators, as well as several national legislators, are elected within these counties.[14]

For both local newspapers and local television news, a major consequence of the changing local media grid is the vanishing metropolitan focus. Because market areas and political units no longer coincide, reporting abandoned traditional emphasis on strictly local problems, shifting to broader topics more likely to be of interest to the entire market area. That shift means less daily provision of information about the important local problems citizens face.[15] This is happening despite nationwide polls still showing heavy reliance on local news, especially news regarding important information affecting the community. For example, in 2020, Pew Research Center reported that nearly half (46%) of Americans said local news outlets were a major source for their news about COVID-19.[16]

Television stations in smaller markets feature more local and less national and international news than their larger cousins.[17] Citizens rely heavily on these broadcasts, but they still tend to be shallow because of time constraints.[18] Many local radio news stations devote more than half of their airtime to local news, but a lot of talk radio content is increasingly made up of nationally syndicated opinion, sports news, or entertainment programs instead of local news or public affairs programming. Stations in smaller radio markets usually present fewer stories simply because the pool of local news is tiny.[19]

Another televised venue for access to local news and public affairs information comes from community access cable channels that allow citizens to watch local government in action. City council meetings, committee hearings, and court procedures have become directly accessible to the public without the intervention of journalists. The suburbs, where such channels have been scarce in the past, are joining the parade, thereby providing more competition for suburban newspapers. However, similar to its national-level cousin, C-SPAN, audiences for live broadcasts of local government activities are generally quite small.

Digital and Web-Native Local News

Though it's often argued that the problem of insufficient local news may be easing because of the arrival of a vast digital media landscape, complete with many new Web-native forms of local news, at least a decade's worth of research suggests this is not true—at least not yet.[20] Beyond the traditional venues establishing a digital presence through websites and social media, few news suppliers are branching out through websites dedicated to local news in specific nearby towns and villages, and only a handful of truly Web-native local news outlets are emerging. In his extensive research on the digital news environment, Matthew Hindman describes the situation as follows:

> The broad landscape of online local news is easy to summarize. Local news is a tiny part of web usage: Collectively, local news outlets receive *less than half a percent of all page views* in a typical market. Newspapers and television stations dominate what local news can be found online. Only a handful of local news websites—seventeen out of 1,074, all detailed later—are unaffiliated with traditional print or broadcast media. Across the one hundred markets, our methodology finds the following:
>
> - 395 television station websites
> - 590 daily newspaper websites
> - 41 weekly news publication websites (nearly all alt weekly newspapers)
> - 31 radio station websites
> - 17 Web-native local news websites unconnected to print, television, or radio outlets
>
> There is surprisingly little evidence in this data that the internet has expanded the number of local news outlets. And while the internet adds only a pittance of new sources of local news, the surprisingly small audience for online local news helps explain the dire financial straits in which local news organizations find themselves.[21]

As Hindman's summary suggests, hyperlocal news sites aiming to fill the gaps in local coverage have simply not emerged in the wake of declining newspaper resources. A few notable exceptions are doing quite well financially; others have partnered with existing local metro papers to offset costs and supplement local news reporting; still others were short-lived. This is unfortunate—more media outlets and platforms offer the potential for more diversity of perspectives and more media reporting on officials at all levels, especially when they can make use of new tools afforded by digital and social media.[22]

According to research by Hindman and others, the disappointing story of local news on the web can largely be explained by two key challenges. One is the more familiar challenge of traffic and referrals—how to draw traffic to local news websites in the first place. The other is a challenge of news site stickiness—how to keep people on local news websites for longer periods of time once they get there—in the effort to compound audience growth. In the earlier days of transitioning to digital, there was little concern about the size of the local news audience online; it was taken for granted. The news industry widely believed that the problem with local news online was simply a matter of getting the sizeable local news audience to pay for locally oriented content. But as researchers learned more about how people spend their time online, it was clear that very little digital attention is spent on news. Instead, most people are shopping, emailing, scrolling and posting on social media, or visiting other sites. Even when we look at traffic for all news sites combined, they only attract about 3% of total web traffic, and a vast majority of that traffic spends its time visiting national news outlets such as CNN or aggregator sites such as Yahoo News. Only about a sixth of all traffic to news sites goes to digital local news outlets. The implication of Hindman's research is clear: Local news cannot earn revenue based on audiences they do not yet have.[23] Compounding the issue is that the algorithms used by search sites such as Google prioritize popularity when returning search results and referring web users to other sites, which means the bulk of traffic is sent to popular and mainstream (i.e., high-traffic) sites focused on national events and issues. Under this infrastructure, local news sites are at a disadvantage because of their relatively small audiences.[24] The traffic challenge is real.

The traffic and stickiness problems are related, but for a long time, news organizations were too focused on the traffic problem, focusing primarily on metrics such as total unique site visitors, without considering the issue of stickiness, which is essential for turning site visits into ad revenues by growing and compounding website audiences. The total number of unique visitors to a site means very little if the *bounce rate* is high, which refers to when website visitors only remain on the page for fractions of a second.[25]

However, research shows there are things local news outlets can do to improve the stickiness of their sites. Because digital local media do not have the bundle-based, built-in audience of traditional local media, they must be attuned to the habits and behaviors of the digital audience. Research suggests several key strategies for doing so. One is to publish lively, ever-changing content—news that is fresh and frequently updated. Convenience matters, too: Sites with good content recommendation systems and faster speeds are more likely to have engaged audiences that won't bounce as quickly; visitors on these sites are more likely to click more news stories and are more likely to revisit the site soon.[26]

Outlets should also continually test what works. According to research by communication scholar Jessica Collier and her colleagues, small differences in things such as how links are labeled to refer readers can influence site users' click-through rates. Their research also suggests that outlets should be mindful of how site behavior varies according to the paths by which users reach the site. People referred to local news sites from social media platforms such as Facebook may have different interests and motivations and therefore may behave differently while on the site relative to users who habitually visit the site by entering its domain name directly into their browser.[27] On the positive side, news organizations are paying more attention to the relevant metrics and doing (or commissioning) more testing. Some of the most successful papers already incorporate analytics into their daily workflow. Also, nonprofit organizations such as the University of Texas Center for Media Engagement will partner with local news organizations to test means by which to improve audience engagement on local news sites. If local news organizations can build and maintain sites in ways that promote sustained online audience growth over time, they will improve their competitive advantage against large news sites such as CNN or aggregators such as Google News.[28] But, at least for now, local news sites' disadvantage against monopolistic competitors such as Google and Facebook is steep, which means Web-based news is not yet a sufficient replacement for declines in traditional forms of local media.

Decline of Mainstream State Venues

As local news organizations continue to lose resources, it is a particular problem for coverage of state politics and governance. Traditionally, most press coverage of state news was found in local newspapers. Local papers staffed news bureaus in capital cities and assigned reporters to serve in statehouse press corps. But these reporting investments—both the infrastructures and the personnel—require investment. Studies reveal that when local media must make budget cuts in response to declining revenues, state capital bureaus are among the first hit. Since 1999, the number of newspaper journalists covering state capitals has significantly decreased, and coverage of state politics continued to suffer.[29] Between 2003 and 2014, state house press corps also declined by 35%.[30] Local news coverage of state government is better in state capital cities but has generally suffered as local newspaper revenues, news investment, and employment have continued to decline.

Neglect of state-level happenings is even a problem on local newspaper op-ed pages. A recent study of the op-ed pages of two local newspapers found that in one paper, during July and August of 2020, state-related events and issues were the focus of only 18% of the syndicated content on the op-ed page.[31] State-related events and issues accounted for 43% of op-eds and editorials and only 41% of letters to the editor. In this local paper, the rest of the content, which made up half or more of each category, focused on national political events and issues for those two months. It was only when the paper instigated a temporary ban on national politics for the month of July that California-focused content comprised 38% of syndicated material, 96% of op-eds and editorials, and 95% of the letters to the editor (see Figure 7-6). Observers of state news bemoan the fact that current levels of coverage are simply not adequate for the sufficient monitoring of state government, especially considering its impact on citizens' lives.[32]

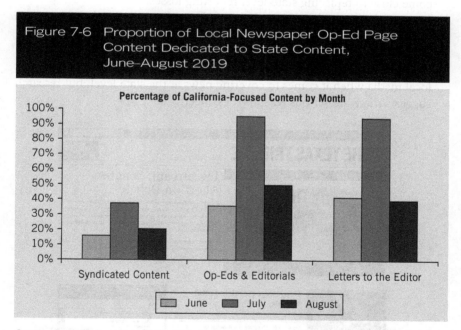

Figure 7-6 Proportion of Local Newspaper Op-Ed Page Content Dedicated to State Content, June–August 2019

Source: Adapted from Darr, J. P., Hitt, M. P., & Dunaway, J. L. (2021). *Home style opinion: How local newspapers can slow polarization.* Cambridge University Press.

Note: The unusually high proportion of state content in July is due to the paper's decision to ban national political content from the op-ed page for the month of July. June and August represent normal levels. Data are based on authors' content analysis of the op-ed page of *The Desert Sun,* the local newspaper serving the California's Palm Springs area and Coachella Valley, June through August, 2019.

The New State Venues

At the same time, new venues for state news are cropping up all over, and they may have the potential to offset losses from traditional subnational media. The presence of citizen journalists, bloggers, and reporters from internet-based news outlets is growing in state press corps. Those tracking state blogs report that there is a political blog covering every state and that there are several in some of the larger states. Nonprofit and mainline news organizations are also partnering with some of these new venues to help ensure their viability and to support investigative reporting at the state level. Thus far, evidence suggests that, in some instances, these organizations are helping bring attention to stories that might have otherwise been missed because of thinning resources for state-level reporting from mainstream media. Yet the emergence of new state-level media has not come close to replacing state-level reporting losses.[33]

Experts cite the *Texas Tribune* (http://www.texastribune.org; see Photo 7-1) as a model for new venues offering quality state-level reporting.[34] Evidence remains mixed on the extent to which digital and social media local news output will fill the gaps left open by declining traditional local media when it comes to covering news at the state level, but research suggests there are serious reasons for concern.[35]

Photo 7-1 Screenshot from *The Texas Tribune*'s website.

Source: The Texas Tribune.

Press–Government Relations

Subnational news is important for setting the public policy agenda at the state and local levels. It helps or hinders politicians in achieving their goals. It influences the election and appointment of public officials. It informs the public and officialdom about political affairs and politicians' wrong-doings. However, there are differences in emphasis between national and subnational political coverage, largely because subnational politics operate on a much smaller scale and in a much clubbier environment. Scholars intermittently neglect the study of subnational media, despite unmistak-able signs of their importance.[36]

How State and Local Officials Use the Press

At the subnational level, public officials find it much easier to stay in touch with each other without relying on news stories. They also remain in closer direct contact with a comparatively tiny corps of reporters, so formal press conferences are less necessary. Moreover, their news is rarely so excit-ing that they can count on decent attendance if they do schedule a news conference. Fewer subnational officials are experts in media relations. The public information and public relations materials they present to the media are often so poorly done that they do more harm than good. Many tasks that mayors and city managers perform are highly technical and difficult to condense into brief news stories suitable for lay publics. When officials do make the effort to tell their stories, reporters generally lack technical expertise to judge the accuracy of the account. Consequently, when the story relates to a policy decision involving important technical issues—for example, whether to start, continue, or stop a sewer project; how to finance it; and similar matters—the official views are likely to define the situation with little media scrutiny.

Media scholar Phyllis Kaniss identified six media styles that are espe-cially common among public figures at the subnational level.[37] The *para-noid media-avoider* fears the press and tries to avoid it as much as possible. Information-hungry journalists are likely to retaliate with unfavorable pub-licity at every opportunity. The *naïve professional* supplies the media with information and talks freely with journalists without realizing that uncon-trolled release of information empowers reporters to determine which top-ics will be highlighted and how they will be framed. The *ribbon cutter* is a media junkie heavily concerned with arranging events, however trivial, that are likely to attract journalists. The ensuing publicity may have few political payoffs. *Dancing marionettes* take their cues from media editorials and take action in areas suggested by newspeople rather than initiating policies independently. The reward is likely to be favorable coverage, although the policy agenda that newspeople favor may be undesirable from the official's perspective. *Colorful quotables* excel in creating sound bites and making sure that these come to the attention of reporters. Like ribbon cutters, their political rewards are apt to be small. Finally, *liars* conceal or slant information or distort it outright to put themselves in a favorable light.

The era of informal, inexpert handling of the press by subnational officials seems to be ending. Currently, all governors and most big-city mayors have press secretaries or public information offices. Similar to their counterparts at the national level, public figures try to use these offices to push their programs through recalcitrant legislative bodies and to disseminate news about their activities to various political elites and interested citizens. However, as on the national level, such efforts often fail. Fearing being hoodwinked by clever professionals, the contemporary media are suspicious, cynical commentators rather than trusting friends.

Elected officials are not alone in craving good media coverage. Appointed officials, too, need favorable images to help them win funding and support for the policies their agencies pursue. Federal officials think positive coverage increases their chances of achieving major policy goals.[38] Legislatures rarely deny support to popular agencies. By the same token, bad publicity hurts. When media frame stories in ways that subvert official goals, public officials may have to reset their own sights. For example, city sanitation departments are forced to concentrate on cleaning minor waste sites and to neglect more serious ones when publicity highlights a particular pollution hazard.

As on the national scene, local strategies designed to win media attention include holding press conferences, issuing press releases, staging newsworthy events, writing op-ed pieces, and writing letters to the editor. Contacting media personnel directly seems to be the best approach, and apparently, it is quite successful. Press releases are least productive. Estimates are that more than half of the content of the print and electronic media originates with publicity seekers rather than journalists.[39] Government officials at all levels provide a large share of these so-called news subsidies.[40]

In the past, most efforts to gain media coverage at the subnational level were directed at the print media, which governors, lieutenant governors, attorneys general, secretaries of state, and various legislative leaders deemed to be the most effective transmitters of state and local political news. That is changing. More local officials realize that television and digital media are most important for mobilizing public opinion. Therefore, they try harder to get coverage from these venues for themselves and their agencies.[41]

How Reporters Operate at Subnational Levels

Reporters are also somewhat different at the subnational level. Taken as a group, they have less formal education and considerably less job experience. Still, the officials' level of education may rank considerably below that of reporters. Turnover rates are high among reporters. They are often forced to move to a different market when they switch jobs because clauses in their contracts forbid them from working for a competitor in the same area. Reporters' unfamiliarity with local politics in their new surroundings may strain relations between reporters and officials when they disagree in their analyses of political events. However, most of the time, personal relations between reporters and officials tend to be more cordial at the subnational level because these people interact more. In fact, ties of friendship are sometimes blamed for the dearth of press criticism of local officials and local businesses.[42]

Aside from media outlets under the wing of metropolitan newspapers, news organizations at the subnational level are usually considerably smaller than their national counterparts. Consequently, reporters have to cover many beats rather than becoming specialists. Roving reporters must depend more heavily on routine sources, such as daily inquiries at the police and fire departments, local newspapers, assorted press releases, tips from viewers, wire service stories, and the wire service "day books" that list significant local events. The quality of local coverage tends to decline without specialized news beats and with skeleton reporting staffs.[43] Because most government business stops in the early evening hours, late evening local news broadcasts depend heavily on the staples supplied by police and fire department records.[44] Serious political news featured on early evening national newscasts is deemed "stale" by nine or ten at night. Stories with the best pictures and best sound bites tend to become leads, even when they are not necessarily the most important stories. Because many state and local stories are technical and undramatic, journalists strive mightily to make them entertaining. That means bypassing opportunities for detailed exposition of problems because that might bore the audience. In the process of tabloidizing news, the importance of events and their broader and long-term consequences are easily lost.

There are also challenges stemming from the geography of news markets. Journalists who work in large metropolitan areas are often accused of ignoring the politics of nearby suburban communities. There are several reasons they favor covering the central city.[45] Among them is the fact that metropolitan newspaper offices usually are closer to the central city hall than to the suburbs. That makes inner-city officials and other news sources located in the inner city easier to reach and more likely to visit news outlets. Inner cities are also more likely to generate the kind of news that political reporters ordinarily cover, such as political wheeling and dealing, ample doses of corruption, racial strife, protest demonstrations, and heavy slices of crime.[46] The shrinking size of the press corps, including the loss of highly experienced journalists, also accounts for the lack of coverage for many important subnational stories and for more pack journalism. The overall quality of news has eroded.

Subnational News Content

What do eager news audiences get when they turn to the nightly local news broadcasts? Several reports by Pew's Project for Excellence in Journalism tell part of the story.[47] Local news tends to be "live, local, and late breaking," with a heavy dose of crime reports. But how much focus does local, community relevant information get? What kinds of information is it? How much local news space is spent covering big national news instead? Also, what about coverage of state politics? When it is covered, what kinds of stories attract media attention? Is the coverage at either level sufficient for holding election officials accountable across states and local communities?

Box 7-1
Local and National Frames in Coverage of an Environmental Disaster

Some events and issues can be viewed from a local perspective or national perspective. Editors, producers, and reporters must make decisions about which will move audiences more profoundly. At times, locally focused frames will have more impact than stories without a local angle. Often, this impact is heightened because audiences trust their local news providers more than outsiders.[48] When resources allow it, subnational journalists choose and write or publish stories based on the needs and preferences of their own audiences. This is rightly so from an economic perspective, but it can mean that national stories at the local level look vastly different than their national counterparts and across localities. For example, local coverage of the 2010 Deepwater Horizon oil gusher looked distinctly different across the Gulf states. The negativity in coverage was heavily dependent on proximity to the rig and the percentage of the local economy dependent on tourism and oil and gas. But there were also similarities: In all but Texas, local governors made the news more than President Obama, a trend not reflected in national coverage. Figures 7-7 and 7-8 show these patterns.

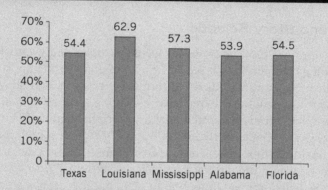

Figure 7-7 Percentage of Negative News Stories by Local News Markets

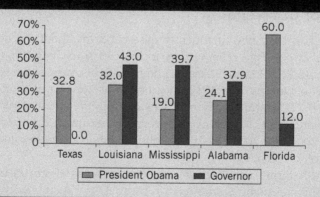

Figure 7-8 President Obama and State Governors as Newsmakers

Source: 100 days of gushing oil. (2010, August 25). *Pew Research Center.* https://www.pewre search.org/journalism/2010/08/25/100-days-gushing-oil/; Turcotte, J., Kirzinger, A., Dunaway, J., & Goidel, R. K. (2017). The many layers of local: Proximity and market influence on news coverage of the Deepwater Horizon oil spill. *Social Science Quarterly, 98*(3), 993–1009.

Local News

Historically, when asked which news topics they follow "very closely," crime, weather, and sports are the favorite topics listed among local news consumers. This highlights the importance local audiences place on the "local" in their news; they also frequently report that news about people and events in their own community is another important reason for tuning in. Topics such as local government and politics are typically ranked lower. The audience appeal of crime, weather, sports, and traffic is reflected in news content, especially as local news doubles down on their efforts to attract and retain audiences.

Topic and Story Selection

A majority of local news stories focus on topics and events from the surrounding community (but see Box 7-1). Proximity is an important local news value. News also tends to be formulaic, reactive, and short. These patterns are not new, but the trends are escalating. Though a lot of time on local news was already dedicated to sports, weather, and traffic, that proportion rose even higher between 2005 and 2012, increasing from 32% to 40% of broadcast time. The largest increase among these categories came from sports, where the airtime percentage rose from 7% to 12%. Crime coverage actually dropped from 29% to 17%, but this drop was somewhat offset by a 7% increase in coverage of accidents, disasters, and unusual events.

Depth of Coverage

Critics of local news frequently raise concerns about the depth and substance of coverage. The average local news story length is declining over time. In Pew Research Center's comparison of coverage between 1998 and 2002 to patterns from 2012, the number of stories over a minute long dropped by 11% and the number of stories shorter than thirty seconds increased by 8%. Coverage of politics and government dropped by 50% between 2005 and 2012. By 2012, political public affairs stories made up only 3% of the broadcast.

News is formulaic. It reports on familiar types of stories in routine ways, night after night. Stories tend to be brief, and such brevity does not permit deep analysis. As a result, local newscasts largely provide a headline service. It provides a news diet of snacks rather than meals and therefore satisfies no one's hunger. The presentation of controversial stories is often one-sided, depriving audiences of the chance to fully assess the merits of different positions. Original investigative stories are rare. On most stations, only 7% of the stories originate from reporters' efforts to cover important issues on their own initiative rather than relying on press releases or merely recording ongoing events.[49] Investigations by local television news reporters fall well short of local newspapers, even in larger television markets.[50]

As part of its mandate to ensure that the electronic media serve the public interest, the Federal Communications Commission (FCC) urges local television and radio stations to gear their programming to local information needs, including covering local politics. Obviously, that mandate is honored more by lip service than by actual performance. Local stations do carry some local political news, but it constitutes only 10% of the average broadcast, if that. This is hardly what the FCC has in mind when it calls for an emphasis on local programming.

Although these figures show that local news is light on politics, one must keep in mind that there are generally multiple nightly local newscasts. The proportion of serious political news available to citizens may therefore be fairly substantial. Several studies of the effects from watching local newscasts indicate that most viewers feel better informed about the local community. They trust and appreciate newscasts more, but they are also more prone to fear crime and develop false stereotypes about the perpetrators and victims of crime. Readers of local print media are more likely to know about and participate in local politics.[51] Whether reading stimulates participation or participation stimulates reading remains an open question.

Just as one cannot lump all national media together for purposes of analysis, so one must differentiate local media along a number of dimensions. Size is one of them. Stations in the largest markets offer considerably more political news than stations in smaller markets.[52] Media outlet ownership characteristics and economic competition also influence the quality of political news coverage from local media outlets. When local news organizations are market-driven because they are owned by shareholders or face stiff competition in the media market, they tend to focus less on substantive political news.[53]

State News: A Neglected Stepchild

All of the news media slight news about state politics. News media situated in state capitals were the only exceptions until they were joined by state-oriented websites, including news and analysis providers such as the Pew Center on the States. Among stories about government and politics in major newspapers and national and local television news, the share of state news is less than 10%. It averages around 6%. The share allotted to local news is better. It garners between one-quarter to close to one-half of the stories in newspapers such as *The New York Times* and *Chicago Tribune* as well as local newscasts.[54]

Why does state news receive the least attention when states play such important roles in politics? Some media, such as the national television networks, specialize in national news, and others specialize in local news—such as the many local television network affiliates. For example, *The Washington Post*, a major national paper, publishes four times more stories on the president than an average local newspaper (15 stories per day vs. 3.5).[55] Even though local media do not specialize in national news, they still cover it. But few daily publications, aside from those located in state capitals, specialize in state news.

One reason state news is neglected is that when it comes to local news outlets, it must compete with the need for a local emphasis. Within states, the media enterprises with enough resources to cover news at all levels of government are usually located in the state's most populous cities (where local news abounds) rather than state capitals.

Another reason is that the flow of state news can be sporadic because most state coverage traditionally focused on the legislature rather than the governor. Because many state legislatures have relatively brief annual sessions or even biennial sessions, the flow of news about legislative activities is often sparse and intermittent. Thus, most daily papers do not make political activities at the state capital a regular full-time beat. In some cases, there is an issue of lack of fit between state boundaries and media markets; New Hampshire is an example—the state's media markets overlap state boundaries, so news must appeal to residents of more than one state. In short, the primary forms of mainstream media prohibit extensive coverage of state politics.[56] See Table 7-1 for an example of spotty local coverage of state legislative elections.

State news is a double loser on the national scene because it is also competing with the need for an emphasis on national politics. State coverage from national media is extremely sparse and spotty. National television normally highlights a small number of states and neglects the rest. Some regions of the country receive more coverage than one might expect from the size of their populations, whereas others receive considerably less. Swing states and states that host early presidential primaries tend to get more coverage because of their role in presidential elections. But national media do not have the time or resources to cover 50 governorships or state legislatures or even the 100 senators who comprise the senate delegation for all 50 states.

Complaints about inadequate coverage must always be evaluated in light of the fact that media space and time are limited. What kinds of stories should the networks have omitted to make room for significant news about the states? There is no good answer. Nonetheless, the growing importance of state politics has made the scarcity and thinness of state news ever more damaging.

Is the Media Environment Nationalizing?

Although the market structures of the U.S. news environment typically map roughly onto national and local political jurisdictions, a growing body of research is pointing to the possibility that the news environment (and news consumption) is nationalizing. Whether this is actually occurring is unclear as of yet; the evidence amassed so far suggest that if the media environment is nationalizing, it's doing so largely in response to market forces: changes in local news supply (i.e., what's available to audiences) and changes in local news demand (i.e., what audiences want). We will start with the supply side.

Mission Creep: National News on Local Media

During the 1990s, ease of access to information about national and global politics contributed to more local coverage of national and world news. New communication technologies allowed local stations to access the pool of national news at will and report it from a local angle. In addition, local stations entered into cooperative news-gathering arrangements that allowed member stations to send their stories to other members in the system via satellite. Local stations consequently became less dependent on network coverage for national and world events and provided it more than before but nowhere close to the amounts reserved for national outlets.

In recent years, those trends reversed, and clear venue jurisdictions between local newspaper coverage and national media outlets largely returned, except for a few notable cases.[57] This is due to the fact that in today's more fragmented and competitive media environment, local outlets realize their bread and butter is in reporting the local news. As national newspapers started to expand their circulation across the country, local news sources doubled down on their niche, leveraging their comparative advantage in the local news marketplace by retaining a strong focus on regional events and politicians.[58] Local newspapers intensified their focus in response to the economic threat from easily accessible national news. For example, the *Richmond Times-Dispatch* featured 60 articles on Eric Cantor's 2014 primary challenger for Virginia's 7th Congressional District compared to the national papers' three articles (*The New York Times*, *The Wall Street Journal*, and *USA Today* combined).[59]

Yet there are exceptions. National newsmakers remain eager to reach the hinterlands, where coverage tends to be gentler and more in tune with the newsmakers' agendas. Presidents tour the country in search of positive news about their policies.[60] It's a win-win for local news reporting; a visit from national political figures provides the opportunity to report on nationally prominent politicians but in the context of a local event. Coverage of members of Congress is similar. They rely heavily on publicity in their home states, at least to the extent that the local media reporting infrastructure will allow for it. Members strive to supply local media with ready-to-use stories posted on websites, blogs, Twitter, or any other platform likely to generate good publicity.[61] In turn, local media tend to pay more attention—and more favorable attention—to their senators and representatives than the national media.[62] Covering the local congressional delegation provides another win-win opportunity because it allows for locally relevant coverage of national politics.

The size and structure of the parent companies that own local newspapers and the size of the market they serve can also affect the ratio of local to national news content newspapers provide. The declining resources described in earlier sections of this chapter matter, too. This is because for national chains, systematizing across outlets and focusing on content common across outlets is cheaper than investing in local reporting at each outlet. Newspapers owned by national chains tend to invest less in their reporting staffs—or make more cuts to newsroom staff—than non–chain owned papers.[63] Similarly, so-called hedge fund media owners—media companies owned and controlled by investment firms—cut newspaper reporting staffs at higher rates relative to more traditional and journalistically oriented ownership types.[64] Research links the purchase of formerly independent media outlets by conglomerates to cost-cutting through disinvestment in local news (i.e., relying on national content instead).[65] Earlier research also shows that media owned by corporations primarily oriented by profit maximization and very large media chains provide less, and less substantive, locally relevant news stories.[66] As long as local newspapers continue to experience steep revenue and staffing declines, pressures to cut costs will likely continue to have a depressive effect on the amount of local coverage provided, with either no news or national news filling in the gap.

In the local television world, local affiliates owned by Sinclair Broadcasting (discussed in Chapter 2) provide another example of when local news venues increase their coverage of national politics. Reflective of some of the trends described above, Sinclair attracted significant public attention for its rapid acquisitions of media properties, widely viewed as accelerating media consolidation. Sinclair is already the second-largest owner of television stations, owning 186 stations in 87 markets across the country with a combined estimated reach of up to 40% of the American public. In 2017, the company tried (and failed) to acquire Tribune media, which would have expanded their level of audience reach to over 70% of Americans.[67]

Perhaps more uniquely for the domain of local news, Sinclair also attracted public attention for its editorial practices. Unlike its national broadcast and cable counterparts, local television has historically remained relatively unmarred by charges of partisan bias. This is likely due to the fact that local television news normally focuses on local politics over national politics, and local politics is less structured by the political debates and acrimony between the two major political parties. Even when local television news does cover national politics, it typically does so through an objective lens. Sinclair represents a departure from both of these norms. According to research from Gregory J. Martin and Joshua McCrain, local news on Sinclair stations covers substantially more national politics than local politics and, when it does, it's from a right-leaning (if not right-wing) point of view. Notably, this editorial slant is not demand-driven; Sinclair stations actually lost audiences in response to the practice, and its owners are quite up front about the overlap between their political objectives and station content.[68] We will return to a discussion of the possible consequences of Sinclair's right-leaning slant in later chapters, but what's relevant here is the editorial practice of prioritizing national political content over coverage of local affairs. Especially given that Sinclair reaches 40% of American households and seems to have plans to acquire as many media properties as it can, the consequence may be a broader return to the mission creep of the 1990s, where local news is increasingly simply another platform for news about national politics. In the next section, we discuss the demand-side drivers of news nationalization. Following that, we will discuss what this trend means for partisanship, polarization, and political accountability.

Audience Creep: Migration From Local to National Venues

The other part of what's driving news nationalization is change on the demand side: namely a reduction in the demand for local news. Some of these shifts in demand are occurring in response to societal changes or political forces; others are occurring in direct response to changes in the supply of local news.

The local news industry struggled following the arrival of digital media. Declining advertising revenues amidst increasingly stiff competition for audience attention continues to accelerate the local news crisis. The impact is felt disproportionately by newspapers, where declines are consistent and fairly drastic, though recently, local television news also declined. As reported elsewhere in this chapter, circulation and revenues continue to drop, and recent increases in newspapers' web traffic are plateauing. The dismal trends in circulation and revenues are reflected in newsroom staffing. While the declines in news resources are troubling, the rapid disappearance of local newspapers is a full-blown disaster. Nearly 2,500 local newspapers closed since 2004, each leaving a former newspaper community without this important resource for local news and information. The growing problem of newspaper closures and the news deserts they leave behind is well-documented. Despite that television is still the most popular media form of news for most Americans and that local television does better than both cable and network television, local television news is also facing the music. In 2018, local television news audiences dropped by 14%.

The migration of local news audiences to national news is both a cause and consequence of these trends. Relatively low demand for local print and television news compared to national news likely explains much of the revenue losses leading to staffing cuts and newspaper closures. On the other hand, when local outlets fail to perform well due to declining resources or when they disappear altogether, formerly loyal local news audiences are forced to seek alternative sources for news. And while local newspapers are disappearing, cable and digital news outlets are proliferating and readily available. The expansion (and fragmentation) of both of these newer media forms also means that news offerings are no longer bundled with local sports, traffic, and entertainment content or tethered by local geographies. People can now find that information from many sources, leaving them free to opt out of local news while getting weather updates from the weather channel and defaulting to national sources for news. When television and newspapers were dominant, local political news was presented alongside other desirable and locally relevant information about local sports, shopping, businesses, and entertainment as well as comics and crossword puzzles. In other words, back then, you had to read the paper or watch the local news to know the weather. The challenge that local news organizations face is that political content is less attractive to many consumers once removed from that bundle. As audiences lose or abandon local newspapers and seek to replace them with local networks such as NextDoor or Facebook groups for other kinds of local information, they are unlikely to seek out local outlets for political information. According to research by Dan Hopkins, this is because audiences prefer stories about national news relative to local news when given the choice, which means they will default to national news outlets with greater reach, if they seek any news replacements at all.[69] The upshot is that as local news availability declines and disappears, regular exposure to national news media is on the rise, leading to the increasingly common prediction that our news environment is nationalizing.[70]

Why News Nationalization Matters

Some may reasonably wonder why we should be concerned about a nationalizing news environment. After all, local newspapers are antiquated and a poor fit with the affordances of the contemporary digital media environment. Local television news has flaws, too: It focuses mostly on traffic, weather, and sports while largely neglecting public affairs. What is so important about local news venues focusing on what's local?

Local news differs from national news, and these differences have important political consequences. First, local news is the only type able to provide the relevant information needed for citizens to hold their state and local political representatives accountable. National news cannot and does not cover all 535 legislative offices of the United States Congress, much less fifty state governments or thousands of municipal governments. Instead, it focuses on the president, Congress, the courts, and federal agencies, with a bias toward emphasizing conflict among those institutions and elites (see Chapters 5 and 6).[71] Second, local news is more trusted relative to its national-level counterparts.[72] This trust gives local news unique influence over citizens' knowledge, attitudes, and behavior, which is critically important in times of crisis. Third, local news is based on relevance to the community rather than partisan conflict, resulting in less-polarizing content relative to that on national news.[73]

Recent evidence shows that healthy local journalism encourages accountability in local government. State government is more corrupt in the absence of robust local news.[74] When local House representatives are not scrutinized by a local press, they exert less effort for their constituencies, are less active in congressional hearings, are more likely to vote the party line, are less likely to serve on district-relevant committees, and appropriate fewer funds to their districts.[75]

Citizens' high trust in local news, relative to national news, makes it more informative.[76] It also encourages state and local political participation. When media cover politics in the surrounding area, citizens' attentiveness, knowledge, and participation are higher for local politics. When local media disappear or decline, so does attentiveness, knowledge, and participation at state and local levels.[77] Local elections are also less competitive in the absence of scrutiny from local media, typically to the benefit of incumbents.[78]

While national news covers officials through a partisan lens, often focusing primarily on extremists or those embroiled in scandal,[79] local coverage of elected officials focuses on their behavior as agents of their constituency. Local news deemphasizes partisanship by covering legislators' locally relevant activities, informing voters about representatives' district performance, and giving officials a platform to discuss local issues. State and local politicians use this coverage to cultivate a "personal vote" based on their service to the local constituency. Local news about how well members of Congress serve their districts most strongly affect voters in the opposing party, allowing for the possibility of performance-based split-ticket voting in lieu of straight-party voting.[80] Research by Joshua Darr, Matthew Hitt, and Johanna Dunaway shows that when local newspapers close, it polarizes voting behavior, and when local newspapers deemphasize national political topics, the rise of affective polarization slows.[81]

The absence of local content and perspectives decreases viewpoint diversity, political accountability, and subnational political knowledge and engagement. If the news environment nationalizes, evidence suggests the possibility of several troubling consequences. Citizens will have fewer opportunities to monitor and influence their elected officials, hindering government performance and accountability. Already rising levels of polarization may also accelerate, along with media mistrust.[82]

The Quality of Subnational News

Maintaining high-quality coverage is often more difficult for local media than for national media. As mentioned, compared with most national television networks, local television has a far greater need for a steady stream of news because it usually has multiple daily newscasts. That puts a premium on broadcasting the latest news rather than repeating more important stories that were featured earlier in the day. It is also more difficult for local newscasters to find interesting political stories and solicit high-quality commentary for them.

The difficulties of maintaining high-quality news have serious conse-quences because local news is the main political information source for many Americans. There are few competing sources of information about local politics, so the local media may be the sole source of information available to interested citizens as well as government officials. It therefore matters if news content is too narrowly focused and reporters are soft on local politicians or spare local projects and policies from criticism out of a sense of local boosterism.

Economics

Lack of economic resources is also a problem for local stations and local newspapers. To maintain profitability through a wide audience reach, local television pitches its programs to a moderately educated audience that presumably is uninterested in sophisticated political analysis. It forces local media to use the most readily available stories, including press releases from the government and the business community, and explains why they seldom feature original, in-depth investigations. Reporters rarely question estimates of costs and benefits of local development projects. They tend to be upbeat in reporting about local business leaders and economic trends. In the words of Phyllis Kaniss, "While there is much in the news and edito-rial columns that is critical of local officials, this criticism is limited when compared with the amount of information that is taken directly, and almost unquestioningly, from official bureaucratic sources."[83] Larger local stations and newspapers with greater financial resources do somewhat better in seeking out important news, providing context for their stories, and resist-ing pressures from advertisers. Smaller news outlets cannot afford to antag-onize the advertising hand that feeds them.

Flaws in Gatekeeping

Besides discouraging hard-hitting investigations or in-depth cover-age of the activities of government officials, the economic pressures facing local news lead to additional flaws in gatekeeping. The old saying "If it bleeds, it leads" tells the story well. Sensational, dramatic, and frightening topics attract and help maintain a wide audience reach among the mod-erately educated local television market audience. Unfortunately, the con-sequences of this are an overemphasis on superficial news, dramatic and sensational crime news, and frequently biased representations of racial and ethnic groups in local news.

Emphasis on Crime News

Local news pressures to attract and retain the interest of local media audiences leads to disproportionate emphasis on crime news. A plentiful diet of crime news is available. On local television news, nearly 32% of the coverage is devoted to the topic. Business and consumer news issues receive less than one-third as much attention.[84] Crime and justice news receives more than triple the news share allotted to any other topic. The trend is pervasive enough to coin the term *crime news script*, which is used to describe the regular and formulaic accounting of violent crime in local television news. The nature of crime news coverage and its prevalence in the media, particularly on television, has long been a matter of concern to public officials and the public. It is widely believed that current coverage practices deflect attention from the social causes of crime and the policies needed to curb it.

Sensational stories about violent crimes also lead to exaggerated fear of crime because the focus is on the most violent incidents, which in fact constitute only a tiny portion of the crime actually committed. Nearly 66% of the crime stories in the *Chicago Tribune* in 2002 dealt with murder or sexual assaults, in a year when these crimes constituted slightly under 2% of the actual crimes in the city. By contrast, white-collar crime, which is more widely prevalent and often threatens public safety, receives little coverage, which conceals its seriousness as a social problem. These figures are typical for crime coverage by local news media.[85] Many experts on criminal behavior contend that extensive, graphic coverage of crime can glamorize it and thereby encourage imitation. News stories that focus selectively on sensational aspects of a case can also mislead the public—and possibly jurors—about who is guilty and who is innocent. When that happens, guilty defendants may escape justice and innocent ones may be convicted.[86]

If there is widespread agreement that current patterns of crime news coverage are excessive and undesirable, why do they continue in daily newspapers and on national and local television throughout the country? There are several reasons. Most importantly, despite their complaints, audiences flock to crime news, partly because it involves personal security but mostly to satisfy a hunger for excitement. This has been the case since the birth of tabloid newspapers more than 150 years ago. When crime news makes huge, front-page headlines, paper sales rise sharply and audience ratings for television news channels skyrocket. The local television news, with its heavy crime component, has eclipsed national news, which carries more serious political stories and less crime, in the battle for high audience ratings. In the entertainment world, crime shows are highly popular. Besides audience appeal, crime news has the advantage of ease of coverage. The police beat can supply a steady diet of new crimes for hungry reporters who prefer to mine a news-rich source rather than work leaner beats.

Biases in Group Representation

Adding to concern about this level of reliance on the crime news coverage tends to overrepresent people of color as perpetrators of crime while underrepresenting them as victims of crime. Both patterns often contribute to audiences' reliance on negative racial stereotypes. Recent research documents that some of the patterns of misrepresentation are changing in ways that reflect the contemporary political context. Latinos, for example, are overwhelmingly overrepresented as undocumented immigrants on news programs, and Muslims are greatly overrepresented as terrorists.[87] We will revisit this topic in Chapter 9.

Subnational Election Coverage

The entire U.S. electoral system is organized to reflect local and statewide politics. All national officials—the president, senators, and representatives—are selected from state-based electoral districts, as are state officials and the half-million local officials who occupy legislative, executive, judicial, and administrative positions throughout the states. Candidates for most of these offices, including scores of positions on local government boards and committees, are of prime interest to geographically limited constituencies. They rarely attract the attention of nationwide broadcasts or the few newspapers that have a nationwide circulation. Their political fate—and that of the areas they serve—therefore depends largely on coverage by local media.

News About the Candidates

The role of the local media in promoting candidates in state and local campaigns is similar to what it is for national campaigns.[88] It is a growing role because state officials are spending more money on their media campaigns now. Because they deal with friendly reporters, they try to obtain news story coverage rather than counting primarily on advertisements.

In the past, subnational officials relied heavily on radio advertisements because of the high costs of television. The new media have changed that pattern. Local officials use them extensively, along with advertisements on local radio stations and old-fashioned flyers and door-to-door campaigning.

Evidence suggests that local stations generally provide citizens with little information about the comparative merits of the candidates. A study of 31 stations in fourteen television markets during the last month of the 2000 presidential election campaign found that local election news broadcasts were much briefer on average, taking up only a 10% slice of the newscast.[89] Studies of senate and gubernatorial races in 2004, 2006, and 2008 showed that local news coverage of these races was less substantive and more negative, especially when produced by local news outlets owned by public shareholders and facing competitive economic pressures.[90]

What's more, these trends are more pronounced when it comes to coverage of nonpresidential politics and elections.[91] News coverage of subnational elections is generally scarce. Table 7-1 shows the percentage of state legislative races that were covered in various amounts from local newspapers in their states in 2012. When offered, only a fraction of stories focus on candidates' policy positions. An Annenberg study on local news coverage of the 2004 campaigns revealed that only 5% of stories focused on local races. Less than a third of that 5% focused on issues. These patterns are especially prevalent among news outlets with parent companies owned and controlled by public shareholders rather than a family or individual and those with low investments in political reporting.[92]

Though useful campaign information is spotty, newspaper endorsements and debates are more important below the national level because most candidates for state and local offices are less familiar to the voters, who therefore turn more to the news media for guidance.[93] When viewers were asked to compare debates among presidential contenders at the national level with debates among candidates for state and local offices, they reported that they found the presidential debates more important and interesting but learned more and were influenced more by the state and local debates.[94] Before watching the debates, 70% of the viewers of the local debates were undecided about their voting choices compared with 40% of viewers of the presidential debates. If lack of information is a disease that plagues national elections, it apparently is far more virulent at state and local levels. Subnational candidate debates and newspaper endorsements are probably not enough to offset what voters could likely access from quality news.

Table 7-1 Local Newspaper Coverage of Selected State Legislative Elections, 2012

State	No Coverage (Percentage)	Number of Article(s) Covering Election					Races	Sources
		1	2	3	4	≥5		
California	15.0	15.0	14.0	10.0	2.0	44.0	100	360
Colorado	30.6	14.1	9.4	10.6	11.8	23.5	85	205
Florida	18.1	19.1	11.4	11.4	7.6	32.4	105	389
Georgia	56.8	14.5	9.4	4.7	3.4	11.1	234	351
Illinois	48.6	13.6	9.6	4.0	4.5	20.8	177	313
Michigan	12.7	4.6	24.6	8.2	15.5	34.5	110	251
Nevada	29.6	27.8	9.3	13.0	5.6	6.7	54	303
New Mexico	62.2	11.7	9.0	5.4	1.8	10.1	111	286
New York	46.0	9.9	11.3	7.5	2.4	33.0	213	355
North Carolina	35.3	12.9	19.4	7.1	4.1	22.2	170	319
Ohio House	43.6	11.1	10.3	11.1	6.0	18.0	117	327
Texas	1.7	4.5	2.2	4.5	4.5	82.7	179	420

Source: Adapted from Sui, M., Paul, N., Shah, P., Spurlock, B., Chastant, B., & Dunaway, J. (2018). The role of minority journalists, candidates, and audiences in shaping race-related campaign news coverage. *Journalism & Mass Communication Quarterly, 95*(4), 1079–1102.

Notes: Election data are from the Candidate Emergence in the States Project; Juenke, E. G., & Shah, P. (2016). Demand and supply: Racial and ethnic minority candidates in white districts. *Journal of Race, Ethnicity, and Politics, 1*(1), 60–90. News content data were obtained from the Access World News archive collection from Newsbank. Ohio data are for the lower chamber only.

News About Referenda

Elections involving local politics often are issue centered. Referenda on prospective policies are examples. Although these political contests have low visibility, their impact on the average citizen can dwarf that of the more publicized contests. Radio and television—the main sources of political information for average voters—carry little news and few editorials about the referenda. Thirty- and sixty-second television advertisements are inadequate to cover the important points of most of these complex issues. However, some radio talk shows give extensive coverage to referenda, albeit often generating more heat than light. Unlike television, major regional newspapers provide comprehensive coverage of referendum issues. They carry extensive background features, pro and con articles and editorials, and news about campaign activities in the urban centers, though not elsewhere in the jurisdiction covered by the referenda.[95]

SUMMARY

The media spotlight falls unevenly on the body politic. In this chapter, we examined institutions that do not receive sufficient light for the U.S. public to adequately assess them and the roles they play in the nation's political life. We also noted problems that arise in reporting about crime, especially when the media focus on sensational events rather than political substance.

Local news is sparse and unevenly distributed at the national level and is chosen by news value rather than political significance criteria. At the subnational level, news about state politics is neglected nearly everywhere in the United States. It is drowned out by national and local news. Hence, most citizens remain uninformed about state politics in their own states as well as sister states. Still, politicians seek it out because reporters at the subnational level rarely scrutinize politicians' performance and policies. News tends to be descriptive rather than provide critical analysis.

News about local politics is far more prevalent than state news. Many regions within metropolitan areas, including suburbs and outlying communities, have local newspapers. Regrettably, the quality of coverage of politics has deteriorated since the beginning of the 20th century. Fewer cities now have their own daily newspapers, and intra-city competition among major dailies has almost vanished. Local television features an average of four hours of news daily, but nearly half of that is an unending tale of weather, crime, and disasters. The political dialogue has suffered. It may be too early, however, to mourn the death of solid local politics coverage. The new technologies that make it affordable to tailor broadcasts to the needs of niche audiences, and the realization that good programming is economically profitable, may restore the vigorous publicity that is essential at all political levels in a democracy.

DISCUSSION QUESTIONS ─────────────────

1. How is the media environment changing in ways that affect the provision and consumption of local and state news? What are the implications for the information provided to citizens? What are the implications for political accountability?

2. How are press–government relations at the state and local levels different from those between press and officials at the national level? How do those differences shape coverage?

3. How are decisions about which stories get covered different at the local level? What are the problems with gatekeeping in local news? How do they impact the quality of the coverage local citizens get and the accuracy of the impressions they form?

4. What does it mean to say that the media environment is nationalizing? Do you think this is actually occurring? Whether you answered yes or no, what are some of the potentially troubling outcomes that we might see arise as a consequence of that trend?

5. Local news obviously has its problems. Is it still sufficient (or sufficient enough) for meeting the information needs of state and local citizens? Why or why not?

6. How well do media cover state and local elections? What factors specific to the provision of local news are shaping coverage of elections at these levels?

READINGS ─────────────────────────────

Abernathy, P. M. (2014). *Saving community journalism: The path to profitability*. University of North Carolina Press.

Abernathy, P. M. (2016). *The rise of a new media baron and the emerging threat of news deserts*. Center for Innovation and Sustainability in Local Media, University of North Carolina at Chapel Hill.

Abernathy, P. M. (2018). *The expanding news desert*. Center for Innovation and Sustainability in Local Media, School of Media and Journalism, University of North Carolina at Chapel Hill.

Abernathy, P. M. (2020). *News deserts and ghost newspapers: Will local news survive?* University at North Carolina at Chapel Hill.

Ali, C. (2017). *Media localism: The policies of place*. University of Illinois Press.

Anderson, C. W., Downie, L., & Schudson, M. (2016). *The news media: What everyone needs to know*. Oxford University Press.

Darr, J. P., Hitt, M. P., & Dunaway, J. L. (2021). *Home style opinion: How local newspapers can slow polarization*. Cambridge University Press.

Harte, D., Howells, R., & Williams, A. (2018). *Hyperlocal journalism: The decline of local newspapers and the rise of online community news*. Routledge.

Hayes, D., & Lawless, J. L. (2021). *News hole: The demise of local journalism and political engagement*. Cambridge University Press.

Hindman, M. (2018). *The internet trap*. Princeton University Press.

Hopkins, D. J. (2018). *The increasingly United States: How and why American political behavior nationalized*. University of Chicago Press.

Kennedy, D. (2018). *The return of the moguls: How Jeff Bezos and John Henry are remaking newspapers for the twenty-first century*. ForeEdge Press.

Napoli, P. M. (2007). *Media diversity and localism: Meaning and metrics*. Erlbaum.

Nielsen, R. K. (2015). *Local journalism: The decline of newspapers and the rise of digital media*. IB Tauris.

Palmer, L. (2019). *The fixers: Local news workers and the underground labor of international reporting*. Oxford University Press.

Ryfe, D. M. (2017). *Journalism and the public: Key concepts in journalism*. Polity Press.

NOTES

1. Lippmann, W. (1965). *Public opinion*. Free Press, p. 229. Originally printed in 1922.

2. Barthel, M., Holcomb, J.., Mahone, J., & Mitchell, A. (2016, November 3). Civic engagement strongly tied to local news habits. *Pew Research Center.* http://www.journalism.org/2016/11/03/civic-engagement-strongly-tied-to-local-news-habits/; Darr, J. P. (2016). *News you use* [Working paper]. Louisiana State University, Baton Rouge, Louisiana, United States.

3. Newman, N., Fletcher, R., Levy, D. A. L., & Nielsen, R. K. (2016). *Reuters institute digital news report 2016*. Reuters Institute for the Study of Journalism. https://reutersinstitute.politics.ox.ac.uk/sites/default/files/research/files/Digital%2520News%2520Report%25202016.pdf

4. Barthel, M. (2016, June 15). 5 key takeaways about the state of the news media in 2016. *Pew Research Center.* http://www.pewresearch.org/fact-tank/2016/06/15/state-of-the-news-media-2016-key-takeaways/; Many would

shrug if their local newspaper closed. (2009, March 12). *Pew Research Center*. http://www.people-press.org/2009/03/12/many-would-shrug-if-their-local-newspaper-closed/; Gronke, P., & Cook, T. E. (2007). Disdaining the media: The American public's changing attitudes toward the news. *Political Communication, 24*(3), 259–281.

5. John J. Pauly and Melissa Eckert (2002) explain why Americans trust local news in "The Myth of 'The Local' in American Journalism," *Journalism and Mass Communication Quarterly, 79*(2), 310–326; also see "Many would shrug if their local newspaper closed." (2009, March 12). *Pew Research Center*. https://www.pewresearch.org/politics/2009/03/12/many-would-shrug-if-their-local-newspaper-closed/

6. Darr, Joshua P., Hitt, M. P., & Dunaway, J. L. (2018). Newspaper closures polarize voting behavior. *Journal of Communication, 68*(6), 1007–1028; Darr, J. P., Hitt, M. P., & Dunaway, J. L. (2021). *Home style opinion: How local newspapers can slow polarization*. Cambridge University Press.

7. Abernathy, P. M. (2018). *The expanding news desert*. Center for Innovation and Sustainability in Local Media, School of Media and Journalism, University of North Carolina at Chapel Hill; Abernathy, P. M. (2020). *News deserts and ghost newspapers: Will local news survive?* University of North Carolina Press. https://www.usnewsdeserts.com/reports/news-deserts-and-ghost-newspapers-will-local-news-survive/

8. Newspapers: Fact sheet. (2019, July 9). *Pew Research Center*. https://www.journalism.org/fact-sheet/newspapers/

9. Newspapers: Fact sheet. (2019, July 9). *Pew Research Center*. https://www.journalism.org/fact-sheet/newspapers/

10. Peterson, E. (2019). Paper cuts: How reporting resources affect political news coverage. *American Journal of Political Science*; Hayes, D., & Lawless, J. L. (2021). *News hole: The demise of local journalism and political engagement*. Cambridge University Press.

11. James N. Rosse coined the term. See Bernstein, J. M., Lacy, S., Cassara, C., & Lau, T-Y. (1990). Geographic coverage by local television news. *Journalism Quarterly, 57*(Winter), 664, Note 4.

12. Hayes, D., & Lawless, J. (2018). The decline of local news and its effects: New evidence from longitudinal data. *The Journal of Politics, 80*(1), 332–336.

13. Peterson, E. (2019). Paper cuts: How reporting resources affect political news coverage. *American Journal of Political Science*.

14. Johnson, M. (2013). Media politics in the states. In R. G. Niemi & J. J. Dyck (Eds.), *Guide to state politics and policy*. CQ Press.

15. Fico, F., & Soffin, S. (1995). Fairness and balance of selected newspaper coverage of controversial national, state, and local issues. *Journalism and Mass Communication Quarterly*, 72(3), 621–633; Bridges, J. A., & Bridges, L. W. (1997). Changes in news use on the front pages of the American daily newspaper, 1986–1993. *Journalism and Mass Communication Quarterly*, 73(4), 826–838; also see State of the news media. (2004). *Pew Research Center.* http://www.journalism.org/topics/state-of-the-news-media/2004/

16. Shearer, E. (2020, July 2). Local news is playing an important role for Americans during the COVID-19 outbreak. *Pew Research Center.* https://www.pewresearch.org/fact-tank/2020/07/02/local-news-is-playing-an-important-role-for-americans-during-covid-19-outbreak/

17. Shearer, E. (2020, July 2). Local news is playing an important role for Americans during the COVID-19 outbreak. *Pew Research Center.* https://www.pewresearch.org/fact-tank/2020/07/02/local-news-is-playing-an-important-role-for-americans-during-covid-19-outbreak/; The state of the news media 2009. (2009, March 16). *Pew Research Center.* http://www.stateofthenewsmedia.org/2009

18. Davie, W. R., & Lee, J-S. (1995). Sex, violence, and consonance/differentiation: An analysis of local TV news values. *Journalism and Mass Communication Quarterly*, 72(1), 128–138; also see Coulson, D. C., Riffe, D., Lacy, S., & St. Cyr, C. R. (2001). Erosion of television coverage of city hall? Perceptions of TV reporters on the beat. *Journalism and Mass Communication Quarterly*, 78(1), 81–92.

19. Riffe, D., & Shaw, E. F. (1990). Ownership, operating, staffing, and content characteristics of "news radio" stations. *Journalism Quarterly*, 67(Winter), 684–691; The state of the news media 2009. (2009, March 16). *Pew Research Center.* http://www.stateofthenewsmedia.org/2009

20. Hindman, M. (2018). *The internet trap: How the digital economy builds monopolies and undermines democracy.* Princeton University Press; Hindman, M. (2008). *The myth of digital democracy.* Princeton University Press.

21. Hindman, M. (2018). *The internet trap: How the digital economy builds monopolies and undermines democracy.* Princeton University Press, p. 110.

22. Johnson, M. (2013). Media politics in the states. In R. G. Niemi & J. J. Dyck (Eds.), *Guide to state politics and policy.* CQ Press.

23. Hindman, M. (2018). *The internet trap: How the digital economy builds monopolies and undermines democracy.* Princeton University Press.

24. Fischer, S., Kokil, K., & Lelkes, Y. (2020). Auditing local news presence on Google News. *Nature Human Behaviour*, 4(12), 1236–1244.

25. Hindman, M. (2018). *The internet trap: How the digital economy builds monopolies and undermines democracy*. Princeton University Press.

26. Hindman, M. (2018). *The internet trap: How the digital economy builds monopolies and undermines democracy*. Princeton University Press.

27. Collier, J., Stroud, N. J., & Dunaway, J. L. (2021). Pathways to deeper news engagement: Factors influencing click behaviors on news sites. *Journal of Computer-Mediated Communication*; Flaxman, S., Goel, S., & Rao, J. M. (2016). Filter bubbles, echo chambers, and online news consumption. *Public Opinion Quarterly, 80*(S1), 298–320.

28. Hindman, M. (2018). *The internet trap: How the digital economy builds monopolies and undermines democracy*. Princeton University Press.

29. This section draws heavily on Johnson, M. (2013). Media politics in the states. In R. G. Niemi & J. J. Dyck (Eds.), *Guide to state politics and policy*. CQ Press.

30. Enda, J., Matsa, K. E., & Boyles, J. L. (2014, July 10). America's shifting statehouse press. http://www.journalism.org/2014/07/10/americas-shifting-state-house-press/

31. Darr, J. P., Hitt, M. P., & Dunaway, J. L. (2021). *Home style opinion: How local newspapers can slow polarization*. Cambridge University Press.

32. Gibbons, G. (2010, June). *Ants at the picnic: A status report on news coverage of state government* [Discussion Paper Series #D-59]. Shorenstein Center on Media, Politics, and Public Policy, Harvard University, Cambridge, MA, United States.

33. Johnson, M. (2013). Media politics in the states. In R. G. Niemi & J. J. Dyck (Eds.), *Guide to state politics and policy*. CQ Press.

34. Grabowicz, P. (2014). Tutorial: The transition to digital journalism. *Berkeley Graduate School of Journalism*. http://www.franglish.fr/NRC/2017_MUC_digital_journalism.pdf; Smith, A. (2010, June 9). Neighbors online. *Pew Research Center*. https://www.pewresearch.org/internet/2010/06/09/neighbors-online/; How news happens: A study of the news ecosystem in one American city. (2010, January 11). *Pew Research Center*. http://www.journalism.org/2010/01/11/how-news-happens/; Spivak, C. (2013). Solving the hyperlocal puzzle. *American Journalism Review, April/May*.

35. Napoli, P. M., Stonbely, S., McCollough, K., & Renninger, B. (2015, June). Assessing the health of local news ecosystems: A comparative assessment of three New Jersey communities. *Rutgers*. http://wp.comminfo.rutgers.edu/mpii-new/wp-content/uploads/sites/129/2015/06/Assessing-Local-Journalism_Final-Draft-6.23.15.pdf; also see Hindman, M. (2011, June 15). Less of the same: The lack of local news on the internet. *Federal Communications Commission*. http://www.fcc.gov/document/media-ownership-study-6-submitted-study/; Local news

in a digital age. (2015, March 5). *Pew Research Center.* https://www.pewre search.org/journalism/2015/03/05/local-news-in-a-digital-age/; Stites, T. (2011, December 8). Layoffs and cutbacks lead to a new world of news deserts. *NiemanLab.* https://www.niemanlab.org/2011/12/tom-stites-layoffs-and-cutbacks-lead-to-a-new-world-of-news-deserts/

36. Shea, D. M. (1999). All scandal politics is local: Ethical lapses, the media, and congressional elections. *Press/Politics, 4*(2), 45–62.

37. Kaniss, P. (1991). *Making local news.* University of Chicago Press, pp. 175–179.

38. Linsky, M. (1986). *How the press affects federal policy making.* Norton, p. 236.

39. Berkowitz, D., & Adams, D. B. (1990). Information subsidy and agenda-building in local television news. *Journalism Quarterly, 67*(Winter), 725.

40. Van Slyke Turk, J., & Franklin, B. (1987). Information subsidies: Agenda-setting traditions. *Public Relations Review, 13,* 29–41; Berkowitz, D. (1987). TV news sources and news channels: A study in agenda-building. *Journalism Quarterly, 64*(Autumn), 508–513.

41. Tsagarousianou, R., Tambini, D., & Brian, C. (Eds.). (1998). *Cyberdemocracy: Technology, cities, and civic networks.* Routledge; Lee, M. (Ed.). (2008). *Government public relations: A reader.* CRC Press; also see Rozell, M. J. (Ed.). (2003). *Media power, media politics.* Rowman and Littlefield.

42. Taylor, C. E., Lee, J-S., & Davie, W. R. (2000). Local press coverage of environmental conflict. *Journalism and Mass Communication Quarterly, 77*(1), 175–192.

43. Kaniss, P. (1991). *Making local news.* University of Chicago Press, p. 107; also see Dunaway, J. (2008). Markets, ownership, and the quality of campaign news coverage. *Journal of Politics 70*(4), 1193–1202.

44. News selection criteria are discussed in Gant, C., & Dimmick, J. (2000). Making local news: A holistic analysis of sources, selection criteria, and topics. *Journalism and Mass Communication Quarterly, 77*(3), 628–638; Rosenstiel, R., Just, M., Belt, T. L., Pertilla, A., Dean, W., & Chinni, D. (2007). *We interrupt this newscast: How to improve local news and win ratings, too.* Cambridge University Press.

45. Kaniss, P. (1991). *Making local news.* University of Chicago Press, p. 126.

46. Kaniss, P. (1991). *Making local news.* University of Chicago Press, p. 76.

47. Project for Excellence in Journalism. (2004). State of the news media 2004. *Pew Research Center.* https://www.pewresearch.org/wp-content/uploads/sites/8/2017/05/State-of-the-News-Media-Report-2004-FINAL.pdf; Pew Project for Excellence in Journalism. (2009). State of the news media, 2009. *Pew Research Center.* https://assets.pewresearch.org/files/journalism/State-of-the-News-Media-Report-2009-FINAL.pdf; Jurkowitz, M., Mitchell, A.,

Santhanam, L. H., Adams, S., Anderson, M., & Vogt, N. (2013, March 17). The changing TV news landscape. *Pew Research Center.* http://www.stateofthe-media.org/2013/special-reports-landing-page/the-changing-tv-news-landscape/.

48. Gartner, S. S. (2004). Making the international local: The terrorist attack on the USS *Cole,* local casualties, and media coverage. *Political Communication,* 21(2), 139–159.

49. Gartner, S. S. (2004). Making the international local: The terrorist attack on the USS *Cole,* local casualties, and media coverage. *Political Communication,* 21(2), 139–159.

50. Hamilton, J. T. (2016). *Democracy's detectives.* Harvard University Press.

51. Moy, P., McCluskey, M. R., McCoy, K., & Spratt, M. (2004). Political correlates of local news media use. *Journal of Communication,* 54(3), 532–546; Gilliam, F. D., Jr., & Iyengar, S. (2000). Prime suspects: The influence of local television news on the viewing public. *American Journal of Political Science,* 44(3), 560–573; Scheufele, D. A., Shanahan, J., & Kim, S-H. (2002). Who cares about local politics? Media influences on local political involvement, issue awareness, and attitude strength. *Journalism and Mass Communication Quarterly,* 79(2), 427–444; Darr, J. P. (2015). *Using the local news: Campaigns, newspapers, and accountability* [Doctoral dissertation]. University of Pennsylvania, Philadelphia, Pennsylvania, United States. https://repository.upenn.edu/edissertations/1036/

52. Hess, S. (1991). *Live from Capitol Hill! Studies of Congress and the media.* Brookings Institution Press, p. 49; also see Taylor, C. E., Lee, J-S., & Davie, W. R. (2000). Local press coverage of environmental conflict. *Journalism and Mass Communication Quarterly,* 77(1), 175–192.

53. Hamilton, J. T. (2004). *All the news that's fit to sell.* Princeton University Press; Dunaway, J. (2008). Markets, ownership, and the quality of campaign news coverage. *Journal of Politics* 70(4), 1193–1202.

54. Graber's research is based on national television news, local news, and newspapers in 2004. National television news data were obtained from the Vanderbilt Television News Archive. ABC local news was obtained from the Museum of Broadcast Communication. CBS and NBC local news were recorded by the author.

55. Darr, J. P. (2015). *Using the local news: Campaigns, newspapers, and accountability* [Doctoral dissertation]. University of Pennsylvania, Philadelphia, Pennsylvania, United States. https://repository.upenn.edu/edissertations/1036/; Cohen, J. E. (2010). *Going local.* Cambridge University Press.

56. Hess, S. (1992, April). *Levels of the game: Federalism and the American news system.* Paper presented at the Hofstra University Conference, Hempstead, NY, United States; Johnson, M. (2013). Media politics in the states. In R. G. Niemi & J. J. Dyck (Eds.), *Guide to state politics and policy.* CQ Press.

57. Carpini, M. X. D., Keeter, S., & Kennamer, J. D. (1994). Effects of the news media environment on citizen knowledge of state politics and government. *Journalism & Mass Communication Quarterly, 71*(2), 443–456.

58. George, L. M., & Waldfogel, J. (2006). *The New York Times* and the market for local newspapers. *American Economic Review, 96*(1), 435–447.

59. Darr, J. P., Hitt, M. P., & Dunaway, J. L. (2018). Newspaper closures polarize voting behavior. *Journal of Communication, 68*(6), 1007–1028.

60. Eshbaugh-Soha, M., & Peake, J. S. (2008). The presidency and local media: Local newspaper coverage of President George W. Bush. *Presidential Studies Quarterly, 38*(4), 609–630; Eshbaugh-Soha, M. (2008). Local newspaper coverage of the presidency. *Press/Politics, 13,* 103–119; Cohen, J. E. (2010). *Going local.* Cambridge University Press.

61. Vinson, C. D. (2003). *Local media coverage of Congress and its members: Through local eyes.* Hampton Press; Fogarty, B. J. (2008). The strategy of the story: Media monitoring legislative activity. *Legislative Studies Quarterly, 33*(3), 445–469; Schaffner, B. F. (2006). Local coverage and the incumbency advantage in the U.S. House. *Legislative Studies Quarterly, 31,* 491–512.

62. Hess, S. (1991). *Live from Capitol Hill! Studies of Congress and the media.* Brookings Institution Press; Vinson, C. D. (2003). *Local media coverage of Congress and its members: Through local eyes.* Hampton Press.

63. Peterson, E. (2019). Paper cuts: How reporting resources affect political news coverage. *American Journal of Political Science*; Hayes, D., & Lawless, J. L. (2021). *News hole: The demise of local journalism and political engagement.* Cambridge University Press.

64. Peterson, E., & Dunaway, J. (2020). *Changing media ownership and new news barons: Implications for news investment?* Paper presented at the Annual Meeting of the American Political Science Association.

65. Martin, G., & McCrain, J. (2021). *The political consequences of media consolidation* [Working paper]. Stanford University, Stanford, California, United States.

66. Dunaway, J. (2008). Markets, ownership, and the quality of campaign news coverage. *Journal of Politics 70*(4), 1193–1202.

67. Sinclair Broadcast Group. (2021). *About.* [Website]. https://sbgi.net/#About; See also Levendusky, M. S. (2021). How does local TV news change viewers' attitudes? The case of Sinclair Broadcasting. *Political Communication.* https://doi.org/10.1080/10584609.2021.1901807

68. Martin, G. J., & McCrain, J. (2019). Local news and national politics. *American Political Science Review, 133*(2), 372–384.

69. Hopkins, D. J. (2018). *The increasingly United States: How and why American political behavior nationalized.* University of Chicago Press.

70. Darr, J. P., Hitt, M. P., & Dunaway, J. L. (2021). *Home style opinion: How local newspapers can slow polarization.* Cambridge University Press.

71. Douglas, A. R. (2004). *Congress, the press, and political accountability.* Princeton University Press.

72. Guess, A., Nyhan, B., & Reifler, J. (2018). *All media trust is local? Findings from the 2018 Poynter Media trust survey.* https://cpb-us-e1.wpmucdn.com/sites .dartmouth.edu/dist/5/2293/files/2021/03/media-trust-report-2018.pdf; Gramlich, J. (2019). Q&Q: What Pew Research Center's new survey says about local news in the U.S. *Pew Research Center.* https://www.pewresearch .org/fact-tank/2019/03/26/qa-what-pew-research-centers-new-survey-says-about-local-news-in-the-u-s/

73. Darr, J. P., Hitt, M. P., & Dunaway, J. L. (2018). Newspaper closures polarize voting behavior. *Journal of Communication, 68*(6), 1007–1028; Padgett, J., Dunaway, J. L., & Darr, J. P. (2019). "As seen on TV? How gatekeeping makes the US House seem more extreme." *Journal of Communication, 69*(6), 696–719.

74. Campante, F. R., & Do, Q-A. (2014). Isolated capital cities, accountability, and corruption: Evidence from US states. *American Economic Review, 104*(8), 2456–2481.

75. Snyder, Jr., J. M., & Strömberg, D. (2010). Press coverage and political accountability. *Journal of Political Economy, 118*(2), 355–408.

76. Fowler, E. F. (2020). Strategy over substance and national in focus? Local television coverage of politics and policy in the United States. In A. Gilyas & D. Baines (Eds.), *The Routledge Companion to Local Media and Journalism* (pp. 185–192). Routledge; Gramlich, J. (2019). Q&Q: What Pew Research Center's new survey says about local news in the U.S. *Pew Research Center.* https://www .pewresearch.org/fact-tank/2019/03/26/qa-what-pew-research-centers-new-survey-says-about-local-news-in-the-u-s/

77. Gentzkow, M., Shapiro, J. M., & Sinkinson, M. (2011). The effect of newspaper entry and exit on electoral politics. *American Economic Review, 101*(7), 2980–3018; Hayes, D., & Lawless, J. (2015). As local news goes, so goes citizen engagement: Media, knowledge, and participation in U.S. House Elections. *Journal of Politics, 77,* 447–462, https://doi.org/10.1086/679749; Hopkins, D. J. (2018). *The increasingly United States: How and why American political behavior nationalized.* University of Chicago Press.

78. Schulhofer-Wohl, S., & Garrido, M. (2013). Do newspapers matter? Short-run and long-run evidence from the closure of *The Cincinnati Post*. *Journal of Media Economics*, 26(2), 60–81; Rubado, M. E., & Jennings, J. T. (2020). Political consequences of the endangered local watchdog: Newspaper decline and mayoral elections in the United States. *Urban Affairs Review*, 56(5), 1327–1356; but also see Gentzkow, M., Shapiro, J. M., & Sinkinson, M. (2011). The effect of newspaper entry and exit on electoral politics. *American Economic Review*, 101(7), 2980–3018.

79. Padgett, J., Dunaway, J. L., & Darr, J. P. (2019). As seen on TV? How gatekeeping makes the US House seem more extreme. *Journal of Communication*, 69(6), 696–719.

80. Darr, J. P., Hitt, M. P., & Dunaway, J. L. (2018). Newspaper closures polarize voting behavior. *Journal of Communication*, 68(6), 1007–1028.

81. Darr, J. P., Hitt, M. P., & Dunaway, J. L. (2021). *Home style opinion: How local newspapers can slow polarization*. Cambridge University Press.

82. Darr, J. P., Hitt, M. P., & Dunaway, J. L. (2018). Newspaper closures polarize voting behavior. *Journal of Communication*, 68(6), 1007–1028; Darr, J. P., Hitt, M. P., & Dunaway, J. L. (2021). *Home style opinion: How local newspapers can slow polarization*. Cambridge University Press.

83. Kaniss, P. (1991). *Making local news*. University of Chicago Press, pp. 90–91.

84. Rosenstiel, R., Just, M., Belt, T. L., Pertilla, A., Dean, W., & Chinni, D. (2007). *We interrupt this newscast: How to improve local news and win ratings, too*. Cambridge University Press; Vinson, C. D., & Ertter, J. S. (2002). Entertainment or education: How the media cover the courts. *Press/Politics*, 7(4), 80–89.

85. Vinson, C. D., & Ertter, J. S. (2002). Entertainment or education: How the media cover the courts. *Press/Politics*, 7(4), 80–89; also see Romer, D., Jamieson, K. H., & Aday, S. (2003). Television news and the cultivation of fear of crime. *Journal of Communication*, 53(1), 88–104.

86. Sotirovic, M. (2003). How individuals explain social problems: The influence of media use. *Journal of Communication*, 53(1), 122–137.

87. Gilliam, F. D., Jr., & Iyengar, S. (2000). Prime suspects: The influence of local television news on the viewing public. *American Journal of Political Science*, 44(3), 560–573; Dixon, T. L. (2015). Good guys are still always in white? Positive change and continued misrepresentation of race and crime on local television news. *Communication Research*. https://doi.org/10.1177%2F0093650215579223; Dixon, T. L., & Williams, C. L. (2015). The changing misrepresentation of race and crime on network and cable news. *Journal of Communication*, 65, 24–39.

88. Schaffner, B. F. (2006). Local coverage and the incumbency advantage in the U.S. House. *Legislative Studies Quarterly, 31*, 491–512.

89. Farnsworth, S. J., & Lichter, S. R. (2004). Increasing candidate-centered television discourse: Evaluating local news coverage of campaign 2000. *Press/Politics, 9*(2), 76–93.

90. Dunaway, J. (2008). Markets, ownership, and the quality of campaign news coverage. *Journal of Politics 70*(4), 1193–1202; Dunaway, J. (2013). Media ownership and story tone in campaign news. *American Politics Research, 41*(1), 24–53; Dunaway, J. L., Davis, N. T., Padgett, J., & Scholl, R. M. (2015). Objectivity and information bias in campaign news. *Journal of Communication, 65*, 770–792.

91. Arnold, R. D. (2004). *Congress, the press, and political accountability*. Russell Sage Foundation.

92. Kaplan, M., Goldstein, K., & Hale, M. (2005). *Local news coverage of the 2004 campaigns: An analysis of nightly broadcasts in 11 markets*. Lear Center Local News Archive. https://www.policyarchive.org/handle/10207/6408; Dunaway, J. (2008). Markets, ownership, and the quality of campaign news coverage. *Journal of Politics 70*(4), 1193–1202.

93. St. Dizier, B. (1985). The effects of newspaper endorsements and party identification on voting choice. *Journalism Quarterly, 62*(Autumn), 589–594.

94. Lichtenstein, A. (1982). Differences in impact between local and national televised political candidates' debates. *Western Journal of Speech Communication, 46*, 291–298; also see Bystrom, D., Roper, C., Gobetz, R., Massey, T., & Beall, C. (1991). The *Effects of a Televised Gubernatorial Debate. Political Communication Review, 16*, 57–80.

95. For an excellent overview of the referendum process, see de Vreese, C. H., & Semetko, H. (2004). *Political campaigning in referendums*. Routledge.

Foreign Affairs Coverage

Learning Objectives

1. Explain whether and how people pay attention to news about foreign affairs, including American media coverage of international events and issues.

2. Discuss journalists' reporting and gatekeeping practices behind news about foreign affairs.

3. Examine how war and international conflict is covered by the press with regard to the tensions between press and government officials over information control.

In late 2019, American news network NBC asked audiences for both NBC and MSNBC to share what they thought were the biggest news stories of the last decade. Data from their submissions, shown in Figure 8-1, reflect how little foreign affairs appears in American press coverage. Among all of the stories shown, only one is about something occurring explicitly outside the United States (U.S.), and only a few, such as climate change, the environment, wildfires, social issues, or technology, can reasonably be classified as addressing truly global issues or events—those affecting or occurring both in the U.S. and other parts of the world. However, because these data are based on audience perceptions of the biggest stories, we cannot tell from them how many international stories were covered. Nor can we know anything about whether audiences would have been interested in stories that were not covered. Perhaps audiences would nominate more international stories if more were covered; it is difficult to know, and evidence for American public interest in global issues is mixed. For example, 2020 Google search trend

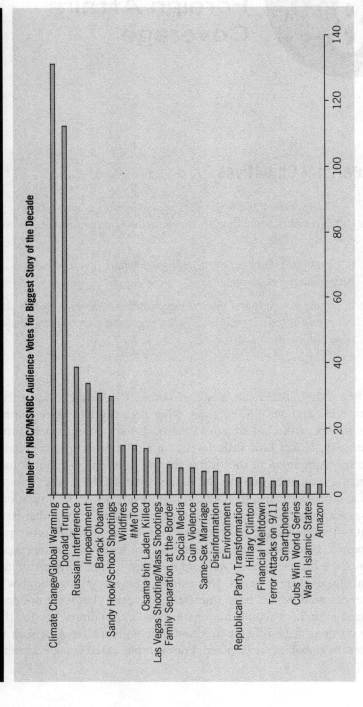

Figure 8-1 The Biggest Stories of the Decade According to NBC/MSNBC Audiences

Number of NBC/MSNBC Audience Votes for Biggest Story of the Decade

Climate Change/Global Warming
Donald Trump
Russian Interference
Impeachment
Barack Obama
Sandy Hook/School Shootings
Wildfires
#MeToo
Osama bin Laden Killed
Las Vegas Shooting/Mass Shootings
Family Separation at the Border
Social Media
Gun Violence
Same-Sex Marriage
Disinformation
Environment
Republican Party Transformation
Hillary Clinton
Financial Meltdown
Terror Attacks on 9/11
Smartphones
Cubs Win World Series
War in Islamic States
Amazon

0   20   40   60   80   100   120   140

Source: Adapted from NBC News. (2019, December 31). *The biggest stories of the decade—according to you.* https://www.nbcnews.com/news/us-news/biggest-stories-decade-according-you-n1106956

data for the U.S. show *Iran* as the 5th most common term searched in news and *Australia fires* as the 10th most common. Yet, in a study of Google search trend data spanning 111 countries and five languages, the U.S. ranked 28th among English-speaking countries in the sample for use of the search term *human rights*. Though the search trend data vary over time and rates for human rights searches are occasionally high in response to salient events, even at its peaks, the evidence suggests that the American public's interest in human rights is comparatively low, a finding consistent with much of the research on public interest in foreign affairs.[1] The market-based media system in the U.S. mandates that coverage typically caters to audience preferences, and decades of research shows a high correlation between issues that earn high levels of media coverage and public perceptions about those issues that are most important. Regardless of whether low interest is driving low foreign affairs coverage or if low coverage is driving low interest, the American media cover foreign affairs only sporadically relative to domestic events and issues, and this generally reflects the audience's relatively low levels of interest.

Without enough coverage, what are the links—if any—between the mass media and the process of creating foreign policies and producing policy outputs? How do governments use the media to further their policy objectives around the world? Do the media perform their watchdog role appropriately in times of war or with respect to foreign affairs more generally? In this chapter, we will try to answer such provocative questions about how the mass media influence U.S. foreign policy.

We will first focus on the overall significance that U.S. media and U.S. citizens assign to news about foreign countries. Then we will point out the main differences between the production of foreign and domestic news. We will consider the unique problems newspeople face in collecting foreign affairs news and shaping it to meet newsworthiness criteria while heeding the canons of journalistic ethics and independence. Producing high-quality foreign news both in times of peace and in times of war is an extraordinarily difficult task. We shall note how well it is currently carried out and point to accomplishments and failures.

The Foreign News Niche

Newspeople commonly assume that the U.S. public is interested primarily in what goes on in the United States. Reports about the public's ignorance of foreign countries and foreign affairs lend credence to these assumptions. Americans profess modest interest in foreign news, but when given a choice, they do not seek it out. When survey researchers asked a randomly selected national sample of people in 2016 about the types of news that they follow routinely, less than a quarter of the respondents (19%) claimed to follow international news "very closely," a marked decline from the 52% who reported following international news "most of the time" in 2004. These numbers tend to fluctuate depending on the overall thrust of the news. How interest in foreign affairs waxes and wanes depends on the visibility of U.S. foreign involvements.[2]

Even when interest rises, it is rarely profound. Most news consumers do not follow stories about international events very closely. Very few are inclined to take actions to foster their beliefs, and if they do, their enthusiasm tends to be short-lived. Interest in news about the weather, crime, sports, the local community, health, local government, the nation, science, and business—in that order—surpasses interest in news from abroad.[3] These patterns reflect the unfortunate irony that citizens neglect the genre of news they arguably need most: Foreign affairs reporting from a robust press is an essential ingredient in the public's ability to exert pressure on leaders and influence foreign policy. Without it, opposition voices are not sufficiently brought to light for the public, and democratic leaders can act at will in foreign policy with little accountability.[4]

Most Americans do not make foreign news a primary focus of attention, and many print and electronic media outlets are providing less international coverage over time. In 2016, a year that included a Syrian refugee crisis, a major terrorism event in Paris, and ongoing unrest in the Middle East, the top ten stories related to foreign policy received only 504 minutes of total coverage on the major broadcast networks' nightly news programs combined, amounting to less than 4% of total coverage. Compared to other networks, CNN generally devotes more time to international news stories and stories concerning U.S. affairs abroad. The format of news websites affords more space for news, which may be one reason why international news typically accounts for a larger percent of the news space on websites relative to their television programming.[5] On social media platforms, news use has increased over time, but the proportion of all social media and other forms of digital news content dedicated to international news is difficult to estimate. However, as the Google search trend data cited above suggest, news engagement measures show some evidence of the popularity of international news topics among digital audiences.[6] Differences in attention to foreign news are significant because the various platforms attract different clientele and vary in overall credibility. It is important to keep in mind that news space percentage figures tell us nothing about actual amounts of news. Ten percent of *The New York Times* news space can accommodate much more information than 10% of the news space of a 15-minute radio show. Furthermore, *The New York Times* remains the preferred information source for "official" Washington news.

Compared with attention to domestic affairs, foreign news is a neglected stepchild in terms of space, time, and prominence of display. Figure 8-2 demonstrates that few of the major networks' foreign news stories earned much airtime in 2019. Only five of the top twenty stories focused on foreign affairs at all, and two of those five stories were related to scandals plaguing the Trump administration—Russia's interference in the 2016 U.S. election and Trump's phone call with Ukraine's Zelensky. A third was about tensions between Iran and the U.S. in the Persian Gulf. In only two stories—one on the Syrian civil war and the other on Hurricane Dorian in the Bahamas—was the U.S. not central to the story.

These patterns in coverage reveal that news selection criteria for international news are far more rigorous; the bar for an international story to be judged newsworthy enough to get aired or printed is much higher. To be published in the mainstream media, foreign news must have a more profound impact on the political, economic, or cultural concerns of the United States than domestic news. It must involve people of more exalted status and/or entail more violence or disaster.[7] During crises, particularly prolonged ones that endanger U.S. lives, foreign coverage may double or even triple; it may even drown out other news. Conversely, the number of stories and their length shrink when times seem unusually calm.[8]

Making Foreign News

Although news making for domestic stories and for foreign stories differ substantially, there are many similarities. First, we will consider the gatekeepers—the corps of foreign correspondents who are the frontline echelon among gatherers of foreign affairs news for the legacy media. Then we will discuss the setting for news selection, the criteria for choosing stories and the means of gathering them, the constraints on news production, and finally the effects of gatekeeping on foreign affairs coverage.

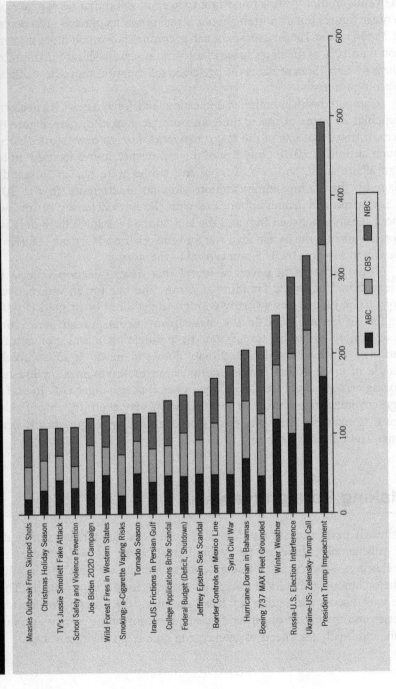

Figure 8-2 Broadcast Network News Minutes Devoted to Top Twenty Stories of 2019

Source: Adapted from Tyndall Report, Year in Review 2019. (2020). *Tyndall Report.* http://tyndallreport.com/yearinreview2019/.

Gatekeepers: The Vanishing News Bureaus

A combination of advancing technology, globalization of news, and efforts to cut costs is changing gatekeeping for foreign news. Most news about events happening throughout the world used to be collected and sold by four major news agencies: the U.S.–owned Associated Press (AP), which leads the pack; Britain's Reuters, which merged with Canada's Thomson Corporation (Thomson-Reuters is now based in New York City); France's Agence France-Presse, the world's oldest news agency, dating back to 1835; and ITAR-Tass, which superseded the Soviet news agency, Tass, in 1992.[9] Among these world-class wire services, AP has historically been the largest and is typically considered the dominant international news agency.[10]

The AP maintains news operations in over 250 locations worldwide.[11] It provides print and broadcast news in multiple languages to clients in 97 countries. The AP produces 2,000 stories a day, 1 million photos and 70,000 videos per year, with 1.7 million video clips stored in archive.[12] AP reporters are initial gatekeepers who ferret out the stories that make up the pool from which other gatekeepers select reports or find leads to pursue stories more fully. Because news agency reporters work for a variety of clients throughout the world, their news reports must be bland so that they do not offend views spanning a wide political spectrum. Wire service news therefore emphasizes fast and ample factual reports of ongoing events. It does not provide interpretations but leaves that to the users of its reports.

Besides the wire service bureaus, much foreign news once came from news bureaus maintained by various other news organizations. That has changed. Permanent international bureaus are no longer the model for handling most international coverage. There are a few notable exceptions, such as National Public Radio (NPR) and *The New York Times,* which recently expanded their foreign correspondent corps abroad. *The Times* can afford to operate its twenty-six bureaus because their cost is defrayed largely by income from selling syndicated stories to other media enterprises. CNN is a major player in international broadcasting and cable news. It has close to forty editorial operations around the globe and approximately 3,000 employees, scattered throughout the world, who collect and report news in multiple languages for worldwide audiences. CNN reports reach viewers in 90 million U.S. households, and CNN International reaches more than 370 million households and hotel rooms across the globe. CNN digital is a top news destination and regularly reaches 200 million unique visitors per month.[13] In part due to the wide audience, CNN's coverage constitutes a mixed bag of events and interviews, ranging from the trivial to the highly significant. It records whatever is readily and inexpensively available, so viewers are the first to see a breaking news event at close range. Table 8-1 shows the types of news that CNN offers to its global audiences on a typical day. It represents an impressive array of newsworthy events happening in diverse locations north and south of the equator.

Gatekeepers: The New Types of Foreign Correspondents

In the past, specially trained, experienced American journalists supplied much of the foreign news in the U.S. press. These elite journalists have become nearly extinct. New types of foreign correspondents are joining and replacing them. Who are these new reporters? Journalism scholars John Maxwell Hamilton and Eric Jenner identify several types.[14] In addition to the traditional U.S. correspondents stationed abroad, many foreign reporters now supply American media with news about other countries and regions. Their stories may lack the traditional U.S. perspective, but they are gathered at a fraction of the cost of stationing a U.S. newspaper correspondent abroad. The price doubles for broadcast correspondents. Given these cost differentials, it should come as no surprise that less than a third of the correspondents reporting news from abroad to the United States are Americans.[15] The belief that only native Americans are capable of reporting news with an appropriate U.S. flavor has given way to the idea that foreign news reported by foreigners may actually be beneficial. It may tell Americans how people in other countries interpret the political scene, which may alleviate concerns that foreign affairs coverage often comes from Westernized or ethnocentric perspectives.

Encouraged by easy international travel and cheap airfare, more and more U.S.–based media are sending correspondents abroad for short jaunts to report about a particular event. These "parachute" journalists travel from the United States or, less commonly, from overseas jumping-off points. *USA Today*, for example, uses its overseas bureaus as regional jumping-off points for parachuters. Parachute journalism has become almost routine for large news organizations and fairly common for smaller ones. The horde of U.S. parachute journalists dispatched to report about the death of Pope John Paul II in 2005 and the selection of his successor is a good example. The majority of the news organizations that sent more than 6,000 journalists to Rome were newcomers to gathering foreign news.[16] Their inexperience was painfully apparent but only to knowledgeable news consumers.

So-called premium service foreign correspondents are another innovation. Hamilton and Jenner cite the example of the Bloomberg subscription news service.[17] Besides its contingent of expert, U.S.–based

Table 8-1 One Day of CNN World News Headlines, April 6, 2021

Europe	Asia
Italy: Italy makes vaccines compulsory for health workers. But some are unconvinced.	**North Korea:** North Korea won't participate in Tokyo Olympic Games.
Russia: Putin signs law allowing him to run for two more terms as Russian president.	**China:** China's plans to "improve" democracy in Hong Kong could spell the end of the city's opposition.
England: UK government proposes pilots for COVID-19 passports as way out of lockdown.	**Myanmar:** Myanmar's military is waging war on its citizens. Some say it's time to fight back.
Hungary: Hungary records the deadliest day of the pandemic, despite its leading vaccine rollout.	**Japan:** Japan's powerful patriarchy often sidelines women. Fixing that won't be easy.

Africa	Middle East
Kenya: Kenya orders closure of two refugee camps, gives ultimatum to UN agency.	**Jordan:** Jordan bans social media chatter on royal family as king tries to draw line under crisis.
Mozambique: Dozens unaccounted for in Mozambique after Islamist attack, rights groups say.	**Israel:** In jarring day for Israel, Netanyahu's corruption trial resumes as coalition talks heat up.
Tanzania: Did Tanzania's COVID-denying leader die of the coronavirus?	**United Arab Emirates:** UAE's tiny lunar rover will face big challenges on the moon.

Americas	United States
Argentina: Argentina's president tests positive for COVID-19 after vaccine.	**California:** VP Harris is the latest White House official to appear with California Gov. Newsom amid recall effort.
Chile: Chile's government distributed faulty birth control pills. Now more than 150 people are pregnant.	**Mississippi:** Mississippi GOP governor pushes back on vaccine passports: "I don't think it's a good thing to do in America."
Brazil: Political turbulence in Brazil overshadows COVID-19 crisis.	**Arkansas:** Arkansas Republican governor vetoes anti-trans health care bill.

Source: World News. (2021, April 6). *CNN.com.*

print and broadcast reporters, who cover economic stories in the United States, Bloomberg has a large number of print and broadcast reporters stationed in more than 70 countries around the globe.[18] A single subscription to Bloomberg news pays for access to global financial news gathered by this international corps of correspondents. News from all over the world may not be a high priority for most Americans, but in the age of globalization, foreign news is essential for large corporations with customers or branches all over the world. Nearly all of these corporations also have their own reporters, who often are professional journalists, located abroad to dispatch salient news to their U.S. bases. Much of this news is not confidential and spreads beyond the confines of the company to the news media.

GlobalPost is a comparatively recent addition to the roster of news services that supply worldwide news to their members. Its reporters live in various parts of the world, including many countries that have received little attention from traditional news agencies. In addition to the usual focus on particular countries or regions, GlobalPost also has specialists who cover particular institutions, such as nongovernmental organizations (NGOs), unique perspectives such as world views, problems such as the environment and health, or activities such as commerce and sports. The GlobalPost business model may herald the emergence of a new business model for news. It consists of a combination of member fees, sales of individual stories, and syndication and advertising fees. The service is designed to meet the needs of media companies, businesses, NGOs, and nonprofit organizations.[19]

Another stream of special interest news comes from public relations agencies hired by foreign countries to promote their images. Public relations campaigns commonly promote tourism and trade (especially special events such as the Olympics) or in the wake of political crises. Many countries contract for professional image management. Citizens for a Free Kuwait, a front organization for the government of Kuwait, for example, spent nearly $11 million with only one public relations firm to burnish Kuwait's image in the months after it had been invaded by Iraq.[20] By stimulating or suppressing media coverage, public relations agencies try to turn the political climate in their clients' favor.[21]

The largest group of foreign correspondents—if that name actually fits—are nonprofessionals who use websites and social media to report their observations from abroad or from U.S. locations. Citizen journalists and bystanders record and stream events as they happen—as was demonstrated in much of the Arab Spring coverage. Technological advances such as the widespread use of mobile devices has also influenced professional journalists' reporting of international events, especially live-event news. In fact, one criticism of the BBC's coverage of the Arab Spring was that the news organization relied too heavily on content generated by nonprofessionals without adequately flagging the content as user-generated material and referencing how it was authenticated.[22] The potential now exists for journalists to rely more on live feeds and crowd-sourcing (the use of submitted content from members of the public at a newsworthy event) and less on the reports and interpretations of officials. In their study of how these technologies are shaping news, media scholars Sean Aday and W. Lance Bennett found that event-driven reporting is now more likely but officials remain heavily relied upon.[23]

Finally, large numbers of Americans now draw their information about events beyond U.S. borders from internet visits to foreign newspapers and foreign broadcasts. They can learn, for example, about turmoil and developments in the Middle East from an Arab perspective by turning to Al Jazeera, or from a French perspective by reading *Le Monde*. Or they can listen to news from Britain's BBC or turn to English-language news from China transmitted by CNN. International news can be scanned easily and inexpensively by anyone who has a computer connected to the internet. How many people use foreign news sources and what the consequences are remains uncertain, but Table 8-2 provides a sense of U.S. audience appetites for international news online based on Web traffic statistics for news sites.

Given that news reporting through diverse cultural lenses varies in perspective, the same raw story materials yield different end products. At times, the versions vary so widely that they seem to cover totally different situations. The language in which news content is offered matters, too. Spanish- and English-language media outlets in the United States, for example, cover immigration using different frames, in different volumes, and using different tones.[24] In a comparison of French and American media depictions of immigration, Rodney Benson finds both similarities and differences in coverage. Structural similarities at the media outlet level, such as commercial pressures, result in similar patterns in coverage while cultural differences explain divergent coverage. Though globalization and media systems and structures exert pressures for particular kinds of content, cultural and political differences across nation-states can still produce divergent coverage of the same events and issues.[25]

It has become impossible to profile the "typical" foreign correspondent because there are so many new types. Foreign correspondents used to be better educated than domestic journalists, more experienced, more worldly wise, and better paid. They were U.S. citizens, and like most

Table 8-2 U.S. Audience Web Traffic on News Sites From Around the World, November 2016

Place	Number of Sites	Total Unique Visitors	Average Daily Visitors	Total Visits	Average Minutes per Visit	Average Visits per Visitor	Example Sites
United Kingdom	21	63,415,000	4,942,000	187,068,000	104	53	telegraph.co.uk theguardian.com bbc.com
Russia	12	3,803,000	309,000	10,696,000	37	45	rt.com sputniknews.com
India	7	3,489,000	451,000	20,661,000	22	51	indianexpress.com
Latin America	11	1,097,000	191,000	8,136,000	42	81	latintimes.com eltiempo.com
China	8	768,000	71,000	13,000	22	32	cctv.com chinadaily.com xinhuanet.com
South Korea	8	539,000	56,000	1,983,000	20	29	koreatimes.com asiae.co.kr
Spain	5	907,000	167,000	5,968,000	22	28	elmundo.es elnuevoherald.com
France	6	825,000	64,000	2,502,000	20	21	lemonde.fr france24.com

Source: Dunaway's research based on comScore Media Metrix Web traffic data from U.S.–based audiences.

Notes: Data are from November 2016. News sites were identified as international if the domain name indicated a different location, if the name of the outlet specifically mentioned the country or region, or by reputation. Any uncertain cases were then cross-checked by visiting the site. Site visit data is based on total U.S. audience, from home or work, on desktops only.

journalists working for elite media, they were politically liberal, taking positions to the left of mainstream views. Nonetheless, they rarely challenged the U.S. government's stance on foreign policy issues, unless prominent leaders questioned the policy. That demographic profile no longer fits most of the women and men who report from abroad.

It is difficult to profile foreign journalists dispatched to the United States by foreign media institutions. A fair amount of information is available about the roughly 1,500 formally accredited correspondents who are stationed in Washington, DC, or New York, but little is known beyond these elites.[26] Historically, accredited foreign reporters have been an exceptionally well-educated and multilingual group from friendly and relatively wealthy countries.[27] The poorer regions of the world find it too costly to send correspondents to Washington, DC.[28] In political orientation, foreign newspeople covering the United States have tended to be further to the left than most U.S. reporters and somewhat critical of U.S. policies and lifestyles.[29]

The foreign reporters are stationed in the nation's capital and find it difficult to cover the whole United States adequately. Thus, the impressions that foreigners receive about U.S. politics largely reflect official Washington perspectives. Many foreign reporters complain that top-level U.S. officials rarely grant them interviews that would allow them to file original reports. The frustrations that such slights produce, coupled with the leftward orientation of many overseas reporters, generate a substantial amount of criticism of U.S. policies. However, the damage done to the conduct of U.S. foreign relations by critical news coverage abroad may be countered by U.S. government broadcasts designed to polish the country's image. Al Hurra, funded by Congress and part of the Middle East Broadcasting Network, airs in twenty-two countries across the Middle East and North Africa (MENA) region, attempting to offer "objective, accurate and relevant news and information" to its audience, while also seeking to "support democratic values."[30] Weekly viewership is estimated at about 25 million, though this number is somewhat in dispute. A wide variety of programs include international news, Washington, DC–based shows where journalists from a range of news organizations are brought in to discuss issues of the day, and nonpolitical shows. Al Hurra offers in-depth reporting with a range of viewpoints not always heard in the MENA region media, but the organization has faced scrutiny due to rising costs and bleeding ratings. In 2008, its management and funding were the source of a joint investigation by ProPublica and 60 Minutes, which ultimately led to congressional inquiries.[31]

The Setting for News Selection

News cannot be gathered and produced in a vacuum. It always reflects the spirit of a particular historical period, political and institutional contexts, and reporters' backgrounds and experiences.

The journalists who gather international news for mainstream U.S. media operate from a perspective developed in the context of U.S. politics and political culture. Besides reflecting the U.S. value structure, stories also tend to conform to established U.S. stereotypes. Leaders widely characterized as either villainous or virtuous are primarily depicted true to their image in news stories. The ready availability of contrary images on the internet may make it more difficult to maintain stereotypes.

Because the major news services perform the initial gatekeeping tasks for most American newspapers and electronic media, topic selection tends to be quite uniform. In the United States, elite papers take the lead in framing the stories, and editors and reporters of old and new media elsewhere follow suit. The result is foreign news that is far more limited in scope than domestic news. However, diligent digital news consumers can broaden their exposure by choosing news from a nearly infinite number of available sources on the internet (see Table 8-2).

Political Pressures

Overt and covert political pressures to publish or suppress news stories play a greater role in foreign news production. Correspondents reporting from various regions of the world often must do their host country's bidding. Many host governments are politically unstable and fear for their survival if they receive unfavorable publicity. Hence, they censor all (or most) news stories. If foreign correspondents want to remain in the country, they must write dispatches acceptable to the authorities or face severe penalties that include confiscation of their notes and pictures, closure of transmission facilities, expulsion, criminal prosecution, or even physical harm. These circumstances produce a strange phenomenon: The most undemocratic countries often receive the least criticism, whereas more open societies are freely reproached.

Scores of countries bar foreign reporters entirely from entering or expel them after entry. Albania, Cambodia, El Salvador, Iran, Nicaragua, North Korea, South Africa, the former Soviet Union, and Vietnam provide vivid examples from recent decades, though most countries have foreign correspondents currently stationed there. Israel routinely imposes tight censorship on its military ventures in the occupied West Bank and Gaza Strip, and large areas of Central

America and of the former Soviet Union have been closed to reporters, making it almost impossible to cover their politics adequately. The United States also uses a variety of tactics to limit reporters' access to sites of ongoing U.S. military operations.[32] Bureaucratic hurdles imposed on journalists range from difficult visa requirements to a failure to provide transportation to outlying areas to hurdles in transmitting the news back home.

Danger to Journalists

Related to the political pressures described above, reporters also often face physical danger. They are frequently jailed or assaulted and sometimes murdered (see Figure 8-3). According to the International Federation of Journalists, 2,680 journalists were killed in connection with their journalistic work since 1990. In 2020, 65 journalists were killed, up 17 from the number reported for 2019. The most lethal countries were Mexico, Afghanistan, Pakistan, India, Philippines, Syria, Nigeria, and Yemen.[33] These problems persist, despite that the Helsinki Accords of 1975 guarantee free and safe access to signatory countries' newspeople.

In some parts of the world, recent trends of intensifying political polarization and populism are driving increases in anti-press sentiment and the rising number of threats to journalists. In 2021, the International Press Institute urgently sought to bring attention to threats and violence against journalists in the Netherlands, a country historically known for high levels of media freedom. The general secretary of the Dutch Association of Journalists pointed to the increasing number of incidents as products of hostility toward the media, which he attributed to a mix of polarization, populism, declining trust in the media, conspiracy theories, and frustration and skepticism related to COVID-19.

Even in the U.S., similar trends of rising polarization, populism, and press hostility are contributing to an increasingly hostile environment for journalists. Press freedom advocates allege that this hostility was accelerated by four years of public press demonization from President Trump (see Chapter 5). While there is no clear causal evidence supporting that contention, domestic incidents against journalists were sharply on the rise during the Trump administration. During his final year in office, journalists were frequently attacked by counter-protest groups and even the police while trying to cover Black Lives Matter (BLM) protests. Between May and November of 2020, more than 370 journalists were physically attacked while covering BLM protests, and more than 121 were arrested or faced criminal charges from law enforcement (see Photo 8-1).

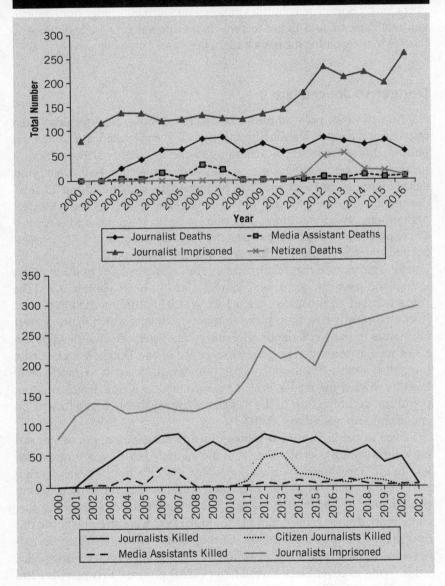

Figure 8-3 Number of Journalists Killed or Imprisoned in Connection With Journalistic Work, 2000–2021

Source: Adapted from Violations of press freedom barometer. (n. d.). Reporters Without Borders. https://rsf.org/en/barometer?year=2021. Figure was created in April 2021 and is therefore based on incomplete data for that year. Imprisonment data are missing for 2018–2020; trend line ignores gaps to connect data points from 2017 and 2021.

Economic Pressures

Economic considerations, similar to cultural and political factors, also influence foreign news selection. When profits are a primary concern, American news media feel pressured to concentrate on audience-appealing stories. In the realm of foreign reporting, audience-appealing content may take the form of soft entertainment content or coverage of sensational/violent events. This constraint is more burdensome for news beyond the nation's borders than for domestic stories because news from abroad must be exceptionally good to attract the large audiences that permit high advertising prices. There is also pressure to minimize production costs. Some stories may be excluded when they cannot be covered cheaply; others may be included merely because they are comparatively inexpensive and convenient to produce. Economic influences on decisions about news selection are also conditioned by the cultural, political, and diplomatic pressures described above as well as the ownership structures of news outlets' parent companies (see Chapter 2 on how ownership influences profit orientation).[34] Governments of all regime types still try to control the press through manipulation of norms, routines, and institutional structures of professional journalism. The U.S. press is dependent on government

Photo 8-1 PORTLAND, OR; SEPTEMBER 26: A member of the Proud Boys tackles a fellow member after he assaulted freelance journalist Justin Katigbak (right) during a Proud Boy rally on September 26, 2020, in Portland, Oregon. Oregon Governor Kate Brown declared a state of emergency prior to Saturday's rally as fears of political violence between Proud Boys and Black Lives Matter protesters grew.

Source: Photo by Nathan Howard/Getty Images.

officials as sources of information and as newsmakers in their own right. This means that even though the American press is generally free of direct censorship from the government, it remains heavily dependent on the government for news gathering. At times, resource-strapped newsrooms are forced to rely too heavily on government resources, essentially peddling official press releases as fully explicated news stories. Media scholars Kirby Goidel, Craig Freeman, and Brian Smentkowski refer to the notion that our press is truly free of government influence as one of the key myths surrounding our rights and liberties.[35] Box 8-1 provides an example of how political and economic cross pressures shape foreign reporting.

Media Diplomacy

The extreme measures that many political leaders take to silence individual reporters or entire media organizations are a sad testimony to the pervasive belief that media can subvert public policies and topple governments.[36] That belief also fuels the many efforts by image-conscious governments around the world to plant favorable stories in the news or to suppress unfavorable ones. At times, political leaders use interviews with foreign journalists to circumvent normal diplomatic channels and instead send messages to other leaders via the published interviews. Alternatively, leaders may send their messages directly to a news channel. For example, Al Qaeda leader Osama bin Laden repeatedly communicated with the United States and other countries by sending taped messages to Al Jazeera. That channel broadcast his words directly rather than merely reporting about them.

Scholars describe an "Al Jazeera effect," referring to the demise of the Western media's virtual monopoly on creating the political images that shape world affairs. New broadcasters and narrowcasters of world news mushroomed in all regions of the globe to report the news from non-Western perspectives.[37] The internet even made it possible to create virtual political enclaves beyond the control of established political powers. For example, the nations of the world do not recognize Al Qaeda as a full-fledged transnational organization. Nonetheless, the internet enables scattered cells to communicate and act as a transnational organization. Similarly, no internationally recognized Kurdish state existed during the first decade of the 21st century. Nevertheless, Kurds dispersed throughout the Middle East made the internet the site of their virtual state, jointly planning its policies. The political consequences of these developments are potentially enormous because people, including political leaders, base their beliefs and actions on the images of the world that they choose to accept. The internet provides them with a broad array of competing choices beyond the Western media's versions that were the major options in the past.

Journalists may even take the initiative in serving as go-betweens for hostile governments. A celebrated incident involved CBS anchor Walter Cronkite, who became a peacemaker in 1977 when he used a television interview to draw a promise from Egypt's president Anwar el-Sadat to visit Jerusalem if it would further peace. In a separate interview, Cronkite secured a pledge from Israeli prime minister Menachem Begin that he would personally welcome Sadat at Ben Gurion Airport. With such mutual commitments, the scene was set for the historic meeting.[38] When Sadat arrived in Israel, flanked by anchors from the three U.S. networks, 2,000 journalists from all over the globe were part of the welcoming crowds. This was media diplomacy in the broadest sense. In the weeks that followed, more than 30 million people in the United States and millions more worldwide watched and judged the peacemaking process. Television alone devoted 24 hours of broadcasts to the spectacle, supplemented by radio and print news.

Even when diplomatic relations are carried out through normal channels, reporters often become part of the political process by choosing the issues to be aired during interviews with political leaders and by selecting activities to cover during negotiating sessions and when leaders travel abroad. Reporters cover these events as they see them.[39] In the long-standing conflict in Northern Ireland, reporters gave voice to formally excluded parties, such as Sinn Fein, the political wing of the Irish Republican Army, by publicizing their views about ongoing negotiations.[40]

Although media diplomacy is often helpful, it also is fraught with disadvantages and dangers. Government officials, who have far more foreign policy expertise than journalists, may be maneuvered into untenable positions. They may have to react to unforeseen developments with undue haste, especially when 24-hour newscasts may arouse interest groups that see peaceful or disruptive protests in front of television cameras as a way to promote their causes worldwide. That has been a common occurrence at the annual economic summit meetings of world leaders.[41] Also, journalists may inadvertently provide a propaganda forum for foreign leaders. This is why many Americans harshly condemned CNN's Peter Arnett when he engaged Iraqi president Saddam Hussein in a long television interview during the Gulf War. The interview permitted the Iraqi leader to broadcast accusations against his antagonists to a worldwide audience.

Gathering the News: The International News Beat

The international beat system is quite similar to local beats. Foreign news bureaus usually are located wherever journalists can expect an abundance of political news. From there, correspondents cover entire countries rather than particular types of stories. However, due to the economic troubles traditional media are facing, international news beats and foreign news bureaus are on the decline. A 2020 report by the Pew Research Center reveals that the number of newsroom employees working for print media outlets dropped significantly between 2008 and 2019, by about 23%. This almost certainly corresponds with the continuing declines in the number of foreign correspondents employed by newspapers around the country. During the last decade, numerous newspapers closed down all their foreign bureaus, while others made substantial cuts. Even in the world of major network television news, declines in foreign affairs reporting persist. According to Pew State of the News Media reports, network coverage of foreign news is a fraction of what it was three decades ago. In 2009, ABC, CBS, and NBC all had news bureaus in London, Moscow, Havana, Baghdad, Beijing, Hong Kong, and Tokyo; even those numbers have since reduced. Several cities are covered by only one or two of these networks. Some of these are one-person bureaus, staffed by a single journalist who performs all the functions needed for modern print and electronic journalism. Advocates of the one-person pattern argue that it works well, thanks to modern technologies such as cell phones that can take excellent videos. That judgment remains controversial.[42] Many experts blame the softening of foreign news and the lack of coverage of many crucial events on shorthanded, inexperienced staffs who are unfamiliar with the countries that they discuss in their reports.

On the brighter side, a few organizations are making the effort to strengthen and protect foreign reporting. The AP still maintains bureaus in more than 80 countries, with Bloomberg not far behind. NPR, *The Wall Street Journal,* and *The Economist* all added bureaus or kept up a strong foreign bureau presence. A handful of successful digital media outlets also profess a commitment to foreign affairs reporting. Jonah Peretti, BuzzFeed's founder and CEO, argues that foreign news investment is critical for the global media brand he is trying to build. The company invested in its news to provide informative, if edgy, reporting in a style that appeals to its 18- to 34-year-old audience as shown in Photo 8-2.[43] In late 2020, *The Washington Post* announced it will take steps in 2021 to increase the global reach of its newsroom. The plans include adding new foreign bureaus in Sydney and Bogota, increasing the paper's international reach to 26 locations across the world, and adding "breaking news" hubs in Europe and Asia. According to *The Post's* PR office, these moves build on a recent effort to develop a European presence to focus on international conflict. The goal is to build up the foreign affairs reporting capacity to enable a provision of rapid and live coverage of breaking news and events 24 hours a day, 7 days a week.[44] Notably, this should probably not be viewed as the harbinger of a broader trend—the fact that *The Post* is owned independently by Amazon founder Jeff Bezos means its financial structure allows for more news investment relative to news outlets with fiduciary obligations to shareholders.

Despite greater ease of travel to all parts of the world, the bulk of foreign affairs news that U.S. media report still originates in Washington, DC, from news beats covering the White House, the State Department, and the Pentagon. When journalists try to cover foreign policy–relevant news, they often face officials who are reluctant to talk because delicate negotiations or the prestige of the United States may be at stake. That makes it difficult for the media to construct cohesive stories about some of the most important political issues facing the nation.

Foreign news bestows unequal attention on regions and countries of the world, just as domestic news covers regions of the United States unequally. There is no correlation between size of population and amount of coverage.

Photo 8-2 Foreign Affairs Stories on Buzzfeed

Source: BuzzFeed.

In general, stories cover the countries with which the United States has its most significant diplomatic contacts. In recent years, that usually meant England, France, Germany, Italy, and Russia in Europe; Egypt, Iran, Iraq, and Israel in the Middle East; the People's Republic of China, Japan, and North and South Korea in East Asia; and India, Pakistan, and Afghanistan in South and Central Asia because of U.S. military presence there. Aside from Canada and Mexico, the western hemisphere is covered lightly, except when Americans become concerned about the production and export of illicit drugs, civil strife, international business issues, climate change and related disasters, human rights abuses, or major regime transitions. Asian coverage was light until the Vietnam War replaced stories from other parts of the world for several years. Overall, foreign coverage dropped off sharply in all types of media since the end of the Cold War. Similar to domestic news, traditional political content is fading, and social and economic news is becoming more plentiful.[45] There is a preference for covering predictable events such as elections or international conferences because coverage can be planned in advance.

As with all types of news coverage, if foreign affairs news bleeds, it definitely leads, thanks to what is often called the news media's "pornographic barbarism."[46] Heaviest coverage goes to areas involved in bloody conflicts that include massive injuries to civilians. However, when the U.S. government is involved in a conflict, the media tend to avoid violent imagery that reflects casualties occurring at the hands of the U.S. military.[47] For example, between 2003 and 2005, the media was criticized by Bush administration officials and others for focusing too much on American deaths and not enough on progress being made in the region in coverage of the Iraq and Afghanistan wars. Critics linked the alleged pattern of negativity with mainstream news media's opposition to the war, but empirical evidence from a study of 2005 Fox News and NBC coverage showed that even though there were plenty of negative stories about the wars, negative information was downplayed rather than amplified.[48]

In general, journalists favor stories with visuals because they are more attractive to viewers than stories that are purely verbal. Pictures are especially important for foreign news because they bring unfamiliar sights, which might be hard to imagine, directly into viewers' homes. Starvation in Sudan and Somalia, the lifestyles of tribes in New Guinea and Australia, and street riots in Spain and China become much more comprehensible if audiences can experience them visually. Still, not even words and pictures combined can tell a whole story if the audience is unfamiliar with the setting in which the reported events are happening. Ugly street scenes of protesters attacking police, torching buildings, and looting stores may be misinterpreted if the audience does not know the even uglier events that might have provoked the protest.[49] Audiences are also more likely to pay attention to stories that are linked explicitly to U.S. interests.

Criteria for Choosing Stories

As the discussion above suggests, foreign news—like domestic news—is selected primarily for audience appeal rather than for political significance. This means that stories must have an angle that interests Americans. Sociologist Herbert Gans examined foreign affairs news in television newscasts and in newsmagazines and identified seven subjects that media favor.[50] Listed in order of frequency of coverage, these are:

1. *U.S. activities in foreign countries*, particularly when the United States faces war with them or when presidents and secretaries of state visit.

2. *Events that affect Americans directly in a major way*, such as oil embargoes and international economic problems.

3. *U.S. relations with potentially hostile states*, especially when they are facing internal political and military problems.

4. *Government upheavals and leadership changes in friendly states*, along with the activities of European royalty.

5. *Dramatic political conflicts*. Most wars, coups d'état, and revolutions are reported; protests, as a rule, are covered only when they are violent.

6. *Disasters*, if they involve great loss of life and destruction of property.

7. *The excesses of foreign dictators*, particularly when they involve brutality against political dissidents. Genocides in Rwanda and Bosnia are examples.

Noticeably absent from U.S. broadcasts and newspapers are stories about ordinary people and ordinary events abroad. These would be news to Americans, but except for occasional special features, they are not "news" in the professional dictionary of journalists. With regard to disasters (see #6 above), there is a rough calculus by which media measure severity: "10,000 deaths in Nepal equals 100 deaths in Wales equals 10 deaths in West Virginia equals one death next door."[51] In general, the more distant a nation, the more frequently a newsworthy event must happen to be reported.

Foreign news stories must be exciting and engaging. Emphasis on violence, conflict, and disaster; timeliness or novelty; and familiarity of persons or situations are the major selection criteria. Stories from areas that are familiar because of ample prior coverage or because they are common travel destinations are more likely to be published than stories from more remote parts of the world. Recent studies of terrorism event coverage reflect these tendencies. An analysis of U.S. broadcast and cable news coverage of terrorism events between 1998 and 2013 shows that both geographic distance and cultural and political affinity with the U.S. were major predictors for which events were covered. Even though 57,628 terrorist events occurred during this time and resulted in 56,534 casualties and 54,829 injuries, only a fraction of events were covered. These terrorism attacks happened in over ninety nations worldwide, concentrating in Iraq (21%), Pakistan (13%), and Afghanistan (10%), followed by India (9%), Thailand (4%), Philippines (4%), Russia (3%), and Colombia (3%). CNN produced the largest volume of terrorism coverage (2,057 stories), followed by CBS (79), Fox News (71), MSNBC (69), ABC (43), and NBC (40). Table 8-3 illustrates the relationship between proximity, affinity, and the likelihood of coverage. Even when controlling for casualties, injuries, and manner of

Table 8-3 Examples of Event Countries' Coverage by Distance to and Affinity With the United States, 1998–2013

	Country	Distance to U.S. (Miles)	Affinity with U.S.	U.S. Coverage
Distant countries with high U.S. affinity	Israel	5,898	0.76	Yes
	Spain	3,788	0.36	Yes
	Greece	5,113	0.35	Yes
	England	3,619	0.27	Yes
	France	3,905	0.26	Yes
Nearby countries with low U.S. affinity	Ecuador	2,799	−0.44	No
	Columbia	2,363	−0.16	No
	Mexico	1,818	−0.14	No

Source: Adapted from Sui, M., Dunaway, J., Sobek, D., Abad, A., Goodman, L., & Saha, P. (2017). US news coverage of global terrorist incidents. *Mass Communication and Society*, *20*(6), 895–908.

Note: Geographic distance is an average of all cities in a given country where terrorism attacks occurred in 1998 to 2013. Event data are from the Global Terrorism Database, https://www.start.umd.edu/gtd/. Affinity scores, where −1 represents "least affinity" and 1 represents "most affinity," were drawn from Bailey, M. A., Strezhnev, A., & Voeten, E. (2017). Estimating dynamic state preferences from United Nations voting data. *Journal of Conflict Resolution*, *61*(2), 430–456.

attack, distance and affinity have the strongest impacts on whether terrorism events were covered. The higher threshold for newsworthiness in the area of international news is evident.[52] When news from countries with unfamiliar cultures is published, the rule of "uncertainty absorption" comes into play. Only plausible stories are acceptable, and they must be cast into a familiar framework, such as the battle against poverty and racism or the moral bankruptcy of military dictators.[53] Such biases make it exceedingly difficult to change images of culturally distant countries. International newspaper reporting biases in coverage of the Libyan civil war reflect the journalistic constraints on foreign news well (see Box 8-1).

Box 8-1

Filtering Revolution: Reporting Bias in International Coverage of the Libyan Civil War

When journalists and news organizations make decisions about covering armed conflict, a lot is at stake. Coverage can influence foreign government intervention, the deployment of humanitarian aid groups, and public opinion on the world stage.[54] Researchers and participants in armed conflict have documented and criticized systematic reporting biases in foreign affairs: News media systematically underreport or overreport certain kinds of international events.

Why is this? Political scientists Matthew A. Baum and Yuri M. Zhukov examine this question using protest and violence data from the 2011 Libyan uprising and daily newspaper coverage of the Arab Spring from 113 countries. They find that reporting biases depend on the political and institutional contexts surrounding news organizations. When news organizations are based in places where there is less government pressure for certain types of coverage (i.e., in democracies), patterns in coverage reflect the usual news values for large-scale dramatic conflict. When outlets are based in nondemocratic regimes, evidence of government pressure is seen in frames that emphasize the legitimacy of the government and the looming restoration of order. In the case of the Libyan uprising, outlets in nondemocratic places underreported protests and nonviolent collective action by opposition voices, ignored government atrocities, and amplified opposition atrocities. According to Baum and Zhukov, coverage from nondemocratic states exhibited a status-quo bias while coverage from democracies contained revisionist bias. Figure 8-4 shows overall patterns of coverage by outlets from democratic and nondemocratic regimes.

(Continued)

(Continued)

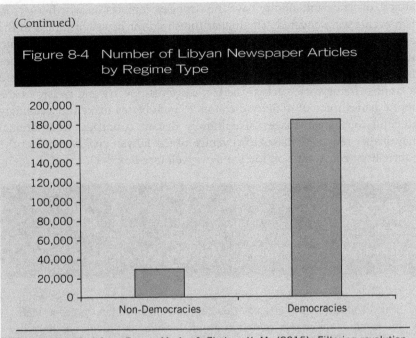

Figure 8-4 Number of Libyan Newspaper Articles by Regime Type

Source: Adapted from Baum, M. A., & Zhukov, Y. M. (2015). Filtering revolution: Reporting bias in international newspaper coverage of the Libyan civil war. *Journal of Peace Research*, *52*(3), 384–400.

The media's preference for news about current happenings leads to concentration on rapidly breaking stories in accessible places. Telling such stories is easier and cheaper than ever because the new technologies spawn ample crops of pictures. They come from bystanders' cell phone photographs and videos, as did much of the imagery for the Arab Spring protests. More significant, long-range developments, such as programs to improve public health or reduce illiteracy or efforts to create new political parties, are more difficult to capture in pictures. When such developments are reported without analysis of the context that spawned them, they acquire an unwarranted air of suddenness and unpredictability. They have no past, and without appropriate follow-ups, they also have no future. They are merely a brief presence in the parade of current events.

Space and time limitations are particularly troubling for reporting foreign events, which are often unintelligible without adequate background information or interpretation. Complexity therefore becomes a major enemy, and avoidance or oversimplification becomes the defensive strategy.

Reporters must write stories simply and logically even if the situation defies logic. Usually, a single theme must be selected to epitomize the entire complex story. This leads to gross oversimplification of multifaceted situations such as China's policies in Tibet or Iran's pursuit of nuclear power. These complexities are often compounded when citizen journalists are providing images or information for stories.

International Conflict in the Modern Age

In the wake of the Vietnam War, many politicians and other political observers believed that fighting lengthy wars was becoming nearly impossible for democratic societies in the age of full-color, battlefront television. Viewing the reality of the horrors of battle presumably would sap public support for wars. To avoid images that could interfere with conducting wars, the United States, like other countries, often restricts war coverage over journalists' strong and vocal objections. Journalists remind military brass that exclusion from battlefronts constitutes undue muzzling of the press at a time when its watchdog functions are especially crucial.[55] In response to these complaints, the military frequently revises its rules to permit journalists more access to ongoing military operations. It is difficult to devise a workable system because it is well-nigh impossible to reconcile journalists' demands for press freedom with the military's security concerns. Whenever such conflicts make it into the courts, judges usually side with the military and public opinion supports their decisions.[56] However, the balance of forces shifted moderately in the media's favor when U.S. civilian and military officials realized Al Jazeera and other Middle Eastern sources would be covering the impending war in Iraq. Media in the U.S. were likely to pick up this coverage in the absence of frontline news from U.S. sources.

A new approach announced in February 2003 therefore provided for a pool of approximately 600 print and broadcast war correspondents from the United States and other countries to accompany troops from all branches of the military. These "embedded" journalists were screened and trained by the Pentagon so they would fit smoothly into the units to which they were assigned (see Photo 8-3). "Embeds" had to sign an agreement on ground rules of coverage and pledge that they would submit potentially sensitive stories to prepublication scrutiny by military censors. The Defense Department promised only light censorship. Journalists who remained outside the embedded group, the so-called unilaterals, were not subject to restrictive rules. But in line with history, their access to frontline operations was severely restricted. Roughly 40% of journalists ultimately chose to be unilaterals.

Photo 8-3 Embedded Reporter Carol Rosenberg of the *Miami Herald*

Source: Photo by Scott Peterson/Getty Images.

Note: Embedded journalists were responsible for much of the coverage of the U.S. conflict in Iraq beginning in 2003. Pictured here is reporter Carol Rosenberg of the *Miami Herald* as she works at a checkpoint on May 1, 2004, on the edge of Fallujah, Iraq.

When the plan was announced, critics immediately questioned whether embedded journalists would be able to retain their objectivity when they shared their lives with the troops and were likely to become close friends with many of them. Embedding might simply be another form of government news management that amounted to journalists being in bed with the military. Judging from the reports of journalists and observers, that apparently happened only rarely and the embedding process received a good deal of praise. One observer noted that "embedding allowed far greater access to the battlefield than the press has enjoyed in more than two decades and has dampened the long hostility between the Pentagon and the press."[57] But another report warned that collaboration with the military comes at a price: "The weakness is that the embeds' accounts necessarily become the story of the war as seen through the eyes of American soldiers. No reporter is going to be 'objective' about those who are protecting his or her life."[58]

It is unlikely that the time will ever arrive when the military and the press will be fully satisfied with each other's conduct. Their respective goals are in conflict. War is a dirty business and can never be photogenic when pictured in all its brutality. As long as "just" wars for "good causes" (whatever they may be) are condoned and even celebrated by the world community, full coverage of the horrors of war remains a sensitive issue. Cries for formal or informal censorship under the banner of patriotism will overwhelm cries for press freedom.

Flaws in Gatekeeping

Foreign affairs coverage is dramatic in the effort to fill the limited interests of most Americans. Still, foreign news buffs rightly complain that it lacks depth and breadth. It stereotypes and oversimplifies, and it often distorts facts by failing to place them in a realistic context. Analysis of forty-six years of news coverage of the Soviet Union between 1945 and 1991 revealed that the lion's share went to military aspects of the Cold War, while economic and science issues were neglected. It is no wonder that most Americans, including political leaders, were taken by surprise when economic deficiencies led to the disintegration and collapse of the Soviet Union in the 1990s.[59] Those deficiencies failed to capture media attention. Below, we describe six major patterns in coverage attributable to flaws in gatekeeping for international news: biased framing, uncritical coverage, news distortions, overemphasis on conflict, support for the status quo, and a bias for sourcing government officials.

Good Frames for Friends, Bad Frames for Foes

The fact that foreign news reported in the U.S. press is based heavily on U.S. sources, which tend to support government policies, explains why the legacy media regularly cast U.S. policies and allies in a favorable light. Coverage of the downing of two planes, one by Soviet fire and the other by U.S. fire, is a good illustration. In 1983, a Soviet fighter plane shot down Korean Airlines Flight 007 with a loss of 269 lives. Five years later, in 1988, the Vincennes, a U.S. Navy ship, shot down Iran Air Flight 655 with a loss of 290 lives. The Soviets justified the shooting by saying that the Korean plane was a hostile target; the Americans made the same claim for their action. Though the cases differed in detail and in the context in which they occurred, they were sufficiently alike that one might expect roughly similar reaction. That did not happen, judging from reports in *Time, Newsweek, The New York Times, The Washington Post,* and the CBS Evening News. As the saying goes, outcomes are judged by whose ox is gored. The framing, language, and pictures used in the stories cast the Soviet action as a moral outrage and the U.S. action as a regrettable technological failure.[60] Similarly, media coverage and framing of crimes and human rights violations at the hands of leaders who have control over resources pertinent for U.S. interests is gentler relative to coverage of their less-relevant-for-U.S. counterparts.

There is no evidence that the distortions that spring from these biased framing examples were deliberate. Rather, the framing reflects their choice of sources—the heavy reliance on U.S. officials—as well as the politically socialized perspectives of the journalists, based on the predispositions with which they approach stories involving countries identified as friend or foe. Nonetheless, many scholars believe that these biases in coverage can have political consequences. A 2014 study of U.S. sanction cases between 1976 and 2000 shows that media coverage of human rights abuses had a stronger positive impact on the likelihood of sanctions for non-allies (foes) than for allies.[61]

Uncritical, Spotty Flashlight Coverage

Reporting of foreign news usually lacks a sense of history and a sense of the meaning of successive events. Therefore, it often confuses the public. The news does not provide sufficient information to permit most Americans to understand the rationale for major foreign policies or events. Some stories, even those directly involving U.S. security, are ignored until events reach crisis proportions or until there is a precipitating incident. *The New York Times* correspondent James Reston put the problem this way:

> We are fascinated by events but not by the things that cause the events. We will send 500 correspondents to Vietnam after the war breaks out . . . meanwhile ignoring the rest of the world, but we will not send five reporters there when the danger of war is developing.[62]

When news about the aftermath of the 2003 Iraq War turned sour in 2004, the news media were chided for neglecting their watchdog role. *The New York Times* and *The Washington Post* apologized for supporting President George W. Bush's policies too wholeheartedly, true to their usual stance in covering news about U.S. military ventures abroad.[63]

They had featured a limited amount of dissent about war strategies with-out questioning the overall goals and the need for war. The criticism and self-criticism regarding the adequacy of prewar debates reflected the fact that the media did not live up to political elites' expectations about their watchdog role in the foreign policy realm. Unfortunately, there are no satisfactory solutions to the dilemmas that journalists face during inter-national crises, when their feelings of patriotism demand support for the government while their journalistic duty calls for raising red flags of caution. Yet research shows that journalistic norms and routines do sometimes cause coverage to deviate from elite debate and that coverage can have an independent influence on the public's response to foreign policy crises.[64]

News Distortions

Just as with domestic news, foreign news neglects major social and economic problems. The reasons are readily apparent. Such problems are difficult to discuss in brief stories, pictures are scarce, and changes come at a glacial pace. Some social problems are extremely complex; most reporters are ill equipped to understand them, let alone report about them. When news stories address economic development issues, the focus is on dramatic negative aspects such as famines, health crises, and conflicts. As Rafael Caldera, former president of Venezuela, told a press conference at the National Press Club in Washington, DC,

> The phrase "no news is good news" has become "good news is no news." . . . Little or nothing is mentioned in American media about literary or scientific achievements . . . [or] about social achievements and the defense against the dangers which threaten our peace and development. . . . [Instead,] only the most deplorable incidents, be they caused by nature or by man, receive prominent attention.[65]

It is small consolation for such ruffled feelings that the news selection criteria applied to events in developing nations are typical for news every-where.[66] The situation is aggravated by the fact that many developing coun-tries depend on Western news media, especially the AP and CNN, for their international news. These countries complain about "media imperialism."[67] Critics in developing nations also decry the corrupting effects of Western programs that feature violence and sexually explicit episodes. Western programs allegedly damage the cultural identity of people in developing nations, drawing them away from their own heritage.[68]

Overemphasis on Conflict

Negative news, including news about violent conflicts, is more prevalent in the U.S. media than in the media of many other societies. Comparisons of news coverage of the Iranian hostage crisis from media in the United States and France are revealing. *The New York Times* coverage featured stereotypical portrayals of Muslims and tales of violence in its depictions of the crisis. Far more peaceful images emerged in the French newspaper *Le Monde*.[69]

By and large, news media in democracies feature more conflict than do media in authoritarian and totalitarian societies. In part, this happens because government-controlled and government-supported news organizations can afford to forgo dramatic negative news, since their financial health is unrelated to audience size. U.S. news media draw attention to conflict rather than to peaceful settlement and make much of the world beyond U.S. borders seem chaotic. Routine foreign news languishes in the back pages or is condensed into news snippets. Issues are often oversimplified, and coverage focuses mainly on what the conflict portends for politics (if anything) rather than what it means to the country and its citizens.

Distortions in domestic news are not likely to mislead most U.S. audiences because past experiences and socialization provide corrective lenses.[70] The foreign scene, by contrast, must be viewed without correction for myopia and astigmatism. Americans may be skeptical about the accuracy of the images, but in the domain of foreign affairs, many may lack the means to judge the nature and degree of distortion.

Support of the Status Quo

Finally, the thrust of most foreign news stories supports government policies. The media usually accept official designations of who are friends and enemies of the United States and interpret these friends' and enemies' motives accordingly. Whenever relationships change, media coverage mirrors the change. Coverage of the Soviet Union's attack on Korean Airlines Flight 007 is a good example of the approach used for disfavored countries. Because the president and the executive branch are the prime sources of foreign affairs news, they can (most of the time) set the agenda of coverage with stories that are framed to reflect official perspectives.[71]

On the whole, despite some coverage that challenges the official version of international politics and U.S. foreign policies, the tenor of news stories in mainstream media and on the internet supports prevailing stereotypes about the world. Preoccupation with the developed world reinforces many Americans' beliefs about the importance of these nations. In the same way, the portrayal of less-developed countries as incapable of managing their own affairs makes it easy to believe that they do not deserve higher status and the media attention that accompanies it.

Newspeople usually are willing to withhold news and commentary when publicity would severely complicate the government's management of foreign policy, and the official sources they rely on certainly do the same. Governments seeking to avoid negative coverage from the Western press will also assist with this by going to great lengths to ensure favorable coverage. For example, Human Right Watch describes Saudi Arabia's global public relations efforts as "image laundering." The Saudi government has a deplorable human rights record, much of which it gets away with through the suppression or manipulation of the press. In the time since Saudi agents killed journalist Jamal Khashoggi in 2018, Saudi Crown Prince Mohammed bin Salman and his government are as of yet unscathed, despite being implicated in the murder. This lack of accountability is due in part to the fact that U.S. officials—including both the Trump and Biden administrations—are restrained in their criticism, no doubt because the U.S. relies on Saudi Arabia for its valuable natural resources. Press coverage naturally reflects the lukewarm response of officials, but it may also be due in part to the crown prince's aggressive public relations efforts since 2018. He paid for high-profile events attended by famous international athletes and celebrities in the hopes of suppressing criticism from celebrities and the press and to draw attention away from his government's record on human rights violations. As the Deputy Middle East Director of Human Rights Watch put it,

> When Hollywood A-listers, international athletes, and other
> global celebrities take government money to perform in Saudi
> Arabia while staying silent on the government's atrocious rights
> record, they are boosting the kingdom's strategy of whitewashing
> Crown Prince Mohammad bin Salman's abuses.[72]

In October 2020, Human Rights Watch announced a new worldwide campaign to try and counter the Saudi government's attempt to whitewash its dismal record on human rights.

The press will often suppress information when releasing it could put sensitive negotiations, civilians, or troops in jeopardy, such as when they refrained from sharply criticizing Iranian leaders during the 1979 hostage crisis to avoid angering them and when an invasion of Haiti by U.S. troops was in the offing in 1994; CNN and the three major television networks pledged to refrain from showing any pictures that might put the troops at risk (see Box 8-2 for more discussion of the potential risks of releasing graphic photos).[73]

Box 8-2
News From the Global Village

To varying degrees throughout the world, the connectivity of new media is superseding the traditional political connections that have brought identity and structure to global politics. This rewiring of the world's neural system is proceeding at remarkable speed, and its reach keeps extending ever further. It changes the way states and citizens interact with each other and it gives the individual a chance at a new kind of autonomy, at least on an intellectual level, because of the greater availability of information. . . . [A] huge universe of new communications and information providers . . . are changing the relationship between those who govern and those who are governed . . . assisting those with previously unachievable political agendas. The advent of television a half-century ago pales in comparison with new media's effects on global political life today.[1]

Fifty years ago, media guru Marshall McLuhan predicted that electronic technology would one day contract the world into a village in which information would instantaneously reach all people. As the above quote from Philip Seib's book about Al Jazeera suggests, that day has arrived. The internet allows people to live in online virtual communities—global villages—that share news topics but have different interests and concerns.

The world as a village in which people are in constant touch and react quickly to each other's behaviors is well illustrated by the torture memo incident that made waves throughout the globe in 2009. The story began when the Justice Department released previously secret U.S. government memoranda that detailed torture tactics authorized for extracting information from suspected terrorists. Debate raged about the possible impact of publication of these documents at home and, far more importantly, abroad. Methods of prisoner interrogation were still a domestic policy issue, but they had become an international issue as well. Policy makers and journalists had to consider that reality. For most social, economic, and political issues, the question "How well will it play in the United States?" had to be permanently amended by adding "How well will it play in the world?"

The torture memo story also illustrates another crucial aspect of telling news stories in our global village world. Pictures are powerful, but their meanings hinge on the captions and the viewers' diverse cultural prisms. Pictures absorb the meanings that accompanying words ascribe to them. Villagers around the globe will attach their own captions; their interpretations will reflect their unique preconceptions.

Concerns about the unique potency of pictures prompted President Obama to balk when asked to release pictures of the shocking torture episodes, even though the Justice Department had previously released the verbal memos that described the torture methods in graphic detail. Military officials had warned him that the pictures—spread throughout the global village by the internet—were likely to infuriate global villagers, who might then attack American soldiers and civilians who happened to be nearby.

1. Seib, P. (2008). *The Al Jazeera effect: How the new global media are reshaping world politics.* Potomac Books, p. 175.

Official-Source Bias and the Indexing Hypothesis

If the media are generally supportive of government policies, how can their adverse comments about the Vietnam War or the Gulf War be explained? The answer is that the media generally emphasize the government's positions until many respected sources voice strong dissent. To use a term popularized by political scientist Lance Bennett, the media "index" their coverage to the degree of disagreement by powerful political leaders with the government's position.[74] The media do not care to lead dissent in this minefield of uncertainties about facts, and they fear that irate audiences will accuse them of a lack of patriotism. Only when respected opposition forces publicly express their concern do the media couple their government accounts with coverage of the dissenting voices.[75]

Tests of the indexing hypothesis in the post–Cold War era suggest that it may apply only in situations when consequential national security interests are at stake.[76] It may also be true that the end of the Cold War marked a break with the past that led to the "cascade" model of foreign affairs coverage identified by Robert Entman. Entman contends that foreign policy consensus among elites has become the exception rather than the norm. That leaves the media free to choose among competing interpretations of events happening abroad. The president's framing still has the best chance to be reflected in the news, but other frames may trump it, depending on how they cascade through communications networks that reach the media. As always, journalistic news selection criteria are also a major selection factor.

The research on indexing and public opinion strongly suggests that Americans' views about foreign policy are shaped by the opinions of U.S. government officials. One reason is because the media source them so heavily. Recent research by political scientists Danny Hayes and Matt Guardino shows that public opinion can also be shaped by the views expressed by foreign elites through the U.S. media. They find that in the absence of domestic opposition to the war in Iraq, public opinion was shaped by the dissenting views of officials from other countries, particularly those countries that are traditional allies to the U.S. The press works best as a tool for public influence over foreign policy when there is extensive domestic partisan opposition to vocalize dissenting views to the press.[77] This illustrates yet another reason that the routines for newsgathering on foreign and international affairs are so important—journalists' decisions about who they should source can have implications for something as important as public support for the decision to go to war.[78]

The Impact of Foreign Affairs Coverage

Is there a "CNN effect"? The idea that graphic media coverage of events abroad can force the U.S. government to engage in unplanned and undesired interventions is dubbed the *CNN effect*. The name was coined by scholars who studied the U.S. intervention in Somalia that began in 1992, shortly after CNN published gruesome pictures of atrocities against civilians in that country. Subsequent analyses suggest that CNN was given undue credit in that case. Officials formulated plans for the humanitarian intervention well ahead of the airing of the CNN stories.[79]

Further investigations suggest that there is, indeed, evidence for a CNN effect in situations in which television pictures of human suffering inflicted by nature or by fellow humans have aroused sympathies for the victims among the U.S. public as well as U.S. officials. But the effect is less automatic than initially postulated, and it seems to be limited to situations involving humanitarian crises.

However, media coverage can influence foreign affairs even when it does not lead to military intervention. Effects include shortening the time for choosing a policy, which in turn shrinks the pool of people regularly consulted prior to decisions and increases the chances for ill-considered policies.[80] Televised coverage of a crisis may pressure the president to react hastily to avoid appearing weak and vacillating. As Lloyd Cutler, White

House counsel to presidents Jimmy Carter and Bill Clinton, put it, "If an ominous foreign event is featured on TV news, the President and his advisers feel bound to make a response in time for the next evening news program."[81] This may leave no time to investigate the news report or for officials of the foreign country to explain it. President John F. Kennedy waited eight days in 1961 before commenting on the construction of the Berlin Wall; President George H. W. Bush had to respond overnight to its destruction.[82] In the instantaneousness of the digital media environment, presidents and press secretaries long for the days in which they had until overnight to respond. Many international crises require immediate responses.

Madeleine Albright, President Clinton's secretary of state, saw advantages and disadvantages with the 24-hour news cycle:

> Some of it is very good, because you know what's going on and there is a real-time sense about things. . . . But, in other ways, it makes you have to respond to events much faster than it might be prudent. . . . So it's a double-edged sword.[83]

SUMMARY

The quality of U.S. foreign policy and the effectiveness of U.S. relations with other countries are crucial to the welfare of people throughout the world. Sound policy and relations require a solid information base. This chapter shows that the foreign affairs information base on which Americans depend leaves much to be desired. The flow of information about our world is enormous and overpowering, but most stories are shallow. They lead audiences into a jungle of diverse perspectives without a road map. Many guideposts are misleading, whether unintentionally or deliberately.

The reasons for these reporting flaws are complex. They include the economics of reporting news from all parts of the globe, the sociopolitical setting in which news gathering takes place, and the audiences to whose worldviews and tastes the news must cater. Foreign affairs news often must be gathered under trying conditions. Strange locations and inadequate technological facilities can make nightmares of the physical aspects of getting to the scene of the action, collecting information, and transmitting it. These technical difficulties are compounded by political difficulties. They include the reluctance of public officials everywhere to commit themselves publicly on foreign affairs matters and the harassment of correspondents venturing into places where they are unwanted. Expulsion, imprisonment, and physical harm are common. With so much territory to cover, professional reporters frequently avoid areas where news is hard to get. This effectively removes many regions of the world from media scrutiny and contributes to unevenness of news flow.

How good is the foreign affairs news presented by traditional U.S. news media? The picture is mixed and must be judged in light of the problems faced in foreign news production. News from around the globe must be at once timely, exciting, personalized, and brief, yet understandable for a U.S. audience that is barely interested in most events abroad. To satisfy these criteria with shrinking resources of time and money, journalists focus on sensational, mostly negative news. They write stories primarily from a U.S. perspective and usually follow the current administration's foreign policy rationale and the public's stereotyped views of the world. Despite these shortcomings, Americans can obtain a rich mixture of stories about political events abroad. The web is a gold mine of information for those who can tell the real metal from the dross. Elite newspapers generally give fairly thorough exposure to U.S. foreign policies. However, U.S. newspapers rarely challenge the objectives of foreign policies unless they can cite support from respected political sources. They may, however, question how effectively the administration is executing these policies.

Occasionally, television commentators serve as active diplomats through interviews that set the stage for subsequent political developments. Graphic accounts of human suffering abroad have, from time to time, spawned humanitarian interventions, but scholars have little predictive evidence about under what circumstances this "CNN effect" occurs. The impact of new media remains unclear as well. We know that the influx of news from all parts of the world is huge. It is dispatched by thousands of amateur journalists who are unrestrained by the legal and ethical shackles that bind professionals. The quality of their reporting ranges from excellent to dismal. But it is unknown how much of their work leaves a mark and who is affected. Do powerful people listen? Are opinions changed? Speculations abound but solid answers are lacking. Many questions remain as well about the circumstances that propel American news media to cover dissenting views about foreign policy that may force a change in the goals and strategies favored by incumbent presidents. One thing is clear: It is no longer heresy in times of foreign crises to criticize the administration's foreign policy rather than rally around the flag. In fact, criticism at such times may ultimately be deemed a hallowed duty. Its potency will depend on its wisdom and the credibility of the source that dispenses it.

DISCUSSION QUESTIONS ──────────────

1. How well do people pay attention to news about foreign affairs? Is the American public interested? Do the media perceive the public to be interested? If so, why don't they cover it more? If not, how does this perception shape newsroom decisions about how much space to devote to covering foreign affairs?

2. How is covering foreign affairs similar to or different from other reporting and journalistic practices, such as those we learned about in earlier chapters? How do the journalists themselves compare to those covering domestic politics? Are the things that shape how (and how much) foreign news is reported the same or different in this important news niche?

3. What are some of the problems with gatekeeping in the category of foreign affairs news? What are the patterns and biases we might see in this kind of coverage as a result? What are the various ways these patterns in coverage could have important implications for governance, diplomacy, and American public opinion about foreign affairs?

READINGS ──────────────

Baum, M. A., & Groeling, T. J. (2010). *War stories: The causes and consequences of public views of war.* Princeton University Press.

Baum, M. A., & Potter, P. B. K. (2015). *War and democratic constraint: How the public influences foreign policy.* Princeton University Press.

Bernard, C. C. (2015). *Press and foreign policy.* Princeton University Press.

Cooper, G. (2018). *Reporting humanitarian disasters in a social media age.* Routledge.

Cottle, S., Sambrook, R., & Mosdell, N. (2016). *Reporting dangerously: Journalist killings, intimidation, and security.* Palgrave Macmillan.

Dell'Orto, G. (2014). *American journalism and international relations: Foreign correspondence from the early republic to the digital era.* Cambridge University Press.

Dell'Orto, G., & Wetzstein, I. (Eds.). (2018). *Refugee news, refugee politics: Journalism, public opinion and policymaking in Europe.* Routledge.

Dubbs, C. (2020). *An unladylike profession: American Women war correspondents in World War I.* University of Nebraska Press.

Fainberg, D. (2021). *Cold War correspondents: Soviet and American reporters on the ideological frontlines.* Johns Hopkins University Press.

Feldman, S. (2015). *Going to war in Iraq: When citizens and the press matter*. University of Chicago Press.

Hamilton, J. M. (2009). *Journalism's roving eye: A history of American foreign reporting*. Louisiana State University Press.

Hamilton, J. M. (2020). *Manipulating the masses: Woodrow Wilson and the birth of American propaganda*. Louisiana State University Press.

Hamilton, J. M., & Lawrence, R. G. (2012). *Foreign correspondence*. Routledge.

Hayes, D., & Guardino, M. (2013). *Influence from abroad: Foreign voices, the media, and U.S. public opinion*. Cambridge University Press.

Lugo-Ocando, J., & Nguyen, A. (2017). *Developing news: Global journalism and the coverage of "third world" development*. Taylor & Francis.

Monshipouri, M. (2016). *Information politics, protests, and human rights in the digital age*. Cambridge University Press.

Moseley, R. (2017). *Reporting war: How foreign correspondents risked capture, torture and death to cover World War II*. Yale University Press.

Palmer, L. (2018). *Becoming the story: War correspondents since 9/11*. University of Illinois Press.

Palmer, L. (2019). *The fixers: Local news workers and the underground labor of international reporting*. Oxford University Press.

Parks, L. (2018). *Rethinking media coverage: Vertical mediation and the war on terror*. Routledge.

Pedelty, M. (2020). *War stories: The culture of foreign correspondents*. Routledge.

Robinson, P. (2005). *The CNN effect: The myth of news, foreign policy, and intervention*. Routledge.

Taylor, J. (2020). *War photography: Realism in the British press*. Routledge.

Zayani, M. (2019). *Al Jazeera phenomenon: Critical perspectives on new Arab media*. Routledge.

NOTES

1. Dancy, G., & Fariss, C. J. (n. d.). *The search for human rights: What Google trends can tell us* [Working paper].

2. Mitchell, A., Gottfried, J., Barthel, M., & Shearer, E. (2016, July 7). The modern news consumer: News attitudes and practices in the digital era. http://www.journalism.org/2016/07/07/the-modern-news-consumer/. Data are quoted directly from the Topline questionnaire from the 2016 Pew Research Center's American Trends Panel; Pew Project for Excellence in Journalism. (2013). *State of news media 2012*. http://www.stateofthemedia.org/2012/.

3. In changing news landscape, even television is vulnerable: News attitudes and habits. (2012, September 27). *Pew Research Center*. http://www.people-press.org/2012/09/27/section-3-news-attitudes-and-habits-2/.

4. Baum, M. A., & Potter, P. B. K. (2015). *War and democratic constraint: How the public influences foreign policy.* Princeton University Press.

5. Data analyzed are from Pew Research Center's 2012 News Coverage Index Dataset, which includes 20,447 stories, including 1,977 newspaper stories, 3,242 online news stories, 5,186 stories from network television, 6,472 stories from the cable news networks, and 3,570 stories from news radio. Figures from CNN's television coverage includes *CNN Daytime*, *The Situation Room*, *Anderson Cooper 360*, *John King USA*, and 23 stories pulled from unspecified shows; CNN.com figures are from website screen captures pulled from the site at 9 a.m. and 4 p.m. daily during the period analyzed.

6. Top ten stories ranked by time on US foreign policy focus 2015. (2021). *Tyndall Report*. http://tyndallreport.com/yearinreview2015/foreignpolicy/; 360 amazing Twitter stats. (2016, November). *Digital Marketing Ramblings*. http://expandedramblings.com/index.php/march-2013-by-the-numbers-a-few-amazing-twitter-stats/.

7. Shoemaker, P. J., Danielian, L. H., & Brendlinger, N. (1991). Deviant acts, risky business, and U.S. interests: The newsworthiness of world events. *Journalism Quarterly*, 68(Winter), 781–795.

8. Norris, P. (1995). The restless searchlight: Network news framing of the post-Cold War world. *Political Communication*, 12(4), 357–370.

9. Hachten, W. A., & Scotton, J. F. (2007). *The world news prism: Global information in a satellite age* (7th ed.). Blackwell. Other important international news suppliers are Germany's Deutsche Press Agentur and Japan's Kyodo News Service as well as China's Xinhua News Agency and United Press International, once second only to the Associated Press among U.S. news agencies.

10. Tuinstra, F. (2004). Caught between the Cold War and the internet. *Nieman Reports*, 58(3), 100–103.

11. Associated Press. (2021). [Website]. http://www.ap.org.

12. Advancing the power of facts. (2020, June 2). *Associated Press*. https://www.ap.org/en-us/

13. CNN Worldwide Fact Sheet. (2021). *CNN*. http://cnnpressroom.blogs.cnn.com/cnn-fact-sheet/.

14. Hamilton, J. M., & Jenner, E. (2004). Foreign correspondence: Evolution, not extinction. *Nieman Reports*, 58(3), 98–100; Hamilton, J. M., & Jenner, E. (2004). Redefining foreign correspondence. *Journalism*, 5(3), 301–321.

15. Hamilton, J. M., & Jenner, E. (2004). Foreign correspondence: Evolution, not extinction. *Nieman Reports, 58*(3), 98–100.

16. Erickson, E., & Hamilton, J. M. (2006). Foreign reporting enhanced by parachute journalism. *Newspaper Research Journal, 27*(1), 33–47.

17. Hamilton, J. M., & Jenner, E. (2004). Foreign correspondence: Evolution, not extinction. *Nieman Reports, 58*(3), 98–100; Hamilton, J. M., & Jenner, E. (2004). Redefining foreign correspondence. *Journalism, 5*(3), 301–321.

18. Hammer, J. (2014, December 11). As legacy news outlets retreat, who will be there to report on the world? *Nieman Reports.* http://niemanreports.org/articles/as-legacy-news-outlets-retreat-who-will-be-there-to-report-on-the-world/.

19. See PRX, https://theworld.org/

20. Manheim, J. B. (1994). Strategic public diplomacy: Managing Kuwait's image during the Gulf Conflict. In W. L. Bennett & D. L. Paletz (Eds.), *Taken by storm: The media, public opinion, and U.S. foreign policy in the Gulf War* (pp. 131–148). University of Chicago Press.

21. Manheim, J. B., & Albritton, R. B. (1984). Changing national images: International public relations and media agenda-setting. *American Political Science Review, 78*(September), 641–657; Albritton, R. B., & Manheim, J. B. (1985). Public relations efforts for the third world: Images in the news. *Journal of Communication, 35*(Spring), 43–59; Manheim, J. B. (1994). *Strategic public diplomacy and American foreign policy: The evolution of influence.* Oxford University Press.

22. Dowell, B. (2012, June 25). BBC trust: Coverage of Arab Spring needed more "breadth and context." *The Guardian.* http://www.guardian.co.uk/media/2012/jun/25/bbc-trust-coverage-arab-spring

23. Livingston, S., & Aday, S. (2003). Gatekeeping, indexing, and live-event news: Is technology altering the construction of news? *Political Communication, 20,* 363–380.

24. Branton, R., & Dunaway, J. (2008). English- and Spanish-language media coverage of immigration: A comparative analysis. *Social Science Quarterly, 89*(4), 1006–1022.

25. Benson, R. (2013). *Shaping immigration news: A French–American comparison.* Cambridge University Press; Baum, M. A., & and Yuri M. Zhukov, Y. M. (2015). Filtering revolution: Reporting bias in international newspaper coverage of the Libyan civil war. *Journal of Peace Research, 52*(3), 384–400.

26. *Editor & Publisher International Yearbook, 1991.* (1991). Editor & Publisher. In the United States, the needs of foreign correspondents are served by the United States Information Agency. It maintains foreign press centers in major

U.S. cities and arranges high-level briefings by government officials and news-gathering tours on major economic, political, and cultural themes. It also provides extensive information services and even helps with arranging appointments and filing facilities at international summits.

27. Wilnat, L., & Weaver, D. (2006). Through their eyes: Foreign correspondents in the United States. *Journalism History, Las Vegas, 32*(2), 116.

28. Wilnat, L., & Weaver, D. (2006). Through their eyes: Foreign correspondents in the United States. *Journalism History, Las Vegas, 32*(2), 116.

29. Ghorpade, S. (1984). Foreign correspondents cover Washington for world. *Journalism Quarterly, 61*(Fall), 667.

30. U.S. Agency for Global Media. (2018, November 3). A new and revitalized Alhurra TV launches across the Middle East. *U.S. Agency for Global Media.* https://www.usagm.gov/2018/11/03/a-new-and-revitalized-alhurra-tv-launches-across-the-middle-east/

31. Linzer, D. (2008, December 24). Where things stand: Alhurra. *Propublica.* https://www.propublica.org/article/where-things-stand-alhurra-1224

32. Nossek, H. (2007). Terrorism and the media: Does the weapon matter to the coverage? In H. Nossek, A. Sreberny, & P. Sonwalkar (Eds.), *Media and political violence.* Hampton Press; Graber, D. A. (2003). Terrorism, censorship, and the First Amendment. In P. Norris, M. Kern, & M. Just (Eds.), *Framing terrorism: The news media, the government, and the public.* Routledge.

33. IJF's 30th annual report on killings of journalists and media staff puts death toll at 65 in 2020. (2021, March 11). *The International Federation of Journalists.* https://www.ifj.org/media-centre/news/detail/category/health-and-safety/article/ifjs-30th-annual-report-on-killings-of-journalists-and-media-staff-puts-death-toll-at-65-in-2020.html

34. Baum, M. A., & Zhukov, Y. M. (2015). Filtering revolution: Reporting bias in international newspaper coverage of the Libyan civil war. *Journal of Peace Research, 52*(3), 384–400.

35. Goidel, K., Freeman, C., & Smentkowski, B. (2015). *Misreading the Bill of Rights: Top ten myths concerning your rights and liberties.* Prager.

36. Gilboa, E. (1998). Media diplomacy: Conceptual divergence and applications. *Harvard International Journal of Press/Politics, 3*(3), 56–75.

37. Seib, P. (2008). *The Al Jazeera effect: How the new global media are reshaping world politics.* Potomac Books.

38. Seib, P. (2008). *The Al Jazeera effect: How the new global media are reshaping world politics.* Potomac Books.

39. For a full discussion of reporting on the Middle East peace negotiations between Israel and the Palestinians, see Wolfsfeld, G. (1997). *Media and political conflict: News from the Middle East*. Cambridge University Press.

40. Sparre, K. (2001). Megaphone diplomacy in the Northern Irish peace process: Squaring the circle by talking to terrorists through journalists. *Harvard International Journal of Press/Politics*, 6(1), 88–104.

41. O'Heffernan, P. (1993). Mass media and U.S. foreign policy: A mutual exploitation model of media influence in U.S. foreign policy. In R. J. Spitzer (Ed.), *Media and public policy*. Praeger.

42. See Cable news: Fact sheet: State of the news media 2016. (2016). *Pew Research Center*. https://assets.pewresearch.org/wp-content/uploads/sites/13/2016/06/30143308/state-of-the-news-media-report-2016-final.pdf; also see Martin, J. D. (2012, April 23). Loneliness at the foreign "bureau": News organizations exaggerate the size of their overseas newsrooms. *Columbia Journalism Review*. http://www.cjr.org/behind_the_news/loneliness_at_the_foreign_bureau.php

43. Wadekar, N. (2015, September 24). State of the media: International coverage in U.S. journalism. http://www.neontommy.com/news/2015/09/state-media-international-coverage-us-journalism; Hammer, J. (2014, December 11). As legacy news outlets retreat, who will be there to report on the world? *Nieman Reports*. http://niemanreports.org/articles/as-legacy-news-outlets-retreat-who-will-be-there-to-report-on-the-world/.

44. *The Washington Post* announces newsroom expansion including new foreign bureaus, breaking news hubs in Europe and Asia. (2020, December 21). *The Washington Post*. https://www.washingtonpost.com/pr/2020/12/21/washington-post-announces-newsroom-expansion-including-new-foreign-bureaus-breaking-news-hubs-europe-asia/

45. Utley, G. (1997). The shrinking of foreign news: From broadcast to narrowcast. *Foreign Affairs*, 76(1), 2–10. Also see Cunningham, B. (2000). The AP now. *Columbia Journalism Review*, 39(4).

46. Taylor, P. (2005). The pornographic barbarism of the self-reflecting sign. In H. Nossek, A. Sreberny, & P. Sonwalkar (Eds.), *Media and political violence* (349–366). Hampton Press.

47. Aday, S. (2011). The real war will never get on television: An analysis of casualty imagery. In D. A. Graber (Ed.), *Media power in politics* (6th ed.). CQ Press.

48. Aday, S. (2010). Chasing the bad news: An analysis of 2005 Iraq and Afghanistan war coverage on NBC and Fox News channel. *Journal of Communication*, 60, 144–164.

49. Fox, R. (2007). Visions of terror: On the use of images in the mass mediated representation of the Bali bombing. In H. Nossek, A. Sreberny, & P. Sonwalkar (Eds.), *Media and Political Violence*. Hampton Press.

50. Gans, H. J. (1979). *Deciding what's news: A study of* CBS Evening News, NBC Nightly News, Newsweek, *and* Time. Pantheon. See also Wolfsfeld, G. (1997). *Media and political conflict: News from the Middle East*. Cambridge University Press; Perlmutter, D. D., & Hamilton, J. M. (Eds.). (2007). *From pigeons to news portals: Foreign reporting and the challenge of new technology*. Louisiana State University Press.

51. Diamond, E. (1975). *The tin kazoo: Television, politics, and the news*. MIT Press, p. 94.

52. Sui, M., Dunaway, J., Soobek, D., Abad, A., Goodman, L., & Saha, P. (2017). US news coverage of global terrorist incidents. *Mass Communication and Society*, 20(6), 895–908. Data source for affinity scores is Bailey, M. A., Strezhnev, A., & Voeten, E. (2017). Estimating dynamic state preferences from United Nations voting data. *Journal of Conflict Resolution*, 61(2), 430–456.

53. Hallin, D. C. (1987). Hegemony: The American news media from Vietnam to El Salvador: A study of ideological change and its limits. In D. L. Paletz (Ed.), *Political communication research: Approaches, studies, assessments*. Ablex, p. 17; Entman, R. M. (1996). Hegemonic socialization, information processing, and presidential news management: Framing the KAL and Iran Air incidents. In A. Crigler (Ed.), *The psychology of political communication*. University of Michigan Press.

54. Peksen, D., Peterson, T. M., & Drury, A. C. (2014). Media-driven humanitarianism? News media coverage of human rights abuses and the use of economic sanctions. *International Studies Quarterly*, 58, 855–866.

55. Gergen, D. R. (1991). Diplomacy in a television age: The dangers of teledemocracy. In S. Serfaty (Ed.), *The media and foreign policy*. St. Martin's.

56. Graber, D. A. (2003). Terrorism, censorship, and the First Amendment. In P. Norris, M. Kern, & M. Just (Eds.), *Framing terrorism: The news media, the government, and the public*. Routledge.

57. Bernhard, N. (2003). Embedding reporters on the frontline. *Nieman Reports*, 57(2), 87–90.

58. Kennedy, D. (2003). Embedded reporting: Is objectivity an acceptable casualty of this kind of reporting? *Nieman Reports*, 57(2), 87; Aday, S., Livingston, S., & Hebert, M. (2005). Embedding the truth: A cross-cultural analysis of objectivity and television coverage of the Iraq War. *Press/Politics*, 10(1), 3–21; Pfau, M., Haigh, M., Gettle, M., Donnelly, M., Scott, G., Warr, D., & Wittenberg, E. (2004). Embedding journalists in military combat units: Impact on newspaper

story frames and tone. *Journalism and Mass Communication Quarterly*, 81(1), 74–88.

59. Doris A. Graber's research.

60. Entman, R. M. (1991). Framing U.S. coverage of international news: Contrasts in narratives of the KAL and Iran Air incidents. *Journal of Communication*, 41(Fall), 6–27.

61. Peksen, D., Peterson, T. M., & Drury, A. C. (2014). Media-driven humanitarianism? News media coverage of human rights abuses and the use of economic sanctions. *International Studies Quarterly*, 58, 855–866.

62. Reston, R. (1967). *Sketches in the sand*. Knopf, p. 195; for supporting evidence in the Gulf War, see Lang, G. E., & Lang, K. (1994). The press as prologue: Media coverage of Saddam's Iraq, 1979–1990. In W. L. Bennett & D. L. Paletz (Eds.), *Taken by storm: The media, public opinion, and U.S. foreign policy in the Gulf War* (pp. 43–62). University of Chicago Press.

63. *The New York Times* Editors. (2004, May 26). *The New York Times* reviews its own coverage of Iraq War. *The New York Times*; Kurtz, H. (2004, August 12). *The Post* on WMDs: An inside story. *The Washington Post*.

64. Lehmann, I. A. (2005). Exploring the transatlantic media divide over Iraq. *Press/Politics*, 10(1), 63–89; Entman, R. (2004). *Projections of power: Framing news, public opinion, and U.S. foreign policy*. University of Chicago Press; Hess, S., & Kalb, M. (Eds.). (2003). *The media and the war on terrorism*. Brookings Institution Press; Groeling, T., & Baum, M. A. (2008). Crossing the water's edge: Elite rhetoric, media coverage, and the rally-round-the-flag phenomenon. *Journal of Politics*, 70(4), 1065–1085.

65. Quoted in Matta, F. R. (1979). The Latin American concept of news. *Journal of Communication*, 29(Spring), 169.

66. Gaddy, G. D., & Tanjong, E. (1986). Earthquake coverage by the Western press. *Journal of Communication*, 36(Spring), 105–112. For a conflicting analysis, see Adams, W. C. (1986). Whose lives count? TV coverage of natural disasters. *Journal of Communication*, 36(Spring), 113–122.

67. For a discussion of media imperialism, see Schiller, H. I. (1989). *Culture, Inc.: The corporate takeover of public expression*. Oxford University Press; Ravault, R. J. (1996). International information: Bullet or boomerang? In D. L. Paletz (Ed.), *Political communication research: Approaches, studies, assessments*. Ablex.

68. The impact of foreign television is assessed in Tan, A. S., Li, S., & Simpson, C. (1986). American TV and social stereotypes of Americans in Taiwan and Mexico. *Journalism Quarterly*, 63(Winter), 809–814.

69. Said, E. W. (1987). *Covering Islam: How the media and the experts determine how we see the rest of the world* (revised ed.). Vintage; also see Gunther, R., &

Mughan, A. (2012). *Democracy and the media: A comparative perspective.* Cambridge University Press.

70. Adoni, H., & Mane, S. (1984). Media and the social construction of reality: Toward an integration of theory and research. *Communication Research, 11*(July), 323–340; see also Graber, D. A. (2001). *Processing politics: Learning from television in the internet age.* University of Chicago Press.

71. Lent, J. A. (1977). Foreign news in American media. *Journal of Communication, 27*(Winter), 46–50. See also Ramaprasad, J., & Riffe, D. (1987). Effect of U.S.–India relations on *New York Times* coverage. *Journalism Quarterly, 64*(Summer/Autumn), 537–543; Hallin, D. C. (1987). Hegemony: The American news media from Vietnam to El Salvador: A study of ideological change and its limits. In D. L. Paletz (Ed.), *Political communication research: Approaches, studies, assessments.* Ablex, p. 17; Altheide, D. (1984). Media hegemony: A failure of perspective. *Public Opinion Quarterly, 48*(Summer), 476–490.

72. Saudi Arabia: "Image laundering" conceals abuses. (2020, October 2). *Human Rights Watch.* https://www.hrw.org/news/2020/10/02/saudi-arabia-image-laundering-conceals-abuses#

73. TV networks say coverage would not endanger troops. (1994, September 19). *The New York Times.*

74. Bennett, W. L. (2010). An introduction to journalism norms and representations of politics. *Political Communication, 13*(4), 373–384.

75. Hallin, D. C. (1984). The media, the war in Vietnam, and political support: A critique of the thesis of an oppositional media. *Journal of Politics, 46*(February); for many examples, see also Mermin, J. (1999). *Debating war and peace.* Princeton University Press; Zaller, J., & Chiu, D. (2000). Government's little helper: U.S. press coverage of foreign policy crises, 1946–1999. In P. I. B. L. Nacos, & R. Y. Shapiro (Eds.), *Decisionmaking in a glass house: Mass media, public opinion and American and European foreign policy in the 21st century.* Rowman & Littlefield.

76. Zaller, J., & Chiu, D. (2000). Government's little helper: U.S. press coverage of foreign policy crises, 1946–1999. In P. I. B. L. Nacos, & R. Y. Shapiro (Eds.), *Decisionmaking in a glass house: Mass media, public opinion and American and European foreign policy in the 21st century.* Rowman & Littlefield, pp. 74–81.

77. Baum, M. A., & Potter, P. B. K. (2015). *War and democratic constraint: How the public influences foreign policy.* Princeton University Press.

78. Hayes, D., & Guardino, M. (2013). *Influence from abroad: Foreign voices, the media, and U.S. public opinion.* Cambridge University Press.

79. Livingston, S. (1996). *Clarifying the CNN effect: An examination of media effects according to type of military intervention.* Harvard University Press.

80. Gilboa, E. (2003). Television news and U.S. foreign policy: Constraints of real-time coverage. *Press/Politics*, 8(4), 97–113.

81. Gilboa, E. (2003). Television news and U.S. foreign policy: Constraints of real-time coverage. *Press/Politics*, 8(4), 97–113.

82. Nicholas O. Berry (1990) makes the same argument in *Foreign policy and the press: An analysis of* The New York Times' *coverage of U.S. foreign policy*. Greenwood Press.

83. Albright, M. (2001). Around-the-clock news cycle a double-edged sword. *Harvard International Journal of Press/Politics*, 6(1), 105–108. Quote is from p. 105.

9

Diversity, Inclusion, and Equality in Media and Politics

Learning Objectives

1. Describe the importance of descriptive representation in democratic governance and its relationship with descriptive representation in the news.

2. Comprehend the importance of descriptive representation in political news coverage.

3. Identify the nature and degree of bias in news depictions of groups based on race, ethnicity, class, sex, or gender identity.

4. Examine the state of diversity in newsrooms around the United States (U.S.) and what diversity (or its absence) in newsrooms means for patterns commonly observed in news content.

5. Assess how alternative media meets the demand for specialized forms of news tailored specifically to address the unmet information needs of groups historically not well served by traditional media.

When Dorothy Byrne, the head of news and current affairs at UK's Channel Four, spoke at a weekly seminar held by the Reuters Institute of Politics in 2019, she summarized her central point with this statement:

> My key message to you today is that if you want a successful newsroom, it has to be representative of the diversity of your population in terms of gender, sexuality, disability and ethnicity. If you yourselves are not representative of your audience or

your readers, then you cannot understand and represent their interests. As society changes, if you don't change with it, you will lose viewers, listeners and readers.[1]

Byrne is not the only prominent news professional urging the news industry to take more drastic action to ensure it is representative of the diverse communities it aims to serve. American journalism has struggled to meet the challenge of increasing diversity and inclusion for more than fifty years, beginning at least as early as 1968 when the findings of the Kerner Commission—a presidential commission established by Lyndon Johnson to examine contributors to racial strife in America—were published in a report from the U.S. National Advisory Commission on Civil Disorders. In a sharply worded critique, the commission rebuked the media for its part in contributing to racial misunderstanding in America through biased, unfair coverage:

> Along with the country as a whole, the press has too long basked
> in a white world, looking out of it, if at all, with white men's
> eyes and a white perspective. That is no longer good enough.
> The painful process of readjustment that is required of the news
> media must begin now.[2]

But how much has changed? According to Reuters Institute Journalism Fellow and *Toronto Star* public editor, Kathy English, the statements in the Kerner Report "ring as true today as they did during that era of civil unrest and a resulting news credibility crisis."[3] In the wake of the commission's report and charges of inaccurate and unfair reporting on the civil rights movement, public trust and confidence in journalism declined. In the 1970s, Americans' media trust rose again, holding at relatively high rates, ranging between 68% and 72%. And although it declined somewhat over the course of the 1980s and in the 1990s, it was not until 2004 that it dropped to 44%. After reaching the 50% mark once more in 2005, in the years between 2006 and 2020, the American public's trust in media never again reached or exceeded 50%. English's point is this: Today's media is still not reflective of the broader population it aims to serve and is once again facing a crisis of credibility.[4]

Besides reaffirming the adage that "past is prologue," what Kathy English tried to highlight in her report on revitalizing the role of public editors is the importance of the link between descriptive representation, perceived legitimacy, and trust in the media. She, Byrne, and others maintain that journalism's lack of diversity is a major contributor to media mistrust, low levels of perceived press credibility, and related declines in news ratings, revenues, and audiences. While the causes of these declines are almost certainly more complex than being solely attributable to a single factor, such criticisms are not off the mark. How can anyone expect newsrooms without personnel who reflect a diversity of experiences and perspectives to anticipate and meet the information needs of communities who do have a diversity of experiences and perspectives? Newsrooms that understand where their audiences are coming from are best equipped to serve them well.

This chapter describes and explains the concept of descriptive representation as applied to media and politics in the United States. It starts with a discussion of the state of descriptive representation in government and politics and examines how that relates to representation in news coverage. In the following section, the chapter explores how often and how equitably various groups are represented in the media, primarily in news coverage. Next, we look to diversity and descriptive representation in newsrooms around the country, examining the extent to which we can understand whether the patterns observed in coverage are in part a product of the demographic make-up of newsrooms. Finally, the chapter explores the availability of various forms of alternative media, considering how well they serve groups and communities not typically well-served by mainstream media.

Descriptive Representation in Politics

Research on diversity and representation in democratic governance makes a distinction between two types of representation: descriptive and substantive. The more intuitive of the two is *descriptive representation*, which is the idea that having representatives in government that resemble the broader population is, in itself, a normatively good thing. Proponents of descriptive representation argue that the importance of having diversity in representative government does not necessarily require or assume that people of various sex, gender, racial, and ethnic identities will behave differently once elected or appointed to office. Instead, the mere fact that they are present is important because it instills a stronger sense of government legitimacy and authority in the view of a diverse citizenry. Research demonstrates this effect for the courts and Congress as well as for perceptions about state and local governments. Members of minority groups, for example, assign greater legitimacy and importance to court opinions when the court is more reflective of the demographics of the broader population.[5] Similarly, research on legislative representation demonstrates that people want, and are more likely to contact, representatives with whom they share characteristics such as race, ethnicity, or religion.[6]

Proponents of descriptive representation in government argue that it is important because it has the potential to diversify the perspectives and experiences held by those governing. Descriptively representative leaders' preferences are ostensibly more reflective of those of a diverse populace. In other words, some would argue that descriptive representation should also improve substantive representation by making the perceptions and behaviors of those in office more in line with the populace. Under this view, if more women, African Americans, Asian Americans, and Latinos are elected and/or appointed to office, the groups they descriptively represent will be better understood and therefore better served.[7]

Despite the many potential benefits of diversity, many characteristics of the American public are not well-reflected by the individuals holding elected and appointed offices across the three major branches of the federal government. This is true even as today's (117th) Congress is more racially and ethnically diverse than ever. More than 120 members identify as Asian/Pacific Islander, Black, Latino or Native American. In total, these members account for 23% of Congress. By chamber, they account for 26% of the House and 11% of the Senate. This is a marked improvement over the last several decades, yet it still falls short of the level of diversity that reflects the nation as a whole. Non-Hispanic whites make up 77% of Congress, but only 60% of the nation's population. Similarly, the proportion of women in the 117th Congress is at record highs. Women make up 27% of members across the House and Senate. However, their representation is somewhat lopsided in terms of partisanship—there are more women Democrats than men, and 27% is an improvement, but obviously this is not reflective of their 51% share of the U.S. population.[8]

Although it, too, has improved over the years, the federal judiciary also faces challenges with respect to diversity. According to a 2019 study from the Center for American Progress, sitting federal judges remain predominately white and male, accounting for nearly 60% of sitting federal judges. Women make up 27% when their population numbers are at 51%, while people of color account for about 20%, despite accounting for 40% of the population. Those who identify as lesbian, gay, bisexual, transgender, and queer/questioning (LGBTQ) only make up 1% of sitting federal judges, despite accounting for 4.5% of the population.[9] Executive and legislative offices and the courts are more diverse at state and local levels, but they generally still fall short of mirroring the communities they represent.

One of many reasons diversity is an ongoing challenge for appointed positions is that there are often diverging views across the two parties (and across presidential administrations and other executive offices, such as gubernatorial offices) about the extent to which descriptive representation is critically important.[10] Those who downplay any urgent need for it maintain that it is not required for good substantive representation and that constituency groups should elect (and choose to re-elect) on the basis of qualifications and performance—rewarding those in office who have served them well. Further complicating the debate is that research on the extent to which descriptive representation is required for (or improves) good substantive representation is mixed.

Nevertheless, evidence of the differences in prioritization across recent presidential administrations is apparent when it comes to efforts to diversify the executive and judicial branches. The Obama administration made diversity a priority, changing the composition of both branches considerably. The nascent Biden administration appears determined to continue in this vein; the all-women team leading Biden's White House communication office has been vocal about the administration's efforts to diversify the judiciary and executive branch, including many top leadership positions. Notably, too, when Biden selected Kamala Harris as his running mate, he positioned her to serve as the not only the first woman but also the first African American, and Asian American vice president in American history. In addition to nominating a diverse slate of judicial nominees, including federal appeals court judges, Biden also nominated several "firsts" as cabinet secretaries and cabinet-level agency leaders (see Table 9-1).

Research on descriptive and substantive representation in American politics suggests that groups in society feel more efficacious, meaning they feel more like their political attitudes and behaviors matter, when they are descriptively represented. When Latinx candidates run for office, for example, more Latinx voters turn out to vote. Similarly, in places where minority candidates have held office in the past, minority group members are more likely to run for office. Next, we related this to diversity in media content and personnel. Do similar relationships hold for descriptive representation in the mass media? Research on the concept and effects of symbolic annihilation suggests they do, as we discuss in the following section.

Table 9-1 Biden Cabinet Secretary Confirmations and "Firsts" to Hold the Office

Position	Nominee Confirmed	First to Hold the Office
Secretary of Defense	Lloyd Austin	African American
Secretary of Treasury	Janet Yellen	Woman
Secretary of State	Antony Blinken	
Secretary of Transportation	Pete Buttigieg	Openly gay man
Secretary of the Department of Homeland Security	Alejandro Mayorkas	Immigrant and Latino
Secretary of Veterans Affairs	Denis McDonough	
Secretary of Agriculture	Tom Vilsak	
Secretary of Energy	Jennifer Granholm	Person born outside the U.S.
Secretary of Education	Miguel Cardona	
Secretary of Commerce	Gina Raimondo	
Secretary of Housing and Urban Development	Marcia L. Fudge	African American woman (since 1979)
Secretary of Justice	Merrick Garland	
Secretary of Interior	Deb Haaland	First Native American
Secretary of Health and Human Services	Xavier Becerra	
Secretary of Labor	Marty Walsh	

Source: Adapted from Biden political appointee tracker. (2021, April 29). *The Washington Post.* https://www.washingtonpost.com/politics/interactive/2020/biden-appointee-tracker/

Note: Buttigieg is the first openly gay man to serve in any cabinet secretary position; Deb Haaland is the first Native American to serve in any cabinet secretary position.

Descriptive Representation in the News

We learned in the previous section that many groups are not well descriptively represented across the major branches and levels of our federal government. Given how much political elites are the drivers of (and primary sources in) the news, it seems like low representation in government would also mean low representation in the news and possibly in mass media content more generally. Which social and demographic groups are not regularly seen in mass media and in the news in particular? Which groups are shown a lot, and how are they depicted? If some groups are not well represented in the news, or if they are only shown in a negative light, what are the implications?

Research suggests that group media representations matter in part because of the important role media plays in socialization (see Chapter 10). Media exposure can influence what people believe about other groups as well as their own group, and these beliefs can influence attitudes and behavior. The concept of *symbolic annihilation* exemplifies the problem well. According to communication scholars George Gerbner and Larry Gross, absence from media "means symbolic annihilation."[11] Because media so heavily shape people's impressions about the world, media representation affirms social and political relevance. When women, members of certain socioeconomic status, or minority groups are ignored by mass media, they are denied their relevance. Group underrepresentation and misrepresentation in media can harm self-esteem and hinder the development of group members' self-concept. It can also affect the attitudes and behaviors of others regarding group members.

Class Representation

A recent study of class depictions on television programs found that a majority of characters appearing on prime-time shows (65%) were middle class, while 21.2% of characters were upper class, and only 11.3% of characters were working class. There were also differences across the prominence of the character roles. Sixty-seven percent of working-class characters had major roles compared to 46% of middle-class characters and 63% of upper-class characters. Among those playing minor roles, 33% were working class, 54% were middle class, and 37% were upper class. A large majority (83%) of the working-class characters portrayed were male and 17% were female. Women were not very present in televised depictions of working-class families and settings.[12] However, several very popular situation comedies depicted middle-class families in prime-time shows over the last few decades. Shows such as *The Connors, Mom, The Goldbergs*, and *Superstore* are some of the most recent examples.[13]

When depicted by news media, people of lower and working classes appear in news stories regularly but are subject to different roles and frames in coverage. Where affluent story subjects play prominent roles as primary subjects or expert sources, lower- and working-class individuals are more likely to be depicted as overly demanding of government benefits and ser-vices, undeserving parties in labor disputes, or victims of crimes or natural disasters.[14]

Racial and Ethnic Group Representation

The frequency with which different racial and ethnic group members appear in media content varies across the group, the platform, and the genre. Broadly speaking, however, studies show that television and film tend to both underrepresent and misrepresent racial and ethnic minority groups. Importantly, this tendency is generally not a response to market demand; shows and movies with diverse casts usually attract more audiences relative to their homogeneous counterparts. While representation improved in some genres, there is still significant variation across groups in terms of how well they are represented in mass media.

Media representation of Black Americans improved during the 1990s, when they started appearing on the screen at rates more reflective of their actual proportion in the U.S. (approximately 13% according to 2015 Census data). While this is good news, the data show that the quantity and value of appearances varies significantly across films and television programs. A five-second screenshot coupled with one line on an obscure off-hour television show is not comparable with a leading role in a prime-time show or heavily streamed Netflix series. For example, Nancy Signorelli's research finds that Black characters more commonly appear in limited networks and genres, often limiting these characters to shows and films with mostly minority characters. Though Black characters are appearing more often in media, the positive benefits are minimized if their appearances remain segregated from mainstream genres, channels, platforms, and networks.

When Black Americans are represented in the news, research suggests the picture is bleak once we consider both the quantity and quality of coverage. Black Americans tend to appear infrequently in the news, but they are overrepresented in stories about crime. Black males are particularly likely to be depicted as perpetrators of violent crime in the news. In the videos and images accompanying these stories, they are often shown in images casting them in a threatening light. Black Americans are also underrepresented as victims of crime and as police officers in news stories. Even though about 16% of law enforcement officers are Black, that's true of only 3% of police officers shown on news programs. Perhaps even more troubling is that the same patterns apply to news stories and Black youths. Though Black youths constitute only about 18% of all juvenile perpetrators, a full 39% of juvenile offenders shown on news programs are Black.[15]

When appearing in news about government, politics, and public policy, Black Americans tend to appear infrequently and primarily in the news conjunction with news about a limited set of events and issues. Given that 2020 was yet another year in which racial tensions were ignited by police killings of unarmed Black men, one of the primary ways in which African Americans were depicted in news was in protest. Perhaps ironically, one of the subtler aspects of the ongoing discontent about police mistreatment of Black Americans is media's failure to fully acknowledge and publicize the sheer number of African Americans who died at the hands of police (see Photo 9-1).

Studies of media representations of Latino/Latinx Americans reveal very different patterns. Though the Latinx population is the largest and fastest growing ethnic group in the U.S., they are dramatically underrepresented in television programs. Though the degree to which members of the Latinx community are represented in television programming waxes and wanes over time, it never comes close to reaching the true proportion of Latinos in the U.S. In 2017, Latinx characters only accounted for about 3% of characters on television, when 2015 Census figures estimated their proportion of the U.S. population at 17.6%. Latinas are more likely to appear in frequent roles on television relative to Latino men, who remain

Photo 9-1 Signs of Protest from Black Lives Matter Plaza in Washington, DC

Source: Author's photo; taken Sunday, July 26, 2020, in Washington, DC.

severely underrepresented. Film and video games reveal similar rates of underrepresentation, with most studies estimating that the proportion of Latinx characters in films and/or video games ranges somewhere between 1.5% and 3%. The frequency of news media representations of Latinx individuals varies considerably across time and media markets. In the coverage there is, Latinos are often portrayed as immigrants—primarily undocumented immigrants—and the tone of coverage is frequently negative.[16]

Representation of Native Americans in the media is rare, especially when it comes to regularly appearing characters on popular programs. The proportion of Native American characters on television does not reach 1.2%, which is the percentage of the U.S. population classified as Native Americans and Alaska Natives. When Native Americans are found in media, their portrayals often fail to reflect the diversity of the many different tribes recognized by the U.S. government today. Instead, mediated depictions of Native Americans are generic and stereotypical.[17]

Mediated depictions of Asian Americans and Pacific Islanders come closer to being accurately representative in terms of quantity, relative to other underrepresented groups. Nearly six percent (5.8%) of the U.S. population is classified as Asian American or Pacific Islander, according to the 2015 Census. They make up nearly four percent (3.8%) of the characters on prime-time television programs. Though this group is still underrepresented, the gap between the proportion of the actual population and the proportion of prime-time characters is much smaller relative to Latinos, for example. However, the positive assessment is limited to quantity. The quality of depictions of Asian Americans and Pacific Islanders is fraught with stereotypes.

Relatively few social scientific studies have investigated how people of Arab or Middle Eastern descent are depicted in U.S. mainstream media, but the studies that do exist document very low levels of representation. According to communication scholars Dana Mastro and David Stamps, one challenge to quantifying coverage of these groups is that media depictions tend to treat people from the Middle East, Arabs, and Muslims as homogeneous, making it difficult to accurately document their media representation. As with other minority groups, research suggests that—to the extent they are depicted at all—Arabs, Middle Easterners, and Muslims are underrepresented or negatively represented in U.S. mass media.[18]

Media Representations of Sex and Gender Identities

Because women make up roughly half of the U.S population—and, for that matter, the global population—one might think they would not be underrepresented in mass media. Yet, a 2015 report by the Global Media

Monitoring Project (GMMP) revealed that a mere 24% of primary news story subjects were women. Even in news stories about topics ostensibly related to issues of sex or gender—such as acts of sexual violence against women—men were the primary subjects and sources.[19] Researchers document decades-long, systematic patterns of underrepresentation and misrepresentation of women in media. Despite some improvement at the margins over time (the GMMP figure in 1995 was 17%) the general pattern persists. Even in digital news content, women are not well represented. The GMMP study found that only 26% of digital news story subjects were women, only a 2% improvement over more traditional media forms.[20]

In entertainment genres, studies of media representations of women often focus on the gendered roles in which they are depicted. Concerns revolve around stereotypes and the quality or accuracy of depictions more than the quantity, though women are still underrepresented in these genres, too. In both news and entertainment, the continual underrepresentation of women is thought to be related to the fact that fewer of the decision makers over content production are women. In newsrooms, the underrepresentation of women is well documented, but fewer studies focus on women's roles in the production of entertainment content. We will return to a discussion of the impact of diversity and content production later in the chapter.

Of course, comparisons between the frequency with which men and women are represented in the media only tell part of the story. Such comparisons are typically based on a binary classification of biological sex, and do not address the frequency (or quality) of media representations of people spanning the array of possible sex and gender identities. Researchers are beginning to recognize this and are taking steps to provide a more nuanced picture of how media portray people with various sex and gender identities. Though currently limited, research conducted so far suggests that while the frequency of media representations of LGBTQ characters and individuals improved in recent years, inclusiveness remains elusive, and this applies to the quantity, quality, and diversity of representation.

According to studies by GLAAD, the percentage of regularly appearing LGBTQ characters on broadcast and cable television programs never quite reached 5% between 2014 and 2017. Moreover, across both cable and broadcast television, a majority of LGBTQ characters were male. Most bisexual characters were female, as were most trans characters. Researchers stress that the lack of diversity among LGBTQ characters and/or their invisibility is particularly important because media often provide role models for young people who lack in-person access to role models with shared identities and experiences. Underrepresentation in media can have substantial influence on younger LGBTQ people looking for media role models or trying to cultivate a sense of community when real-world alternatives are not immediately available to them.[21]

Media Representations of Disability

Mass media portrayals of people with disability do not accurately reflect their numbers in society. According to data from the International Labor Organization, people with disability account for 15% of the world's population. Though people with disability are often depicted in television programs, advertisements, and film, their presence does not come close to accounting for 15% of all characters across these platforms and genres. When disabled people are represented in mass media, they often only appear in minor roles, further contributing to their invisibility in the media; they are also frequently misrepresented and are portrayed in negative ways. Researchers studying media and disability maintain that this underrepresentation is especially problematic because it reflects (and therefore reinforces) the lack of inclusiveness people with disability endure in the real world.[22] Media misrepresentations through stereotypical portrayals are equally problematic, but they will be revisited later in the chapter.

Multiple and Intersecting Identities

It may be that some of the most egregious examples of underrepresentation occur for people who share two or more of these group identities. It is difficult to know, because most of the research documenting representation in media tends to study one group at a time. One reason for that is that media depictions homogenize. Another reason is the difficulty of identifying, much less quantifying, more complex identity structures in analyses of media content. Thus, we know far less about the frequency of representation of people of mixed race, Blacks who also identify as Latinx, Asians who are also LGBTQ+, Latinas and Black women, and Native Americans with disability, and so on. As with many of the identities and groups addressed earlier in this section, stereotypes and misrepresentations are still common, even as the overall quantity of portrayals remains small.

Stereotypes and Unequal Treatment

As the sections above indicate, research shows that mass media depictions of many groups are not of sufficient quantity to reflect their true numbers in society. Other research focuses instead on the quality of media portrayals, examining the extent to which the media convey stereotypes or otherwise misrepresent groups. Some researchers are also interested in the effects of misrepresentations when they occur.

Racial and Ethnic Groups

Mainstream media in the U.S. primarily cater to white English-speaking audiences. As the section above details, one consequence of this is that racial and ethnic minority groups are routinely left out of coverage. When these groups do appear in mainstream English-language mass media, they are portrayed negatively, most often with negative stereotypes. Media watchers have complained for decades that racial and ethnic stereotypes are far too common in mass media. Numerous studies show evidence supporting the legitimacy of such complaints. Despite the fact that the frequency and degree of bias varies widely across programs, stations, newspapers, and parts of the country, racial and ethnic minorities are commonly depicted as unsophisticated and foolish, violent criminals, overly demanding "problem" people, or hypersexual nonprofessionals.[23]

Crime News

Heavy reliance on what's known as the *crime news script* is one of the primary means by which negative racial stereotypes appear so frequently in the news. The crime news script refers to the tendency television news programs have in opting to air sensational and dramatic stories about violent crime, so much that they overrepresent the proportion and frequency of violent crimes actually occurring in the real world. Not only does this emphasis on violent crime create the impression that people have a higher chance of being a victim of a crime than they actually do, these stories also disproportionately portray non-whites as the perpetrators of these violent crimes and disproportionately portray whites as victims.

African Americans, for example, are commonly depicted as not only the perpetrators but also as violent, threatening, and usually unkempt in appearance. Some research also suggests that more prejudicial information is included in news stories when the criminal defendant is Black relative to white counterparts. This unevenness in coverage does not accurately reflect crime statistics. African Americans are portrayed as perpetrators at higher proportions than their actual numbers in real world crime-related statistics such as arrest reports. In studies comparing department of justice statistics to news coverage, researchers found that although 39% of juvenile suspects that were shown were Black, in reality, Black youths only accounted for

18% of suspects. Coverage of whites was much more reflective of the real-world data. Twenty-four percent of juvenile perpetrators depicted were white compared to 22% in the data from the Department of Justice.[24]

As we will discuss at length in Chapter 10, such distortions are harmful because mass media play a key role in forming people's impressions about the world. People learn through the media. When the news distorts reality, it distorts public impressions of the real world. Research demonstrates this. When people are exposed to high rates of stories about violent crime, they think crime is more common than it really is. Studies show that these patterns in coverage increase audiences' likelihood of expressing preferences for punitive crime punishments and, among white audiences, they intensify negative attitudes about African Americans.[25] People are also more likely to express a great deal of concern about crime when it is covered extensively in the news. This is due to a process called *agenda setting*, which refers to the process by which the news media influences public perceptions about what issues are most important by covering some much more than others. The public reads increased media attention as an indicator of issue importance.

News media portrayals that encourage reliance on negative stereotypes are problematic because research also indicates how pervasive stereotypes are in society and shows that they can influence people's attitudes towards (and beliefs about) other groups. When people rely on stereotypes to form their impressions of other groups, it can also shape their political attitudes and behaviors, especially with respect to policies perceived to affect specific group outcomes. For example, in the case of immigration, subtle negative cues in the news can activate racial attitudes and boost opposition to new immigrants.[26]

Racialized Issues

As the discussion in the previous section reveals, political issues often become narrowly associated with certain groups in politics, media, and public opinion, even if they affect numerous groups in reality. When this kind of association happens for policy issues that become tied to racial or ethnic groups, researchers describe them as *racialized issues*. Even in circumstances in which an issue is not racialized in a broader sense, media coverage of an issue can still be racialized. For example, media coverage of immigration is racialized. Despite the fact that immigration policy is applicable to and affects groups from nations of origin all around the world, it is mainly people from Mexico, Central, and South America—Latinx communities—who have been the primary focus of immigration-related news coverage in the U.S. since the 1990s.[27] During this same time period, individual-level attitudes about Latinos also became a better predictor of public opinion on immigration policy, revealing how closely immigration policy area is associated with Latinx immigrants specifically in people's minds.[28] Immigration coverage also tends to be negative and primarily focused on illegalities associated with immigrants and immigration, either focusing on illegal border crossings or immigrants who are undocumented. Proximate coverage of border-related issues is also negative and sensational, fixating on crimes such as sex trafficking and drug trafficking.[29]

Research demonstrates the racialization of other policy issues as well. Several policy issues are linked with "symbolic group cues." Welfare is widely considered a racialized policy issue, and research attributes this in part to how media portray it.[30] For example, despite that white women are more likely receive welfare than Black women, welfare is most often depicted in association with Black women in news coverage and in political ads.[31] When African Americans are present in political news coverage, it is often only in association with racialized policy issues such as welfare, affirmative action, crime, law enforcement, police shootings, or proximate events such as the Black Lives Matter protests. Research suggests that by highlighting the particular aspects associated with racialized issues— whether it is through negative stereotypes or criminality—news media can increase the salience of these issue attributes for citizens. When this occurs, it influences their evaluation of the issue as a whole.

Framing People as Problems

In racialized policy contexts, Blacks, Latinos, and other groups are also often framed in news coverage as "problem people," either as violent or overly demanding of government and services. Such frames reinforce stereotypical associations about criminality, a lack of harmony between groups, and public misperceptions about which groups benefit most from government programs.[32] Minority group members are often depicted in the news as self-interested and "demanding of the body politic—continually causing or being victimized by a problem that seems endless."[33] A study of national network news by the National Association of Hispanic Journalists (NAHJ) found that Latinos are underrepresented in national news, and when covered, the primary topics with which Latinos were associated were immigration and crime. These two topics accounted for 36% of the news stories in which Latinos were a major subject. The NAHJ report concluded that "too often Latinos are portrayed as a problem people living on the fringes of U.S. society. Rarely do we see stories about the positive contributions of Latinos."[34] Mainstream news commonly reflects dramatic and episodic framing of race and ethnicity. It also tends to focus heavily on interracial conflict and violence. These patterns downplay evidence of racial comity and neglects other institutional and societal factors.[35]

Racial and Ethnic Stereotypes

Aside from characterizing African Americans as a problem people and associating them with criminality or racialized issues, media portrayals commonly include several other kinds of stereotypes. Early television, radio, and film often represented African Americans as a few basic archetypes, casting them as servants, buffoons, or objects of ridicule. The civil rights movement improved media portrayals at the margins, but the media still often depicted Blacks in negative and stereotypical ways. It was not until the 1980s that African Americans appeared in professional capacities and roles roughly on par with other groups in media. Even then, they were still portrayed poorly and their appearances were isolated to limited programs, stations, and genres. When Black Americans are in the news, the predominant stereotype is still that of criminality, a common pattern that unfortunately persists today.[36]

Latinx Americans are also regularly subject to a range of stereotypical portrayals in mass media. They are portrayed as criminals and as sex objects. Media representations of Latinos often convey poor work ethic, a lack of intelligence, and poor English-language skills. When portrayed as sex objects, the depictions often reflect a hot-tempered "Latin lover" stereotype, where characters are sexually attractive but prone to angry outbursts. Media representations of Latinos typically portray Latinos as low in socio-economic status, despite the fact that Latinos in the U.S. are a broad and heterogeneous group. Some of the more recent research suggests that things may be improving in entertainment television, though language-based stereotypes remain.[37] In the news, Latinos most often appear in stories about immigration, with a majority focusing on the negative aspects of immigration or criminality associated with immigration such as border arrests of (or unrest about) undocumented immigrants. Undocumented immigrants are depicted in the news at a rate much higher than their size in the U.S. population, and they are vastly overrepresented as criminals.[38]

When Asians and Pacific Islanders appear in mass media, they are frequently portrayed as the "model minority" stereotype. They are associated with high academic achievements, strong work ethic, traditional family values, and high skill levels in the areas of math and science. Despite the positive elements of these stereotypes, researchers maintain that these stereotypes are still harmful as misrepresentations. Stereotypes can create pressure to maintain the model status; they can foster tension with other groups based on perceptions of competitive threat, and such generalizations also homogenize across groups in ways that overrepresent some subgroups while symbolically annihilating others. Recently, researchers have also identified patterns in which stereotypical media depictions of Asian Americans play differently across women and men. Asian women are frequently portrayed as obedient, quiet, and exotic; alternatively, they are represented as ruthless, sneaky, and seductive. Asian men, on the other hand, are depicted as effeminate, nerdy, and asexual or alternatively as martial arts experts.[39]

Mass media portrayals of Native Americans—aside from being relatively infrequent—usually include stereotypes based on notions about the historical traditions associated with certain tribes, emphasizing ceremonial garb and spiritual ceremonies. When depicted in modern contexts, media portrayals still utilize stereotypes, but they revolve around alcoholism, drug use, poverty, corruption, and associations with casinos. Both types of portrayals also homogenize across the many different cultures and tribes that exist within the broader classification of Native American or Alaska Native in the United States. Compared to larger groups such as African Americans and Latinos, relatively few empirical studies about mass media portrayals of Arab or Middle Eastern Americans have been conducted. Researchers have, instead, tended to focus more narrowly on mediated depictions of Muslims. Those studies provide ample evidence suggesting that Muslims are depicted in negative and stereotypical ways, as violent and aggressive, and usually in the context of being associated with terrorism. Studies of Western media images of Arab women reveal they are typically depicted as passive and oppressed. These stereotypes span genres and platforms.[40]

Class Stereotypes

According to research, televised portrayals of the working class on entertainment programs commonly convey negative stereotypes. One stereotype frequently included in mediated portrayals of working-class television characters is that they are unintelligent. Working-class characters (especially males) are depicted as having very basic tastes, being lazy, exhibiting poor parenting skills, having drug or alcohol problems, and having little work ethic.[41] Overall, television provides a more flattering account of wealthy characters and families, and most entertainment television tends to cast low-socioeconomic status as a product of being irresponsible or lacking initiative, as if it is somehow deserved.[42] These trends are problematic in that they contribute to reliance on negative stereotypes and foster class biases based on notions of deserv-ingness. However, despite a common criticism that working-class peo-ple are underrepresented on television, they are more misrepresented than underrepresented. Intersectional variants of working-class people are, however, underrepresented. Most of the popular television sitcoms about working-class people, for example, are about white, blue-collar, heterosexual couples with children.[43]

Instead of examining how working-class individuals are depicted in the news, more of the recent work related to news media and class focused on how media target content toward working-class audiences (or how media is framed in ways appealing to different levels of socio-economic status) and how the framing of economic issues influences perceptions of working-class audiences. For example, Reese Peck's book on Fox News argues that Fox News combines populism with journalism in ways that link conservatism with white working-class taste. This includes the dismissal of the arts, literature, music, and fine dining and embracing their alternatives—pop culture staples such as "bro country," reality TV, NASCAR and monster trucks, and chain res-taurants. Peck argues that by appealing to blue-collar Americans, Fox News sets itself apart from elite, professional, news sources (such as *The New York Times*). One way this is achieved is through opinion con-tent, where Fox News hosts claim that these outlets and their allies treat non–college educated, conservatives as know-nothing rednecks.[44] While part of the aim is undoubtedly to attract and retain the loyalty of this particular audience, an unfortunate by-product of pitting these outlets and their audiences against each other is that it is likely one of the mechanisms driving the rise in affective partisan polarization. The U.S. is not the only place where media frames are contributing to class-based political conflict. In a focus-group based study conducted in Brazil and Sweden, the data reveal how the processes through which young people are socialized into the world of news tend to validate and encourage social differences: The modern day news environment allows media choice and news use to encourage moral and cultural boundaries between groups.[45] Matt Guardino's book, *Framing Inequality*, examines why low- and middle-income citizens support economic policies that in their personal economic self-interest. Based on a theory of "media refraction," Guardino argues that these policies were more popular than they should have been among these groups because news coverage was biased in their favor, which made them more appealing to middle- and low-income individuals.[46]

Sex and Gender Identities

Research on media representations of women reveals heavy use of stereotypes, many based on traditional gender roles. Women are often characterized as primarily relevant in the domestic sphere, playing roles focused on family as mothers, sisters, and wives, while men are cast in roles as breadwinners who are focused on work, politics, and other serious matters. A broad conclusion from much of the work on gender and media is that other than the general underrepresentation of women across various programs and roles, there is a lack of multidimensional portrayals of women in mass media. In more recent research, especially as the diversity of content offerings has increased, researchers have explored how depictions of women and gender representations vary according to the target audience of the program or channel. This research reveals that programming targeting women seems to offer more nuance in gender portrayals (across different identities) while content aimed at men tends to revert to older stereotypes associated with traditional gender roles. The quality of media representations also depends heavily on the type of media content examined. Television advertising, for example, is inundated with gender stereotypes and has been for decades. And, while entertainment media such as television and films are increasingly diversifying assignment of major and lead roles across sex, gender, race, and ethnicity, news media coverage of politicians remains uneven across sex and gender, as do assignments of men and women as sports journalists, play-by-play announcers, and game day commentators.[47]

Despite that over the last few decades, the rights of LGBTQ people have improved in the U.S. and other places, negative stereotypes of LGBTQ individuals still shape the impressions of significant portions of the American public. Partly because many people have limited direct experience with LGBTQ individuals, it is thought that media representations play a large role in shaping public opinion toward the group as a whole. Hence, many place a lot of the blame for lingering and widely held stereotypes on the media.[48] In addition to shaping perceptions of the public, research shows that media depictions of issues related to sexuality can influence the self-concept of people in regard to their own sexual identity.[49] However, as of yet, there is not much direct evidence to suggest that negative or stereotypical public views about LGBTQ issues and individuals are primarily a result of media influence. Yet the mere potential of any influence makes it important to understand both the quantity and quality of LGBTQ media depictions.

Media representations of LGBTQ people have changed over time, improving in terms of both quality and quantity. Depictions in entertainment media are significantly less disparaging than they were many years ago, and portrayals are also increasingly diverse and less homogenizing. The frequency of news coverage of LGBTQ individuals and issues has also increased over time, beginning with the 1980s, during which the HIV/AIDS epidemic raised the salience of the gay community and issues of sexual identity more generally. In the time since, policy debates around eligibility for military service and legal marriage have also kept the LGBTQ community in the purview of news media. One study of both entertainment and news media between 2000 and 2014 found that articles about LGBTQ issues and individuals became significantly more positive in the time period between 2010 and 2014.[50] This comports with other research suggesting that for most of the 20th century, mainstream news media depicted LGBTQ communities as outsiders, portraying them as a problematic and deviant group and reflecting older negative stereotypes that nonnormative identities are borne from psychological disorders. Though media portrayals have clearly improved in very recent years, they were severely problematic for decades, and stereotypes have shifted in nature and tone more than they've disappeared altogether.[51]

Disability

Research demonstrates that media representations of people with disabilities have generally been negative, inadequate, and inaccurate, creating and reinforcing stereotypes and disability stigma. Researchers have identified several common frames used to depict individuals with disability. They all tend to represent disability as something negative that needs to somehow be overcome as opposed to a valuable asset that can contribute to a positive source of personal identity. For example, in medical and social pathology frames, media depict people with disability as dependent on society for help and support. In some media portrayals, people with disability are depicted as using those disabilities as a means by which to game the system and gain unfair access to special accommodations. In the super-crip frame, they are depicted as superhuman for achieving normal or high accomplishments despite having a disability. Even when not overtly negative, all of these frames are problematic because of how media messages can influence self-esteem and self-identities. Disability advocates argue that these representations are negative and stereotypical and that they contribute to a misunderstanding of life with disability among people with and without disability.[52]

Differential Treatment in Election News

Media coverage is critical for politicians and political candidates. As a result, a significant amount of research has examined whether the press cover women candidates and candidates of color differently than their white and male counterparts. The press visibility of political candidates (i.e., the quantity of their coverage) influences voting behavior; when voters are more aware of a politician, they are typically more recognizable and determined to be more viable by the electorate, leading to higher turnout among supporters.[53] The quality of coverage, of course, is also important. The tone and focus of coverage (whether stories emphasize traits or issues and what kind of issues) and stories with information speaking to the viability of the candidate (their prospects for electoral success) are all aspects of campaign news coverage considered to be influential in voting decisions.[54] Thus, researchers continue to assess whether and how campaign news could be biased according to group status. If election coverage influences electoral prospects, poor media representation for women and minority candidates in campaign news could hinder descriptive representation in government.

Racial and Ethnic Minority Candidates

Given the importance of descriptive representation in government, it is important to ask whether minority candidates get a fair shake from the press. Previous research on campaign news coverage spanning the last several decades generally finds coverage of racial/ethnic minority candidates to be steeped in negativity and stereotypes—that is, if they get much coverage at all.[55] Minority candidates often receive very little news coverage during campaigns. When they are covered, the press tends to focus disproportionately on candidate race or ethnicity. In elections where one candidate is a minority and the other white, the news media tend to place a great deal of emphasis on the race or ethnicity of the minority candidate.[56] Journalists often consider candidates' characteristics such as race, sex, gender, and ethnicity to be novel and newsworthy; however, intense focus on these aspects can create the impression of white and male candidates as the default political candidate.[57] Media also commonly limit the campaign stories about minority candidates to race-related issues, even if those are not the campaign issues on which the candidate is focused.[58] In one study, when Black congressmen described themselves as having diverse interests and making the effort to represent the interests of all their constituents, the media depicted them as narrowly focused on racialized issues.[59] Some research suggests that these patterns in coverage are conditional on the political context. In an analysis of media coverage from the 2008 Canadian federal election, for example, there were no significant differences between the way white and non-white incumbent candidates were depicted. However, in open seat races, only the white candidates received positive coverage related to their qualifications.[60]

Women Candidates

How are women covered by the news media as political candidates? Research on this question examines whether there are gender differences in media coverage of political candidates and office holders. Specifically, these studies investigate the extent to which women are treated differently in press coverage—both in terms of quantity of coverage and in terms of its quality. Early research on media depictions of women as political candidates concluded that women endure a double bind, facing penalties for being too feminine (and therefore not qualified because they lack traits stereotypically associated with males) or not feminine enough (and therefore violating gendered expectations in ways that negatively affect voter assessments). Gendered stereotypes are also commonly used in framing about women candidates. In news stories, women candidates often get pigeonholed such that they are only associated with a narrow set of policy areas in which women are believed to be more qualified. In addition, women typically earn more trait coverage than issue coverage, and the traits covered are often those not relevant for politics, focusing on family life, hairstyles, or clothing. Research also suggests that depending on the context, women candidates are often treated as novelties. Because their status as "firsts" is newsworthy, it tends to eclipse many other aspects of the coverage women candidates receive. Yet some studies find that women candidates are not treated differently by the press and that voters do not treat them differently regardless, at least in the years since partisanship and polarization have been on the rise. According to this work, partisan bias trumps sex and gender bias at the ballot box.

In a recent meta-analysis, which included 90 studies on press coverage of over 4,000 men and women political candidates in over 750,000 news stories, the authors conclude, "About an equal number of studies show that . . . there is no difference in the tone of coverage between male and female candidates." They also find no evidence that country, region, type and level of office, or the type of media outlet moderates the relationship. These findings confirm the unresolved state of the literature with respect to tone in candidate coverage. The authors do find limited evidence to indicate that men candidates get more favorable coverage with respect to their viability as candidates (see Box 9-1), but the size of the difference is small, and the evidence is still somewhat mixed in that "even though men and women politicians receive the same amounts of horse race coverage and possibly also equal amounts of professional background coverage, the findings show that men are portrayed more positively in viability assessments and are quoted more often."[61]

In line with earlier research, findings from the meta-analysis show that stories about women politicians focus more often on their family life, appearance, and the fact that they are running as a woman, but coverage does not focus more on the personality of women candidates. All told, women receive more personal coverage than their male counterparts. Importantly, however, the authors do not find clear evidence to suggest that more personal coverage comes at the expense of issue coverage. Evidence from the meta-analysis suggests that men might have a slight advantage of more issue coverage but women candidates earn roughly equal amounts. On the question of trait stereotypes, the evidence suggests only a weak gender bias, where politicians are primarily covered in association with traits belonging to their gender stereotypes. This is thought to disadvantage women candidates because so many leadership traits are associated with male gender stereotypes. When the authors examined leadership traits in particular, the evidence was also mixed but with a slight advantage for men politicians. The authors offer a cautious conclusion that men are more often covered in association with leadership traits relative to women candidates. As all this evidence from the meta-analysis suggests, the existing research has not yet fully resolved questions about the extent to which media coverage of women as political candidates and officeholders is biased.[62]

LGBTQ Candidates

Research on differences in media treatments of men and women candidates provides some insight into what we might expect from news media depictions of LGBTQ political candidates. Researchers point out that, here too, the novelty of covering candidates who are running as potential "firsts" contributes to the tendency for journalists to place heavy emphasis on sexual identity, which may serve to downplay candidates' qualifications or other relevant information. Alternatively, other frames, such as those framing LGBTQ candidates as "threats to the norm," contain more implicit biases. Questioning the viability of an LGBTQ candidate in press coverage, for example, suggests that viability hinges on conformity with dominant sexual roles. Even when such frames are not overtly or intentionally negative, they may draw attention to sexuality in ways that disadvantage candidates. When candidates are covered as being openly gay, viability frames often pit their sexual orientation against receptivity among party leaders and voters based on the notion that their sexual orientation is unrepresentative of traditional family values. Media prime character-related considerations during evaluations of political candidates and stereotypes about the gay community are often negative. They frequently imply a lack of morals and/or stereotypically apply masculine traits to lesbians and feminine traits to gay men.[63]

Media depictions of LGBTQ candidates can also question their ability to provide substantive representation to the broader public. By painting LGBTQ candidates as interested in only a limited set of issues—those primarily of interest to LGBTQ communities—these depictions paint LGBTQ candidates as one-dimensional figures who are willing to discard the preferences of their constituencies for a narrowly defined political agenda. Though these frames are not applied to all LGBTQ candidates, they appear frequently and seem to be dependent in part on other characteristics of the candidate and their background and experiences. For example, some evidence suggests that candidates with other background characteristics that indicate respectability or normativity can more easily avoid being framed as incapable of representing general interests or as being a threat to the norm.

Research suggests that negative stereotypes continue to influence voters' perceptions of LGBTQ political candidates. According to the literature on stereotyping—which suggests that individuals rely on stereotypes in the absence of individuating information—candidates do not benefit from media coverage and frames that emphasize their sexual identities to the exclusion of all else. With more comprehensive and less stereotypical campaign news coverage, voters will be less reliant on negative stereotypes and should place greater weight on other, more relevant candidate characteristics such as issue positions and experience.[64]

Intersectional Candidates

Research on intersectionality in the American political context shows that gender and race/ethnicity are interactive and equally important when it comes to influencing electoral politics. This work suggests that intersectionality—at least as applied to the case of women of color running for office—is likely to influence multiple aspects of electoral politics: political ambition, voter impressions, candidate strategies, and press coverage to name a few.[65] Despite recent interest in intersectional candidacies and concerns by scholars about unfavorable news coverage about women and minority political candidates and officeholders, relatively fewer studies examine the effects of intersectionality on news coverage of political candidates.[66]

The recent research that is available suggests that the racial or gendered patterns previously identified in research on coverage of women and minority candidates is not enough to anticipate press treatment of intersectional candidates. For example, coverage of women of color as candidates or officeholders is especially biased.[67] When women candidates of color are winning according to polling data, they are less likely to enjoy the spike in positive coverage enjoyed by most white candidates, and they are more likely to be covered with racialized frames.[68] Similarly, Sarah Gershon's research found that House members who were white men, white women, and minority men earned almost an equal amount of positive coverage when they ran for re-election during the 2006 midterms, while women of color received disproportionally more negative coverage compared to the other groups. The double barrier of race and gender (being intersectional as both women and members of Congress) contributed to unfavorable press coverage.[69]

In her content analysis of newspaper coverage of the UK's 2010 general election, media scholar Orlanda Ward finds that the newsworthiness of women candidates' intersectional identities was both positive and negative. While intersectional candidates earned more coverage than white female candidates, but their coverage was also very negative and hyper focused on ethnicity and gender. Such coverage is problematic because it comes possibly at the expense of more politically relevant information, such as policy. In a study examining coverage of intersectional candidates in the 2012 general elections for the U.S. House, Ward compares newspaper coverage of minority women House candidates to matched samples of minority men, and white men and women running. Her analyses and findings reveal that minority women received less positive and more negative coverage relative to all other racial and gender groups in the study. Ward's findings also identified intersectional differences in coverage of women. Minority women received less coverage than their white female counterparts, but when they did, it was twice as likely to make gender central to the story. Jennifer Lucas's analysis of the 2008 election showed that Black women members of congress received increased media attention due to the spotlight on gender and race in the presidential primary election between Democratic candidates Hillary Clinton and Barack Obama.[70] As the nuanced findings from these studies suggest, more research is needed to understand the complexities of how intersectionality affects press coverage of electoral candidates.[71]

Box 9-1
Viability Frames in the 2020 Presidential Election

The findings from a recent study on viability frames in press coverage of the 2020 presidential election highlight the press-related challenges candidates with unique backgrounds face when seeking electoral office. In the study, communication scholar Jason Turcotte and his colleagues find that novelty frames remain prevalent for women and racial minorities running for office. However, they also find that novelty frames are not prevalent at the expense of more substantive coverage of policy issues, suggesting that novelty frames and policy frames can coexist in coverage of historically underrepresented candidates (see Figure 9-1).

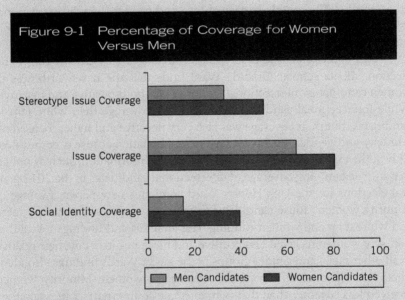

Figure 9-1 Percentage of Coverage for Women Versus Men

Novelty frames were fairly even for women and men, but social identity frames were heavy for minority candidates at nearly 40%, relative to white candidates at just over 15%. Though these frames did not cost non-white candidates coverage about policy issues, policy coverage related to candidates of color focused heavily on immigration and race relations, reflecting issue stereotypes in which candidates of color are perceived to have strengths in racialized issue domains (see Figure 9-2).

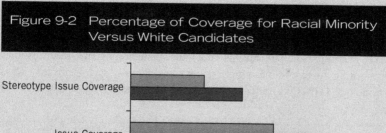

Figure 9-2 Percentage of Coverage for Racial Minority Versus White Candidates

While the authors state clearly that they do not want to generalize from their findings about Pete Buttigieg, because he is the first and only gay candidate for president, they note that he did receive less policy coverage relative to his opponents (see Figure 9-3). However, they note that Buttigieg's

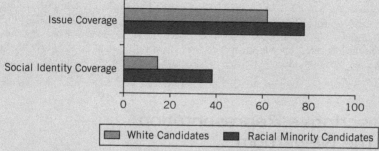

Figure 9-3 Percentage of Coverage for LGBTQ Versus Straight Candidates

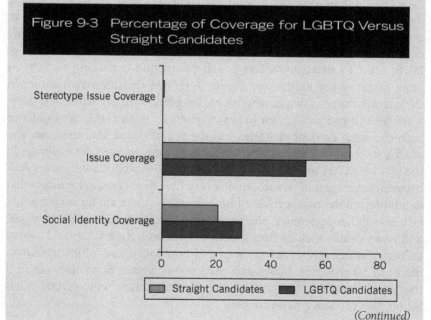

(Continued)

relative inexperience in the public sector (in addition to his youth) could have been a factor. The authors conclude by suggesting that future studies examining novelty frames emphasizing social identity seek innovative ways to include LGBTQ candidates, perhaps even on state-level or local races if necessary.

Source: Figures and write-up adapted from Turcotte, J., Furey, L., Garcia-Ortega, J. O., Hernandez, N., Siccion, C., & Stephenson, E. (2021). The novelty news frame: How social identity influences policy attention of minority presidential candidates. *Newspaper Research Journal*, 42(1), 95–110.

Descriptive Representation in the Newsroom

What explains such differential treatment in coverage? Many argue that one key contributing factor is a lack of diversity in the newsroom. These patterns in coverage are often attributed to the predominance of white, male culture in newsrooms,[72] or the preferences of white, English-speaking mainstream audiences.[73] As of 2018, minority journalists make up an average of 22.6% of workers in U.S. newsrooms. Out of the 293 news organizations the American Society of News Editors (ASNE) surveyed in 2018, only 15 newsrooms had a staff population consisting of 50% or more minority journalists (see Figure 9-4).[74] As the discussion earlier in the chapter suggests, when newsrooms are predominately white and male, it can lead to various implicit biases in coverage. Such biases can influence both the angle or slant of stories and the sources used, and they can also affect gatekeeping, determining which stories are selected for coverage in the first place. Yet research has not been able to establish a consistent link between coverage and newsroom diversity. One likely reason for that is that in addition to the perspectives of news workers, there are numerous other factors—audience demographics and preferences, salient events and issues, and news values such as timeliness and proximity (see Chapter 3)—that influence which stories are covered and how journalists ultimately cover them. In other words, biases and perceptions among news staff—even if they do influence coverage—operate in conjunction with several other factors that influence news content.

Racial and Ethnic Newsroom Diversity

Advocates of diversity in journalism regularly complain about slow progress in traditional media. With the arrival of the digital media, they fervently hoped for a new wave of more diversity-minded management. Until recently, there was not much evidence to suggest that digital newsrooms are any more diverse when compared to mainstream media. One problem is that many news organizations are unwilling to report the demographics of their newsrooms, making it difficult to track progress. However, the ANSE Newsroom Diversity Survey attempts to collect such data.[75] Newsrooms made slight gains in racial and ethnic diversity, increasing diversity and growing more representative of the cities they cover, on average, by 6.6% (see Figure 9-4).

Data from the 2019 ASNE survey suggest that it is the digital-only platforms that are driving race and gender inclusion in newsrooms. Just over 30% of news workers at digitally native publications are people of color, and this reflects a 5% increase over the previous year. Online-only outlets also appear to be doing better in terms of gender inclusion, where women make up 50% of the newsroom work force on average. Though these data suggest a positive trajectory, they must be interpreted with caution because news organizations participate on a voluntary basis, which means we cannot assume the newsrooms in the sample are representative of newsrooms nationally.[76]

In a recent study of 441 full-time workers in 14 Gannett newspaper newsrooms, data suggest that newsroom employees in more traditional newspapers continue to be overwhelmingly male and white. In the Gannett newsrooms studied, approximately 78% of the newsroom employees were white and 59% were men. White men made up nearly 50% of the whole group; white women accounted for about 30% of newsroom employees. Non-white employees only accounted for about 22% of workers, breaking evenly across men and women (see Figure 9-5).

From the perspective of descriptive representation, a potentially more important thing to consider is whether newsrooms are as diverse of the communities they serve. Can community groups expect to have descriptive representations in their newsrooms? The Gannett study also examined this question, comparing each paper's newsroom demographics to those of the county in which it is located. The results were mixed, with some papers more representative of their communities than others, but on the whole, newsrooms do not very accurately reflect the diversity of the local markets they serve (see Figure 9-6).

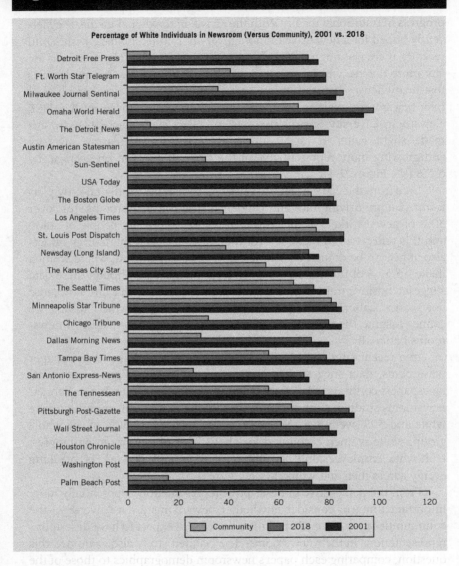

Figure 9-4   Racial and Ethnic Diversity in Newsrooms

Percentage of White Individuals in Newsroom (Versus Community), 2001 vs. 2018

Detroit Free Press
Ft. Worth Star Telegram
Milwaukee Journal Sentinal
Omaha World Herald
The Detroit News
Austin American Statesman
Sun-Sentinel
USA Today
The Boston Globe
Los Angeles Times
St. Louis Post Dispatch
Newsday (Long Island)
The Kansas City Star
The Seattle Times
Minneapolis Star Tribune
Chicago Tribune
Dallas Morning News
Tampa Bay Times
San Antonio Express-News
The Tennessean
Pittsburgh Post-Gazette
Wall Street Journal
Houston Chronicle
Washington Post
Palm Beach Post

0   20   40   60   80   100   120

Community   2018   2001

Source: American Society of News Editors. (n. d.). *Census data, 2001–2018.* https://googletrends.github.io/asne/?view=3&filter=race.

Note: Data provided in partnership with Google News initiative; 105 of 292 newsrooms are compared to a geography larger than a city. These geographies were approximated using public data.

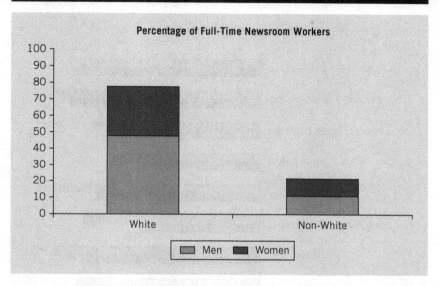

Figure 9-5 Gannett Newsroom Workers by Race and Gender, 2020

Percentage of Full-Time Newsroom Workers

White   Non-White

☐ Men   ■ Women

Source: NewsGuild-CWA and Gannett. Adapted from NewsGuild-CWA Study of Pay Equity in 14 Gannett Newsrooms. Graph is based on data on annual pay for 441 full-time workers in 14 NewsGuild newsrooms as of fall 2020.

Gender Diversity in the Newsroom

Currently, gender diversity in newsrooms faces numerous challenges. First, women journalists globally are facing increasing levels of threats and violence online. On the various digital platforms on which women journalists report or post their content and engage with audiences, they must confront misogyny, gaslighting, and threats of sexual violence and murder. This trend has been accelerating since at least 2016, with the rise of digital misinformation, conspiracy peddling, and political extremism online. According to an April 2021 report from UNESCO, more than 40% of women journalists responding to their survey reported being targeted online as part of a disinformation campaign. One in five reported being attacked offline in connection with online threats of violence. The report identified more than 10,000 obvious instances of abuse on Twitter, a great

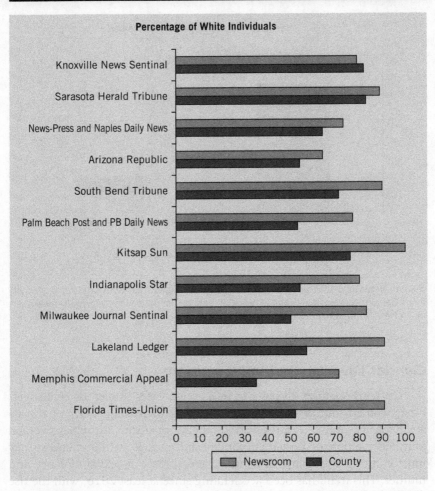

Figure 9-6 Comparing Community Diversity to Newsroom Diversity

Percentage of White Individuals

Knoxville News Sentinal
Sarasota Herald Tribune
News-Press and Naples Daily News
Arizona Republic
South Bend Tribune
Palm Beach Post and PB Daily News
Kitsap Sun
Indianapolis Star
Milwaukee Journal Sentinal
Lakeland Ledger
Memphis Commercial Appeal
Florida Times-Union

0 10 20 30 40 50 60 70 80 90 100

Newsroom County

Source: NewsGuild-CWA and Gannett. Adapted from NewsGuild-CWA Study of Pay Equity in 14 Gannett Newsrooms. Graph is based on data on annual pay for 441 full-time workers in 14 NewsGuild newsrooms as of fall 2020.

deal of which contained sexist and misogynistic language. According to the report, "Online violence against women journalists is designed to belittle, humiliate, and shame; induce fear, silence, and retreat; discredit them professionally, undermining accountability, journalism and trust in facts."

Its authors added that these tactics are also designed to drive women away from public debate.[77]

During the same month, April 2021, another report was released, one documenting dramatic gender pay gaps between men and women working for Gannett, America's largest newspaper company. The report was based on a study commissioned by Gannett and conducted by NewsGuild-CWA, an international union of journalists. In 2020, Gannett vowed to hire and encourage professional development among more women and people of color so that they could better reflect diverse audiences. Yet, according to an internal company report from 2021, Gannett's executives were 84% white and 73% male; its newsrooms were 58% male and 79% white. Similarly, the NewsGuild-CWA study found that 59% of newsroom workers were male and 78% were white. According to other key findings, experienced women journalists—those with more than 30 years of experience in working for a newspaper—earned 63% of the annual median salary of their male peers. Overall, women earned only 83% of men's median salary; women of color earned only 73% of men's median salary.[78] To women journalists, the back-to-back release of these reports must have felt like a double-gut punch. How can we expect to increase gender diversity in newsrooms when women are not paid equitably, even as they face increasing danger merely for doing their work?

For most of the newspapers in the Gannett study sample, newsrooms were dominated by men; only *The Arizona Republic* came close to reaching a near-even distribution of women and men, at 45% and 46%, respectively. In the newsroom of *The Milwaukee Sentinel*, the number of male employees more than doubled the number of women, and at the much smaller *Florida Times-Union*, there were more than three times as many men working in the newsroom as women. Looking at longer trends with the data from ASNE, between 2001 and 2018, the proportion of women in the newsroom increased by 3.7% overall. Thirty-two percent of newsrooms gained in gender diversity, while 21% lost diversity (Figures 9-4 and 9-7).

Newsroom Diversity and Content

What effect do demographic characteristics have on the news product? As described above, the evidence is inconclusive, making it debatable whether adequate coverage of the nation's problems requires media organizations that are a microcosm of the larger society.[79] Nevertheless, scholars and professional journalism organizations offer newsroom

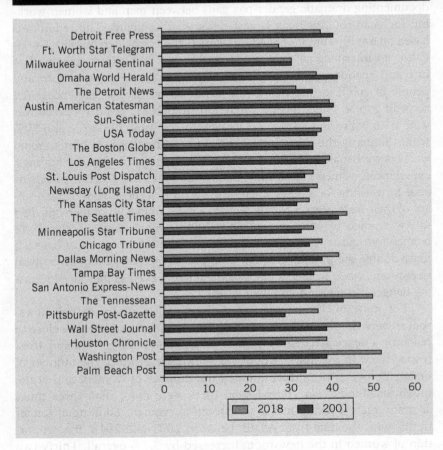

Figure 9-7 Percentage of Women on Newsroom Staff, 2001 Versus 2018

Source: American Society of Newspaper Editors. (n. d.). *Census data, 2001–2018.* https://googletrends.github.io/asne/?view=3&filter=gender.

Note: Data provided in partnership with Google News initiative; 105 of 292 newsrooms are compared to a geography larger than a city. These geographies were approximated using public data.

diversity as the central strategy to combat problematic media coverage of minority groups.[80] The expectation is that "female and minority reporters are able to provide a non-white or non-male perspective in the news."[81]

Proponents of newsroom diversity stress that mainstream media emphasize white, middle-class values while neglecting the interests of minorities and people of lower socio-economic status. Some research supports this view. For example, some studies show that journalists belonging to racial or ethnic minority groups possess a strong sense of racial identity and are driven by the need to represent their in-group members.[82] Reporters of color are also more likely than their white counterparts to include non-white sources in stories.[83]

It is important to recall, however, that at the aggregate level, minority journalists contribute to a small portion of news stories; this may be due in part to the limited editorial freedom reporters have in selecting stories or determining their placement.[84] Numerous studies show that minorities remain underrepresented in the news, a fact widely attributed to biases in news production. Both producers of content and owners of news media are predominantly male, middle aged, and white, and this is reflected in gatekeeping practices and story selection as well as frames and sources used in stories.[85]

Newsroom culture and journalistic training may be other factors working to prevent minority journalists from changing traditional patterns in coverage. Black and Latino journalists are still subject to traditional journalistic norms established by decades of customary practices in journalistic training. Most work in white-majority newsrooms and may fear being perceived as unprofessional or that they might harm their prospects for career advancement if their stories reflect the perspective of an advocate instead of a neutral observer and reporter of facts.[86]

Economic constraints may also play a role. Faced with ever-shrinking newsroom resources, journalists have less time for the community outreach needed to build a network of diverse sources.[87] Newsroom budget and staffing cuts in recent years have offset prior gains in newsroom diversity, stalling the trend in diversity growth and producing a plateau between 2012 and 2015. The commercially oriented media system in the U.S. coupled with the increasingly competitive media landscape and the need to cater to audiences adds complexity to newsroom diversity as a solution to inequities in coverage.[88]

Market Representation and Service to Diverse Audiences

The widely unanticipated popular support for insurgent candidates such as Bernie Sanders and Donald Trump in 2016 raises questions about important gaps in reporting. Why were mainstream journalists so off the mark when it came to anticipating public support for candidates who were able to tap into streams of public discontent across income, education, class, sex, and age? The gaps suggest that news reflects reporters' backgrounds and interests to a degree, but also that mainstream journalists' backgrounds and perspectives are very different from large portions of the American public.[89] Hundreds of specialized media address information needs that are neglected or poorly served by the regular media. They are a partial antidote to the general mass media's failure to cover many important groups and issues.

Racial and Ethnic Media

Media serving African American and Hispanic communities are good examples of outlets classified as racial or ethnic media. Besides having their own print media, large subcultural groups in the United States are also served by radio, television, and digital news media tailored to their special concerns. Over-the-air and cable television and radio stations geared to the needs of subcultures, especially Spanish speakers, are multiplying and flourishing throughout the country (Figure 9-8). There are more than 400 Hispanic newspapers and two major television networks, Univision and Telemundo. In Los Angeles, Univision is now the leading supplier of television news.[90]

Ethnic networks serve relatively youthful populations who are hungrier for televised news than is the general population. They are a growing media force bound to carry increasing weight in U.S. politics, especially in urban areas. In New York City, for example, a dozen ethnic press ventures (out of fifty) claim circulations of more than 100,000. The five largest among them serve Jewish, Chinese, Hispanic, African American, and Korean populations.[91] Just as with alternative media described above, racial and ethnic media often follow a civic or public journalism model. They may try to generate support for issues favored by their audiences, and they may advocate for candidates or issues during crises and events or facilitate community organizing. Previous content-analytic research reveals, for example, that due to differences in preferences of the audiences they serve, Spanish language media outlets often cover political issues they perceive to be relevant to Latinx communities at higher volumes than English-language media, and they often cover those issues—such as immigration—with a more positive tone relative to mainstream English-language media.[92] However, as Box 9-2 explains, there may be harmful spillover effects.

Figure 9-8   Growth of Spanish-Language News Availability,
2000–2008

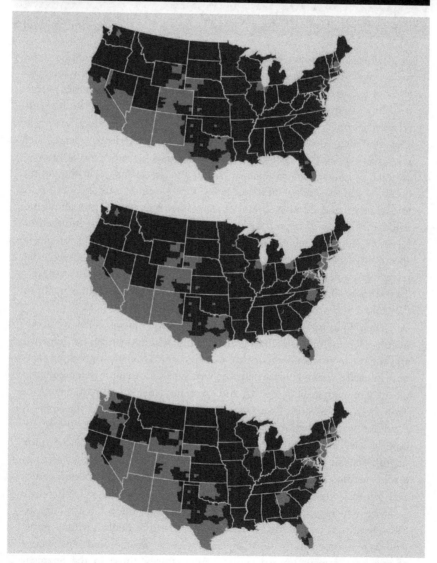

Source: Darr, J. P., Perry, B. N., Dunaway, J. L., & Sui, M. (2020). Seeing Spanish: The effects of language-based media choices on resentment and belonging. *Political Communication, 37*(4), 488–511. Map shows counties with Spanish language television outlets and/or newspapers. Data compiled from Broadcasting and Cable Yearbooks (2000–2001, 2004–2005, 2008–2009).

Box 9-2
The Effect of Seeing Spanish on Resentment and Belonging

In 2018, researchers set out to test the spillover effects from exposure to media offered in different languages. The authors hypothesized that the effect of seeing news stories offered in Spanish might have differential effects on white English-speaking audiences versus bilingual Latinos. Along with relevant theories, previous research, survey data, and anecdotal evidence suggested that some white English-speaking media audiences might feel resentment when they encounter Spanish language, whether in the form of options or instructions in Spanish, say at the gas pump or in the voting booth. Given that today's news media options are numerous and offered in several forms and through several platforms one encounters throughout the day, the researchers wanted to know if we might observe the same effect for news stories. Their study found that the language of news articles—specifically, seeing news stories offered in Spanish—can increase racial resentment among English-speaking white Americans while inducing feelings of inclusion and belonging among Spanish-speaking Latinos living in the United States.

Their findings are based on two online experiments. One was conducted with a sample of 620 English-speaking white American participants, and the other was conducted with a sample of 362 Spanish-speaking Latinos. In each experiment, participants were shown a total of nine news stories dealing with politics, sports, and entertainment. For all participants, at least seven of the stories were in English, but participants in the Spanish condition were shown up to two Spanish language articles. After seeing the news articles, participants were asked to answer questionnaires. Those in the English-speaking sample were asked a series of questions about their feelings toward Latinos, and those in the Latino sample were asked about whether they feel welcome in the United States.

The language in which the news stories were offered had a statistically significant effect on both groups. Those in the English/white sample who were exposed to Spanish-language news stories reported higher rates of racial resentment toward Latinos. Alternatively, those in the Spanish-speaking/Latino sample were more likely to report feeling they belong in the United States if they were exposed to news stories in Spanish. Interestingly, the effect held for political news but not for sports stories, indicating there is something about the language of political information in particular that matters. Party affiliation also mattered. Because Republicans had much higher levels of resentment at the study's outset, exposure to Spanish-language news had no effect. But among Democrats, where resentment started on average at much lower levels, the effect of seeing Spanish language news increased their likelihood of feelings of racial resentment toward Latinos. While Spanish-language media clearly provided a highly valued service to Spanish-speaking audiences and even provide an additional benefit of fostering feelings of inclusion, those positives are somewhat offset by Spanish exposure's effect of stoking resentment among English-speaking whites.

Source: Darr, J. P., Perry, B. N., Dunaway, J. L., & Sui, M. (2020). Seeing Spanish: The effects of language-based media choices on resentment and belonging. *Political Communication*, 37(4), 488–511. See also Manninen, V. (2020, February 19). *Seeing news in a foreign language can stoke racial resentment*. https://journalismresearchnews.org/seeing-news-in-a-foreign-language-can-stoke-racial-resentment/

The Alternative Press

In addition to the press serving racial and ethnic groups, there is also an alternative press at the national level and in local communities. These outlets tend to keep a relatively narrow focus on issues of interest to minority political cultures or people with distinctive lifestyles and cultural and political tastes. Many specialized media are targeted to groups such as LGBTQ communities. Examples of popular alternative papers include Boston's weekly *Dig*, San Francisco's *Bay Guardian*, and the *Isthmus* in Madison, Wisconsin. From time to time, specialized media try to generate support for issues favored by their audiences. They may try to influence elections or advocate for social change in other ways. Although these media provide in-depth coverage of local, national, and international news of interest to their clientele, they omit news covering broader concerns. Their readers may therefore live in narrow communications tunnels that keep them from fully understanding their surroundings.

Oppositional Media

Specialized media also encompass the politically radical, iconoclastic, and counterculture media that flourish in times of social and political stress, such as the late 1960s and early 1970s. These media feature the flagrant opposition to government policy that is permitted in the United States but often forbidden in other countries. At the height of underground press popularity, during the Vietnam War era and its aftermath, readership was estimated at 10 million. The rise of the underground print and electronic press during troubled times demonstrates that mass media can be started and operated with modest means. Similar to most alternative media, the counterculture media of the 1960s were financed through small-scale local advertising and through classified ads. Staffs were paid meager salaries or no salaries at all.[93] At one time, there were nearly 1,000 underground newspapers and 400 counterculture radio stations. Such vitality attests to the vigor and flexibility of the mass media system.[94] The abrupt decline of underground media with the end of the Vietnam War also shows that the system can prune its unneeded branches when demand ends.

Waning public support rather than official censorship led to the steep decline in this genre of journalism. It has been revived with the advent of the internet, where thousands of vitriolic anti-government sites urge opposition to established authorities and their policies and often suggest ways to implement radical ideas. Authoritarian governments seek to suppress these information channels; today, our own government worries about the role digital media play in the recruitment of terrorists. Mao Tse-tung's admonition to "let a thousand flowers bloom," ignored in China, has come to fruition on the U.S. alternative media scene. However, given the explosive growth of electronic soapboxes from which citizens can broadcast their views, the competition for attention has become extraordinarily fierce.

Public Media

As discussed in Chapter 2, public television was organized to provide an alternative to the typical programming available on the three commercial networks that were the sole providers of televised news at the time. Although some portion of public broadcast programming is geared to minorities, disadvantaged or underrepresented groups are not actually the primary audience for its programming. Instead, public broadcasting audiences tend to be relatively well educated, well-to-do, and (aside from those who watch the children's programs) quite small.

Proponents of the public broadcasting system argue that it still fills an important need that merits public support. Poor families need access to the rich cultural programs that are a hallmark of public television. They cannot afford to pay for access to the likes of the History, Discovery, Learning, and National Geographic channels, which cover important realms of information in depth. Because sophisticated cultural and educational programming attracts only small audiences, it is unlikely that the other free television channels will feature such fare in the future, even when digital technology increases the number of available channels.[95] The difficulty of keeping the public broadcasting system solvent without government subsidy may sound its death knell (though, at present, only a small percentage is funded by the government). The European practice of funding public broadcasting principally through consumer fees has never been considered a realistic option in the United States,[96] though funds raised from voluntary subscribers and donors constitute the major part of its funding.

In the context of today's high-choice digital media environment, some readers might question the importance of traditional forms of niche media—those described above as serving specialized audiences.

SUMMARY

This chapter defines the concept of *descriptive representation* and explains why it is important for democratic governance. It also examines the relationship between descriptive representation in government and descriptive representation in the news. Studies of media content and stories disseminated by the news media demonstrate the extent to which different racial and ethnic groups, people of different levels of socioeconomic status, and people of different sex and gender identities receive different amounts of coverage in the news. On the whole, research demonstrates that, as with government, mass media content is not very representative in a descriptive sense. One of many reasons that is true for news content is because journalists rely very heavily on public officials as journalistic sources and cover politics and government affairs heavily.

Perhaps more worrisome than underrepresentation is the extent to which some groups in society are *mis*represented in mass media, especially those groups that are already marginalized in society or occupy a minority status. Research on the nature and degree of bias in mediated depictions of groups and biases based on race, ethnicity, class, sex, or gender identity is revealing. It shows that other than relatively affluent white males, depictions of people often reflect negative stereotypes or stereotypes that homogenize groups instead of accurately depicting within-group heterogeneity. Such misrepresentations are important, especially because so many people in American society rely on mass media instead of their own direct experiences to shape their understanding about the world. Though research cannot always establish a causal relationship between mediated depictions of group members and public opinion, evidence suggests that unflattering media portrayals can influence people's perceptions of in-groups and out-groups alike.

Scholars, activists, and journalism professionals have worried for a long time about the lack of diversity in newsrooms around the United States. They assume, perhaps correctly, that the underrepresentation and/or mis-representation of groups in news content occurs primarily because the pro-totypical newsroom is still predominately white and male. Yet, researchers have had a difficult time empirically linking newsroom diversity to patterns in content. A likely reason for this is that news media are facing challenges on many fronts—increased competition, shrinking budgets, and declining credibility—all of which are limiting their ability to allocate the time, effort, and resources required to diversify their organizations in ways more reflec-tive of the population.

As media choices and offerings have expanded with the arrival of the digital news environment, more and more alternative forms of media are available to those with access. Researchers have documented several kinds; one example is the expanding role of ethnic media. These outlets provide an abundance of detailed news about the many regions from which U.S. immigrants hail and offer different perspectives about numerous politi-cal events and policy issues. But one thing not yet well understood by researchers is the extent to which the array of alternative media meet the demand for specialized forms of news—the publications, programs, and websites tailored specifically to address the unmet content needs of groups historically not well served by traditional media.

DISCUSSION QUESTIONS

1. Why is descriptive representation in democratic government important? What is its relationship with descriptive representation in the news?

2. Why is descriptive representation in political news coverage important? Which groups in society are best (and least) descriptively represented in mass media and the news? What about their treatment when covered? What is the nature and extent of bias in media depictions of groups and biases based on race, ethnicity, class, sex, or gender identity?

3. What is the state of diversity in newsrooms around the U.S.? What does diversity (or its absence) in newsrooms mean for patterns commonly observed in news content?

4. How well do alternative media meet the demand for specialized news outlets? Are they sufficient to address the unmet content needs of groups historically not well served by traditional media?

READINGS

Boczkowski, P. J., & Papacharissi, Z. (Eds.). (2018). *Trump and the media*. MIT Press.

Brock, A., Jr. (2020). *Distributed Blackness: African American cybercultures* (Vol. 9). NYU Press.

Callison, C., & Young, M. L. (2019). *Reckoning: Journalism's limits and possibilities*. Oxford University Press.

Carroll, F. (2017). *Race news: Black journalists and the fight for racial justice in the twentieth century*. University of Illinois Press.

Cheers, I. M. (2017). *The evolution of Black women in television: Mammies, matriarchs and mistresses*. Routledge.

Dell'Orto, G., & Wetzstein, I. (Eds.). (2018). *Refugee news, refugee politics: Journalism, public opinion and policymaking in Europe*. Routledge.

Dunn, T. R. (2018). *Talking white trash: Mediated representations and lived experiences of white working-class people*. Routledge.

Ellcessor, E. (2016). *Restricted access: Media, disability, and the politics of participation*. NYU Press.

Fishman, M. (2018). *Entertaining crime: Television reality programs*. Routledge.

Fraga, B. L. (2018). *The turnout gap: Race, ethnicity, and political inequality in a diversifying America*. Cambridge University Press.

Franks, S. (2013). *Women and journalism*. Reuters Institute for the Study of Journalism.

Fullerton, R. S., & Patterson, M. J. (2021). *Murder in our midst: Comparing crime coverage ethics in an age of globalized news*. Oxford University Press.

Georgiou, M., & Zaborowski, R. (2017). *Media coverage of the "refugee crisis": A cross-European perspective*. Council of Europe.

Guardino, M. (2019). *Framing inequality: News media, public opinion, and the neoliberal turn in US public policy*. Oxford University Press.

Hanitzsch, T., Hanusch, F., Ramaprasad, J., & de Beer, A. S. (Eds). (2019). *Worlds of journalism: Journalistic cultures around the globe*. Columbia University Press.

Hayes, D., & Lawless, J. L. *Women on the run: Gender, media, and political campaigns in a polarized era*. Cambridge University Press.

Hughey, M. W., & González-Lesser, E. (Eds.). (2020). *Racialized media: The design, delivery, and decoding of race and ethnicity*. NYU Press.

Jewkes, Y., & Linnemann, T. (2017). *Media and crime in the US*. SAGE.

Lind, R. A. (Ed.). (2016). *Race and gender in electronic media: Content, context, culture*. Routledge.

Luther, C. A., Lepre, C. R., & Clark, N. (2017). *Diversity in US mass media*. John Wiley & Sons.

Mattoni, A. (2016). *Media practices and protest politics: How precarious workers mobilise*. Routledge.

Mendelberg, T. (2017). *The race card: Campaign strategy, implicit messages, and the norm of equality*. Princeton University Press.

Monteverde, G., & McCollum, V. (2020). *Resist! Protest media and popular culture in the Brexit–Trump era*. Rowman & Littlefield Publishers.

Page, B. I., & Gilens, M. (2020). *Democracy in America? What has gone wrong and what we can do about it*. University of Chicago Press.

Parks, L. (2018). *Rethinking media coverage: Vertical mediation and the war on terror*. Routledge.

Piston, S. (2018). *Class attitudes in America: Sympathy for the poor, resentment of the rich, and political implications*. Cambridge University Press.

Richardson, A. V. (2020). *Bearing witness while Black: African Americans, smartphones, and the new protest #journalism*. Oxford University Press.

Rodríguez, C. E. (2018). *Latin looks: Images of Latinas and Latinos in the US media*. Routledge.

Ryan, M. E. (2018). *Lifestyle media in American culture: Gender, class, and the politics of ordinariness*. Routledge.

Ryfe, D. (2016). *Journalism and the public*. Polity Press.

Segal, M. T., & Demos, V. (Eds.). (2018). *Gender and the media: Women's places*. Emerald Group Publishing.

Sobieraj, S. (2020). *Credible threat: Attacks against women online and the future of democracy*. Oxford University Press.

Tremblay, M. (Ed.). (2019). *Queering representation: LGBTQ people and electoral politics in Canada*. UBC Press.

Trimble, L. (2018). *Ms. Prime Minister: Gender, media, and leadership*. University of Toronto Press.

VanSickle-Ward, R., & Wallsten, K. (2019). *The politics of the pill: Gender, framing, and policymaking in the battle over birth control*. Oxford University Press.

White, I. K., & Laird, C. N. (2020). *Steadfast democrats: How social forces shape Black political behavior*. Princeton University Press.

Willnat, L., Weaver, D. H., Wilhoit, G. C. (2017). *The American journalist in the digital age: A half-century perspective*. Peter Lang.

Worrell, T. R. (2018). *Disability in the media: Examining stigma and identity*. Lexington Books.

Yu, S. S., & Matsaganis, M. D. (Eds.). (2018). *Ethnic media in the digital age*. Routledge.

NOTES

1. Byrne, D. (2019, October 31). If your newsroom is not diverse, you will get the news wrong: Dorothy Byrne on why a diverse newsroom is always better. *Reuters Institute.* https://reutersinstitute.politics.ox.ac.uk/risj-review/if-your-newsroom-not-diverse-you-will-get-news-wrong

2. National Advisory Commission on Civil Disorders. (1968). *Kerner report.* National Advisory Commission on Civil Disorders. https://press.princeton.edu/books/hardcover/9780691174242/the-kerner-report

3. English, K. (2020, December). *A reckoning for relevance: Redefining the role of a public editor* [Journalist Fellowship Paper]. Reuters Institute, University of Oxford; https://reutersinstitute.politics.ox.ac.uk/how-revitalised-public-editor-role-could-solve-two-journalisms-biggest-crises

4. Brenan, M. (2020, September 30). Americans remain distrustful of mass media. *Gallup.* https://news.gallup.com/poll/321116/americans-remain-distrustful-mass-media.aspx.

5. Scherer, N., & Curry, B. (2010). *Does descriptive race representation enhance institutional legitimacy? The case of the U.S. Courts, 72 J. POL. 90*; For an excellent analysis of judicial diversity more generally, see Sen, M. (2017). Diversity, qualifications, and ideology: How female and minority judges have changed or not changed, over time. *Wisconsin Law Review,* 367–399.

6. Bianco, W. T. (1994). *Trust: representatives and Constituents.* University of Michigan Press; but also see Gay, C. (2002). Spirals of trust? The effect of descriptive representation on the relationship between citizens and their government. *American Journal of Political Science,* 717, 721–29.

7. Sen, M. (2017). Diversity, qualifications, and ideology: How female and minority judges have changed or not changed, over time. *Wisconsin Law Review,* 367–399.

8. Schaeffer, K. (2021, March 10). The changing face of Congress in 7 charts. *Pew Research Center.* https://www.pewresearch.org/fact-tank/2021/03/10/the-changing-face-of-congress/

9. Root, D., Faleschini, J., & Oyenubi, G. (2019, October 3). Building a more inclusive federal judiciary. *Center for American Progress.* https://www.american-progress.org/issues/courts/reports/2019/10/03/475359/building-inclusive-federal-judiciary/

10. Rhinehart, S., & Geras, M. J. (2020). Diversity and power: Selection method and its impacts on state executive descriptive representation. *State Politics & Policy Quarterly,* 20(2), 213–233.

11. Gerbner, G., & Gross, L. (1976). Living with television: The violence profile. *Journal of Communication,* 26(2), 172–199, p. 182.

12. Behm-Morawitz, E., Miller, B. M., & Lewallen, J. (2018). A model for quantitatively analyzing representations of social class in screen. *Medical Communication Research Reports*, *35*(3), 210–221. https://doi.org/10.1080/088 24096.2018.1428544

13. VanArendonk, K. (2018, May 18). A timeline of TV's working-class sitcoms. *Vulture.* https://www.vulture.com/2018/05/working-class-sitcoms-timeline.html

14. Kane, J. V., & Newman, B. K. (2019, July). Organized labor as the new underserving rich? Mass media, class-based anti-union rhetoric and public support for unions in the United States. *British Journal of Political Science*, *49*(3), 997–1026.

15. For an excellent review of research on race and ethnicity in the media, see Mastro, D., & Stamps, D. (2018). Race/Ethnicity and media. In P. Napoli (Ed.), *Mediated communication* (pp. 341–358). De Gruyter Mouton.

16. Branton, R. P., & Dunaway, J. (2009). Spatial proximity to the US—Mexico border and newspaper coverage of immigration issues. *Political Research Quarterly*, *62*(2), 289–302.

17. Mastro, D., & Stamps, D. (2018). Race/Ethnicity and media. In P. Napoli (Ed.), *Mediated communication* (pp. 341–358). De Gruyter Mouton.

18. Dixon, T. L., & Williams, C. L. (2015). The changing misrepresentation of race and crime on network and cable news. *Journal of Communication*, *65*, 24–39; Nacos, B. L., & Torres-Reyna, O. (2007). *Fueling our fears: Stereotyping, media coverage, and public opinion of Muslim Americans*. Rowman & Littlefield; Powell, K. A. (2011). Framing Islam: An analysis of US media coverage of terrorism since 9/11. *Communication Studies*, *62*(1), 90–112; Alsultany, E. (2012). *Arabs and Muslims in the media: Race and representation after 9/11*. NYU Press; Van Buren, C. (2006). Critical analysis of racist post–9/11 Web animations. *Journal of Broadcasting & Electronic Media*, *50*(3), 537–554; Šisler, V. (2008). Digital Arabs: Representation in video games. *European Journal of Cultural Studies*, *11*(2), 203–220; Behm-Morawitz, E., & Ortiz, M. (2013). Race, ethnicity, and the media. *The Oxford handbook of media psychology*. Oxford University Press, pp. 252–266; Tukachinsky, R., Mastro, D., & Yarchi, M. (2015). Documenting portrayals of race/ethnicity on primetime television over a 20-year span and their association with national-level racial/ethnic attitudes. *Journal of Social Issues*, *71*(1), 17–38; Alsultany, E. (2013). Arabs and Muslims in the media after 9/11: Representational strategies for a "postrace" era. *American Quarterly*, *65*(1), 161–169; Saleem, M., &. Anderson, C. A. (2013). Arabs as terrorists: Effects of stereotypes within violent contexts on attitudes, perceptions, and affect. *Psychology of Violence*, *3*(1), 84; Saleem, M., Yang, G. S., & Ramasubramanian, S. (2016). Reliance on direct and mediated contact and public policies supporting outgroup harm. *Journal of Communication*, *66*(4), 604–624.

19. Global Media Monitoring Project (GMMP). (2015). *GMMP 2015 global report*. http://whomakesthenews.org/gmmp

20. Horowitz, M. (2018). Gender and media. In P. Napoli (Ed.), *Mediated communication* (pp. 395–409). De Gruyter Mouton.

21. Charmaraman, L., Richer, A., Ruffin, B., Ramanudom, B., & Madsen, K. (2017). Escaping from worries or facing reality: A survey study of adolescent attitudes about sexist and homophobic stereotypes in mainstream US media. *Beyond the Stereotypes? Images of Boys and Girls, and Their Consequences*, 213–224.

22. Worrell, T. R. (2018). *Disability in the media: Examining stigma and identity*. Lexington Books.

23. Mastro, D. (2009). Racial/ethnic stereotyping and the media. *Media Processes and Effects*, 377–391; Tukachinsky, R., Mastro, D., & Yarchi, M. (2015). Documenting portrayals of race/ethnicity on primetime television over a 20-year span and their association with national-level racial/ethnic attitudes. *Journal of Social Issues*, 71(1), 17–38.

24. Dixon, T. L., & Azocar, C. L. (2007). Priming crime and activating Blackness: Understanding the psychological impact of the overrepresentation of Blacks as lawbreakers on television news. *Journal of Communication*, 57(2), 229–253.

25. Gilliam, F. D., Jr., & Iyengar, S. (2000). Prime suspects: The influence of local television news on the viewing public. *American Journal of Political Science*, 560–573.

26. Brader, T., Valentino, N. A., & Suhay, E. (2008). What triggers public opposition to immigration? Anxiety, group cues, and immigration threat. *American Journal of Political Science*, 52(4), 959–978; Mendelberg, T. (2017). *The race card: Campaign strategy, implicit messages, and the norm of equality*. Princeton University Press; Valentino, N. A., Hutchings, V. L., & White, I. K. (2002). Cues that matter: How political ads prime racial attitudes during campaigns. *American Political Science Review*, 75–90.

27. Chavez, L. R. (2001). *Covering immigration: Popular images and the politics of the nation*. University of California Press; Huntington, S. P. (2004, March/April). The Hispanic challenge. *Foreign Policy*, 30–45; Santa Ana, O. (2002). *Brown tide rising: Metaphors of Latinos in contemporary American public discourse*. University of Texas Press; Waldman, P., Ventura, E., Savillo, R., Lin, S., & Lewis, G. (2008). Fear and loathing in prime time: Immigration myths and cable news. *Media Matters*.

28. Valentino, N. A., Brader, T., & Jardina, A. E. (2013). Immigration opposition among US whites: General ethnocentrism or media priming of attitudes about Latinos? *Political Psychology*, 34(2), 149–166.

29. Branton, R. P., & Dunaway, J. (2009). Slanted newspaper coverage of immigration: The importance of economics and geography. *Policy Studies Journal*, 37(2), 257–273.

30. Gilens, M. (2009). *Why Americans hate welfare: Race, media, and the politics of antipoverty policy*. University of Chicago Press.

31. Valentino, N. A. (1999). Crime news and the priming of racial attitudes during evaluations of the president. *Public Opinion Quarterly*, 293–320.

32. Sears, D. O. (1988). Symbolic racism. In P. A. Katz & D. A. Taylor (Eds.), *Eliminating racism* (pp. 53–84). Springer; Entman, R. M. (1990). Modern racism and the images of Blacks in local television news. *Critical Studies in Media Communication*, 7, 332–345.

33. Entman, R. M., & Rojecki, A. (1998). Minorities in mass media: A status report. *Investing in Diversity: Advancing Opportunities for Minorities and Media*, 67–85.

34. Branton, R., & Dunaway, J. (2009). Spatial proximity to the U.S.–Mexico border and newspaper coverage of immigration issues. *Political Research Quarterly*, 62, 289–302; Subervi, F., Torres, J., & Montalvo, D. (2005, June). *Network brownout report 2005: The portrayal of Latinos & Latino issues on network television news, 2004, with a retrospect to 1995*. National Association of Hispanic Journalists. https://nahj.org/wp-content/uploads/2021/01/2005-NAHJ-Network-Brownout-Report.pdf

35. Entman, R. M., & Rojecki, A. (2001). *The Black image in the White mind: Media and race in America*. The University of Chicago Press; Iyengar, S. (1990). Framing responsibility for political issues: The case of poverty. *Political Behavior*, 12, 19–40.

36. Mastro, D., & Stamps, D. (2018). Race/Ethnicity and media. In P. Napoli (Ed.), *Mediated communication* (pp. 341–358). De Gruyter Mouton.

37. Mastro, D., & Stamps, D. (2018). Race/Ethnicity and media. In P. Napoli (Ed.), *Mediated communication* (pp. 341–358). De Gruyter Mouton.

38. Branton, R., & Dunaway, J. (2009). Spatial proximity to the U.S.–Mexico border and newspaper coverage of immigration issues. *Political Research Quarterly*, 62, 289–302; Dixon, T. L., & Williams, C. L. (2015). The changing misrepresentation of race and crime on network and cable news. *Journal of Communication*, 65, 24–39.

39. Mastro, D., & Stamps, D. (2018). Race/Ethnicity and media. In P. Napoli (Ed.), *Mediated communication* (pp. 341–358). De Gruyter Mouton; Zhang, Q. (2010). Asian Americans beyond the model minority stereotype: The nerdy and the left out. *Journal of International and Intercultural Communication*, 3(1), 20–37.

40. Mastro, D., & Stamps, S. (2018). Race/Ethnicity and media. In P. Napoli (Ed.), *Mediated communication* (pp. 341–358). De Gruyter Mouton.

41. Matheson, S. A. (2007). The cultural politics of *Wife Swap*: Taste, lifestyle media, and the American family. *Film & History: An Interdisciplinary Journal of Film and Television Studies, 37*(2), 33–47; Fairclough, K. (2005). Women's work? *Wife Swap* and the reality problem. *Feminist Media*; Leistyna, P. (2009). Social class and entertainment television. *Media/Cultural Studies: Critical Approaches,* 339; Alper, L., & Leistyna, P. (2005). *Class dismissed: How TV frames the working class.* Media Education Foundation.

42. Working-class poverty is often characterized as the inability of people to take responsibility for their lives and reinforces negative stereotypes of the poor. See Kindinger, E. (2016). The paradoxical class politics in *Here Comes Honey Boo Boo.* In S. Lemke & W. Schniedermann (Eds.), *Class divisions in serial television* (pp. 65–87). Palgrave Macmillan; also see Owen, D. (2016). "Hillbillies," "welfare queens," and "teen moms": American media's class distinctions. In S. Lemke & W. Schniedermann (Eds.), *Class divisions in serial television* (pp. 47–63). Palgrave Macmillan.

43. VanArendonk, K. (2018, May 18). A timeline of TV's working-class sitcoms. *Vulture.* https://www.vulture.com/2018/05/working-class-sitcoms-timeline.html

44. Peck, R. (2019). *Fox populism: Branding conservatism as working class.* Cambridge University Press.

45. Lindell, J., & Sartoretto, P. (2018). Young people, class and the news: Distinction, socialization and moral sentiments. *Journalism Studies, 19*(14), 2042–2061.

46. Guardino, M. (2019). *Framing inequality: News media, public opinion, and the neoliberal turn in US public policy.* Oxford University Press.

47. Horowitz, M. (2018). Gender and media. In P. Napoli (Ed.), *Mediated communication* (pp. 395–409). De Gruyter Mouton.

48. Hicks, G. R. (2020). Beliefs and stereotypes about LGBT people. In *Oxford Research Encyclopedia of Politics.* Oxford University Press. https://doi.org/10.1093/acrefore/9780190228637.013.1240

49. Bond, B. J., & Compton, B. L. (2015). Gay on-screen: The relationship between exposure to gay characters on television and heterosexual audiences' endorsement of gay equality. *Journal of Broadcasting & Electronic Media, 59*(4), 717–732; Calzo, J. P., & Ward, L. M. (2009). Media exposure and viewers' attitudes toward homosexuality: Evidence for mainstreaming or resonance? *Journal of Broadcasting & Electronic Media, 53*(2), 280–299.

50. Chen, Y. A. (2018). Media coverage and social changes: Examining valence of portrayal of the LGBT community from 2000 to 2014 in two US magazines. *Intercultural Communication Studies, 27*(1).

51. Lee, B. (2018). Pop out! Mass media and popular culture. In M. J. Murphy & B. Bjorngaard (Eds.), *Living Out Loud*. Routledge.

52. Zhang, L., & Haller, B. (2013). Consuming image: How mass media impact the identity of people with disabilities. *Communication Quarterly, 61*(3), 319–334.

53. Aaldering, L., van der Meer, T., & Van der Brug, W. (2018). Mediated leader effects: The impact of newspapers' portrayal of party leadership on electoral support. *The International Journal of Press/Politics, 23*(1), 70–94; Kiousis, S., & McCombs, M. (2004). Agenda-setting effects and attitude strength: Political figures during the 1996 presidential election. *Communication Research, 31*(1), 36–57.

54. McCombs, M., Llamas, J. P., Lopez-Escobar, E., & Rey, F. (1997). Candidate images in Spanish elections: Second-level agenda-setting effects. *Journalism & Mass Communication Quarterly, 74*(4), 703–717; Soroka, S., Bodet, M. A., Young, L., & Andrew, B. (2009). Campaign news and vote intentions. *Journal of Elections, Public Opinion and Parties, 19*(4), 359–376; Schmitt-Beck, R. (1996). Mass media, the electorate, and the bandwagon. A study of communication effects on vote choice in Germany. *International Journal of Public Opinion Research, 8*(3), 266–291; Van der Meer, T. W. G., Hakhverdian, A., & Aaldering, L. (2016). Off the fence, onto the bandwagon? A large-scale survey experiment on effect of real-life poll outcomes on subsequent vote intentions. *International Journal of Public Opinion Research, 28*(1), 46–72.

55. Caliendo, S. M. (2018). Grabbing the reins: Media and the politics of groups and identity. *Politics, Groups, and Identities, 6*(4), 852–866; Wilson, C. C., II, Gutierrez, F., & Chao, L. (2003). *Racism, sexism, and the media: The rise of class communication in multicultural America*. SAGE.

56. Schaffner, B. F., & Gadson, M. (2004). Reinforcing stereotypes? Race and local television news coverage of Congress. *Social Science Quarterly, 85*(3), 604–623; Terkildsen, N., & Damore, D. F. (1999). The dynamics of racialized media coverage in congressional elections. *The Journal of Politics, 61*(3), 680–699.

57. Ward, O. (2016). Media framing of Black women's campaigns for the US House of Representatives. In N. E. Brown & S. A. Gershon (Eds.), *Distinct identities: Minority women in US politics* (pp. 153–170). Routledge.

58. McIlwain, C. D. (2011). Racialized media coverage of minority candidates in the 2008 Democratic presidential primary. *American Behavioral Scientist, 55*(4), 371–389; Wu, D., & Lee, T.-T. (2005). The submissive, the calculated, and the American dream: Coverage of Asian American political candidates in the 1990s. *The Howard Journal of Communications, 16*(3), 225–241.

59. Zilber, J., & Niven, D. (2000). Stereotypes in the news: Media coverage of African-Americans in Congress. *Harvard International Journal of Press/Politics,* 5(1), 32–49.

60. Tolley, E. (2015). Racial mediation in the coverage of candidates' political viability: A comparison of approaches. *Journal of Ethnic and Migration Studies,* 41(6), 963–984.

61. Van der Pas, D. J., & Aaldering, L. (2020). Gender differences in political media coverage: A meta-analysis. *Journal of Communication,* 70(1), 114–143, pp. 130–131.

62. Van der Pas, D. J., & Aaldering, L. (2020). Gender differences in political media coverage: A meta-analysis. *Journal of Communication,* 70(1), 114–143.

63. Mendelsohn, M., & Nadeau, R. (1996). The magnification and minimization of social cleavages by the broadcast and narrowcast news media. *International Journal of Public Opinion Research,* 8(4), 374–389; Bailey, M. B., Nawara, S. P., & Burgess, S. (2017). Gay and lesbian candidates, group stereotypes, and the news media: An experimental design. In M. Brettschneider, S. Burgess, & C. Keating (Eds.), *LGBTQ Politics* (pp. 334–350). New York University Press.

64. Lalancette, M., & Tremblay, M. (2019). Media framing of lesbian and gay politicians: Is sexual mediation at work?" In M. Tremblay (Ed.), *Queering representation: LGBTQ people and electoral politics in Canada.* UBC Press.

65. Shah, P., Scott, J., & Juenke, E. G. (2019). Women of color candidates: Examining emergence and success in state legislative elections. *Politics, Groups, and Identities,* 7(2), 429–443; Brown, N. E. (2014). Political participation of women of color: An intersectional analysis. *Journal of Women, Politics & Policy,* 35(4), 315–348; Holman, M. R., &. Schneider, M. C. (2018). Gender, race, and political ambition: How intersectionality and frames influence interest in political office. *Politics, Groups, and Identities,* 6(2), 264–280.

66. Ward, O. (2017). Intersectionality and press coverage of political campaigns: Representations of Black, Asian, and minority ethnic female candidates at the UK 2010 general election. *The International Journal of Press/Politics,* 22(1), 43–66.

67. Gershon, S. (2012). When race, gender, and the media intersect: Campaign news coverage of minority congresswomen. *Journal of Women, Politics & Policy,* 33(2), 105–125; Lucas, J. C. (2017). Gender and race in congressional national news media appearances in 2008. *Politics & Gender,* 13(4), 569–596; Towner, T. L., & Clawson, R. A. (2016). A wise Latina or a baffled rookie? Media coverage of Justice Sonia Sotomayor's ascent to the bench. *Journal of Women, Politics & Policy,* 37(3), 316–340; Ward, O. (2016). Seeing double: Race, gender, and coverage of minority women's campaigns for the US house of representatives. *Politics & Gender,* 12(2), 317–343; Ward, O. (2016). Media framing of Black

women's campaigns for the US House of Representatives. *Distinct Identities: Minority Women in US Politics*, 153–170; Ward, O. (2017). Intersectionality and press coverage of political campaigns: Representations of Black, Asian, and minority ethnic female candidates at the UK 2010 general election. *The International Journal of Press/Politics*, 22(1), 43–66.

68. Besco, R., Gerrits, B., & Matthews, J. S. (2016). White millionaires and hockey skates: Racialized and gendered mediation in news coverage of a Canadian mayoral election. *International Journal of Communication*, 10, 4641–4660.

69. Gershon, S. (2012). When race, gender, and the media intersect: Campaign news coverage of minority congresswomen. *Journal of Women, Politics & Policy*, 33(2), 105–125.

70. Lucas, J. C. (2017). Gender and race in congressional national news media appearances in 2008. *Politics & Gender*, 13(4), 569–596.

71. Ward, O. (2016). Seeing double: Race, gender, and coverage of minority women's campaigns for the US house of representatives. *Politics & Gender*, 12(2), 317–343; Gershon, S. A. (2013). Media coverage of minority congresswomen and voter evaluations: Evidence from an online experimental study. *Political Research Quarterly*, 66(3), 702–714.

72. Bravo, V., & Clark, N. (2019). Diversity in news organizations. *The International Encyclopedia of Journalism Studies*. John Wiley & Sons, pp. 1–9; Luther, C. A., Lepre, C. R., & Clark, N. (2017). *Diversity in US mass media*. John Wiley & Sons.

73. Abrajano, M., & Singh, S. (2009). Examining the link between issue attitudes and news source: The case of Latinos and immigration reform. *Political Behavior*, 31(1), 1–30; Hamilton, J. (2004). *All the news that's fit to sell: How the market transforms information into news*. Princeton University Press.

74. American Society of News Editors. (n. d.). *Census data, 2001–2018.* https://googletrends.github.io/asne/?view=3&filter=race.

75. James, B. (2015, August 17). How white and male are digital newsrooms? New media's old diversity problem. *International Business Times*. http://www.ibtimes.com/how-white-male-are-digital-newsrooms-new-medias-old-diversity-problem-2056843

76. See 2019 Diversity Survey. (2019, September 10). *News Leaders Association*. https://www.newsleaders.org/2019-diversity-survey-results.

77. Posetti, J., Shabbir, N., Maynard, D., Bontcheva, K., & Aboulez, N. (2021, April). *The chilling: Global trends in online violence against women journalists* [Research discussion paper]. UNESCO. https://www.icfj.org/sites/default/files/2021-04/The%20Chilling_POSETTI%20ET%20AL_FINAL.pdf

78. NewsGuild-CWA. (2021, April 27). *Study of pay equity in 14 Gannett newsrooms*. https://newsguild.org/study-shows-gannett-underpays-women-and-journalists-of-color-as-much-as-27000/

79. Peiser, W. (2000). Setting the journalist agenda: Influences from journalists' individual characteristics and from media factors. *Journalism and Mass Communication Quarterly*, 77(Summer), 243–257.

80. Caliendo, S. M. (2018). Grabbing the reins: media and the politics of groups and identity. *Politics, Groups, and Identities*, 6(4), 852–866; Nishikawa, K. A., Towner, T. L., Clawson, R. A., & Waltenburg, E. N. (2009). Interviewing the interviewers: Journalistic norms and racial diversity in the newsroom. *The Howard Journal of Communications*, 20(3), 242–259; Saldaña, M., Sylvie, G., & McGregor, S. C. (2016). Journalism–business tension in Swedish newsroom decision making. *Journal of Media Ethics*, 31(2), 100–115.

81. Zeldes, G. A., & Fico, F. (2005). Race and gender: An analysis of sources and reporters in the networks' coverage of the 2000 presidential campaign. *Mass Communication & Society*, 8(4), 373–385.

82. Weaver, D. H., & Wilhoit, G. C. (1996). *The American journalist in the 1990s: US news people at the end of an era*. Psychology Press.

83. Zeldes, G. A., & Fico, F. (2005). Race and gender: An analysis of sources and reporters in the networks' coverage of the 2000 presidential campaign. *Mass Communication & Society*, 8(4), 373–385.

84. Ziegler, D., & White, A. (1990). Women and minorities on network television news: An examination of correspondents and newsmakers. *Journal of Broadcasting & Electronic Media*, 34(2), 215–223; Weaver, D. H., & Wilhoit, G. C. (1996). *The American journalist in the 1990s: US news people at the end of an era*. Psychology Press.

85. Bravo, V., & Clark, N. (2019). Diversity in news organizations. *The International Encyclopedia of Journalism Studies*. John Wiley & Sons, pp. 1–9; Clark, B. (2017). Applied diversity: A normative approach to improving news representations of ethno-cultural minorities based on the Canadian experience. *Journal of Applied Journalism & Media Studies*, 6(2), 245–267.

86. Johnston, A., & Flamiano, D. (2007). Diversity in mainstream newspapers from the standpoint of journalists of color. *The Howard Journal of Communications*, 18(2), 111–131; Nishikawa, K. A., Towner, T. L., Clawson, R. A., & Waltenburg, E. N. (2009). Interviewing the interviewers: Journalistic norms and racial diversity in the newsroom. *The Howard Journal of Communications*, 20(3), 242–259; Wilson, C. C. (2000). The paradox of African American

journalists. In S. Cottle (Ed.), *Ethnic minorities and the media: Changing cultural boundaries* (pp. 85–99). Open University Press.

87. Clark, B. (2014). "Walking up a down-escalator": The interplay between newsroom norms and media coverage of minority groups. *InMedia. The French Journal of Media Studies, 5*, 1–24.

88. Sui, M., Paul, N., Shah, P., Dunaway, J. (n. d.). *Is more better? Effects of newsroom and audience diversity on trait coverage of minority candidates* [Working paper].

89. For recent public arguments about why diversity in the newsroom influences reporting, see Truong, D. (2016). Connecting with diverse perspectives. *NiemanLab.* http://www.niemanlab.org/2016/12/connecting-with-diverse-perspectives/?utm_source=Daily+Lab+email+list&utm_campaign=d202ffee08-dailylabemail3&utm_medium=email&utm_term=0_d68264fd5e-d202ffee08-396025145.

90. The state of the news media 2009. (2009, March 16). *Pew Research Center.* http://www.stateofthenewsmedia.org/2009

91. The state of the news media 2009. (2009, March 16). *Pew Research Center.* http://www.stateofthenewsmedia.org/2009

92. Branton, R., & Dunaway, J. (2008). English- and Spanish-language media coverage of immigration: A comparative analysis. *Social Science Quarterly*, 1006–1022.

93. Johnstone, J. W., Slawski, E. J., & Bowman, W. W. (1976). *The newspeople.* University of Illinois Press, pp. 157–179; State of the news media 2016. (2016, June). *Pew Research Center.* http://www.stateofthemedia.org/2005/ethnical-ternative-intro/alternative/.

94. They are described more fully in Johnstone, J. W., Slawski, E. J., & Bowman, W. W. (1976). *The newspeople.* University of Illinois Press, pp. 157–181; Leamer, L. (1972). *The paper revolutionaries: The rise of the underground press.* Simon and Schuster; Nelson, J. A. (1972). The underground press. In M. C. Emery & T. C. Smythe (Eds.), *Readings in mass communication.* W. C. Brown.

95. The reasons for this situation are explained by Waterman, D. (1986). The failure of cultural programming on cable TV: An economic interpretation. *Journal of Communication, 36*(Summer), 92–107. Also see Entman, R. M., & Wildman, S. S. (1992). Reconciling economic and non-economic perspectives in media policy: Transcending the "marketplace of ideas." *Journal of Communication, 42*(Winter), 5–19.

96. Tierney, J., & Steinberg, J. (2005, February 17). Conservatives and rivals press a struggling PBS. *The New York Times.*

Media Effects

10 Political Socialization and Learning

Learning Objectives

1. Explain the role mass media play in political socialization.

2. Identify all the ways in which mass media contribute to learning about politics.

3. Summarize the cognitive processes through which people learn about politics via mass media.

4. Assess whether and how exposure to mass media affects citizens' levels of political knowledge, including relevant information for making voting decisions.

5. Discuss the various factors that help or hinder citizens' abilities to acquire political knowledge from mass media.

6. Describe what sorts of behavioral effects we might expect to observe in response to mass media exposure.

D o adults learn from media exposure? Research shows that they do and that even entertainment programs and video games with informative messages can serve as potent knowledge transmitters. A study of the impact of health messages embedded in a first-person shooter video game is a good illustration.[1] When researchers measured the effect of embedding graphic anti-DUI (driving under the influence of alcohol) messages in the background of a first-person shooter video game, results indicated that when players felt "transported into the virtual experiences in the game," their willingness to drive under the influence of alcohol was reduced by the graphic anti-DUI message. A study on the impact of health messages in entertainment programs shows similar influence: Health knowledge surveys show that a mere 15% of viewers of *Grey's Anatomy* knew that simple treatments can prevent mother-to-child transmission of HIV. When this message was embedded in one episode of the show, 61% of the viewers learned the information. A follow-up survey six weeks later showed that 45% of the audience still remembered the information.[2] That is an astoundingly high number, considering that few viewers were likely to be affected by the problem and that many were multitasking while watching the show.

How representative are these examples? Can media really shape the knowledge and behavior patterns of countless Americans? Are people's awareness about social and political issues influenced substantially by what they read, hear, and see? Do desirable and undesirable behaviors observed through media produce imitations in real life? How much do people learn from the media, and what, precisely, do they learn?

In this chapter, we will examine these questions, beginning with the shaping of attitudes that occurs as an unintended by-product of media exposure. Aside from programs directed at children, journalists usually do not see themselves as the audience's teachers nor do audiences regard themselves as pupils. Rather, exposure to individual, dramatic events or to the incremental impact of the total flow of information over prolonged periods leads to incidental learning about the political world. We also will consider how the ways in which people choose media shapes the information to which they are exposed and the sorts of things they learn. Finally, we will address the question posed at the start: To what degree does exposure to the mass media influence behavior in politically and socially significant ways?

Mass Media and Political Socialization

Political socialization—learning about political life and internalizing its customs and rules—affects the quality of interactions between citizens and their government. To operate smoothly, political systems need the support of most of their citizens, who must be willing to abide by the laws and to sustain government by performing duties such as voting, paying taxes, or serving in the military. Citizens are more likely to support their government if they are convinced of its legitimacy and capability and if they feel strong emotional ties to it.

Childhood Socialization

Political socialization starts in childhood. Children usually learn basic attitudes toward authority, property, decision making, and veneration of political symbols from their families during early childhood. When they enter school, teaching about political values becomes more systematic. At school, children learn new facts about their political and social world, much of it based on information from mass media.[3]

Children's direct contacts with the media are equally abundant.[4] Millions of babies watch television. In the winter, young children in the United States spend an average of 31 hours a week in front of the television set—more time than in school. Between the ages of 12 and 17, weekly television and digital media consumption can run up to 48 hours (see Photo 10-1).[5] Eighty percent of the content that children see is intended

Photo 10-1 Preteen Girl Lying on Sofa Watching TV in the Living Room With Her Younger Brother Sitting on Her Back

Source: iStockphoto.com/monkeybusinessimages

for adults and shows incidents that differ substantially from those in the child's immediate environment. Children watch military combat, funerals, rocket launchings, courtships, seductions, and childbirth. If they can understand the message, the impact is potentially powerful because children's brains are primed for learning and they are apt to take such presentations at face value.

Teen Socialization

When asked the sources of information on which they base their attitudes about the economy or race or about war and patriotism, high school students mention the mass media far more often than they mention their families, friends, teachers, or personal experiences.[6] Young frequent media users gain substantial information from the media. Compared with infrequent users, they show greater understanding of and support for basic American values, such as the importance of free speech and the right to equal and fair treatment.[7] At the same time, family experiences in early childhood have indirect influence by shaping news habits later in life (Photo 10-2). Research finds that even today, the news habits of parents and the discussion of news in the home have a positive influence on youths' news consumption, which itself has a longer-term impact on news habits.[8]

What children and teens learn from the mass media and how they evaluate what they learn depends on their stage of mental development. According to child psychologist Jean Piaget, children between two and seven years of age do not detect the connections among various phenomena or draw general conclusions from specific instances. Many of the lessons presumably taught by media stories therefore elude young children. Complex reasoning skills develop fully only at the teenage level. Children's interest in certain types of stories also changes sharply with age, as do their attention and information retention spans.[9] Most children strongly support the political system during their early years but become disillusioned about authority figures during their teenage years. Their skepticism diminishes as they finish their education and enter the workforce. What role the media play in this transformation is unclear.[10] Knowledge is also slim about children's and adolescents' imitation of behavior that media stories depict, about the duration of memories, and about the persistence of media effects on learning, behavior, and social relationships.[11]

Family Versus Media as Chief Socializer

The finding that mass media strongly influence socialization runs counter to earlier studies that showed parents and teachers as the chief socializers. Several reasons account for the change. The first is the pervasiveness of television, which exposes even the youngest children to a wealth of images depicting their world. The second reason involves deficiencies in measurement. Much of the early research discounted all media influence unless it came through direct contact between the child and the media. That excluded indirect media influence, such as contacts with parents and teachers who conveyed media information to the child. Finally, research designs have become more sophisticated. In the

Photo 10-2 **Family Having Breakfast in Kitchen Together Reading Newspaper**
Source: iStockphoto.com/monkeybusinessimages

early studies, children were asked to make their own general appraisal of learning sources. A typical question might have been, "From whom do you learn the most: your parents, your school, or newspapers and television?" The questions used in recent studies have been more specific, inquiring first what children know about particular subjects, such as immigration or nuclear energy, and then asking about the sources of their information. In many cases, the mass media are named as the chief sources of information and evaluations. Recent research shows that for adolescents, many political socialization agents are at play: Peers and voluntary associations have the most significant impact on political participation, but higher levels of news consumption and internet use also contribute to higher rates of political participation.[12]

Social and Mobile Media as Agents of Socialization

The fact that today's teens spend so much time on social media is blurring researchers' ability to distinguish between political socialization effects from their social networks and exposure to news and political information. As their name suggests, social media platforms blend nearly all aspects of social life with media exposure, making it difficult to understand the learning and socialization effects of each. However, some research shows that endorsement cues such as sharing or liking can carry as much or more weight than traditional media cues.[13] The proliferation of smartphones has only intensified teen immersion in digital spaces by enabling a nearly constant ability to text, chat, or engage with social media. A 2018 study by the Pew Research Center found that among the 95% of teens who report having access to a smartphone, 45% admit to being "almost constantly" online. A 2021 study reveals that 18- to 29-year-olds are more likely to favor sites and apps such as Snapchat and Instagram relative to adults over the age of 30 (see Figure 10-1). However, the shift to mobile does not appear to be changing the general processes political of news socialization. In their study, Stephanie Edgerly and her colleagues found that parental modeling is still an important factor shaping news consumption, even if the modeling is occurring through the use of mobile devices.[14]

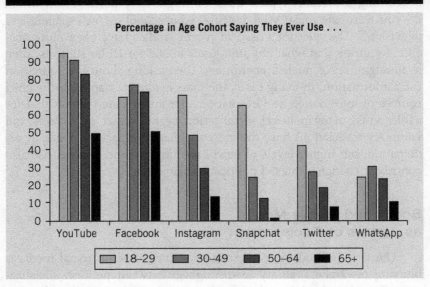

Figure 10-1   Social Media and Messaging App Use by Age Cohort, 2021

Source: Age gaps in Snapchat, Instagram use are particularly wide, less so for Facebook. (2021, April 6). *Pew Research Center.* https://www.pewresearch.org/internet/2021/04/07/social-media-use-in-2021/pi_2021-04-07_social-media_0-02a/

Adult Socialization

The pattern of heavy reliance on media exposure for political news continues into adulthood, though it has been declining sharply in recent decades. Media reliance on the whole is substantial, though forms of consumption are changing. For instance, during June of 2020, 23% of adults in the United States (U.S.) consumed news about the 2020 election on a news website or app, and 44% consumed news about COVID-19 on news sites and apps. Fewer American adults closely followed stories about the election and COVID-19 on social media, at 8% and 23%, respectively. Those who relied on social media tended to exhibit lower levels of knowledge about these subjects relative to those following via every other format, with the exception of local television news (see Figure 10-2).

Figure 10-2   Attention to Election and COVID-19 Among American Adults, 2020

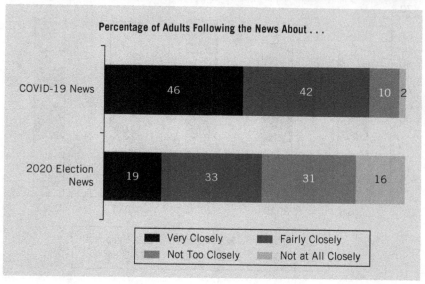

Percentage of Adults Following the News About . . .

COVID-19 News: Very Closely 46, Fairly Closely 42, Not Too Closely 10, Not at All Closely 2

2020 Election News: Very Closely 19, Fairly Closely 33, Not Too Closely 31, Not at All Closely 16

Legend: Very Closely, Fairly Closely, Not Too Closely, Not at All Closely

Source: Jurkowitz, M. (2020, May 22). Americans are following news about presidential candidates much less closely than COVID-19 news. *Pew Research Center.* https://www.pewresearch.org/fact-tank/2020/05/22/americans-are-following-news-about-presidential-candidates-much-less-closely-than-covid-19-news/

Typically, most American adults spend around five hours per day watching live or time-shifted television, and their remaining time is spread across tablets, smartphones, and other media devices. Of course, the total time spent watching and listening to non-news offerings is much greater than for news.[15] The average time adults spend on social networks daily is also on the rise (see Figure 10-3).

All of that exposure to news and to the political information embedded in entertainment programs and on social media platforms contributes to the lifelong process of political socialization and learning.[16] The mass media form

the mainstream of the common symbolic environment that cultivates the most widely shared conceptions of reality. We live in terms of the stories we tell, stories about what things

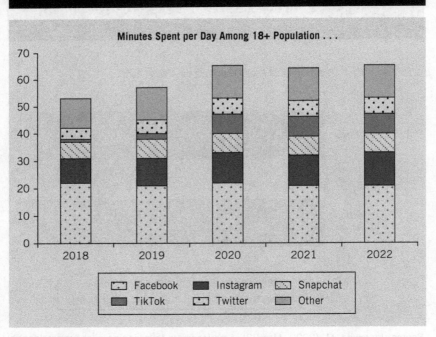

Figure 10-3   Average Time Spent on Social Networks Among 18+ Years of Age by Platform, 2018–2022

Source: Adapted from Insider Intelligence Editors. (2021, January 26). US adults added 1 hour of digital time in 2020. *Insider Intelligence.* https://www.emarketer.com/content/us-adults-added-1-hour-of-digital-time-2020

exist, stories about how things work, and stories about what to do. . . . Increasingly, media-cultivated facts and values become standards by which we judge.[17]

Once people have formed their basic attitudes toward the political system, their attitudes usually stabilize, so later learning largely supplements and refines earlier notions. The need to cope with information about new events and shifting cultural orientations force the average person into continuous learning and gradual readjustments, although people's basic value structures generally remain intact, even when attitudes are modified.[18] However, major personal or societal upheavals may lead to complete resocialization and revised political ideas.[19]

Demographics, Media Use, and Socialization

Race, ethnicity, gender, age, income, education, region, and city size generate differences in habits of media consumption. For instance, African Americans rely more on television and less on high-speed internet for online news than whites. Age has a bearing on newspaper reading, with older people reading more than younger ones. Young media users rely more heavily on social media, tablets, and smartphones for access to information relative to older people. Program preferences vary as well. Older men and women are the heaviest viewers of television news. Younger age cohorts are the lightest news watchers.[20]

Differences in patterns of media use are particularly pronounced among income levels, in part because the more serious news media cater primarily to the interests of the wealthier segments of the public. High-income families, who usually are better educated than poor families, use print media more and television less than the rest of the population. Upper-income people also use a greater variety of media than lower-income groups. Being better informed helps the information-rich maintain and increase their influence and power in U.S. society.[21] Income also influences access to high-speed internet at home, which is a key predictor of online news consumption. Many citizens report that the cost of broadband services is prohibitive and is the reason for their choice to rely on mobile devices and wireless services for access to the internet. At the same time, they complain that the lack of this important service makes it more difficult to keep up with public affairs.[22] See Figure 10-4.

Different media exposure and use patterns partly explain differences in knowledge and attitudes, but historically, the notion of vastly different communications environments for various population groups was farfetched because the bulk of media entertainment and information was similar throughout the country and shared by all types of audiences. Specific stories varied, of course, depending on regional and local interests. Newspapers on the West Coast are more likely to devote their foreign affairs coverage to Asian affairs than are newspapers on the East Coast, which concentrate on Europe and the Middle East. Tabloids put more stress on sensational crime and sex stories than elite papers like the staid *New York Times*. But even though most mainstream news media now cover basically the same categories of stories in the same proportions, the fragmented media environment means that the focus and proportion of news to which people are exposed can differ more than ever before. Though most mainstream news sources from around the country provide a large common core of information and interpretation that imbues their audiences with a shared structure of knowledge and basic values, the contemporary high-choice media environment means that audience predispositions—such as party affiliation or religious orientation—can influence the content audiences see, often producing wide disparities of views on many issues and divergent expressions of facts.[23]

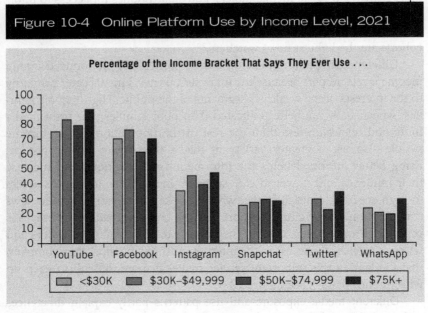

Figure 10-4   Online Platform Use by Income Level, 2021

Source: Auxier, B., & Anderson, M. (2021, April 7). Social media use in 2021. *Pew Research Center.* https://www.pewresearch.org/internet/2021/04/07/social-media-use-in-2021/

Mass Media and Political Learning

People learn about political norms, rules, values, events, and behaviors from both fictional and factual mass media stories. Personal experiences are severely limited when compared with the range of experiences the media offer to us explicitly or implicitly about the social order and political activities. An accident report, for example, besides telling what happened, may suggest that police and fire forces respond too slowly and that emergency facilities in the local hospital are inadequate. When societal problems such as poverty or pollution are framed as discrete events and reflect one family's starvation or a particular oil spill, attention is likely to be focused on individual solutions, obscuring the larger societal problems.[24] Television soap operas may persuade audiences that most politicians are corruptible—after all, the majority of those shown on television are.[25] In fact, fictional stories are the most widely used sources for political information. Surveys show that only one-half to two-thirds of the adult television audience regularly exposes itself to explicitly political news (see Box 10-1).[26]

Box 10-1

From Individual Learning to Informed Public Opinion: Is the Whole Greater Than Its Parts?

E Pluribus Unum—"out of many, one"—is a hallowed motto in the United States. Among other meanings, it symbolizes that individual voices become truly powerful only when they blend and become the public's opinion. Does individual learning about politics aggregate into informed, collective public opinion that shapes public policies in the United States?

The answer is yes. Studies about learning across several policy areas find that public opinions fluctuate in reaction to ongoing political happenings, suggesting that collectively, publics were learning from the news and expressing rational responses.[1]

As Benjamin Page and Robert Shapiro concluded nearly two decades ago in *The Rational Public,* when the opinions of individual Americans meld into collective public opinions, they constitute reasonable responses to current information and changing circumstances; they also reflect the American public's basic values and beliefs.[2] That finding bodes well for the future

(Continued)

(Continued)

of democratic governance. Coherent collective responsiveness is a sign of an attentive, intelligent public that learns from the most readily available sources of current information. U.S. democracy may be muddling through, as democracies are wont to do. But it is adequately, if not imperfectly, supported by the combined learning of citizens who join their voices into a multitonal public opinion chorus.

1. Graber, D. A. (Assisted by C. Griffiths, M. G. Mierzejewski, & J. M. Smith). (2008). *Re-measuring the civic IQ: Decline, stability, or advance?* [Paper presentation]. The American Political Science Association, Boston, MA, United States; also see Wlezien, C. (1995). The public as thermostat: Dynamics of preferences for spending. *American Journal of Political Science, 39,* 981–1000; Soroka, S. N., & Wlezien, C. (2010). *Degrees of democracy: Politics, public opinion and policy.* Cambridge University Press.

2. Page, B. I., & Shapiro, R. Y. (1992). *The rational public: Fifty years of trends in Americans' policy preferences.* University of Chicago Press.

People's opinions, feelings, and evaluations about the political system may spring from their own thinking about facts supplied by the media; from attitudes, opinions, and feelings explicitly expressed in news or entertainment programming; or from a combination of the two.[27] When audiences have direct or vicarious experiences to guide them, and particularly when they have already formed opinions grounded firmly in their personal values, they are least likely to be swayed by the media. Many people who use the media for information and as a point of departure for formulating their own appraisals nonetheless reject or ignore attitudes and evaluations that media stories supply explicitly or implicitly.[28] For example, the public gave little credence to the widely publicized predictions by media pundits that proof of President Bill Clinton's affair with White House intern Monica Lewinsky would end the Clinton presidency.

People are prone to accept journalists' views about national and international issues absent personal experience or guidance from social contacts. Even when people think they are forming their own opinions about familiar issues, they often depend on the media more than they realize. Extensive television exposure has been shown to lead to "mainstreaming," making people's outlook on political life "congruent with television's portrayal of life and society."[29]

The media's persuasiveness does not mean that exposure is tantamount to learning and mind changing. Multiple studies show that two-thirds of newspaper readers generally do not know their paper's preferred position on specific economic, social, and foreign policy issues.[30] Most media stories are promptly forgotten. Stories that become part of an individual's fund of knowledge tend to reinforce existing beliefs and feelings. This may be even more true in the contemporary fragmented media environment, where people can actively choose to follow content already in line with existing predispositions. Acquisition of new knowledge or changes in attitude are the exception rather than the rule. Still, they occur often enough to be significant.

How People Learn

How do audiences interpret the stories that they have selected? The early models that depicted a straight stimulus–response relationship have been disproved. There is no "hypodermic needle effect": The media do not inject information unaltered into the minds of audiences. Rather, the images that media convey stimulate perceptions in audience members that meld the media stimuli with each individual's perceptual state at the time they receive the message.

Blending New and Old Information

From childhood on, people develop ideas and feelings about how the world operates. When those ideas relate to politics, they are usually grounded in information drawn from the mass media. Cognitive psychologists call these mental configurations by various names, including *schemas* and *scripts*.[31] They serve as organizing devices that help people assimilate new information. As the journalist Walter Lippmann explained it,

> For the most part we do not first see, and then define, we define
> first and then see. In the great blooming, buzzing confusion
> of the outer world, we pick out what our culture has already
> defined for us, and we tend to perceive that which we have
> picked out in the form stereotyped for us by our culture.[32]

For example, media crime stories and statistics condition most Americans to consider African Americans as more likely perpetrators of violent crimes. Numerous experiments accordingly show that whites who witness a white person wielding a murder weapon later on mistakenly identify a Black person as the assailant.[33] Their image is *perceiver determined*, meaning that it is shaped by what they already believe, rather than *stimulus determined*, meaning that the image reflects the actual stimulus that their senses have absorbed. Similar media misattributions are applied to whites and to other minority groups such as Latinos. For example, news media portrayals overwhelmingly depict Latinos in the context of immigration or illegal immigration, ignoring all other aspects of Latinos in America. Coverage of Latinos also often disproportionately reflects criminality.[34] Recent work based on news coverage in the Los Angeles television market identifies some improvement in the accuracy of media representation of African Americans as perpetrators, victims, and officers, while Latinos were underrepresented as victims and officers and whites were overrepresented as victims and officers (see Chapter 9).[35]

Research shows that images of political candidates are largely perceiver determined for those aspects for which the audience already has developed complex schemas. For instance, people assume that Democratic presidential candidates will pursue policies typically associated with Democrats. They read or view the news in that vein, picking up bits of information that fit while rejecting, ignoring, or reinterpreting those that do not fit.

Information about aspects of events or people not widely known or stereotyped leads to stimulus-determined images. How the media frame these political issues and depict the people involved largely determines what the audience perceives. Perceptions about the personalities of newcomers to the political scene, assessments of their capabilities, and appraisals of the people with whom they surround themselves, for example, usually are stimulus determined.[36] Likewise, when the media describe present-day China, when they cast doubt on the safety of nuclear energy production, or when they praise the merits of a newly developed drug, they create images that are apt to dominate people's schemas.

Numerous studies show that political elites and other well-informed people develop exceptionally large arrays of schemas, allowing them to absorb many stories that are beyond the reach of the poorly informed.[37] They are more physically stimulated by new information and therefore are more likely to remember it.[38] The knowledge gap between the well informed and the poorly informed widens as a result. Those with the least political knowledge are likely to remain politically unsophisticated and impotent. The knowledge gap between the information rich and the information poor also makes mutual understanding of political views more difficult.

Transient Influences

Many transitory factors impinge on learning from news. People are intermittently attentive or inattentive and inclined or disinclined to learn. Up to half of television viewers eat dinner, wash dishes, read, or text their friends while watching television. Examination time at school, illness in the family, or the year-end rush at work may preempt time normally devoted to media. Though contemporary levels of media choice mean that news is available at all times, so too are entertainment programs, YouTube clips, and social media platforms that compete with news. Researchers cannot predict the effect of media messages without knowing the group context in which the exposure or conversation took place. For instance, if one watches or talks about a presidential inauguration with friends who are making fun of the way the president talks and acts, the occasion loses its solemnity and becomes banal. How a person interacts with information also depends on the format of that information. If news reports present conflicting facts or opinions; if they are too long or too short; or if they are repetitious, dull, or offensive; their effect is apt to be diminished. Mobile devices and social media platforms present information in ways that can also affect attention and processing.[39] Moreover, the total communications matrix affects the influence of its parts, so the impact of print news may be blunted by prior or subsequent presentations on television, radio, or digital media platforms or by interpersonal conversations.[40]

Learning From Partisan Media

Source credibility and appeal are also significant factors in news processing. People find television news more believable than comparable print news because seeing news anchors on their living room television screens makes them familiar and trustworthy. Recent trends in declining network audiences and overall levels of trust in the media may diminish television news's "credibility advantage." Partisanship, too, plays an important role in source appraisal. People are more likely to trust the partisan news network that matches their own partisanship.

The expansion of media choice that has come with dramatic changes to news media in recent decades prompted new questions about how we learn from partisan media. Media bias is widely debated, and elite cues about the partisan leanings of media outlets are abundant for news consumers—especially in the case of media with partisan brands and even in cases where partisan slant is arguable (see Photo 10-3). Citizens have ideas about partisan slant from news organizations even when they

Photo 10-3 Democratic presidential hopeful Senator Amy Klobuchar waits to speak with MSNBC journalist Chris Matthews in the spin room following the ninth Democratic primary debate of the 2020 presidential campaign season

Source: BRIDGET BENNETT/AFP via Getty Images.

Note: The debate was co-hosted by NBC, MSNBC, Noticias Telemundo, and *The Nevada Independent* at the Paris Theater in Las Vegas, Nevada, on February 19, 2020.

are not heavy news consumers. Since source credibility is important for whether audiences process or discount media messages, perceptions of partisan media slant may influence whether and how audiences learn from news.

Other factors influence learning from partisan media as well. Partisan media often provide different accounts of events and political issues as part of their partisan spin. In doing so, they may fail to provide full or accurate information and distort the knowledge of their audiences. Partisan media messages may also depress knowledge because they receive less scrutiny from like-minded audiences. Messages processed with less care may result in lower levels of recall. Partisan media messages also have the potential to enhance political knowledge. Specifically, they may do so by providing an organizational framework for thinking about the event or issue being covered. Because humans process information schematically, partisan presentations of news may foster understanding. Natalie (Talia) J. Stroud's research investigates these questions by examining whether choosing like-minded news media depresses or enhances political knowledge and finds some evidence that partisan selective exposure raises rather than depresses political knowledge. Other work suggests that news stories with partisan slant sometimes contain more substantive information.[41]

Learning Effects on Political Knowledge

What kinds of politically relevant knowledge and actions spring from people's contacts with the media? Because of the limitations of measuring instruments, the answer to that question is difficult. In Chapter 1, we pointed out the impossibility of isolating media influence when it is one of many factors in a complex environment. For example, when samples of citizens are asked why they worry about certain events or issues, a significant proportion often cites more media coverage as one of the reasons, and we know people tend to care more about issues the media covers intensely. However, these kinds of measures do not indicate the precise impact of media attention. Until researchers can trace an individual's mental processes and isolate and appraise the significance of each of the components that interact and combine to form mental images, media's influence on knowledge and attitudes cannot be fully assessed. Nor can researchers understand completely exactly what is learned from media.

Measurement Problems

Research tends to focus on very small facets of learning, such as testing what specific facts individuals learn about political candidates or about a few public policies. Even within such narrow areas, testing is severely limited. It often zeroes in on memorizing factual details from stories rather than on total knowledge gains. For instance, election coverage of a presidential candidate teaches more than facts about the candidate. It may also inform the audience about the role played by White House correspondents in campaign coverage and about living conditions in other cities. Such knowledge gains often are far more valuable for the news consumer than the story details, but they are usually overlooked.

Much learning occurs at the subconscious level. People are unaware of it when they learn something new and therefore fail to mention it when asked what they learned. At times, people may temporarily forget new information, only to have it reenter consciousness a short while later.[42] In fact, people are generally bad at accurately describing much at all about their media use experiences. Some problems relate to response bias; study respondents tend to drastically overreport the amount of news they follow. Other problems relate to the difficulty respondents have in remembering details about their news consumption and exposure.

As a result, several studies attempt to improve on existing methods for measuring media exposure.[43] Some efforts involve trying to improve survey-based self-report through various means,[44] and other approaches avoid self-reporting problems altogether by relying on observational audience tracking data or eye-tracking data.[45] Eye-tracking measures of media exposure are beneficial because they avoid error and can discern nuances in attention that occur while consuming media content; this is one reason they are widely employed by media industry testing. However, eye-tracking measures focus narrowly on attention and reactions to content and cannot broadly track overall media exposure. This illustrates one way that eye-tracking studies are limited by low external validity. We can learn very precise information about individual media use sessions, but not much about mass audience habits in the real world.

Measures based on passively collected audience behavior data have the benefit of high external validity in that they show real-world, real-time data on what news is being consumed and by what types of people and in various places. However, these data provide little information about how much attention people are paying to media, specifics of what they are seeing, or what they might learn. Approaches tied to improving self-report biases often employ the internal validity strength of experimental design and provide the additional benefit of revealing clues about the reasons people cannot accurately report their media exposure. Each of these approaches to improving our measures of media exposure have benefits and limitations but, combined across numerous studies and replications, they should make headway toward a better collective understanding of media effects.

Many assumptions about learning that seem intuitively correct remain untested; nonetheless, they are widely accepted as true. For example, news reports and dramatic television programs presumably teach audiences how lawyers or police officers or hospitals conduct their business. Media researcher Joshua Meyrowitz argues that television radically changed social roles so that women working in the home, who were previously isolated, learned about the attractive roles traditionally open only to men in U.S. society. News stories motivated them to compete for those jobs. Along with other shows and movies, popular mainstream television shows such as NBC's *Will and Grace* and ABC's *Modern Family* challenged and changed perceptions about gay and lesbian individuals and their roles in society.

Forgetting remains a neglected research sphere. Much learning gleaned from news stories is evanescent. When China is rocked by a devastating earthquake or the governor of New York resigns in the middle of a sex scandal, the salient names and facts are on many lips. But after the events pass, the knowledge evaporates rapidly. How rapidly seems to depend on several factors, most importantly people's ability to store and retrieve information. After three months of inattention, ordinary stories are hard to recall, even for people with good memories. If media periodically revive stories with follow-ups or with closely related stories, memory becomes deepened and prolonged. In fact, the media rehashed a few crucial incidents so often that they are now permanent memories. The Great Depression, World War II, the assassination of President John F. Kennedy, the horrors of the 2001 collapse of the World Trade Center towers, and extensive coverage of the COVID-19 pandemic are examples.[46]

Factual Learning

Given these limitations on initial learning and on remembering, what can be said about the extent of political learning from the mass media? Average people are aware of an impressive array of politically important topics that the media covered. However, they do not master many details. They recognize information if it is mentioned to them but fail to recall it without such assistance.[47] When John Robinson and Dennis Davis tested recall of specific facts mentioned in thirteen television news stories within hours of viewing, accuracy scores hovered around 40%, with only minor differences among age groups. Education and prior information levels produced the largest variations in scores, with the best-informed people scoring 13.8 percentage points higher than those who were poorly informed; 11.2 percentage points separated the scores of college graduates and the scores of people who ended their education in grade school.[48]

Many people are shocked by low recall scores because they believe that stories cannot be fully understood without memorizing factual details. For example, political scientists Scott Keeter and Cliff Zukin titled their study of voter knowledge gains during the 1976 and 1980 presidential elections *Uninformed Choice* because recall scores were low. Keeter and Zukin argued that most citizens are too uninformed to make intelligent political choices.[49] Such judgments may be unduly harsh, because these studies gauge knowledge solely by a citizen's ability to recall facts such as the names of prominent officeholders and figures about the length of their terms of office or the growth rate of budget deficits. Such factual information tests are inadequate for judging political knowledge and competence. What really matters is that citizens understand what is at stake in major political issues and what policy options are available for coping with problems. An extensive repertoire of factual detail is not essential for that. Political scientist Arthur Lupia argues that media and elites should refine communication techniques so that it is presented in ways that are better at facilitating audience attention and learning.[50] As media scholar Michael Schudson puts it, "There's a difference between the 'informational citizen,' saturated with bits and bytes of information, and the informed citizen, the person who has not only information but a point of view and preferences with which to make sense of it."[51]

Are people aware of major political issues and their significance? Are they able to place them in the general context of current politics? When researchers ask these genuinely important questions, the picture of the public's political competence brightens considerably. People may not remember the content of political speeches very well, but as already mentioned, they are aware of a wide range of current issues. Moreover, when interviewers probe for understanding rather than for knowledge of specific facts, they often discover considerable political insight. For instance, people who cannot define either *price deregulation* or *affirmative action* may still have fairly sophisticated notions about these matters. They know about government price controls on some goods and services and fully understand the burdens that minorities face in finding a job.[52]

Learning General Orientations

Some media stories leave the audience with politically significant feelings that persist long after facts fade from memory. Although many details of the 2001 terrorist strike are faded in memory, Americans still retain vivid feelings of horror, sympathy, and grief. News may leave people with generalized feelings of trust or distrust, even when it etches few facts into their memories. For instance, prominently featured stories of serious corruption in government may lower the public's esteem for the integrity of government. People who read newspapers that are severely critical of government actions express significantly less trust in government than do those exposed to favorable views. People who did not go beyond grade school seem to be particularly susceptible to erosion of trust in the wake of mass media criticism.[53] Cynical people, in turn, tend to participate less than others in such civic activities as voting and lobbying.[54]

As political scientist Murray Edelman pointed out, news stories may make people quiescent because they become fearful of interfering with crucial government actions or because they become complacent about the need for public vigilance. Fear that dissension weakens the government may decrease tolerance for dissidents. Edelman also warns that political quiescence has significant downsides. It may lead to acceptance of faulty public policies, poor laws, and ineffective administrative practices.[55]

On a more personal level, millions of people use the media to keep in touch with their communities. Their contacts help to counter feelings of loneliness and alienation because information becomes a bond among individuals who share it.[56] The models of life that the media depict create wants and expectations as well as dissatisfactions and frustrations. These feelings may become powerful stimulants for social change for the society at large or for selected individuals within it. Alternatively, the feelings may bolster support for the political status quo and generate strong resistance to change. Whether media-induced orientations and actions are considered positive, negative, or a mixture of both depends, of course, on one's sociopolitical preferences.

Deterrents to Learning

Lack of interest in politics and distaste for media offerings, as well as deficiencies in the supply of information, deter many people from keeping up with politics. Rather than discussing politics, which they see as a sensitive topic, they prefer to talk about sports or the weather or local gossip. In fact, as the level of abstract, issue-oriented content in political news rises, the attentive audience shrivels. People scan the news for major crises without trying to remember specific facts. Political interest and learning perk up quickly and often dramatically whenever people sense that events will greatly affect their lives or when they need information for their jobs or for social or political activities.[57] For example, media coverage of the disputed outcome of the 2000 presidential election fired up public interest that had smoldered during the campaign. The postelection events received more public attention in five weeks than the entire primary campaign had received during a five-month span.[58] A similar sharp rise in public attention to news followed the 2001 terrorist attack, the 2004 tsunami in Asia, and Hurricane Katrina in 2005.[59] The 2016 and 2020 presidential elections drew enormous audience interest, including televised debates for which ratings far outstripped those of previous recent election cycles.[60]

Widespread public interest in most political crises flares up like a straw fire and then dies quickly. Attention spans for news are erratic and brief, even though most Americans believe that as good citizens, they ought to be well informed about political news. They feel guilty, or at least apologetic, if they are not. The alienation of many population groups from the media further inhibits learning. Many members of the public consider mass media hostile. They often believe that the media lie and distort the news, casting police as trigger-happy oppressors of the disadvantaged or unions as corrupt and a barrier to economic progress. Public opinion polls in recent decades show considerable erosion of public confidence in the trustworthiness of the media in general. The media now rank near the bottom of trustworthiness, along with Congress and the legal profession.[61] Public distrust in the media is so pervasive that politicians regularly utilize an effective strategy of attacking the media when they or their co-partisans receive unfavorable coverage. Political incivility depicted on news programs also substantially erodes trust (see Chapter 12).[62]

How the media present information also affects learning. The media bombard the public daily with more news than it can handle, given the pressures of daily living. Most of the news is touted as significant, even though much is trivial. The constant crisis atmosphere numbs excitement and produces boredom. Audiences are not likely to try hard to learn a wealth of factual information that is of no immediate use and provides little gratification. Moreover, "happy talk" television news formats and exciting film footage encourage the feeling that news is a lighthearted diversion.

The presentation of stories in disconnected television snippets complicates the task of making sense out of news stories and integrating them with existing knowledge. This is especially true when stories are complex, as are most reports about controversial public policies. People who feel that they cannot understand what is happening are discouraged from spending time reading or listening. Learning also suffers when media present conflicting stories and interpretations without giving guidance to the audience. Journalists working for ostensibly neutral outlets hesitate to take sides in controversies, fearing accusations of unacceptable editorializing. If people watch several newscasts, hoping for an enriched news diet, they find that roughly half the material is repetitive. Even within a single newscast, a large proportion of every story is rehashed background information that puts the story into perspective for viewers who are seeing it for the first time.

The internal structure of television newscasts also impedes learning. Most news stories (74%) take up less than two-and-a-half minutes, yet they are crammed with information that people cannot possibly absorb in that time. Fully 30% of the stories exhibit more than ten pictures in addition to the verbal text, which is usually out of sync with the pictures. The pictures tend to remain on the screen too briefly to extract the full range of their messages. Two-thirds flash by in ten seconds or less. Furthermore, most news programs tightly package disparate items without the pauses that are essential for viewers to absorb information. Hence, it is not surprising that half the audience after the lapse of a few hours cannot recall a single item from a television newscast. Distracting activities that viewers combine with watching television aggravate the problem.

As we described in Chapter 4, the manner in which some forms of digital news are produced and disseminated also present challenges for learning from news. Websites displaying content in text-heavy formats do not direct users' attention in ways to facilitate learning and recall.[63] Screen size and manner of display on mobile devices also influence the amount of attention users are willing and able to spend on news content and may even influence the choice of whether to attend news on their device in the first place. Though many Americans visit news sites, digital news faces many challenges to attracting users who will spend enough attention and time on digital platforms to become engaged enough to learn. Unique visitors and audience reach often show high levels of traffic, but measures of time spent on site show that these visits are fleeting. Short-lived attention is especially true for mobile news consumers, and data show that people are increasingly getting more and more news from computers, tablets, and smartphones (see Figure 10-5).[64]

Despite all of the deterrents to learning, Americans still learn much about politics from their many thousands of hours of news consumption over a lifetime. During childhood and adolescence, much news exposure is indirect, conveyed by caregivers and teachers. It usually does a good job of socializing youths into the U.S. political system. As adults, they may be disappointed and cynical about particular leaders or policies, but relatively few individuals question the legitimacy of the government, object to its basic philosophy, or reject its claims. The dire predictions about

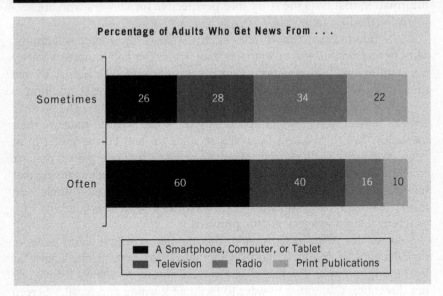

Figure 10-5 Preferred Platforms for News, 2020

Percentage of Adults Who Get News From . . .

Sometimes
| 26 | 28 | 34 | 22 |

Often
| 60 | 40 | 16 | 10 |

■ A Smartphone, Computer, or Tablet
■ Television ■ Radio ■ Print Publications

Source: Shearer, E. (2021, January 12). More than eight-in-ten Americans get news from digital devices. *Pew Research Center.* https://www.pewresearch.org/fact-tank/2021/01/12/more-than-eight-in-ten-americans-get-news-from-digital-devices/

television-induced deterioration of political life and rampant political alienation among citizens have not materialized.[65] In fact, if the media improve political reporting and political leaders arouse the public's interest, knowledge levels could rise sharply.

Conditional Learning Effects

Most Americans are exposed to the combined effects of traditional and digital media either directly or indirectly through contact with people who tell them what they have heard, seen, or read. They may know that President Joe Biden selected Pete Buttigieg, former mayor of South Bend, Indiana, as his secretary of transportation. They may feel reassured or disturbed by the appointment and might believe that it is either good or bad to have Buttigieg serving in that position. But which of these thoughts and feelings come from television, newspapers, conversations, online social networks, or a combination of these? It is nearly impossible to disentangle such strands of information.[66]

Print Versus Audiovisual Forms of News

Each medium makes unique contributions to learning. For example, television, because of its visuals, is especially powerful in transmitting realism and emotional appeal. Print media excel in conveying factual details. Because most tests of learning from the media focus on the kinds of facts that print media emphasize, they are generally credited with conveying more knowledge than audiovisual media do.[67] Television bashing is popular when social critics search for a scapegoat for the ills of society.[68] The critics downplay the learning opportunities provided by seeing events unfold on the television screen. Media scholar Neil Postman, for example, warns that massive use of television will turn the United States into a nation of dilettantes who avoid serious thinking because television trivializes the problems of the world.[69] Rod Hart calls it a "seductive" medium that turns people into passive watchers of the political scene rather than active participants.[70]

The claim that audiences who are print reliant—rather than audiovisual reliant—are better informed and that this proves the superiority of print news must be put into the appropriate context. As a group, print-reliant people differ from those who depend mostly on televised media in important ways. These differences make factual learning easier. Print aficionados generally enjoy higher socioeconomic status and better formal education. Their mid- and upper-level jobs provide above-average incentives for learning the factual details by which social scientists judge citizens' knowledge. Attitudes toward the media matter as well. Most people who view print media as primary information sources think of electronic media largely as sources of entertainment. These differences, rather than the nature of each medium, may explain some of the disparities in the effects of various types of media.[71] Television emerges as the most instructive medium if one tests for information that is best conveyed audiovisually, such as impressions of people and dramatic events.[72] Television is also the most readily comprehensible medium for millions of people with limited education. That includes the 32 million U.S. adults who are functionally illiterate and, therefore, almost entirely beyond the reach of print media (even in its digital forms).[73] In other words, television can reach a wider audience. One of the most important benefits of the broadcast era was that it helped reduce information inequalities between those in the public who were interested in public affairs and those who were not, which is also correlated with income and educational status.[74] What the poorly educated learn about politics from audiovisuals may be fragmentary and hazy, but it represents a quantum leap over the knowledge available to pre–television-age generations.

Television's greatest political impact, compared with nonvisual media, springs from its ability to reach millions of people simultaneously with the same images. Although the traditional networks are losing substantial portions of their nightly news viewers, they remain extremely influential.[75] Televised events still share experiences nationwide. Millions of Americans saw the September 11, 2001, terrorist attack and its aftermath on television. They watched U.S. troops fight in Iraq and Afghanistan and joined in vicarious visits to the Vatican during the papal transition in 2005. They witnessed the 2008 presidential campaign that broke through the dikes of race and gender prejudice by featuring, for the first time, a white woman and an African American man as the major parties' standard-bearers. In 2016, 84 million television viewers tuned in for the first presidential debate between the two major party nominees, one of which was the first woman in American history to be nominated to lead a major party ticket.[76] On January 6, 2021, millions of television audiences watched an insurrection unfold at the Capitol. Just days later, on January 20, 33.8 million people tuned in to watch President Joe Biden's inauguration; it drew the third-highest viewership among presidential inaugurations over the last forty years.[77] U.S. print media have never equaled the reach of television and the power that flows from it, including the power to shape collective memories.[78]

Conditional Effects Across Platforms and Devices

As we mentioned in Chapter 4, researchers are only now beginning to understand how some digital platforms influence the public's ability to learn from news. Learning from Web-based news platforms is conditioned heavily by the manner in which the information is presented, but evidence suggests there is nothing about computing platforms themselves that prohibit learning. Learning is simply different online. In fact, learning and recall can be enhanced by communication strategies that take advantage of the affordances of digital news platforms, such as picture-based page layouts and interactive features. News websites with contemporary image-based displays promote recall (see Figure 10-6). Interactive features enhance recognition and recall of information associated with the interactive feature but diminish recall on other parts of the site.[79] News audience behaviors also weigh in—reliance on news aggregators and searching for news in filter bubbles may omit important sources from one's news menu. However, just as with newspaper, radio, and television, the bulk of evidence indicates that when it is used for news and information seeking, the internet has pro-civic consequences, such as higher levels of learning and engagement.[80]

Learning from social media is also conditional. News exposure on social media is heavily determined by both individual user behaviors (such as choices about which people to friend and follow) and the interests; preferences; and sharing, following, and commenting behaviors within one's social network. On the positive side, social media users don't appear to select into networks that are entirely one-sided and attitudinally congruent, and incidental exposure to both attitudinal and counter-attitudinal news does occur. Unfortunately, sharing and clicking behaviors do result in more exposure to like-minded news than cross-ideology content, and incidental exposure occurring on social media has not yet produced verifiable increases in political knowledge.[81] There is some evidence that opinion leaders who are politically active offline are also active in their online social networks, which tend to be large, suggesting a potential for influence. Political elites such as candidates and party leaders are also among the most heavily followed on social media, which provides a healthy dose of information but one not vetted through fact-checking processes of institutional journalism.[82]

As we described in Chapter 4, the explosive growth of mobile news consumption is the most dramatic shift currently affecting the information environment. Mobile devices present challenges to learning from news. Several studies show that learning from the small screen, even from video, is challenging relative to large screens and that it curbs recall and requires more cognitive processing effort. When wireless service is spotty, slow-loading content also discourages news consumption; users defect after waiting only a second or two for content to load. Commercial Web traffic data patterns suggest that mobile users spend far less time on news pages compared to desktop and laptop users. Though reach is high, mobile attention rates are fleeting. The exception is among mobile users of news apps, who spend a long time on news content but unfortunately constitute a very tiny fraction of the online public audience. Presentation of content in mobile-friendly ways will undoubtedly help; news outlets are currently working on best practices for optimizing news content for mobile screens. It is not yet clear what implications these adaptations will have for the informative content in news.[83]

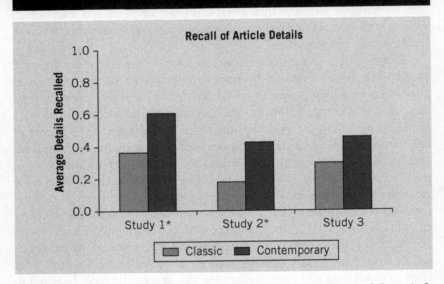

Figure 10-6   Recall of Information by Classic Versus Contemporary Webpage Layout for News Sites

Recall of Article Details

Average Details Recalled

Study 1*   Study 2*   Study 3

Classic   Contemporary

Source: Reprinted with permission from Stroud, N. J., Curry, A., Cardona, A., & Peacock, C. (2015). *Homepage layout.* Engaging News Project. https://engagingnewsproject.org/wp-content/uploads/2015/07/Online-News-Presentation-White-Paper2.pdf.

Note: * = Statistically significant difference

In short, the research on the differential effects of media reveals that different types of platforms and devices present stimuli that vary substantially in nature and content. It would be surprising, therefore, if their impact were identical, even when they deal with the same subjects. However, "there is no evidence of *consistent* significant differences in the ability of different media to persuade, inform, or even to instill an emotional response in audience members."[84]

Behavioral Effects

Because the media shape people's knowledge, attitudes, and feelings, they obviously can influence behavior. Two areas illustrate the extent of concern about behavioral effects: imitation of violence and crime (particularly among adolescents) and stimulation of economic and political development in underdeveloped regions. In addition, in Chapter 11, we will discuss the effects of media coverage on voting behavior.

Crime and Violent Behavior in Children

Many social scientists believe that portrayals of violence and crime in the media, particularly on television, lead to imitation, especially by children and young adults. Research thoroughly investigates the possible link between television exposure and deviant behavior. The Surgeon General's office produced a bookshelf of information on the topic over the last several decades.[85] Congressional committees spent countless hours listening to conflicting testimony by social scientists about the impact of television violence; it is commonly seen as an important issue. Meanwhile, the amount of violent content, particularly in fictional programs, has escalated, though numbers vary widely depending on the definition of *violence*. A 1996 study that defined *violence* broadly as "any overt depiction of the use of physical force or the credible threat of such force intended to physically harm an animate being or group of beings" found the most violence on premium cable channels. On HBO and Showtime, 85% of programming contained violence. The rate was 59% for basic cable channels and 44% for broadcast television.[86]

The Parents Television Council, a nonprofit watchdog group, studied several prime-time shows rated TV-PG and TV-14. Their report shows a substantial increase in violence on PG rated programs over the last decade (28%). The violence included graphic killings and/or injuries by gunfire and stabbings, blood, death, and scenes of decapitation and dismemberment. On programs rated TV-14, the study found that during the 2017–2018 seasons, there was more than twice as much violence than on the 2008–2008 television seasons.[87] The trends also affect programs on the broadcast networks; they are not limited to cable. The escalation of crime and violence incidents on television is an ongoing matter of widespread public concern.[88]

What do studies of the impact of television violence reveal? Despite the strong inclination of many researchers to find that crime fiction causes asocial behavior, the evidence is inconclusive because many other factors influence behavior and cannot be ruled out. Some children do copy violent behavior, especially when they watched aggression that was left unpunished or rewarded and when countervailing influences from their parents and their teachers are lacking.[89] But aside from imitating television examples when tempted to do so, very few children become violent after exposure to violence in the mass media. Most children lack the predisposition and the opportunity for violence, and most do not live in an environment that encourages asocial behavior.[90] A number of studies tracked the behavior of children exposed to a great deal of violence on television during their early years. As adults, these individuals display a higher incidence of asocial behaviors. Still, that does not point definitively to television as the cause, given the complexity of the environments that mold children and young adults.[91]

Age-linked comprehension differences further confound the situation. Younger children may not be able to comprehend many of the events presented by the media in the same way that adolescents do. The complex social reasoning that adults often ascribe to even young children does not develop until youngsters reach their teenage years. Several studies of children in preschool and early grade school suggest that much of what adults consider to be violent does not seem so to children. Cartoon violence is an example.[92] Therefore, many of the programs that adults consider as glorifications of violence may actually suggest more benign behavior to children.

The proportion of preadolescents and adolescents in the United States who are prone to imitate crime is unknown. However, the wide dispersion of television throughout U.S. homes makes it almost certain that the majority of children susceptible to imitating violence will be exposed. Even if the actual number of highly susceptible preadolescents and adolescents is tiny and statistically insignificant, the social consequences can be profound. Such considerations prompted Congress to mandate in the Telecommunications Act of 1996 that television sets should include a "V-chip" to enable adults to block violent television programs from transmission to their homes. The device has not been used extensively, and probably least often in the kinds of homes where the most vulnerable youngsters are likely to live, considering the correlation between child delinquency and flawed home environments. Likewise, in 2000, Congress passed the Children's Internet Protection Act (CIPA), which mandated that schools and libraries install technology to protect children from obscene and violent content on the internet, but some local systems have chosen to forgo federal funds and leave their computers unfiltered. In 2011, the Federal Communications Commission (FCC) provided updates to the rules for implementing CIPA, which included a requirement to monitor the online activity of minors and educate them regarding appropriate online behaviors, such as responses to cyberbullying.

Behavior Change in Adults

What about imitation of socially undesirable behavior by adults? The same considerations apply. Imitation depends on the setting at the time of media exposure and on the personality and attitudes that viewers bring to a situation. Widespread societal norms seem to be particularly important. For instance, the 1986 report of the Attorney General's Commission on Pornography noted that exposure to aberrant sexual behavior led to comparatively little imitation. In fact, there was some evidence that greater availability of obscene and pornographic materials reduced sex crimes and misdemeanors because vicarious experiences substituted for actual ones.[93] There was a great deal more evidence that exposure to criminal behavior encourages imitation. The difference may be more apparent than real, however, because crime is more likely to be reported whereas sexual perversions usually remain hidden.

In sum, the precise link between exposure to media images and corresponding behavior remains uncertain. Attempts by government bodies to regulate media offerings that might stimulate undesirable behavior therefore lack a firm scientific basis. Even if that hurdle can be overcome, it is questionable whether a democratic society should attempt to manipulate the minds of its citizens to protect them from temptations to violate social norms. It seems best to leave control of the content of entertainment programs to widely based informal social pressures. The question of whether social pressures should be allowed to interfere with reporting real-world violence poses even more difficult dilemmas. The possibly adverse effects on behavior must be balanced against the public's need to keep informed about the real world.

Socioeconomic and Political Modernization

The potential of the media to guide people's behavior prompted great efforts to use them as tools for social and political development. The results produced some successes and many failures.

Social and Political Development

Hope that using the media could bring about industrialization, improved social services, and democratization ran very high in the decades following World War II. A personality characteristic that political scientist Daniel Lerner labeled "empathic capacity" was called the key to human and material development. The idea behind this theory was that when the media present new objects, ideas, and behaviors, audiences presumably empathize with what is happening in the story and try to imitate it. For instance, when the media show how slum dwellers have built new housing or how flood victims have purified their polluted water supply, audience members will apply the information to their own lives.

Crediting the media with a major role in modernization and democratization rests on three assumptions: (1) that the mass media can create interest and empathy for unfamiliar experiences; (2) that the mass media can provide graphic audiovisual examples of new practices, which audiences can readily understand and imitate; and (3) that development, once started, encourages people to increase their knowledge and skills. Where formal education is not readily available, the media provide information and enhance the capacity to learn. Progress in industrialization, living standards, and political advancement that has followed the spread of media to many formerly information-deficient regions is cited as proof that the assumptions are correct.[94]

Psychological Barriers to Development

Although many technologically and politically underdeveloped regions showed measurable progress, with the media apparently serving as catalysts, social and political change was far slower and more sporadic than development theorists expected. Many psychological and physical obstacles stood in the way, including the hostility of individuals or communities to change and their unwillingness to alter long-established patterns. Mass media may actually become a negative reference point when people condemn the lifestyles that the media depict. In fact, various fundamentalist groups around the world mobilized to bar mass media offerings in their communities and stop social and political innovations.

People who are not overtly hostile to change still may be uninterested in altering their lifestyles. To persuade them to adopt innovations may require the intervention of a trusted person, such as a clergy member, a health care provider, or a family member. The influence of the mass media then becomes a "two-step flow," moving from the media to opinion leaders and then to their followers.

Adoption of Changes

Although it is difficult to use the mass media to change people's basic attitudes and ingrained behaviors, many mass media campaigns succeeded. Five steps are important. The first step is this: People must become aware of the possibility for change. Here, the media are especially helpful. Radio can inform people about new energy-saving devices or new child-rearing methods. Television and movies can demonstrate new behaviors and new technologies. The internet offers many previously unavailable, inexpensive opportunities for political participation. Second is understanding how to accomplish the suggested changes. For example, people may be aware that public assistance is available, but they may not know how to apply for it. Mass media usually fail to supply detailed information, although the internet can fill some information gaps. On average, only one-third of all stories that might inspire action, such as environmental protection or energy conservation, contain information about implementation.[95] Unless this gap is filled, the chain leading to the adoption of innovations is broken.

Third is evaluation. People assess the merits of an innovation and decide whether they want to adopt it. Innovations often fail to take root because prospective users reject them as bad, inappropriate, too risky, or too difficult. Media messages alone may not be persuasive enough. It may also be crucial to have a trusted person urge or demonstrate adoption of the innovation. Fourth is trial. The effect of the media in getting people to try innovations is limited. Factors beyond media control are more important, such as the social and financial costs of the change as well as the audience's willingness to change. Some individuals are more receptive to innovations; others are skeptical and cautious. Fifth is adoption. The media contribute most to this phase by encouraging people to stick with the changes that have become part of their life and work styles. For example, the adoption of birth control practices is useless unless they are kept up. The same holds true for many health and sanitation measures or improved work habits. To ensure persistence, mass media must cover a topic regularly, stressing long-range goals and reporting progress.

It is difficult to predict which media campaigns designed to reform behavior will succeed and which will fail.[96] Douglas S. Solomon, who studied health campaigns conducted by private and public institutions, believes that four factors account for success or failure. To succeed, campaigns must set well-specified, realistic goals that are tailored to the needs of the target groups. They must carefully select appropriate media and media formats and present their message at key times and intervals. Messages must be properly designed for the greatest persuasiveness. Successful campaigns also must include continuous evaluation and appropriate readjustments.[97]

Above all, the success of the mass media in bringing about change hinges on receptivity to reforms. Ongoing efforts to use the media to modernize developing areas; to turn former communists into democratic citizens; or to bring socially helpful information to individuals who are poor, elderly, and handicapped must concentrate on identifying the specific circumstances most likely to bring success. Responding to requests initiated locally (rather than designing information campaigns from the outside) and integrating local traditions into new approaches seem to hold the most promise.[98]

SUMMARY

The mass media play a major role in political socialization and in learning and accepting the beliefs, norms, and rules that govern political life. Contrary to earlier findings that indicated limited impact, the media are very influential in this process. Consequently, they represent a tremendously powerful political force.

However, the impact of the media on political socialization and other aspects of political learning varies, depending on people's lifestyles and circumstances. Psychological, demographic, and situational factors influence perceptions, as do the manner of news presentation and framing. Although many factors contribute to diversity in socialization and learning, there are powerful unifying forces as well. Most Americans are exposed to similar political information and develop roughly similar outlooks on what it means (and ought to mean) to be an American both politically and socially. Fragmenting media may be eroding some of the unifying aspects of mass media.

Various theories explain why and how individuals select their information sources, process the available information, and commit facts and opinions to memory. Overall, memory for specific facts that the media present is spotty because most people forget the details after they have drawn conclusions from them. Through repeated exposure to news over time, many people become aware of significant political problems and appreciate their basic significance. Equally important, exposure to the media can produce a range of politically relevant moods, such as apathy, cynicism, fear, trust, acquiescence, or support. These moods condition participation in the political process, which may range from no participation at all to efforts to overthrow the government by force.

The media may also produce or attenuate behavior that affects the quality of public life. We assessed the role of the media in fostering socially undesirable behaviors, especially crime and violence. We also explored the ways in which the media influence the political and social development of various population groups. The media are most successful in informing people and creating initial attitudes. They are least effective in changing established attitudes and ingrained behaviors.

Given the many largely uncontrollable variables that determine media influence, efforts to manipulate media content to foster societal goals are risky at best. They could set dangerous precedents for inhibiting the free flow of controversial ideas or for using the media as channels for government propaganda.

DISCUSSION QUESTIONS ———————————

1. What roles do mass media play in political socialization? How does socialization occur, and during what life stages do media play a significant role in political learning and socialization?

2. What are some of the processes through which mass media contribute to learning about politics?

3. How do mass media messages and patterns of media consumption affect citizens' political knowledge?

4. What kinds of things increase citizens' likelihood of gaining political knowledge from mass media? What kinds of things are harmful or hinder the ability to gain political knowledge from media?

5. Can we expect to observe many behavioral effects in response to mass media exposure? If so, what kind? If not, why not?

READINGS ————————————————————

Albertson, B., & Gadarian, S. K. (2015). *Anxious politics: Democratic citizens in a threatening world.* Cambridge University Press.

Clark, L. S., & Marchi, R. (2017). *Young people and the future of news: Social media and the rise of connective journalism.* Cambridge University Press.

Dunaway, J. L., & Searles, K. (forthcoming). *News attention in a mobile era.* Oxford University Press.

Ellcessor, E. (2016). *Restricted access: Media, disability, and the politics of participation* (Vol. 6). NYU Press.

Ellis, A. C. (Ed.). (2020). *Impact of political socialization on the support for democratic principles: Emerging research and opportunities.* IGI Global.

Gierzynski, A. (2018). *The political effects of entertainment media: How fictional worlds affect real world political perspectives.* Rowman & Littlefield.

Good, K. D. (2020). *Bring the world to the child: Technologies of global citizenship in American education.* MIT Press.

Graber, D. A. (2012). *Processing politics: Learning from television in the Internet age.* University of Chicago Press.

Kavenaugh, J., Marcellino, W., Blake, J. S., Smith, S., Davenport, S., & Tebeka, M. G. (2019). *News in a digital age: Comparing the presentation of news information across time and across media platforms.* Rand Corporation.

Lahikainen, A. R., Mālkiā, T., & Repo, K. (Eds.). (2017). *Media, family interaction and the digitalization of childhood*. Edward Elgar Publishing.

Lemish, D., Jordan, A., & Rideout, V. (Eds.). (2018). *Children, adolescents, and media: The future of research and action*. Routledge.

Lupia, A. (2016). *Uninformed: Why people know so little about politics and what we can do about it*. Oxford University Press.

Perse, E. M., & Lambe, J. (2016). *Media effects and society*. Routledge.

Potter, W. J. (2018). *Media literacy*. SAGE.

Settle, J. E. (2018). *Frenemies: How social media polarizes America*. Cambridge University Press.

Sinclair, B. (2012). *The social citizen: Peer networks and political behavior*. University of Chicago Press.

Strasburger, V. C., Wilson, B. J., & Jordan, A. B. (2013). *Children, adolescents, and the media* (3rd ed.). SAGE.

Trūltzsch-Wijnen, C. W. (2020). *Media literacy and the effect of socialization*. Springer International Publishing.

Van Dijk, J. (2020). *The digital divide*. John Wiley & Sons.

Wahl-Jorgensen, K. (2019). *Emotions, media and politics*. Wiley.

Watkins, S. C., & Cho, A. *The digital edge: How Black and Latino youth navigate digital inequality* (Vol. 4). NYU Press.

Woolley, S. C., & Howard, P. N. (Eds.). (2018). *Computational propaganda: political parties, politicians, and political manipulation on social media*. Oxford University Press.

NOTES

1. Burrows, C. N., & Blanton, H. (2016). Real-world persuasion from virtual-world campaigns. *Communication Research*, *43*(4), 542–570.

2. White, G. B. (2008). Capturing the ethics education value of television medical dramas. *The American Journal of Bioethics, 8*(12), 13–14.

3. Shah, D. V. (1998). Civic engagement, interpersonal trust, and television use: An individual-level assessment of social capital. *Political Psychology, 19*, 469–496; Uslaner, E. M. (1998). Social capital, television, and the "mean world": Trust, optimism, and civic participation. *Political Psychology, 19*, 441–467; Lemish, D. (2007). *Children and television: A global perspective*. Blackwell.

4. Watkins, B. (1985). Television viewing as a dominant activity of childhood: A developmental theory of television effects. *Critical Studies in Mass Communication, 2*(1985), 323–337. Average high school graduates have spent 15,000 hours watching television and 11,000 hours in the classroom. They have seen 350,000 commercials. For an excellent discussion of various aspects of youth socialization, see McLeod, J. M., & Shah, D. V. (Eds.). (2009). Communication and political socialization. *Political Communication, 26*(1), especially pp. 65–117.

5. *Connected to the future: A report on children's internet use from the corporation for public broadcasting.* (2003). Corporation for Public Broadcasting. http://www .grunwald.com/pdfs/Connected-to-the-Future_GRUNWALD-CPB%20Study .pdf

6. Sears, D. O., & Valentino, N. (1997). Politics matters: Political events as catalysts for pre-adult socialization. *American Political Science Review, 91*, 45–65; Sears, D. O., & Funk, C. L. (1999). Evidence of the long-term persistence of adults' political predispositions. *Journal of Politics, 61*, 1–28; Calavita, M. (2005). *Apprehending politics: News media and individual political development.* State University of New York Press.

7. Pingree, S. (1983). Children's cognitive processes in constructing social reality. *Journalism Quarterly, 60*(Fall), 415–422; also see Demaine, J. (Ed.). (2005). *Citizenship and political education today.* Palgrave Macmillan; Sugarman, S. (2007). *If kids could vote: Children, democracy, and the media.* Lexington Books.

8. York, C., & Scholl, R. M. (2015). Youth antecedents to news media consumption: Parent and youth newspaper use, news discussion, and long-term news behavior. *Journalism & Mass Communication Quarterly, 92*(3), 681–699.

9. Piaget, J. (1962). *The language and thought of the child* (3rd ed.). Harcourt Brace; Conover, P. J. (1991). Political socialization: Where's the politics? In W. Crotty (Ed.), *Political science: Looking to the future; political behavior* (Vol. 3). Northwestern University Press.

10. A study of prime-time values on television showed that less than 4% featured citizenship values, such as patriotism or citizen duties. Selnow, G. W. (1990). Values in prime-time television. *Journal of Communication, 40*(Summer), 69.

11. Kubey, R. (1994). Media implications for the quality of family life. In D. Zillmannn, J. Bryant, & A. C. Huston (Eds.), *Media, children, and the family.* Erlbaum; Comstock, G. A., & Scharrer, E. (2007). *Media and the American child.* Elsevier. For a more recent account, also see Edgerly, S., Thorson, K., Thorson, E., Vraga, E. K., & Bode, L. (2018). Do parents still model news consumption? Socializing news use among adolescents in a multi-device world. *New Media & Society, 20*(4), 1263–1281.

12. Quintelier, E. (2015). Engaging adolescents in politics: The longitudinal effect of political socialization agents. *Youth & Society*, *47*(1), 51–69.

13. Messing, S., & Westwood, S. J. (2014). Selective exposure in the age of social media: Endorsements trump partisan source affiliation when selecting news online. *Communication Research*, *41*(8), 1042–1063.

14. Edgerly, S., Thorson, K., Thorson, E., Vraga, E. K., & Bode, L. (2018). Do parents still model news consumption? Socializing news use among adolescents in a multi-device world. *New Media & Society*, *20*(4), 1263–1281.

15. The total audience report: Q1 2016. (2016, June 27). *Nielsen*. https://www.nielsen.com/us/en/insights/report/2016/the-total-audience-report-q1-2016/

16. Baum, M. A. (2003). *Soft news goes to war: Public opinion and American foreign policy in the new media age*. Princeton University Press. This article explains the important role played by soft news in informing the public; Key news audiences now blend online and traditional sources. (2008, August 17). *Pew Research Center*. http://www.people-press.org/2008/08/17/key-news-audiences-now-blend-online-and-traditional-sources/.

17. Gerbner, G., Gross, L., Jackson-Beeck, M., Jeffries-Fox, S., & Signorielli, N. (1978). Cultural indicators: Violence profile No. 9. *Journal of Communication*, *28* (Summer), 178, 193; see also Gerbner, G., Gross, L., Morgan, M., & Signorielli, N. (1984). Political correlates of television viewing. *Public Opinion Quarterly*, *48*(Summer), 283–300; Prior, M., & Lupia, A. (2008). Money, time, and political knowledge: Distinguishing quick recall and political learning skills. *American Journal of Political Science*, *52*(1), 169–183; Lay, J. C. (2006). Learning about politics in low-income communities: Poverty and political knowledge. *American Politics Research*, *34*(3), 319–340.

18. The importance of pre-adult political learning for subsequent political orientations is discussed in Jennings, K., & Stoker, L. (2008). Of time and the development of partisan polarization. *American Journal of Political Science*, *52*(July), 619–635; Jennings, K. (2004). Political participation as viewed through the lens of the political socialization project. In M. Herman (Ed.), *Advances in political psychology*. Emerald Group; Graber, D. A. (1993). *Processing the news: How people tame the information tide* (2nd ed.). University Press of America; Graber, D. A. (2012). *Processing politics: Learning from television in the internet age*. University of Chicago Press, Chapter 2.

19. Stoker, L., & Jennings, M. K. (2008). Of time and the development of partisan polarization. *American Journal of Political Science*, *52*(3), 619–635.

20. Mitchell, A., Gottfried, J., Barthel, M., & Shearer, E. (2016, July 7). Pathways to news. *Pew Research Center*. http://www.journalism.org/2016/07/07/pathways-to-news/; Horrigan, J. B., & Duggan, M. (2015, December 21). Home broadband 2015. *Pew Research Center*. http://www.pewinternet

.org/2015/12/21/home-broadband-2015/; The total audience report: Q1 2016. (2016, June 27). *Nielsen.* https://www.nielsen.com/us/en/insights/report/2016/the-total-audience-report-q1-2016/

21. However, the benefits derived from the use of a particular medium vary for demographic groups. For example, while use of local news media coincides with civic participation for most audiences, this does not hold true for African Americans, for whom civic participation is encouraged more by interpersonal networks. Mastin, T. (2000). Media use and civic participation in the African-American population: Exploring participation among professionals and non-professionals. *Journalism and Mass Communication Quarterly, 77*(1), 115–127.

22. Mossberger, K., Tolbert, C., & Franko, W. W. (2013). *Digital cities: The internet and the geography of opportunity.* Oxford University Press; Horrigan, J. B., & Duggan, M. (2015, December 21). Home broadband 2015. *Pew Research Center.* http://www.pewinternet.org/2015/12/21/home-broadband-2015/

23. Bullock, J. G., Gerber, A. S., Hill, S. J., & Huber, G. A. (2015). Partisan bias in factual beliefs about politics. *Quarterly Journal of Political Science, 10*(4), 519–578.

24. Iyengar, S. (1991). *Is anyone responsible? How television frames political issues.* University of Chicago Press, pp. 136–143.

25. Rothman, S., Lichter, S. R., & Lichter, L. (1992). Television's America. In S. Rothman (Ed.), *The mass media in liberal democratic societies* (pp. 221–266). Paragon House.

26. Poindexter, P. M. (1980). Non-news viewers. *Journal of Communication, 30*(Fall), 58–65; Delli Carpini, M. X., & Williams, B. A. (1996). Constructing public opinion: The uses of fictional and nonfictional television in conversations about the environment. In A. N. Crider (Ed.), *The psychology of political communication* (pp. 149–175). University of Michigan Press.

27. For examples of various types of general and specific information supplied by entertainment programming, see Childs, D. (2008, September 16). *Grey's Anatomy* lesson? ABC News. https://abcnews.go.com/Health/MindMoodNews/story?id=5818221&page=1; Funkhouser, G. R., & Shaw, E. F. (1990). How synthetic experience shapes social reality. *Journal of Communication, 40*(Summer), 75–87; Potter, W. J., & Ware, W. (1989). The frequency and context of prosocial acts on primetime TV. *Journalism Quarterly, 66*(Summer), 359–366.

28. Graber, D. A. (1993). *Processing the news: How people tame the information tide* (2nd ed.). University Press of America, pp. 90–93.

29. Gerbner, G., Gross, L., Morgan, M., & Signorielli, N. (1984). Political correlates of television viewing. *Public Opinion Quarterly, 48*(Summer), 283–300, p. 286.

30. Jordan, D. L. (1993). Newspaper effects on policy preferences. *Public Opinion Quarterly, 57,* 191–204; Schneider, W., & Lewis, A. I. (1985). Views on the news. *Public Opinion, 8*(August–September), 5–11, 58–59.

31. Graber, D. A. (1993). *Processing the news: How people tame the information tide* (2nd ed.). University Press of America, pp. 27–31 (for details on learning processes, see Chapters 7–9). Also see Wicks, R. H. (1991). Schema theory and measurement in mass communication research: Theoretical and methodological issues in news information processing. *Communication Yearbook, 15,* 115–154. SAGE. An excellent discussion of processing of audiovisual information research, including a lengthy bibliography, is presented by Lang, A. (2000). The limited capacity model of mediated message processing. *Journal of Communication, 50*(1), 46–70. How learning goals affect processing is reported by Huang, L-N. (2000). Examining candidate information search processes: The impact of processing goals and sophistication. *Journal of Communication, 50*(1), 93–114.

32. Lippmann, W. (1922). *Public opinion.* Harcourt Brace, p. 31.

33. See, for example, Oliver, M. B. (1997). Caucasian viewers' memory of Black and white criminal suspects in the news. *Journal of Communication, 49*(3), 46–60 (and references cited therein); Entman, R. M., & Rojecki, A. (2001). *The Black image in the white mind: Media and race in America.* University of Chicago Press.

34. Branton, R. P., & Dunaway, J. (2009). Spatial proximity to the US–Mexico border and newspaper coverage of immigration issues. *Political Research Quarterly, 62*(2), 289–302; Branton, R. P., & Dunaway, J. (2009). Slanted newspaper coverage of immigration: The importance of economics and geography. *Policy Studies Journal, 37*(2), 257–273.

35. Dixon, T. L. (2015). Good guys are still always in white? Positive change and continued misrepresentation of race and crime on local television news. *Communication Research.* https://doi.org/10.1177%2F0093650215579223

36. Iyengar, S. (1987). Television news and citizens' explanations of national affairs. *American Political Science Review, 81*(September), 815–831. The impact of stereotyped beliefs on public policy is discussed in detail in Gilens, M. (1999). *Why Americans hate welfare: Race, media, and the politics of antipoverty policy.* University of Chicago Press.

37. Price, V., & Zaller, J. (1993). Who gets the news? Alternative measures of news reception and their implications for research. *Public Opinion Quarterly, 57*(1), 133–164; Gaziano, C. (1997). Forecast 2000: Widening knowledge gaps. *Journalism and Mass Communication Quarterly, 74*(2), 237–264. For evidence of shared reactions to television programs, irrespective of educational level, see Neuman, W. R. (1982). Television and American culture: The mass medium and the pluralist audience. *Public Opinion Quarterly, 46*(Winter), 471–487.

38. Grabe, M. E., Lang, A., Zhou, S., & Bolls, P. D. (2000). Cognitive access to negatively arousing news: An experimental investigation of the knowledge gap. *Communication Research*, 27(1), 3–26.

39. Dunaway, J., Searles, K., Sui, M., & Paul, N. (2018). News attention in a mobile era. *Journal of Computer-Mediated Communication*, 23(2), 107–124.

40. Burriss, L. L. (1987). How anchors, reporters, and newsmakers affect recall and evaluation of stories. *Journalism Quarterly*, 64(Summer/Fall), 514–519. The impact of framing on the perception of the legitimacy of social protest is discussed in McLeod, D. M., & Detenber, B. H. (1999). Framing effects of television news coverage of social protest. *Journal of Communication*, 49(3), 3–23; also see Lang, A. (2000). The limited capacity model of mediated message processing. *Journal of Communication*, 50(1), 46–70; Buscemi, W. L. (1997). Numbers? Borrinnnggg!!! *PS: Political Science and Politics*, 30(4), 737–742; Valkenburg, P. M., Semetko, H., & de Vreese, C. H. (1999). The effects of news frames on readers' thoughts and recall. *Communication Research*, 26(5), 550–569.

41. Stroud, N. J. (2011). *Niche news: The politics of news choice*. Oxford University Press.

42. An overview of hyperamnesia research is presented in Wicks, R. H. (1995). Remembering the news: Effects and message discrepancy on news recall over time. *Journalism and Mass Communication Quarterly*, 72(3), 666–682.

43. Althaus, S. L., & Tewksbury, D. H. (2007). *Toward a new generation of media use measures for the ANES* [Report to the board of overseers]. American National Election Studies, Ann Arbor, MI, United States; Dilliplane, S., Goldman, S. K., & Mutz, D. C. (2013). Televised exposure to politics: New measures for a fragmented media environment. *American Journal of Political Science*, 57, 236–248; Mutz, D. C. (2011). *Population-based survey experiments*. Princeton University Press; Guess, A. M. (2015). Measure for measure: An experimental test of online political media exposure. *Political Analysis*, 23, 59–75; Feldman, L., Stroud, N. J., Bimber, B., & Wojcieszak, M. (2013). Assessing selective exposure in experiments: The implications of different methodological choices. *Communication Methods and Measures*, 7, 172–194.

44. Jerit, J., Barabas, J., Pollock, W., Banducci, S., Stevens, D., & Schoonvelde, M. (2016). Manipulated vs. measured: Using an experimental benchmark to investigate the performance of self-reported media exposure. *Communication Methods and Measures*, 10(2–3), 99–114.

45. Guess, A. M. (2021). (Almost) Everything in moderation: New evidence on Americans' online media diets. American Journal of Political Science. https://doi.org/10.1111/ajps.12589; Hindman, M. (2011). Less of the same: The lack of local news on the internet. FCC. http://www.fcc.gov/document/media-ownership-study-6-submitted-study; Dunaway, J., Searles, K., Sui, M., & Paul, N. (2018). News attention in a mobile era. *Journal of Computer-Mediated*

Communication, 23(2), 107–124; Vraga, E., Bode, L., & Troller-Renfree, S. (2016). Beyond self-reports: Using eye tracking to measure topic and style differences in attention to social media content. *Communication Methods and Measures, 10*(2–3), 149–164; Nielsen Norman Group. (2021). *How people read online: The eyetracking evidence* (2nd ed.). Author. https://www.nngroup.com/reports/how-people-read-web-eyetracking-evidence/#:~:text=Content%20is%20the%20core%20of%20building%20positive%20relationships%20with%20users.&text=The%20findings%20in%20this%20412,hours%20of%20testing%20session%20time

46. Stauffer, J., Frost, R., & Rybolt, W. (1983). The attention factor in recalling network television news. *Journal of Communication, 33*(Winter), 29–37. Also see Graber, D. A. (2012). *Processing politics: Learning from television in the internet age.* University of Chicago Press.

47. Graber, D. A. (2012). *Processing politics: Learning from television in the internet age.* University of Chicago Press, Chapter 2; Van Dijk, T. A. (1988). *News as discourse.* Erlbaum; Robinson, J. P., & Levy, M. R. (1986). *The main source: Learning from television news.* SAGE; also see Popkin, S., & Dimock, M. A. (1999). Political knowledge and citizen competence. In S. L. Elkin & K. E. Soltan (Eds.), *Citizen competence and democratic institutions* (pp. 117–146). Pennsylvania State University Press.

48. Robinson, J. P., & Davis, D. (1990). Television news and the informed public: An information-processing approach. *Journal of Communication, 40*(3), 106–119; also see Robinson, J. P., & Davis, D. (1989). News flow and democratic society in an age of electronic media. In G. Comstock (Ed.), *Public communication and behavior* (Vol. 2). Academic Press.

49. Keeter, S., & Zukin, C. (1983). *Uninformed choice: The failure of the new presidential nominating system.* Praeger. But see Lupia, A., & McCubbins, M. D. (1998). *The democratic dilemma: Can citizens learn what they need to know?* Cambridge University Press; Delli Carpini, M. X., & Keeter, S. (1996). *What Americans know about politics and why it matters.* Yale University Press.

50. Lupia, A. (2016). *Uninformed: Why people know so little about politics and what we can do about it.* Oxford University Press.

51. Michael Schudson, M. (1995). *The power of news.* Harvard University Press, p. 27.

52. V. O. Key, with the assistance of Milton C. Cummings Jr., reached the same conclusion in *The Responsible Electorate* (Harvard University Press, 1965), p. 7. Regarding the wisdom inherent in public opinion, see Page, B. I., & Shapiro, R. Y. (1992). *The rational public: Fifty years of trends in Americans' policy preferences.* University of Chicago Press, pp. 383–390; Anderson, D. R. (1998). Educational television is not an oxymoron. *Annals of the American Academy of Political and Social Science, 557*(May), 24–38.

53. Miller, A. H., Goldenberg, E. N., & Erbring, L. (1979). Type-set politics: Impact of newspapers on public confidence. *American Political Science Review*, 73(March), 67–84.

54. Cappella, J. N., & Jamieson, K. H. (1997). *The spiral of cynicism: The press and the public good*. Oxford University Press.

55. Edelman, M. (1976). *Politics as symbolic action*. Academic Press; Edelman, M. (1988). *Constructing the political spectacle*. University of Chicago Press.

56. Hearold, S. (1986). A synthesis of 1043 effects of television on social behavior. In G. A. Comstock (Ed.), *Public communication and behavior* (Vol. 1). Academic Press. Also see Marcus, G. E., Neuman, W. R., & MacKuen, M. (2000). *Affective intelligence and political judgment*. University of Chicago Press; Damasio, A. R. (1994). *Descartes' error: Emotion, reason, and the human brain*. Grosset/Putnam.

57. The desire to be politically informed varies widely. News selection criteria are discussed in Graber, D. A. (1993). *Processing the news: How people tame the information tide* (2nd ed.). University Press of America, Chapter 4.

58. Center for Media and Public Affairs. (2000, December 20). *Florida trouble triples TV attention*. Author. http://cmpa.gmu.edu/wp-content/uploads/2013/10/prev_pres_elections/2000/2000.12.20.Florida-Trouble-Triples-TV-Attention.pdf.

59. Check Chapter 5 for sources for these events; for Hurricane Katrina, see Two-in-three critical of Bush's relief efforts. (2005, September 8). *Pew Research Center*. https://www.pewresearch.org/politics/2005/09/08/two-in-three-critical-of-bushs-relief-efforts/

60. Katz, B. (2016, October 10). NFL's "Sunday Night Football" gets crushed in ratings by presidential debate. *Forbes*. http://www.forbes.com/sites/brandonkatz/2016/10/10/nfls-sunday-night-football-gets-crushed-in-ratings-by-presidential-debate/#6f96c8b12186.; Q3: CNN has best quarter in eight years. (2016, September 26). *CNN*. http://cnnpressroom.blogs.cnn.com/2016/09/26/q3-cnn-has-best-quarter-in-eight-years/.

61. Stanley, H. W., & Niemi, R. G. (2008). *Vital statistics on American politics, 2007–2008*. CQ Press. For a comprehensive examination of public distrust in the media, see Ladd, J. (2012). *Why Americans hate the media and how it matters*. Princeton University Press.

62. Mutz, D. C. (2015). *In-your-face politics: The consequences of uncivil media*. Princeton University Press.

63. Stroud, N. J., Curry, A., Peacock, C., & Cardona, A. (2015, July). Contemporary vs. classic design. *Center for Media Engagement*. https://engagingnewsproject.org/research/news-presentation/

64. Hindman, M. (2011). *Less of the same: The lack of local news on the internet. FCC.* http://www.fcc.gov/document/media-ownership-study-6-submitted-study; Dunaway, J., Searles, K., Sui, M., & Paul, N. (2018). News attention in a mobile era. *Journal of Computer-Mediated Communication, 23*(2), 107–124.; Dunaway, J. (2016, August). *Mobile vs. computer: Implications for news audiences and outlets* [Discussion Paper Series #D-103]. Shorenstein Center, Harvard University, Cambridge, MA, United States. https://shorensteincenter.org/mobile-vs-computer-news-audiences-and-outlets/

65. For dire predictions, see Manheim, J. B. (1991). *All of the people all the time: Strategic communication and American politics.* Routledge; Sharpe, M. E., & & Entman, R. (1990). *Democracy without citizens: Media and the decay of American politics.* Oxford University Press, Chapter 7. For a more positive view, see Graber, D. A. (2004). Mediated politics and citizenship in the twenty-first century. *Annual Review of Psychology, 55,* 545–571; Graber, D. A. (2004). Framing politics for mass consumption: Can American news media meet the challenge? In M. G. Hermann (Ed.), *Advances in Political Psychology* (Vol. 1). Elsevier; Page, B. I., & Shapiro, R. Y. (1992). *The rational public: Fifty years of trends in Americans' policy preferences.* University of Chicago Press, pp. 383–390.

66. Impact differences between print and electronic media are discussed in Neuman, W. R., Just, M. R., & Crigler, A. N. (1992). *Common knowledge: News and the construction of political meaning.* University of Chicago Press; the political impact of conversations is addressed in Walsh, K. C. (2004). *Talking about politics: Informal groups and social identity in American life.* University of Chicago Press. For the view that differences in media modality are very important, see Moy, P., & Pfau, M. (2000). *With malice toward all? The media and public confidence in democratic institutions.* Praeger.

67. Hart, R. P. (1994). *Seducing America: How television charms the modern voter.* Oxford University Press; Delli Carpini, M. X., & Keeter, S. (1996). *What Americans know about politics and why it matters.* Yale University Press.

68. Putnam, R. D. (2000). *Bowling alone: The collapse and revival of American community.* Simon and Schuster; Norris, P. (1996). Does television erode social capital? A reply to Putnam. *PS: Political Science and Politics, 29:* 474–480; Norris, P. (2001). *Digital divide: Civic engagement, information poverty, and the internet worldwide.* Cambridge University Press.

69. Postman, N. (1985). *Amusing ourselves to death: Public discourse in the age of show business.* Viking Penguin; Hart, R. P. (1994). *Seducing America: How television charms the modern voter.* Oxford University Press. For a good discussion of the differences between the effects of print and television news on people's behavior, see Meyrowitz, J. (1985). *No sense of place: The impact of electronic media on social behavior.* Oxford University Press, 94–106.

70. For a succinct discussion of the controversy about the scope of learning from television, see Leighley, J. E. (2004). *Mass media and politics: A social science*

perspective. Houghton Mifflin, Chapter 6; Sugarman, S. (2007). *If kids could vote: Children, democracy, and the media*. Lexington Books.

71. The advantages of learning from audiovisuals are detailed in Graber, D. A. (2001). *Processing politics: Learning from television in the internet age*. University of Chicago Press.

72. Graber, D. A. (2001). *Processing politics: Learning from television in the internet age*. University of Chicago Press, Chapter 3.

73. Britt, R. R. (2009, January 10). 14 percent of U.S. adults can't read. *Live Science*. http://www.livescience.com/culture/090110-illiterate-adults.html

74. Prior, M. (2007). *Post-broadcast democracy: How media choice increases inequality in political involvement and polarizes elections*. Cambridge University Press.

75. Webster, J. G. (2016). *The marketplace of attention: How audiences take shape in a digital age*. MIT Press.

76. Katz, B. (2016, October 10). NFL's "Sunday Night Football" gets crushed in ratings by presidential debate. *Forbes*. http://www.forbes.com/sites/brandonkatz/2016/10/10/nfls-sunday-night-football-gets-crushed-in-ratings-by-presidential-debate/#6f96c8b12186.

77. Gordon, B. (2021, January 28). Fact check: Joe Biden's inauguration didn't have the lowest-ever TV ratings. *USA Today*. https://www.usatoday.com/story/news/factcheck/2021/01/28/fact-check-joe-bidens-inauguration-viewership-ranks-3rd-since-1981/4302498001/

78. The importance of collective memories is spelled out in Edy, J. A. (2006). *Troubled pasts: News and the collective memory of social unrest*. Temple University Press; Peri, Y. (1999). The media and collective memory of Yitzhak Rabin's remembrance. *Journal of Communication, 49*(3), 106–124.

79. Xu, Q., & Sundar, S. S. (2016). Interactivity and memory: Information processing of interactive versus non-interactive content. *Computers in Human Behavior, 63*, 620–629; Stroud, N. J., Curry, A., Peacock, C., & Cardona, A. (2015, July). Contemporary vs. classic design. *Center for Media Engagement*. https://engagingnewsproject.org/research/news-presentation/

80. Shah, D. V., Cho, J., Eveland, W. P., Jr., & Kwak, N. (2005). Information and expression in a digital age: Modeling internet effects on civic participation. *Communication Research, 32*(5), 531–565.

81. Bakshy, E., Messing, S., & Adamic, L. A. (2015). Exposure to ideologically diverse news and opinion on Facebook. *Science, 348*(6239), 1130–1132; Feezell, J. T., & Ortiz, B. (2015, August). *"I Saw It on Facebook": An experimental study of learning political information through social media* [Paper presentation]. The Political Communication Pre-Conference at the annual meeting of the American Political Science Association, San Francisco, CA, United States.

82. Karlsen, R. (2015). Followers are opinion leaders: The role of people in the flow of political communication on and beyond social networking sites. *European Journal of Communication, 30*(3), 301–318; Gainous, J., & Wagner, K. M. (2014). *Tweeting to power: The social media revolution in American politics*. Oxford University Press.

83. Dunaway, J. (2016, August). *Mobile vs. computer: Implications for news audiences and outlets* [Discussion Paper Series #D-103]. Shorenstein Center, Harvard University, Cambridge, MA, United States. https://shorensteincenter.org/mobile-vs-computer-news-audiences-and-outlets/.

84. Neuman, W. R. (1991). *The future of the mass audience*. Cambridge University Press, p. 99 (emphasis added); Pan, Z., Ostman, R., Moy, P., & Reynolds, P. (1994). News media exposure and its learning effects during the Persian Gulf War. *Journalism Quarterly, 71*(1), 7–19; Preiss, R. W. (Ed.). (2007). *Mass media effects research: Advances through meta-analysis*. Erlbaum.

85. None of these studies focuses on the effects of exposure to nonfictional violence in the media. The series began with a report by the surgeon general on television violence effects; see Surgeon General's Scientific Advisory Committee on Television and Social Behavior. (1971). *Television and growing up: The impact of televised violence*. National Institutes of Health. https://www.ncjrs.gov/pdffiles1/Digitization/147171NCJRS.pdf; for a critical review of one of the follow-up reports, see Cook, T. D., Kendzierski, D. A., & Thomas, S. V. (1983). The implicit assumptions of television research: An analysis of the 1982 NIMH report on "television and behavior." *Public Opinion Quarterly, 47*(Spring), 161–201.

86. Violence dominates on TV, study says. (1996, February 7). *Chicago Tribune*.

87. Parents Television Council. (2019). *A decade of deceit: How TV content ratings have failed families*. Author. https://go.parentstv.org/decades-report/documents/Decades-Report.pdf.

88. Parents Television Council. (2009). *The alarming family hour . . . no place for children*. Author. https://issuu.com/parentstv.org/docs/familyhour-study07-final2

89. Geen, R. G. (1994). Television and aggression: Recent developments and theory. In B. Zillmann, J. Bryant, & A. C. Huston (Eds.), *Media, children, and the family*. Routledge; Singer, J. L., Singer, D. G., & Rapaczynski, W. S. (1984). Family patterns and television viewing as predictors of children's beliefs and aggression. *Journal of Communication, 34*(Summer), 73–89. The politics of research on the effects of television violence are discussed by Rowland, W. D., Jr. (1983). *The politics of TV violence: Policy uses of communication research*. SAGE.

90. Carlson, J. M. (1985). *Prime time law enforcement: Crime show viewing and attitudes toward the criminal justice system.* Praeger; Heins, M. (2000). Blaming the media: Would regulation of expression prevent another Columbine? *Media Studies Journal, 14*(3), 14–23; Heins, M. (2001). *Not in front of the children: Indecency, censorship and the innocence of youth.* Hill and Wang.

91. Hamilton, J. T. (Ed.). (1998). *Television violence and public policy.* University of Michigan Press; Comstock, G., & Paik, H. (1994). The effects of television violence on antisocial behavior: A meta-analysis. *Communication Research, 21,* 516–539; Gauntlett, D. (2005). *Moving experiences: Media effects and beyond* (2nd ed.). J. Libbey.

92. Snow, R. P. (1974). How children interpret TV violence in play context. *Journalism Quarterly, 51*(Spring), 13–21.

93. *Attorney general's commission on pornography: Final report.* (1986). Government Printing Office; Dienstbier, R. A. (1977). Sex and violence: Can research have it both ways? *Journal of Communication, 27*(Summer), 176–188; Presidential Commission on Obscenity and Pornography. (1970). *Report of the commission on obscenity and pornography.* Bantam Books; Greenfield, P. M. (2004). Inadvertent exposure to pornography on the internet: Implications of peer-to-peer file-sharing networks for child development and families. *Applied Developmental Psychology, 25,* 741–750.

94. Edeani, D. O. (1981). Critical predictors of orientation to change in a developed society. *Journalism Quarterly, 58*(Spring), 56–64. The carefully measured impact of the introduction of television into a Canadian community is presented in *The Impact of Television: A Natural Experiment in Three Communities,* edited by Tannis MacBeth Williams (Academic Press, 1985).

95. Weiss, J. A., & Tschirhart, M. (1994). Public information campaigns as policy instruments. *Journal of Policy Analysis and Management, 13*(1), 82–119; Lemert, J. B., Mitzman, B. N., Seither, M. A., Cook, R. H., & Hackett, R. (1977). Journalists and mobilizing information. *Journalism Quarterly, 54*(Winter), 721–726.

96. Rice, R. E., & Atkin, C. K. (Eds.). (2001). *Public communication campaigns* (3rd ed.). SAGE. Also see Odugbemi, S., & Jacobson, T. (Eds.). (2008). *Government reform under real-world conditions: Citizens, stakeholders and voice.* World Bank.

97. Solomon, D. S. (1982). Health campaigns on television. *Television and behavior: Ten years of scientific progress and implications for the eighties* (Vol. 2, pp. 308–321). National Institute of Mental Health; Backer, T. E., Rogers, E. M., & Sopory, P. (1992). *Designing health communication campaigns: What works?* SAGE.

98. Crompton, J. L., & Lamb, C. W., Jr. (1986). *Marketing government and social services.* Wiley; Lame, M. L. (1997). Communicating in the innovation process: Issues and guidelines. In J. L. Garnett & A. Kouzmin (Eds.), *Handbook of administrative communication.* Marcel Dekker.

Persuasion, Campaigns, and Advertising

Learning Objectives

1. Explain the role media play in modern-day campaigns and elections.

2. Discuss the political implications of a media-centered campaign system.

3. Describe how candidates and campaigns are depicted by news media and the reasons behind the patterns we observe in coverage.

4. State the various ways the arrival and proliferation of digital and social media are shaping campaigns and elections today.

5. Assess how and how much people learn from campaigns and election news.

D igital media came of age in the 2008 campaigns, as did data analytics in 2012.[1] In 2016, campaigns invested heavily in digital communication strategies and analytic staffing, continuing to innovate and further developing the precision of their analytics. Advances in digital message testing and data gathering paid off, especially for the Trump campaign. However, 2016 was not solely about digital analytics. A major lesson from the 2016 campaign was that there is still much to learn about how politics and personality interact with the logics of digital and traditional forms of media to moderate the effectiveness of campaign messages. Projections for spending on digital messages for the 2020 presidential election were off the charts.[2] According to reliable estimates, spending reached nearly $1.8 billion.[3] What advantages does such spending on digital communications afford for candidates and campaigns? How much of this spending is displacing spending on more traditional formats, such as mailers and television and radio advertising? What are the implications for what voters learn about candidates and who turns out to vote? In this chapter, we will discuss the major features of modern campaigns and press coverage of contemporary campaigns and how both have evolved from campaigns of the past.

Political Campaigns in a Digital Era

In 1952, television became the main battlefield for presidential contests. In the time since, campaigns have made strategic communication decisions about how to use messaging and media to give their candidates the best chance of winning. Campaigns must decide which likely voters to target, what message to use, and how to reach them. The expansion of news and entertainment choices that characterizes the current media landscape has implications for these decisions. Campaigns can pinpoint voter groups based on the demographics of the people tuning in to various niche programs or networks. Additionally, recent advances in technology and data gathering and analysis allow campaigns to microtarget voters by matching individual-level voter characteristics with media and internet behaviors.

In the wake of recent election cycles, modern presidential campaigns realize the importance of data analytics. Analytics teams are now permanent and central fixtures in the hierarchy of major election campaigns. Analytics teams are responsible for using large data sets to predict the individual-level behavior of millions of Americans to aid in campaign message testing and microtargeting and to run predictive election models state by state throughout the campaign. The Biden and Trump campaigns of 2020 were no exception; spending from each reflected the importance of digital investment.

In the presidential election of 2016, both major party campaigns invested heavily in digital strategies but employed different tactics. According to Donald Trump's digital director, Brad Parscale, a key reason for the Trump victory was the nearly $90 million the campaign invested in digital advertising. Though Hillary Clinton's campaign generated more content across all the popular social media platforms, it continued to invest heavily in televised political ads, spending more than $200 million in the later stages of the campaign. Trump's campaign spent less than $100 million on televised ads during the same time and instead invested heavily in digital ads. The advantage of investing in digital ads is the enormous message-testing capabilities digital platforms provide[4] while providing the same, if not better, allowances for microtargeting. The analytics people working on the Trump campaign tested thousands of ad variants on Facebook. They A/B tested differences in overall format, in the effectiveness of video versus stills, presence or absence of subtitles, and so on. The more versions they tested, the more likely it was that ads would be presented to Facebook users because Facebook wants to use ads that generate the most engagement.[5]

Clinton's campaign actually generated more content on social media platforms than Trump's, as Figure 11-1 suggests. The Clinton team also invested in digital advertising, spending approximately $30 million in the final weeks of the campaign (about one-third of what Trump spent).[6] Even though a common news media narrative in 2016 was how Clinton's ad spending vastly outweighed Trump's, in digital advertising, the lopsidedness was reversed. The vast uptick in use of social media for news and politics that cycle, coupled with the message-testing capabilities of digital advertising, meant digital ad investment was apparently money well spent.

Spending was not the only critical difference for the ultimate successes of the 2016 campaigns' digital tactics. The politics of the times and fundamental differences between the candidates' public personas and their relative ability to effectively leverage particular attributes of Facebook and Twitter meant that the candidates' messages were perceived and received differently by both the public and the press. Simply put, even though the Clinton campaign generated more social media content relative to the Trump campaign,[7] its efforts were not as effective, at least on Facebook and Twitter. Unfortunately for Clinton, the interaction between the political context and the peculiarities of certain social media platforms did not serve her well. First, Clinton was running in a race that privileged political outsiders, insurgents, and authenticity. Public esteem for politics-as-usual and political institutions was at historic lows. The voting public craved authenticity. Though Clinton's long time in public service helped her tout experience, she was part of the political establishment and struggled to overcome the public's perception that she was a prototypical strategic politician. As a candidate, she struggled to convey authenticity to voters. Second, Twitter and Facebook also privilege authenticity. These platforms are social and personal, and campaign messages must be crafted with the particular characteristics of the various platforms in mind. Users are conditioned to more personalized views—effective messaging on these platforms often requires candidates to personalize their messages by showing different sides of themselves and their issue positions than the smooth polish historically required for televised political ads.[8] Even as Clinton's digital messaging team crafted loads of content, rapid-response messages, and well-crafted attacks and issued positions, they seem to have ultimately lacked the personalization, authenticity, and audience appeal to attract and maintain the attention of the public and the press.

Based on coverage by the mainstream press, one would never expect that Clinton's campaign generated more social media content than Trump's. Whether by accident or strategic genius, the most effective element of Trump's Twitter communication was all the free media attention his tweets earned for the campaign. Even though the size of Trump's Twitter following was purportedly inflated by bots, the initial impression of his growing traction and the reactionary and controversial nature of his tweets was enough to attract and sustain the attention of the media, which only served to grow his actual public following.[9] The postelection public discussions of many political strategists, journalists, and social scientists suggests the importance of social media platforms as part of future candidates' earned media strategies.[10]

Figure 11-1   Twitter Messages From the Final Week of the 2016 Campaign

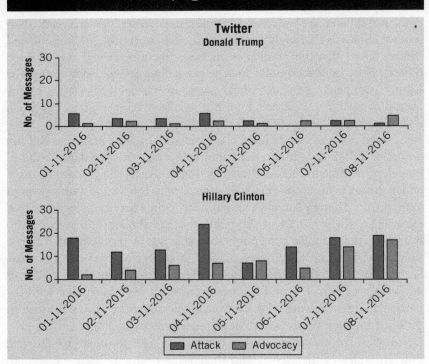

Source: Zhang, F., Stromer-Galley, J., Tanupabrungsun, S., Hegde, Y., McCracken, N., & Hemsley, J. (2017). Understanding discourse acts: Political campaign messages classification on Facebook and Twitter. In D. Lee, Y. R. Lin, N. Osgood, & R. Thomson (Eds.), *Social, cultural, and behavioral modeling* (Vol. 10354). Springer. http://illuminating.ischool.syr.edu/#/platforms/1,2/dates/2016-11-01,2016-11-08/candidates/10,5/types/8&9,5&6. Licensed under Creative Commons Attribution 4.0 International: https://creativecommons.org/licenses/by/4.0/.

By the presidential election of 2020, the importance of investing in digital communications and analytics was not lost on anyone—especially the major primary and general election contenders. Though the digital spending strategies of the two major candidates in the general election differed, both revealed heavy investment in digital advertising. According to data and reports from the Wesleyan Media Project, the Trump campaign outspent Biden's campaign on Facebook and Google ads over the course of the campaign, but Biden's campaign invested more heavily in digital ads during later months, gaining the edge on Facebook ads and a substantial lead in spending on Snapchat late in the campaign cycle. Biden's campaign also spent late on over-the-air television advertising, out-airing Trump ads by a rate of four to one by mid-October.[11]

Box 11-1
Understanding Online Political Advertising

Spending on political advertising in the United States (U.S.) has quickly been shifting from television to digital and online platforms over the past decade. In 2020, about 24% of ad spending in the presidential general election was on digital advertising, with the Trump campaign estimated to have put 39% of its ad spending online. Yet that shift to online ads raises many questions about how political ads themselves may have changed. Campaigns are not simply taking their 30-second ads created for television and putting them on YouTube or Facebook. Rather, the content of political advertising has altered, as has how campaigns use them.

For one, online ads do a lot more than persuade, which is the primary goal of almost every political ad on television. One study found that only 35% of Facebook ads that were distributed in U.S. Senate races in 2018 had persuasion as a primary focus. Just over 30% were focused on "acquisition," that is, gathering a user's email address and other contact information so that the campaign could follow up. Another 21% of ads focused primarily on raising money, while a small percentage (2%) were geared toward mobilization—convincing people to attend a campaign event or vote.

Online ads are also somewhat different than television ads in their content. A study that compared Facebook and television ads in federal, statewide, and

(Continued)

(Continued)

down-ballot races in 2018 discovered that Facebook ads were less nega-tive and less focused on policy issues but more partisan in their language. That last finding has implications for the American electorate. If citizens are increasingly exposed to digital ads that emphasize partisan language, that could speed up partisan polarization among the public.

Yet online ads may be welcomed by underdogs and poorly funded can-didates. Because online ads can be much more targeted than television ads, the incumbent's advantage in ad spending is less on Facebook than it is on television. In fact, in state house and state senate races, challengers spent more on online ads than did incumbents.

Notes: Fowler, E. F., Franz, M. M., Martin, G. J., Peskowitz, Z., & Ridout, T. N. (2021). Political advertising online and offline. *American Political Science Review, 115*(1), 130–149; Ridout, T. N., Fowler, E. F., & Franz, M. M. (2021). Spending fast and furious: Political advertising in 2020. *The Forum, 18*(4), 465–492; Fowler, E. F., Franz, M. M., Martin, G. J., Peskowitz, Z., & Ridout, T. N. (2021). Political advertising online and offline. *American Political Science Review, 115*(1), 130–149; Ridout, T. N., Fowler, E. F., & Franz, M. M. (2021). The influence of goals and timing: How campaigns deploy ads on Facebook. *Journal of Information Technology & Politics,* 1–17.

As Box 11-1 reveals, the strategies and practices of contemporary polit-ical campaigns are in flux. Digital media tools make up an increasing share of campaign weapon arsenals, yet traditional media are still central to the strategic efforts of most major political campaigns. As long as aired televi-sion advertisements retain the potential to shift electoral margins by one or two percentage points—especially in key presidential battleground states—traditional media will warrant significant investment. In fact, comparisons of spending between 2016 and 2020 show that most Americans saw more television ads in 2020 relative to 2016. While it remains unclear as of yet whether or when digital media campaigning will eclipse traditional media campaign strategies, mass media (of whatever sort) will remain central to American campaigns and elections for a long time to come.[12]

The Consequences of Media-Dominated Politics

The availability of television in nearly every home, the pervasiveness of public opinion polling, and access to the internet, where election-related websites abound, guarantee that the news media will play a major role in presidential elections. What exactly does that role entail? We will consider three main facets: the power of journalists to influence the selection of candidates, the requirement for candidates to televise well, and the explosive growth and diversification of made-for-media campaigns.

Media as Kingmakers

Before television, voters had little chance to assess the candidates on their own. The political parties controlled nominations, and voters made their choices based largely on party labels. Party affiliation remains important at the state and local levels, where media information about candidates is scant, particularly on television. The exceptions are nonpartisan local elections (when candidates run without party designation and endorsement) or primary elections (in which candidates of the same party compete against each other). With the arrival of the television age, journalists became the chief influence in the selection of candidates and the key issues of the campaign. Television brought candidates, especially presidential contenders, directly into the nation's living rooms, giving voters information for making choices based on the media's menu. Candidates, like actors, depend on their acting ability for success. In the television age, media people did most of the casting for presidential hopefuls, whose performance was then judged according to the assigned role.

News media exhibited this clout as the 2016 primary election approached. During this crucial pre-primary season, the news media gave substantial amounts of free airtime and mostly positive coverage to candidate Trump, despite little funding and (at the time) little political following. The earned media attention from mainstream outlets is largely credited with building his momentum leading up to and during the early primaries.[13] Only later did the press work more aggressively to investigate his credibility as a candidate.

Casting occurs early in the primaries when newspeople, on the basis of as yet slender evidence, predict winners and losers to narrow the field of eligible candidates who must be covered. Concentrating on the frontrunners in public opinion polls makes newspeople's tasks more manageable, but it often forces trailing candidates out of the race prematurely. In the 2016 contest, primary candidate and former governor of Florida Jeb Bush was an example of how poll slippage can affect candidates' fortunes. Though he enjoyed a strong standing in the polls in early 2015, once that began to slip, his press coverage got increasingly negative. This reflects the typical press framing of candidates who are losing ground in the polls. The story of why they are losing ground dominates the coverage, which results in an unflattering portrayal.[14]

Early, highly speculative calculations become self-fulfilling prophecies because designated winners attract supporters whereas losers are abandoned. For example, as Donald Trump continued to rise in the polls, he benefited from the "gaining ground" frame, which typically leads to more coverage overall and coverage that is relatively favorable. Through the end of 2015, Trump earned close to twice the coverage of Jeb Bush, and more than twice the coverage of other leading contenders such as Marco Rubio and Ted Cruz.[15] During the 2020 Democratic primary election, as Joe Biden's lead steadily increased, his coverage did, too. Coverage imbalances throughout the primary season can seriously handicap campaigns.

Candidates who exceed expectations in garnering votes are declared winners; candidates who fall short are losers.[16] When journalist Pat Buchanan finished sixteen points behind George H. W. Bush in the 1992 New Hampshire Republican presidential primary, the media declared Buchanan the winner because he had exceeded their expectations. They did the same for Bill Clinton, who had trailed former Massachusetts senator Paul Tsongas in the 1992 Democratic primary in New Hampshire. The candidacy of Republican senator Bob Dole during the 1996 primaries was prematurely declared dead when he finished behind his competitors in a few early contests. In 2020, Mayor Pete Buttigieg earned positive coverage for exceeding expectations in some of the early Democratic primary states. His rise in polls in Iowa and New Hampshire started in September and October, leading to a competitive contest across against better-known candidates Elizabeth Warren, Bernie Sanders, and Joe Biden.[17]

Media coverage and public opinion polls tend to move in tandem in the early months of a campaign. Candidates who receive ample media coverage tend to perform well in the polls. Good poll ratings then bring more media coverage. Once the caucus and primary season has started in the spring of the presidential election year, the outcomes of these contests become more important predictors of media attention. One other pattern is common, though not universal. The substance of stories tends to be favorable for trailing candidates in the race and is often unfavorable for front-runners. Recent primary seasons have exhibited this trend: Opposing candidates often employ an attack-the-front-runner strategy; media coverage and sometimes the polls follow suit. For example, shortly after Mitt Romney officially announced his bid for the presidency, it was clear why the presumed front-runner had waited so long to announce. His opponents attacked him from all angles; the media reported these attacks and noted that they were reflective of his standing as front-runner.[18] When Joe Biden entered the Democratic primary race as a healthy favorite to win the nomination in 2020, the other Democratic candidates' campaign rhetoric—as well as President Trump's—clearly reflected an attack-the-front-runner strategy.[19]

The media's role as kingmaker—or killer of the dreams of would-be kings—is often played over a long span of time. Image making for presidential elections now begins on a massive scale more than a year before the first primary. The "pre–pre-campaign," on a more limited scale, begins shortly after the previous election (if not before it, in some respects, especially as vice presidential candidates are considered), with newspaper and magazine stories about potential presidential candidates. Senators and governors who have received favorable publicity over many years may gradually come to be thought of as likely presidential nominees. Losers in the previous campaign who were bruised but not badly beaten remain on the possibilities list.

Media coverage can destroy candidacies. This happened to two Democratic presidential candidates in 1988. Delaware Senator Joe Biden was forced out of the campaign by widely publicized charges that his speeches contained plagiarized quotations from other political leaders. Twenty years later, the stain had faded enough to permit Barack Obama to make him vice president. Media attention to this choice was negligible, and now Biden is president. The second media casualty in 1988 was Senator Gary Hart of Colorado, who withdrew after charges of philandering—he had dared reporters to follow and scrutinize him when questioned about adultery, and they did so. Recurrent media references to the Chappaquiddick incident, which linked Senator Edward Kennedy (D–MA) to the drowning of a young woman on his staff, also kept his supporters from drafting him as a presidential contender. In the 1992 campaign, Bill Clinton was accused of adultery and draft dodging, charges that caused his poll ratings and positive media appraisals to plummet. Despite the bad publicity, Clinton managed to win major primaries and the presidency, earning the title "The Comeback Kid." In 2016, Donald Trump's candidacy exhibited resilience in the face of bad publicity, surviving public outcry over controversial statements about Mexican immigrants, allegations of questionable business dealings, a publicly released recording of sexually lewd remarks about women, and allegations of sexual assault from women who stepped forward during the campaign. Though the ongoing stream of scandals and gaffes sometimes produced dips and drops in Trump's poll standings, his popularity remained high and he ultimately won the nomination and the presidency.[20] During the 2020 election cycle, and for most of his presidency, Trump largely remained immune to long-term effects from bad press. Clearly, adverse publicity can be overcome.

Television images can be important in making a candidate electable or unelectable. For instance, the televised Kennedy–Nixon debates of 1960, the Reagan–Mondale debates of 1984, and the Bush–Gore debates of 2000 helped to counter the public's impressions that John F. Kennedy, Ronald Reagan, and George W. Bush were unsuited for the presidency.[21] Kennedy was able to demonstrate that he was capable of coping with the presidency despite his youth and relative inexperience, and Reagan in 1984 conveyed the impression that he remained mentally fit for a second term. Bush's performance in the second debate counteracted charges that he lacked sufficient intellect and debating skills to become an effective president.[22]

When the media chose certain policy issues to emphasize during crucial phases of the campaign, they sharply diminished the chances of presidents Jimmy Carter and George H. W. Bush to win second terms, and they ravaged John McCain's presidential aspirations. In Carter's case, shortly before the 1980 presidential election, the country—and the media—commemorated the anniversary of a major foreign policy failure: Carter's inability to win the release of U.S. hostages in Iran. Disapproval of Bush in the 1992 election was directed mainly at his highly publicized failure to solve major domestic economy problems during the last year of his term. In McCain's case, reminders about his support of the Iraq War and his admission that he knew little about economics reinforced voters' beliefs that it was time for a change to a Democratic administration. Relentless media coverage of the ongoing COVID-19 crisis and the Trump administration's handling of it was quite likely a deciding factor in his 2020 electoral defeat.

Media-operated public opinion polls are also a source for media king-making. The major television networks, in collaboration with such newspapers as *The New York Times, The Washington Post,* and *USA Today,* all conduct popularity ratings and issue polls throughout presidential elections. The results are publicized extensively and then become benchmarks for voters, telling them who the winners and losers are and what issues are crucial to the campaign. Depending on the nature and format of the questions the pollsters ask and the political context in which the story becomes embedded, the responses can spell fortune or misfortune for the candidates.

Television-Age Recruits

Another important consequence of broadcast and digital campaigning is the change it has wrought in the types of candidates likely to be politically successful. Because television broadcasts and streaming videos and images on digital and social media can bring the images of candidates for office directly into the homes of millions of voters, a candidate's ability to look impressive and perform well before the cameras has become crucial. People who are not videogenic have been eliminated from the pool of available recruits. Abraham Lincoln's rugged face probably would not have passed muster in the digital media age. President Truman's "Give 'em hell, Harry" homespun style would have backfired had it been presented on the nation's television and mobile screens rather than to small gatherings.

Actors and other celebrities who are adept at performing before the public now have a much better chance than ever before to be recruited for political office. Ronald Reagan and Arnold Schwarzenegger, who were seasoned actors; John Edwards and Barack Obama, powerful orators; Al Franken, a comedian; and Donald Trump, former star of the NBC reality hit *The Apprentice* are examples of television-age recruits, whose chances for public office would have been much slighter in an earlier era. As columnist Marquis Child put it, candidates no longer "run" for office; they "pose" for office (Photo 11-1).[23] Currently, word has it that Austin, Texas–based actor Matthew McConaughey is considering a run for the Texas governorship—despite that his politics are largely unknown (according to *The Texas Tribune*),[24] he might win if he can play governor as well as he played Louisiana State Police homicide detective Rust Cohle in the first season of HBO's *True Detective*.

In fact, good pictures can counterbalance the effects of unfavorable verbal comments. When CBS reporter Leslie Stahl verbally attacked President Reagan for posturing as a man of peace and compassion during the 1984 presidential campaign, a Reagan assistant promptly thanked her for showing four-and-a-half minutes of great pictures of the president. He was not in the least concerned about Stahl's scathing remarks. The pictures had shown the president

> basking in a sea of flag-waving supporters . . . sharing concerns
> with farmers in a field, picnicking with Mid-Americans, pumping
> iron . . . getting the Olympic torch from a runner . . . greeting
> senior citizens at their housing project, honoring veterans who
> landed on Normandy, honoring youths just back from Grenada,
> countering a heckler . . . [and] wooing black inner-city kids.[25]

Media advisers have become year-round members of presidential and gubernatorial staffs. These experts coach candidates about proper dress and demeanor for various occasions, create commercials for the candidates, and handle general news coverage of the campaign. Presidential contenders spend roughly two-thirds of their budgets on television. In 2016, the Clinton campaign outraised and outspent the Trump campaign, even when taking into account the more than $55 million Trump invested in his own campaign and the millions he raised from small contributions from individual donors. Clinton's campaign invested far more in television advertising than Trump's, but his campaign concentrated investments in digital advertising. Both candidates relied heavily on social media platforms as ways to communicate directly with potential supporters.[26] In election campaigns, funding disparities usually are a grave handicap for the financial underdog, whose messages are drowned out by the opposition. The 2016 election year was anomalous given that Hillary Clinton lost the election after she outraised Donald Trump, in part due to a notable shift in funding from outside groups on the Democratic side, which was a reversal from the previous cycle. In the 2020 presidential election, Joe Biden raised $1,044,187,828 from candidate committee money and $580,113,800 from outside sources. President Trump raised $773,954,550 from candidate committee money and $313,954,719 from outside sources.[27] That time around, the higher amounts of money raised and spent were correlated with winning.

Conventional notions about what campaign funding should pay for may keep shifting as the implications from the *Citizens United v. Federal Election Commission* decision continue to unfold.[28] Given the high cost of advertising and of gaining news exposure, a candidate's ability to raise money remains an important consideration, even when federal funding is available and email and social networks provide cheap, candidate-controlled access to potential voters. The political consequences in recruitment and in postelection commitments that spring from such financial considerations are huge, and donors are more partisan.

Media-Centric Campaign Strategies

Twenty-first-century election campaigns are structured to garner the most favorable media exposure, reaching the largest number of prospective supporters with the greatest degree of candidate control over the message. Candidates concentrate on photo opportunities, talk show appearances, or trips to interesting events and locations. Even when candidates meet voters personally at rallies, parades, or shopping centers, they generally time and orchestrate the events to attract favorable media coverage. Today, candidates target their appearances across multiple venues.

Photo 11-1 CLEVELAND, OH - JULY 21, 2016: Republican presidential candidate Donald Trump delivers a speech during the evening session on the fourth day of the Republican National Convention on July 21, 2016 at the Quicken Loans Arena in Cleveland, Ohio. Republican presidential candidate Donald Trump received the number of votes needed to secure the party's nomination. An estimated 50,000 people were expected in Cleveland, including hundreds of protesters and members of the media. The four-day Republican National Convention kicked off on July 18.

Source: Alex Wong/Getty Images.

Entertainment Venues

Appearances on entertainment shows, once considered unpresidential, have become routine. Maverick candidate Ross Perot started the pattern during the 1992 presidential race by announcing his presidential aspirations on CNN's *Larry King Live* call-in television show. Other candidates flocked to the talk show trek, preferring the light banter and respectful questions of callers to the pointed inquisition in interviews by the national press. By 2000, it seemed almost obligatory for presidential contenders to appear on talk shows hosted by major television personalities. John McCain first announced his entry into the 2008 presidential contest on David Letterman's show. Such appearances make strategic sense; voters under age 30 frequently claim that late-night talk shows and comedy programs such as *Saturday Night Live* are their major sources of campaign information (see Box 11-2 for more on this trend).[29] Candidates' escape from the highly critical national press to friendlier environments also takes the form of interviews on political satire shows and morning talk shows.

Network morning news shows now devote entire hours to conversations with the candidates and accept telephoned questions from viewers during the show. All in all, the trend seems to be toward candidates having more direct contact with voters and increased control over campaign messages, all at the expense of campaign coverage control by the major media.

Party-Friendly Venues

Surveyed voters increasingly reveal that they engage in partisan media selectivity. As Figure 11-2 shows, partisans on either side of the aisle often make distinctly different media choices. During the 2020 election,

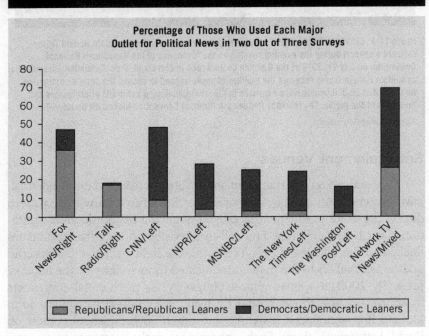

Figure 11-2 Voters' Main Source for Election News by Audience Lean

Source: Adapted from Pew Research Center. (2021, February 19). How Americans navigated the news in 2020: A tumultuous year in review. *Pew Research Center.* https://www.journalism.org/2021/02/22/about-a-quarter-of-republicans-democrats-consistently-turned-only-to-news-outlets-whose-audiences-aligned-with-them-politically-in-2020/pj_2021-02-22_navigating-news-2020_1-06/

Note: Data based on U.S. surveys of adults conducted October 29–November 11, 2019; August 31–September 7, 2020; and November 18–19, 2020.

Republicans most often selected Fox News for election news, while many Democrats chose CNN. When audiences are distinctly partisan, it shapes campaigns' decisions about which news networks and programs on which to appear as guests for interviews. When candidates appear on programs with audiences friendly to their party and issue stances, hosts and reporters are less likely to be hostile and aggressive, lest they offend their viewers.

The upshot from this is that candidates are increasingly likely to favor party-friendly and/or neutral networks over those they perceive to be hostile. As both candidate and president, Obama was more likely to grant interviews to hosts and anchors on networks such as MSNBC, CNN, or the major broadcast networks, while Trump typically favored Fox News and later Newsmax, while sometimes guesting with the broadcast networks. Biden's appearances exhibit a similarly selective pattern thus far, at least in terms of making fewer appearances on or avoiding outlets such as Fox News or Newsmax and other right-leaning organizations.

Local Venues

As we reported in Chapter 5, the relationship between the president and the press varies from one part of the country to another. Because tensions are usually higher between the White House and the Washington, DC, press corps, incumbent presidential candidates and their electoral challengers favor friendlier local and regional media outlets with appearances and interviews, outlets more distant from the harsh northeastern seaboard press. And, due to the manner in which primary contests are run and the structure of the electoral college, attention from state and local media can be critical for presidential contenders currying favor in strategically important states. Presidential candidates visit small communities throughout the country to bask in the admiration of local audiences and local media. This might be especially useful in early primary states for building momentum as primary candidates or in swing states during the general election. After all, they can make or break the electoral college vote. Taking advantage of advances in communication technology, candidates can grant interviews to local television and radio stations throughout the country, even when they cannot physically leave Washington, DC.

Attracting Coverage

Candidates maximize their chances of receiving media attention by planning their schedules around events that are known to attract reporters. They spend disproportionate amounts of time during the primary season campaigning in Iowa and New Hampshire, where media coverage of the earliest contests is usually heavy. In a typical presidential campaign, coverage of Iowa's caucuses and New Hampshire's primary election overshadows television news coverage of later primaries. Historically, it has done so by a ratio of more than four to one.[30] To keep a favorable image of candidates in front of the public, campaign managers arrange newsworthy events to familiarize potential voters with their candidates' best aspects. Managers show candidates dressed informally, mixing with enthusiastic crowds of average people and looking relaxed, happy, and confident. During the 2016 pre-primary season, 34% of Donald Trump's coverage focused on activities and events he performed and attended.[31] Activities and events accounted for roughly 15% of Trump and Biden's general election coverage in 2020.[32]

Incumbents have a distinct advantage over challengers. Although they may attract about the same number of campaign stories, incumbents receive additional attention through coverage of their official duties. Incumbents may also be able to dictate the time and place of media encounters. When a president schedules a meeting for reporters in the White House Rose Garden, ample coverage is certain. Once promising challengers have attained wide recognition as front-runners, newspeople compete for their attention as well. These candidates' power to grant or withhold attention can be translated into influence over the quality and quantity of coverage.

Media judge the newsworthiness of campaign stories by general news criteria. Therefore, they pay little attention to minor candidates and newcomers whose chances for success are small. Lack of coverage, in turn, makes it extremely difficult for unknowns to become well known and increase their chances of winning elections. This is one of many examples of unintentional media bias that redounds to the benefit of established politicians.

Journalistic norms about newsworthiness and the need for candidates to attract coverage can also create incentives. Negative campaign ads are increasingly frequent in presidential races; this trend continued through recent election cycles and now extends to negative messaging in digital media.[33] Political scientist John Geer argues that the news media are partially to blame for this because of the way journalists cover campaigns. Conflict and negativity are deemed newsworthy by journalists and, for that reason, they cover negative political ads extensively. Given the need for candidates to attract advantageous coverage, campaign strategists have noticed that one way to get news coverage is to produce and air the kinds of ads that will attract news media. If an ad is picked up by the news, it can work as free advertising for the campaign and allows the sponsor of the ad to dictate the narrative around the campaign. Following the most recent campaign cycles, we now know this extends to messages sent over social media. Mainstream journalists frequently cover candidate posts, especially if they are negative. This is another way candidates and campaigns try to manipulate journalistic norms to attract coverage for their campaigns.[34]

Digital Campaigning

Electoral campaigns have been mightily influenced by advances in digital and social media. Campaign operations are investing significantly more resources in developing their digital presence and messaging strategies.[35] One need not look further than the 2020 presidential campaign to see evidence of how digital media have permeated the campaign strategy repertoire.

Campaign Websites and Blogs

Now thought of as a requirement, candidate websites first began to emerge in the mid-1990s. Since that time, they have evolved a great deal from essentially serving as online campaign brochures to being very interactive. Campaign websites of today collect as much information as they share and are constantly updated to reflect the fluidity of issues and events during the campaign. When information is shared with would-be supporters, it is not simply through a biographical sketch or a list of issue positions, though incumbent candidates typically include more background information than challengers. Many sites allow space for candidates and campaign staff to engage in exchanges with potential voters. However, the open access, broad audience, and reproduction potential of digital content limits its potential for nuance. Risk-averse campaigns keep their websites free of exchanges that would alienate potential voters or that would reflect badly on the campaign if reproduced and disseminated.[36]

Campaign websites are widely viewed as essential for soliciting funds, recruiting volunteers, and developing communication networks with supporters. The campaign website revolution in fundraising was largely pioneered by Howard Dean's 2004 primary campaign. The Dean campaign completely changed the way campaign fundraising was structured by demonstrating that fundraising did not have to rely on large, expensive fundraising events. Rather, with the internet's allowances for inexpensive channels of communication, smaller donations could be solicited from exponentially more donors. Candidates learned that their websites could be a place for supporters to donate money easily and cheaply.[37] We still see evidence of those early lessons today. For example, the homepage of Joe Biden's 2020 campaign website featured "Donate" and "Volunteer" buttons at the top of the page. Under the donate tab, visitors could find one-click buttons with suggested amounts for small donations (Photo 11-2).

Campaign blogs can also serve as effective strategic communication tools when used effectively. They provide the space and structure for constructing and sharing narratives around the candidate and campaign while also allowing for interactive features and two-way communications between campaigns and supporters. Candidates have taken variable approaches with campaign blogs; some campaigns have welcomed interactions with the public through comment features and other means of inviting feedback, while others have avoided these options, fearing blowback for nonresponsiveness or potential corrosiveness, vitriol, or internet trolls.[38] The Biden/Harris 2020 campaign website featured blog-like entries called "Notes from Joe" (see Photo 11-3).

Campaigns and Social Media

If the 2008 election cycle is largely identified with breakout use of social media in political campaigns, the 2016 cycle asserted its dominance, only to continue through 2020. The 2006 midterms were a testing ground

Photo 11-2 Screenshot of Homepage of Joe Biden's 2020 Campaign Website
Source: joebiden.com.

for some limited social media use, but it wasn't until the 2008 cycle that campaigns fully embraced these technologies and developed sophisticated digital and social messaging strategies. When 2012 arrived, social media was a substantial part of any campaign strategy. By 2016, candidates at all levels invested heavily in their digital campaign strategies. In fact, one of the major lessons of the 2016 presidential contest was the need for digital-first campaign strategies.[39] In the 2016 general election presidential contest, both candidates made heavy use of social media platforms.[40] This trend persisted through 2020; both campaigns allocated nearly half or more of their campaign funds toward digital messaging.

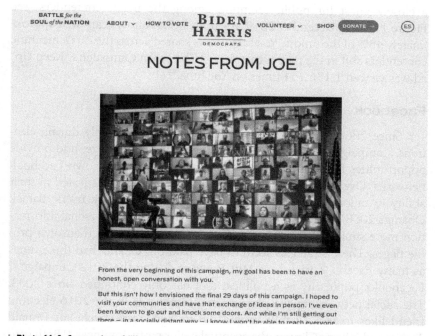

Photo 11-3 Screenshot of "Notes From Joe" Page on Biden/Harris Campaign Website

Source: joebiden.com.

YouTube

YouTube was embraced earlier than Facebook or Twitter; it had some usage by candidates in 2006 as an additional place to post political advertising or unflattering videos of the opponent. YouTube campaign material received a lot of attention from voters even in the 2006 cycle. However, in 2008, campaign activity on YouTube grew significantly. The campaigns for both presidential contenders posted political ads, videos, and personal statements on YouTube. Notable videos were also posted from people outside the campaigns; the best known was probably the "Yes We Can" video from entertainer will.i.am.[41] Three political ads ranked among YouTube's ten most-watched ads during the 2016 presidential elections, drawing several million more views to political ads than campaigns of the past would have ever imagined. The 2016 Trump campaign's digital-first strategy was evident in streaming, too—his campaign led the pack in number of YouTube videos and views, followed by Bernie Sanders, Hillary Clinton, and Ted Cruz.[42] During the 2020 Democratic primary, YouTube data revealed a close contest for public attention among the major contenders (see Figure 11-3). In December 2019, the three front-runners captured approximately 45% of the unique YouTube Views shared across the 10 Democratic contenders still in the race at that time.[43] The Biden Campaign's "Keep Up" ad was viewed 1,136,154 times on YouTube.[44]

Facebook

Since 2008, candidates have utilized Facebook heavily during elections. Campaigns create and maintain their own profile pages and provide opportunities for supporters to share materials with their own Facebook networks. Over time, campaigns have become more sophisticated in their ability to tailor content to the interests of social network users. Barack Obama's 2008 Facebook profile, for example, contained personal information more similar to what regular Facebook users post on their own profile pages. These strategies seem to have paid off; Obama had three times as many Facebook friends as Mitt Romney during the 2012 campaign.[45] Facebook's popularity as a political tool has only continued since 2008. The social networking site played a significant role in the 2016 election; friend likes totaled 12 million and 7.8 million, respectively, for Donald Trump and Hillary Clinton, the eventual major party nominees.[46] Both candidates invested heavily in social media strategies, but Trump is credited with the foresight to adopt a digital-first strategy by investing more heavily in digital advertising than televised political advertising.[47] However, Hillary Clinton and her campaign were more active across all social media sites in terms of total volume relative to the Trump campaign, despite lopsided mainstream media coverage of their posted content.[48]

In the years since 2016, much debate and speculation focused on the question of whether and to what extent Facebook was responsible—at least in part—for Trump's electoral upset in 2016. Post-election revelations of Russian

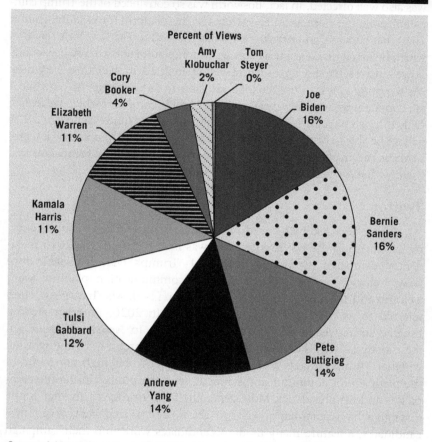

Figure 11-3 2020 Democratic Primary Candidates' Share of Unique YouTube Views

Percent of Views

Amy Klobuchar 2%
Tom Steyer 0%
Cory Booker 4%
Elizabeth Warren 11%
Joe Biden 16%
Kamala Harris 11%
Bernie Sanders 16%
Tulsi Gabbard 12%
Pete Buttigieg 14%
Andrew Yang 14%

Source: Adapted from Feng, B. (2019, December 8). Does YouTube's data tell us a story about the 2020 democratic candidates? *Towards Data Science.* https://towardsdata science.com/does-youtubes-data-tell-us-a-story-about-the-2020-democratic-candidates-69568d2b0ce5

Note: Data are from YouTube Data API; methods and analysis conducted by Bryan Feng. See article for details on methodology.

interference and rampant circulation of misinformation through the platform catapulted the network into the midst of several public scandals in which Facebook was accused of helping to elect Trump as the president. While the debates are nowhere near resolved, one would have to search far and wide to find someone doubting Facebook's potential as a campaign tool when used effectively. According to Andrew Bosworth of Facebook, Trump's 2016 digital campaign on Facebook was successful not only because it was well funded; it was also well directed. In fact, Bosworth was so convinced of the Trump campaign's ability to once again effectively use the platform for electoral gain in 2020 that he wrote an internal memo (later leaked to *The New York Times*) in which he urged his colleagues to resist any temptation to try to use Facebook's power and reach to prevent a Trump victory in 2020. In the memo, he writes, "As tempting as it is to use the tools available to us to change the outcome, I am confident we must never do that or we will become that which we fear."[49] Only through ongoing research, experimentation, and future campaign cycles will we be able to better understand Facebook's role in 2016 and how it might be most effectively used in future elections both by political campaigns and those with more nefarious goals to achieve their ends.

Twitter

Twitter was also being used in a limited fashion in 2008, but its enormous growth in the last several years was first evident in the 2016 presidential campaign. Obviously, Donald J. Trump's (@realDonaldTrump) heavy reliance on Twitter as a political communication platform went well beyond the 2016 campaign (see Photo 11-4); Mr. Trump's is often referred to as "the first Twitter presidency." In 2020, President Trump tweeted or retweeted 12,234 times, according to *Newsweek*, based on their analysis with data from the Trump Twitter archive.[50] Time will tell whether Trump remains an outlier with respect to his high utilization of the platform for communicating directly with the public during the campaigns and his presidency. More generally, Twitter provides another venue through which potential voters can get a personalized view of political candidates, a feature many modern candidates work into their campaign communication strategies.[51] Twitter allows a constant feed of information about how candidates are responding to events and issues in real time and allows the instantaneous sharing of information with ordinary voters, including press releases, official reports, or news stories.

Whatever the Kids Are On

Campaigns capitalize on the digital reach of Instagram, Snapchat, and TikTok, which have more recently gained popularity, especially among the young voter cohorts. All are different in features and format from Facebook and Twitter. It is important to understand that candidates' strategic use of each of these platforms is heavily dependent on both the composition of

Photo 11-4 A Trump tweet from the early days of the 2016 Democratic Party Presidential Primaries.

Source: President Donald J. Trump/Twitter.

the user audiences and the functions and features afforded by the particular technology.[52]

Mobile devices are also playing a more prominent role in campaign strategy. In 2010, congressional candidates were creating campaign apps—software applications that may be downloaded onto mobile devices and smartphones— to improve mobilization and ground-game efforts. The campaign world has several apps designed to help voters find their polling locations or to report problems at the polls; Google data suggests that mobile devices were heavily used by voters to search for voting information on Election Day in 2012.[53] The explosive growth of mobile and social media since 2010 meant that by 2016— and certainly by 2020—savvy candidates and campaigns were designing messages optimal for mobile consumption and sharing on social media platforms.[54]

Impact

For all the strategic adaptation the expansion of social media use has prompted, evidence is still somewhat new on the question of whether social media messages can persuade voters to change their vote choice. While use and popularity on social media seem to be linked to general election performance, social media strategies are often used in tandem with traditional campaign strategies,[55] making it more difficult to discern their impact. There is better evidence that social media messages can mobilize or demobilize voters—raising or lowering the propensity to vote. For example, social cues on Facebook can increase turnout.[56] Digital and social media are also effective for raising funds, attracting traditional media attention, or organizing rallies or protests. However, social media's full impact remains to be seen. Given that social media use for news is now common for over 60% of U.S. adults, current trends suggest we will continue to see growing influence of social media and digital campaign strategies in political elections.[57]

The 2008 campaign saw the debut of social websites as major outlets for candidates' messages, and this trend continued through the 2020 election.[58] Now, many messages first aired on television or news websites are rebroadcast on social media venues and capture as many or more viewers there than when they aired originally. The reach on these platforms is vast. For example, more than 13 million people viewed NBC's posting of the first Clinton–Trump debate on YouTube. Of course, more than 23 million viewed *SNL's* spoof on the debate.[59]

Though digital and social media allow new levels of interactivity between candidates and voters, campaigns engage in strategies of what Jennifer Stromer-Galley refers to as *controlled interactivity*. Campaigns utilize the interactive affordances of digital and social media only insofar as they help the strategic aims of the campaigns.[60] Primarily, campaigns seek to use digital communication technologies in ways that enlist the help of their supporters through the use of their own social networks. Meanwhile, campaigns collect data on which messages are most effective at doing so and for which type of supporter.

For the average voter, the consequences of the availability of these fine-tuned and more candidate-centered approaches to campaigning are not entirely clear. Unquestionably, more people than ever before have been exposed to them since 2008. The blogosphere and online news sites also continue to expand their reach. Compared with the 2000 presidential election, use of the internet as a mainstay of election information has more than quadrupled (Table 11-1). Still, television remains the chief source of election news, although fewer people tuned in to cable, network, and local news television sources for election news in 2020 compared with earlier cycles. Among cable channels, political orientation arcs from conservative Fox News to liberal MSNBC, with CNN in the middle. It is unclear how such choices affect election outcomes, as people tend to choose news venues in tune with their existing political orientations.

Although the Web remains a secondary source of campaign information for the general public, and although the 2020 presidential candidates still budgeted vast sums of money for over-the-air television, the digital communication environment was tremendously helpful for raising funds. It is a major source of money from millions of citizens who responded to website appeals.[61] The Web also served as a virtual pied piper for all candidates, luring thousands of supporters to the campaigns. Web appeals enlisted them in email recruiting efforts and mobilized them to go to the polls and bring their friends and neighbors along. That feat would have been impossible to achieve through direct mail or phone calls.

The Web also served as a rallying tool for political activists and political action committees (PACs) who would have found it difficult to be heard otherwise. MoveOn.org, for example, used its website and email blitzes to raise millions of dollars and mobilize more than 2 million liberals to the cause of removing Republicans from office (Photo 11-5). Large civic organizations such as MoveOn also retain the digital staff and expertise to continually develop their messaging strategies.[62] These digital fundraising and mobilization efforts can exert a crucial impact on election outcomes, especially in close elections. In 2016 and 2020, websites remained a central point of new media campaign activity and emails were still a heavily utilized campaign tool. The traditional media picked up many of the messages circulated by activists on the Web and in emails, giving their sometimes extreme views a huge national audience. In addition, hundreds of websites, including blogs, provided a rich menu of information to voters who wanted to explore election issues in depth. Emails by the millions sent by personal friends and celebrities, often stimulated by website appeals, may well be the most potent electioneering weapon of the 21st century.

Both old and new campaign media venues are important for the microtargeting practices described at the beginning of this chapter. In the 2016

Dear MoveOn member,

Red alert: Polls are neck-and-neck. If we don't get progressives and Democrats out to vote, 48 hours from now we could end up with president-elect Donald Trump. But if we knock on more doors, make more calls, and get our people to the polls, we can send Trump packing, elect Hillary Clinton, and take back the Senate on Tuesday.

It's really that simple. So.....

Click anywhere on this giant red button to start making calls to voters in swing states.

Studies prove that making calls to have critical conversations with voters is one of the MOST POWERFUL THINGS you can do between now and Election Day. And it'll be fun! You'll get to join other committed MoveOn members on the phones as soon as you click.

Go ahead, scroll back up, and click the big red button.

Just click here if you like this link more than big red buttons (or if, for some reason, don't see a big red button above).

So what are you waiting for? Let's go!

—MoveOn Elections Team

Want to support MoveOn's work? Senator Elizabeth Warren says, "I'm so enthusiastic about MoveOn's smart and targeted plan to hire a network of organizers in key battleground states to mobilize and train volunteers to knock on hundreds of thousands of doors. It's bold and ambitious—and exactly what is needed to help swing Senate races, resoundingly defeat Donald Trump, and build the power we need to win progressive change after the election." Will you chip in to help make it all possible?

Click here to chip in $2.70, or whatever you can afford.

Photo 11-5 Mobilization Email From MoveOn.org From the Final Days of 2016

Source: MoveOn.org.

election cycle, $1 billion was spent on digital ads, an 8% increase since 2012. Yet these figures pale in comparison to the estimated $6 billion political candidates spent on television advertising in 2016.[63] As of October 25, 2020, the Trump campaign spent just over 47% of its funding ($201,460,242) on digital messaging compared to the Biden campaign's 29.4% ($166,118,753). The Trump campaign spent $224,802,892 across broadcast, cable, and satellite television and radio combined; the Biden campaign spent $393,637,209 across these media (see Figure 11-4).[64]

The effectiveness of both types of ads was enhanced by the use of data on individual voters, which has become a key part of narrowly targeting digital ads, television ads, and personalized appeals sent via email, text, and social media.[65] Table 11-1 shows the platforms people relied on most for campaign news in the last few cycles. Digital forms

Figure 11-4   2020 Presidential Campaign Spending by Medium

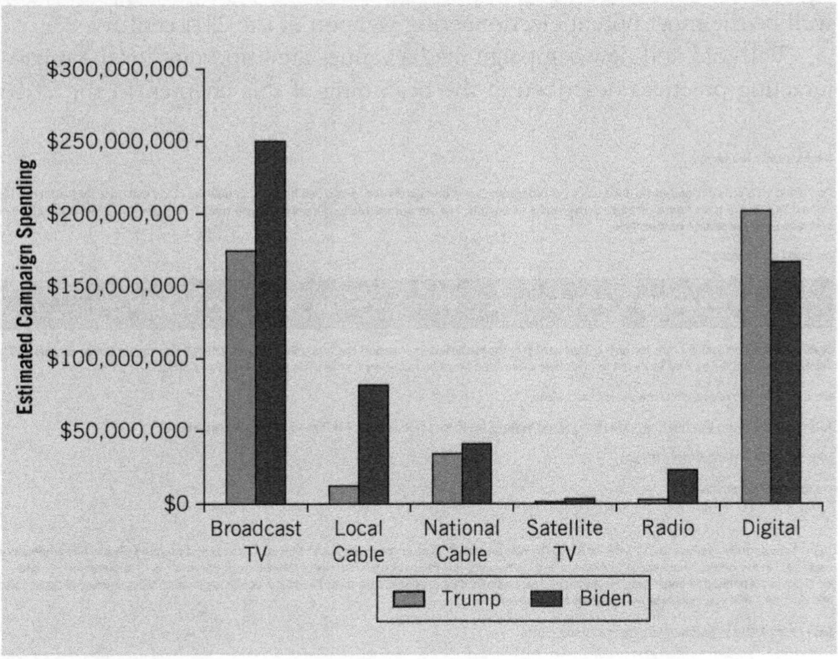

Source: Figure is adapted from Wesleyan Media Project. (2020, October 29). *Presidential general election ad spending tops $1.5 billion.* Author, Table 2.

News Source	2000	2004	2008	2012	2016	2020
Television	70	76	72	67	78	47
Cable TV	36	42	46	42	54	27
Network TV	22	33	24	19	49	36
Local TV	21	12	13	11	57	41
Newspapers/Print Publications	39	46	29	27	36	14
Radio	15	22	21	20	44	13
Internet/Smartphone, Computer, or Tablet	11	21	33	47	65	78

Sources: Low marks for the 2012 election. (2012, November 15). *Pew Research Center.* http://www.people-press.org/2012/11/15/low-marks-for-the-2012-election/. Figures for 2012 based on combined surveys of 1,206 voters conducted November 8–11, 2012; Gottfried, J., Barthel, M., Shearer, E., & Mitchell, A. (2016, February 4). The 2016 presidential campaign: A news event that's hard to miss. *Pew Research Center.* http://www.journalism.org/2016/02/04/the-2016-presidential-campaign-a-news-event-thats-hard-to-miss/; Assessing different survey measurement approaches for news consumption. (2020, December 7). *Pew Research Center.* http://www.journalism.org/2020//12/08/assessing-different-survey-measurement-approaches-for-news-consumption/pj_2020-12-08_news-consumption_2-04/

Note: Figures add up to more than 100% because multiple answers were allowed.

continue to grow, while television remains the most widely used. Pew Research Center studies frequently ask respondents how many sources they typically use; in recent years, many respondents report getting news from five or more sources. Among those citing digital platforms, as often relied on in 2020, 31% relied on news websites and apps; 22% often relied on social networking sites; 23% reported relying on internet searches; and 6% reported using podcasts.[66]

Election News Content

What kinds of news media coverage have recent elections received? Did the media sufficiently cover the issues likely to require the new president's attention? Did they supply adequate criteria to enable voters to decide which policy options would best suit their priorities and which candidate would be most likely to govern successfully? Following some general comments about the media mix, we will address these questions and assess the adequacy of the information supply for making sound voting choices.

Although the link between the media and election outcomes has been studied more thoroughly than other links between media and politics, many unanswered questions remain because the dynamics of the process are always in flux. Moreover, the evidence suggests that the media's role varies substantially, depending on the influence of such factors as incumbency, the candidates' personalities and histories, and major national crises such as wars or economic tsunamis. Obviously, the effects and effectiveness of the media will vary depending on the changing political scene, the type of coverage chosen by newspeople, and the fluctuating interests of voters.[67]

Unscrambling the Message

The impact of campaign media messages is difficult to determine. Campaign commercials, for instance, have become a major ingredient of contemporary campaigns and often give them a distinctive flavor. But it is well-nigh impossible to isolate their contribution because all of the ingredients—print and electronic news stories, editorials, talk show banter and punditry, internet messages, advertisements, even political jokes and skits on entertainment shows—mix inextricably with one another and become transformed in the process. Ads generate and influence news stories and news stories induce and influence ads, which in turn lead to other ads and news stories and editorials.[68]

That is why we discuss campaign information as a whole, usually without isolating the unique contributions of different media. Distinctions exist, of course. Studies show, for example, that cable television and brief video formats are superior to newspapers for conveying particular messages and that the content of advertising messages is often discounted because they are regarded as self-serving propaganda, even though they provide more information about policy issues than most campaign news stories (though this varies by the funding source or sponsorship of the advertisement).[69] A shortage of good data has prevented researchers from intensive analysis of the role that commercials play when they are carried by venues other than television. Therefore, we know far less about the impact of messages displayed on bumper stickers or billboards, printed in newspaper advertisements, disseminated through video, or shown as banner ads on mobile devices. However, newer research utilizing field experiments in the campaign environment is making headway in explaining the impact of various types of political messages that are delivered in ways other than through television advertisements. For example, scholars are investigating the effects of campaign messages left on voicemail, radio advertisements, and direct mail campaigns.[70] Research on digital forms of campaign news and advertising is also emerging at a quick pace, and digital forms allow for message testing in ways that prior forms of media made more difficult.

For the many candidates the news media ignore, direct messages through television commercials, candidate websites, email, and social media often provide a better chance to gain attention.[71] That includes the vast majority of "also-rans" for national office, who seem unelectable to the major media, as well as most candidates competing for local and even state offices. Locally, the impact of commercials and other forms of direct messaging can be decisive. Indeed, wisely spent advertising funds can buy elections, even for congressional candidates who receive news story coverage.[72] To quote political scientist Michael Robinson, commercials for congressional candidates "can work relative wonders," especially when they are not challenged by the other side. "A well-crafted, heavily financed, and uncontested ad campaign does influence congressional elections."[73] This fact raises the chilling specter that wealthy candidates may be able to buy major public offices by investing their fortunes in expensive advertising campaigns. That fear escalated with the entry of such multimillionaires as Ross Perot and Steve Forbes into the presidential sweepstakes. Perot bought large blocks of television time for infomercials—data-packed commercials—in the 1992 presidential campaign. Forbes used personal funds to finance an expensive advertising blitz in the 1996 Republican primaries. Speculations that New York's billionaire mayor, Michael Bloomberg, might run for president in 2008 raised fears that money might be the trump card for winning the presidency. Historically, superior funding has not guaranteed victory, at least at the presidential level.

The candidacy of Donald Trump revived debates about billionaire candidates, at least in early stages of the campaign. Campaign finance data released by the Federal Election Commission in February 2017 showed that, indeed, Trump self-financed nearly 23% of his campaign in the amount of just over $56 million. Other accounts report that he invested up to $66 million of his own funds. Yet Trump was able to raise approximately

$280 million from small donors giving individual donations of $200 or less. Hillary Clinton outraised Trump, and she was advantaged by heavier contributions from super-PACs. Clinton spent more heavily on traditional campaign tactics such as television ads and get-out-the-vote efforts, while Trump relied heavily on earned media and invested heavily in digital advertising. Both candidates made heavy use of social media platforms to disseminate direct messages.[74] That Clinton outraised Trump in 2016 and that Biden defeated Trump in 2020 despite his ability to invest heavily in his own campaigns may ease concerns about presidential office buying.

Patterns of Coverage

Any evaluation of how the media perform their tasks must also take into consideration the commercial pressures that journalists face. It is extremely difficult to mesh the public's preference for simple, dramatic stories with the need to present ample information for issue-based election choices. Information that may be crucial for voting decisions often is too complex and technical to appeal to much of the audience. Hence, newspeople feel compelled to write breezy infotainment stories that stress the horse race and skim over policy details.[75]

Prominence of Election Stories

In a typical presidential election year, election stories constitute roughly 13% of all newspaper political coverage and 15% of televised political news. That puts these stories on par with foreign affairs news or coverage of crime. Election news receives average attention in terms of headline size, front-page or first-story placement, and inclusion of pictures, but stories are slightly longer than average. Although election stories are quite prominent when primaries, conventions, and significant debates are held, they have not historically dominated the news. Normally it is quite possible to read the daily paper without noticing election news and to come away from a telecast with the impression that election stories are merely a minor part of the day's political developments. This has changed in recent cycles. Election news, which filled 10% of cable news in 2007, jumped to 41% in 2012, far exceeding the second most covered news story of the year: the Florida shooting of teenager Trayvon Martin, which accounted for 7% of cable news.

By July 2016, even when the presidential election was still several months away, nearly 60% of respondents reported they were "exhausted" by the amount of election coverage. Earlier in the campaign, 91% of Americans reported learning about the election from at least one type of news source in the prior week. Campaign coverage of the 2016 presidential contest took up a substantial portion of news, and interest was relatively higher, despite reports of fatigue.[76] Coverage, interest, and fatigue were also high for the 2020 election cycle, though COVID-19 related coverage sometimes eclipsed campaign news in terms of both volume and attention. Campaign coverage was substantial, nevertheless. However, as reported in Chapter 7, while presidential races receive significant attention from the news media, coverage of subnational races is scarce—even for competitive statewide elections for senate seats or the gubernatorial office.

Uniformity of Coverage

Patterns of presidential election coverage are remarkably uniform, regardless of a venue's partisan orientation. The major difference generally is the breadth of coverage, measured by the number and length of stories, and the favorable ratings of candidates and issues.[77] There are noteworthy coverage variations among media sectors, platforms, and business models. Compared to newspaper coverage, the usual one- or two-minute television story gives little chance for in-depth reporting and analysis. To conserve limited time, television newscasters create stereotypes of the candidates early in the campaign and then build their stories around these stereotypes by merely adding new details to the established image. Once established, stereotypes stubbornly resist change; there is a feeling that leopards never change their spots.[78] Issue positions and experience is also more common early in the campaign as candidates are still introducing themselves and their positions to the public. As the campaign proceeds, those stories become old news, and stories recounting the horse race—who is winning and who is losing—emerge as a dominant theme in coverage.[79]

Content analysis studies during congressional, state, and local campaigns show similar patterns. The political portraits that various media paint of each candidate match well in basic outline and in most details. But the time and space allotted to various aspects and the tone of evaluations can vary significantly. Generally, election news patterns are quite stable in successive elections, and all venues cover the major happenings and offer similar categories of coverage such as issues, traits, experience, horse race, and strategy. But no longer does this necessarily mean that Americans receive similar types of information on which to base their political decisions. It depends on their media selections. Mainstream media that are not ideologically branded offer similar patterns in coverage. Partisan venues online and on cable sometimes choose different traits, issues, and events on which to focus. Similarity in coverage of election campaigns has benefits as well as drawbacks. The large degree of homogeneity introduced into the electoral process is an advantage in a heterogeneous country such as the United States, where it can be difficult to develop political consensus. But it also means uniform neglect of many topics and criteria for judging candidates. Shared ignorance mars shared knowledge. A uniform information base obviously has not produced uniform political views throughout the country. Differences in political evaluations must be attributed to varying framing and interpretations of the same facts and to the different outlooks that audiences bring to the news. The impact of news usually is perceiver determined rather than stimulus determined.

Of the factors that encourage uniform coverage, journalists' professional socialization appears to be the most important. Newspeople share a sense of what is newsworthy and how it should be presented. Reporters cover identical beats in a fashion that has become routine for election coverage. That means keeping score about who is winning and losing and reporting dramatic incidents and juicy personal gossip. It means avoiding dull facts as much as possible without totally ignoring essential, albeit unglamorous, information. However, content is becoming more diverse in certain areas as news content becomes more common across digital platforms. A 2012 report on YouTube by the Pew Project for Excellence in Journalism shows that news content on YouTube is more conversational and fluid, with a significant amount of audience-contributed content. As media consumers continue to expand their news use across various types of digital media, patterns of uniformity in content are likely to continue to change, even for election news.[80]

Coverage does not strictly follow the campaign model of reporting. In that model—the utopia of campaign managers—the rhythm of the campaign, as produced by the candidates and their staffs, determines what news media cover. Reporters dutifully take their cues from the candidates. Some research shows a relationship between the strategic efforts of campaign and the flow of election news.[81] However, most press coverage has largely conformed to an incentive model. Whenever exciting stories provided an incentive for coverage, the media published them, in a rhythm dictated by their needs and the tastes of their audiences. The needs and tastes of the candidates are often ignored unless they manage to generate the kinds of stories and pictures that journalists find irresistible. In some ways, declining news resources and digital media have revived campaigns' ability to structure the media narrative of campaigns. Covering campaign communications is relatively cheap and easy, which makes campaign ads, emails, and social media posts ripe for providing the basis of a news article storyline. As a result, coverage of direct candidate communications now occupies a substantial portion of campaign news (Photo 11-6).[82]

Though campaign coverage is not entirely dictated by the candidates, the campaign process and the strategic decisions of the candidates can shape coverage. For example, another reason polling gets covered so frequently is that newly released polling data are timely and newsworthy relative to biographical information and issue stances introduced early in the campaign. As a result, early in the campaign, we see more campaign news stories focused on traits and issues associated with the candidate while polling coverage remains throughout the campaign cycle.[83] Patterns in coverage are also driven by the strategic decisions of the campaigns themselves. Candidates' ads are often issue- and trait-based early in the campaign to serve as an introduction to voters; news stories reflect this early in the cycle. Likewise, strategy-framed stories pick up along with horse race coverage as Election Day nears and get-out-the-vote efforts of the campaigns are underway. The increase in news coverage of political ads and campaigns' social media posts in recent years also contributes to coverage patterns being somewhat campaign driven.[84]

Substance of Coverage

Candidate Qualifications: The candidate qualifications that media highlight fall into two broad groups: those that are generally important in judging a person's character and those specifically related to the tasks of the office. Included in the first group are personality traits (integrity, reliability, compassion), style characteristics (forthrightness, folksiness), and image characteristics (confidence, level-headedness). Professional qualifications at the presidential level include the capacity to develop and execute effective foreign and domestic policies, the ability to mobilize public support, and a flair for administration. The candidate's political philosophy is also a professional criterion. Presidential candidates over the years have most frequently been assessed in terms of their trustworthiness, strength of character, leadership capabilities, and compassion. Media have covered professional capacities—the very qualities that deserve the fullest discussion and analysis— only scantily and often vaguely even when an incumbent is running.[85]

The handful of professional qualifications that news stories mention from time to time include general appraisals of the capacity to handle foreign affairs, which has been deemed crucial in a global society, and the capacity to sustain an acceptable quality of life for all citizens by maintaining the economy on an even keel and by controlling crime and internal disorder. The same types of qualities reappear from election to election but not necessarily in every candidate's profile. Disparate coverage then makes it very difficult for the electorate to compare and evaluate the candidates on important dimensions. Effective comparisons are also hindered by contradictions in remarks reported about the candidates. Bound by current codes of objective reporting and neutrality in electoral contests, the media rarely give guidance to the audience for judging conflicting claims. The exception is the trend toward fact-checking, which involves analyzing candidates' claims and reporting the extent to which they are true or false.[86]

Verbal news commentary about the political candidates tends to be negative, so voters' choices have seemed dismal in recent elections. The high praise that Barack Obama earned throughout his 2008 campaign was a notable exception. Overall, only 18% of newspaper coverage about him was negative, but that figure jumped to 28% in 2012. In the 2016 presidential election contest, the tone of overall news coverage for both candidates proved markedly negative. A study from the Shorenstein Center on Media, Politics and Public Policy reveals the ugly details. The tone of coverage Clinton received varied widely, ranging from negative to positive even at the earliest stages of the campaign. Trump's coverage was consistently more negative than positive during the general election but had a run of positive coverage during the pre-primary and primary seasons. Tone of coverage depended heavily on the topic at hand. Both candidates endured controversies and scandals, earning negative coverage. The campaign was heavily covered through the lens of the horse race, which is positive for the candidate winning and usually negative for the candidate losing. For example, because Clinton was leading in the polls for most of the race, the tone of her horse race coverage was positive. Coverage of the debates was more positive for Clinton than Trump, but because the proportion of Clinton's scandal coverage began a slow but steady increase in late September, her negative coverage grew to 37% in early November. Neither Trump's nor Clinton's positive coverage breached 50% for any outlet in the study. The negativity in 2016 reflects a broader trend: Since 2004, presidential campaign coverage has grown increasingly negative.[87]

However, things are not all bad. Mainstream news coverage of the 2020 election was anomalous in one key respect. According to an analysis from media scholar Thomas E. Patterson, Joe Biden's coverage on CBS, a major national news network, was "the most positive ever recorded for a television-age presidential nominee." A full 89% of stories were positive and only 11% were negative. Trump's pattern was the reverse, with 5% positive and 95% negative.[88]

Box 11-2
Political Humor in Campaigns

Humor has always been a potent political tool in society, from ancient times onward. In the Middle Ages, rulers employed court jesters to talk freely and frankly about flawed policies and politicians at a time when it was a capital crime to mock the high and mighty. The inexcusable could be excused if, by definition, it was merely a "jest."

In modern times, truths told in jest (or satirized) and jokes about political leaders still are powerful weapons in political contests. They leap across the barriers of political correctness and chisel their message into human minds. Satire attracts huge audiences, especially among the best-informed segments of the public, who know enough about the political scene to understand the full meaning of veiled messages.

The 2016 presidential election was yet another exhibition of the popularity and power of political humor. Humorous messages took many forms, ranging from political cartoons in newspapers and on the Web to newspaper comic strips and televised satirical animated shows such as *Family Guy* and *The Simpsons*. Comedic news programs such as John Oliver's *Last Week Tonight* and *Full Frontal with Samantha Bee*, *Saturday Night Live*, and the satirical newspaper *The Onion* are household names. Their barbs circulated widely in 2016. The late-night talk shows, including *The Late Late Show* with James Corden, *The Tonight Show* with Jimmy Fallon, and *Jimmy Kimmel Live!* added to the feast of political jokes. They made fun of the candidates' performance and skills, and occasionally their policies. Only people familiar with ongoing news developments could relish the humor, but judging from their viewership, this constituted many millions of people.

As is common during elections, a large number of jokes during the 2016 campaign referred to personal traits and the performances of the candidates. For example, Hillary Clinton's longtime political ambition and practiced performances were a common source of humor. Donald Trump endured many barbs about his overall manner, his bluntness, and his dealings with women. The various scandals each candidate was involved in also provided plenty of material.

Both candidates endured quite a bit of grief from the late-night shows after their debate performances. Though Clinton was widely perceived as the net winner across their debate contests, both candidates' performances provided

(Continued)

(Continued)

fodder for late-night comedy. From reenactments of Trump looming directly behind Clinton as she answered a question during a town hall debate to replicating Clinton's giddy shimmy in response to an off-putting remark by Trump, comedy writers' rooms had plenty to work with (see Photo 11-6). Throughout the 2016 campaign season, *SNL*'s Kate McKinnon and frequent *SNL* guest host and *30 Rock* star Alec Baldwin delighted audiences with their depictions of the two major party candidates. Later, *SNL* mocked the candidates in a tweet.

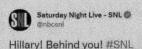

Hillary! Behind you! #SNL

12:15 AM · Oct 16, 2016 · Twitter Media Studio

4,272 Retweets   **465** Quote Tweets   **7,505** Likes

Photo 11-6 Days after Donald Trump loomed directly behind Hillary Clinton during the town hall presidential debate, *Saturday Night Live* cast member Kate McKinnon and guest star Alec Baldwin parodied the moment; it was an example of the show's running commentary on the election. After *Saturday Night Live* tweeted about the moment, it began an extended conversation across social media.

Source: Twitter, @nbcsnl

Such jokes may seem pretty tame, but repeated over and over again, they become part of the candidate's image that voters internalize and carry to the voting booth. No wonder *Newsweek* featured *The Daily Show*'s Jon Stewart on its cover shortly before the 2004 presidential election, calling him one of the most powerful media figures in that contest. In the same year, Stewart's parody of an American government textbook, *America (The Book): A Citizen's Guide to Democracy Inaction*, placed fifteenth on *The New York Times* list of best-selling books. Social media extends the far-reaching impact of these jokes and thus, continues to influence a candidate's image.

The typical negativity in election coverage is epitomized by the lead paragraph in a *Time* magazine story at the end of the 1980 race between Reagan and Carter: "For more than a year, two flawed candidates have been floundering toward the final showdown, each unable to give any but his most unquestioning supporters much reason to vote for him except dislike of his opponent."[89] The negative characterizations, which are increasing and mar most presidential and subnational elections, are hardly fair to capable candidates, who often possess great personal strengths and skills that should be praised rather than debased. However, the level of journalistic negativity is variable across news media outlets and can also vary with candidate strategies and electoral contexts.[90]

Issues and Events: Journalists' overriding consideration in reporting about particular issues, as in all political coverage, is newsworthiness rather than intrinsic importance. That is why happenings on the campaign trail, however trivial, receive extended coverage. Rather than exploring policy issues in depth, news stories emphasize rapidly paced, freshly breaking events. In fact, the amount of coverage for particular issues often seems to be in inverse proportion to their significance. For instance, during the 1992 primaries, one of every six campaign stories on the television networks referred to Governor Bill Clinton's personal life. Sexual foibles, reputed drug use during college days, slips of the tongue, and bad jokes all made headlines and were repeated endlessly on various entertainment programs. In the 2000 campaign, a story about George W. Bush's arrest on drunk driving charges twenty-four years earlier received more coverage during the last three days of the campaign than all foreign policy issues had received since Labor Day.[91] When Hillary Clinton choked up a tiny bit in responding to questions during the New Hampshire primary campaign in 2008, it became a major media focus, as did an out-of-wedlock pregnancy in candidate Sarah Palin's family that same year. The 2016 campaigns were populated by gaffes and scandals provided by both candidates, which occupied much press attention and served both candidates with plenty of negative coverage.[92] During the 2020 election, we witnessed President Trump's efforts to return to his favorite means of attracting coverage: tweets and rallies. Though in-person rallies were stalled for a time due to the COVID-19 pandemic, Trump resumed in-person rallies sooner, eager to attract supporters and coverage, while the Biden campaign held drive-in rallies in which people attended but remained in their cars. Both attracted event-style campaign coverage.

Three features stand out in coverage of issues and events. First and most significant, the media devote a large amount of attention to horse race aspects of campaigns. During the 2020 election, the Shorenstein Center on Media, Politics and Public Policy tracked and examined all general election campaign stories from two major news outlets through Election Day. According to the study, during the general election campaign, 74% of CBS coverage about Joe Biden focused on the horse race; horse race stories comprised 35% of Trump's CBS coverage. Horse race stories encompass campaign strategies, polls, fundraising, and advertising. On the Fox News network, the horse race accounted for 51% of Biden's coverage and 28% of Trump's. CBS covered the Biden and Trump issue positions only 10% and 12% of the time, respectively. On Fox News, issue coverage reached nearly 20% for Biden and 25% for Trump. Neither network covered candidates' leadership experience more than 10% of the time.[93] Although the horse race bias is an ongoing problem in campaign coverage, 2016 horse race content was up from 2012 and remained high in 2020. The explosion of public opinion polling since 2004 explains the prevalence of horse race coverage, as polls are welcome grist for the 24/7 cable news mill and for political websites, which need a constant stream of newly minted stories.

All this enlarges a particular media syndrome that might be best described as the *media echo effect*. The expansion of polls and the media's fascination with seeing the race through their strategic lens create a pattern in which the media reinforce and magnify the phenomena they observe. The press covers what the candidate does that day. The polls measure the political impact of that behavior. The media then analyze whether the latest campaign performance is helping in the polls. That in turn influences the candidate's behavior. Winning in the polls begets winning coverage.[94]

There are also economic incentives for news organizations to cover polling and the horse race. Scholars and observers of campaigns have been saying for years that horse race coverage is dominant because of its audience appeal. In 2004, media scholar Shanto Iyengar and colleagues empirically investigated this question and found that campaign news audiences do in fact prefer horse race to issue stories; their study concludes that "the horse race sells." This means that, from the perspective of news organizations, horse race stories are doubly appealing—they are newsworthy and they are pleasing to audiences.[95] Table 11-2 provides a breakdown of horse race coverage and its relationship with tone toward the candidates in the 2020 election.

Second, information about issues is patchy because the candidates and their surrogates try to concentrate on issues that help their campaigns and to avoid issues likely to alienate any portion of the huge and diverse electorate from whom all are seeking support. Third, there is more issue coverage, albeit unsystematic, than scholars have acknowledged in the past. Audiences often overlook commentary about issues because it is embedded in many horse race stories and discussions of candidates' qualifications. For example, the claim that a candidate is compassionate may be linked to their concern about health care laws. When the design of content analyses focuses narrowly on recording only one issue per news story, multifaceted stories are forced into a single category and important facets become obscured.

In recent elections, some twenty-five issues, such as taxes, Social Security, or education, have usually surfaced intermittently in the press; for television, the number hovers around twenty. Typically, only half of these receive extensive and intensive attention. Many important policy questions likely to arise during the forthcoming presidential term are entirely ignored. Although candidates like to talk about broad policy issues, such as war and peace or the health of the economy, newspeople prefer to concentrate on narrower, specific policy positions on which the candidates disagree.

As is the case for coverage of presidential qualifications, issues discussed in connection with individual candidates vary. Voters thus receive little aid from the media in appraising and comparing the candidates on the issues. Compared with print media, television news usually displays more uniform patterns of issue coverage for all the candidates and involves a more limited range of issues. Television stories are briefer, touch on fewer aspects of each issue, and contribute to the stereotypic images developed for particular candidates. Events are often fragmented and barren of context, but what is left is dramatized to appeal to the audience. No wonder most people turn to television for news about the candidates and their campaigns.

We should assess media coverage not only in terms of the numbers of stories devoted to various topics but also in terms of political impact. There are times when election politics is particularly volatile and a few stories may carry extraordinary weight. Rapid diffusion of these stories throughout the major media enhances their impact. Michael Robinson calls such featured events *medialities*—"events, developments, or situations to which the media have given importance by emphasizing, expanding, or featuring them in such a way that their real significance has been modified, distorted, or obscured."[96] Medialities usually involve policy scandals, economic disasters, and personal foibles. Such key stories can have a far more profound impact on the campaign than thousands of routine stories and should be appraised accordingly. Examples from the 2016 election included the echo chamber coverage of Hillary Clinton's "basket of deplorables," and Donald Trump's "They're bringing drugs. They're bringing crime. They're rapists. And I assume some are good people," comments in reference to people coming to the United States from Mexico.[97] In prominent examples from the 2020 campaign, Biden said he would consider a Republican running mate at a New Hampshire campaign event in December 2019; in a televised debate in July, he encouraged voters to visit the wrong campaign website.[98] Neither of these were comparable in impact to the examples from 2016. As shown in Figure 11-5, controversy coverage was relatively low in 2020.

Political and Structural Bias: Does election coverage give a fair and equal chance for all viewpoints to be expressed so that media audiences can make informed decisions? Are the perennial charges of bias that disappointed candidates level evidence that newspeople always show favoritism? Or are they merely reactions to coverage that did not advance those candidates'

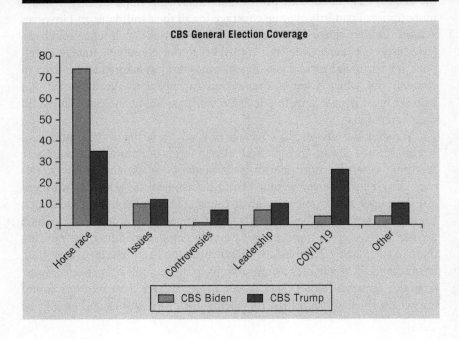

Figure 11-5   Presidential Campaign News Topics as a Percentage of Campaign News, 2020

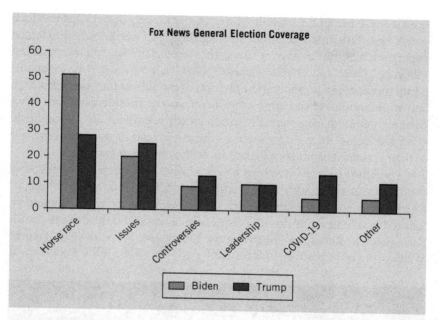

Fig. Fox News General Election Coverage

Source: Adapted from Patterson, T. E. (2020, December). A tale of two elections: CBS and Fox News' portrayal of the 2020 presidential campaign. *Shorenstein Center on Media, Politics and Public Policy.* https://shorensteincenter.org/patterson-2020-election-coverage/. Licensed under CC BY 3.0. https://creativecommons.org/licenses/by/3.0/

Notes: Data collected by Media Tenor. Other category includes stories about things such as events, staffing, and logistics.

causes? In general, journalists working for mainstream news outlets—not the branded partisan cable news networks—try to balance coverage of all major candidates for the same office. They aim for rough parity in the number of stories about each candidate and in the balance of favorable and unfavorable stories.

Nevertheless, imbalances in coverage occur frequently, even if not systematically. When they do, it raises the question as to whether political or structural bias is involved. Political bias reflects ideological judgments, whereas structural bias reflects the circumstances of news production. Balanced reporting may be impossible when candidates' newsworthiness and willingness to talk to reporters vary or when their campaigns are linked to different issues. Structural bias, even though it lacks partisan motivation, nonetheless may profoundly affect people's perceptions about campaigns.[99]

Editorials, of course, are intrinsically biased because their primary purpose is to express opinions. As part of the editorial function, many news media endorse candidates. That has little impact at the presidential level but does seem to matter for lower-level offices, particularly in elections in which voters have little information for making their own decisions.[100] Influential papers, such as the *Los Angeles Times, The Washington Post,* and the small but influential *Union Leader* of Manchester, New Hampshire, can be extraordinarily successful in promoting the election of candidates they have endorsed and in defeating unacceptable contenders. At the presidential level, news coverage tends to be essentially evenhanded, regardless of the candidate endorsed. Below the presidential level, the media tend to give more coverage to their endorsed candidates than to those they have not endorsed.

The effort to keep coverage balanced does not extend to third-party candidates. Anyone who runs for president who is not a Republican or Democrat is out of the mainstream of newsworthiness and is slighted or ignored by the news profession. Especially newsworthy third-party candidates, such as Robert La Follette of the Progressive Party in 1924, George Wallace of the American Independent Party in 1968, John Anderson of

Table 11-2 Volume and Tone of General Election Coverage by Topic, 2020

	CBS		Fox News	
	Trump	Biden	Trump	Biden
Horse race				
Positive	8%	98%	44%	80%
Negative	92%	2%	56%	20%
Non–Horse race				
Positive	5%	39%	42%	15%
Negative	95%	61%	58%	85%
Amount of Coverage				
Percentage of Statements	68%	32%	56%	41%

Source: Adapted from Patterson, T. E. (2020, December). A tale of two elections: CBS and Fox News's portrayal of the 2020 presidential campaign. *Shorenstein Center on Media, Politics and Public Policy.* https://shorensteincenter.org/patterson-2020-election-coverage/. Licensed under CC BY 3.0. https://creativecommons.org/licenses/by/3.0/

Note: Data are from Media Tenor, collected from weekday evening broadcasts from June 22–November 3, 2020.

the National Unity Campaign in 1980, independent Ross Perot in 1992, and the Green Party's Ralph Nader in 2000, have been notable exceptions. Newsworthiness considerations also account for the sparse coverage of vice presidential candidates, despite the importance of the office and the possibility that the vice president may have to replace a deceased incumbent. A total of 95% of the coverage in a typical presidential election goes to the presidential contenders and only 5% to their running mates. This disparity is also noteworthy because recent research illustrates that when vice presidential contenders are the subjects of more election coverage, they have a stronger impact on vote choice.[101] For lower-level races, coverage of candidates is determined by news media assessments of competitiveness, which, in turn, has an effect on competitiveness.

Adequacy of Coverage

How adequate is current election coverage? Do the media help voters make decisions according to commonly accepted democratic criteria? As discussed, the media do not make comparative appraisals of candidates and issues easy for voters. In presidential contests, information is ample about the major mainstream candidates and about day-to-day campaign events. It is sketchy and often confusing about the candidates' professional qualifications and about many important policy issues. Most primary contenders, candidates of minor parties, and vice presidential candidates are largely ignored. This is not surprising because the field of candidates usually is quite large, with several hundred individuals registering as formal candidates for the presidency. The prevalence of negative information about the candidates makes it seem that all of them are mediocre or even poor choices. This negative cast can be a major factor in many voters' decisions to stay home on Election Day. It also undermines the ability of newly elected officials to command support after the election, especially from members of the opposing party.

Voters gave election news record low marks for the 2016 cycle, as Figure 11-6 shows. There are more D and F grades than A, B, and C grades combined. Usually, voters think that Republican candidates (more than Democrats) are treated unfairly. In 2016, that trend continued in the sense that Clinton supporters graded the press more positively than did Trump supporters, 60% of whom gave the press a failing grade. Nearly 60% of all voters gave the press a D or an F for its performance during the 2016 cycle. Fifty-nine percent reported being worn out by so much coverage of the 2016 presidential campaign and candidates. A full 90% of voters felt there was more mudslinging in the 2016 campaign, and 73% said there was less

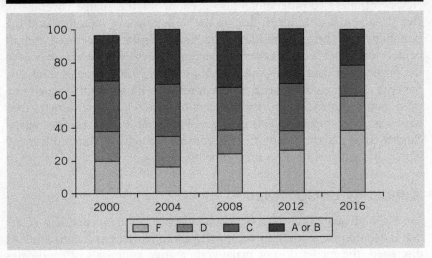

Figure 11-6   Voters' Evaluations of Election News

Source: Adapted from Low marks for major players in 2016 election—including the winner: Voters' evaluations of the campaign. (2016, November 21). *Pew Research Center.* http://www.people-press.org/2016/11/21/voters-evaluations-of-the-campaign/

issue coverage than usual.[102] This is striking compared to assessments in the 1996, 2000, 2004, 2008, and 2012 presidential campaigns, where at least three out of four voters felt adequately informed.

Americans' frustration with and fatigue from political and election news does not seem to be abating, either. Pew Research Center follow-up studies in 2018 and 2019 reveal that the proportion of Americans who report being worn out by the news was at 68% and 66%, respectively (see Figure 11-7).

Following the tumultuous 2020 presidential campaign and its aftermath, voters gave low marks to social media in particular. According to Pew Research Center, approximately 64% of U.S. adults say social media is having a mostly negative effect on the way things are going in America today, and among those respondents, nearly 30% cite misinformation problems as the reason. Respondents also cited problems with hate, harassment, and extremism on social networking sites as well as problems with digital literacy and the difficulty of knowing what sources to trust in such an overwhelming tide of information.[103] Other Pew Research Center data lend credence to these concerns. Americans who rely heavily on social media as a means by which to access the news know less about politics. More specifically, social media news users were more likely to believe incorrect

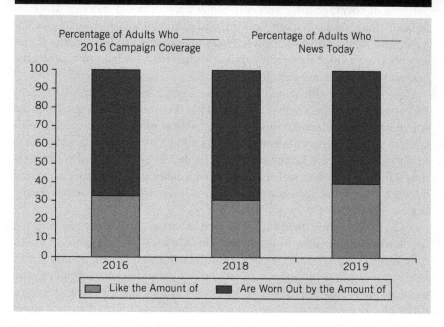

Figure 11-7   American News Fatigue Since 2016

Percentage of Adults Who _____
2016 Campaign Coverage

Percentage of Adults Who _____
News Today

Like the Amount of   *Are Worn Out by the Amount of*

Source: Adapted from Gottfried, J. (2020, February 26). Americans' news fatigue isn't going away—about two-thirds still feel worn out. *Pew Research Center.* https://www .pewresearch.org/fact-tank/2020/02/26/almost-seven-in-ten-americans-have-news -fatigue-more-among-republicans/.

Note: "No answer" is not shown.

factual information about COVID-19 and were more often exposed to unproven or exaggerated claims. People who mainly consume news on social media sites are also less likely to be politically engaged. News and political information consumed on social media does not seem to be any less exhausting for Americans, either. In 2019, 46% of social media users reported feeling worn out by political posts and discussions; by 2020, this number rose to 55%.

Many scholars and pundits would agree with the poor grades given for election news—whether consumed on social or traditional media— because citizens do not match the high standards of civic knowledge that democratic theory prescribes. The most serious deficiency in the news supply is inadequate analysis of policy issues, often neglected in exchange for more horse race coverage, which means that voters do not learn about the key points at stake, the scope and nature of various trade-offs, and the impact of their votes on the resolution of major political problems. The patterns of coverage force voters to make choices based more on the candidates' traits, partisan identification, and campaigning skills than on their governing skills and policy preferences. These are valid criticisms if one accepts the premise that policy issues, rather than leadership characteristics, should drive voting choices.

If the public's chief role is to choose a good leader, along with a general sense of the directions this leader will take, then judgments about the adequacy of the information supply become far more positive. The proliferation of news venues in the internet age allows average people easy access to a vast variety of information at diverse levels of depth and sophistication. Links on election websites are an especially rich source for facts and interpretations that facilitate in-depth analyses, whenever voters feel the need—which they rarely do.[104]

The mainstream media do fall short when it comes to supplying the needs of political elites in ready fashion. Opinion leaders would benefit from more complete coverage of the candidates' stands on major and minor issues, more point-by-point comparisons of candidates and policies, and more ample evaluations of the political significance of differences in candidates and their programs. Stories covering important topics that candidates neglect would be useful, as would more coverage of third-party candidates and vice presidential contenders. In the end, though, no news consumer need hunger for information in the internet age. With a little effort, a global cornucopia of facts and opinions is readily available to anyone with access to a computer and the internet, should they want news.

In presidential contests, the deficiencies of media coverage are most noticeable during the primaries, when large slates of same-party candidates are competing in each. The media meet this challenge by giving uniformly skimpy treatment to all candidates except those designated as front-runners. It is not uncommon for two or three front-runners to attract 75% or more of the coverage, leaving a pack of trailing contenders with hardly any attention at all. As political scientist Thomas Patterson has noted, "Issue material is but a rivulet in the news flow during the primaries, and what is there is almost completely diluted by information about the race."[105] One problem is that in primaries, candidates often agree on a larger number of issues, which means differences are stretched and highlighted, and coverage focuses on viability and likeability as opposed to issues. While the quality of coverage during the primaries may be thin, the quantity is substantial, although it is unequally distributed, so the races in well-covered states become disproportionately influential. By the middle of the primary season, interest in these contests dwindles. Coverage shrivels. It perks up slightly during the conventions and when the final campaign starts, following the Labor Day holiday in September.

Campaign News Negativity

News media have also received criticism in recent years for the negativity of election coverage. Though much negativity in campaign news comes from the campaigns themselves, campaign news negativity is also a product of journalists' norms and routines for deciding what is newsworthy. Negativity in presidential campaigns has been on a fairly consistent upswing since about the mid-1980s and with it, the volume of negative campaign coverage.[106] Generally speaking, there is more political news today containing criticism of government, politicians, and their policies and fewer news stories focusing on substantive issues. Audiences more frequently encounter a journalistic tone of cynicism and negativity in political news coverage. Political news often focuses on journalists' analysis, and much less of the coverage is about what the candidates are saying. Even when journalistic commentators are generally neutral in the sense of being nonpartisan, they are usually broadly critical and negative in their comments.[107]

These trends in negativity are thought to have significant implications for political attitudes and behavior. Common conjecture and scholars alike argue that negative media coverage of politics has contributed to an overall decline in citizens' trust in government and participation in politics.

Table 11-3 Tone of Candidates' General Election Coverage by Source (Percentage)

	CBS		Fox News	
	Trump	Biden	Trump	Biden
Positive	5%	89%	42%	41%
Negative	95%	11%	58%	59%

Source: Adapted from Patterson, T. E. (2020, December). A tale of two elections: CBS and Fox News' portrayal of the 2020 presidential campaign. *Shorenstein Center on Media, Politics and Public Policy.* https://shorensteincenter.org/patterson-2020-election-coverage/. Licensed under CC BY 3.0. https://creativecommons.org/licenses/by/3.0/

Note: Data are from Media Tenor, collected from weekday evening broadcasts from June 22–November 3, 2020.

Negative political news content has been linked to decreases in several forms of political participation, generally negative attitudes toward government, more distrust in government, cynicism, and negative evaluations of political institutions.[108]

What is driving the increase in negative news coverage of politics? Many suggest it can be explained by the economic structure of the media. The public as a news audience responds well to general negativity in political news coverage. Given that most news organizations' revenue is dependent on attracting audiences, if negativity appeals to audiences, it should appeal to market-driven news media. In 2016, both presidential candidates were covered more negatively than positively, and social media content was even more negative about the candidates.[109] During 2020, negative tone was still quite common, but it was not as uniformly distributed between the two major candidates relative to 2016 (see Table 11-3).

What People Learn From Campaign Coverage

What do people learn from campaign coverage? The answer varies, of course, depending on their interest in the campaign, prior political knowledge, desire for certain information, and political sophistication. Good published research remains sparse, especially when it comes to the effects of advertising. Nonetheless, several general trends emerge from national surveys, such as those conducted biannually by the Survey Research Center at the University of Michigan and from intensive interviews of smaller panels of voters.

Learning About Candidates and Issues

A serious obstacle to understanding media influence on elections is the dearth of analyses of media content. Only rarely have researchers examined the content of election news, including commercials, and the context of general news in which it is embedded. That makes it impossible to test what impact—if any—diverse messages have on viewers' perceptions. In general, researchers have also failed to ascertain media exposure accurately. They frequently assume that people have been exposed to all election stories in a particular news source without checking precisely which stories have come to the attention of which individuals and what the individuals learned.[110]

The foremost impression from interviews with voters is that they can recall very little specific campaign information. That does not necessarily mean that they have not learned anything. When people are confronted with factual information, such as news about a particular presidential candidate, they assess how it fits into their established view of that candidate. If it is consonant, the information strengthens that view and the person's feelings about the candidate. If it is dissonant, the person is likely to reject it outright or note it as a reasonable exception to their established schema. The least likely result is a major revision of their established beliefs about the candidate. Once people have processed the news, they forget most of the details and store only their summary impression in memory. That approach is called *online processing*. When people are later quizzed about details, they are likely to recall only what was frequently repeated in recent news stories. Online processing thus creates the false impression that the average person has formed opinions about the candidate without having learned the appropriate facts.[111]

Voting Behavior

Do media-intensive campaigns change votes? The answer to this perennial question, so dear to the hearts of campaign managers, public relations experts, and social scientists, hinges on the interaction between audiences and messages. Crucial variables include the voters' receptivity to a message urging change, the potency of the message, the appropriateness of its form, and the setting in which it occurs. For most voters, the crucial attitudes that determine voting choices are already firmly in place at the beginning of the campaign, so their final vote is a foregone conclusion. Vote changes are most likely when voters pay fairly close attention to the media and are ambivalent in their attitudes toward the candidates. Campaign messages are most potent if they concern a major and unexpected event, such as a successful or disastrous foreign policy venture or corruption in high places, and if individuals find themselves in social settings where a change of attitude will not constitute deviant behavior. Campaign messages are also more potent when issues candidates emphasize are reflected in campaign coverage. These circumstances are fairly rare, which explains why changes of voting intention are comparatively uncommon. Fears that televised campaigns can easily sway voters and amount to "electronic ballot box stuffing" are therefore unrealistic.[112]

However, even small numbers of media-induced vote changes might be important. Tiny percentages of votes, often less than 1%, decide many elections at all levels. That was demonstrated dramatically in the 2000 presidential election, where vote totals in Florida were extremely close and their validity was questioned—yet the electoral votes of that state determined the victor. The media may also skew election outcomes when they can stimulate or depress voter turnout; a difference in turnout is more likely to occur than changes in voting choices. Do broadcasts that predict election results before voting has ended affect turnout? The answer remains moot despite several investigations of the problem. Current evidence indicates that the effects, if they do occur, have rarely changed election outcomes.[113]

Attempts to stop the media from projecting winners and losers while voting is still in progress have run afoul of First Amendment free speech guarantees. This may explain why the laws passed in more than half of the states to restrain exit polling are seldom enforced.[114] Congress has tried since 1986 to pass a Uniform Poll Closing Act. Although the measure has thus far failed to pass, prospects for ultimate success are good, especially after the presidential election of 2000, in which the issue of broadcasting election results while polling places remained open in parts of the United States became a huge political controversy. A smaller dispute arose in 2004 when media published exit polls that wrongly suggested a Kerry victory before the polls had closed. The concern about the impact of exit polls and early forecasts may be overdrawn. Voters are bombarded throughout the election year with information likely to determine their vote and turnout. Why should the media be squeamish on the campaign payoff day?

The most important influence of the media on voters does not lie in changing votes once predispositions have been formed but in shaping and reinforcing predispositions and influencing the initial selection of candidates. When newspeople sketched out the image of Bill Clinton and held him up as a potential winner during the 1992 primaries, ignoring most of his rivals, they morphed the obscure governor of a small southern state into a viable candidate. Millions of voters would never have cast their ballots for the unknown Arkansas politician had the media not thrust him into the limelight as a likely winner.

By focusing the voters' attention on selected individuals, their characteristics, and issue stands, the media also determine (to a large extent) the issues by which the public will gauge the competence of the candidates. Very early in the campaign, often long before formal campaigning starts, media interpretations of the significance of issues can shape the political and emotional context of the election. As Leon Sigal noted many years ago, the media

> play less of an independent part in creating issues, sketching imagery, and coloring perceptions of the candidates than in getting attention for their candidacies. Newsmen do not write the score or play an instrument; they amplify the sounds of the music makers.[115]

SUMMARY

The media's role in campaigns is powerful and pervasive. Campaigns have become battles for spreading favorable and unfavorable messages about candidates and issues through traditional and digital media venues. The main quest is for a place in the limelight and a winning image. Candidates expect that public recognition and support—or opposition—are likely to follow, particularly at the presidential level.

In this chapter, we have scrutinized newspaper, television, and digital media election coverage, considering general coverage patterns, the substance and slant of coverage, and the manner of presentation. The evidence shows that the media place heavy emphasis on the candidates' personal qualifications for office and on the ups and downs of the race. They often mention policy issues but rarely explore them in depth. Mainstream media stories are chosen primarily for their newsworthiness; digital messages are more likely to caricature the contrasts between candidates' qualifications and policies, with one side as veritable angels and the other as Satan's disciples or dunces. Structural biases abound and have important political consequences, but outright political bias is uncommon from mainstream news outlets such as the broadcast television networks.

Although the public claims, off and on, to be very interested in learning about the election, it absorbs only a small portion of the considerable amount of available information. Nonetheless, the bits of information that people absorb create sufficient political understanding to permit sound voting choices based primarily on whether the chosen candidate seems trustworthy and capable of leading the country. Although news stories rarely change people's minds, they can influence undecided voters. Along with media impact on turnout, shaping the views of even small numbers of voters can determine the outcome in close elections and change the course of political life.

Before television, research and conventional wisdom suggested that news media impact on elections was minimal because election stories persuaded few people to change their votes. Television and digital age research has cast the net much wider to include the media's effects on all phases of the election campaign, from the recruitment and nomination stages to the strategies that produce the final outcome. In addition to studying the media's impact on the final choices of voters, social scientists now look at political learning during campaigns and at the information base that supports voting decisions. Television news stories and massive numbers of highly sophisticated commercials have changed the election game, especially at the presidential level. The affordances of digital communication technologies have made retail politicking possible again and have personalized appeals to individual voters. Personalization is taking place on a scale that was unimaginable before the internet.

Despite its innovations, even the 2020 campaign was guided by the familiar principles that candidates must communicate with their bases as well as attract new voters who have weak—or no—ties to the opposition party or who are likely to stay away from the polls. The digital media environment provides a range of new, inexpensive channels that candidates can use to distribute messages of their choice to audiences around the clock, around the country, and around the world. The target audiences, as before, are potential voters, who are a bit easier to pinpoint because of platform diversity and sophisticated digital analytics. In their messages, essentially, was old wine in new bottles, much of it branded more heavily than before by the candidates rather than the thinning ranks of professional journalists. The digital media did not crowd out the familiar old-timers; the old-timers fueled the reach and meaning of digital platforms in ways that will continue to shape the strategic practices of campaigns. One thing is certain: Candidates and media remain inextricably intertwined. Those who aspire to elective office must play the media game by rules that continue to evolve.

DISCUSSION QUESTIONS

1. How central are media to the conduct and impact of modern-day political campaigns?

2. What are some of the political implications of the U.S. having such a media-centered campaign system?

3. How are candidates and campaigns depicted by news media? Why do we observe these patterns in coverage? Are there problems with campaign news or is coverage adequate from a democratic perspective?

4. What are some of the consequential ways that digital, social, and mobile media are shaping campaigns and elections today? What do these new tools mean for how campaigns are operated and the strategies candidates employ? What do they mean for citizen exposure to news and information about the campaigns? Are they more harmful or more helpful?

5. Do people learn from campaigns and related media? How well do they learn? What are the impediments to learning from media about candidates and campaigns?

READINGS

Achen, C., Bartels, L., Achen, C. H., & Bartels, L. M. (2017). *Democracy for realists*. Princeton University Press.

Barber, J. D. (2017). *The pulse of politics: Electing presidents in the media age*. Routledge.

Bode, L., Budak, C., Ladd, J. M., Newport, F., Pasek, J., Singh, L. O., Soroka, S. N., & Traugott, M. W. (2020). *Words that matter: How the news and social media shaped the 2016 presidential campaign*. Brookings Institution Press.

Cushion, S., & Thomas, R. (2018). *Reporting elections: Rethinking the logic of campaign coverage*. John Wiley & Sons.

Fowler, E. F., Franz, M. M., & Ridout, T. N. (2018). *Political advertising in the United States*. Routledge.

Hibbing, J. R. (2020). *The securitarian personality: What really motivates Trump's base and why it matters for the post-Trump era*. Oxford University Press.

Jamieson, K. H. (2020). *Cyberwar: How Russian hackers and trolls helped elect a president: What we don't, can't, and do know*. Oxford University Press.

Karpf, D. (2016). *Analytic activism: Digital listening and the new political strategy*. Oxford University Press.

Klar, S., & Krupnikov, Y. (2016). *Independent politics*. Cambridge University Press.

Kreiss, D. (2016). *Prototype politics: Technology-intensive campaigning and the data of democracy*. Oxford University Press.

Lawless, J., & Fox, R. L. (2015). *Running from office*. Oxford University Press.

Lupia, A. (2016). *Uninformed: Why people know so little about politics and what we can do about it*. Oxford University Press.

McKenna, E., & Han, H. (2014). *Groundbreakers: How Obama's 2.2 million volunteers transformed campaigning in America*. Oxford University Press.

Nelson, C. J., & Thurber, J. A. (Eds.). (2018). *Campaigns and elections American style: The changing landscape of political campaigns*. Routledge.

Panagopoulos, C. (2017). *Political campaigns*. Oxford University Press.

Scammell, M., & Semetko, H. (2017). *The media, journalism and democracy*. Routledge.

Sides, J., Tesler, M., & Vavreck, L. (2019). *Identity crisis: The 2016 presidential campaign and the battle for the meaning of America*. Princeton University Press.

Stromer-Galley, J. (2019). *Presidential campaigning in the Internet age*. Oxford University Press.

Vaidhyanathan, S. (2018). *Antisocial media: How Facebook disconnects us and undermines democracy*. Oxford University Press.

White, I. K., & Laird, C. N. (2020). *Steadfast democrats: How social forces shape Black political behavior*. Princeton University Press.

Woolley, S. C., & Howard, P. N. (Eds.). (2018). *Computational propaganda: Political parties, politicians, and political manipulation on social media*. Oxford University Press.

NOTES

1. For a description of early developments in modern campaign analytics and how they emerged, see Issenberg, S. (2012). *The victory lab: The secret science of winning campaigns*. Crown. For an interesting perspective on the degree to which Obama's campaign tactics ultimately mattered, see John Sides's series of blog posts about election 2012 on https://themonkeycage.org/search/?_categories=2012-election

2. We say *estimations* because current FEC laws do not require specific details about sub-vendors in campaign spending disclosure reports. See Holliday, K., & Liberman, J. (2020, November 30). Digital political advertising in 2020: What we learned. *Campaigns & Elections*. https://www.campaignsandelections.com/campaign-insider/digital-political-advertising-in-2020-what-we-learned.

3. Kantar Media is widely cited as being among the most reliable sources for ad spending data. See Holliday, K., & Liberman, J. (2020, November 30). Digital political advertising in 2020: What we learned. *Campaigns & Elections*. https://www.campaignsandelections.com/campaign-insider/digital-political-advertising-in-2020-what-we-learned

4. Karpf, D. (2016). *Analytic activism*. Oxford University Press.

5. Lapowsky, I. (2016, November 15). Here's how Facebook *actually* won Trump the presidency. *Wired*. https://www.wired.com/2016/11/facebook-won-trump-election-not-just-fake-news/.

6. Lapowsky, I. (2016, November 15). Here's how Facebook *actually* won Trump the presidency. *Wired*. https://www.wired.com/2016/11/facebook-won-trump-election-not-just-fake-news/.

7. Zhang, F., Stromer-Galley, J., Tanupabrungsun, S., Hegde, Y., McCracken, N., & Hemsley, J. (2017). Understanding discourse acts: Political campaign messages classification on Facebook and Twitter. In D. Lee, Y. R. Lin, N. Osgood, & R. Thomson (Eds.), *Social, cultural, and behavioral modeling* (Vol. 10354). Springer. http://illuminating.ischool.syr.edu/#/platforms/1,2/dates/2016-11-01,2016-11-08/candidates/10,5/types/8&9,5&6.

8. See McGregor, S. C., Lawrence, R. G., & Cardona, A. (2017). Personalization, gender, and social media: Gubernatorial candidates' social media strategies. *Information, Communication, and Society*, 20(2), 264–283; McGregor, S. C. (2017). Personalization, social media, and voting: Effects of candidate self-personalization on vote intention. *New Media & Society*. https://doi.org/10.1177/1461444816686103; Enli, G. (2015). *Mediated authenticity: How the media constructs reality*. Peter Lang.

9. Stromer-Galley, J. (2017, February 4). *Trump's tweets and other tremendous tales: What the illuminating 2016 project reveals about social media in 2016*. Presentation

at the Texas A&M University conference on Making Sense of the 2016 Elections. Though Trump reportedly had more Facebook and Twitter followers than Clinton during the campaign, a large proportion were *bots* (fake accounts); see Salkowitz, R. (2017, January 17). Trump's 20 million twitter followers get smaller under the microscope. *Forbes.* http://www.forbes.com/sites/robsalkowitz/2017/01/17/trumps-20-million-twitter-followers-get-smaller-under-the-microscope/#6256e134675b; for data and figures comparing Trump and Clinton activity on Facebook and Twitter, see Zhang, F., Stromer-Galley, J., Tanupabrungsun, S., Hegde, Y., McCracken, N., & Hemsley, J. (2017). Understanding discourse acts: Political campaign messages classification on Facebook and Twitter. In D. Lee, Y. R. Lin, N. Osgood, & R. Thomson (Eds.), *Social, cultural, and behavioral modeling* (Vol. 10354). Springer. http://illuminating.ischool.syr.edu/#/platforms/1,2/dates/2016-11-01,2016-11-08/candidates/10,5/types/8&9,5&6.

10. Lapowsky, I. (2016, November 15). Here's how Facebook *actually* won Trump the presidency. *Wired.* https://www.wired.com/2016/11/facebook-won-trump-election-not-just-fake-news/.

11. Wesleyan Media Project. (2020, October 29). *Presidential general election ad spending tops $1.5 billion.* Author. https://mediaproject.wesleyan.edu/releases-102920/

12. Wesleyan Media Project. (2020, October 29). *Presidential general election ad spending tops $1.5 billion.* Author. https://mediaproject.wesleyan.edu/releases-102920/

13. Patterson, T. E. (2016, June). *Pre-primary news coverage of the 2016 presidential race: Trump's rise, Sanders' emergence, Clinton's struggle.* Shorenstein Center on Media, Politics and Public Policy. https://shorensteincenter.org/pre-primary-news-coverage-2016-trump-clinton-sanders/.

14. Patterson, T. E. (2016, June). *Pre-primary news coverage of the 2016 presidential race: Trump's rise, Sanders' emergence, Clinton's struggle.* Shorenstein Center on Media, Politics and Public Policy. https://shorensteincenter.org/pre-primary-news-coverage-2016-trump-clinton-sanders/.

15. Patterson, T. E. (2016, June). *Pre-primary news coverage of the 2016 presidential race: Trump's rise, Sanders' emergence, Clinton's struggle.* Shorenstein Center on Media, Politics and Public Policy. https://shorensteincenter.org/pre-primary-news-coverage-2016-trump-clinton-sanders/.

16. Bartels, L. M. (1985). Expectations and preferences in presidential nominating campaigns. *American Political Science Review*, 79(September), 804–815. The importance of the winner image is discussed in Brady, H. E., & Johnston, R. (1987). What's the primary message: Horse race or issue journalism? In G. R. Orren & N. W. Polsby (Eds.), *Media and momentum: The New Hampshire primary and nomination politics.* Chatham House.

17. Skelley, G. (2019, December 9). Who's leading the democratic primary in the first four states? *FiveThirtyEight*. https://fivethirtyeight.com/features/whos-leading-the-democratic-primary-in-the-first-four-states/

18. As frontrunner, Romney attacked from all sides. (2011, June 10). *Fox News*. http://www.foxnews.com/politics/2011/06/10/romneys-frontrunner-status-draws-attacks-from-all-sides.html

19. Madhani, A., Albertson, T. K., & Norvell, K. (2019, April 30). Joe Biden is the 2020 Democratic front-runner. Now he has a target on this back. *USA Today*. https://www.usatoday.com/story/news/politics/elections/2019/04/30/joe-biden-enters-2020-frontrunner-top-democratic-target/3617895002/

20. Walsh, D. (2016, September 20). Donald Trump, the unsinkable candidate. *The New York Times*. https://www.nytimes.com/2016/09/21/world/americas/donald-trump-the-unsinkable-candidate.html?_r=0.

21. For analysis of the impact of debates, see Lanoue, D. J., & Schrott, P. (1991). *The joint press conference: The history, impact, and prospects of American presidential debates* Greenwood. Also see Trent J. S., & Friedenberg, R. V. (2008). *Political campaign communication: Principles and practices* (6th ed.). Rowman and Littlefield; Kraus, S. (2000). *Televised presidential debates and public policy* (2nd ed.). Erlbaum. Full texts of presidential debates can be found on the website of the Commission on Presidential Debates, http://www.debates.org.

22. The importance of looking "presidential" on the campaign trail, especially during debates, is discussed in Grabe, M. E., & Bucy, E. P. (2009). *Image bite politics: News and the visual framing of elections*. Oxford University Press. Also see Adato, K. (2008). *Picture perfect: Life in the age of the photo op*. Princeton University Press.

23. Quoted in Diamond, E. (1982). *Sign-off: The last days of television*. MIT Press, p. 175.

24. Svitek, P. (2021, March 18). Matthew McConaughey is flirting with a run for governor. But his politics remain a mystery. *The Texas Tribune*. https://www.texastribune.org/2021/03/15/matthew-mcconaughey-texas-governor/

25. Schram, M. (1987). *The great American video game: Presidential politics in the television age*. Morrow, p. 26.

26. Allison, B., Rojanasakul, M., Harris, B., & Sam, C. (2016, December 9). Tracking the 2016 presidential money race. *Bloomberg*. https://www.bloomberg.com/politics/graphics/2016-presidential-campaign-fundraising/; Donald Trump (R) winner. (2017, November 27). *Open Secrets*. http://www.opensecrets.org/pres16//candidate.php?id=N00023864; Zhang, F., Stromer-Galley, J., Tanupabrungsun, S., Hegde, Y., McCracken, N., & Hemsley, J. (2017). Understanding discourse acts: Political campaign messages classification on Facebook and Twitter. In D. Lee, Y. R. Lin, N. Osgood, & R. Thomson (Eds.),

Social, cultural, and behavioral modeling (Vol. 10354). Springer. http://illuminat
ing.ischool.syr.edu/#/platforms/1,2/dates/2016-11-01,2016-11-08/candi
dates/10,5/types/8&9,5&6.

27. 2020 presidential race. (2021, March 22). *Open Secrets.* https://www.opense
crets.org/2020-presidential-race/

28. Baum, L. (2012, October 24). 2012 shatters 2004 and 2008 for total ads aired.
Wesleyan Media Project. https://mediaproject.wesleyan.edu/2012-shatters-
2004-and-2008-records-for-total-ads-aired/

29. Campaign 2004 final. (2004). *Media Monitor, 18*(6), 9; Holmwood, L. (2008,
October 20). Sarah Palin helps *Saturday Night Live* to best ratings in 14 years.
The Guardian. http://www.guardian.co.uk/media/2008/oct/20/ustelevision-
tvratings

30. Campaign 1996: The primaries. (1996). *Media Monitor* (March–April), 2.

31. Patterson, T. E. (2016, June). *Pre-primary news coverage of the 2016 presidential
race: Trump's rise, Sanders' emergence, Clinton's struggle.* Shorenstein Center on
Media, Politics and Public Policy. https://shorensteincenter.org/pre-primary-
news-coverage-2016-trump-clinton-sanders/.

32. Patterson, T. E. (2020, December). A tale of two elections: CBS and Fox News'
portrayal of the 2020 presidential campaign. *Shorenstein Center on Media,
Politics and Public Policy.* https://shorensteincenter.org/patterson-2020-elec
tion-coverage/.

33. Patterson, T. E. (2016, December 7). News coverage of the 2016 general election: How the press failed the voters. *Shorenstein Center on Media, Politics and
Public Policy.* https://shorensteincenter.org/news-coverage-2016-general-
election/.

34. Geer, J. G. (2012). The news media and the rise of negativity in presidential
campaigns. *PS: Political Science & Politics, 45*(3), 422–427; Kreiss, D. (2016).
Prototype politics: Technology-intensive campaigning and the data of democracy.
Oxford University Press; Stromer-Galley, J. (2017, February 4). *Trump's tweets
and other tremendous tales: What the illuminating 2016 project reveals about social
media in 2016.* Presentation at the Texas A&M University conference on
Making Sense of the 2016 Elections.

35. See more detailed discussion of elections in Chapter 12; for in-depth treatments of the evolving power of digital campaign strategies and their impact,
see Kreiss, D. (2012). *Taking our country back: The crafting of networked politics
from Howard Dean to Barack Obama.* Oxford University Press; Stromer-Galley, J.
(2019). *Presidential campaigning in the internet age.* Oxford University Press;
Kreiss, D. (2016). *Prototype politics: Technology-intensive campaigning and the
data of democracy.* Oxford University Press.

36. Druckman, J. N., Kifer, Martin, J. K., Parkin, M., & Montes, I. (2017). An inside view of congressional campaigning on the Web. *Journal of Political Marketing*, 442–475. https://doi.org/10.1080/15377857.2016.1274279

37. Edgerly, S. L., Bode, L., Kim, Y. M., & Shah, D. V. (2013). Campaigns go social: Are Facebook, YouTube and Twitter changing elections? In T. Ridout (Ed.), *New directions in media and politics*. Routledge; Kreiss, D. (2012). *Taking our country back: The crafting of networked politics from Howard Dean to Barack Obama*. Oxford University Press.

38. Stromer-Galley, J. (2019). *Presidential campaigning in the Internet age*. Oxford University Press.

39. Lapowsky, I. (2016, November 15). Here's how Facebook *actually* won the Trump presidency. *Wired*. https://www.wired.com/2016/11/facebook-won-trump-election-not-just-fake-news

40. For evidence and examples from the 2016 election cycle, see Lapowsky, I. (2016, November 15). Here's how Facebook *actually* won the Trump presidency. *Wired*. https://www.wired.com/2016/11/facebook-won-trump-election-not-just-fake-news

41. Wallsten, K. (2010). "Yes We Can": How online viewership, blog discussion, campaign statements, and mainstream media coverage produced a viral video phenomenon. *Journal of Information Technology & Politics*, 7, 161–181; this section draws heavily on Edgerly, S. L., Bode, L., Kim, Y. M., & Shah, D. V. (2013). Campaigns go social: Are Facebook, YouTube and Twitter changing elections? In T. N. Ridout (Ed.), *New directions in media and politics*. Routledge

42. Harwell, D. (2016, March 25). How YouTube is shaping the 2016 presidential election. *The Washington Post*. https://www.washingtonpost.com/news/the-switch/wp/2016/03/25/inside-youtubes-explosive-transformation-of-american-politics/?utm_term=.bd1760d93dd0.

43. Feng, B. (2019, December 8). Does YouTube's data tell us a story about the 2020 democratic candidates? *Towards Data Science*. https://towardsdatascience.com/does-youtubes-data-tell-us-a-story-about-the-2020-democratic-candidates-69568d2b0ce5

44. Biden, J. (2020, August 27). *Keep up* [Video]. YouTube. https://www.youtube.com/watch?v=C3UsWMbUpF4

45. Moire, J. (2012, November 26). Facebook by the numbers: The 2012 presidential race. *AdWeek*. http://www.adweek.com/digital/facebook-by-the-numbers-the-2012-presidential-race/?red=af.

46. Goidel, K., & Gaddie, K. (2016, November 3). The Wildcatters: The Twitter candidate, social media campaigns, and democracy. *HuffPost*. http://www

.huffingtonpost.com/entry/the-wildcatters-the-twitter-candidate-social-media_us_581b5211e4b0f1c7d77c968d

47. Lapowsky, I. (2016, November 15). Here's how Facebook *actually* won the Trump presidency. *Wired.* https://www.wired.com/2016/11/facebook-won-trump-election-not-just-fake-news

48. Stromer-Galley, J. (2017, February 4). *Trump's tweets and other tremendous tales: What the illuminating 2016 project reveals about social media in 2016.* Presentation at the Texas A&M University conference on Making Sense of the 2016 Elections.

49. Bosworth, A. [Andrew Bosworth (Boz)]. (2020, January 7). *The NYT recently obtained a copy of a post I made to the wall of my internal profile within Facebook.* [Facebook post]. Facebook. https://www.facebook.com/boz/posts/10111288357877121

50. Cole, B. (2021, January 1). Donald Trump sent record 12,200 tweets in 2020, ends year with stock market boast. *Newsweek.* https://www.newsweek.com/donald-trump-record-12200-tweets-2020-stock-market-boast-1558415

51. MacGregor, S. C., Lawrence, R. G., & Cardona, A. (2017). Personalization, gender, and social media: Gubernatorial candidates' social media strategies. *Information, Communication, and Society, 20*(2), 264–283.

52. Stromer-Galley, J. (2017, February 4). *Trump's tweets and other tremendous tales: What the illuminating 2016 project reveals about social media in 2016.* Presentation at the Texas A&M University conference on Making Sense of the 2016 Elections.

53. Gross, J. (2012, November 12). 2012 was the breakthrough year for digital persuasion across 4 screens. *Google Politics and Elections Blog.* http://google-politics.blogspot.com/2012/11/2012-was-breakthrough-year-for-digital.html.

54. 2016 will be remembered as the first mobile election. (2016, September 15). *Forbes.* http://www.forbes.com/sites/quora/2016/09/15/2016-will-be-remembered-as-the-first-mobile-election/#f72903a5c505.

55. Bode, L., Lassen, D. S. Kim, Y. M., Shah, D. V., Fowler, E. F., Ridout, T., & Franz, M. (2016). Coherent campaigns? Campaign broadcast and social messaging. *Online Information Review, 40*(5), 1468–4527.

56. Bond, R. M., Fariss, C. J., Jones, J. J., Kramer, A. D. I., Marlow, C., Settle, J. E., & Fowler, J. H. (2012). A 61-million-person experiment in social influence and political mobilization. *Nature, 489*(7415), 295–298.

57. Edgerly, S. L., Bode, L., Kim, Y. M., & Shah, D. V. (2013). Campaigns go social: Are Facebook, YouTube and Twitter changing elections? In T. N. Ridout (Ed.), *New directions in media and politics.* Routledge.

58. Mitchell, G. (2009). *Why Obama won: The making of a president.* BookSurge; Zhang, E, Stromer-Galley, J., Tanupabrungsun, S., Hegde, Y., McCracken, N., & Hemsley, J. (2017). Understanding discourse acts: Political campaign messages classification on Facebook and Twitter. In D. Lee, Y. R. Lin, N. Osgood, & R. Thomson (Eds.), *Social, cultural, and behavioral modeling* (Vol. 10354). Springer. http://illuminating.ischool.syr.edu/#/platforms/1,2/dates/2016-11-01,2016-11-08/candidates/10,5/types/8&9,5&6.

59. YouTube. (n.d.). *2016 debates on YouTube* [YouTube search]. YouTube. https://www.youtube.com/results?search_query=2016+debates+on+youtube.

60. Stromer-Galley, J. (2019). *Presidential campaigning in the internet age.* Oxford University Press; Kreiss, D. (2016). *Prototype politics: Technology-intensive campaigning and the data of democracy.* Oxford University Press.

61. The Federal Election Commission reports precise numbers about campaign fundraising (http://www.fec.gov/disclosurep/pnational.do;jsessionid=70C52D202F168DEDA36F15C70CBA7B1F.worker3). It recorded roughly $722 million for Barack Obama and $449 million for Mitt Romney for the 2012 election.

62. Karpf, D. (2016). *Analytic activism.* Oxford University Press.

63. Digital political ad spending to skyrocket in 2016. (2016, April 21). *Insider Intelligence.* https://www.emarketer.com/Article/Digital-Political-Ad-Spending-Skyrocket-2016/1013861

64. Wesleyan Media Project. (2020, October 29). *Presidential general election ad spending tops $1.5 billion.* Author, Table 2. https://mediaproject.wesleyan.edu/releases-102920/#table2. Estimates for TV, cable and radio are from Kantar/CMAG with analysis by the Wesleyan Media Project. Digital spending totals come from Wesleyan Media Project analysis of the Facebook Ad Library, Google Transparency Reports, and the Snapchat Political Ads Library.

65. Kaye, K. (2012, August 19). Obama outspends Mitt Romney on digital ads 4:1. *HuffPost.* http://www.huffingtonpost.com/2012/08/19/2012-ads_n_1808383.html; Stampler, L. (2012, November 5). Obama spent more on online ads than it cost to build the Lincoln Memorial. *Business Insider.* http://www.businessinsider.com/infographic-obama-romney-final-ad-spend-2012-11; Geer, J. G. (2012, November 9). Were the Romney and Obama TV ads a total waste? *Daily Beast.* http://www.thedailybeast.com/articles/2012/11/09/were-the-romney-and-obama-tv-ads-a-total-waste.html

66. Barthel, M., Mitchell, A., Asare-Marfo, D., Kennedy, C., & Worden, K. (2020, December 7). Assessing different survey measurement approaches for news consumption. *Pew Research Center.* https://www.journalism.org/2020/12/08/assessing-different-survey-measurement-approaches-for-news-consumption/pj_2020-12-08_news-consumption_2-04/

67. Extensive election data are archived at the Annenberg School for Communication in Philadelphia, the Shorenstein Center at Harvard University's Kennedy School, the Brookings Institution, and the Pew Internet and American Life Project. In addition, the Cooperative Campaign Analysis Project undertook a six-wave panel study of the 2008 campaign, conducting more than 100,000 online interviews. It is part of the YouGov/Polimetrix cooperative studies. For one of the first major attempts to study the full campaign cycle, covering multiple phases of the 1992 presidential campaign, see Just, M. R., Crigler, A. N., Alger, D. E., & Cook, T. E. (1996). *Crosstalk: Citizens, candidates, and the media in a presidential campaign.* University of Chicago Press.

68. For a useful discussion of the interplay between news media and political advertising contexts, see Geer, J. G. (2012, June 12). The news media and the rise of negativity in presidential campaigns. *PS: Political Science & Politics, 45*(3).

69. Weber, C. R., Dunaway, J., & Johnson, T. (2012). It's all in the name: Source cue ambiguity and the persuasive appeal of campaign ads. *Political Behavior, 34*(3), 561–584; Brooks, D. J., & Murov, M. (2012, May). Assessing accountability in a post–citizens united era: The effects of attack ad sponsorship by unknown independent groups. *American Politics Research, 40,* 383–418.

70. Daron R. Shaw, Green, D. P., & Gimpel, J. G. (2012). Do robotic calls from credible sources influence voter turnout or vote choice? Evidence from a large-scale randomized experiment. *Journal of Political Marketing, 11*(4), 231–245; Panagopoulos, C., & Green, D. P. (2008). Field experiments testing the impact of radio advertisements on electoral competition. *American Journal of Political Science, 52*(1), 156–168.

71. Neuman, W. R., Just, M., & Crigler, A. (1992). *Common knowledge: News and the construction of political meaning.* University of Chicago Press, pp. 39–59; Just, M. R., Crigler, A. N., Alger, D. E., & Cook, T. E.(1996). *Crosstalk: Citizens, Candidates, and the Media in a Presidential Campaign.* University of Chicago Press, pp. 62–66; West, D. M. (2009). *Air wars: Television advertising in election campaigns, 1952–2008* (5th ed.). CQ Press; Stromer-Galley, J. (2017, February 4). *Trump's tweets and other tremendous tales: What the illuminating 2016 project reveals about social media in 2016.* Presentation at the Texas A&M University conference on Making Sense of the 2016 Elections; Kreiss, D. (2016). *Prototype politics: Technology-intensive campaigning and the data of democracy.* Oxford University Press.

72. Gronbeck, B. E. (1989). Mythic portraiture in the 1988 Iowa presidential caucus bio-ads. *American Behavioral Scientist, 33,* 351–364; Payne, J. G., Marlier, J., & Baucus, R. A. (1989). Polispots in the 1988 presidential primaries. *American Behavioral Scientist, 33,* 365–381; Ridout, T. N., & Franz, M. (2011). *The persuasive power of campaign advertising.* Temple University Press.

73. Robinson, M. J. (1981). The media in 1980: Was the message the message? In A. Ranney (Ed.), *The American elections of 1980*. American Enterprise Institute, p. 186.

74. Allison, B., Rojanasakul, M., Harris, B., & Sam, C. (2016, December 9). Tracking the 2016 presidential money race. *Bloomberg*. https://www.bloomberg.com/politics/graphics/2016-presidential-campaign-fundraising/; Donald Trump (R) winner. (2017, November 27). *Open Secrets*. http://www.opensecrets.org/pres16//candidate.php?id=N00023864

75. Iyengar, S., Norpoth, H., & Han, K. S. (2004). Consumer demand for election news: The horse race sells. *Journal of Politics*, 66(1), 157–175.

76. Gottfried, J. (2016, July 14). Most Americans already feel election coverage fatigue. *Pew Research Center*. http://www.pewresearch.org/fact-tank/2016/07/14/most-americans-already-feel-election-coverage-fatigue/.

77. For comparisons of coverage in Boston; Los Angeles; Fargo–Moorhead, North Dakota; and Winston-Salem, North Carolina, see Just, M. R., Crigler, A. N., Alger, D. E., & Cook, T. E.(1996). *Crosstalk: Citizens, candidates, and the media in a presidential campaign*. University of Chicago Press, pp. 92–96; also see State of the news media 2009. (2010). *Pew Project for Excellence in Journalism*. http://www.stateofthemedia.org/2009.

78. Dunaway, J., & Stein, R. M. (2013). Early voting and campaign news coverage. *Political Communication*, 30(2), 278–296; Darr, J. P. (2016). Presence to press: How campaigns earn local media. *Political Communication*, 33(3), 503–522.

79. Dunaway, J. (2008). Markets, ownership, and the quality of campaign news coverage. *Journal of Politics*, 70(4), 1193–1202; Dunaway, J., & Lawrence, R. G. (2015). What predicts the game frame? Media ownership, electoral context, and campaign news. *Political Communication*, 32(1), 43–60; Iyengar, S., Norpoth, H., & Han, K. S. (2004). Consumer demand for election news: The horse race sells. *Journal of Politics*, 66(1), 157–175.

80. YouTube: A new kind of visual news. (2012, July 17). *Pew Project for Excellence in Journalism*. https://www.youtube.com/watch?v=SpvwpYKFzuY.

81. Dunaway, J., & Stein, R. M. (2013). Early voting and campaign news coverage. *Political Communication*, 30(2), 278–296; Darr, J. P. (2016). Presence to press: How campaigns earn local media. *Political Communication*, 33(3), 503–522.

82. Ridout, T. N., & Smith, G. R. (2008). Free advertising: How the media amplify campaign messages. *Political Research Quarterly*, 61(4), 598–608; Dunaway, J., & Stein, R. M. (2013). Early voting and campaign news coverage. *Political Communication*, 30(2), 278–296.

83. Dunaway, J., & Stein, R. M. (2013). Early voting and campaign news coverage. *Political Communication*, 30(2), 278–296. Rosenstiel, T. (2005). Political polling

and the new media culture: A case of more being less. *Public Opinion Quarterly*, 69(5), 698–715.

84. Geer, J. G. (2012, June 12). The news media and the rise of negativity in presidential campaigns. *PS: Political Science & Politics, 45*(3). For an example of campaign coverage of Trump's tweets, see Jacobs, J., & Cirilli, K. (2016, September 30). Trump tweets about sex tape as campaign struggles to regroup. *Bloomberg.* https://www.bloomberg.com/news/articles/2016-09-30/trump-tweets-about-sex-tape-as-campaign-struggles-to-regroup

85. Graber, D. A., & Weaver, D. (1996). Presidential performance criteria: The missing element in election coverage. *Harvard International Journal of Press/Politics, 1*(Winter), 7–32. A companion analysis of the 2000 election yielded similar findings.

86. Scriber, B. (2016, September 8). Who decides what's true in politics? A history of the rise of political fact-checking. http://www.poynter.org/2016/who-decides-whats-true-in-politics-a-history-of-the-rise-of-political-fact-check ing/429326/; Nyhan, B., & Reifler, J. (2015). Displacing misinformation about events: An experimental test of causal corrections. *Journal of Experimental Political Science, 2,* 81–93; Nyhan, B., & Reifler, J. (2010). When corrections fail: The persistence of political misperceptions. *Political Behavior, 32*(2), 303–330; Nyhan, B., & Reifler, J. (2012). Misinformation and fact-checking: Research findings from social science. New America Foundation; Nyhan, B., Reifler, J., & Ubel, P. (2013). The hazards of correcting myths about healthcare reform. *Medical Care, 51*(2), 127–132. Dunaway, J. L., Davis, N. T., Padgett, J., & Scholl, R. M. (2015). Objectivity and information bias in campaign news. *Journal of Communication, 65*(5), 770–792.

87. Winning the media campaign 2012. (2012, November 2, 2012). *Pew Research Center.* https://www.pewresearch.org/journalism/2012/11/02/winning-media-campaign-2012/; Patterson, T. E. (2016, December 7). News coverage of the 2016 general election: How the press failed the voters. *Shorenstein Center on Media, Politics and Public Policy.* https://shorensteincenter.org/news-coverage-2016-general-election/.

88. Patterson, T. E. (2020, December). A tale of two elections: CBS and Fox News' portrayal of the 2020 presidential campaign. *Shorenstein Center on Media, Politics and Public Policy.* https://shorensteincenter.org/patterson-2020-elec tion-coverage/

89. Quoted in King, A. (1982). How not to select presidential candidates: A view from Europe. In A. Ranney (Ed.), *The American elections of 1980.* American Enterprise Inst. for Public Policy Research, p. 305.

90. Dunaway, J. (2013). Media ownership and story tone in campaign news coverage. *American Politics Research, 41,* 24–53; Geer, J. G. (2012, June 12). The news media and the rise of negativity in presidential campaigns. *PS: Political Science & Politics, 45*(3).

91. Lichter, S. R. (2001). A plague on both parties: Substance and fairness in TV election news. *Press/Politics*, 6(3), 12.

92. Patterson, T. E. (2016, December 7). News coverage of the 2016 general election: How the press failed the voters. *Shorenstein Center on Media, Politics and Public Policy*. https://shorensteincenter.org/news-coverage-2016-general-election/.

93. Patterson, T. E. (2016, December 7). News coverage of the 2016 general election: How the press failed the voters. *Shorenstein Center on Media, Politics and Public Policy*. https://shorensteincenter.org/news-coverage-2016-general-election/.

94. Patterson, T. E. (2016, December 7). News coverage of the 2016 general election: How the press failed the voters. *Shorenstein Center on Media, Politics and Public Policy*, p. 12. https://shorensteincenter.org/news-coverage-2016-general-election/.

95. Iyengar, S., Norpoth, H., & Han, K. S. (2004). Consumer demand for election news: The horse race sells. *Journal of Politics*, 66(1), 157–175.

96. Robinson, M. J. (1981). The media in 1980: Was the message the message? In A. Ranney (Ed.), *The American elections of 1980*. American Enterprise Institute, p. 191.

97. Chozick, A. (2016, September 10). Hillary Clinton calls many Trump supporters "deplorables," and GOP pounces. *The New York Times*. https://www.nytimes.com/2016/09/11/us/politics/hillary-clinton-basket-of-deplorables.html?_r=0; Lee, M. Y. H. (2015, July 8). Donald Trump's false claims linking Mexican immigrants and crime. *The Washington Post*. https://www.washingtonpost.com/news/fact-checker/wp/2015/07/08/donald-trumps-false-comments-connecting-mexican-immigrants-and-crime/?utm_term=.09d39656b9b6

98. Crowley, J. (2020, January 15). Joe Biden's biggest gaffes in his 2020 campaign. *Newsweek*. https://www.newsweek.com/joe-biden-2020-gaffes-campaign-1482189

99. For an interesting discussion of the special concerns involved in covering African American candidates, see Dates, J. L., & Gandy, O. H., Jr. (1985). How ideological constraints affected coverage of the Jesse Jackson campaign. *Journalism Quarterly*, 62(Autumn), 595–600.

100. St. Dizier, B. (1985). The effect of newspaper endorsements and party identification on voting choice. *Journalism Quarterly*, 62(Autumn), 589–594.

101. Ulbig, S. G. (2013). *Vice presidents, presidential elections, and the media*. First Forum Press.

102. Low marks for major players in 2016 election—including the winner: Voters' evaluations of the campaign. (2016, November 21). *Pew Research Center*. http://www.people-press.org/2016/11/21/voters-evaluations-of-the-campaign/

103. Auxier, B. (2020, October 15). 64% of Americans say social media have a mostly negative effect on the way things are going in the U.S. today. *Pew Research Center.* https://www.pewresearch.org/fact-tank/2020/10/15/64-of-americans-say-social-media-have-a-mostly-negative-effect-on-the-way-things-are-going-in-the-u-s-today/

104. For a more detailed discussion of the quality of the information supply and its adequacy for informing voters, see Graber, D. A. (2003). The media and democracy: Beyond myths and stereotypes. *Annual Review of Political Science*, 6, 139–160; Graber, D. A. (2004). Mediated politics and citizenship in the twenty-first century. *Annual Review of Psychology*, 55, 545–571.

105. Patterson, T. E. (1988). *The mass media election: How Americans choose their president* (3rd ed.). Praeger, p. 250; also see Smith, E. R. A. N. (1989). *The unchanging American voter.* University of California Press.

106. Geer, J. G. (2012, June 12). The news media and the rise of negativity in presidential campaigns. *PS: Political Science 7 Politics, 45*(3).

107. Patterson, T. E. (1994). *Out of order*. Vintage Press; Cappella, J. N., & Jamieson, K. H. (1997). *Spiral of cynicism: The press and the public good.* Oxford University Press.

108. Farnsworth, S. J., & Lichter, S. R. (2007). *The nightly news nightmare: Network television's coverage of U.S. presidential elections, 1988–2004* (2nd ed.). Rowman and Littlefield; Patterson, T. E. (1994). *Out of order.* Vintage Press; Cappella, J. N., & Jamieson, K. H. (1997). *Spiral of cynicism: The press and the public good.* Oxford University Press.

109. Hamilton, J. T. (2004). *All the news that's fit to sell: How the market transforms information into news.* Princeton University Press; Mutz, D. C., & Reeves, B. (2005). The new videomalaise: Effects of televised incivility on political trust. *American Political Science Review, 99*(1), 1–16; Dunaway, J. (2013). Media ownership and story tone in campaign news coverage. *American Politics Research, 41*, 24–53.

110. Prior, M. (2009). Improving media effects research through better measurement of news exposure. *Journal of Politics, 71*(3), 893–908; Prior, M. (2009). The immensely inflated news audience: Assessing bias in self-reported news exposure. *Public Opinion Quarterly, 73*(1), 130–143.

111. Graber, D. A. (1988). *Processing the news: How people tame the information tide* (2nd ed.). Longman; Lodge, M., & Stroh, P. (1993). Inside the mental voting booth: An impression-driven process model of candidate evaluation. In

S. Iyengar & W. J. McGuire (Eds.), *Explorations in political psychology*. Duke University Press.

112. Hayes, D. (2008). Does the messenger matter? Candidate-media agenda convergence and its effect on voter issue salience. *Political Research Quarterly*, *61*(1), 134–146; Ridout, T. N., & Smith, G. R. (2008). Free advertising: How the media amplify campaign messages. *Political Research Quarterly*, *61*(4), 598–608.

113. For a wealth of detailed analyses of various aspects of the 2012 presidential election, especially outcome forecasts, see Wilson, P. (1983). Election night 1980 and the controversy over early projections. In W. C. Adams (Ed.), *Television coverage of the 1980 presidential campaign* (pp. 152–153). Ablex; Tannenbaum, P. H., & Kostrich, L. J. (1983). *Turned-on TV/turned-off voters: Policy options for election projections*. SAGE; Lavrakas, P. J., & Holley, J. K. (Eds.). (1988). *Polls and presidential election campaign news coverage*. Northwestern University Press.

114. For a discussion of how state laws have fared in the courts, see Bates, S. (1986). Lawful exits: The court considers election day polls. *Public Opinion*, *8*(Summer), 53–54.

115. Sigal, L. V. (1978). Newsmen and campaigners: Organization men make the news. *Political Science Quarterly*, *93*(Fall), 465–470; also see Hillygus, D. S., & Shields, T. G. (2008). *The persuadable voter: Wedge issues in presidential campaigns*. Princeton University Press.

CHAPTER 12

Incivility, Negativity, and Bias in the Media

Learning Objectives

1. Define the three major types of media bias and how common perceptions about media bias differ from reality.

2. Describe affective bias, where it comes from, and how commonly it is observed.

3. Identify information biases and their underlying causes.

4. Examine the various kinds of political media bias and their effects.

5. Indicate the root causes of media bias to understand when, where, and why they occur.

6. Explain the major societal consequences of media bias.

In February 2020, Bryce Randall, a contributing writer for *The Commonwealth Times*, wrote an opinion piece in which he lamented the vast amount of negativity in news. From too much front-page focus on Donald Trump to local news overemphasis on crime, corruption, and poverty, Randall described an all-too-familiar response to today's news:

> In the mass media, it feels like the front-page news stories are consistently tethered to President Donald Trump. I went to read *The New York Times*, and one of the first things I saw on their homepage was an article covering the president's impeachment sandwiched between one [article] on a doctor who studied the coronavirus and another about Pete Buttigieg at the Iowa caucus. Although these articles are covering relevant material, they present the same narrow selection of topics that the media has chosen to focus consistently on—politics and tragedy.

Randall also highlighted the scope of the negativity bias in news, noting that it is not limited to the major national news outlets but is present in local news, too. "*The Richmond Times-Dispatch* is flooded with the same negative energy. I used to be a regular reader of the newspaper, but reading the same articles about local government and crime gets stale and, quite frankly, exhausting."[1]

Past research identifies similar trends, but the digital media environment is still in flux and is constantly changing in its diversity of content offerings, and the fluid digital media marketplace often obscures patterns of supply and demand. Is negativity in politics and news on the rise? Is political bias? If so, what are the causes and effects? Though many people perceive more negativity, incivility, and bias in political news today, these remain open questions in research on media and politics. In this chapter, we will examine what research reveals about patterns of negativity, incivility, and bias in the media and attempt to shed light on these important questions.

Perceptions About Media Bias

Research highlights three major types of media bias that are relevant to the interests of news consumers: *affective biases*—those having to do with the tone or emotional content of news, such as the negativity bias just discussed; *ideological* or *partisan bias*; and what political scientist W. Lance Bennett has called *informational biases*. First, we will discuss commonly held perceptions about media bias, and then we will examine each major type of media bias in turn.

When most people encounter the term *media bias*, they think about partisan media bias. Indeed, there is widespread debate about the extent to which there is ideological or partisan slant in the media. Citizens, the punditry, and journalists themselves have much to say on the topic. Many argue that the media have a liberal bias. This contention is usually based on the notion that most journalists are liberal. Others claim that the media have a conservative bias, citing corporate media ownership and assumed corporate (that is, conservative) policy interests. Yet much of these public discussions about pervasive ideological or partisan bias in the media are not supported by evidence. Prominent examples of the ideologically branded major cable networks aside, most claims about systematic, surreptitious media bias from the ostensibly neutral mainstream press are based on little supporting evidence.[2]

Even though a majority of journalists rate themselves as more liberal than the general public and even though corporations have conservative interests, the simple fact is that many of the norms and routines of making the news prevent opportunities for individual journalists, editors, or media owners to systematically slant the news. As media scholar Timothy E. Cook put it, "As scholarship has generally concluded, news making is a collective process more influenced by the uncritically accepted routine workings of journalism as an institution than by attitudes of journalists."[3] In short, the news values discussed at length in Chapters 2 and 3, rather than political values, shape the news. As a result, the two other major types of bias make it into the news on a more regular basis: affective and informational biases. More often than not, in mainstream news outlets, these biases are due to the effort in making the news more attention grabbing and appealing to audiences rather than to deliberate efforts of journalists to color the news with their own political perspectives. In the next sections, we will discuss affective and informational biases. We will then examine political—i.e., partisan and ideological—bias in the news.

Affective Biases

Politics seems to be increasingly negative and uncivil; news often reflects this. Pressure to grab the attention of distracted audiences and would-be political supporters reinforces the tendency of news media and politicians to rely on the human negativity bias when they want to be heard in the cacophony of the information environment. Cable news channels adopt opinion-based formats and deep benches of partisan pundits and guests who replay the contentiousness of national party politics in their televised exchanges. On the news, they rely most heavily on congressional leaders and members with polarized political views for quotes.[4] The politicians themselves engage in negative and uncivil exchanges through these quotes and on-air performances when given the opportunity. At other times, they make use of political ads and digital platforms to launch their attacks or defend their claims, hoping all the while that their posturing will earn attention from the mass public and free coverage from the press. Popular entertainment programs depict the nation's leaders as inept and morally bankrupt or as buffoons in political satire on television and social media (Photo 12-1). Meanwhile, when members of the public are asked about politics, they are increasingly likely to express hostility and anger toward people and politicians on the other side of the political spectrum.[5] These trends lead us to wonder: How much of the negativity originates with decision making by the media? How much comes from politicians themselves? Do affective biases in the news foster contentious politics, or do they simply reflect current trends in elite politics? How much of what we see across the many forms of news is actually negative?

Saturday Night Live - SNL ✓
@nbcsnl
···

Joe and Kamala have a message for Donald Trump.

🔗 **Watch now at youtube.com**

▶ 7.7M views   0:27 / 0:28 🔊 ⤢

12:39 AM · Nov 8, 2020 · Twitter Media Studio

43.5K Retweets   **15.2K** Quote Tweets   **184.7K** Likes

Photo 12-1 *SNL* **tweets about their election parody with Jim Carrey as Joe Biden and Maya Rudolph as Kamala Harris**

Saturday Night Live tweeted their parody of the 2020 election results. The tweet, which went viral, included a video of Jim Carrey as Joe Biden and Maya Rudolph as Kamala Harris, mocking Donald Trump in a ludicrous manner. Political satire like this can still affect the candidate's image despite the lack of truth in the parodied or exagerrated actions.

Source: Twitter, @nbcsnl

Negativity and Incivility in the News

The muddying of public figures is only one of the problems that stem from overly negative and cynical political news coverage. Stories about Hunter Biden's history of struggles with substance abuse, charges against Patriot's owner Robert Kraft for paying for sex, or House representative Ilhan Omar's divorce and alleged affair—all of these are part of the epidemic of scandals, controversy, and mudslinging that mars the nation's political landscape.[6] In each case, the media examined, interpreted, and judged incidents in the lives of the individuals, often regardless of the story's significance, truth, or private nature. Although the press in the United States (U.S.) is entitled to probe the lives and reputations of such public persons and the American public has a right to know about matters that are politically relevant, there is widespread agreement that the press is often overzealous in such investigations and destroys reputations needlessly. Newspeople have leverage over politicians and other public figures, and they can pressure public officials into action by threatening to publicize stories that these targets would prefer to conceal. Threats of unfavorable coverage can have major political consequences. Politicians often act or refrain from acting because they know that newspeople might publish damaging information. They especially dread adverse publicity from influential columnists. Threat of such coverage is one reason former president Trump's associate Michael Cohen paid $130,000 in hush money to adult film actress Stormy Daniels during the 2016 campaign. The payment was an attempt to keep her from disclosing a prior affair with Trump in the crucial final two weeks of the campaign.[7]

Attack journalism raises a number of important ethical and political issues, and it is only one source of news negativity. From the perspective of the people whose reputations and careers are dragged through the mud and often ruined, attack journalism raises questions about the privacy rights of public figures and the ethics of journalists who publish such stories even when the subject matter has no relevance to current or future job performance. Some journalists justify focusing on such incidents by claiming that they illuminate the individual's character. But many others admit that they are merely jumping on the bandwagon of competition. If others exploit the story, they feel compelled to feature it as well. That is hardly the epitome of ethical behavior.

Beyond injury to individual public figures, there are broader consequences. The risk of having long-past or more recent indiscretions exposed to public view or having offhand remarks elevated into major pronouncements sharply reduces the pool of people willing to make their careers in politics. Many talented people are likely to prefer the safety of private life over the merciless glare of unstoppable publicity in the public sector. For example, recent research shows that women in particular are less likely to run for office because of their perceptions about the harshness of the political environment; this contributes to the already disproportionately low levels of women in elected office. Recent research shows a similar effect among young Americans.[8]

"Gotcha" journalism and the cynical commentary and analysis often accompanying it also contribute to the public's growing cynicism about politics and politicians and erodes its respect for the news profession.[9] Finally, the extraordinary amount of media time and space devoted to mudslinging frenzies comes at the expense of other, more worthwhile news that may never be published. The old Greek admonition "everything in moderation" is relevant. Whenever attack journalism seems appropriate, the media should practice it. But there is never a need for feeding frenzies of journalists in sorry displays of pack journalism.

Experts blame news economics and the increasingly stiff competition among media outlets for rising negativity and incivility. The need to attract and retain audiences and the need for enough content required on round-the-clock radio and television fills long hours with emotional audience bait.[10] Economic pressures facing media organizations in the U.S. have only increased over time. The immediacy and availability of digital media platforms have only accelerated the pace of economic competition, potentially contributing to rising negativity.[11] Not only to do they add to the field of competition; citizen journalists, bloggers, and citizens who generate content are less bound by news norms of objectivity and their content is often more partisan in nature. But is it actually more negative?

Trends and Causes

Many people believe that negativity in media coverage of politics is on the rise. For example, media scholar W. Lance Bennett identifies two trends, one in which news content is more critical of government, politicians, and their policies while providing fewer news stories focusing on substantive issues. Another is more frequent exposure to journalistic tones of cynicism and negativity in political news coverage. Mark Rozell documents patterns of increasingly hostile news coverage of government since the late 1970s and refers to this time period as an "era of cynicism." Larry Sabato referred to the same time period as one of "junkyard journalism."[12]

However, recent research from political scientists Stuart Soroka and Yanna Krupnikov suggests reasons for optimism. Their work documents trends in negativity in news spanning the last two decades, as Figure 12-1 shows. Looking at the valence of over 300,000 news stories occurring over a period of thirty years, they find that preferences for negativity varies both over time and across people. Even as humans do have a negativity bias (which often leads to a preference for negative, sensational, and conflict-ridden news), contexts and individual differences can create demand for positive news. The demand for neutral or positive content tends to act as a counterweight to the demand for negativity, which results in a pattern of political news tone that tends to be self-correcting. Valence is very negative at times for sure, but it returns to periods of only mild negativity later. The authors conclude that despite frequent upticks in negativity, we are not in a downward spiral where the future of news is destined to be increasingly and overwhelmingly negative.

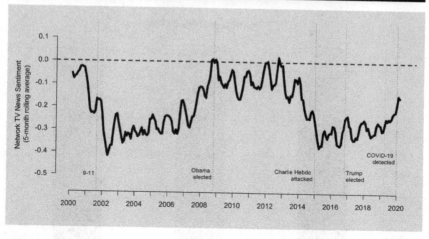

Figure 12-1   Negativity in News, 2000-2020

Source: Adapted from Soroka, S. N., & Krupnikov, Y. (2021). *The increasing viability of good news.* Cambridge University Press.

Note: The line shows a rolling center-weighted five-month average for all stories on national nightly news programs on ABC, CBS, and NBC. Sentiment is based on positive and negative word counts in the Lexicoder Sentiment Directory, as implemented in quanteda in R. Net sentiment is calculated as follows: log[(pos counts + 0.05) / (neg counts + 0.05)]. Graphic is adapted from data and analysis by Soroka and Krupnikov (2021).

Negative Campaigning

Besides perceptions of audience demand for it, what explains some of these periods of intensely negative political news? Political scientist John Geer attributes rising negativity in political news in part to increasing negativity in campaign messaging and political advertising. News media cover campaigns and elections and are likely drawn to more competitive—and often more negative—campaigns. However, he also notes that the media's penchant for focusing on the negative only further incentivizes negative campaign tactics for candidates seeking to earn free airtime.[13] Interestingly, despite high rates of attack advertising in the 2012 and 2016 presidential elections, the 2020 election saw a significant drop in the proportion of attack ads, despite a high volume of ads overall, as Figure 12-2 shows.[14]

In election coverage, news programs, commentary, and analyses now spend more time on what journalists are saying about races and candidates

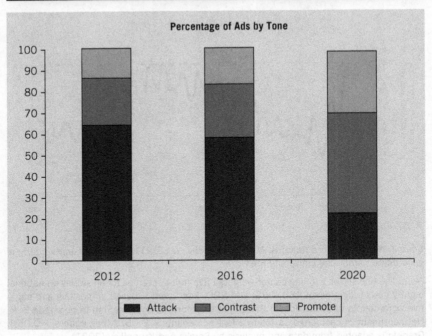

Figure 12-2 Tone in Presidential Advertising, 2012–2020

Percentage of Ads by Tone

Attack Contrast Promote

Source: Adapted from, Ridout, T. N., Fowler, E. F., & Franz, M. M. (2020). Spending fast and furious: Political advertising in 2020. *The Forum, 18*(4), 465–492. https://mediapro ject.wesleyan.edu/103018/

Note: Based on initial Wesleyan Media Project coding of Kantar/CMAG data. Totals include all sponsors, including outside groups.

while offering much less coverage of what the candidates are actually saying. Even when journalistic commentators (relative to partisan pundits) offer generally neutral analyses on mainstream news outlets, they are usually broadly negative in their comments and tend to make sweeping judgments about the statements and actions of public officials and candidates.[15]

Another reason for negativity and cynicism is the emergence and predominance of game frame campaign news coverage. *Game frame coverage* is news coverage of electoral campaigns and political issues cast in mainly strategic terms, focusing on who is winning and losing. Most game frame campaign news coverage focuses on conflict as part of the strategy or game, and much of it is also negative in the sense that it portrays candidates as scheming politicians willing to do nearly anything to win. As the game or strategy frame continues to dominate as a common campaign frame, we are likely to continue to see more emphasis on conflict and negativity in political news coverage.[16] Recent research also suggests another negative consequence of horse race coverage—as the analysis of polling is becoming more sophisticated, horse race coverage increasingly tends to confuse the public. The costs associated with the horse race do not seem offset by much informational benefit provided to voters.[17]

Some of the uptick in political news negativity can certainly be attributed to increasingly negative actions and statements of candidates, campaigns, and those already holding public office. Political scientists Daniel M. Shea and Alex Sproveri find that our history shows distinct periods of intensely negative politics, often coinciding with critical elections or times of economic crisis. In terms of the recent trends, each of their measures shows that descriptions of negativity in politics climbed since the 1980s. Susan Herbst argued that one explanation for historical surges in negativity and incivility is their use as strategic weapons to gain political advantage (on both sides of the aisle).[18] Mudslinging, after all, has been a staple in American political history, but then, what explains the apparent rise in negativity from political news media?

Other research examines more closely the relationship between politicians' strategic behaviors and political news. For example, research conducted by political scientist John G. Geer shows that negativity in presidential campaigns increased markedly during the time since the 1960s and that this uptick in negativity also coincided with rising party polarization. This seems to suggest that negativity in political news simply reflects the actions and statements of politicians, candidates, and campaigns. On the other hand, more recent evidence shows that broadcast and cable national news media provide speaking opportunities to extreme members of Congress much more often than to moderates, and cable news is especially guilty of this practice.[19] Obviously, newsworthiness and the effort to produce cost-effective and appealing political stories share some of the blame as well.

News coverage of political ads also increased sharply over time, and this is especially true for negative ads. Media scholars argue that the change in attention to ads (and negative ads in particular) can be attributed to the journalistic shift to analysis and interpretation, increases in game/strategy/horse race frames, and how well negative advertising lends itself to these types of coverage. In short, a main reason for the increase in political attack ads is that news media now cover these ads at such high volumes that in doing so, they actually create the incentive to produce more of these ads. As long as campaigns know they can earn free advertising through the media by generating outrageous attack ads, we should continue to see an increase in negative campaign strategy.[20] The 2016 and 2020 election cycles indicate that social media platforms such as Twitter can be used in much the same way. Outrageous and negative tweets from the major candidates were heavily reflected in mainstream news coverage.

Based on findings from statewide elections in the 2004, 2006, and 2008 election cycles, Figure 12-3 shows the relationship between the volume of attack ads in media markets and the likelihood of campaign news stories having a negative tone; the more candidates air attack advertising, the more likely that news stories about the race will be negative. Clearly, there is a reciprocal relationship between the strategic actions of campaigns and negativity, cynicism, and incivility in election news coverage. The cycle is supported by the economic pressures facing news organizations and the norms and routines of journalism that favor negativity, political analysis, and game frame news. Further exacerbating these trends are the emergence of super PACs (political action committees) as well-funded participants in the political advertising game and candidates' ability to raise unprecedented amounts of money, especially at the presidential level (see Photo 12-2).[21]

News Economics and Cognitive Biases

Negativity in political news coverage is also on the rise because it is appealing to audiences—put simply, it sells. Audiences are attracted to negativity for psychological reasons widely demonstrated across several fields, including economics and evolutionary and cognitive psychology. This negativity bias has implications for both media selectivity—the choice

Photo 12-2 Screenshots From 2020 Campaign Attack Ads

Source: The Museum of the Moving Image, The Living Room Candidate Archive of Presidential Campaign Commercials, 1952–2020. Ad attacking Biden (left) was paid for by Donald J. Trump for President. Ad attacking Trump (right) was paid for by Biden for President.

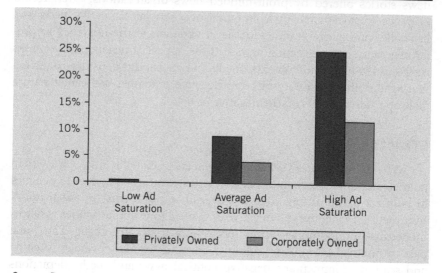

Figure 12-3 Probability of Negativity in Campaign News Stories by Volume of Attack Ads in the Media Market

Source: Dunaway's research, with Jason Turcotte, J. (2013, August/September). *Political advertising context and campaign news coverage* [Paper presentation]. The annual meeting of the American Political Science Association, Chicago, Illinois, United States. Based on analysis of 5,222 campaign news stories.

of what stories media promote from which sources—and for how much attention people pay to specific media messages once they are encountered. Research demonstrates that negative information has a more powerful influence on individuals than neutral or positive information. Generally speaking, individuals pay more attention to negative information for longer periods of time and give it more consideration than positive information when making decisions. Negative information is also more likely to grab the attention of most individuals than nonnegative information. Negative information is more memorable for most people. Research by political scientist Stuart Soroka and his colleagues demonstrates that this human negativity bias exists even cross-nationally—it is not specific to American or Western cultures.[22] From this perspective, it makes sense that newsmakers routinely focus on the negative. They need to attract and retain audiences and if negative news attracts and holds attention longer, it is better for the bottom line.

Not all the blame for news negativity should be placed at the feet of the news media, however; at least some of the blame should be reserved for the audience and their preferences. As long as negativity is more noticed, attended to, and recalled by audiences, it will be the dominant focus of news stories offered by profit-minded news organizations.[23] Yet, recent evidence from research by communication scholar Sarah Bachleda and her colleagues suggests individual-level variation in the tendency to prefer negativity when selecting news.[24] If the appeal of negative news varies across individuals and contexts, media outlets should consider balancing that against the possibility of other negative outcomes associated with a disproportionate focus on the negative in news.

Effects

Why does it matter? What are the effects of incivility and negativity in political news? Research links negative news coverage of politics to declines in political participation, trust in government, and trust in the media.[25] Information that conveys a negative or cynical tone about politics is harmful because it undermines citizen motivations to become engaged and take part in political life. From feeding frenzies to scandal coverage to snide and scathing commentary, negative political news and media depictions of political incivility are thought to have serious repercussions for the way citizens think about governmental actors and institutions.[26]

Though scholars acknowledge that negativity and incivility are common to American political life when viewed from a historical perspective, the advent of audio and visual media brings political conflict, negativity, and incivility much closer to our own experiences and emotions, making them much more likely to have an impact on our impressions. Several studies demonstrate that because media portrayals of political conflict are often viewed at close range, they generate emotional and negative responses among audiences, thereby lowering public opinions of leaders and government.[27] Research by Diana Mutz, for example, finds that even though political television provides the best opportunities for citizen exposure to oppositional viewpoints, the uncivil and "in-your-face" manner in which these viewpoints are often expressed detracts from the credibility of the speaker. Because of the uncivil presentation of information and the up-close intimacy afforded through political television and strategic camera angles, viewers have intensified negative reactions to political advocates from the other side. This intensified negative reaction reduces the likelihood of citizen viewers finding legitimacy in oppositional arguments.[28]

Until recently, researchers were surprisingly unified in their assessments that political incivility seen in the media has a negative impact on our evaluations of leaders and government. Other research also suggests that changes in the modern media landscape are apt to make this worse, such as the increasing economic competition among news firms, the emergence of 24-hour cable news networks, their branded ideological positioning, and popular opinion-show formats. Sociologist Sarah Sobieraj and political scientist Jeffrey M. Berry find that discourse intended to provoke a visceral response from audiences is extensive on political blogs and cable news analysis programs. Political scientists Richard Forgette and Jonathan S. Morris find that the high-conflict news formats commonly found on cable networks contribute to lower levels of public approval toward political institutions, lower trust in government, and lower levels of support for the political system (see Photo 12-3).[29] Samara Klar and Yanna Krupnikov describe how the constant media exposure to partisan disagreement means that many Americans are unwilling to admit to their partisan identities. Rather, they hide under the cloak of political independence in social settings and suppress their political preferences to withdraw from political engagement. Jennifer Lawless and Richard L. Fox find a potentially devastating consequence from the toxicity in the contemporary political information environment: Young people have high disdain for politics and vociferously deny any willingness to run for future office.[30]

However, evidence also suggests that the negativity bias—the human tendency to notice and pay attention to negative information more than neutral and positive information—manifests differently across individuals and contexts, producing nuanced political effects that can sometimes even be positive. Stuart Soroka demonstrates that people are more engaged and more attentive when news is negative. He downplays assessments that negativity is all bad, highlighting its use as a simple human mechanism for prioritizing information. Because democratic institutions are designed to capitalize on citizens' attention to negative information, negativity biases can produce reasonable political outcomes. Bethany Albertson and Shana Kushner Gadarian identify a nuanced process where in the face of constantly negative and threatening news, anxiety motivates learning by making people value information more heavily, prompting more intensive information seeking. In effect, negativity and anxiety can get a typically uninformed and unengaged citizenry closer to the democratic ideal, but it can also motivate anxious citizens to place trust in strategic politicians competing to offer policy solutions. That trust is vulnerable to manipulation and is sometimes misplaced.[31]

Information Biases

Information biases are also present in political news coverage; these biases—part of a larger category of selection biases—are important because they have to do with the quality of information citizens are getting from the news. Selection biases are those biases in coverage that come from decisions journalists make about what to emphasize in coverage, what information gets covered, and what information gets ignored. Political communication scholar W. Lance Bennett identifies four information biases commonly found in the American news product: personalization, dramatization, fragmentation, and the authority-disorder bias. Essentially, these biases matter because they have the net effect of removing important information, context, and perspectives from the news. Generally speaking, they all stem from the structure of our privately owned media system, which transforms political news and information into a consumer product.[32]

Personalization Bias

One way to make serious news stories more appealing to audiences is to personalize them, focusing on the human-interest side of a story through the lens of the individual rather than policy or political processes. This tendency is what Bennett refers to as the *personalization bias*. There are countless examples of the personalization of political news stories—one example is in coverage of a 2013 U.S. Supreme Court decision that struck down part of the Defense of Marriage Act, which defined marriage in a way that excluded gay couples from recognition.[33] Stories about the Court's decision often centered on interviews with individual gay or lesbian couples and focused on what the ruling would mean for their own personal circumstances. The angle of coverage was appealing and emotional, but most stories focusing heavily on personalized interpretations of the Court's decision missed the opportunity to discuss the broader societal consequences and what that meant going forward at the state and federal levels.

Dramatization Bias

Another common information bias Bennett identifies is the *dramatization bias*. Dramatization emphasizes the most sensational elements of a story over contextualized details about an event or issue. Personalization of a story often goes hand in hand with dramatization because the plights of individuals or groups are usually more easily dramatized than persistent political problems or complex policy processes. An example of dramatization is illustrated with this headline on the controversial immigration ban imposed by President Trump in early 2017: "Top Diplomats, Tech Giants Blast Immigration Order as Court Showdown Looms." The story attached to the headline was not heavily dramatized, but the body of many news stories are as dramatic as headlines such as these suggest. They often describe politics in terms of winning and losing political battles rather than focusing on the details of the policy proposal or issues that were in contention.[34]

Fragmentation Bias

One consequence of personalizing and dramatizing news stories is that related stories are often told in a manner that isolates them from one another; this is known as the *fragmentation bias*. Fragmentation is problematic because it can prevent citizens from having useful opportunities to fully consider the implications of broader issues and events. Coverage of the economy during the economic downturn of 2008—also known as the Great Recession—was heavily fragmented. For example, coverage of the subprime mortgage market often centered on individuals and families stuck in upside-down mortgages and facing foreclosure. Such stories were moving and compelling but failed to explain the mortgage market infrastructure and lending practices or connect these problems to the rest of the economy and the potential for recovery.

Media scholar Shanto Iyengar describes a phenomenon similar to fragmentation as "episodic coverage." According to Iyengar, episodic news stories are those that provide only a snapshot of an issue or event. He compares episodic news against "thematic news," which is more contextual, providing a broader view of problems, events, or issues. Illustrations of both types were found in coverage of two tragic examples of gun violence, the shooting of Congresswoman Gabrielle Giffords and several others at a public event in Arizona in 2011 and the 2012 mass shooting of students and teachers at Sandy Hook Elementary School in Newtown, Connecticut. Episodic coverage of these events entailed dramatic accounts of the events themselves and personal stories of individual victims and their families. Both events also prompted thematic stories; examples of these focused on the broader trends of mass shootings, state and federal gun laws, and the successes and failures of mental health diagnosis and treatment in the U.S. Iyengar's work on thematic versus episodic coverage links episodic news stories to the inability of citizens to accurately hold government and leaders accountable for causing or solving societal problems.[35]

Authority-Disorder Bias

The final information bias in Bennett's typology is the *authority-disorder bias*. This bias is concerned with leaders' ability to retain or restore order and is often seen in the context of a political event or natural disaster. Two prominent examples are from disasters that struck the Gulf Coast: Hurricane Katrina and the 2010 Deepwater Horizon oil rig explosion and gusher. As the devastation and aftermath of Katrina unfolded, coverage of President George W. Bush's response to the event raised questions about his ability to govern and restore order in the Gulf Coast. In 2010, questions about President Barack Obama's ability or inability to stop the Deepwater Horizon gusher and deal with its aftermath were central to an overwhelming proportion of national news stories about the event. The extended nature of the disaster made it particularly amenable to news frames about Obama's performance regarding the disaster—including whether, when, and how he would be able to stop the leak and deal with the environmental repercussions facing the Gulf Coast.

Political Bias

Political media bias is what most people think of when they hear the phrase *media bias*. Political media bias, or politically slanted news, refers to news content that appears to be partisan or ideological, leaning in one direction more than the other instead of being objective or neutral.

Media Bias in the Broadcast Era

Until the late 1990s and the rise of cable news, most news audiences and professional journalists viewed partisan or ideological news as something to disdain. Objectivity in reporting was central to the canons of American professional journalism and considered essential to being viewed as a credible and respected news organization. Partisan news, in other words, was not generally seen as a good thing. And research showed that mainstream media, for the most part, was free from systematic bias, despite rhetoric from pundits and politicians suggesting otherwise. Yet, what many people do not know is that historically, partisan media was not always viewed in a negative light. In fact, it has come full circle in the American press system. Newspapers first began as partisan papers, only to later move to the objective style of reporting we usually see today. The change was not prompted by the societal ills of partisan news. Rather, the movement away from the partisan press was inspired largely by the invention of high-speed presses and commercial pressures to appeal to the widest possible audience. Economist James T. Hamilton documents the shift as follows:

> To reach more readers, and therefore spread the high fixed costs across many consumers, newspapers stopped talking about politics in an explicitly partisan manner. Independent papers could draw readers from across the political spectrum. At the same time, advertising became an important way for companies with nationally and locally distributed brands to raise awareness about their products. Papers with larger audiences attracted more attention from advertisers, another incentive to increase readership. As a result, papers began to drop overt political bias and proclaim their independence in covering news of government and politics.[36]

During the broadcast era, research on media effects found biases emerging from the economic structure of the media (primarily information biases) much more often than it found bias from partisan or ideological slant in the news. When partisan slant was observed, it was usually in response to market demand for it. In other words, even when partisan bias emerged, it arose from market-based economic pressures rather than from the surreptitious persuasive efforts of journalists, editors, and media owners. Though researchers were still interested in understanding when and for whom media effects could be persuasive, polarization was not yet on the rise and research showed little evidence of media exposure producing major attitude change. And because most news outlets at the time were mainstream and operating under the norms of journalistic objectivity, research downplayed the need for a great deal of concern about systematic partisan news bias.

Partisan Cable News and the Internet

The broadcast era, however, was a very different technological and political context when compared to today.[37] The media environment offered much less choice—not only for channels and programs but also for platforms and devices with which to encounter and/or consume news. At that time, the combined national television market share of the three major broadcast networks comprised nearly 90% of the national television audience. And, at least in terms of news, they shared similar programming schedules. For several hours of the day, there was nothing but news to watch on television. The significant market share also meant relatively little competitive threat or need for content differentiation. The national news available to audiences across the three networks—and across most newspapers and radio programs, for that matter—was uniform relative to today. Mainstream news really was mainstream and, for the most part, objective. Additionally, polarization had not yet taken root to the extent it has today. At that time, the characteristics of the media environment and existing evidence about media bias presented no real urgency for researchers to be overly concerned about effects from partisan media bias.

The arrival and proliferation of cable, and with it the reemergence of partisan news, changed much of that. When cable arrived, it vastly expanded the choices available to media consumers. This had several important effects. First, it increased competition for audiences. Television news and newspapers were suddenly competing with countless entertainment offerings and cable news networks who could offer updated news on a 24-hour cycle. This newly fragmented market environment also created pressure for specialized or niche content offerings, including news. On the entertainment side, channels such as Comedy Central, HGTV, and

MTV emerged to meet the preferences of audiences who favor comedy, home improvement projects, and music videos. On the news side, first was CNN, which offered more international news and live late-breaking news and coverage on a 24-hour basis. Eventually, it was clear the market could accommodate specialized news, too. Rupert Murdoch capitalized on long-standing complaints about liberal media from politicians and pundits on the right and marketed the Fox News network as a "Fair and Balanced" alternative. In the wake of Fox News's enormous success, MSNBC, which originally began as a cable news network simply part of the NBC family, followed suit, making a significant left turn in programming and commentary, aiming to be the liberal cable counterweight to Fox News.[38]

The reemergence of partisan news, both in the form of cable television networks and via the numerous content offerings now provided by the arrival and proliferation of the internet, revived researchers' interests in persuasive media effects, especially with respect to the effects of partisan media bias. Partisan-leaning news is not only available in the expanded media environment; it is often actively sought out, especially by more partisan news consumers. These changes reinvigorated concerns about the ability for partisan media messages to persuade, in part because the fragmented media environment encouraged "echo chambers" in which individuals choose to consume news they agree with, limiting their exposure to news that is consistent with the prevailing attitude. In part because partisan polarization was on the rise by this point, many were concerned that echo chambers would encourage further polarization by reinforcing existing partisan attitudes and reducing exposure to arguments from the other side.[39]

Worry about these developing trends spawned scores of studies on the effects of selective exposure and partisan news consumption, many of which provided evidence showing that such concerns were warranted. The tendency to make media selections based on partisan preferences was demonstrated in many studies based on lab-based experiments. Still, evidence was inconclusive as to the extent to which people consistently seek pro-attitudinal information and avoid attitude-discrepant information.[40] Studies based on cable and network television audience data showed little evidence of isolated echo chambers, suggesting that people do not always select their party's brand of news, even if they do much of the time. And when it came to online news instead of television news, research based on Web traffic data showed quite a bit of diversity in the news sources consulted by online news audiences across the ideological spectrum; Web traffic was heavy and concentrated on popular, relatively neutral sites.[41] Other research emphasized how high levels of media choice also provide people who are not interested in news with something else to watch. So many entertainment channels meant that, unlike the broadcast days with only a few channels from which to choose, the fragmented media environment always provided something other than news to watch, read, or listen to. Because so many Americans prefer entertainment over news programming, this research suggested there was little reason to be concerned about the public exposure to biased, partisan news.[42]

Social Media

Even as research on the effects of partisan cable news and news websites seemed to downplay concerns about massive effects from exposure to politically biased news, ongoing changes to the digital media environment and still-rising levels of polarization retained researchers' interest in effects from partisan news. Algorithmic filtering via search engines, news aggregators, and social networking sites also contributed concerns about partisan echo chambers. These platforms are known for personalized content and their potential to create echo chambers or "filter bubbles." But research showed that evidence for filter bubbles and their effects was also mixed. Some studies showed partisan enclaves in the digital media environment, but others showed that high levels of choice and social networks actually encouraged exposure to more diverse content. For example, in their study of exposure to political information on Facebook, Etan Bakshy and colleagues found that exposure to agreeable information is more common than exposure to information from the opposition, but they also found significant amounts of exposure to cross-party content. Other research suggests that the social nature of these networking and peer endorsements help encourage exposure to diverse political perspectives and sources of news. The upshot of the research is that despite substantial evidence that echo chambers and filter bubbles exist to some extent, they are not complete partisan silos. Instead, these silos are prevalent but permeable when it comes to cross-ideological content, and they may even facilitate exposure to diversity. Nevertheless, research on media effects from social media exposure is still emerging and is not yet conclusive on the conditions under which effects from exposure to media bias—whether affective, informational, or partisan—are most likely to occur. Much of the developing research on effects from exposure to political information on social media is currently focused on misinformation, a topic to which we will return in Chapter 14.

Partisan Media Bias: Covert or Cognitive?

Although the public and many politicians seem quite convinced that the news media regularly and systematically exhibit covert partisan bias, scholars studying this question are not. The discrepancy can be explained in part by the numerous studies showing that political elites' claims about media bias contribute to the public perceptions about media bias.[43] It can also be explained in part by a phenomenon known as the *hostile media effect*, the tendency for partisans to view news coverage as biased against their own viewpoint.[44] The hostile media effect suggests that perceptions of media bias are often simply in our heads—a product of our own cognitive biases. As humans, we are more sensitive to perceiving information counter to our views as "biased" because we take information we agree with as simply being the truth. Cognitive biases make it difficult to take accusations about media bias at face value, but they also explain a lot about discrepancies between people's impressions about systematic media bias and actual evidence for it.

Much of the research on media effects focuses on cognitive explanations—perhaps as much as on media bias itself—when trying to understand whether and how exposure to news makes people more partisan and polarized. A lot of this work draws heavily from theories of motivated reasoning, which explain how our motives shape how we seek news and political information, what news sources we choose, and how we evaluate the information once exposed. According to motivated reasoning, people process information in ways that help them grapple with it, especially if the information seems contradictory to their previously held beliefs. Motivated reasoning suggests that for most people with strong partisan views, exposure to biased media messages will have minimal effects on attitudes because media messages slanted in an agreeable direction will simply be accepted and disagreeable information will be avoided or dismissed. Motivated reasoning theories cast some doubt on the ability for covert media bias to change hearts and minds—though because it might be less noticeable for those who are less informed, covert bias is more likely than overt bias (from branded cable news outlets) to have persuasive effects.[45]

Claims about pervasive effects from covert media bias also face skepticism from political communication researchers who no longer think media audiences are passive, a key factor underlying the concern that audiences are naïve and vulnerable to persuasion as receivers of partisan messages in the news. Of late, researchers are less convinced that people are passively persuaded by partisan messages. The dominant view now is that the effects of partisan media are more likely to occur through selective exposure behaviors (that is, actively seeking out like-minded news), which reinforce existing political predispositions. The active audience view also suggests that people who already hold partisan views are not easily moved to the other side. Those who may be politically agnostic and more persuadable actively avoid political information by taking advantage of the expansion of entertainment choices afforded through the current media landscape. Simply put, the active audience exhibits many characteristics and behaviors that suggest outright persuasion by partisan news messages is rare.[46]

Another reason why researchers have not broadly concluded that covert partisan media bias is pervasive is the difficulty in studying media bias and demonstrating it empirically. There are varying definitions and interpretations of partisan news bias, and there are also numerous mechanisms through which partisan media bias can occur—including selection bias, editorial bias, framing, terminology, agenda convergence, negativity, criticism, and narratives. Despite the lack of a scholarly consensus on the existence and effects of covert partisan media bias, recent findings suggest some patterns about the most common and persuasive types of partisan bias.

Editorial Bias

Several interesting studies have examined editorial bias, wherein bias in coverage about candidates, parties, and officeholders is linked to whether they were endorsed by news organizations.[47] In 2002, Kim Fridkin Kahn and Patrick Kenney showed that newspaper coverage of Senate races was slanted in favor of the candidate who received the editorial endorsement made by the paper and that the slant in coverage influenced voters' perceptions of candidates. In a 2006 study, Adam J. Schiffer also found evidence of editorial bias affecting news coverage, even after controlling for several other structural factors that could influence campaign coverage. A 2011 study by Valentino Larcinese and colleagues shows that newspapers that regularly endorsed Democratic candidates were less likely to provide coverage of bad economic news during the Bill Clinton administration than during the George W. Bush administration. On the other hand, a study by Daniel Butler and Emily Schofield found that newspapers were more likely to print letters from candidates they had not endorsed.

Selection Bias

Political news coverage is also often biased in terms of whose narrative or agenda is advantaged in the framing or placement of news coverage or commentary. Tim Groeling and Matthew Baum find that bias can occur through the selections news organizations make in terms of which partisan elites to quote. They examined which partisan statements from the Sunday news talk shows were cited in networks' nightly news programs. Matthew Gentzkow and Jesse Shapiro demonstrate that newspapers can exhibit partisan bias by adopting one party's preferred terminology in their coverage of issues. Research by Tim Groseclose produces estimates of news organizations' partisanship by tracking the frequency with which they refer to partisan policy groups, think tanks, and speeches by members of Congress. In a well-known study of the editorial and op-ed pages of *The New York Times*, political scientist Benjamin Page shows how selection bias in the editorial and op-ed pages can be constructed so that it falls in line with the editorial position of the paper. The findings from Page's study also illustrate how elite major papers such as *The New York Times* can shape major policy debates by constructing debate on opinion pages in ways that exert influence over public opinion and the nature and direction of national debate on critical issues facing the country, even ones as important as the decision to do to war.[48] These examples represent narrative or agenda partisan biases, where news organizations exhibit bias by letting one side frame the debate or shape the agenda or narrative more frequently than the other.[49]

Causes of Bias

The causes of all three main types of media bias (affective, informational, partisan) can be easily grouped into two categories, ideological and structural, though they sometimes bleed together, as in cases where it is financially beneficial to offer partisan news.

Political Causes of Media Bias

When ideology or partisanship is the sole cause of bias, it conjures the common image of media bias occurring through individual journalists slanting the news by inserting their own partisan views into the stories they submit or letting their partisanship influence what stories to cover. Bias can occur through journalists' choices about what to cover (selection bias) or through decisions about how to cover it (presentation bias).[50] Though research has shown this does not occur commonly or systematically, it certainly happens. When partisanship enters the news this way, it could be because reporters are biased and want to persuade readers to their viewpoint. Reporters may write with an ideological slant because they feel pressure to do so from colleagues or superiors such as their editors, producers or publishers, or company owners. Some research has shown that the culture within news organizations can sometimes shape the news through hiring, firing, or the editorial process wherein stories are rejected by editors until they reflect the preferred viewpoint.[51] This might be true of news organizations who've adopted clear partisan brands. Still, most of the research empirically documenting media biases highlights structural influences when it comes to mainstream news outlets.[52]

Structural Causes of Media Bias

There is more empirical evidence for structural bias in the news than political bias. Structural biases are those that occur because of the way our media system operates or the changing features of the media landscape. Earlier sections in this chapter suggested several of the structural causes for affective and informational biases commonly found in political news; we will elaborate further here.

The American media system is primarily market based. Most news organizations rely on revenue from advertisers trying to sell their products to consumers. This economic link between audience preferences and the economic success of news organizations is at the heart of structural contributors to media bias. Because they are market-audience driven, structural media biases are also referred to as *demand-side* explanations of media bias. Several prominent studies support demand-side explanations of news biases by linking economic motives and economic competition to news content.[53] This work identifies two specific media market characteristics that often influence news content: market competition for audiences and audience characteristics.

Market competition for audiences influences news content because more competition means that news organizations must work harder to retain their share of the market audience. As a result, the competition within media markets often produces more sensational and negative news as competitors scramble to appeal to the audience's tastes. John Zaller and R. Douglas Arnold find that market competition adversely affects the quality of information available in the news. John McManus demonstrates that because audiences have a preference for less-substantive news, journalistic quality runs counter to efforts toward profit maximization. In the electoral arena, Shanto Iyengar and colleagues demonstrate how the dominance of horse race coverage in election news is attributable to an audience preference for horse race election frames. Most work on this focuses on how audience demand and competition between news organizations influence the quality of political news content. The bulk of the evidence shows that the market incentives created by our media system are major contributors to the informational biases described above.[54]

Audience characteristics affect news coverage because certain groups have known preferences for news, and news content varies according to the programming preferences of these groups. This means that news organizations' attempts to please certain segments of their media markets could produce informational, affective, or partisan news bias. If a news organization is targeting younger viewers within its market, informational biases and affective biases may dominate because younger audiences often prefer more entertainment-based and more negative and sensational news. On the other hand, if it is targeting older, rural viewers in a southern market, news content may be information rich but slanted toward the conservative end of the ideological spectrum.[55]

Some research demonstrates these structural influences on partisan news bias by showing that political preferences among media market audiences contribute to politically slanted news coverage. David Baron's research describes a demand-side bias perspective, explaining how, with profit maximization in mind, news organizations may produce ideologically slanted news coverage in an effort to appeal to certain audience groups within the market.[56]

Similarly, research by several economists reveals that newspapers respond to audience demand for partisan or ideologically slanted news coverage, especially when they are facing competition within their markets.[57] Matthew Gentzkow and Jesse Shapiro demonstrate newspapers' responsiveness to audience demand for politically slanted news coverage by showing that papers are likely to adopt one party's terminology in their coverage when their media market is dominated by that party; they find that the newspapers' slant matches the partisan preferences of their market pool of potential readers. Sendhil Mullainathan and Andrei Shleifer suggest that economic competition between newspapers often increases political bias, arguing that under conditions of high competition, newspapers are more likely to cater to the political predispositions of their readers. They also contend that reader heterogeneity plays a role in determining slant in political news coverage. Specifically, they find that news slant is less likely to occur in diverse media markets because the preferences of the majority of the market are not as obvious, while in markets with clearly dominant political preferences, news organizations slant their news in a manner that caters to those preferences.[58]

Effects of Bias

Two major effects arise from the biases we have discussed: a general dissatisfaction with the media and decreasing trust in the media.

Dissatisfaction With the Media

The pace and direction of changes in the framing and distribution of news hinge heavily on how satisfied journalists and their audiences are with the current product. Dissatisfaction with U.S. mass media runs deep and wide. Journalists are increasingly disenchanted with their efforts, pundits regularly voice their disapproval, and audience voices also contribute the chorus of complaints.

The Journalists' Perspective

According to two surveys of journalists, most think that the profession is going in the wrong direction. Earlier surveys of journalists reflected this, too—for a long time, news professionals working for print, television, radio, and internet organizations expressed concerns about the steadily narrowing scope of news dictated by economic pressures. Today, they report that the three biggest problems they face are related to the economics of news. The first is a broken business model that leaves journalists insufficiently funded to do good work. The second is the same business model that causes media to pander to audiences. The third is the need to entertain or sensationalize in order to keep audiences interested. News investment is clearly a problem; ranks of legacy media have thinned markedly, and reporting staffs have been decimated, which is an ongoing trend. Fewer reporters with fewer resources equates to fewer news stories and a focus on simple stories, cheaply gathered close to home. It is no wonder that journalists also report lower levels of autonomy and job satisfaction. Pandering to audiences is frustrating for journalists because it usually means they cannot give much attention to complex stories and that they must entertain or sensationalize to keep readers interested. The lack of attention to complex and serious issues leaves journalists feeling as if they are less able to perform the watchdog function by holding the powerful accountable. Journalists also complain that there is a tendency to highlight or inflate conflict and showboating or "gotcha" journalism. In terms of credibility, they worry about the overreliance on anonymous sources and information that cannot be corroborated. Perhaps surprisingly, the answer provided least often was bias. In sum, journalists blame the economic model of news for most of what's plaguing journalism. The constant quest for audience attention leads to simplistic reporting and a demand for scandal, sensationalism, and conflict. Journalists also lament prioritization of speed over accuracy.[59] They want fewer factual errors and less sloppy reporting—wishes that are unlikely to be fulfilled in a digital media setting with a "publish first, edit later" mentality geared to giving voice to nonprofessional citizen reporters and to comments by random members of the audience.[60]

Declining Media Trust

A major consequence of all three types of bias is decreasing levels of public trust in the media. Political comedy shows, while entertaining and even informative, are cynical and often cast leaders and the media in an extremely unfavorable light. In addition, negative and vitriolic news coverage, partisan coverage, and politicians' attacks on the media contribute to a public distrust of the news. Declines in media trust were somewhat steady over the last two decades, as Figure 12-4 shows.

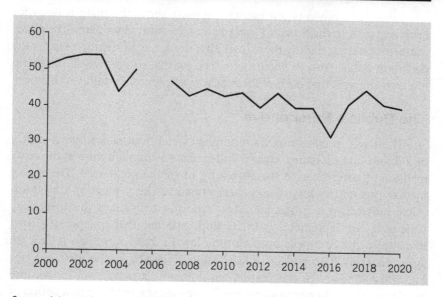

Figure 12-4   Americans' Trust in Mass Media

Source: Adapted from Brenan, M. (2020, September 30). Americans remain distrustful of media. *Gallup.* https://news.gallup.com/poll/321116/americans-remain-distrustful-mass-media.aspx

Note: Missing data point is because Gallup did not ask the question in 2006.

Table 12-1 News Professionals' View of No. 1 Reason People Distrust the Media More Now

	Percentage Giving Response
The media gets so much wrong	5.31%
Our public discourse is more politically organized	49.56%
General distrust of most institutions these days	20.35%
People think the media is in the pocket of corporate interests	5.31%
Other	20.35%

Source: 113 journalists surveyed on why they're so despised. (2016, July 24). *New York Magazine.* http://nymag.com/daily/intelligencer/2016/07/media-survey.html

Note: Based on a survey of 113 journalists working in print, television, and digital media; this sample is unscientific in that the editors sent the survey to a list of colleagues and selection methods are unreported.

Table 12-1 presents journalists' opinions about the main reasons for declining trust in the press.[61] Nearly half of the journalists blame the polarization of politics; slightly more than 20% think it is a function of generally declining public trust in institutions. The journalists are not off the mark; research suggests that both of these factors are almost certainly to blame.

The Public's Perspective

The flaws in current news reporting, which journalists blame largely on bottom-line pressures, clearly undermine the public's trust in the news media and contribute to the shrinking of media audiences. The legacy media's precipitous loss of audiences enhances the perception that traditional journalism is in trouble. Most crucially, consumers find news less believable. In September 2016, Gallup reported that the public's trust in news media dropped to an all-time low of 32%. Although it shot up again between 2016 and 2018, 2019 and 2020 saw further declines (see Figure 12-4). Though the drop is not dramatic, it is noteworthy because media trust was already low and has (for the most part) been in a period of decline over the last 20 years. Large portions of audiences believe that stories are often inaccurate and that journalists do not care about the people whose stories they report. Furthermore, the majority of audiences regard the news media as politically biased.[62]

The sizable discrepancies in believability assessments by Democrats and Republicans are also alarming. According to recent research by Pew Research Center, partisanship is the strongest determinant of people's trust and confidence in the news media. Republicans and those who lean Republican are less trusting of the news media overall, are more likely to express negative views about news media, and have low confidence in the news media relative to Democrats and those who lean Democratic. Republicans distrust news venues more than Democrats do thanks, in part, to the widespread and long-held belief among conservatives that the news bears a liberal imprint, as seen in Figure 12-5. Poll numbers from surveys of professional journalists add fuel to the fire. When asked about their ideological orientation, roughly six in ten journalists call themselves moderates, another three claim to be liberals, and only one in ten professes to being a conservative.[63] Justified or not, these answers support the fears of conservatives and make them prone to criticize the press. Ideology also plays a growing part in choosing particular news outlets. For example, Republicans flock to the conservatively oriented Fox News channel, while Democrats avoid it.

Using multiple data sources, research by Jonathan Ladd shows how public confidence in the news media declined at a faster rate over the last few decades relative to the average level of confidence in all other institutions combined; this decline occurred for both Republicans and Democrats. Research suggests that this declining trust in the media has consequences for the way people seek information.[64] As distrust in media increases, so does *partisan selective exposure*, the audience behavior of seeking like-minded political perspectives in news (introduced in Chapter 4). As one might expect, Democrats flock to news organizations accused of liberal bias; Republicans avoid those and obtain news from outlets charged with having a conservative bias.[65]

Ladd argues that several of the structural changes to the news media environment and the resulting informational, affective, and partisan biases are linked to declining levels of media trust. Declining levels of trust in the media coincide with the stiffening economic competition news media have faced since the 1970s. As discussed in Chapter 4, competition among news organizations typically yields lower levels of quality in political news and less media professionalism, opening the door for more criticism from political elites. This process is cyclical. As the public experiences more low-quality news and more media criticism from elites, they become distrustful of mainstream institutional media and begin to seek out more partisan news, which only serves to foster media distrust, partisan information seeking, and political behavior.[66] As changes to the

Figure 12-5 Partisan Differences in Trust and Confidence in News Media

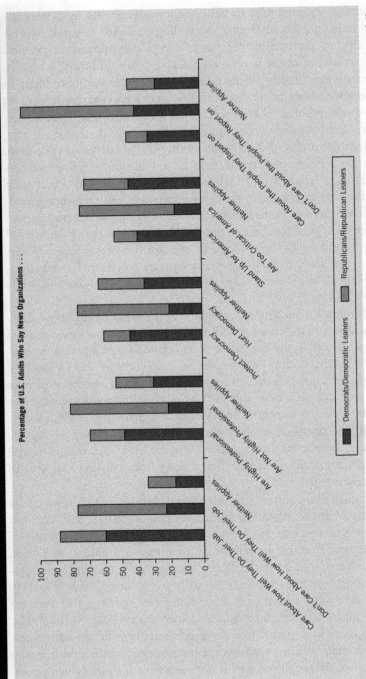

Percentage of U.S. Adults Who Say News Organizations . . .

Democrats/Democratic Leaners
Republicans/Republican Leaners

Source: Adapted from Gottfried, J., Walker, M., & Mitchell, A. (2020, August 31). Partisans remain sharply divided in many views toward the media; stark differences between Trump's strongest supporters, critics. *Pew Research Center.* https://www.journalism.org/2020/08/31/partisans-remain-sharply-divided-in-many-views-toward-the-news-media-stark-differences-between-trumps-strongest-supporters-critics/

Note: Data are from a Pew Research Center survey of U.S. adults conducted February 18–March 2, 2020.

Photo 12-4 Tweet from President Trump saying negative presidential approval numbers reported by mainstream media were nothing but fake news.

Source: President Donald J. Trump/Twitter.

media environment continue to unfold, research should have much to say about the implications of distrust in the media.

Campaigning Against the Media

To make matters worse, politicians are well aware of the public's declining trust in the media and take every available opportunity to gain voters' favor by campaigning against the media. Though this is a common rhetorical strategy of politicians, the 2016 presidential election and primary season was crowded with examples of candidate complaints about the behavior of the news media. As a presidential candidate, Donald Trump had numerous contentious public exchanges with the press, including a series of incidents in which he lobbed accusations of bias and unfair treatment against Fox News anchor Megyn Kelly. The saga began during the first Republican primary debate when Kelly, acting as debate moderator, asked Trump tough questions about whether "his history with women would be fodder for Hillary Clinton's claims that he was part of a 'war on women.'" Later, Trump publicly insinuated that Kelly was hostile during the debate because she was menstruating, and he spent the next several months launching sporadic tirades against her on Twitter and in live interviews in which she was referred to as a bimbo, a liar, and crazy.

The attacks on Kelly reflect an increasingly common strategy employed by politicians as public trust in the press continues to decline: attack the media in the face of scrutiny or unfavorable coverage. This particular feud was amplified by a context in which Trump was periodically accused of treating women badly while running a campaign against the first woman in American history to ever receive a major party nomination for the presidency. It pushed the bounds of acceptable levels of incivility (even by today's standards), was steeped in sexism, and extended to campaign surrogates and into the ranks of the Fox News network and political journalism more broadly. Given the context of the campaign and the ongoing allegations, Kelly not asking tough questions would have been seen as seriously neglecting her job, especially considering Fox News's position as a right-leaning news outlet. And yet, against the backdrop of today's

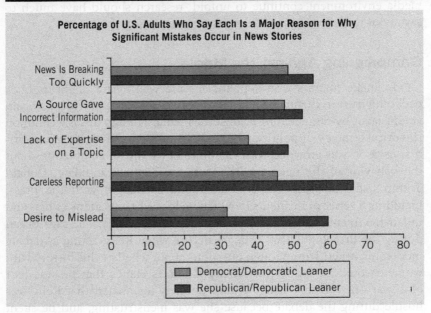

Figure 12-6 Republican and Democratic Assessments of Mistakes in News

Percentage of U.S. Adults Who Say Each Is a Major Reason for Why Significant Mistakes Occur in News Stories

Source: Adapted from Gottfried, J., Walker, M., & Mitchell, A. (2020, August 31). Partisans remain sharply divided in many views toward the media; stark differences between Trump's strongest supporters, critics. *Pew Research Center.* https://www.journalism.org/2020/08/31/partisans-remain-sharply-divided-in-many-views-toward-the-news-media-stark-differences-between-trumps-strongest-supporters-critics/

Note: Data are from a Pew Research Center survey of U.S. adults conducted February 18–March 2, 2020.

media environment and increasingly acrimonious politics, Kelly's reward for doing her job well was a series of publicly delivered insults.[67]

As the Trump administration transitioned into the White House, tensions with the press were still high. The early weeks of 2017 were marked by Trump accusing several news outlets of engaging in fake news (see Photo 12-4); President Trump's tirades against the press persisted throughout his entire term in office. In part a result of decades of these kind of cues from elite politicians and pundits (primarily from those on the right), media distrust is increasingly asymmetrical and reflective of negative partisan affect. Not only do Republicans have less confidence and trust in the news, but they are also more likely to think mistakes in news stories are intentional (see Figure 12-6).

Media distrust matters from a democratic perspective. Those who distrust the media are also less likely to turn to the media for new information. Rather, they rely on what they already think and their own long-held political beliefs, which fosters further reliance on news from their own partisan persuasion. Perhaps not surprisingly, then, media distrust also increases partisan voting and susceptibility to misinformation from political elites.

SUMMARY

There are three major categories of bias in the media: affective, informational, and political (i.e., partisan or ideological). Though the public is primarily concerned with partisan bias in the news, research identifies more systematic evidence for effects from affective biases and informational biases.

Affective media biases are those that have to do with the emotional tone or content found in political news, including negativity, incivility, and cynicism, all of which seem to be on the upswing in our political news. Affective biases are problematic because they foster disdain for our leaders and government and a general distrust of the political process, and they contribute to low levels of political engagement among citizens.

There are two main challenges to purging affective biases from political news. The first is their appeal to audiences, which is based on a human bias for paying attention to negative information. The second challenge to getting rid of affective biases is their link to the economic performance of news organizations. As long as news organizations are concerned about their financial health and as long as they perceive audience preferences for negativity, incivility, and cynicism, we are likely to continue to see affective biases in political news.

Informational biases are also pervasive; most stem from structural aspects of our media system and the norms and routines of news making. For that reason, informational biases are also likely to remain a staple of American political news. News that is personalized, dramatized, fragmented, and told within the framework of order versus chaos fulfills news production objectives and is easily digestible and appealing to audiences. The storytelling devices that result in these biases support the financial goals of news organizations on two fronts: They promote cheaply and efficiently made news and they attract and retain mass audiences. Unfortunately, these benefits normally outweigh the average news organizations' parallel goal of informing the public, which means the civic journalism model of news is rarely reflected in our political news content.

Partisan media bias may not be as much of a problem as public hand-wringing suggests, at least in terms of the secret partisan persuasion of audiences. First, the existing research suggests that systematic covert media bias is not as common as affective or informational biases. Second, even though the modern media landscape has fostered a newly emerging class of ideology- and partisan-branded news outlets, overt media bias is not entirely different from the opinion sections of newspapers—audiences know what they are getting. In fact, audience perceptions about the biases of ideological news organizations are so ingrained that audiences perceive bias from these outlets even when it is not present. More importantly, the preexisting preferences of audiences are strong enough to make outright persuasion difficult.

If we do see negative societal effects from partisan news, it is much more likely to appear in the form of political polarization and dissatisfaction with and distrust of the media.[68] To be sure, these are big problems to confront, but public worries about mass surreptitious persuasion by partisan media are probably not warranted. At the same time, changes to the information environment are happening so rapidly that research does not yet tell us definitively how concerned we should be about effects from the mass public's exposure to negative, superficial, or partisan news.

DISCUSSION QUESTIONS

1. How do common perceptions about media bias differ from reality? What are the major types of media bias, and which are most common? What is affective bias, and where does it come from? How commonly is it observed?

2. What are information biases? What kinds do we most commonly see? Why do they occur?

3. What is political media bias? What causes it? How well can we know it when we see it? How common is political media bias, and from what kinds of news organizations are we most likely to see it?

4. What are the root causes of media bias?

5. What are some of the important societal consequences of media bias?

READINGS ———————————————————————————

Albertson, B., & Gadarian, S. K. (2015). *Anxious politics: Democratic citizenship in a threatening world*. Cambridge University Press.

Arceneaux, K., & Johnson, M. (2013). *Changing minds or changing channels? Partisan news in an age of choice*. University of Chicago Press.

Baldwin, T. (2018). *Ctrl alt delete: How politics and the media crashed our democracy*. Oxford University Press.

Bednarek, M., & Caple, H. (2017). *The discourse of news values: How news organizations create newsworthiness*. Oxford University Press.

Bennett, W. L. (2016). *News: The politics of illusion* (10th ed.). University of Chicago Press.

Bode, L., Budak, C., Ladd, J. M., Newport, F., Pasek, J., Singh, L. O., Soroka, S. N., & Traugott, M. W. (2020). *Words that matter: How the news and social media shaped the 2016 Presidential campaign*. Brookings Institution Press.

Chadwick, A. (2017). *The hybrid media system: Politics and power*. Oxford University Press.

Dimaggio, A. R. (2017). *The politics of persuasion: Economic policy and media bias in the modern era*. SUNY Press.

Forgette, R. (2018). *News grazers: Media, politics, and trust in an information age*. CQ Press.

Hayes, D., & Lawless, J. L. (2021). *News hole: The demise of local journalism and political engagement*. Cambridge University Press.

Iyengar, S. (2018). *Media politics: A citizen's guide* (4th ed.). Norton.

Kerbel, M. R. (2018). *Remote and controlled: Media politics in a cynical age*. Routledge.

Klar, S., & Krupnikov, Y. (2016). *Independent politics: How American disdain for parties leads to political inaction*. Cambridge University Press.

Kuypers, J. A. (2020). *President Trump and the news media: Moral foundations, framing, and the nature of press bias in America*. Lexington Books.

Ladd, J. M. (2012). *Why Americans hate the media and how it matters*. Princeton University Press.

Levendusky, M. (2013). *How partisan media polarize America*. University of Chicago Press.

Mutz, D. C. (2016). *In-your-face politics: The consequences of uncivil media*. Princeton University Press.

Nadler, A. (2019). *News on the right: Studying conservative news cultures*. Oxford University Press.

Papacharissi, Z. (2015). *Affective politics: Sentiment, technology, and politics*. Oxford University Press.

Paul, R., & Elder, L. (2019). *The thinker's guide for conscientious citizens on how to detect media bias and propaganda in national and world news: Based on critical thinking concepts and tools*. Rowman & Littlefield.

Prior, M. (2018). *Hooked: How politics captures people's interest*. Cambridge University Press.

Peck, R. (2019). *Fox populism: Branding conservatism as working class*. Cambridge University Press.

Schiffer, A. J. (2018). *Evaluating media bias*. Rowman & Littlefield, 2018.

Schudson, M. (2020). *Journalism: Why it matters*. John Wiley & Sons.

Soroka, S. N. (2014). *Negativity in democratic politics: Causes and consequences*. Cambridge University Press.

Stroud, N. J. (2011). *Niche news: The politics of news choice*. Oxford University Press.

Sydnor, E. (2019). *Disrespectful democracy: The psychology of political incivility*. Columbia University Press.

Wahl-Jorgensen, K. (2019). *Emotions, media and politics*. Polity Press.

NOTES

1. Randall, B. (2020, February 11). Opinion: If politics and negativity are all the news media has to offer, I don't want it anymore. *The Commonwealth Times*. https://commonwealthtimes.org/2020/02/11/if-politics-and-negativity-is-all-the-media-has-to-offer-i-dont-want-it-anymore/

2. McManus, J. H. (1994). *Market-driven journalism: Let the citizens beware?* SAGE; Shoemaker, P. J., & Reese, S. D. (2014). *Mediating the message in the 21st century: A media sociology perspective*. Routledge; Bennett, W. L. (2012). *News: The politics of illusion* (9th ed.). Longman.

3. Cook, T. E. (2005). *Governing with the news: The news media as a political institution* (2nd ed.). University of Chicago Press, p. 71; Dunaway, J. (2013, August 28). *Media markets and campaign news slant* [Paper presentation]. The Annual Political Communication APSA Pre-Conference, Chicago, Illinois, United States.

4. Padgett, J., Dunaway, J. L., & Darr, J. P. (2019). As seen on TV? How gatekeeping makes the US House seem more extreme. *Journal of Communication*, 69(6), 696–719.

5. Mutz, D. C. (2016). *In-your-face politics: The consequences of uncivil media*. Princeton University Press; Soroka, S. (2014). *Negativity in democratic politics: Causes and consequences*. Oxford University Press; Padgett, J., Dunaway, J. L., & Darr, J. P. (2019). As seen on TV? How gatekeeping makes the US House seem more extreme. *Journal of Communication*, 69(6), 696–719; Dunaway, J. (2013). Media ownership and story tone in campaign news. *American Politics Research*, 41(1), 24–53.

6. Sabato, L. J., Stencel, M., & Lichter, S. R. (2000). *Peepshow: Media and politics in an age of scandal*. Rowman and Littlefield. This book discusses many cases of scandal reporting along with guidelines that media should follow in publishing or ignoring such incidents.

7. Shepard, K. (2021, May 6). Democrats on FEC blast decision to drop probe into Trump hush-money payment to Stormy Daniels: "Defies reality." *The Washington Post*. https://www.washingtonpost.com/nation/2021/05/06/fec-trump-stormy-daniels-cohen/

8. Fox, R. L., & Lawless, J. L. (2011). Gendered perceptions and political candidacies: A central barrier to women's equality in electoral politics. *American Journal of Political Science*, 55(1), 59–73; Lawless, J. L., & Fox, R. L. (2015). *Running from office: Why young Americans are turned off to politics*. Oxford University Press.

9. Muddiman, A., Pond-Cobb, J., & Matson, J. E. (2017). Negativity bias or backlash: Interaction with civil and uncivil online political news content. *Communication Research*. https://doi.org/10.1177/0093650216685625

10. Sabato, L. (1991). *Feeding frenzy: How attack journalism has transformed American politics*. Free Press, p. 53.

11. Hasell, A. (2020). Shared emotion: The social amplification of partisan news on Twitter. *Digital Journalism*, 1–18; Stella, M., Ferrara, E., & De Domenico. M. (2018). Bots increase exposure to negative and inflammatory content in online social systems. *Proceedings of the National Academy of Sciences*, 115(49), 12435–12440.

12. Sabato, L. J. (1992). Open season: How the news media cover presidential campaigns in the age of attack journalism. In M. D. McCubbins (Ed.), *Under*

the watchful eye: Managing presidential campaigns in the television era. CQ Press, p. 128; Bennett, W. L. (2012). *News: The politics of illusion* (9th ed.). Longman; Rozell, M. J. (1996). *In contempt of Congress: Postwar press coverage on Capitol Hill.* Praeger, p. 53; this section draws heavily on Dunaway, J. (2013). Media ownership and story tone in campaign news. *American Politics Research, 41*(1), 24–53.

13. Geer, J. G. (2012). The news media and the rise of negativity in presidential campaigns. *PS: Political Science and Politics, 45*(3), 422–427.

14. Ridout, T. N., Fowler, E. F., & Franz, M. M., Spending fast and furious: Political advertising in 2020. *The Forum, 18*(4), 465–492.

15. Patterson, T. E. (1994). *Out of order.* Knopf; Patterson, T. E. (1996). Bad news, period. *PS: Political Science and Politics, 29*(1), 17–20.

16. Gross, K., & Brewer, P. R. (2007). Sore losers: News frames, policy debates, and emotions. *Harvard International Journal of Press/Politics, 12*(1), 122–133; Bennett, W. L. (2012). *News: The politics of illusion* (9th ed.). Longman; Iyengar, S., & McGrady, J. A. (2007). *Media politics: A citizen's guide.* Norton; Lawrence, R. G. (2000). Game-framing the issues: Tracking the strategy frame in public policy news. *Political Communication, 17,* 93–114; Fallows, J. M. (1996). *Breaking news: How the media undermine American democracy.* Pantheon Books.

17. Westwood, S. J., Messing, S., & Lelkes, Y. (2020). Projecting confidence: How the probabilistic horse race confuses and demobilizes the public. *The Journal of Politics, 82*(4), 1530–1544.

18. Shea, D. M., & Sproveri, A. (2012). The rise and fall of nasty politics in America. *PS: Political Science, 45*(3), 416–421; Herbst, S. (2010). *Rude democracy: Civility and incivility in American politics.* Temple University Press.

19. Padgett, J., Dunaway, J. L., & Darr, J. P. (2019). As seen on TV? How gatekeeping makes the US House seem more extreme. *Journal of Communication, 69*(6), 696–719.

20. Geer, J. G. (2012). The news media and the rise of negativity in presidential campaigns. *PS: Political Science and Politics, 45*(3), 422–427; Ridout, T. N., & Smith, G. R. (2008). Free advertising: How the media amplify campaign messages. *Political Research Quarterly, 61,* 598–608; Fowler, E. F., & Ridout, T. N. (2009). Local television and newspaper coverage of political advertising. *Political Communication, 26*(2), 119–136; Patterson, T. E. (1994). *Out of order.* Knopf; Patterson, T. E. (1996). Bad news, period. *PS: Political Science and Politics, 29*(1), 17–20; Iyengar, S., Norpoth, H., & Hahn, K. S. (2004). Consumer demand for election news: The horse race sells. *Journal of Politics, 66*(1), 157–175.

21. Geer, J. G. (2012). The news media and the rise of negativity in presidential campaigns. *PS: Political Science and Politics, 45*(3), 422–427; see also Ridout,

T. N., & Smith, G. R. (2008). Free advertising: How the media amplify campaign messages. *Political Research Quarterly, 61,* 598–608; Fowler, E. F., & Ridout, T. N. (2009). Local television and newspaper coverage of political advertising. *Political Communication, 26*(2), 119–136.

22. Soroka, S., Fournier, P., & Nir, L. (2019). Cross-national evidence of a negativity bias in psychophysiological reactions to news. *Proceedings of the National Academy of Sciences, 116*(38), pp. 18888–18892.

23. Baumeister, R. F., Bratslavsky, E., & Finkenauer, C. (2001). Bad is stronger than good. *Review of General Psychology, 5*(4), 323–370; Bless, H., Hamilton, D. L., & Mackie, D. M. (1992). Mood effects on the organization of person information. *European Journal of Social Psychology, 22,* 497–509; Ohira, H., Winton, W. M., & Oyama, M. (1997). Effects of stimulus valence on recognition memory and endogenous eyeblinks: Further evidence for positive–negative asymmetry. *Personality and Social Psychology Bulletin, 24,* 986–993; Pratto F., & John, O. P. (1991). Automatic vigilance: The attention-grabbing power of negative social information. *Journal of Personality and Social Psychology, 61*(3), 29–58; Robinson-Reigler, G. L., & Winton, W. M. (1996). The role of conscious recollection in recognition of affective material: Evidence for a positive–negative asymmetry. *Journal of General Psychology, 123*(2), 93–104; Soroka, S. (2014). *Negativity in democratic politics: Causes and consequences.* Oxford University Press.

24. Bachleda, S., Neuner, F. G., Soroka, S., Guggenheim, L., Fournier, P., & Naurin, E. (2020). Individual-level differences in negativity biases in news selection. *Personality and Individual Differences, 155,* 109675.

25. Lichter, R., & Noyes, R. (1996). *Good intentions make bad news.* Rowman and Littlefield; Miller, A. H., Wattenberg, M. P., & Malanschuk, O. (1986). Schematic assessments of presidential candidates. *American Political Science Review, 80*(2), 521–540; Patterson, T. E. (1994). *Out of order.* Knopf; Mutz, D. C. (2016). *In-your-face politics: The consequences of uncivil media.* Princeton University Press.

26. Garment, S. (1991). *Scandal: The crisis of mistrust in American politics.* Random House; Rozell, M. J. (1996). *In contempt of Congress: Postwar press coverage on Capitol Hill.* Praeger, p. 53; Patterson, T. E. (1996). Bad news, period. *PS: Political Science and Politics, 29*(1), 17–20; Sabato, L. J. (1992). Open season: How the news media cover presidential campaigns in the age of attack journalism. In M. D. McCubbins (Ed.), *Under the watchful eye: Managing presidential campaigns in the television era.* CQ Press, p. 128; Bennett, W. L. (2012). *News: The politics of illusion* (9th ed.). Longman; Dunaway, J. (2013). Media ownership and story tone in campaign news. *American Politics Research, 41*(1), 24–53.

27. Mutz, D. C. (2016). *In-your-face politics: The consequences of uncivil media.* Princeton University Press; Mutz, D. C., & Reeves, B. (2005). The new videomalaise:

Effects of televised incivility on political trust. *American Political Science Review*, 99(1), 1–15; Druckman, J. N. (2003). The power of television images: The first Kennedy–Nixon debate revisited. *Journal of Politics*, 65(May), 559–571; Funk, C. (2001). Process performance: Public reactions to legislative policy debate. In J. R. Hibbing & E. Theiss-Morse (Eds.), *What is it about government that Americans dislike?* Cambridge University Press; Hart, R. P. (1994). *Seducing America: How television charms the modern voter*. Oxford University Press; Hibbing, J. R., & Theiss-Morse, E. (1998). The media's role in public negativity toward Congress: Distinguishing emotional reactions and cognitive evaluations. *American Journal of Political Science*, 42(April), 475–498; Keeter, S. (1987). The illusion of intimacy: Television and the role of personal qualities in voter choice. *Public Opinion Quarterly*, 51(Autumn), 344–358; Lang, A. (2000). The limited capacity model of mediated message processing. *Journal of Communication*, 50(March), 46–70; Lombard, M., Reich, R. D., Grabe, M. E., Bracken, C. C., & Ditton, T. B. (2000). Presence and television: The role of screen size. *Human Communication Research*, 26(January), 75–98; Reeves, B., & Naas, C. (1996). *The media equation: How people treat computers, television, and new media like real people and places*. Cambridge University Press.

28. Mutz, D. (2007). Effects of "in-your-face" television discourse on perceptions of a legitimate opposition. *American Political Science Review*, 101(4), 621–635; Mutz, D. C. (2016). *In-your-face politics: The consequences of uncivil media*. Princeton University Press.

29. Sobieraj, S., & Berry, J. M. (2011). From incivility to outrage: Political discourse in blogs, talk radio, and cable news. *Political Communication*, 28, 19–41; Forgette, R., & Morris, J. S. (2006). High-conflict television news and public opinion. *Political Research Quarterly*, 59(3), 447–456.

30. Klar, S., & Krupnikov, Y. (2016). *Independent politics: How American disdain for parties leads to political inaction*. Cambridge University Press; Lawless, J. L., & Fox, R. L. (2015). *Running from office: Why young Americans are turned off to politics*. Oxford University Press.

31. Soroka, S. (2014). *Negativity in democratic politics: Causes and consequences*. Oxford University Press; Albertson, B., & Gadarian, S. K. (2015). *Anxious politics: Democratic citizenship in a threatening world*. Cambridge University Press.

32. Bennett, W. L. (2012). *News: The politics of illusion* (9th ed.). Longman; Hamilton, J. T. (2004). *All the news that's fit to sell: How the market transforms information into news*. Princeton University Press.

33. *United States v. Windsor, Executor of the Estate of Spyer, et al.*, No. 12–307 (2013).

34. Zapotosky, M., Barnes, R., & Murphy, B. (2017, February 6). Top diplomats, tech giants blast immigration order as court showdown looms. *The Washington Post*. https://www.washingtonpost.com/politics/trump-administration-appeals-to-restore-travel-ban-says-earlier-ruling-was-second-guessing-the-

president/2017/02/05/6fcdbb5a-eb4c-11e6-80c2-30e57e57e05d_story
.html?utm_term=.c27d460ddde6

35. Iyengar, S. (1990). *Is anyone responsible?* University of Chicago Press.

36. Hamilton, J. T. (2004). *All the news that's fit to sell: How the market transforms information into news.* Princeton University Press, p. 3.

37. This section draws heavily on Dunaway, J. L., & Settle, J. E. (2021). Opinion formation and polarization in the news feed era: Effects from digital, social, and mobile media. In D. Osborne & C. Sibley (Eds.), *The Cambridge handbook of political psychology.* Cambridge University Press.

38. Martin, G. J., & Yurukoglu, A. (2017). Bias in cable news: Persuasion and polarization. *American Economic Review, 107*(9), 2565–2599.

39. Stroud, N. J. (2011). *Niche news: The politics of news choice.* Oxford University Press.

40. Stroud, N. J. (2011). *Niche news: The politics of news choice.* Oxford University Press; Levendusky, M. S. (2013). Why do partisan media polarize viewers? *American Journal of Political Science, 57*(3), 611–623.

41. Hindman, M. (2018). *The internet trap.* Princeton University Press; Flaxman, S., Goel, S., & Rao, J. M. (2016). Filter bubbles, echo chambers, and online news consumption. *Public opinion quarterly, 80*(S1), 298–320.

42. Prior, M. (2007). *Post-broadcast democracy: How media choice increases inequality in political involvement and polarizes elections.* Cambridge University Press; Arceneaux, K., & Johnson, M. (2013). *Changing minds or changing channels? Partisan news in an age of choice.* University of Chicago Press.

43. Watts, M. D., Domke, D., Shah, D. V., & Fan, D. P. (1999). Elite cues and media bias in presidential campaigns. *Political Communication, 26,* 144–175; Smith, G. R. (2010). Politicians and the news media: How elite attacks influence perceptions of media bias. *International Journal of Press/Politics, 15,* 319–343; Ladd, J. M. (2012). *Why Americans hate the media and how it matters.* Princeton University Press; Groeling, T. (2013). Media bias by the numbers: Challenges and opportunities in the empirical study of partisan news. *Annual Review of Political Science, 16,* 129–151.

44. Gunther, A. C., & Schmitt, K. (2006). Mapping of the hostile media effect. *Journal of Communication, 54*(1), 55–70.

45. Dunaway, J. L., & Settle, J. E. (2021). Opinion formation and polarization in the news feed era: Effects from digital, social, and mobile media. In D. Osborne & C. Sibley (Eds.), *The Cambridge handbook of political psychology.* Cambridge University Press.

46. Arceneaux, K., & Johnson, M. (2013). *Changing minds or changing channels? Partisan news in an age of choice.* University of Chicago Press.

47. Kahn, K. F., & Kenney, P. J. (2002). The slant of the news: How editorial endorsements influence campaign coverage and citizens' views of candidates. *American Political Science Review*, 96(2), 381–394; Schiffer, A. J. (2006). Assessing partisan bias in political news: The case of local senate election coverage. *Political Communication*, 23, 23–39; Larcinese, V., Puglisi, R., & Snyder, J. M. (2011). Partisan bias in economic news: Evidence on the agenda setting behavior of U.S. newspapers. *Journal of Public Economics*, 95, 1178–1189; Butler, D. M., & Schofield, E. (2010). Were newspapers more interested in pro-Obama letters to the editor in 2008? Evidence from a field experiment. *American Politics Research*, 38, 356–371.

48. Page, B. I. (1996). *Who deliberates? Mass media in modern democracy*. University of Chicago Press.

49. Groseclose, T., & Milyo, J. (2005). A measure of media bias. *Quarterly Journal of Economics*, 120, 1191–1237; Groseclose, T. (2011). *Left turn: How liberal media bias distorts the American mind*. St. Martin's Press.

50. Groeling, T. (2013). Media bias by the numbers: Challenges and opportunities in the empirical study of partisan news. *Annual Review of Political Science*, 16, 129–151.

51. Sigelman, L. (1973). Reporting the news: An organizational analysis. *American Journal of Sociology*, 79, 132–151.

52. Cook, T. E. (2005). *Governing with the news: The news media as a political institution* (2nd ed.). University of Chicago Press; Shoemaker, P. J., & Reese, S. D. (2014). *Mediating the message in the 21st century: A media sociology perspective*. Routledge.

53. Zaller, J. R. (1999, October 24). A theory of media politics: How the interests of politicians, journalists, and citizens shapes the news [Unpublished manuscript]; Arnold, R. D. (2004). *Congress, the press, and political accountability*. Princeton University Press; Hamilton, J. T. (2004). *All the news that's fit to sell: How the market transforms information into news*. Princeton University Press; McManus, J. H. (1994). *Market-driven journalism: Let the citizens beware?* SAGE.

54. McManus, J. H. (1994). *Market-driven journalism: Let the citizens beware?* SAGE; Zaller, J. R. (1999, October 24). A theory of media politics: How the interests of politicians, journalists, and citizens shapes the news [Unpublished manuscript]; Arnold, R. D. (2004). *Congress, the press, and political accountability*. Princeton University Press; Iyengar, S., Norpoth, H., & Hahn, K. S. (2004). Consumer demand for election news: The horse race sells. *Journal of Politics*, 66(1), 157–175; Dunaway, J. (2008). Markets, ownership, and the quality of campaign news coverage. *Journal of Politics*, 70(4), 1193–1202; Dunaway, J., & Lawrence, R. G. (2015). What predicts the game frame? Media ownership, electoral context, and campaign news. *Political Communication*, 32(1), 43–60.

55. Hamilton, J. T. (2004). *All the news that's fit to sell: How the market transforms information into news*. Princeton University Press.

56. Baron, D. P. (2006). Persistent media bias. *Journal of Public Economics, 90*, 1–36.

57. Gentzkow, M., & Shapiro, J. M. (2010). What drives media slant? Evidence from US daily newspapers. *Econometrica, 78*(1), 35–71.

58. Mullainathan, S., & Shleifer, A. (2005). The market for news. *American Economic Review, 95*(4), 1031–1053.

59. 133 journalists surveyed on why they're so despised. (2016, July 24). *New York Magazine* http://nymag.com/daily/intelligencer/2016/07/media-survey.html

60. Financial woes now overshadow all other concerns for journalists. (2008, March 17). *Pew Research Center.* http://www.people-press.org/2008/03/17/financial-woes-now-overshadow-all-other-concerns-for-journalists/.

61. Financial woes now overshadow all other concerns for journalists. (2008, March 17). *Pew Research Center.* http://www.people-press.org/2008/03/17/financial-woes-now-overshadow-all-other-concerns-for-journalists/; the survey was conducted September 17–December 3, 2007.

62. Financial woes now overshadow all other concerns for journalists. (2008, March 17). *Pew Research Center.* http://www.people-press.org/2008/03/17/financial-woes-now-overshadow-all-other-concerns-for-journalists/

63. The Web: Alarming, appealing and a challenge to journalistic values. (2008, March 17). *Pew Research Center for the People and the Press.* https://assets.pewresearch.org/wp-content/uploads/sites/4/2011/01/Journalist-report-2008.pdf

64. This section draws heavily on Ladd, J. M. (2013). The era of media distrust and its consequences. In T. N. Ridout (Ed.), *New directions in media and politics.* Routledge; Ladd, J. M. (2012). *Why Americans hate the media and how it matters.* Princeton University Press.

65. Ladd, J. M. (2013). The era of media distrust and its consequences. In T. N. Ridout (Ed.), *New directions in media and politics.* Routledge; see also, Mutz, D. C. (2016). *In-your-face politics: The consequences of uncivil media.* Princeton University Press, Chapter 4.

66. Ladd, J. M. (2012). *Why Americans hate the media and how it matters.* Princeton University Press.

67. Chavez, P., Stracqualursi, V., & Keneally, M. (2016, October 26). A history of the Donald Trump–Megyn Kelly feud. *ABC News.* http://abcnews.go.com/Politics/history-donald-trump-megyn-kelly-feud/story?id=36526503; Hampson, R. (2016, November 15). Exclusive: Fox anchor Megyn Kelly describes scary, bullying "year of Trump." *USA Today.* http://www.usatoday.com/story/news/politics/elections/2016/11/15/megyn-kelly-memoir-donald-trump-roger-ailes-president-fox-news/93813154/.

68. As discussed in Chapter 4, evidence for a causal link between partisan news content and mass polarization remains mixed; see Prior, M. (2013). Media and political polarization. *Annual Review of Political Science, 16*, 101–127.

Media Effects: Then and Now

R obust, accessible, and uncensored media are widely viewed as essential to a healthy democracy. Yet this once-basic assumption is now at the center of public debate in America. Critics question whether the media in the United States (U.S.) can fulfill this role, and many doubt whether they even aspire to do so. The credibility of traditional media is under attack, while their ability to serve as a watchdog is threatened by economic competition and declining newsroom investment. Social media makes media messages more accessible for the public, but they also blur the lines between hearsay, journalism, and misinformation in ways that exacerbate mistrust in media. Polarization is on the rise, a trend many attribute to the partisanship and showmanship ever-present on partisan cable news. Despite that media messages broadcast via television and radio were once feared as potential tools for propaganda and government control, the power of mainstream media is no longer evident to many people. Those concerned about declining and ineffective media long for the heyday of the broadcast era, when three major mainstream television news networks had the power to set the agenda for politicians and the mass public alike.[1] Is such nostalgia warranted? Have once-powerful mainstream media lost the ability to influence? Did they ever really have it? If so, what changed? Are we better or worse off than before the arrival of digital and social media?

In Chapter 4, we explained how changing media technologies expanded the market for news, consumer choice, and the array and types of people producing and sharing news content. We also examined how these changes influenced the public's news habits and the means by which they encounter and consume news and political information. In this chapter, we will explain researchers' decades-long and evolving view of media effects on the political knowledge, attitudes, and behavior of the mass public. We will then focus on many of the implications of the shift toward a digital media environment and what these changes mean for how we understand media effects. Specifically, we will examine how changes in communication technology altered, and continue to shape, media effects on citizens' political learning, attitudes, and behavior.

History and Theories of Media Effects

Researchers studied how print and broadcast media presentations shaped the beliefs, attitudes, and behavior of audiences for decades.[2] Research on the subject began with the arrival of radio and television and concerns about the reach and power of broadcast media and government propaganda. Research from this time focused on direct effects, examining whether exposure to media messages produced mass persuasion and attitude change. Initially, media effects researchers thought media were all-powerful, capable of drastically changing public opinion. Subsequently, scholars evolved toward a view of media effects as minimal. Much of the evidence researchers produced suggested that media were capable of exerting only very little influence. Later—following improvements in theories and methodological techniques researchers used—the accumulated evidence suggested the answer was somewhere in between. The consensus was that media messages had powerful but limited effects. But that consensus—reached in the heyday of print and broadcast media—was based on a media environment very different from today.

When print and broadcast media were dominant, the media environment was smaller and more uniform. The three major broadcast networks combined regularly reached nearly 90% of the national television audience.

The three networks also had fairly synchronized programming schedules across them. The significant market share also meant the three networks held a monopoly; they faced relatively minimal competition for mainstream audiences. The networks saw little need for content differentiation to appeal to niche audiences. The power, reach, and uniformity of the messages meant that even if major mainstream media outlets lacked the ability to persuade, they could influence public attitudes and behaviors in other ways. For example, researchers discovered the media had agenda-setting powers—the ability to influence what the people think *about* and consider to be important—even if they did not have the power to change deeply held attitudes and opinions.

The political context was also different. Partisan polarization had not yet taken root, and what societal divisions did exist were not linked as tightly with political preferences, nor were political identities as central to most Americans. Despite that media persuasion was limited by partisan predispositions even then, evidence suggests that people were more open to persuasion than today. During the broadcast era, partisan-motivated reasoning was probably not as overwhelming an influence during that time. Today, both the technological and political contexts are different. The media environment has vastly expanded content offerings through cable and satellite subscription services and streaming services on the internet. Digital platforms (websites and social media) provide countless opportunities for consuming media content, despite being delivered in slightly different configurations. At the same time, politicians and the public are increasingly sorted and polarized along partisan and ideological lines. Though there is some debate as to the nature and drivers of these divisions, researchers generally agree that Americans are simply less tolerant of partisans on the other side than they once were, and partisanship and ideology are more tightly intertwined than in the past, a fact that strengthens the salience, intensity, and influence of citizens' political identities. In the wake of these dramatic changes, media influence is uncertain once more, motivating researchers to redouble their efforts to understand under what conditions media effects occur.

The Arrival of Broadcast and the Era of Powerful Media Effects

The 1920s arrival of radio (and later television) broadcasting brought with it cause for concern. Many people feared that messages delivered through these new entertaining and accessible technologies were too powerful and too persuasive for exposed audiences to resist.[3] These concerns were reinforced by fears about the influence of government propaganda following World Wars I and II.[4] Researchers of the time held the same expectation—that exposure to mediated messages results in strong persuasive effects. These "magic bullet" or "hypodermic needle" theories (which essentially theorized that audiences would uniformly accept and be influenced by the information conveyed in mass media messages) were based on two key assumptions. The first was that media audiences were homogeneous; the second was that they were passive. The implication was that the new levels of audience reach afforded by broadcast technology allowed for persuasive control over a vast and vulnerable citizen audience.[5] At the same time, the entertainment-based formats raised concerns about whether broadcast forms of media could meet the obligation to provide quality public affairs information.[6]

The Minimal Effects Era

By the middle of the 20th century, however, research showed that media exposure did not determine political attitudes, behaviors, or beliefs.[7] This work called into question assumptions underlying the idea of all-powerful media and suggested new assumptions instead. Studies showed that audiences had diverse preferences and were quite capable of making independent choices about what media they consume, according to their individual preferences and tastes. Evidence also showed that pre-existing conditions such as one's contexts, relationships, and predispositions were the main determinants of attitudes and behaviors—not media messages. During this time, audiences were no longer viewed as passive receptors capable of being converted by media persuasion. These new assumptions would guide the next phase of work, which later became known as the era of minimal effects.[8] Three traditions in minimal effects research developed.

The Columbia School

Unable to demonstrate massive media effects, scholars turned to news theories to explain the role media played, if any, in shaping attitudes and behaviors. Columbia researchers Lazarsfeld, Berelson, and Gaudet are credited with the "two-step flow" model, which argued that ideas flowed "from radio and print to the opinion leaders and from them to the less active sections of the population."[9] This theory documented the importance of interpersonal influence for understanding media effects and showed how media messages could have indirect effects through people's interpersonal contexts. By demonstrating how media effects might be indirect, the two-step flow model further downplayed the idea of direct and powerful media effects. Columbia scholars also focused on what occurs before individuals are exposed to media messages, such as factors that influence selections about which media to consume. On this point, Lazarsfeld and colleagues found that people engaged in selective exposure, the behavior of deliberately choosing specific media messages to attend.[10] Though now familiar to media researchers, selective exposure—active decisions by audience members to consume specific types of messages—was, during this time, a radical departure from assumptions of uniform exposure that characterized "magic bullet" and "hypodermic needle" theories from the era of direct and powerful effects.[11] During the period of minimal effects, selective exposure was cited as one of the primary explanations for why media effects were minimal.[12]

The Michigan Tradition

Research from scholars at the University of Michigan were primarily interested in voting behavior and therefore were focused largely on persuasion and attitude change during campaigns. For this reason, they focused more on explanatory factors such as party identification, political attitudes, and policy-based issue positions. As a result, those working in the Michigan tradition paid little attention to media consumption in the studies they conducted, but inferences were possible based on the evidence they produced. Their evidence suggested that voting decisions were largely already in place by the end of the party convention and before the actual general election campaigns began; this indicated that voting decisions were primarily driven by partisan loyalty and incumbent performance rather than messages received during the political campaign. Though their findings and conclusions still allowed for the fact that campaigns could stimulate interest and possibly even influence votes, the primary evidence demonstrated that such effects were secondary relative to party identification and evaluations of the incumbent's performance in office. The Michigan tradition is credited with perpetuating the minimal effects model (albeit inadvertently) because they did not specifically account for media influence in their research. Without new evidence, the scientific consensus that media were only capable of producing minimal effects on attitudes and behaviors remained in place.[13]

Minimal Effects in Psychology

The psychological tradition in media effects was focused on persuasion and attitude change more generally. This tradition emphasized that anchoring attitudes could condition media effects. Influential work by Carl Hovland and his colleagues discovered that persuasion depended on perceptions of source credibility—how much people believe a source of information is a credible one—through a series of experiments to identify conditions under which persuasion occurred. Their primary contribution was the insight that individuals vary in the degree to which they are susceptible to persuasion. William J. McGuire's psychological research was also highly influential. His primary contribution was to point out that the distinction between exposure to a message and acceptance of a message is critical in persuasion. Being exposed to a message is not enough to guarantee that people pay attention to the message and receive it or that they accept it. People can ignore or refute messages, which blunts persuasive effects. McGuire also demonstrated that political interest and awareness are important for understanding media effects because the degree to which someone is interested in politics is likely to influence whether they are exposed to political media messages or news in the first place. With no exposure, there can be no persuasion. Both of these insights would later help advance the literature on media effects.

Generally speaking, research in the psychology tradition revealed that people could learn information from media messages, but that the messages have little or no effect on deeply entrenched beliefs and attitudes. Though this work suggested learning effects, those were largely ignored during this time due to a primary focus on persuasion among effects researchers. The main conclusion drawn from the media effects tradition in psychology was that expectations for powerful media effects were far-fetched.[14] Despite these conclusions, critical insights provided during this time—from McGuire's research in particular—would go on to inspire a few major studies that bridged the path from the minimal effects era to the era of powerful but limited effects.[15]

Not-So-Minimal Effects

Despite early failures to demonstrate direct and powerful media effects, some researchers remained convinced that mass media could have powerful influence over attitudes and behavior—especially as television proliferated in American households.[16] These researchers focused on the possibility of important indirect effects from exposure to media messages, looking for effects from media production processes such as story selection, presentation, and distribution. They learned that these news-making processes not only had influence over the news content itself but also on its impact on public opinion.

Persuasive Effects

Researchers from the minimal effects period made a significant research advance when they discovered the importance of the distinction between exposure to media messages and the acceptance of media messages. Political scientist John R. Zaller was one of the first to later reassert this argument, applying it to political persuasion. Reflecting McGuire's ideas of minimal effects, Zaller argued that persuasion requires both receipt and acceptance of messages. He also maintained that although exposure was not a sufficient condition for persuasion, it was a necessary condition, highlighting the role that motivation plays in exposure to political information. The desire to consume news or learn about politics is important because it influences how likely and how often people are to be exposed to news. Exposure is much more likely to occur for people highly interested in politics, but for these individuals, exposure is not likely to lead to persuasion. That is because the highly interested are typically partisans who have relatively strong existing political attitudes, beliefs, and identities. People with high levels of political interest might regularly be exposed to news, but they are not likely to accept information with which they disagree. Those low in interest would be high on acceptance but low on exposure, rarely motivated to pay attention to political information much at all.[17]

Despite articulating how narrow the circumstances are for persuasion, Zaller's work still helped refute the view of minimal effects because he showed a path through which persuasive media effects were possible. In his model, the volume of media messages can broaden exposure such that low interest people are exposed, and acceptance is more likely to happen among this group. Zaller also pointed out the need to account for crosscutting messages, especially those that are equally intense but from opposing sides, such as in electoral campaigns between competing candidates. Where people previously interpreted a lack of opinion change as the absence of a persuasive media effect, Zaller argued that indecision from crosscutting competing messages can result in defaulting to one's original position. According to this explanation, an apparent lack of persuasion could be the result of crosscutting messages that are equally intense. The implication was that persuasion was more likely with an imbalance in the volume of messages and enough volume to reach some of those low- or mid-awareness people for whom opinions are not already set in stone.

Zaller's reassertion of the crucial distinction between message exposure and message acceptance and his identification of the information environment conditions under which persuasion would occur were fundamental in refuting minimal effects.

The early traditions in media effects research produced several important conclusions among researchers. It debunked massive media influence theories such as "magic bullet" and "hypodermic needle." Based on this research, we learned that audiences are active and selective, and that their choices (and thus rates of media exposure) depend on political interest, psychological traits, predispositions, and interpersonal contexts.[18] We also learned that media effects are often strong, but they are still limited and mainly indirect. They usually stop short of direct persuasive effects, except for certain individuals and under very limited conditions. Rather, media persuade mainly through their ability to set the agenda and prime considerations that serve as the basis for political decision making, such as voting. This is largely because simple message exposure is not the same as message attention or acceptance. Those who are highly attentive to news and political information are rarely persuaded because of previously held political predispositions (i.e., affiliation with a party) and those who are uninterested are rarely exposed to political news and information in the first place. When they are, they may not be attentive to persuasive information because they lack interest.[19] Zaller was not the only holdout still convinced that media could exert powerful effects. Broadcast-era media effects researchers made advances in demonstrating media effects by accepting that media can exert important effects through means other than persuasion and opinion change. Agenda-setting effects provide one example.

Agenda-Setting Effects

If personal needs and pleasures entirely determined choices of news items, news selection patterns would show infinite variations. This was not the case during the broadcast era. Similarities in the information environment of average Americans produced common patterns in news exposure during that time. Gatekeeping practices across monopoly-holding media outlets produced a high level of similarity in news supply. The American public relied on a shared base of information, which gave the nation a shared sense about what issues were most important. Media monopolies and news uniformity generated powerful agenda setting effects.

Bernard Cecil Cohen provided the earliest well known articulation of agenda-setting theory by stating it as follows: The media "may not be successful much of the time in telling people what to think, but it is stunningly successful in telling its readers what to think about."[20] Soon after, a famous study conducted by Maxwell McCombs and Donald L. Shaw showed a high degree of similarity about which issues were covered by a variety of media sources; it established the existence of strong correlations between voter attention to key issues and the volume of news coverage dedicated to those issues.[21] A few years later, research from political scientists Shanto Iyengar and Donald R. Kinder provided robust evidence for agenda-setting effects through the use of several lab-based experiments; the use of experiments to demonstrate media effects helped researchers overcome methodological challenges from the previous era.[22]

Generally, agenda-setting theories suggest that when it comes to drawing public attention to events and issue areas of the most importance, mass media tell people in fairly uniform fashion which individual issues and activities are most significant and deserve to be ranked highly on the public's agenda of political concerns.[23] Importance is indicated through media cues such as banner headlines, front-page placement in newspapers, or first-story placement on television. Frequent and ample coverage also implies significance. The stories news editors select for the front page of a major national newspaper or the lead story of the national news broadcast—or even those stories covered at high volumes—are those most likely to be named by members of the public as important.

The agenda-setting hypothesis was tested and replicated in hundreds of studies during the decades following its first articulation. Agenda-setting studies are still ongoing and represent a significant subset of media effects research. Researchers in this area are currently trying to understand whether agenda-setting is less common today because the media environment is fragmented, potentially creating differing perceptions of reality among audiences who seek only their preferred brand of partisan news and avoid other perspectives. Some research suggests that the media's agenda-setting power is weaker today as a result. Other work suggests that because many Americans are still exposed regularly to mainstream news, major media still largely set the agenda for much of the populace.

Still, many people readily adopt the mainstream media's judgment of importance, often inadvertently. When we look at the front page of the newspaper or the top of a news webpage, we expect to find the most important stories there. We may watch the opening minutes of a telecast eagerly to catch the big stories and then allow our attention to wander. As a result, agenda setting by the media leads to uniformities in exposure and in significance ratings of news items. When the media make events seem important, the general public as well as politicians discuss them and form opinions. This enhances the perceived importance of the events and ensures even more public attention and possibly political action.

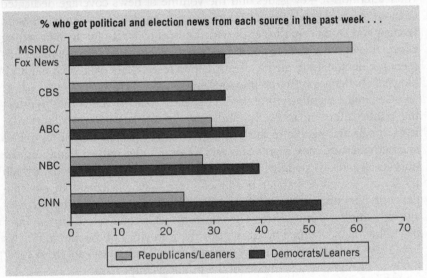

Figure 13-1   Political and Election News Sources by Party, 2020

% who got political and election news from each source in the past week . . .

Source: Adapted from Jurkowitz, M., Mitchell, A., Shearer, E., & Walker, M. (2020, January 24). U.S. media polarization and the 2020 election: A nation divided. *Pew Research Center.* https://www.journalism.org/2020/01/24/u-s-media-polarization-and-the-2020-election-a-nation-divided/.

Numerous studies confirm the agenda-setting influence of the media.[24] When people are asked which issues are most important to them personally or to their communities, their lists tend to correspond to cues in the news sources that they use. However, agenda setting varies in potency. Audiences follow media guidance but not slavishly. Past and current experiences, conversations with others, and independent reasoning provide alternatives to media guidance.[25] Comparisons of media agendas with public opinion polls and reports about political and social conditions show that media guidance is most important for new issues that have not been widely discussed and for issues beyond the realm of personal experience.[26] The need for raw material for conversations with friends and associates is a particularly strong force when people select stories. Prominent media coverage ensures that an issue will be noticed, but it does not guarantee that citizens will weight it as heavily as the media. Likewise, people will note information that is useful or gratifying to them, even if it is on the back pages, receives minuscule headlines, or is briefly reported at the tail end of a newscast.[27]

As noted above, current research examines how changes to the media environment will impact the agenda-setting power of traditional media. Questions range from whether mainstream media agenda-setting power has been completely overturned to which forms of digital media and social media have agenda-setting potential. To date, the bulk of evidence reveals a reciprocal process in which digital and social media can shape the traditional media agenda and traditional media can shape the content and flow of digital and social media.[28] The two-way agenda-setting potential reflects the hybridity of the media system (discussed in Chapter 4). The intersection of digital media logics and traditional media logics means that, at times, digital media will set the agenda and at other times, traditional media will set the agenda.

Priming Effects

The research conducted by Shanto Iyengar and Donald R. Kinder also demonstrated important priming effects. *Priming* is a process in which media emphasis causes people to assign weights to particular issues when they make summary political evaluations—such as voting decisions. A number of experimental studies have found, for example, that television news coverage of specific events primes audiences to appraise politicians in light of these events. Viewers' political perspectives narrow, so a single phenomenon deflects attention from the broader context.[29] It is not surprising that experiments indicate that a president's popularity ratings fare better when the audience has been primed with questions about his political successes rather than his failures.[30]

Priming emerged from studies of agenda setting because researchers realized that whatever emerged as the political agenda could also influence attitudes. Priming works when coverage of a particular subject or issue alters the criteria by which people evaluate public officials.[31] Priming effects are also well demonstrated in both experiments and surveys. They can affect voter evaluations of presidents, legislators, and other public officials. They have also been applied to assessments of candidate traits.

Priming studies uncover fascinating media effects. One recent example finds that political ads using imagery of the American flag primes symbolic patriotism and other responses electorally favorable for Republican candidates.[32] But thus far, experiments tell us little about how long priming effects persist or their likely political impact. Further testing in natural settings is required to judge under what conditions and for what length of time priming persists.

Framing Effects

Similar to priming effects, the media also exert effects on public opinion and political attitudes through *framing*—reporting the news from a certain perspective so that some aspects of the situation are more noticeable than others. For example, in a study of immigration news stories printed in *The New York Times* between 1980 and 2011, Marisa Abrajano and Zoltan Hajnal reported that the framing of immigration as an economic concern had been used with frequency only since 2000. The authors associated the increased use of the economic frame for immigration stories with a drop in public support for the Democratic Party. Similar in some ways to agenda setting, the use of frames can influence the way the public thinks about issues and views of issues (see Figure 13-2).[33]

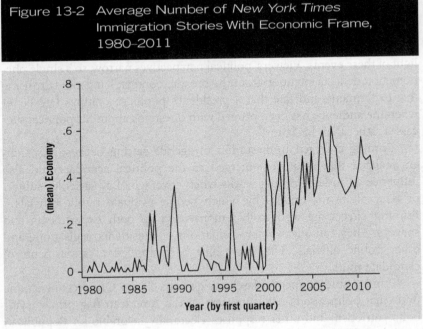

Figure 13-2   Average Number of *New York Times* Immigration Stories With Economic Frame, 1980–2011

Source: Abrajano, M. A., & Hajnal, Z. (2015). *White backlash*. Princeton University Press.
Note: Based on content analysis of 6,778 *New York Times* articles printed from 1980–2011.

Framing occurs through media presentations of messages. Framing was first studied extensively following Tversky and Kahneman's famous studies on how gain/loss framing affects choice.[34] Sometimes framing and framing effects occur due to news values and norms and routines of professional journalism (see Chapter 3). Other times, frames emerge from strategic political rhetoric uses by politicians. How much control journalists have over framing varies widely. Framing occurs when reporters adopt the frames chosen by regular beat sources; it can also happen when reporters choose sources who share their framing preferences or express their own frame choices in editorials and editorialized news. Journalists tend to exercise the least control over the framing of uncontroversial news coming from official sources and the most control over the framing of news about unexpected events or events unearthed by journalists' efforts.

When it comes to influencing debate and action on public policies, it is extraordinarily important whether journalists choose to frame issues in terms of the substance of the policy or in terms of the strategies used in battles about the policy. For example, as Figure 13-3 shows, reporting about the Hurricane Katrina disaster in *The New York Times, The Washington Post,* the New Orleans *Times-Picayune,* and the Baton Rouge *Advocate* stressed government failures in the relief process rather than the substance of essential reforms. Of 1,590 articles, 78% dealt with process issues. They appeared in the most prominent spots in the papers. Substance stories, dealing with the dimensions of the disaster and preventive measures, fared much less well. Scholars contend that the predominance of "process frames" in most public policy stories marginalizes the substance of political issues and prevents political leaders from explaining policy substance to the public prior to the adoption of laws. Lack of intelligent public dialogue about public policies is one of the damaging consequences of such framing. Public cynicism is another.[35]

Recent research on framing investigates the extent to which competing frames cancel each other out and/or the conditions under which one strategic frame wins out over another. In electoral contexts, for example, competing frames from rival candidates often do cancel out, with the result being that voters will fall back on initial predispositions, such as party identification.[36] Such an effect might first appear as a "non effect," but it suggests that competing frames are operating to cancel each other out. Regardless of origin, frames can have substantial implications for audience interpretation, evaluation, and decision making. Research on framing has shown, too, that whether framing effects occur depends on many factors, such as the type of frame, the source promoting the frame, characteristics of the audience exposed to the frame, and the context and timing of the frame's delivery.[37]

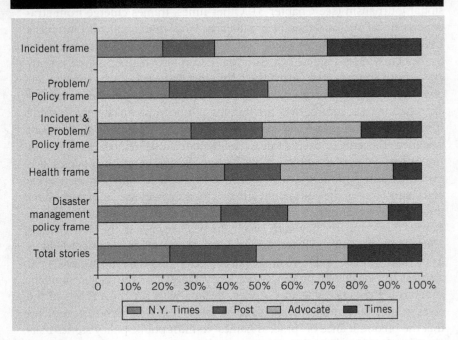

Figure 13-3 Framing Categories for Hurricane Katrina (Percentage of Newspaper Stories Featuring the Theme)

Source: Adapted from Barnes, M. D., Hanson, C. L., Novilla, L. M. B., Meacham, A. T., McIntyre, E., & Erickson, B. C. (2008). Analysis of media agenda setting during and after Hurricane Katrina: Implications for emergency preparedness, disaster response, and disaster policy. *American Journal of Public Health, 98*(4), 604–610.

Other Theories of Media Effects

Cultivation Theory: Despite early research showing that there was no real need for concerns about media exerting strong direct effects over the public, the popularity and perceived power of television was still a source of concern for researchers worried about the long-term effects of television exposure. Some were particularly concerned about the potential effects from exposure to violent images. Cultivation theory emerged in response to these concerns. Its main supposition was that television portrayals about the world would taint public perceptions of the real world, especially among those who consumed high volumes of television programming. Specifically, concerns were that exposure to violent images—especially over the long term—would lead to public fear, social conflict, and power struggles. Cultivation was hypothesized to occur through two mechanisms: mainstreaming and resonance. *Mainstreaming* suggests that television cultivates by homogenizing portrayals in ways that generate common perspectives. *Resonance* is something akin to a reinforcing effect—it intensifies cultivation effects when television portrayals are consistent with everyday, real-world experiences.[38] Savvy readers of this text may realize that, similar to agenda setting, cultivation on a broad scale would require mass media to regularly reach a very large proportion of the public. The emergence of the contemporary, more fragmented digital media environment thus raises the question of whether cultivation will hold now that the traditional mainstream television audience is splintered across a much larger and more diverse array of channels and platforms. Only time will tell. Despite that internet usage often enhances and reinforces the reach of traditional media and that there is still a great deal of audience overlap for major outlets and platforms, selective exposure patterns are fluid. In recent election cycles, media and fragmentation patterns suggest the persistence of distinct audience publics forming different perceived political realities.[39]

Narcotizing Effects: Cultivation effects were not the only negative media effects worried about during the early stages of effects research. Over the years, several different arguments were advanced about the potential dampening effects from high levels of media consumption on political and civic life. In 1948, Paul Lazarsfeld and Robert Merton cautioned about a "narcotizing dysfunction" from mass media exposure. According to their explanation, media consumption can have a narcotizing effect on the public, one that results in withdrawal from political and civic life.[40] Various iterations of this argument have appeared in research on political participation and engagement in the time since. Robert Putnam's *Bowling Alone* offered increased proliferation of televisions into homes and higher rates of entertainment-based television programming as at least one explanatory factor in part of a broader explanation for declines in social capital—a trend beginning in the 1950s.[41] According to communication scholar Nojin Kwak and his colleagues, even the so called slacktivism hypothesis—which expects digital communication technologies and digital media activism to have detrimental effects on in-person or offline political participation and engagement—is simply a contemporary, digital iteration of the mass media's narcotizing effect.[42]

The Sleeper Effect: Studies of attitudes date back to at least the 1930s. One of the most robust findings from the vast body of research on attitudes and persuasion is that if attitude change occurs; it usually happens to a greater degree in the time most immediately following an attempt at persuasion, only to later start shifting back toward the original attitudinal state. This process is known as *attitude decay*. The *sleeper effect* describes a departure from this pattern, where the persuasive impact of media exposure increases over time. Various explanations for the sleeper effect have been offered. The most convincing of these was that source effects hamper persuasion at the time of the attempt, but as source and message are separated in memory over time, learning that occurred from exposure to the message itself can remain in memory, unfettered by negative orientations toward the source or its credibility. The explanation characterized the consensus for a time during the 1950s and 1960s, but scholarly debates around the sleeper effect emerged during the 1970s, lasting through the decade. By the late 1980s, researchers addressed criticisms about the sleeper effect by convincingly replicating sleeper effects across several studies, and more robustly demonstrating the source and message conditions under which sleeper effects were likely to occur.[43] However, even the most recent research on the sleeper effect is still trying to understand how the interplay among source and message credibility, argument strength, topics, and timing operate in tandem to produce it.[44]

Spiral of Silence Theory: The argument central to Noelle-Neumann's spiral of silence theory is that news media and interpersonal context can produce silencing spirals by creating the impression among some that their views are in the minority. This impression, in turn, prompts self-perceived minority opinion individuals to keep quiet about their views and perspectives instead of expressing them. An underlying assumption in the theory is that the news media are a main source of information for learning about public opinion, including which views are minority or majority, making them central to producing such an effect. The theory emerged when broadcast television news channels still held a monopoly market share of the American viewing audience and began to cover public opinion polls extensively in their news programs. Though numerous studies show that news media do in fact shape people's perceptions of the political world, evidence for spiral of silence effects has been inconsistent. Researchers question whether spiral of silence theory is still viable. It relies on assumptions that were characteristic of the broadcast era (homogeneous and monopolistic media), which is not commensurate with today's fragmented media landscape.[45]

Media Dependency Theory: The central argument of media dependency theory is that the strength of media effects is conditioned by the degree to which individuals regularly rely on the media. Under this theory, researchers expect to observe strong media effects on those people who consume a great deal of media. With this theory, researchers intuited that individual-level differences might help explain some of the variation in media effects studies being conducted at the time. It was one of the first theories that sought to grapple with the complexities of not only individual-level differences but also contextual factors such as interpersonal social networks and other cultural and societal influences. Because this theory is capable of dealing with contextual complexity and media dependency, researchers find it relevant for understanding media effects today. Media dependency theory has even been extended to encompass dependency on a particular medium, device, or platform, which is critical in an era where internet, social media, and smartphone addictions are of growing concern.[46] Table 13-1 provides a summary of major theories and effects from the broadcast era.

Table 13-1   Chronology and Origins of Broadcast-Era Media Effects

Expected/Observed Effect	Theory/Effect	Timing/Early Works
Powerful, Direct, Uniform	Hypodermic Needle Theory and Magic Bullet Theory	1920s concerns over media technology and propaganda
Minimal, Limited, Indirect	Two-Step Flow	Lazarsfeld, Berelson, & Gaudet (1948)
Powerful	Narcotizing Effect	Lazarsfeld & Merton (1948)
Minimal	Sleeper Effect	Hovland, Lumsdaine, & Sheffield (1949)
Moderate, Conditional	Preference-Based, Reinforcement	Hovland (1949; 1953), McGuire (1968)
Minimal	Selective Exposure	Festinger (1957)
Powerful	Cultivation Theory	Gerbner (1967)
Minimal	Uses and Gratifications	Lundberg & Hulton (1968)

(Continued)

(Continued)

Expected/Observed Effect	Theory/Effect	Timing/Early Works
Powerful, Limited	Agenda-Setting Effect	McCombs & Shaw (1972)
Powerful	Spiral of Silence Theory	Noelle-Neumann (1974)
Powerful, Conditional	Media Dependency Theory	Ball-Rokeach & DeFleur (1976)
Powerful, Limited	Framing Effect	Tversky & Kahneman (1981), Iyengar & Kinder (1987)
Powerful, Limited	Priming Effect	Iyengar, Peters, & Kinder (1982), Iyengar & Kinder (1987)
Powerful, Conditional	Receive-Accept-Sample Model	Zaller (1992)

Source: Compiled by J. L. Dunaway from Iyengar, S. (2017). *A typology of media effects.* In K. Kenski & K. H. Jamieson (Eds.), *The Oxford handbook of political communication* (pp. 59–68). Oxford University Press; Jamieson, K. H. (2017). Creating the hybrid field of political communication: A five-decade long evolution of the concepts of effects. In K. Kenski & K. H. Jamieson (Eds.), *The Oxford handbook of political communication.* Oxford University Press; Stroud, N. J. (2017). Selective exposure theories. In K. Kenski & K. H. Jamieson (Eds.), *The Oxford handbook of political communication.* Oxford University Press; Elasmar, M. G. (2018). Media effects. In P. M. Napoli (Ed.), *Mediated communication* (Vol. 7, pp. 29–53). Walter de Gruyter GmbH & Co KG; Cacciatore, M. A., Scheufele, D. A., & Iyengar, S. (2016). The end of framing as we know it . . . and the future of media effects. *Mass Communication and Society, 19*(1), 7–23.

The Arrival of Cable and the Internet: The Expansion of Media Choice

In the 1980s, more technological innovation—this time, the satellite—changed audiences' access to mass media. Cable channels proliferated and Americans' choices for content expanded; the cost of entry for new media outlets was lowered, disrupting the news economy by creating more competition. The broadcast television monopoly over the share of the American audience started to decline. New cable news entrants, such as CNN, filled the airwaves on a 24-hour basis, providing constant news coverage and political commentary. The arrival of cable and the internet only increased economic threat and competition for traditional print and broadcast news organizations, exacerbating economic stress and limiting the amount of resources available for investing in newsroom personnel and other tools required for in-depth reporting. The quality of content suffered under these economic pressures.[47]

The expansion of media choice also significantly shifted the focus of research on media effects by reviving interest in selective exposure theories. Earlier media effects research demonstrated that audiences are active and have heterogeneous preferences. Audience preferences and predispositions guide both media selections and audience responses to media messages. The active and heterogeneous nature of audiences meant that the most significant change wrought by the arrival of cable and the internet was how it reshaped the structure of market offerings. Cable produced a gradual expansion of channel offerings into households, and as high-speed internet proliferated, we saw those same options expand to their online formats, as well as the introduction of thousands of additional outlets for entertainment and news. The arrival of the internet in particular lowered barriers to entry; both cable and internet meant a growing rush of new competitors offering content in the media field, creating pressure for content providers to seek and meet unmet needs for niche programming. Shortly, more narrowly casted options emerged in the domains of both news and entertainment. These structural variations allowed different patterns of media exposure.

In contrast to their discovery during the era of minimal effects, when interest in selective exposure theories first resurged with the arrival of cable and the internet, they were not typically thought of as a means by which media effects are limited. In the face of expanding media choice, the importance of selective exposure took on new meaning. Many commentators and researchers were concerned about the effect of partisan selective exposure behaviors. They expected that when given the choice, people would choose only to consume political information with perspectives similar to their own, leading to the formation of attitudinal echo chambers that would serve to strengthen and polarize political attitudes.[48]

Concerns about partisan selective exposure were reasonable. Not only was polarization on the rise and largely concurrent with cable and internet proliferation trends,[49] self-report and audience data reflected at least some fragmentation among audiences for partisan cable media outlets, though perhaps not to the level of completely isolated echo chambers.[50] Media selectivity along ideological lines is still common. For example, conservatives typically flock to Fox News while liberals choose CNN or MSNBC (see Figure 13-1). Where the political orientations of these cable channels differ, their audiences' opinions often reflect the cleavages.[51] Partisans and partisan leaners also tend to trust attitude-agreeable outlets more (see Figure 13-4). The individual-level tendency to engage in selective exposure is demonstrated in numerous empirical research studies. In controlled experiments, for example, subjects tend to choose news articles aligned with their political opinions over those that do not.[52]

Other research highlighted different concerns about media choice and some even downplayed worries about the potential for persuasive and polarizing effects in a high-choice media environment. Markus Prior's research, for example, suggested that the primary cause for concern about expanding media choice was not about partisan attitudes but what it meant for citizen exposure to (or avoidance of) news and political information.[53]

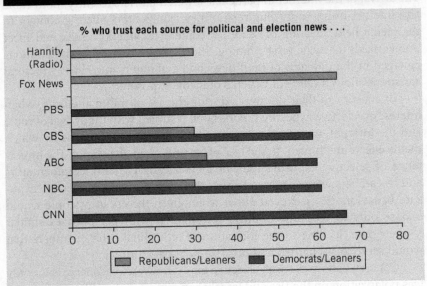

Figure 13-4 Trust in Political and Election News Sources by Party, 2020

% who trust each source for political and election news . . .

Republicans/Leaners   Democrats/Leaners

Source: Adapted from Jurkowitz, M., Mitchell, A., Shearer, E., & Walker, M. (2020, January 24). U.S. media polarization and the 2020 election: A nation divided. Pew Research Center. https://www.journalism.org/2020/01/24/u-s-media-polarization-and-the-2020-election-a-nation-divided/

Note: Missing data for outlet indicates it was not listed among top five trusted for partisans and leaners on that side.

Prior pointed out that it was not only options for news that expanded with higher media choice. The expansion of entertainment options was even greater than that for news. In the broadcast era, the average home had only five to ten channels from which to choose. Today, the average number of channels per household is somewhere closer to 160. Prior argued that because a healthy contingent of the American public has a preference for entertainment media over news, the fact that with cable and the internet there was always something else to read, listen to, or watch would mean that many people would take those opportunities and opt out of news consumption all together. On the one hand, this was good news from the perspective of concern about echo chambers and partisan polarization. If people are choosing to watch ESPN instead of Fox News or MSNBC, they are not being exposed to potentially polarizing partisan news. On the other hand, the fact that so many people are opting out of news has other detrimental effects. Those citizens who typically prefer entertainment over news will no longer be exposed to news regularly on an incidental basis, which contributes to declines in their political knowledge and participation.

Prior's research showed that both access to more cable channels and access to the internet decrease political knowledge and participation among those who are not very interested in news and politics. However, access to high choice for those who are interested in news meant increases in political knowledge and participation. While that is good news for some, it also widened the political knowledge gap between those who are interested in news and politics and those who are not. Because those with lower levels of news interest and political knowledge were dropping out of opportunities for political participation, Prior noted that over time, the electorate would be increasingly made up primarily of strong partisans, which would ultimately produce more polarized voting behavior in the aggregate.

From this perspective, the active and heterogeneous nature of audiences meant that high-choice environments would produce selections based on a preference for entertainment over news as often (or more often) than they would produce choices among in-party and out-party partisan news channels, rendering any polarizing effects on the mass public as minimal. So just as in earlier phases of media effects research, initial concerns about exposure to persuasive political information were offset by the fact that audiences are active and selective. Research from Markus Prior— and later, Vin Arceneaux and Martin Johnson—demonstrated that audiences often actively avoid political programing in lieu of entertainment, dampening the possibility of widespread persuasive and polarizing effects from selective exposure to partisan news.[54] And, just as researchers learned from early work in minimal effects, those audience decisions depended on interest in politics and strength of existing political attitudes and beliefs.

A key aspect of the broad debate over the polarizing effects of a high-choice media environment involves the role of motivated reasoning. Researchers have known for quite some time that motivated reasoning guides media selections for many people, especially partisans. Yet a great deal of research on media effects and information processing shows that motivated reasoning does more than simply shape choices about what media to consume. Instead, it also influences audiences' reactions to news and political information once exposure to it occurs. For example, research shows that *fact polarization*, where partisans on two sides of the political continuum seem to be operating with a different set of facts, is on the rise. Naturally, this has many people concerned about whether media selectivity and partisan news sources are to blame.[55] What a lot of research suggests, however, is that fact polarization, persuasion, and even misperceptions can also occur because people often simply ignore or reject information they disagree with, even if they are exposed to diverse viewpoints. Partisan-motivated reasoning shapes audiences' reactions to political information as much as it shapes their choices about media sources. The availability of partisan news sources and audience preferences for agreeable news are not the only drivers of polarization.

Digital, Social, and Mobile Media Effects

One of the reasons the arrival of cable and the internet was so disruptive to researchers' efforts to understand media effects is because it so vastly expanded media choice available to audiences. Initially, internet optimists assumed that the availability of so much more information would lead to higher rates of political knowledge among citizens and higher rates of voter turnout and other forms of political engagement. After all, news consumers now had the option of anywhere from three to ten (or more) 24-hour cable news networks from which to choose, not to mention countless websites offering various forms of news and political information from around the globe. While the arrival of cable doubled or tripled the number of news options provided by the major television networks, the internet exponentially expanded media offerings. Not only did every existing traditional media outlet eventually have a digital version of itself, countless Web-native sources of political information—interest group websites, campaign and party websites, new news sources, news aggregator sites, and blog sites—emerged at a rapid pace. The optimistic view was that so much political information available from so many sources should help democratize the information environment, at least among those with internet access.

However, once again, as with cable, so much choice—coupled with people's tendency to engage in selective exposure—also created the potential for partisan echo chambers. *Echo chambers* was a term used to describe a state in which people only choose media sources they agree with politically, creating an echo chamber of similar views, thoughts, and opinions. Terms such as *partisan enclaves, information silos,* and *filter bubbles* mean essentially the same thing. All of these concepts reflect efforts to articulate the concern that in the newer, highly fragmented media environment, people will no longer be exposed to views and information they do not agree with. People worried that echo chambers would remove common understanding about the important issues of the day, reduce opportunities for democratic deliberation and debate, and contribute to partisan polarization, which was already on the rise by this point in time. Partisan selective exposure—the act of choosing politically agreeable media sources—was not the only problem. Algorithmic filtering—when news aggregators and search engines use algorithms to direct people to websites and news stories based on their already-known political preferences, creating what filter bubbles—presented another challenge. The so-called pessimist's take was that even as high media choice created more opportunities for exposure to political information, there was also potential for exacerbating political divisions.

Research conducted over the next several years following the arrival and proliferation of the internet further informed debates about exposure diversity on the Web and persuasive media effects in the digital media environment. Yet, even now, evidence is still inconclusive as to the extent to which people consistently seek political information sources they know they agree with and avoid those with which they do not agree. This is true both for how people behave online and offline.[56] Studies based on digital audience and Web-tracking data show low levels of online ideological segregation (i.e., online echo chambers), significant overlap in online news audiences across the ideological spectrum, and that web traffic is highly concentrated on popular, relatively neutral mainstream news sites.[57]

Algorithmic filtering conducted by search engines, news aggregators, and social networking was also a source of concern about the persuasive and polarizing effects of partisan enclaves and ideological segregation in digital media contexts. These platforms personalize content,[58] but evidence for the prevalence of filter bubbles is also mixed, as is evidence about their effects.[59] Some studies find that digital media encourage partisan enclaves or information silos,[60] but other research finds that high-choice environments encourage exposure diversity.[61] As researchers continued to grapple with understanding persuasive media effects from the vast expansion of media on the Web, the arrival and proliferation of social media platforms added even more complexity to the digital media environment, which was not yet well understood in the first place.

Social media platforms are simply another part of the digital media environment, so why would media effects be different on social networking sites such as Facebook, Twitter, Instagram, and the like? Research points to several features of social media that make these platforms unique or likely to produce different kinds of effects relative to simply seeking news on a website such as CNN.com. News exposure on social media is heavily determined by both individual user behaviors (such as choices about people to friend and follow) and the interests, preferences, and sharing, following, and commenting behaviors within one's social network. On the positive side, social media users do not appear to select networks that are entirely one-sided and attitudinally congruent, and incidental exposure to both attitudinal and counter-attitudinal news does occur. Unfortunately, sharing and clicking behaviors do result in more exposure to like-minded news than cross-ideology content, but incidental exposure to attitude-inconsistent and neutral information does occur frequently. Though Etan Bakshy and colleagues find that exposure to like-minded information is more frequent relative to counter-attitudinal information, they find significant amounts of exposure to cross-ideological content on Facebook.[62]

A clear implication of research on social media effects is that the "social" in social media actually matters for whether influence occurs. Social networks were designed with social (not political) aims in mind, and the network structures providing the scaffolding of these sites are social too, comprised of both strong and weak ties. People are most persuaded by sources they trust, especially people they know personally—such as those in their networks. A key feature of social media is the ability for people to share their personal views and to share and re-share news stories or links to other kinds of political information. On social media sites, friends or followers displace news editors as the curators and gatekeepers of what is considered newsworthy. What is deemed credible on social media is therefore different and based more on social considerations than on expertise or political considerations. Such social considerations are likely to drive sharing and re-sharing behaviors, which are akin to endorsement on social media sites. Several prominent recent studies suggest that the amplifying effect of social networks and their affordances for sharing and re-sharing information sharply increases the likelihood that media messages can have substantial effects by activating attitudes and motivating behavior.[63]

As a positive take from the perspective of concerns about echo chambers and filter bubbles as drivers of polarization, evidence suggests that the social nature of networking ties and endorsements encourages cross-ideology exposure. Because people have network ties crossing the ideological spectrum, social sharing and peer endorsements work to increase exposure diversity.[64] Though there is substantial evidence of partisan enclaves, echo chambers, and filter bubbles, they do not create complete silos on social media. Instead, these silos are prevalent but porous to cross-ideological content, and they may even facilitate exposure diversity.

Research shows that patterns of information processing and exposure are different on mobile devices compared to traditional computers, such as laptops and desktops. Most of the research conducted so far has focused on how mobile devices affect learning or the ability to feel immersed in media content to the extent one often does when consuming media on larger screens. Several of these studies find that information seeking and processing is much harder with smaller screens, even from video content. When information exposure occurs on mobile devices, recall is lower and cognitive processing requires more effort. What this means, of course, is that people generally learn less from video when they watch on a small screen,[65] and when it comes to text-based content, screen size is negatively correlated with ease of reading, clarity of information organization, and reading time.[66] Not surprisingly, consuming information on mobile phones also requires more time spent scrolling for information.[67] Attention to media content itself is generally more limited on mobile devices.

Whether the evidence on mobile media effects is good news or bad probably depends on the media effect at hand. From the perspective of learning from news and the acquisition of political knowledge, low attention and more effortful cognitive processing means less meaningful engagement with news on mobile devices. At the same time, fleeting attention spans and less time with news and political information likely means the effects of persuasive or polarizing information or even misinformation are minimal on mobile devices.[68]

Understanding Differential Effects

The research on media effects reveals that the different types of media available today—where messages are delivered by all kinds of platforms and devices—present media content in ways that vary substantially. It would be surprising, therefore, if their impact were identical, even when they deal with the same subjects or contain the same informational content. Current research does not provide uniform answers about the precise effects of these variations.[69] We focus on what is known about the differential impact spanning several modes of content delivery—differential influences from print, broadcast, and digital media stimuli on mass audiences.

News on the Web

Early projections about the effect of the internet on political knowledge predicted that because the internet provided more information from many venues at a low cost, it would naturally enhance levels of political knowledge. For many people, this is true—those who are interested in politics become better informed and exhibit higher levels of political knowledge as choice expands. However, as we described above, the expansion of choice provided by the many outlets on cable and the internet also expands the number of outlets offering entertainment content. The implication of this is that for many, namely those uninterested in politics, the expansion of choice decreases the likelihood of encountering political information incidentally and becoming more informed as a result. Instead, the high-choice environment provides many alternatives to public affairs content. The end result is that with more content choices comes a widening gap in political knowledge between those who are interested in politics and those who are not.[70]

Besides effects from the changing market structure for news and the expansion of choice, researchers are only now beginning to understand how digital platforms influence media effects and the public's ability to learn from news when they are exposed to it. Political learning and persuasion depend in part on the way information is presented and the way people process information. For example, some research suggests learning from digital media may be more difficult. Traditional media provide cues about where to look first, such as the main headline on the front page.[71] The way information is presented on the internet actually facilitates whether learning occurs. On news websites, image-heavy layouts encourage more learning and recall than classic print-heavy displays. The complexity of the information on the page in print displays hampers the search for information and inhibits object recognition and recall. Simple page layouts are preferred to noisy, distracting designs. News audiences' increasing reliance on digital and social media for news underscores the urgency for a better understanding of learning, recall, and engagement when news is presented in different displays across various platforms.[72]

Social Media

Exposure patterns and learning are also different on social media when compared to other forms of digital information consumption, such as from news websites. First, while social media offers an array of platforms from which to choose, choice is sometimes limited once users are on the site. Newsfeeds and posts from people in one's network often produce incidental exposure to political information even for those not interested in politics. Candidates and political organizations are also using social networking sites to send messages and share information. Hence, social media users often get exposed to political information even when they do not seek it. This is one reason the savviest political operations make use of individuals' existing social networks to encourage more message exposure.[73]

Research shows that political use of Facebook has the potential to influence political attitudes, learning, and behavior.[74] As we noted above, incidental exposure occurs through social networks—those who are politically interested often share information with their networks on sites such as Facebook or Twitter. If online networks operate similarly to the way research suggests traditional social networks function, we would expect online interaction about that shared information to stimulate conversation and the exchange of information. Even though people often have like-minded online social networks, that would not prohibit (and may possibly help) those who are less politically interested to become politically engaged and learn from those in their social networks who are more interested. Indeed, some research suggests that possibilities for learning from this sort of incidental exposure through social networks are promising.[75] However, much of the political information shared on social media is shared with strategic goals in mind, not democratic values. Campaigns dole out heavy volumes of banal announcements and policy-free attacks, providing clear evidence that a lot of political communication on social networks is not informative.[76] This provides one explanation for why research identifying healthy rates of incidental exposure to political information on Facebook does not reveal correlated improvements in user political knowledge.[77]

Mobile Media Effects

Research on digital news consumption and information processing shows that mobile platforms present challenges to learning from news. Several studies show that learning from the small screen, even from video, is challenging relative to large screens and that it curbs recall and requires more cognitive processing effort. People learn less from video when they watch on a small screen,[78] and screen size is negatively correlated with ease of reading, clarity of information organization, and reading time;[79] small screens also require more time spent scrolling for information.[80] There is also some evidence that attention itself is limited on mobile devices. Recent experimental studies using eye-tracking software to monitor news consumption on computers, tablets, and smartphones found that relative to mobile users, computer users spent more time reading news content and were more likely to notice links on the page.

Web traffic data for news sites reveals similar patterns.[81] Large commercial Web traffic data patterns show that mobile users spend far less time on news websites compared to desktop and laptop users. Though audience reach is high on mobile devices (see Table 13-2)—meaning that many people use them to seek and consume news—mobile attention rates are low. The exception is among mobile users of news apps, who spend a long time on news content but who constitute a very tiny fraction of the online public audience. Presentation of content in mobile-friendly ways will undoubtedly help; news outlets are currently working on best practices for optimizing news content for mobile viewing. It is not yet clear what implications these adaptations will have for the informative content in news.[82]

Research on lingering digital divides also casts doubt on the informative potential of news on mobile devices. Karen Mossberger and colleagues find that the likelihood of seeking news online drops significantly absent high-speed internet access in the home.[83] Pew Research Center data show similar evidence: Between 2010 and 2015, respondents grew increasingly likely to report that not having broadband at home is a major disadvantage in key areas such as finding new job opportunities, gaining new career skills, learning about or accessing government services, and getting health information. Respondents were 13% more likely to report not having broadband at home as a major impediment to keeping up with the news. This is because mobile internet is not as fast or stable as wired internet, making searches and consumption of certain kinds of Web content relatively inconvenient. For example, when wireless service is spotty, slow-loading content discourages news consumption on mobile devices. Four out of five users click away if a video stalls while loading. If content is slow to load, users defect after only a second or two of waiting. News providers are doing whatever they can to avoid the problem of making people have to click and wait in the mobile environment, such as Facebook's agreement with news outlets to put news stories directly into news feeds and Gmail's

Table 13.2 Top Digital Destinations for News, July–September 2020

News Site	Web Traffic Share	Monthly Visitors	% Desktop	% Mobile
yahoo.com	17.07%	1.916 Billion	62.2%	34.8%
cnn.com	4.78%	537.2 Million	43.2%	56.8%
foxnews.com	3.16%	354.5 Million	43.7%	56.3%
msn.com	2.96%	332.0 Million	50.5%	49.5%
nytimes.com	2.70%	303.5 Million	51.5%	48.5%
news.google.com	1.93%	217.0 Million	77.7%	22.3%
washingtonpost.com	1.58%	177.7 Million	45.4%	54.6%
cnbc.com	1.09%	122.0 Million	39.1%	60.9%
dailymailco.uk	1.03%	115.7 Million	46.9%	53.1%
usatoday.com	1.02%	115.0 Million	38.1%	61.9%

Source: Similarweb Research Intelligence, News and Media Industry. [Website]. https://pro.similarweb.com/#/research/marketresearch/webmarketanalysis/mapping/News_and_Media/840/2020.07-2020.09?webSource=Total

Note: Data are from news industry in the United States.

efforts to facilitate saving linked content to read later.[84] Though high-speed wireless has improved exponentially, even the fastest wireless is relatively slow when compared to high-speed internet on a traditional computer and is not likely to catch up to wired internet.[85]

The upshot of all of this is that although mobile provides more opportunity for internet access for many who might not otherwise have it, there are important differences in access and utility relative to what high-speed internet on computers provides. From an information-seeking and learning perspective, mobile-only internet access does not operate interchangeably with high-speed computer access. However, research on how mobile access affects civic and political engagement finds that use of mobile technology can enhance engagement for some, depending on user competence with mobile technology and the size and composition of their social network.[86]

Political Discourse, Deliberation, and Mobilization

Optimism about the democratic effects of media technology also centers on the degree to which the nearly endless sources of political information and the increased affordances for interactivity will enhance political engagement and participation more generally. Researchers have asked questions about whether features of modern media increase more campaign contributions, stimulate higher voting rates, and raise the quality of democratic deliberation. In this area, the optimists' views are supported in that there does seem to be a positive relationship between access to the internet and political engagement.[87] Participation online has increased since 2008, and the political engagement of those involved in social networking sites often extends to offline behaviors. While some evidence suggests that the effects of the internet on engagement seem to be conditioned on political interest, the choice of content, and political and structural contexts, other evidence shows that social influence through networks can exert rather powerful mobilization effects.[88]

Media Effects on Discourse and Deliberation

Fears about political affect and polarization aside, structurally, the contemporary digital media environment certainly provides new channels through which individuals can share political information and opinions. If nothing else, these channels (emails, texts, instant messages, social media networks, online discussion groups) are tools that can potentially be used for democratic discourse and deliberation. Social media provide spaces for the open exchange of ideas and information. Social network sites have the potential to provide opportunities to engage those who are politically less interested and to foster political knowledge through information exposure. In fact, some research already shows evidence of these trends, and their use is growing among all age cohorts.[89]

Because social media networks are primarily social, they are often politically diverse even though some ideological clustering occurs.[90] The exposure to diverse political information in a social network setting allows for political discussion and the potential for engagement and political learning. In fact, when studying online discussion spaces, media scholars Magdalena Wojcieszak and Diana C. Mutz find that the "potential for deliberation occurs primarily in online groups where politics comes up only incidentally, but is not the central purpose of the discussion space." Their findings suggest that the interaction of the social network and the occasional piece of political information is precisely the kind of situation likely to allow political deliberation and discussion.[91] More recent research raises questions about whether ideologically diverse networks mean more exposure to cross-ideological information. Social network users are less likely to be exposed to cross-ideological content on social media and are less likely to engage with cross-ideological content.[92] However, low levels of exposure do not prohibit meaningful deliberation when incidental exposure does occur.

Other research investigates whether social media networks should function similarly to the way face-to-face networks operate by fostering the exchange of information, trust, and social capital. Leticia Bode examines this contention and finds that intense engagement with one's Facebook network encourages behaviors that stimulate political participation of all kinds. Other research shows that opinion leaders are highly engaged in social media networks and finds high levels of correlation between social network political engagement and offline political engagement.[93] Research by Jacobs, Cook, and Delli Carpini suggests that the positive effects of online deliberation are much weaker than the effects found for in-person deliberation.[94] In short, social media behaviors may foster habits that encourage consideration of diverse viewpoints, the exchange of political information, and political participation, but more research is still needed for meaningful conclusions. Research in this area is difficult because social media platforms become quickly outmoded. Friendster and MySpace faded fast; Facebook, Twitter, Instagram, and Snapchat are hugely popular now, but they may not last. Researchers have to move quickly to keep pace with trends in digital and social media to truly understand their influence.

Effects on Political Mobilization and Organizing

Digital and social media have played a major part in many recent instances of political activism. A survey-based study of 2003 anti–Iraq War protesters demonstrates that mobilizers rely heavily on electronic media, websites, and listservs, finding that 48% of people involved with the Global Social Justice movement relied on digital or electronic sources for political information daily, while 73% of protestors reported relying on electronic or digital media for routine political activities.[95] As the Mubarak government was beginning to fail in Egypt in 2011, digital media allowed coordinated communication with people outside Egypt, and the government was concerned enough with the potential of digital media to shut down the internet nationwide.

Modern communication technologies allow a speed of mobilization previously unheard of, and the networks of communication and mechanisms of delivery enable communication with people across a range of interest or involvement, allowing communicators to tap groups beyond tight-issue publics. This means that even fleeting interest in an issue or cause, or simply a social connection, can prompt individuals' involvement in high levels of political participation such as protests, walkouts, or boycotts. According to political communication scholars, these changes enabled by technology represent a drastic shift in how mobilization occurs. Essentially, the result is more fluid organizational forms that require less infrastructure, membership, and funding but can nonetheless be very successful in mobilizing interest and action.[96]

Despite all the recent attention to social media, email is still an enormously powerful tool for online organizing, and advocacy groups are constantly honing their use of email to become more efficient. Organizations such as MoveOn communicate with huge memberships to advance political causes and mobilize support for issues (Photo 13-1).[97] During the 2012 election cycle, President Obama's campaign sent more than 1,700 variations of emails and raised over $600 million, primarily from fundraising messages.[98] At the same time, Johnson and Bimber find that the internet is good for raising funds and short-term engagement but seems ill equipped to foster meaningful offline mobilization. Echoing several other studies, they note that online organizing today adopts a "postbureaucratic" form of diffused hierarchy and less centralized leadership, but they suggest this lack of infrastructure and hierarchy renders long-term mobilizing difficult.[99]

A debate over "clicktivism" or "slacktivism" also persists. It focuses on whether the ease of sending political appeals and clicking to join, sign, volunteer, or donate removes the impassioned intensity and desire to act from political activism, diminishing its meaning and impact. Several examples of poorly coordinated e-petitions and petered-out mini-movements demonstrate that meaningful organizing and action still require a significant amount of sophisticated forethought and planning. Still, most evidence suggests that the impact of communication and information technologies has vast potential for mobilization and political organizing.[100]

As technologies evolve, so does research on their role in civic engagement and mobilization. Recent research investigating when online spaces and digital communications facilitate mobilization and when they do not reveals several conditioning factors. In her investigation of four online

Dear MoveOn member,

We're teaming up with our friends at the Progressive Change Campaign Committee to host a special emergency conference call TONIGHT featuring Senators Elizabeth Warren and Chuck Schumer, who will lay out the Senate Democrats' strategy for stopping Republicans from dismantling the Affordable Care Act and discuss the role all of us can play.

Click here to RSVP for tonight's call that will start at 10 p.m. ET/9 CT/8 MT/7 PT, and we'll send you the dial-in information.

Can't join the call? Click here to sign the petition telling Congress: Don't take away our health care.

Senate Democrats are going to hold the Senate floor late into the night tonight, to fight against Republican efforts to repeal the Affordable Care Act. Tonight's Senate action will challenge Republicans to not "Make America Sick Again"—and is a sign that Democrats are gearing up to resist the Trump/Republican agenda with every tool at their disposal.

Already, MoveOn members have flooded Senate offices with phone calls and attended speak-outs at Senate offices around the country to tell Republicans, "Don't take away our health care." Now, we are gearing up to fight the nomination of Tom Price who is committed to repealing the ACA and attacking Medicare and Medicaid as head of Health and Human Services.

This is the first big fight of 2017 against the Trump and Republican legislative agenda. It's imperative that we give it our all so that Trump and the GOP experience the full force of progressive organizing. We'll all need to keep up the pressure to keep Democrats united in defense of health care and push a few Republicans to stop plans that would strip health care from tens of millions of Americans.

Tonight's late-night debate is one sign that Democrats are ready to fight. Join us on tonight's call to hear more about their plans and ours.

Click here to RSVP, and join us on tonight's call at 10 ET/ 9 CT / 8 MT / 7 PT.

Can't join the call? Click here to sign the petition telling Congress: Don't take away our health care.

Thanks for all you do.

—Ben W., Emma, Justin, Jo, and the rest of the team

Photo 13-1 Sample of MoveOn.org call-to-action email

Source: MoveOn.org.

spaces, Jessica Beyer finds that the rules and structures governing these spaces influence the degree to which they foster mobilization. Features such as anonymity, low levels of formal regulation, limited access to small-group interaction, and the cohesiveness of the group all have an impact on the likelihood of political action.[101] Zizi Papacharissi argues that affect and emotion afforded through the narrative and network structure of social media are key to activating latent ties that foster digital mobilization.[102] Chris Wells's study of civic organizations' attempts to engage youths identifies particular patterns of digital communications to be (in)effective among the digital youth culture, who have developed new norms of citizenship that embrace civic communications different than those used by most civic organizations. Young digital citizens prefer civic communication styles matching their preference for the self-expression and participatory experiences that populate their networks through diverse and sharable content. The success of civic organizations' efforts to engage the youth will depend on whether they adopt new forms of civic communication.[103]

New forms of digital analytics are also shaping the effectiveness of digital media activism. Digital communication strategies are governed by different logics than traditional media, and civic organizations are still learning what strategies work well in the digital environment. Civic organizations with the know-how have developed sophisticated logics underlying the use of a new class of digital analytic tools. Ranging from online video platforms designed to go viral and automated tactical optimization systems, these tools allow for a strategy of what Dave Karpf refers to as "digital listening."[104] For civic groups and organizations with resources, staff, and skills, these digital tactics allow constant feedback on message effectiveness. Using analytics, civic organizations can constantly monitor and improve their success in attracting the attention and engagement of the mass public. This form of activism relies on three distinct features: a culture of digital message testing as a means to inform strategic decisions about ongoing tactics; reliance on data from social networking sites, email, and website traffic data; and analytic strategies using large amounts of data. These strategies undoubtedly provide insight into ways of improving engagement but also come with the potential to distract from the original civic aims of the organization and prioritize what is clickable over what is critical to the mission of the organization.

SUMMARY

The early research on media effects began by focusing on direct and consequential effects; researchers thought media messages would have substantial effects on persuasion and attitude change. Research later moved toward the view that media effects were minimal. By the time the broadcast era came to a close, accumulated evidence had moved consensus once again, this time toward a middle ground. Media effects were direct and significant but limited, landing somewhere in between massive and minimal effects. Nevertheless, those conclusions were based on a media environment very different from today. The media environment is high choice. There are countless content offerings through cable, satellite, and the internet. Digital platforms (websites and social media) also provide nearly endless opportunities for consuming media content, despite being delivered in slightly different configurations. This high-choice setting allows for many opportunities for political learning, but selective exposure behaviors and a highly polarized political setting also stoke concerns that people will only choose to consume ideologically flavored news they already agree with. Research on cable and internet echo chambers remains mixed. Evidence about polarizing effects they might encourage is inconsistent. Social and mobile media present even more new challenges for researchers—for both these media forms, we know much less about persuasive and polarizing media effects.

Early projections about the effect of the internet on political learning knowledge were optimistic. They predicted that because the internet provided more information from many venues at a low cost, it would naturally enhance levels of political knowledge. This was the case for politically interested people. However, the expansion of choice provided by the many outlets on cable and the internet also expanded the number of outlets offering entertainment. This meant that for those uninterested in politics, the expansion of choice allowed constant access to entertainment programming, which decreased the likelihood of incidental exposure to political information, leaving them less informed. The end result was a widening gap in political knowledge between those who are politically interested and those who are not.[105]

Media exposure is different on social media. While social media offers an array of platforms from which to choose, choices about what you see are limited once users are on the sites. Newsfeeds and posts from people in a social network often force incidental exposure to political information even for those not interested in politics. Candidates and political organizations also use these sites to share information, producing even more instances of incidental exposure. Social media incidental exposure may produce by-product political learning. The negative implication is that exposure to misinformation may contribute to the development of political misperceptions; at the same time, studies find that users often do not learn from corrections to misinformation. Researchers have much more to learn about the conditions under which exposure to political information or misinformation leads users to recall information and update their knowledge or beliefs.

The mobile setting presents challenges for a mass public with already low levels of interest in political news. Mobile news seeking and consumption are limited by problems with functionality and connectivity. Smaller screens are prohibitive for learning and information seeking. Larger screens equate to more time spent in applications and more data downloads.[106] Mobile connection speeds present another hurdle for news seekers. Mobile users are notorious for how quickly they abandon slow-loading content. However, research on how mobile access affects civic and political engagement finds that use of mobile technology can enhance engagement for some, depending on user competence with mobile technology and the size and composition of their social network.

Social media use can encourage consideration of diverse viewpoints, the exchange of political information, and political participation, but more research is needed. Research on how social media are affecting political discourse and deliberation is difficult because social media platforms become outmoded quickly. Friendster and MySpace faded fast; Facebook, Twitter, Instagram, and TikTok are popular now, but for whom and how long? Researchers must move quickly to keep pace with changes in digital and social media in order to truly understand their influence.

Though digital technologies provide low-cost opportunities and information tools for individuals with shared goals, there are constraints on digital mobilization. Nevertheless, they appear surmountable relative to the historical barriers to entry that constrained achieving collective goals, such as locating a core group with shared interests, coordinating actions, fundraising, and sharing materials. Evidence suggests that under certain conditions, these major obstacles are reduced by advances in communication technology. The digital and social media environment allows multiple opportunities for the routine exchange of ideas, interests, and connections. While these changes may have other implications less beneficial to civic life, it cannot be denied that these technologies lower many of the initial barriers for collective action and organization.[107]

DISCUSSION QUESTIONS ————————————

1. What were the major eras of early media effects research? How did the view of media effects change during the print and broadcast eras? What theories emerged from the eras of media effects?

2. How is the arrival of digital, social, and mobile media changing what researchers know about media effects? How are persuasive effects different? How are learning effects different? Are media effects really pretty much the same?

3. Why do people learn differently from different kinds of media messages? Is information recall, political learning, and/or knowledge easier or more difficult since the arrival of digital media? Or does it depend on something else? If so, explain how and why.

4. How do media affect political discourse, deliberation, and mobilization? Has anything changed since the arrival of digital media? If so, how so?

READINGS

Arceneaux, K., & Johnson, M. (2013). *Changing minds or changing channels? Partisan news in an age of choice*. University of Chicago Press.

Baldwin, T. (2018). *Ctrl alt delete: How politics and the media crashed our democracy*. Oxford University Press.

Bednarek, M., & Caple, H. (2017). *The discourse of news values: How news organizations create newsworthiness*. Oxford University Press.

Bennett, W. L. (2016). *News: The politics of illusion* (10th ed.). University of Chicago Press.

Bode, L., Budak, C., Ladd, J. M., Newport, F., Pasek, J., Singh, L. O., Soroka, S. N., & Traugott, M. W. (2020). *Words that matter: How the news and social media shaped the 2016 Presidential campaign*. Brookings Institution Press.

Chadwick, A. (2017). *The hybrid media system: Politics and power*. Oxford University Press.

Darr, J. P., Hitt, M. P., & Dunaway, J. L. (2021). *Home style opinion: How local newspapers can slow polarization*. Cambridge University Press.

Donner, J. (2015). *After access: Inclusion, development, and a more mobile internet*. MIT Press.

Dunaway, J. L., & Searles, K. (forthcoming). *News attention in a mobile era*. Oxford University Press.

Dimaggio, A. R. (2017). *The politics of persuasion: Economic policy and media bias in the modern era*. SUNY Press.

Forgette, R. (2018). *News grazers: Media, politics, and trust in an information age*. CQ Press.

Hayes, D., & Lawless, J. L. (2021). *News hole: The demise of local journalism and political engagement*. Cambridge University Press.

Hindman, M. (2018). *The internet trap: How the digital economy builds monopolies and undermines democracy*. Princeton University Press.

Iyengar, S. (2018). *Media politics: A citizen's guide* (4th ed.). Norton.

Jamieson, K. H. (2020). *Cyberwar: How Russian hackers and trolls helped elect a president: What we don't, can't, and do know*. Oxford University Press.

Kerbel, M. R. (2018). *Remote and controlled: Media politics in a cynical age*. Routledge.

Margetts, H., John, P., Hale, S., & Yasseri, T. (2016). *Political turbulence: How social media shape collective action*. Princeton University Press.

Nadler, A. (2019). *News on the right: Studying conservative news cultures*. Oxford University Press.

Napoli, P. M. (2019). *Social media and the public interest: Media regulation in the disinformation age.* Columbia University Press.

Nielsen, R. K. (2015). *Local journalism: The decline of newspapers and the rise of digital media.* IB Tauris.

Paul, R., & Elder, L. (2019). *The thinker's guide for conscientious citizens on how to detect media bias and propaganda in national and world news: Based on critical thinking concepts and tools.* Rowman & Littlefield.

Peck, R. (2019). *Fox populism: Branding conservatism as working class.* Cambridge University Press.

Robinson, S. (Ed.). (2016). *Community journalism midst media revolution.* Routledge.

Schudson, M. (2020). *Journalism: Why it matters.* John Wiley & Sons.

Sinclair, B. (2012). *The social citizen: Peer networks and political behavior.* University of Chicago Press.

Stroud, N. J. (2011). *Niche news: The politics of news choice.* Oxford University Press.

Wallis, C. (2015). *Technomobility in China: Young migrant women and mobile phones.* NYU Press.

Webster, J. (2016). *The marketplace of attention: How audiences take shape in a digital age.* MIT Press.

Wells, C. (2015). *The civic organization and the digital citizen.* Oxford University Press.

West, D. M. (2015). *Going mobile: How wireless technology is reshaping our lives.* Brookings Institution.

Wu, I. S. (2015). *Forging trust communities: How technology changes politics.* Johns Hopkins University Press.

NOTES

1. Gentzkow, M. (2017). Small media, big impact. *Science, 358*(6364), 726–727; King, G., Schneer, B, & White, A. (2017). How the news media activate public expression and influence national agendas. *Science, 358*(6364), 776–780.

2. This section draws heavily on Dunaway, J. L., & Settle, J. E. (2021). Opinion formation and polarization in the news feed era: Effects from digital, social, and mobile media. In D. Osborne & C. Sibley (Eds.), *The Cambridge handbook of political psychology.* Cambridge University Press.

3. Bineham, J. L. (1988). A historical account of the hypodemic model in mass communication. *Communication Monographs, 55*(3), 230–246.

4. Elasmar, M. G. (2017). Cross-border mediated messages. In L. Chen (Ed.), *Intercultural communication* (pp. 503–528). de Gruyter Mouton.

5. Iyengar, S. (2017). *A typology of media effects.* In K. Kenski & K. H. Jamieson (Eds.), *The Oxford handbook of political communication* (pp. 59–68). Oxford University Press; Jamieson, K. H. (2017). Creating the hybrid field of political communication: A five-decade long evolution of the concepts of effects. In K. Kenski & K. H. Jamieson (Eds.), *The Oxford handbook of political communication.* Oxford University Press.

6. Prior, M. (2005). News vs. entertainment: How increasing media choice widens gaps in political knowledge and turnout. *American Journal of Political Science, 49*(3), 577–592.

7. Katz, E. (1957). The two-step flow of communication: An up-to-date report on an hypothesis. *Public Opinion Quarterly, 37*(4), 61–78.

8. Iyengar, S. (2017). *A typology of media effects.* In K. Kenski & K. H. Jamieson (Eds.), *The Oxford handbook of political communication* (pp. 59–68). Oxford University Press; Jamieson, K. H. (2017). Creating the hybrid field of political communication: A five-decade long evolution of the concepts of effects. In K. Kenski & K. H. Jamieson (Eds.), *The Oxford handbook of political communication.* Oxford University Press.

9. Lazarsfeld, P. F., Berelson, B., & Gaudet, H. (1968). *The people's choice.* Columbia University Press, p. 151.

10. Iyengar, S. (2017). *A typology of media effects.* In K. Kenski & K. H. Jamieson (Eds.), *The Oxford handbook of political communication* (pp. 59–68). Oxford University Press; Jamieson, K. H. (2017). Creating the hybrid field of political communication: A five-decade long evolution of the concepts of effects. In K. Kenski & K. H. Jamieson (Eds.), *The Oxford handbook of political communication.* Oxford University Press.

11. Smith, S. M., Fabrigar, L. R., & Norris, M. E. (2008). Reflecting on six decades of selective exposure research: Progress, challenges, and opportunities. *Social and Personality Psychology Compass, 2*(1), 464–493.

12. Iyengar, S. (2017). *A typology of media effects.* In K. Kenski & K. H. Jamieson (Eds.), *The Oxford handbook of political communication* (pp. 59–68). Oxford University Press; Jamieson, K. H. (2017). Creating the hybrid field of political communication: A five-decade long evolution of the concepts of effects. In K. Kenski & K. H. Jamieson (Eds.), *The Oxford handbook of political communication.* Oxford University Press.

13. Iyengar, S. (2017). *A typology of media effects.* In K. Kenski & K. H. Jamieson (Eds.), *The Oxford handbook of political communication* (pp. 59–68). Oxford University Press; Jamieson, K. H. (2017). Creating the hybrid field of political communication: A five-decade long evolution of the concepts of effects. In K. Kenski & K. H. Jamieson (Eds.), *The Oxford handbook of political communication.* Oxford University Press.

14. Iyengar, S. (2017). *A typology of media effects*. In K. Kenski & K. H. Jamieson (Eds.), *The Oxford handbook of political communication* (pp. 59–68). Oxford University Press; Jamieson, K. H. (2017). Creating the hybrid field of political communication: A five-decade long evolution of the concepts of effects. In K. Kenski & K. H. Jamieson (Eds.), *The Oxford handbook of political communication*. Oxford University Press.

15. Zaller, J. R. (1992). *The nature and origins of mass opinion*. Cambridge University Press; Iyengar, S., & Kinder, D. R. (1987). *News that matters: Agenda-setting and priming in a television age*. University of Chicago Press.

16. Iyengar, S., & Kinder, D. R. (1987). *News that matters: Agenda-setting and priming in a television age*. University of Chicago Press.

17. McGuire, W. J. (1968). The nature of attitudes and attitude change. In G. Lindzey & E. Aronson (Eds.), *Handbook of social psychology* (2nd ed., Vol. 3, pp. 136–314). Addison Wesley; Zaller, J. R. (1992). *The nature and origins of mass opinion*. Cambridge University Press; Iyengar, S. (2017). *A typology of media effects*. In K. Kenski & K. H. Jamieson (Eds.), *The Oxford handbook of political communication* (pp. 59–68). Oxford University Press; Jamieson, K. H. (2017). Creating the hybrid field of political communication: A five-decade long evolution of the concepts of effects. In K. Kenski & K. H. Jamieson (Eds.), *The Oxford handbook of political communication*. Oxford University Press.

18. Iyengar, S. (2017). *A typology of media effects*. In K. Kenski & K. H. Jamieson (Eds.), *The Oxford handbook of political communication* (pp. 59–68). Oxford University Press; Jamieson, K. H. (2017). Creating the hybrid field of political communication: A five-decade long evolution of the concepts of effects. In K. Kenski & K. H. Jamieson (Eds.), *The Oxford handbook of political communication*. Oxford University Press.

19. Zaller, J. R. (1992). *The nature and origins of mass opinion*. Cambridge University Press.

20. Cohen, B. C. (1963). *The press and foreign policy*. Princeton University Press.

21. McCombs, M. E., & Shaw, D. L. (1972). The agenda-setting function of mass media. *Public Opinion Quarterly, 36*(2), 176–187.

22. Shanto I., & Kinder, D. R. (1987). *News that matters: TV and American opinion*. University of Chicago Press.

23. For a discussion of replacement of older issues by newer ones, see Brosius, H-B., & Kepplinger, H. M. (1995). Killer and victim issues: Issue competition in the agenda-setting process of German television. *International Journal of Public Opinion Research, 7*(3), 211–231.

24. McCombs, M. E. (2004). *Setting the agenda: The mass media and public opinion*. Polity Press; Iyengar, S., & Kinder, D. R. (1987). *News that matters: TV and*

American opinion. University of Chicago Press; Page, B. I., & Shapiro, R. Y. (1991). *The rational public: Fifty years of trends in Americans' policy preferences.* University of Chicago Press; Wanta, W. (1997). *The public and the national agenda.* Erlbaum; Kiousis, S., McDevitt, M., & Wu, X. (2005). The genesis of civic awareness: Agenda setting in political socialization. *Journal of Communication, 55*(4), 756–774.

25. Mutz, D. (1998). *Impersonal influence: How perceptions of mass collectives affect political attitudes.* Cambridge University Press; Barabas, J., & Jerit, J. (2009). Estimating the causal effects of media coverage. *American Journal of Political Science, 53*(1), 73–89; Craig, S. C., Kane, J. G., & Gainous, J. (2005). Issue-related learning in a gubernatorial campaign: A panel study. *Political Communication, 22*(October–December), 483–503; Graber, D. A. (2004). Mediated politics and citizenship in the twenty-first century. *Annual Review of Psychology, 55*(January), 545–571.

26. Druckman, J. N. (2005). Does political information matter? *Political Communication, 22*(October–December), 515–519; Gaines, B. J., Kuklinski, J. H., Quirk, P. J., Peyton, B., & Verkuilen, J. (2007). Same facts, different interpretations: Partisan motivation and opinion on Iraq. *Journal of Politics, 69*(November), 957–974; Prior, M. (2007). *Post-broadcast democracy: How media choice increases inequality in political involvement and polarizes elections.* Cambridge University Press.

27. The importance of personal and contextual factors in news selection and evaluation is discussed in Erbring, L., Goldenberg, E., & Miller, A. (1980). Front-page news and real-world cues: Another look at agenda-setting by the media. *American Journal of Political Science, 24*(February), 16–49; Hill, D. B. (1985). Viewer characteristics and agenda setting by television news. *Public Opinion Quarterly, 49*(Fall), 340–350. Also see Walsh, K. C. (2003). *Talking about politics: Informal groups and social identity in American life.* University of Chicago Press.

28. See Conway, B. A., Kenski, K., & Wang, D. (2015). The rise of Twitter in the political campaign: Searching for intermedia agenda-setting effects in the presidential primary. *Journal of Computer-Mediated Communication, 20*(2015), 363–380; Sayre, B., Bode, L., Shah, D., Wilcox, D., & Shah, C. (2010). Agenda setting in the digital age: Tracking attention to California Proposition 8 in social media, online news, and conventional news. *Policy & Internet, 2,* 7–32; also see Bennett, W. L., & Iyengar, S. (2008). A new era of minimal effects? The changing foundations of political communication. *Journal of Communication, 58*(4), 707–731.

29. Iyengar, S. (1994). *Is anyone responsible? How television frames political issues.* University of Chicago Press; Iyengar, S., & Kinder, D. R. (1987). *News that matters: TV and American opinion.* University of Chicago Press.

30. For an example of corroborative research, see Krosnick, J. A., & Kinder, D. R. (1990). Altering the foundations of support for the president through priming. *American Political Science Review, 84*(June), 497–512.

31. Iyengar, S., & Simon, A. (1993). News coverage of the Gulf crisis and public opinion: A study of agenda-setting, priming, and framing. *Communication Research, 20*(3), 365–383; Weaver, D. H. (2007). Thoughts on agenda setting, framing, and priming. *Journal of Communication, 57*(1), 142–147; Scheufele, D. A., & Iyengar, S. (2012). The state of framing research: A call for new directions. *The Oxford handbook of political communication theories*, pp. 1–26.

32. Kalmoe, N. P., & Gross, K. (2016). Cueing patriotism, prejudice, and partisanship in the age of Obama: Experimental test of U.S. flag imagery effects in presidential elections. *Political Communication, 37*(6), 883–899.

33. Abrajano, M. A., & Hajnal, Z. (2015). *White backlash*. Princeton University Press.

34. Tversky, A., & Kahneman, D. (1981). The framing of decisions and the psychology of choice. *Science, 211*(4481), 453–458.

35. Lawrence, R. G. (2000). Game-framing the issues: Tracking the strategy frame in public policy news. *Political Communication, 17*(2), 93–114; Cappella, J. N., & Jamieson, K. H. (1997). *Spiral of cynicism*. Oxford University Press, Chapters 3 and 8.

36. Chong, D., & Druckman, J. N. (2007). Framing theory. *Annual Review of Political Science, 10*, 103–126; Chong, D., & Druckman, J. N. (2007). Framing public opinion in competitive democracies. *American Political Science Review, 101*(4), 637–655; Chong, D., & Druckman, J. N. (2007). A theory of framing and opinion formation in competitive elite environments. *Journal of Communication, 57*(1), 99–118.

37. Leeper, T. J., & Slothuus, R. (2018). How the news media persuades: Framing effects and beyond. *Oxford Handbook of Electoral Persuasion*, 1–26; For comprehensive reviews, also see Busby, E., Flynn, D. J., & Druckman, J. N. (2018). Studying framing effects on political preferences: Existing research and lingering questions. In P. D'Angelo (Ed.), *Doing news framing analysis II* (pp. 27–50). Routledge; De Vreese, C. H., & Lecheler, S. (2012). News framing research: An overview and new developments. *The SAGE handbook of political communication*, pp. 292–306.

38. Gerbner, G. (1988). *Violence and terror in the mass media*. Greenwood Press; Gerbner, G., Gross, L., Morgan, M., Signorielli, N., & Shanahan, J. (2002). Growing up with television: Cultivation processes. In M. B. Oliver, A. A. Raney, & J. Bryant (Eds.), *Media effects* (pp. 53–78). Routledge; Elasmar, M. G. (2018). Media effects. In P. M. Napoli (Ed.), *Mediated communication* (Vol. 7, pp. 29–53). Walter de Gruyter GmbH & Co KG.

39. Elasmar, M. G. (2018). Media effects. In P. M. Napoli (Ed.), *Mediated communication* (Vol. 7, pp. 29–53). Walter de Gruyter GmbH & Co KG.

40. Lazarsfeld, P. F., & Merton, R. K. (1948). Mass communication, popular taste and organized social action. In L. Bryson (Ed.), *The communication of ideas* (pp. 238–239). Harper & Bros; Kwak, N., Lane, D. S., Weeks, B. E., Kim, D. H., Lee, S. S., & Bachleda, S. (2018). Perceptions of social media for politics: Testing the slacktivism hypothesis. *Human Communication Research, 44,* 197–221.

41. Putnam, R. D. (2000). *Bowling alone: The collapse and revival of American community.* Simon and Schuster.

42. Kwak, N., Lane, D. S., Weeks, B. E., Kim, D. H., Lee, S. S., & Bachleda, S. (2018). Perceptions of social media for politics: Testing the slacktivism hypothesis. *Human Communication Research, 44,* 197–221.

43. Priester, J., Wegener, D., Petty, R., & Fabrigar, L. (1999). Examining the psychological process underlying the sleeper effect: The elaboration likelihood model explanation. *Media Psychology, 1*(1), 27–48.

44. Albarracín, D., Kumkale, G. T., & Poyner-Del Vento, P. (2017). How people can become persuaded by weak messages presented by credible communicators: Not all sleeper effects are created equal. *Journal of Experimental Social Psychology, 68,* 171–180; Heinbach, D., Ziegele, M., & Quiring, O. (2018). Sleeper effect from below: Long-term effects of source credibility and user comments on the persuasiveness of news articles. *New Media & Society, 20*(12), 4765–4786.

45. Elasmar, M. G. (2018). Media effects. In P. M. Napoli (Ed.), *Mediated communication* (Vol. 7, pp. 29–53). Walter de Gruyter GmbH & Co KG.

46. Elasmar, M. G. (2018). Media effects. In P. M. Napoli (Ed.), *Mediated communication* (Vol. 7, pp. 29–53). Walter de Gruyter GmbH & Co KG.

47. Hamilton, J. (2004). *All the news that's fit to sell: How the market transforms information into news.* Princeton University Press; Starr, P. (2004). The creation of the media: Political origins of modern. *Communications.* Basic Books; Prior, M. (2007). *Post-broadcast democracy: How media choice increases inequality in political involvement and polarizes elections.* Cambridge University Press.

48. Jamieson, K. H., & Capella, J. N. (2008). *Echo chamber: Rush Limbaugh and the conservative media establishment.* Oxford University Press; Levendusky, M. S. (2013). Why do partisan media polarize viewers? *American Journal of Political Science, 57*(3), 611–623; Sunstein, C. R. (2017). *#Republic.* Princeton University Press.

49. Davis, N. T., & Dunaway, J. L. (2016). Party polarization, media choice, and mass partisan ideological sorting. *Public Opinion Quarterly, 5*(1), 770–792;

Prior, M. (2013). Media and political polarization. *Annual Review of Political Science*, *16*, 101–127.

50. Bakshy, E., Messing, S., & Adamic, L. A. (2015). Exposure to ideologically diverse news and opinion on Facebook. *Science*, *348*(6239), 1130–1132.

51. The state of the news media 2008. (n. d.). *Project for Excellence in Journalism*. http://assets.pewresearch.org/wp-content/uploads/sites/13/2017/05/24141607/State-of-the-News-Media-Report-2008-FINAL.pdf

52. Iyengar, S., & Hahn, K. S. (2009). Red media, blue media: Evidence of ideological selectivity in media use. *Journal of Communication*, *59*(1), 19–39; Munson, S. A., & Resnick. P. (2010). Presenting diverse political opinions: How and how much. In E. Mynatt, G. Fitzpatrick, S. Hudson, K. Edwards, & T. Rodden (Eds.), *CHI '10: Proceedings of the SIGCHI conference on human factors in computing systems* (pp. 1457–1466). Association for Computing Machinery; Stroud, N. J. (2011). *Niche news*. Oxford University Press.

53. Prior, M. (2007). *Post-broadcast democracy: How media choice increases inequality in political involvement and polarizes elections*. Cambridge University Press.

54. Prior, M. (2007). *Post-broadcast democracy: How media choice increases inequality in political involvement and polarizes elections*. Cambridge University Press; Arceneaux, K., & Johnson, M. (2013). *Changing minds or changing channels?* University of Chicago Press.

55. Bullock, J. G., Gerber, A. S., Hill, S. J., & Huber, G. A. (2013, May). Partisan bias in factual beliefs about politics. *Quarterly Journal of Political Science*, *10*(4), 519–578.

56. Gentzkow, M., & Shapiro, J. M. (2011). Ideological segregation online and offline. The *Quarterly Journal of Economics*, *126*(4), 1799–1839.

57. Gentzkow, M., & Shapiro, J. M. (2011). Ideological segregation online and offline. *The Quarterly Journal of Economics*, *126*(4), 1799–1839; Nelson, J. L., & Webster, J. G. (2017). The myth of partisan selective exposure: A portrait of the online political news audience. *Social Media + Society*, *3*(3); Flaxman, S., Goel, S., & Rao, J. M. (2016). Filter bubbles, echo chambers, and online news consumption. *Public Opinion Quarterly*, *80*(S1), 298–320; Hindman, M. (2018). *The internet trap: How the digital economy builds monopolies and undermines democracy*. Princeton University Press.

58. Pariser, E. (2011). *The filter bubble: How the new personalized web is changing what we read and how we think*. Penguin.

59. Weeks, B. E., Lane, D. S., Kim, D. H., Lee, S. S., & Kwak, N. (2017). Incidental exposure, selective exposure, and political information sharing: Integrating online exposure patterns and expression on social media. *Journal of Computer-Mediated Communication*, *22*(6), 363–379; Flaxman, S., Goel, S., & Rao, J. M.

(2016). Filter bubbles, echo chambers, and online news consumption. *Public Opinion Quarterly, 80*(S1), 298–320; Peterson, E., Goel, S., & Iyengar, S. (2019). Partisan selective exposure in online news consumption: Evidence from the 2016 presidential campaign. *Political Science Research and Methods, 9*(2), 242–258.

60. Adamic, L. A., & Glance, N. (2005, August). The political blogosphere and the 2004 US election: Divided they blog. In J. Adibi, M. Grobelnik, D. Mladenic, & P. Pantel (Eds.), *LinkKDD '05: Proceedings of the 3rd international workshop on Link discovery* (pp. 36–43). Association for Computing Machinery.

61. Gil de Zúñiga, H., Weeks, B., & Ardèvol-Abreu, A. (2017). Effects of the news-finds-me perception in communication: Social media use implications for news seeking and learning about politics. *Journal of Computer-Mediated Communication, 22*(3), 105–123.

62. Bakshy, E., Messing, S., & Adamic, L. A. (2015). Exposure to ideologically diverse news and opinion on Facebook. *Science, 348*(6239), 1130–1132.

63. King, G., Schneer, B., & White, A. (2017). How the news media activate public expression and influence national agendas. *Science, 358*(6364), 776–780; Gentzkow, M. (2017). Small media, big impact. *Science, 358*(6364), 726–727.

64. Goel, S., Mason, W., & Watts, D. J. (2010). Real and perceived attitude agreement in social networks. *Journal of Personality and Social Psychology, 99*(4), 611; Messing, S., & Westwood, S. J. (2014). Selective exposure in the age of social media: Endorsements trump partisan source affiliation when selecting news online. *Communication Research, 41*(8), 1042–1063.

65. Nipan, M., Emily, B., Hand, S., & George, A. (2008). The effect of mobile phone screen size on video-based learning. *Journal of Software, 3*(4), 51–61.

66. Al Ghamdi, E., Yunus, G., Da'ar, O., El-Metwally, A., Khalifa, M., Aldossari, B., & Househ, M. (2016). The effect of screen size on mobile phone user comprehension of health information and application structure: An experimental approach. *Journal of Medical Systems, 40*(1). https://pubmed.ncbi.nlm.nih.gov/26573648/; Molyneux, L. K. (2015). *Civic engagement in a mobile landscape: Testing the roles of duration and frequency in learning from news* [Doctoral dissertation]. The University of Texas at Austin. https://repositories.lib.utexas.edu/handle/2152/32197

67. Chae, M., & Kim, J. (2004). Do size and structure matter to mobile users? An empirical study of the effects of screen size, information structure, and task complexity on user activities with standard Web phones. *Behaviour & Information Technology, 23*(3), 165–181.

68. Dunaway, J., & Searles, K. (forthcoming). *News attention in a mobile era.* Cambridge University Press.

69. Pan, Z., Ostman, R., Moy, P., & Reynolds, P. (1994). News media exposure and its learning effects during the Persian Gulf War. *Journalism Quarterly, 71*(1), 7–19; Preiss, R. W. (Ed.). (2007). *Mass media effects research: Advances through meta-analysis.* Erlbaum.

70. Prior, M. (2007). *Post broadcast democracy: How media choice increases inequality in political involvement and polarizes elections.* Cambridge University Press.

71. Althaus, S. L., & Tewksbury, D. (2002). Agenda setting and the "new" news: Patterns of issue importance among readers of the paper and online versions of *The New York Times. Communication Research, 29,* 180–207.

72. Bode, L., Edgerly, S., Vraga, E., Sayre, B., & Shah, D. (2012). Digital democracy: The influence of new media production and consumption in politics. In E. Scharrer (Ed.), *Media effects and media psychology.* Wiley; Vraga, E., Bode, L., & Troller-Renfree, S. (2016). Beyond self-reports: Using eye tracking to measure topic and style differences in attention to social media content. *Communication Methods and Measures, 10*(2–3), 149–164; see also *How people read on the Web: The eyetracking evidence* (2nd ed.). (2021). https://www.nngroup.com/reports/how-people-read-web-eyetracking-evidence/#:~:text=Content%20is%20the%20core%20of%20building%20positive%20relationships%20with%20users.&text=The%20findings%20in%20this%20412,hours%20of%20testing%20session%20time

73. Stromer-Galley, J. (2014). *Presidential campaigning in the internet age.* Oxford University Press; Kreiss, D. (2016). *Prototype politics: Technology-intensive campaigning and democracy.* Oxford University Press.

74. Ferrucci, P., Hopp, T., & Vargo, C. J. (2020). Civic engagement, social capital, and ideological extremity: Exploring online political engagement and political expression on Facebook. *new media & society, 22*(6), 1095–1115.

75. McClurg, S. (2003). Social networks and political participation: The role of social interaction in explaining political participation. *Political Research Quarterly, 56*(4), 449–464; Bode, L., Edgerly, S., Vraga, E., Sayre, B., & Shah, D. (2012). Digital democracy: The influence of new media production and consumption in politics. In E. Scharrer (Ed.), *Media effects and media psychology.* Wiley.

76. For evidence and examples from the 2016 election cycle, see Stromer-Galley, J., Hemsley, J., Rossini, P., McKernan, B., McCracken, N., Bolden, S., Korsunska, A., Gupta, S., Kachhadia, J., Zhang, W., & Zhang, F. (2020). Candidate total message activity. *The illuminating project: Helping journalists cover social media in the presidential campaign, 2020.* http://illuminating.ischool.syr.edu/?_ga=1.102502530.2075366977.1486241395#/platforms/1,2/dates/2016-11-01,2016-11-08/candidates/10,5/types/8&9,5&6.

77. Feezell, J. T., & Ortiz, B. (2015, August). *"I Saw It on Facebook": An experimental study of learning political information through social media* [Paper presentation]. The Political Communication Pre-Conference at the annual meeting of the American Political Science Association, San Francisco, CA, United States.

78. Nipan, M., Emily, B., Hand, S., & George, A. (2008). The effect of mobile phone screen size on video-based learning. *Journal of Software, 3*(4), 51–61.

79. Al Ghamdi, E., Yunus, G., Da'ar, O., El-Metwally, A., Khalifa, M., Aldossari, B., & Househ, M. (2016). The effect of screen size on mobile phone user comprehension of health information and application structure: An experimental approach. *Journal of Medical Systems, 40*(1). https://pubmed.ncbi.nlm.nih .gov/26573648/; Molyneux, L. K. (2015). *Civic engagement in a mobile landscape: Testing the roles of duration and frequency in learning from news* [Doctoral dissertation]. The University of Texas at Austin. https://repositories.lib.utexas .edu/handle/2152/32197

80. Chae, M., & Kim, J. (2004). Do size and structure matter to mobile users? An empirical study of the effects of screen size, information structure, and task complexity on user activities with standard Web phones. *Behaviour & Information Technology, 23*(3), 165–181.

81. Dunaway, J., Searles, K., Sui, M., & Paul, N. (2018). News attention in a mobile era. *Journal of Computer-Mediated Communication, 23*(2), 107–124.

82. Dunaway, J. (2016, August). Mobile vs. computer: Implications for news audiences and outlets [Discussion Paper Series #D-103]. *Shorenstein Center on Media, Politics and Public Policy.* https://shorensteincenter.org/mobile-vs-com puter-news-audiences-and-outlets/.

83. Mossberger, K., Tolbert, C., & Franko, W. W. (2013). *Digital cities: The internet and the geography of opportunity.* Oxford University Press.

84. Wang, S. (2016, April 21). Saved you a tap: Gmail's inbox now lets you email links to stories to read later, streamlines newsletters. *NiemanLab.* http://www .niemanlab.org/2016/04/saved-you-a-tap-gmails-inbox-now-lets-you-email- links-to-stories-to-read-later-streamlines-newsletters.

85. Napoli, P. M., & Obar, J. A. (2014). The emerging mobile internet underclass: A critique of mobile internet access. *The Information Society, 30*(5), 323–334.

86. Campbell, S. W., & Kwak, N. (2010). Mobile communication and civic life: Linking patterns of use to civic and political engagement. *Journal of Communication, 60*, 536–555; Campbell, S. W., & Kwak, N. (2011). Political involvement in "mobilized" society: The interactive relationships among mobile communication, network characteristics, and political participation. *Journal of Communication, 61*, 1004–1024.

87. Neuman, W. R., Bimber, B., & Hindman, M. (2011). The internet and four dimensions of citizenship. In R. Y. Shapiro & L. R. Jacobs (Eds.), *The Oxford handbook of American public opinion and the media*. Oxford University Press.

88. Jenny Xie, J. (2013, May 14). Pew: Online political activism grows, but "slacktivism" problem remains. *MediaShift*. http://mediashift.org/2013/05/pew-online-political-activity-is-growing-but-slacktivism-and-class-related-gaps-loom/; also see Karlsen, R. (2015). Followers are opinion leaders: The role of people in the flow of political communication and beyond social networking sites. *European Journal of Communication*, *30*(3), 301–318; Beyer, J. (2016). *Expect us*. Oxford University Press. For evidence of mobilizing effects, see Bond, R. M., Fariss, C. J., Jones, J. J., Kramer, A. D., Marlow, C., Settle, J. E., & Fowler, J. H. (2012). A 61-million-person experiment in social influence and political mobilization. *Nature*, *489*(7415), 295–298.

89. Edgerly, S. L., Bode, L., Kim, Y. M., & Shah, D. V. (2013). Campaigns go social: Are Facebook, YouTube and Twitter changing elections? *New directions in media and politics* (pp. 82–99). Taylor and Francis; Mascaro, C. M., & Goggins, S. P. (2011). Brewing up citizen engagement: The coffee party on Facebook. *C&T '11: The 5th international conference on communities and technologies*. Association for Computing Machinery; Bode, L. (2012). Political information 2.0: A study in political learning via social media [Doctoral dissertation]. University of Wisconsin, Madison, Wisconsin, United States.

90. Gaines, B. J., & Mondak, J. J. (2009). Typing together? Clustering of ideological types in online social networks. *Journal of Information Technology & Politics*, *6*, 216–231; Bakshy, E., Messing, S., & Adamic, L. A. (2015). Exposure to ideologically diverse news and opinion on Facebook. *Science*, *348*(6239), 1130–1132.

91. Wojcieszak, M. E., & Mutz, D. C. (2009). Online groups and political discourse: Do online discussion spaces facilitate exposure to political disagreement? *Journal of Communication*, *59*, 40–56.

92. Bakshy, E., Messing, S., & Adamic, L. A. (2015). Exposure to ideologically diverse news and opinion on Facebook. *Science*, *348*(6239), 1130–1132.

93. Karlsen, R. (2015). Followers are opinion leaders: The role of people in the flow of political communication and beyond social networking sites. *European Journal of Communication*, *30*(3), 301–318.

94. Jacobs, L. R., Cook, F. L., & Delli Carpini, M. X. (2009). *Talking together: Public deliberation and political participation in America*. University of Chicago Press.

95. Bennett, W. L., Breunig, C., & and Terri Givens, T. (2008). Communication and political mobilization: Digital media and the organization of anti-Iraq War demonstrations in the U.S. *Political Communication*, *25*(3), 269–289.

96. Bennett, W. L., Breunig, C., & and Terri Givens, T. (2008). Communication and political mobilization: Digital media and the organization of anti–Iraq War demonstrations in the U.S. *Political Communication*, 25(3), 269–289; Chadwick, A. (2007). Digital network repertoires and organization hybridity. *Political Communication*, 24(3), 283–301; Bimber, B., Flanagin, A. J., & Stohl, C. (2012). *Collective action in organizations: Interaction and engagement in an era of technological change*. Cambridge University Press; Bennett, W. L., & Segerberg, A. (2013). *The logic of connective action: Digital media and the personalization of contentious politics*. Cambridge University Press.

97. Karpf, D. (2012). *The MoveOn effect: The unexpected transformation of American political advocacy*. Oxford University Press.

98. Green, J. (2012, November 29). The science behind those Obama campaign e-mails. *Business Week*. http://www.businessweek.com/articles/2012-11-29/the-science-behind-those-obama-campaign-e-mails; Larson, J., & Shaw, A. (2014, February 15). Message machine: Reverse engineering the 2012 campaign. *ProPublica*. http://projects.propublica.org/emails

99. Johnson, D., & Bimber, B. (2004). The internet and political transformation revisited. In A. Feenberg & D. Barney (Eds.), *Community in the digital age: Philosophy and practice*. Rowman & Littlefield; Bennett, W. L., Breunig, C., & Givens, T. (2008). Communication and political mobilization: Digital media and the organization of anti–Iraq War demonstrations in the U.S. *Political Communication*, 25(3), 269–289; Chadwick, A. (2007). Digital network repertoires and organization hybridity. *Political Communication*, 24(3), 283–301.

100. Bond, R. M., Fariss, C. J., Jones, J. J., Kramer, A. D., Marlow, C., Settle, J. E., & Fowler, J. H. (2012). A 61-million-person experiment in social influence and political mobilization. *Nature*, 489(7415), 295–298; King, G., Schneer, B., & White, A. (2017). How the news media activate public expression and influence national agendas. *Science*, 358(6364), 776–780; Gentzkow, M. (2017). Small media, big impact. *Science*, 358(6364), 726–727; Zhuravskaya, E., Petrova, M., & Enikolopov, R. (2020). Political effects of the internet and social media. *Annual Review of Economics*, 12, 415–438.

101. Beyer, J. (20141). *Expect us*. Oxford University Press.

102. Papacharissi, Z. (2015). *Affective publics*. Oxford University Press.

103. Wells, C. (2015). *The civic organization and the digital citizen*. Oxford University Press.

104. Karpf, D. (2016). *Analytic activism*. Oxford University Press.

105. Prior, M. (2007). *Post broadcast democracy: How media choice increases inequality in political involvement and polarizes elections*. Cambridge University Press.

106. Nielsen, R. K. (2015). *Local journalism: The decline of newspapers and the rise of digital media*. IB Tauris.

107. Bimber, B., Flanagin, A. J., & Stohl, C. (2012). *Collective action in organizations: Interaction and engagement in an era of technological change*. Cambridge University Press; Karpf, D. (2012). *The MoveOn effect: The unexpected transformation of American political advocacy*. Oxford University Press; Zhuravskaya, E., Petrova, M., & Enikolopov, R. (2020). Political effects of the internet and social media. *Annual Review of Economics, 12*, 415–438.

Current Trends and Future Directions

Current Trends and Future Directions

Learning Objectives

1. Classify the different forms of polarization and which forms are truly on the rise in the United States today.

2. Discuss the implications of declining local news for political accountability, citizen political knowledge and engagement, and rising polarization.

3. Explain what we know about the spread, causes, and effects of misinformation and disinformation in politics.

4. Describe today's global digital information inequalities, their different forms, and their impact on citizens' access to media for political power or critical services and information.

5. Assess what, if any, regulatory solutions exist for current trends and challenges in media politics, including the feasibility and effectiveness of such policy solutions.

On November 11, 2016, Facebook CEO Mark Zuckerberg found himself in the unexpected position of defending Facebook's editorial policies, despite the fact that Facebook is not a news organization. Zuckerberg's defense was necessary because of Facebook's lingering "fake news" problem, which drew intense public scrutiny in the final stages of the 2016 presidential election. Several fake news stories were posted and shared widely on Facebook during the campaign, and even though Facebook was not founded as a news company, the large number of people reporting to get their news from the site effectively makes it one. According to a 2020 Pew Research Center study, 36% of adults in the United States (U.S.) regularly get news on Facebook.[1] Initially, Zuckerberg responded to fake news criticisms by citing an internal study showing that the fake news stories amounted to only a small fraction of Facebook's content and claiming the idea that fake news could influence the election was "a pretty crazy idea." Yet several fake news stories went viral during the campaign. As the election came to a close, revelations that Russian television network RT was among the several outlets producing fake news stories underscored the severity of the problem. Eventually Facebook, along with Google, announced plans to combat fake news (Photo 14-1).[2]

In the time since the 2016 election, scrutiny on social media companies only increased, along with pressure for more oversight of the platforms' content. Fairly or unfairly, many people place much responsibility for the rise of populist and other fringe movements, rising polarization, and divisive and uncivil online behavior in the hands of platforms such as Facebook and Google. Whether it is due to their monopolistic, anticompetitive practices, because the infrastructures on these sites encourage the posting and sharing of inflammatory content, or because platform companies have resisted banning false information, hate speech, and other undesirable and often dangerous material, critics regularly condemn the major platform companies and call for more regulation. Those pressures and circumstances surrounding the conclusion of 2020—in the U.S., the events leading up to the January 6 insurrection at the U.S. Capitol, in particular—apparently yielded a turning point in relations between major social media platform companies and democratic governments. Though the U.S. typically has a relatively lighter regulatory hand than its European counterparts, the Justice Department recently decided to pursue antitrust suits against Google and Facebook. In late 2020, the Big Tech companies were also investigated by at least two congressional committees for their influence on Americans' information diets. The Senate Commerce Committee and the Senate Judiciary Committee focused on the platforms' policies for moderating content, grilling the CEOs of Google, Twitter, and Facebook about their failure to adequately perform their role as information gatekeepers.[3]

One of the most appealing features of digital and social media is that capturing and sharing news and information is cheap and easy—enabling ordinary citizens to share information with wide audiences anywhere. Yet the dissemination and sharing of fake news and misinformation raises serious concerns. Social media are not merely a tool for sharing stories; they are also a sourcing tool for traditional and digital journalists.[4] Ease of access means that digital and social media provide additional channels through which news consumers can be duped with false information shared by anyone. The digital media environment provides audiences with many affordances, such as convenience and access; the fake news examples highlight the serious misinformation challenges imposed by the contemporary media environment.[5]

THE SHOVEL

BUSINESS

Mark Zuckerburg – Dead At 32 – Denies Facebook Has Problem With Fake News

BY THE SHOVEL
NOVEMBER 16, 2016

Photo 14-1 Screenshot From a Satirical Fake News Story Announcing Zuckerberg's Death Amidst His Repeated Denials of a Fake News Problem at Facebook
Source: The Shovel.

In this concluding chapter, we will outline the current trends that are most relevant for researchers and students of media and politics in America. Presently, these include rising polarization among both political elites and the mass public, declines in local news and an increasingly nationalized news environment, political mis- and disinformation, and lingering information inequalities that still plague the digital media environment. We will end with discussions about possible policy solutions and a look at what the future might hold.

Rising Polarization

The discussion about the expansion of media choice in Chapter 4 suggested that worries about partisan echo chambers are somewhat overstated, but the media's role in driving polarization is still a topic of public concern. Pundits, journalists, and politicians frequently complain about the polarizing effects of the fragmented media environment. This is understandable because rising polarization—whatever its cause—is something to be concerned about. But what have researchers actually concluded about the relationship between media and political polarization? This is a tricky question for several reasons. First, for a long time, researchers could not agree on whether polarization was actually rising in the mass public. They recognized that elite polarization was on the rise (among partisan members of Congress, for example), but they disagreed on whether the public was also polarizing. Second, the information environment kept changing, making it difficult to get and keep a handle on understanding the effects. Just as researchers started to gain some leverage on questions about the effects of the arrival of cable and the internet, the proliferation of social media and smartphones added new complexities to these relationships. Third, as researchers continued to try and understand the effects of media fragmentation and selective exposure, they uncovered other means by which changes to the information ecology might have polarizing effects. This added confusion to their studies and explanations, not to mention affecting their ability to confidently draw conclusions. To complicate matters even further, research on information processing continued to illustrate many ways in which cognitive biases condition any effects that might occur as a result of structural changes to the media environment.

Is Polarization on the Rise?

Even after there was consensus among researchers about the fact that elites and political activists were more polarized than they used to be and that the trend was getting worse, evidence about whether the opinions of mainstream Americans were growing more polarized was still open to debate. There was not much evidence to suggest, for example, that the issue positions of partisans in the electorate were increasingly divergent from those of partisans on the other side of the aisle.[6] But according to accumulated evidence today, it is clear that there are at least some ways in which partisans in the mass public are growing further apart. For example, presidential approval data reveal a widening rift between partisans on both sides, and this rift is greater than at any time in our history. Also, partisans simply dislike their out-party counterparts more than they used to, and they are less likely to tolerate out-partisans, even in social settings. Recent research appears to be coming to a consensus that even if political or ideological polarization is not on the rise, affective and social forms of polarization are, as is partisan ideological sorting. Even though policy positions remain moderate for most Americans, these forms of polarization are sharply rising, and people are sorting along partisan and ideological lines as their political identities are becoming more organized and consistent.[7]

Affective polarization describes the growing gap between in- and out-party affect—regard for one's own party and dislike for the other party. As partisan affect has intensified over time, in-group favoritism has become increasingly associated with out-group dislike.[8] Partisan out-group dislike now surpasses in-group favoritism as the primary driver of political behavior, which means that for some partisans, the motivation to beat the other party is more relevant than party policy proposals or their performance at governance. Dislike for out-partisans is so strong that partisan identification has surpassed all others to be the first characteristic people discriminate against.[9] Rising affective polarization is troubling for several reasons. It encourages citizens to evaluate politicians and policies emotionally, reducing their ability to hold elected leaders accountable on legitimate grounds, and encourages voters to support politicians who refuse to compromise in the name of partisan grandstanding.[10] Recent research also points to problems negative partisan affect creates even outside the realm of politics. It has a hand in encouraging social segregation along party lines; some evidence suggests it may even distort economic markets.[11]

Social polarization is similar to affective polarization in the sense that it is more about feelings and emotions than policy positions or political ideology. Social polarization reflects the fact that social relationships between Democrats and Republicans are becoming less frequent and increasingly strained: Partisans hold less favorable views of the opposing party, are less comfortable being friends with out-party members, and are more reluctant to see their children marry members of the out-party.[12] A question commonly used to capture social polarization asks, "How do you think you would react if a member of your immediate family told you they were going to marry a [Democrat/Republican]?" Respondents are typically given three options: "Happy," "Unhappy," or "Wouldn't matter at all."[13] In response to this question, partisans are more likely than ever before to say that they would be unhappy—meaning they do not want their child to marry someone of the opposing party. Social forms of polarization are also observed in studies of mate selection and online dating.[14] Married couples, for example, tend to have similar political ideologies and attitudes; those who do are more likely to stay married for a longer period of time. Researchers attribute this to a form of social sorting, where people purposefully seek partners with similar political views. In recent years, social polarization has apparently gotten even worse. A 2020 study found that 63% of people said they would not date someone who's views on Trump were in contrast with their own.[15] If people do not even want their children to marry out-partisans, it is little wonder that they may not want to date or marry out-party members themselves.

Partisan-ideological sorting is related to affective and social forms of polarization, but it is different. *Sorting* describes the degree to which individuals' party and ideological identities have converged or become more related in expected ways.[16] Sorting refers to how one's party identification is aligned with ideologically consistent issue positions. For example, in decades past, it was common to encounter more conservative Democrats and liberal Republicans than it is today. When we describe the electorate as more sorted, it means, for example, it is much harder to find a Republican who wants to raise taxes and increase federal spending on healthcare or a Democrat who wants to lower corporate tax rates and cut spending on healthcare or education. Today, partisan identities are also more likely to converge with religious and other social identities, as in the case of evangelical Christians who disproportionately report being ideologically conservative and identify as Republican. A more-sorted electorate has several important implications for political attitudes and behavior. First, differences in party affiliation today go hand in hand with differences in world view and sense of social and cultural identity.[17] As a result, partisans are stronger identifiers, and partisan identities are wrapped up in and aligned with their other social identities as well. The implication is that today's strongly identified partisans have stronger emotional reactions to political information and circumstances relative to weaker partisans.[18] Some researchers have treated partisan sorting as a key cause of affective polarization, but recent research finds that affective polarization is increasing as much among those who are not well-sorted as it is among those who are. Sorting and affective polarization are correlated for people with high levels of political knowledge, but affective polarization is occurring across people with different levels of political knowledge. The evidence also suggests that affective polarization can drive sorting, complicating researchers' ability to understand which of these phenomena is cause and which is effect.[19] What's clear is that both are rising and complicating democratic responsiveness, policy compromise, and political accountability.[20]

Where evidence for a causal influence from the media environment on mass political polarization has been difficult to pin down, some studies provide convincing evidence that changes to the media environment may be contributing to negative political affect and sorting.[21] Others find evidence to the contrary. Numerous studies have investigated whether the expansion of media choice—and the re-emergence of partisan cable news in particular—are especially to blame. The logic underlying many of these studies is that exposure to partisan news—with its derogatory portrayals of the other side and imbalanced accounts of political events—stimulates and reinforces party identity, producing negative emotional reactions and hostility toward members of the other party and out-party leaders.[22] The imbalanced and negative content is also thought to contribute to extremity in partisan attitudes and issue positions, fueling affective polarization.[23] Though there is good evidence from experiments and surveys in support of these conclusions, it stops short of being sufficient to allow researchers to conclude that partisan news actually causes affective polarization or sorting. After all, it is those who are most interested in news and therefore the most partisan news viewers who are most likely to choose partisan news in the first place, providing little opportunity for much attitude change.[24] Research also shows that even in a high-choice environment, people are not exclusively exposed to attitude-consistent sources of political information. People seek and are exposed to news and political information for many different reasons,[25] and exposure to neutral and opposition-party sources occurs regularly.[26] Enough people also avoid news altogether to minimize the potential for massive effects from partisan news, casting doubt on media choice as the sole driver of affective polarization.[27]

For years, the mixed findings from this area of research were attributable at least in part to differences in methodology and challenges with measurement. As we described in earlier chapters, experimental work was limited in that many early studies failed to adequately capture the high-choice environment in their studies of exposure to partisan news. Forced-choice designs were low on external validity because they measured effects from exposure to partisan news even on people who, in the real world, would not be very likely to consume partisan news.[28] Studies based on observational data were high on external validity but were often unable to identify a causal relationship between choice or consumption of partisan news and persuasion or polarization.

Two recent studies with innovative research designs deal more effectively with these limitations and show relatively convincing evidence of persuasive and polarizing effects. Greg Martin and Ali Yurukoglu use data on cable system channel ordering to create an instrument to capture exposure to Fox News. They find a persuasive Fox News effect in presidential elections, one which grew between 2000 and 2008 due to rising Fox News ratings and an increasingly conservative slant on Fox News. They also find that partisan slant across cable channels increased between 2000 to 2012, with MSNBC moving more to the left and Fox News moving more to the right. Their findings also suggest that the cable channels could explain the increase in political polarization at rates similar to those in the U.S. occurring over the same time period.[29]

To overcome the problems of forced-choice experimental designs and to try an understand whether partisan media could have persuasive and polarizing effects among those who are not interested in news, Justin De Benedictis-Kessner and his colleagues implemented a new experimental design called the Preference-Incorporating Choice and Assignment (PICA) design. The PICA design incorporates both free media choice and forced exposure to news. With it, they estimated both the degree of polarization caused by selective exposure and the persuasive effect of partisan media. Their study revealed that partisan media can polarize both regular partisan news consumers and those audiences who would otherwise avoid it. They also found that exposure to ideologically opposing media can potentially reduce existing levels of polarization.[30] Though evidence still stops short of being conclusive, replication and ongoing innovations and improvement in research design will continue to advance the research on and our understanding about the polarizing effects of the high-choice media environment and exposure to partisan news.

Research on whether internet access is contributing to affective polarization and sorting has also produced mixed evidence. Yphtach Lelkes and colleagues find that higher levels of news consumption enabled by high-speed access to the internet encourages negative political affect by increasing media choice, which results in more time spent online and more exposure to partisan news cues. Meanwhile, Levi Boxell and colleagues identify a somewhat counterintuitive effect, finding that affective polarization is rising most among those least likely to spend time online or using social media. Research by political scientist Andrew Guess might suggest why: His work demonstrates that most people have fairly mainstream online media consumption habits. About 25% of media content to which people are exposed comes from mainstream websites and portals. In addition, there is a significant amount of overlap (or similarity) in online media exposure patterns between Democrats and Republicans. However, the overlap was smaller in 2016 relative to 2015, and Guess finds that a small set of strong partisans are responsible for driving an outsized share of web traffic to ideologically extreme sites. But for most, online media diets are moderate more than anything else.

Several other studies also show how the fact that popularity drives most Web traffic means that online exposure to mainstream and relatively neutral sources of content will continue to comprise a healthy proportion of online news exposure.[31] However, recent research by Yotam Shmargad and Samara Klar shows how algorithmic news ranking by popularity—which, partially determines the order in which news stories are presented—can also polarize. When online networks are like-minded in a partisan sense, ranking increases the tendency to like or endorse stories that reflect the in-party bias of the dominant group. The more the slanted stories are liked, the more they remain at the top of the ranking. In mixed networks, attitude-incongruent information rises to the top, which helps with exposure to new information but discourages engagement.[32] It is too early to determine whether internet usage (and the availability of the wider array of information the internet provides) is the primary contributor to the growth of affective polarization.

At least some evidence suggests that the rise in sorting is related to changes in the media environment. Nicholas Davis and Johanna Dunaway find that cable and internet proliferation operate in conjunction with elite polarization to encourage sorting because high-choice media environments offer more exposure to explicit partisan cues about the differences between the two parties and their positions. They find this effect primarily among the politically interested. Other research also shows that partisans who consume partisan news are better able to identify Democratic candidates as more liberal and Republican candidates as more conservative.[33] These findings support the idea that more exposure to explicit partisan cues can help ordinary Americans differentiate between the parties. Fragmented and more-partisan media may operate through elite polarization to drive sorting, which is thought to be an important precursor to polarization.

All of this is to say that earlier research was slow to reach a consensus as to whether mass polarization was on the rise in part due to limitations in design and methodology, but it was also because researchers did not yet understand and differentiate between these various ways in which the public is growing apart. Now, political communication scholars better understand that even if Americans are not more polarized in terms of their policy positions, they can still be growing apart in terms of political affect, candidate evaluations, and partisan ideological sorting. Some research suggests that polarization—even as traditionally conceived—may also be on the rise but that it is more difficult to demonstrate with common research methodologies. It might be that it is easier to measure and observe affective and social forms of polarization, trait polarization, and sorting because partisans in the public are simply better able to articulate social, emotional, and evaluative differences relative to complex differences in party-issue positions. In short, changes in sorting and affect may simply be easier to detect and measure than changes in more traditional conceptualizations of polarization.[34] Nevertheless, as researchers continue to hone their definitions of these various forms of political division—even if we do not want to refer to them as *polarization*—they should be better able to determine the extent to which patterns of media exposure afforded by today's media environment are contributing and the extent to which other factors are driving these trends.

Other Explanations

As outlined in Chapter 4, many scholars initially attributed trends in rising polarization with changes to the media environment, chiefly blaming the higher levels of media choice that allowed for niche partisan media and partisan selective exposure behavior in audiences.[35] It certainly is the case that consumption of partisan-leaning media was more pervasive than during the broadcast era once cable arrived and that audiences engage in partisan selective exposure across a host of media types, including online. Given that these trends of rising polarization and the fragmenting of the media environment were largely concurrent, it is no wonder that many drew a causal conclusion: As media choices expanded, audiences fragmented.[36] Yet, as we also explained in Chapter 4, empirical evidence linking changes in the media environment to widespread audience fragmentation and polarization is inconclusive.[37] Though several experimental studies provide good evidence suggesting a causal relationship where selective exposure to partisan news enhances polarization, ratings and Web traffic data suggest otherwise, and researchers continue to grapple with longer-term questions about whether widespread polarization occurred primarily as a result of the expansion of media choice and partisan selective exposure behaviors.[38] As part of that ongoing research effort, studies shored up more evidence of a role for media, but they also identified several additional possible drivers of polarization. Some of these other factors are thought to work in tandem with the structural changes to the media environment; others are considered as alternative explanations for why polarization is on the rise.

Elite Polarization

While changes to the media landscape and increased selective exposure coincide with mass polarization, some research finds evidence suggesting that elite polarization is the key driver of mass polarization. Early work on the resurgence of mass partisanship and numerous subsequent studies demonstrate that strength of partisanship in the mass public increases in response to higher levels of polarization between partisan officeholders in Washington. Political scientists Marc Hetherington and, later, Matthew Levendusky argued that polarization among elites has the same effect among the electorate because it helps voters make clearer distinctions between the two parties. Equipped with a better understanding of how the two parties differ from a policy perspective makes it easier for ordinary Americans to choose which party best matches their own issue positions.[39] Other work suggests that elite polarization affects mass voting behavior because it means the pool of candidates from which voters choose is made up of more extreme partisans. The argument is that if political elites are more polarized, this is reflected in the slate of candidates holding and running for office.

Recent studies highlight other important elite-level effects emerging from changes to the media environment, namely, the rise of partisan media. Kevin Arceneaux, Martin Johnson, René Lindstädt, and Ryan Vander Wielen examined whether the arrival of the Fox News network to congressional districts influenced members' legislative voting behavior, and they identified more than a simple "Fox effect" on legislative votes. Members representing Fox News districts voted more conservatively relative to members representing non–Fox News districts, but—as clear evidence of the strategic basis of these changes—Fox News district members closer to reelection were those most likely to change their votes. The Fox effect held for Republicans and Democrats alike.[40] Officeholders have a set of clear expectations about partisan news coverage. Based on those expectations, they make inferences about the effects of partisan coverage on constituents' evaluations and adjust their behavior accordingly. In a subsequent study, Arceneaux and his colleagues found another Fox News effect on congressional political elites. Using congressional district-level data on the local availability of Fox News, in this study, they demonstrated how the presence of Fox News influenced the strategic entry decisions of would-be challenger candidates considering a run for congressional office. Specifically, the presence of Fox News in a district affected Republican potential candidates' perceptions about the vulnerability of Democratic incumbents—Fox News made these potential challengers think Democratic incumbents might be more electorally vulnerable, which changed their decisions about whether to enter races and run for congressional office.[41] In districts with Fox News, Democratic incumbents in mixed or right-leaning districts were more likely to face quality challengers in upcoming elections. These are important elite-level effects from the arrival and proliferation of partisan news, and they may have downstream consequences—and produce indirect media effects—on the mass public.

Declining Media Trust and Oppositional Media Hostility

Declining levels of trust in the media also coincide with mass polarization. Jonathan Ladd argues that this is because those who distrust the media rely on their own existing political predispositions to form opinions in lieu of new information supplied by the media. His research suggests a conditional relationship wherein media distrust is fueled by media polarization and distrust leads to mass polarization. Ladd's argument suggests a different process than what is evidenced by demonstrating that partisan selective exposure can stimulate more extreme views at the individual level in the short term.[42]

Obviously, a great deal of media mistrust is driven by out-party responses to the perspectives and slant provided by partisan media. According to research by Erik Peterson and Ali Kagalwala, partisans view out-party media in highly unfavorable terms, even if they have never been exposed to or are only rarely exposed to its content. Partisans view out-party media through the lenses of inaccurate stereotypes. Accusations of extreme bias, for example, are common from partisans even though content differences between major partisan news outlets are often fairly modest. When people are actually exposed to nonpolitical or neutral stories from oppositional media, hostility is reduced. Their findings illustrate another means by which selective exposure might be encouraging affective polarization: Avoiding out-party sources for news encourages negative partisan affect and mistrust (i.e., oppositional media hostility) toward out-partisan media sources because people assume oppositional media is more slanted than it actually is.[43]

However, low levels of media trust might also limit the media's ability to polarize. A rich history of research documents the importance of credibility in persuasion. Today's media lack the credibility they held in the past. Jonathan Ladd and Alexander Podkul argue that several unique factors of mid-20th century America encouraged high trust in the media. These included low media competition, low polarization, little economic inequality, and high economic growth. More recently, partisan attacks on the media—primarily from political elites on the right—are chipping away at public trust in the media and the credibility of individual news outlets. To the extent that people no longer find the media credible, media have a reduced capacity to influence.[44]

Nationalizing News Environment

Some evidence suggests that the news environment is nationalizing in response to expanding media choice in the U.S. and that this is another trend contributing to rising polarization. Research by Dan Hopkins argues that the American political environment is nationalizing. He attributes the nationalization trend, in part, to the changing media environment. As readers know well by now, the arrival of cable and the internet vastly expanded the media content choices available to American audiences. As it did so, it also largely untethered the provision of local and regional news and public affairs information from geographic boundaries. Cable made 24-hour news available for all of its subscribers, most of which focuses primarily on national or international news. The internet allowed for access to every national and international news source, not to mention every local news source no matter where people live. This shift suddenly allowed people in Los Angeles to read the *Houston Chronicle* online and people in Houston to read the digital version of the *Los Angeles Times*. It also made countless additional national sources available through digital platforms, including the major broadcasting and cable news networks and the digital versions of major national papers such as the *USA today* and *The New York Times*.

This geographically unfettered access to so many news options had several implications. The primary implication was a dramatic decline in local newspaper audiences, which spurred several other important effects. One was that it presented economic challenges to local newspapers and television news outlets who previously earned most of their advertising revenue because people had to watch a whole program or buy a whole paper to get the classifieds, the sports news, traffic reports, movie listings, and so on. Local media could guarantee eyeballs on their ads, even the eyeballs of people who did not care about news. But with cable came ESPN, and with the internet came ESPN.com, Craigslist, and digital movie listings. People no longer needed local media for access to much of the community-level information they sought. And unfortunately, when it comes to news, state and local political information is not much of a draw on its own. When given the choice, audiences prefer to consume national news over local news.[45] This meant that when the local news became separate from the bundle of other local information papers and local television news used to provide, they lost readers and viewers. And as newspapers disappeared or declined in quality, many news consumers replaced it with national news.[46] The upshot is that in the absence of local news, national news is often the default source of political information on which most Americans rely.

Why would the mass audience shifting to national news contribute to rising polarization? Mainly it's because the coverage of politics and government is more partisan. Local public affairs coverage is selected based on relevance to the community. For example, unlike national outlets, local newspapers are interested in the statements and actions of elected officials' primarily because they are relevant to the local community, not because of their party leadership status, ideology, or significance in Congress. Local newspaper coverage of legislators and their service to the district most strongly affect voters in the opposing party, often drawing cross-party votes from constituents when coverage is favorable.[47] This kind of watchdog coverage provided by local media has, historically, helped to keep incumbent performance in the district at the top of voters' considerations, even over partisanship.[48] By covering legislators' activities and quality of service to the local district, local newspapers deemphasize partisanship and give those officials a platform to discuss local issues.[49] By contrast, national news media tend to cover politics almost exclusively through the lens of the partisan conflict in Washington. A recent study by mass communication scholar Jeremey Padgett and his colleagues showed, for example, that the national broadcast and cable news networks give more airtime to the most polarized members of Congress—those House members with the most consistently partisan and most extreme partisan voting records.[50] Because we know the public takes cues from political elites to understand differences between the parties, such biases in coverage likely contribute to public perceptions that the parties are even more polarized than they actually are.

Building on this, political communication scholar Joshua Darr and his colleagues intuited that the dramatic loss of local newspapers across the United States might be producing a polarizing effect of its own. To investigate this question, they studied the effects of local newspaper closures on voting behavior. They did this by collecting a national sample of newspaper closures from 2009 to 2012 to examine if areas where a newspaper closed had higher rates of split-ticket voting relative to areas without a newspaper closure. After matching counties according to race, voting-age population, gender, income, and education, they compared presidential/Senate split-ticket voting before (2008) and after (2012) a newspaper left a community. Darr and colleagues found a 1.9% decrease in split-ticket voting in counties that lost a local newspaper. *Split-ticket voting* refers to when voters in a political geography such as a county or state elect people from different parties at different levels of government—for example, a Democrat for president and Republican for senator. The alternative is *straight-ticket voting*, where people tend to more often check the box electing everyone from the party of their choice, irrespective of issue positions or performance in office. When more people are voting on a party basis alone—as in straight ticket voting—it is more reflective of partisan polarization. Split-ticket voting, on the other hand, is less partisan and polarized. Their findings show that less local news in the marketplace or at least the disappearance of a local newspaper encourages a greater reliance on national news and more emphasis on national and partisan considerations in voting at all levels, which polarizes voting behavior.[51]

In a subsequent study, Darr and colleagues analyzed the effects of a local newspaper experiment in which the paper suspended all reference to national politics on its op-ed pages for the month of July. The findings, based on analysis of pre- and post-surveys of community members in the community the paper served and a matched (untreated) community where the paper retained national politics on the op-ed page, indicated that the simple act of removing reference to national politics from the opinion page for a month was enough to slow the rise in affective polarization.[52] In another recent study, political scientist Daniel Moskowitz argues that local news coverage reduces nationalization by providing information allowing voters to evaluate down-ballot candidates separately from those of candidates for national office, which are typically more partisan. He finds that higher levels of local news coverage is associated with greater knowledge about state and local candidates and officeholders. Watching local television news is related to gains in split-ticket voting (reducing more polarized voting) in gubernatorial and senatorial races. These results suggest that local news curbs the nationalization of elections even in a polarized setting, but this effect is contingent on more traditional forms of local news, which traditionally adhere to the professional norm of objectivity in journalism. Current trends in media consolidation suggest that this model may not remain dominant forever. A recent study of Sinclair Broadcasting—a media company purchasing local television media outlets—showed two significant biases in coverage. Sinclair stations provided more national coverage at the expense of local coverage, and the political coverage provided by their television stations has a right-leaning slant.[53] More research is needed, but evidence is accumulating to suggest that declining local news is yet another contributor to rising polarization.[54]

Ongoing Changes in Digital Media

The co-occurrence of increasing polarization alongside a rapidly evolving media environment encouraged widespread speculation that the two phenomena are related.[55] Since the arrival of cable, media have served as a default explanation for growing societal divisions. Opinion echo chambers and filter bubbles, whether due to selective exposure behavior or algorithmic processes, were widely considered as pervasive drivers of polarization because they discourage regular, inadvertent exposure to oppositional views—exposure that is thought to increase tolerance for opposing views, common ground, and support for compromise.[56] As readers of this text realize by now, research studying this association revealed a more nuanced picture. We know that partisan selective exposure and partisan-motivated reasoning are not automatic. Research based on the expansion of choice due to the arrival of cable and the internet showed several ways in which individual differences and the informational and political context shape information seeking and processing in ways that can moderate the effects of the information environment.[57] Research showed that although the high-choice media environment provides the *opportunity* for motivated information seekers to engage in partisan-selective exposure, they will not always do so.

Even though researchers understand much more than they did ten to twenty years ago, research on the relationship between the changing media environment and polarization continues to produce mixed findings. One reason for this is that changes in communication technology continue to evolve. Just as researchers were gaining some leverage on questions about effects from high levels of media choice from cable and the internet, the emergence and proliferation of social media and smartphones added even more complexity to the high-choice digital media landscape. People's exposure to political news while using digital, mobile, and social media is not only more frequent than in the days of broadcast and cable, but it is also of a qualitatively different nature. Evidence about how digital, social, and mobile media might polarize users shows it is more complicated than typical accounts suggest. Though digital and social media users are exposed to more attitude-consistent than oppositional political information, exposure to cross-party and cross-ideology information is common; nearly half of content to which people are exposed on social media crosses party or ideological lines.[58] Web traffic is also highly concentrated on mainstream sites, further indicating exposure to diversity online.[59]

Also, the things that drive exposure to political information are increasingly complex across digital and social media. Many sites and platforms are social more than political, and they are designed accordingly, which encourages exposure to diverse content through social network ties, posting, and sharing.[60] This is one reason cross-party exposure to information is more common than once anticipated. At the same time, a recent study by Ariel Hasell shows that partisan news stories are shared more frequently on Twitter than nonpartisan stories, and that they are more likely to be emotionally charged relative to nonpartisan news. This suggests that Twitter tends to amplify partisan and emotional news.[61] Even if exposure to partisan information is diverse, its volume and intensity might have disproportionate and polarizing effects.

Evidence for the process through which exposure to partisan information through digital, social, and mobile media polarizes users is also more complicated than typically thought. Though the opportunity for exposure to polarizing information is high, the power and nature of its impact remains in question. First, already high rates of social and affective polarization might be one reason there is not a great deal of evidence for the polarizing effects of echo chambers—attitudes might be near the ceiling of extreme attitudes already.[62] In a recent study by Andrew Guess and colleagues, they find evidence of short-term increases in political interest and knowledge in response to more exposure to partisan news on social media but little evidence of a direct impact on attitudes or political affect.[63] The only long-term impact they observe is a substantial and long-lasting decrease in media trust. Similarly, a study by Jessica Feezell and her colleagues reveal that algorithm-based news exposure can lead to higher rates of political participation, but neither non–algorithm-based or algorithm-based exposure to news increases partisan polarization.[64]

Second, recent research suggests that exposure to oppositional views on social media among partisans actually strengthens existing predispositions; it does not increase tolerance and compromise as commonly theorized.[65] Especially in today's context of high affective polarization and partisan-ideological sorting, motivated processing of political information is strong. It affective and social forms of polarization continue to rise; it seems less and less likely that consumers of political news will be persuaded much by anything.

Third, the conditions under which political views dictate exposure are more complex (and therefore not yet well understood) for many newer media forms.[66] Social sharing and endorsements often weigh more heavily to drive attention and exposure than partisan brands on social media, for example. At the same time, social characteristics and cues are often erroneously interpreted as indicative of political preferences on social media. Source cues operate differently on social media, too, and this is further complicated by high levels of media mistrust and high rates of misinformation circulation on social platforms.

Finally, the effects of cognitive biases are conditioned by information complexities in how information is shared and presented in the digital media environment, such as on the various social media platforms or mobile devices.[67] Newer structural formats such as news feeds on Facebook affect information exposure and processing. They restrict choice and selectivity through algorithmic filtering and network effects. Studies suggest that by increasing incidental exposure, restricted choice through news feeds increases learning and agenda-setting effects.[68] News feeds also tend to blend and display social and political information in ways that encourage polarization.[69] At the same time, other evidence suggests that attention scarcity in the digital media environment may limit the impact of exposure.[70] Facebook referrals drive most traffic to news websites, but referred users only stay for seconds. Mobile news consumers spend far less time reading news stories, even when exposed to them several times a day.[71] What effects should we expect from such fleeting exposure? In order for media messages to affect learning attitudes or behavior (including polarization), they must first attract attention, and researchers are only now beginning to understand limits to attention in the digital media environment. More research is needed before we will fully understand the extent to which and the conditions under which digital and social media have polarizing effects.

Declining Local News

As part of the discussion in the previous section suggests, local news is declining in America. Local newspapers are enduring the worst of it. The American news industry lost 2,100 newspapers over the past 15 years. During that time, newspaper readership and staffing fell by half, and many of the newspapers that remain are struggling, operating at a much weaker capacity relative to their former selves. Circulation and revenues continue to decline, and newspapers' Web traffic leveled off after a period of sharp growth. Between 2000 and 2018, weekday newspaper circulation dropped by nearly 30 million American households, and circulation dropped by 12% from 2017 to 2018 alone. Over the same two years, newspapers also experienced a 13% drop in revenues.[72] Local television news is beginning to suffer, too. Despite that television is still the most popular media form of news for most Americans, local television news lost 14% of its audience in 2018. Local television newsrooms are producing more news with fewer resources, and economic pressures forced many stations into mergers and acquisitions. According to Pew Research Center, more than 140 stations changed owners in 2018.[73]

Local newspapers are essential for local communities. They are the outlets typically producing stories that address residents' critical information needs. Newspaper coverage often sets the agenda for other local news outlets; their reporting often provides stories for local television news, for example. Despite their importance, newspapers are failing.[74] This is a trend that has many public officials, journalists, and educators concerned. Still, we know that even while acknowledging that newspapers provide the most comprehensive news coverage, many readers of this text will be both unsurprised and unmoved by the plight of the newspaper industry. After all, newspapers are viewed by many people (younger people in particular) as antiquated, especially amidst the conveniences of today's digital media environment. Readers may equally question the need for concern about declining local television news. Local TV news certainly has its faults. Years of research reveals many problems with local news. It is often overly sensational and superficial and focuses on traffic, weather, crime, and sports, with little air time for news about local politics and government. With all of this in mind, why are people so worried about the declines in local news?

The primary answer is that local news differs from national news in several important ways, ones that suggest that its continuing decline will have serious consequences for American democracy. Local news outlets exist for the primary purpose of serving local and regional audiences. The American press system is structured so that local news outlets are the only ones in a position to cover local and regional issues well enough to meet the critical information needs of local communities. Recall the important media watchdog function described in Chapter 1. Without local and regional coverage, there is no watchdog over state and local government. Research demonstrates the negative effects: State government is more corrupt when local press is not monitoring and covering local public officials. For example, poorly covered House representatives do not work as hard for their local home-district constituencies. They are less active in congressional hearings, less likely to serve on committees relevant to their constituency, and they appropriate fewer funds for their districts.[75] Subnational government spending is more likely to be fiscally irresponsible in the absence of local press. Less local coverage also makes local elections less competitive, typically to the benefit of incumbents.[76] In other words, local and regional news coverage is really important for political accountability at state and local levels. Information is necessary for citizens to hold their state and local officials and House representatives accountable.[77]

Local news outlets are also more trusted than national news outlets.[78] As described in Chapter 12, media trust is on a downward trajectory and it has been for several years. Not only that, but trust in institutions is declining more generally; institutional mistrust is a problem that will only be made worse in the absence of government accountability. If local media retain more audience trust, they are in a unique position to successfully perform their role as watchdog. Citizens' trust in local news also makes it particularly informative to voters.[79] Local media coverage typically means that citizens' attention to subnational politics is higher. As a result, when local news is robust, political knowledge and engagement are higher for state and local politics.[80] Without healthy local news, citizens cannot effectively monitor and influence their elected officials, which harms government performance and citizen satisfaction.

Grappling with Mis- and Disinformation

While polarization and declines in local news are certainly troubling, ongoing problems with political mis- and disinformation in the digital media environment are probably the most worrisome. Several recent trends—diverging factual beliefs between the public and the scientific community, between partisans on either side of the aisle, and salient examples of fake news—have renewed interest in the role that misinformation plays in public affairs.[81] Misinformation can come from any source, but mass media almost certainly play a role in determining whether and how much misinformation is fed to the mass public. Some accounts attribute misinformation problems to changes in the media environment and the polarized state of national politics. In a world where political elites are increasingly polarized, efforts to persuade the public rely heavily on painting distinctly different pictures of what's wrong with the world, who or what is to blame, and how to fix it. Niche media outlets may be more inclined than traditional media to paint these one-sided views, but more important is that public audiences seek confirmation of their beliefs through media accounts and tend to reject information that would counter those beliefs. Partisan swaths of the public are both vulnerable to misinformation coming from their own side and less willing to believe corrections to that misinformation, especially when it comes from the other end of the political spectrum.[82]

Media-Based Explanations

According to journalist and media critic Craig Silverman, these problems of misinformation are especially likely on digital platforms, and the structures of the digital media environment contribute to misinformation spread more broadly. News organizations often play a role in spreading hoaxes, rumors, and false claims. They are too quick to move on unverified information, and sometimes news media are the reason content goes viral, which is dangerous when information is unverified. Though, in the rush to publish, they cover themselves by using qualified language such as *reportedly* and *claiming*, the simple act of publishing the information gives false content credibility (see Table 14-1). News sites also try to cover their bases by simply linking back to another source for the information, such as the original story. However, following chains of these links reveals that the original source is often something like a post on Facebook rather than a legitimate and verified source of information.[83] Table 14-1 shows results from Silverman's study. The data show how frequently certain kinds of hedging language is used when news outlets want to publish unverified information. The dissemination of misinformation and fake news is a huge problem. Hedging language often goes unnoticed by news audiences, which means they may not notice the nuances of verified versus unverified information.

Table 14-1	Frequency of Hedging Language Tactics Used for False Claims	
Hedging Tactic(s)	**Occurrences**	**Sample Headline**
Report (and variations)	191	Amazon Reportedly Planning an Ad-Supported Video Service That Will Be Cheaper Than Netflix
Use of quotes on claim	77	ISIS "Behead Their Own Fighters" for Spying and Embezzlement in Syria
Say (and variations)	73	Doctor Took Selfie With Joan Rivers While Star Was Under Anesthesia, CNN says
Use of a question	68	Woman With Three Breasts: Real or Hoax?

(Continued)

(Continued)

Hedging Tactic(s)	Occurrences	Sample Headline
Claim (and variations)	57	Boy Who Suffered Power Electrical Shock Claims He Now Has "Superpowers" Like X-Men's Magneto as Metal Objects Stick to Him
May	32	6 Hidden Mass Graves May Hold Missing Mexican Students
Allege (and variations)	31	Audio Recording Allegedly Captures Moment Michael Brown Was Shot
Rumor	29	Rumor: Apple in Late-Stage Talks to Buy Path Social Platform
Source or official	16	Source: Pot in NYC May Soon Net Just a Ticket, Not Arrest
Could	8	Exclusive: Lenovo Could Make an Offer for BlackBerry as Early as This Week
Appears	6	Crabzilla: Photo Appears to Show Giant, 50-Foot Crab Lurking in British Waters
Believed	5	James Foley Killer "Jihadi John" Believed to Be Former London Rapper Abdel-Majed Abdel Bary
Possible	5	Nicaraguan Commission on Possible Meteorite Crash Presents Rock Samples
Purported	3	Purported Lisa Bonet Twitter Account Suspended After Cryptic Cosby Tweet

Source: Adapted from Silverman, C. (2015). Lies, damn lies, and viral content: How news websites spread (and debunk) online rumors, unverified claims, and misinformation. Tow Center for Digital Journalism, Columbia University. http://towcenter.org/wp-content/uploads/2015/02/LiesDamnLies_Silverman_TowCenter.pdf

Note: Data are from Emergent Database of media claims.

Cognitive Biases

There are many media-based explanations for problems of misinformation and political misperceptions. Research demonstrates that high volumes of misinformation circulate through digital and social media; circulation is more frequent than exposure to factual or accurate information.[84] Exposure to it is almost certainly high. Yet a lot of existing research dispels the notion that changes to the media environment are primarily responsible for the many political misperceptions people hold or the rumors and lies they share or endorse. These studies rely on cognitive explanations to explain how exposure to misinformation shapes the development of misperceptions and/or the endorsement or sharing of mis- and disinformation.[85] These accounts portray the media environment as more of an incubator for than a primary driver of political misperceptions.[86]

Recent research seeking to understand media influence on attitudes and behavior draws heavily on theories of motivated reasoning, which explain how people's motives heavily influence the processes by which they seek and process information.[87] Motivated reasoning theories indicate that information seeking and processing is dictated by different goals. Accuracy-based goals aim to correctly inform decisions. Directional goals prioritize finding and processing information in support of already-held beliefs. When it comes to political information, directional goals are heavily guided by partisanship. This logic is important for understanding the effects of misinformation today, with high levels of elite polarization, strengthening affective and social polarization, and an increasingly fragmented media environment.[88]

Motivated reasoning strategies are considered a primary cause in the development of political misperceptions.[89] The logic is that misinformation is processed in ways that allow individuals to draw conclusions consistent with their beliefs.[90] There is evidence to support this logic. Americans interpret factual information about the economy differently according to their partisanship and in ways that defend their partisan identities.[91] Predispositions also predict which conspiracies partisans endorse.[92] Similarly, in work on correcting misinformation, partisans are reluctant to dismiss misinformation that reinforces their preexisting attitudes. Consistent with motivated reasoning, attitudes influence partisans' willingness to accept misinformation as fact rather than exposure to misinformation shaping their political perceptions.[93] The same was true when citizens were exposed to corrective information about weapons of mass destruction (WMDs) in Iraq.[94]

Some motivated reasoning research casts doubt on the idea that the media environment and its allowances for selective exposure are primarily to blame for a more misinformed electorate. Under motivated reasoning, people will either tune out information counter to their beliefs or they will counter-argue it upon exposure, with the effect of only reinforcing their existing attitudes. In other words, when partisans are exposed to misinformation, they are unlikely to be persuaded by it. They will reject misinformation they disagree with. If the misinformation is agreeable, they might believe it or endorse it, but because it is already consistent with their beliefs, this kind of exposure is unlikely to result in true attitude change.[95] An obvious conclusion from research in this area is that directional-motivated reasoning goals will influence the acceptance of attitude-consistent misinformation and resistance to disagreeable misinformation. All of this suggests that there is both good news and bad in the research on misinformation and the development of misperceptions. Cognitive biases and partisan identities can both intensify and serve as a safeguard against persuasive media effects in the contemporary information environment, including effects from exposure to mis- and disinformation.

Fact-Checking

Fact-checking is a long-standing central part of journalism, but recent years saw a rise in political fact-checking. Its recent growth is due in part to the need to counter misinformation, which is not always immediately apparent, especially when emerging from "he said, she said"–style objective political reporting. Fact-checking is especially important in the contemporary high-choice media environment in which audiences can selectively search across an array of media for claims matching their beliefs. Politicians and their strategists have long been able to exploit journalists' commitment to accurately reporting claims from both sides of any dispute—even false claims; they are adept at making effective use of ideologically friendly news outlets. Fact-checking aims to distinguish between objective truth and political spin (see Figure 14-1).[96]

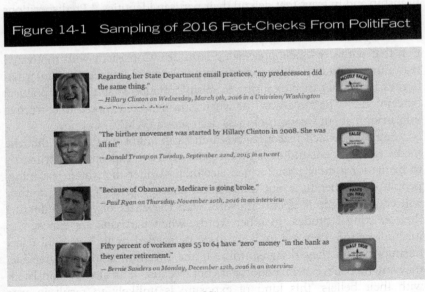

Figure 14-1   Sampling of 2016 Fact-Checks From PolitiFact

Regarding her State Department email practices, "my predecessors did the same thing."
— Hillary Clinton on Wednesday, March 9th, 2016 in a Univision/Washington Post Democratic debate

"The birther movement was started by Hillary Clinton in 2008. She was all in!"
— Donald Trump on Tuesday, September 22nd, 2015 in a tweet

"Because of Obamacare, Medicare is going broke."
— Paul Ryan on Thursday, November 10th, 2016 in an interview

Fifty percent of workers ages 55 to 64 have "zero" money "in the bank as they enter retirement."
— Bernie Sanders on Monday, December 12th, 2016 in an interview

Source: Politifact.com (2016, December 28).

Despite its ostensibly noble purpose, fact-checking is controversial. Due to the cognitive biases described above, misinformation is very difficult to correct in people's minds, even after false claims are debunked, raising questions about fact-checking effectiveness.[97] Worse, there is some evidence that fact-checks can have an effect that is the reverse of what is intended: They sometimes make people cling to false beliefs even more strongly than before. Clearly, there are hazards that come with providing corrective information to the public. On the other hand, there is a recent rise in the dissemination (and sharing) of fake news stories, and the public is ill informed about even basic matters of scientific consensus.[98] For example, 26% of the public believes there is no solid evidence that the earth's temperature is getting warmer.[99]

Fortunately for fact-checkers, recent research suggests that fact-checking can be effective under certain circumstances. Brendan Nyhan, Jason Reifler, Thomas Wood, and Ethan Porter examined the effectiveness of corrective information during the 2016 election cycle by looking at the effects of corrections to Donald Trump's convention speech claims about rising crime. The false claim in question was that violent crimes were up significantly. When respondents were asked to read a news article about the speech that included Federal Bureau of Investigation (FBI) statistics showing that crime has actually dropped sharply, misperceptions went down.[100] In addition, communication scholars Leticia Bode and Emily K. Vraga find that social media can expose people to more accurate (i.e., corrective) information, and under some circumstances, it can even reduce misperceptions. Specifically, they examined whether information delivered via social media algorithm is more useful for countering misinformation because it is more likely to be viewed as credible and objective. The results of their study revealed that when linked "related stories" corrected a post that included misinformation, people with misperceptions were more likely to accept it as accurate relative to information from friends, followers, or other site users, and misperceptions were significantly reduced.[101]

The enduring challenge fact-checking faces is how to retain credibility in a polarized political climate, rampant perceptions of media bias, and historically low levels of trust in the media. Fact-checking is least effective when it belies one's preexisting beliefs about a fact, an issue, or a candidate or when it comes from a news source one perceives to be biased.[102] Politicians and campaigns are attuned to this and are skilled at dismissing unflattering media coverage under cover of media bias; the same strategy can be used to deflect fact-checking. The best hope for fact-checking credibility as an effective watchdog tool is to develop and stick with a systematic and unbiased method for the selection and evaluation of claims and to be transparent about those methods.

The Future of Research on Mis- and Disinformation

Researchers remain very interested in the roles that both polarization and misinformation play in the formation of misperceptions and inaccurate beliefs.[103] This is especially true against a backdrop of rising populism, in which political leaders utilize misinformation tactics meant to divide and breed mistrust. Because of its common association with polarization and exposure to misinformation, the contemporary digital media environment is a natural place to look for explanations for widely held political misperceptions. Existing evidence suggests there is more to the story.

Despite that expanding media choice and a growing array of social media platforms provide ample opportunity to avoid facts and encounter misinformation, it is important to recall that existing beliefs and predispositions motivate both information seeking and processing. Put differently, beliefs and predispositions drive information processing at least as much as they are shaped by them. And as demonstrated by the case in the U.S.—a context of growing affective polarization and elite polarization—the effects of motivated reasoning and political identities are likely to increase their influence over how partisans seek and process information. If partisan identity is so powerful that it can drive even how we evaluate information, the likelihood that misinformation has much potential for persuasive effects among out-group partisans may be minimal in this kind of context.[104]

Researchers also know relatively little about whether there are significant behavioral effects from misinformation exposure. Evidence suggests that exposure to misinformation can make people more likely to endorse or embrace misinformation even when fully aware of its basis on incorrect facts.[105] Yet, research reveals little evidence of effects on voting behavior or electoral outcomes. However, even though research suggests that the direct effects of factual misinformation might be minimal—despite high rates of mass exposure—our ability to make this kind of conclusion depends on several questions that are as of yet unanswered by existing scientific studies.

Digital Information Inequalities

Digital information inequalities present an ongoing challenge to the world of media and politics. Media representation and access to media as sources of information are critically important, but we must also consider who as access to media as a platform for airing perspectives. Having a voice is an important source of political power. Ideally, government "by the people" means that the people have a right to express their views and opinions about any and all issues, whether political, religious, social, and so on. In practice, this requires that people must be able to use the mass media to publicize their views. Before the arrival of the internet and digital media technology, media personnel decided what stories to publicize and whose views to present, leaving many views without a public forum. There was simply not enough time and space available to accommodate all who want to be heard. Average citizens seeking to exercise their First Amendment right spoke before crowds, wrote letters to editors, paid for print ads in newspapers, or posted flyers. Basically, they relied on word of mouth to disseminate important information unless they could somehow gain access to media as a platform.

Public officials who want access to the news media to explain their views face problems similar to those of private individuals. Although the media are likely to be more sympathetic to their requests, on many occasions, coverage was denied or was granted only outside prime time. Several speeches by Presidents Ronald Reagan, Bill Clinton, and others were not broadcast at all because the media considered them partisan political statements or claimed that they contained nothing new. Some speeches were carried by only a few stations, sharply reducing the presidents' audience. Presidents prevent access problems by tailoring their requests for media time to the needs of the media. They particularly avoid schedule conflicts with major sports events. As we discussed at length in other chapters, digital and social media platforms have reduced—but not eliminated—public officials' dependence on traditional media as a means by which to communicate their messages to the public.[106]

Irrespective of technological advancements, there will never be enough channels to publicize all the important views to large audiences nor enough audiences willing and able to pay attention. As explained in Chapter 4, the internet may give everyone a public voice, but it does not guarantee that anyone will listen. Digital communication technologies have somewhat alleviated the problem of unequal access to traditional forms of media, but so much of the digital information landscape is a wilderness that devours voices, leaving them bereft of listeners; information is also still highly concentrated in the hands of major media institutions.[107] Even with the advent of blogs and other means to produce and share user-generated content, the linked structure of the internet means that the endless volumes of information require retrieval rather than perusal when seeking information, which ultimately results in users looking for information in places they are already aware of. Filtering algorithms also bias searches toward well-known high-traffic sites.[108]

However, extant research shows that the lowered barriers to entry for media access serve some traditionally disadvantaged parties and groups well by providing easier access to communicate with potential supporters. Small and niche political parties can take advantage of the affordances of digital communication technologies to increase their vote shares, depending on the political and institutional context, namely the permissiveness of the electoral system.[109] Ultimately, evidence suggests that the internet gives more access and voice to prominent activists and political professionals (i.e., political elites) rather than to ordinary citizens.

At the global level, lingering digital divides mean that access to public voice and access to media as an important source for critical information is still limited in many parts of the world. The proliferation and usage trends for computers, mobile networks, and high-speed internet illustrate some of the reasons why the arrival of the digital era is limited so far in its ability to democratize the global information environment. Figures 14-2 through 14-5 highlight trends and disparities in the changing availability and use of digital communication technologies.

Figure 14-2   Worldwide Percentage of Households With Computers, 2005–2019

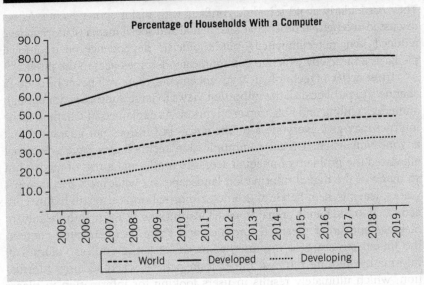

Source: 2005–2019 ICT data. (2021). *ITU.* http://www.itu.int/en/ITU-D/Statistics/Pages/stat/default.aspx

Figure 14-3   Worldwide Percentage of Households With Internet Access, 2005–2019

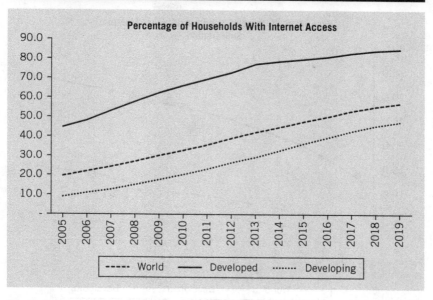

Percentage of Households With Internet Access

Source: 2005–2019 ICT data. (2021). *ITU.* http://www.itu.int/en/ITU-D/Statistics/Pages/stat/default.aspx

In the rare instance that ordinary citizens can reach a vast audience through digital channels, depending on one's location in the world, the digital audience may represent only a fraction of the populace. As Figure 14-4 shows, there are large differences in access to high-speed internet at home between the developed and developing world. Importantly, access to a computer and the internet does not automatically translate into exposure to news or other sources of public affairs information. Speed and reliability of connection are important predictors of whether individuals and households use the internet for news and political information.[110] If quality and speed of internet access is predictive of its use for news, the evidence in Figure 14-4 is highly problematic.

The percentage of U.S. adults with home broadband internet subscriptions dropped from 73% in 2016 to 65% in 2018. Over the same time period, there was a corresponding 12% increase in the percent of U.S. adults using a smartphone as their primary source for internet access. By 2018, smartphone-only internet users made up 20% of the U.S. adult

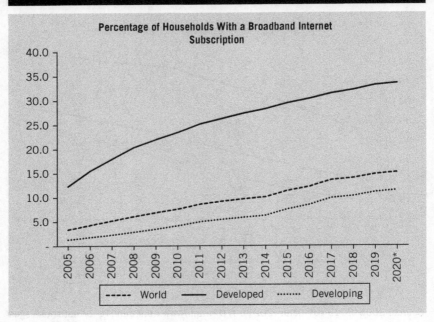

Figure 14-4 Worldwide Percentage of Households With Broadband, 2005–2020

Percentage of Households With a Broadband Internet Subscription

Source: 2005–2020 ICT data. (2021). *ITU*. http://www.itu.int/

population.[111] The research showing that mobile internet use does not provide the same informational benefits as high-speed broadband internet access raises important questions about the implications of smartphone dependency for an informed citizenry. In 2015, for example, many cord-cutting Pew Research Center survey respondents reported that the decision to cut broadband service was a major impediment to keeping up with the news. Similarly, research shows that high-speed internet in the home is a major determinant of online news-seeking while mobile access is not.[112]

Another issue with the speed and quality of internet access is that it varies systematically across groups, even in the U.S., potentially exacerbating existing information inequalities. In the U.S., Latinos and African Americans make up the two largest groups of smartphone-only internet users, at 35% and 24% respectively.[113] Most people in the world have access to some form of the internet, and this is especially true in the U.S., thanks largely to mobile devices, as shown in Figure 14-5. However, it is

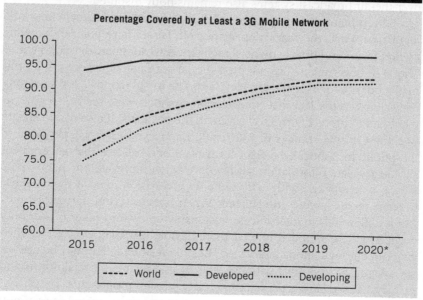

Figure 14-5 Worldwide Percentage Covered by at Least a 3G Mobile Network, 2005–2020

Percentage Covered by at Least a 3G Mobile Network

----- World ⎯⎯ Developed ⋯⋯ Developing

Source: 2005–2020 ICT data. (2021). *ITU.* http://www.itu.int/

important to understand that divides in the speed and quality of that access will continue to produce many of the same kinds of inequalities in access to information, services, and opportunities that characterized the early days of the internet, back when *digital divide* only referred to the difference between people who had any access to the internet and those who did not. Though researchers are shifting their focus to recognize the information inequalities arising from differences in the speed and quality of access, we still have much more to learn about information seeking and consumption across different tiers of access and across various platforms and devices.[114]

Regulatory Solutions?

How (if at all) should government regulate the news media—and the digital media environment more generally—to ensure that the liberty of the press and the people does not become a license for socially harmful behaviors on digital and social media? The explosive growth of unregulated information channels on the internet makes it necessary to raise that perennial question once again.[115] The wisdom of the current regulations that apply to legacy over-the-air broadcast systems also remains hotly disputed.

Governments have several broad policy options for dealing with media regulation. First, they can adopt hands-off, laissez-faire policies, allowing market forces and private owners' preferences to dominate development.[116] The U.S. government has adopted the laissez-faire philosophy for print media but not for over-the-air television. The initial rationale for regulating television was the fact that transmission channels were scarce, so government had to protect fairness of access to the channels. It also had to ensure that these prime sources of information conveyed essential messages to the public in politically correct formats. If one believes that government should regulate information supply only when transmission channels are scarce, as happened with early radio and television, then it makes sense to leave media largely unregulated. When broadcast and narrowcast outlets are plentiful, market forces presumably come into play so necessary services will be supplied in a far more flexible way than is possible when government regulations intervene. The only restraints that may be needed are safeguards to protect national security and maintain social norms and privacy. Laissez-faire is the mantra of deregulation proponents.

Second, information transmission systems can be treated as common carriers, similar to the telephone or rail and bus lines. Common carrier status makes transmission facilities available to everyone on a first-come, first-served basis. Cable broadcast stations (and later the internet) were classified as common carriers of information rather than as creators of information whose messages had to be monitored to guarantee a rich information supply for all sectors of the American public. Owners of cable facilities presumably did not broadcast their own programs. Rather, they leased their channels to various broadcasters for fees regulated by government or by market forces. Under common carrier rules, they could not selectively exclude any programs.

The Federal Communications Commission (FCC) and many local governments prefer the common carrier concept. Even though the U.S. Supreme Court decided in 1979 that cable systems could not be considered common carriers under federal law, Congress and some state and local governments have treated the industry as a common carrier.[117] When Congress ordered cable systems to broadcast all local over-the-air programs, the industry filed a lawsuit. It won judgments in 1985 and again in 1987 that the "must carry rule" violated the First Amendment rights of cable companies.[118] The victory for cable systems was a defeat for champions of broad public access rights to the media. In sum, the application of common carrier rules has been confusing because the substance of the rules is disputed. Cable systems have become a poorly defined, mixed breed that resembles over-the-air television in some ways and traditional common carriers in others.

By comparison, the internet system is subject to very few rules, in part because it is deemed a common carrier and in part because its nature and structure make enforcement of regulations extremely difficult. The Obama years were characterized by debates about regulating the internet. Some camps favor total net neutrality and the avoidance of regulating such things as the amount broadband companies can charge for services; others maintain that the internet is now so essential for education, emergency information and services, and public affairs information that it should be regulated as a utility. In 2015, the FCC passed regulations to prevent companies from charging higher rates for faster "lanes" of internet traffic, a movement toward regulation. Opponents to the change warn it is a move toward government control of the internet, while proponents maintain that the rules are essential to ensure open access to the internet for everyone.[119]

Third, the government can confer public trustee status on communication enterprises. Owners then have full responsibility for programming but are required to meet certain public service obligations. Examples are adherence to equal-time provisions, limitations on materials unsuitable for children or offensive to community standards of morality, providing periodic evidence of service to the community in the way of providing public affairs information, and rules about access to broadcast facilities. Access rules are designed to ensure that there are channels available to governments and various publics to broadcast information about such public issues as education, public safety, and medical and social service programs. Over-the-air television in the United States typically operates under trustee rules.

Periodically, trustee norms clash with the First Amendment. That is why free press purists are so alarmed about the increasingly strict enforcement of social and political correctness norms. They shudder to think that the majority of Americans applaud when journalists in the United States are fired for saying some terrorist actions might be fueled by legitimate grievances or when the FCC imposes heavy fines on a network because a female entertainer's breast was accidentally bared during a Super Bowl broadcast. Given majority approval of such restraints on the press, especially in times of crisis, it is difficult to predict how much freedom the trustee system will grant to the press in the future. The thrust of social pressures will decide that issue.[120]

Areas Most in Need of Reform

Digital communication technologies require a far more complete rethinking of the scope and purpose of federal regulation of broadcast media than has happened thus far. The Telecommunications Act of 1996 is inadequate for dealing with revolutionary technological changes. There is a dire need for major policy innovations.

In the traditional media realm, the difference in treatment between the unregulated print media and the regulated electronic media is highly questionable. It was based on the assumption that there would be numerous competing newspapers in the United States, while broadcast channels were scarce so the forces of competition could not work properly to make the airways an open marketplace of ideas. In reality, competition rose among broadcasters, especially with the proliferation of cable television and internet sources. Meanwhile, competition among daily newspapers lessened over time.

There is no longer any merit in the argument that the scarcity of a particular type of news transmission, along with its importance to the public good, should be the litmus test for determining regulation policies. The distinctions made among publication formats are equally outdated. For example, many newspapers are now available in print and electronic versions. Should the print version be free from controls while the Web version is regulated or vice versa? If the latter, the price of progress in electronic transmission of printed news could be the loss of freedom from government regulation.

Total deregulation of television broadcasts and reliance on traditional First Amendment values is not a realistic policy option in the United States for the foreseeable future. Opponents of deregulation contend that the impact of television on public life in the United States is so profound that the public interest requires controls. Even when competition is ample, it may be necessary to mandate access for neglected viewpoints and to provide programming for ignored audiences, such as children, who also need protection from unwholesome information. Insurmountable opposition to total deregulation makes it essential to think in terms of an overhaul of the policies adopted in the 1996 Telecommunications Act.

The outcome of such an overhaul is impossible to predict because the forces favoring regulation and the forces favoring deregulation are fairly evenly matched, but the camps may be shifting as broadcast media are under increasingly competitive threats. It is even hazardous to predict that the regulatory system will be revised to deal with public needs in the internet age. After all, there was a 62-year gap between the Communications Act of 1934 and the 1996 Telecommunications Act. The only safe prediction is that piecemeal skirmishes and full-scale assaults on regulatory policies will continue apace in the years to come.[121] The back and forth over net neutrality seems destined to continue over the short term. The Trump administration had very different views on how the internet should (or shouldn't) be governed.[122] Biden's administration seems poised to more aggressively take steps toward regulation, especially with policy efforts aimed at curbing monopolistic behaviors by digital mega entities such as Google and the major, widely used social media platforms.

Control Over Digital Media

Digital media enjoy an uncontrolled status similar to the printed press and are free from many government controls, such as the need to provide equal time or to guarantee rights of rebuttal. The digital media environment presents serious challenges for lines between freedom and privacy and between freedom and security. As of yet, in the United States, digital news media are not subject to any more formal government control than unregulated print media. However, it is reasonably safe to predict that there will be some regulation to cope with unsavory developments on the internet.[123] The battles for regulation are already underway in the courts. Publishers of music videos sue, for example, claiming violations of copyrights and piracy of their works.[124] The government also allows legal action against individuals or groups accused of viral attacks on email messages, spamming, and fraud committed with internet tools.

There is also a good chance that new rules may make big social media platforms responsible for the information that they allow to appear on their sites. Big players such as Facebook, for example, have instituted certain rules to prohibit sexual images of children. While the concept of a limited number of curbs on internet freedom of information has become accepted, the ongoing discussion about net neutrality principles means we can expect lengthy and heated battles over the nature and extent of what rules to govern the internet are appropriate and the means for enforcing them.[125] But what that ultimately means for the Web is presently hard to guess.

Global companies such as Facebook, Twitter, Google, and YouTube are facing mounting pressure from many governments around the world—not to mention from citizen groups—to do more to control the content on their sites. In 2016, for example, several of the major tech companies agreed to a European Union code of conduct aiming to stop online hate speech. The code of conduct commits the companies to reviewing most requests for removal of illegal language within 24 hours. Evidence suggests that they are not keeping up with this goal as of yet.[126] In Germany, Angela Merkel's government passed laws that came into effect in 2017 and required companies such as Facebook and Twitter to take a more active role in addressing illegal hate speech on their sites. Among the included stipulations were requirements for the companies to establish channels through which users can report illegal speech, to openly report the number of complaints they get, and to employ ombudsmen who will be charged with rapidly deleting posts containing illegal speech. Companies that fail to meet these stipulations and fail to get the necessary deletions done within 24 hours would face steep fines. Germany has some of the most restrictive hate speech laws in the world.[127] In 2020, the German parliament passed yet another reform to beef up its existing rules. It employs a reporting requirement on the major platforms; they must report any criminal content found on the platform directly to the federal police.[128]

In many places, including the United States, concerns about abridging freedom of speech will limit opportunities to pursue legal means of curbing hate speech online. In addition, peculiarities of the digital realm make it difficult to legally manage hate speech. This is one reason why a recent report by UNESCO proposes several social (rather than legal) means of countering online hate speech, which may ultimately prove more effective. As the European Union code of conduct and German laws illustrate, internet intermediaries are playing an increasingly important role in speech and expression online. Many use their terms of service agreements to set rules or develop user reporting mechanisms. Tactics for dealing with online hate speech largely depend on national and international rules as well as government (legal) intervention and pressure from the public. Organizations such as UNESCO take the position that social and informal interventions rather than formal legal intervention are preferable because legal interventions will result in fragmentation of the internet whereas states and groups favor rules that mean the internet is experienced differently in different locations.[129]

At the same time, private companies express discomfort with being charged with authority over what stays online, and many in civil society are also concerned with private companies serving in those roles. Debate and experimentation are still ongoing, but intermediary companies seem to prefer adopting informal, user-based approaches to dealing with expression-related complaints and requests. Examples include Facebook's social reporting function or systems where users have a process by which they can ask that things be taken down or oppose decisions to remove certain instances of expression. The limitation of the informal processes by intermediaries is that they are piecemeal and variable, leaving gaps that advocacy by civil society, counter-speech, collective action, and improvements in education for digital literacy and ethics will need to fill.[130]

The growing popularity of social media, especially as sources for news, introduces a new and interesting set of questions related to governance. As we discussed at length in earlier chapters, social media platforms are now widely used for news. On these platforms, information of significant importance for public affairs is produced, shared, and consumed. Even the 2016 election cycle highlights how misuse of these platforms for "fake news" and political misinformation can have broad consequences. Historically, news providers in broadcasting were required to perform their role with the public interest in mind. In the case of broadcast news, these public interest rules are the basis of media being allowed to use the broadcast spectrum for free. How should the government think about news and the public interest in the realm of social media? Phil Napoli argues that two features currently characterize public interest in the social media space. First, views of public interest on social media are currently restrictive, focusing only on curbing harmful content rather than on what kinds of content should be encouraged; examples include Facebook and Google deciding to take action to prevent the dissemination of fake news on their sites. Second, Napoli explains that existing notions of public interest on the internet are individualist in that they are in the hands of individual users (as both consumers and producers of information).[131]

The fake-news-on-Facebook problems and the misinformation being peddled by political leaders and other popular figures highlight the fact that social media companies may increasingly find themselves in positions historically reserved for producers and editors and that they will certainly be pressured into thinking about the public interest, even if they are not mandated to think about it on a regular basis. The scant evidence we have so far shows that the digital information environment lacks the negative as well as the positive aspects of journalistic gatekeeping. For all its faults, traditional news media serve the public interest rather well, especially considering the rapid rate at which their resources are declining.

Unfortunately, research underscores the fact that the institutional evolution underlying technology firms does not shape them into the same kind of public interest–minded intermediary that is institutionalized professional journalism. At least in the realm of providing advice and services to campaigns, technology firms developed consultant-type roles aimed at solidifying their worth rather than the public interest.[132] The fake news scandal described at the beginning of this chapter revealed that Mark Zuckerberg was only grudgingly willing to make an effort to stop fake news—and only after public scrutiny. In the time since, Zuckerberg and his counterparts at Twitter and Google grappled with increasing pressure and scrutiny from policymakers concerned about the effects of mis- and disinformation on digital and social media, not to mention the distasteful problems of hate speech, recruitment of domestic terrorists, and cyberbullying.

SUMMARY

Many people are dissatisfied with the performance of the mass media and the internet. Critics can and do air their dissatisfaction through formal and informal channels, but criticism usually has had limited success in bringing about reforms. To fill the gaps left by the major legacy media, numerous alternative media have been created. These media either serve demographically distinct populations or cater to particular substantive concerns or political orientations.

In this chapter, we explored the social and political consequences of technological advances affecting mass media and outlined the areas in which new public policies are needed. We also outlined several looming problems such as rising affective, social, and political polarization and the many challenges associated with mis- and disinformation. The impact of these changes on life and politics in the United States could be enormous unless resistance to the pace of change slows progress. Fragmentation of the broadcast audience has raised fears of political balkanization and the breakdown of the national political consensus that has been deemed essential for successful democratic governance. The reality has been far less grim thus far, but partisan ideological sorting and negative political affect continue to increase among the populace, following in the wake of an extremely polarized contingent of partisan elites. Whether media fragmentation is largely to blame is as of yet unknown, but research is ongoing.

Changes in regulatory policy are in progress to integrate the new broadcast and narrowcast technologies into the existing mass media regulatory structure. But a total overhaul of the current policy regime is unlikely. The forces favoring greater government control of media content continue to be strong because the public is afraid that some news providers will abuse their powers and harm public interests. Whatever the outcome, the debate about media regulation and deregulation needs to safeguard First

Amendment rights in the century that lies ahead. Freeing the electronic media from government supervision will undoubtedly lead to some misbehaviors and abuses, but that may be the lesser evil if more government regulation is the alternative. As Thomas Jefferson wrote to his colleague Edward Carrington in 1787, "Were it left to me to decide whether we should have a government without newspapers or newspapers without a government, I should not hesitate a moment to prefer the latter."[133]

DISCUSSION QUESTIONS

1. What do researchers mean when they say polarization is on the rise in the United States? Are all forms of polarization the same? If not, which type of polarization are they referring to? Researchers debate the extent to which changes to the media environment are driving the various forms of polarization. During the course of that debate, what have they learned?

2. Why should we care about declining local news? What are the implications for political accountability, citizen political knowledge, and political engagement with state and local politics? What about for rising polarization?

3. Researchers are very interested in the spread, causes, and effects of mis- and disinformation in politics. What have they learned?

4. To what extent do global digital information inequalities still exist today? What are the different forms they can take, and which of these forms are most relevant to consider today? How important is it that we address digital inequalities? Why do they matter?

5. What regulatory solutions exist for dealing with the current trends and challenges identified in this chapter? Which are most likely to be feasible and/or effective?

READINGS

Arceneaux, K., & Johnson, M. (2013). *Changing minds or changing channels? Partisan news in an age of choice*. University of Chicago Press.

Baldwin, T. (2018). *Ctrl alt delete: How politics and the media crashed our democracy*. Oxford University Press.

Bednarek, M., & Caple, H. (2017). *The discourse of news values: How news organizations create newsworthiness.* Oxford University Press.

Bennett, W. L. (2016). *News: The politics of illusion* (10th ed.). University of Chicago Press.

Bode, L., Budak, C., Ladd, J. M., Newport, F., Pasek, J., Singh, L. O., Soroka, S. N., & Traugott, M. W. (2020). *Words that matter: How the news and social media shaped the 2016 presidential campaign.* Brookings Institution Press.

Chadwick, A. (2017). *The hybrid media system: Politics and power.* Oxford University Press.

Cushion, S. (2012). *The democratic value of news: Why public service media matter.* Palgrave Macmillan.

Darr, J. P., M. P., & Dunaway, J. L. (2021). *Home style opinion: How local newspapers can slow polarization.* Cambridge University Press.

Donner, J. (2015). *After access: Inclusion, development, and a more mobile internet.* MIT Press.

Dunaway, J. L., & Searles, K. (forthcoming). *News attention in a mobile era.* Oxford University Press.

Dimaggio, A. R. (2017). *The politics of persuasion: Economic policy and media bias in the modern era.* SUNY Press.

Forgette, R. (2018). *News grazers: Media, politics, and trust in an information age.* CQ Press.

Hayes, D., & Lawless, J. L. (2021). *News hole: The demise of local journalism and political engagement.* Cambridge University Press.

Hindman, M. (2018). *The internet trap: How the digital economy builds monopolies and undermines democracy.* Princeton University Press.

Iyengar, S. (2018). *Media politics: A citizen's guide* (4th ed.). Norton.

Jamieson, K. H. (2020). *Cyberwar: How Russian hackers and trolls helped elect a president: What we don't, can't, and do know.* Oxford University Press.

Kerbel, M. R. (2018). *Remote and controlled: Media politics in a cynical age.* Routledge.

Margetts, H., John, P., Hale, S., & Yasseri, T. (2016). *Political turbulence: How social media shape collective action.* Princeton University Press.

Nadler, A. (2019). *News on the right: Studying conservative news cultures.* Oxford University Press.

Napoli, P. M. (2019). *Social media and the public interest: Media regulation in the disinformation age.* Columbia University Press.

Nielsen, R. K. (2015). *Local journalism: The decline of newspapers and the rise of digital media.* IB Tauris.

Pickard, V. (2019). *Democracy without journalism? Confronting the misinformation society.* Oxford University Press.

Robinson, S. (Ed.). (2016). *Community journalism midst media revolution.* Routledge.

Schlosberg, J. (2016). *Media ownership and agenda control: The hidden limits of the information age.* Routledge.

Schiffer, A. J. (2018). *Evaluating media bias.* Rowman & Littlefield.

Schudson, M. (2020). *Journalism: Why it matters.* John Wiley & Sons.

Sinclair, B. (2012). *The social citizen: Peer networks and political behavior.* University of Chicago Press.

Stroud, N. J. (2011). *Niche news: The politics of news choice.* Oxford University Press.

Wallis, C. (2015). *Technomobility in China: Young migrant women and mobile phones.* NYU Press.

Webster, J. (2016). *The marketplace of attention: How audiences take shape in a digital age.* MIT Press.

West, D. M. (2015). *Going mobile: How wireless technology is reshaping our lives.* Brookings Institution.

Williams, B. A., & Delli Carpini, M. X. (2011). *After broadcast news: Media regimes, democracy, and the new information environment.* Cambridge University Press.

Wu, I. S. (2015). *Forging trust communities: How technology changes politics.* Johns Hopkins University Press.

NOTES

1. Shearer, E., & Mitchell, A. (2021, January 12). News use across social media platforms in 2020. *Pew Research Center.* https://www.journalism.org/2021/01/12/news-use-across-social-media-platforms-in-2020/.

2. Folkenflik, D., & Wertheimer, L. (2016, November 19). Mark Zuckerberg addresses fake news on Facebook. *NPR.* http://www.npr.org/2016/11/19/502717970/mark-zuckerberg-addresses-fake-news-on-facebook.

3. Wareham, J. (2020, February 10). Should social media platforms be regulated? *Forbes.* https://www.forbes.com/sites/esade/2020/02/10/should-social-media-platforms-be-regulated/?sh=4b5e4b2b3370; O'Carroll, E. (2020, November 19). Why Big Tech faces rising pressure in Congress and courts. *The Christian Science Monitor.* https://www.csmonitor.com/Technology/2020/1119/Why-Big-Tech-faces-rising-pressure-in-Congress-and-courts

4. Kreiss, D. (2016). *Prototype politics: Technology-intensive campaigning and the data of democracy.* Oxford University Press.

5. Silverman, C. (2015, February 10). Lies, damn lies, and viral content: How news websites spread (and debunk) online rumors, unverified claims, and misinformation.

Tow Center for Digital Journalism, Columbia University. http://towcenter.org/research/lies-damn-lies-and-viral-content.

6. Prior, M. (2013). Media and political polarization. *Annual Review of Political Science, 16,* 101–127.

7. Iyengar, S., Sood, G., & Lelkes, Y. (2012). Affect, not ideology: A social identity perspective on polarization. *Public Opinion Quarterly, 76*(3), 405–431; Lelkes, Y., Sood, G., & Iyengar, S. (2017). The hostile audience: The effect of access to broadband internet on partisan affect. *American Journal of Political Science, 61*(1), 5–20; Iyengar, S., & Krupenkin, M. (2018). The strengthening of partisan affect. *Political Psychology, 39,* 201–218; Mason, L., & Wronski, J. (2018). One tribe to bind them all: How our social group attachments strengthen partisanship. *Political Psychology, 39,* 257–277; Mason, L. (2015). "I disrespectfully disagree": The differential effects of partisan sorting on social and issue polarization. *American Journal of Political Science, 59*(1), 128–145.

8. Iyengar, S., & Krupenkin, M. (2018). The strengthening of partisan affect. *Political Psychology, 39,* 201–218; Mason, L., & Wronski, J. (2018). One tribe to bind them all: How our social group attachments strengthen partisanship. *Political Psychology, 39,* 257–277.

9. Iyengar, S., Sood, G., & Lelkes, Y. (2012). Affect, not ideology: A social identity perspective on polarization. *Public Opinion Quarterly, 76*(3), 405–443; Iyengar, S., & Westwood, S. J. (2015). Fear and loathing across party lines: New evidence on group polarization. *American Journal of Political Science, 59*(3), 690–707.

10. Martherus, J. L., Martinez, A. G., Piff, P. K., & Theodoridis, A. G. (2021). Party animals? Extreme partisan polarization and dehumanization. *Political Behavior, 43,* 517–540. https://doi.org/10.1007/s11109-019-09559-4; Hetherington, M. J., & Rudolph, T. J. (2015). *Why Washington won't work.* University of Chicago Press.

11. McConnell, C., Margalit, Y., Malhotra, N., & Levendusky, M. (2018). The economic consequences of partisanship in a polarized era. *American Journal of Political Science, 62*(1), 5–18; Settle, J. E., & Carlson, T. N. (2019). Opting out of political discussions. *Political Communication, 36*(3), 476–496; Dias, N., & Lelkes, Y. (2021). The nature of affective polarization: Disentangling policy disagreement from partisan identity. *American Journal of Political Science.*

12. Iyengar, S., Lelkes, Y., Levendusky, M., Malhotra, N., & Westwood, S. J. (2019). The origins and consequences of affective polarization in the United States. *Annual Review of Political Science, 22,* 129–146.

13. Mason, L. (2018). *Uncivil agreement: How politics became our identity.* University of Chicago Press.

14. Alford, J. R., Hatemi, P. K., Hibbing, J. R., Martin, N. G., & Eaves, L. J. (2011). The politics of mate choice. *The Journal of Politics, 73*(2), 362–379.

15. Cox, D. A., Clemence, J., & O'Neil, E. (2020, February 6). Partisan attachment: How politics is changing dating and relationships in the Trump era. *AEI.* https://www.aei.org/research-products/report/partisan-attachment-how-politics-is-changing-dating-and-relationships-in-the-trump-era/

16. Mason, L. (2015). "I disrespectfully disagree": The differential effects of partisan sorting on social and issue polarization. *American Journal of Political Science, 59*, 128–145.

17. Mason, L. (2016). A cross-cutting calm: How social sorting drives affective polarization. *Public Opinion Quarterly, 80*(S), 351–377.

18. Huddy, L., Mason, L., & Aarøe, L. (2015). Expressive partisanship: Campaign involvement, political emotion, and partisan identity. *American Political Science Review, 109*(1), 1–17; Iyengar, S., & Krupenkin, M. (2018). The strengthening of partisan affect. *Political Psychology, 39*, 201–218.

19. Lelkes, Y. (2018). Affective polarization and ideological sorting: A reciprocal, albeit weak, relationship. *The Forum, 16*(1), 67–79.

20. Iyengar, S., Lelkes, Y., Levendusky, M., Malhotra, N., & Westwood, S. J. (2019). The origins and consequences of affective polarization in the United States. *Annual Review of Political Science, 22*, 129–146; Hetherington, M. J., & Rudolph, T. J. (2015). *Why Washington won't work.* University of Chicago Press.

21. Lelkes, Y., Sood, G., & Iyengar, S. (2017). The hostile audience: The effect of access to broadband internet on partisan affect. *American Journal of Political Science, 61*(1), 5–20; Davis, N. T., & Dunaway, J. L. (2016). Party polarization, media choice, and mass partisan-ideological sorting. *Public Opinion Quarterly, 80*, 272–297; for a discussion of difficulty in establishing a causal relationship between media and polarization and unresolved debate, see Prior, M. (2013). Mass media and political polarization. *Annual Review of Political Science, 16*, 101–127.

22. Berry, J. M., & Sobieraj, S. (2013). *The outrage industry: Political opinion media and the new incivility.* Oxford University Press; Puglisi, R., & Snyder, J. M., Jr. (2011). Newspaper coverage of political scandals. *The Journal of Politics, 73*(3), 931–950.

23. Levendusky, M. (2013). *How partisan media polarize America.* University of Chicago Press; Rogowski, J. C., & Sutherland, J. L. (2016). How ideology fuels affective polarization. *Political Behavior, 38*(2), 485–508; Webster, S. W., & Abramowitz, A. I. (2017). The ideological foundations of affective polarization in the US electorate. *American Politics Research, 45*(4), 621–647.

24. Arceneaux, K., & Johnson, M. (2013). *Changing minds or changing channels? Partisan news in an age of choice*. University of Chicago Press.

25. Arceneaux, K., Johnson, M., & Cryderman, J. (2013). Communication, persuasion, and the conditioning value of selective exposure: Like minds may unite and divide but they mostly tune out. *Political Communication, 30*(2), 213–231.

26. Webster, J. G., & Ksiazek, T. B. (2012). The dynamics of audience fragmentation: Public attention in an age of digital media. *Journal of Communication, 62*(1), 39–56; Nelson, J. L., & Webster, J. G. (2017). The myth of partisan selective exposure: A portrait of the online political news audience. *Social Media + Society, 3*(3).

27. Prior, M. (2007). *Post-broadcast democracy: How media choice increases inequality in political involvement and polarizes elections*. Cambridge University Press; Arceneaux, K., & Johnson, M. (2013). *Changing minds or changing channels? Partisan news in an age of choice*. University of Chicago Press.

28. Arceneaux, K., & Johnson, M. (2013). *Changing minds or changing channels? Partisan news in an age of choice*. University of Chicago Press; Arceneaux, K., & Johnson, M. (2016). Using experiments to understand how agency influences media effects. *Oxford Research Encyclopedia of Politics*.

29. Martin, G. J., & Yurukoglu, A. (2017). Bias in cable news: Persuasion and polarization. *American Economic Review, 107*(9), 2565–2599.

30. De Benedictis-Kessner, J., Baum, M. A., Berinsky, A. J., & Yamamoto, T. (2019). Persuading the enemy: Estimating the persuasive effects of partisan media with the preference-incorporating choice and assignment design. *American Political Science Review, 113*(4), 902–916. Also see Arceneaux, K., & Johnson, M. (2016). Using experiments to understand how agency influences media effects. *Oxford Research Encyclopedia of Politics*.

31. Hindman, M. (2018). *The internet trap*. Princeton University Press; Flaxman, S., Goel, S., & Rao, J. M. (2016). Filter bubbles, echo chambers, and online news consumption. *Public Opinion Quarterly, 80*(S1), 298–320.

32. Shmargad, Y., & Klar, S. (2020). Sorting the news: How ranking by popularity polarizes our politics. *Political Communication, 37*(3), 423–446.

33. Darr, J. P., & Dunaway, J. L. (2018). Resurgent mass partisanship revisited: The role of media choice in clarifying elite ideology. *American Politics Research, 46*(6), 943–970.

34. Hetherington, M. J., Long, M. T., & Rudolph, T. J. (2016). Revisiting the myth: New evidence of a polarized electorate. *Public Opinion Quarterly, 80*, 321–350.

35. Iyengar, S., & Hahn, K. S. (2009). Red media, blue media: Evidence of ideological selectivity in media use. *Journal of Communication, 59*(1), 19–39.

36. Stroud, N. J. (2011). *Niche news: The politics of news choice*. Oxford University Press.

37. Arceneaux, K., & Johnson, M. (2013). *Changing minds or changing channels? Partisan news in an age of choice*. University of Chicago Press; Prior, M. (2013). Mass media and political polarization. *Annual Review of Political Science, 16*, 101–127; Webster, J. G. (2016). *The marketplace of attention: How audiences take shape in a digital age*. MIT Press.

38. Stroud, N. J. (2010). Polarization and partisan selective exposure. *Journal of Communication, 60*, 556–576; Levendusky, M. (2013). *How partisan media polarize America*. University of Chicago Press.

39. Hetherington, M. J. (2001). Resurgent mass partisanship: The role of elite polarization. *American Political Science Review, 95*(3), 619–631; Levendusky, M. (2009). *The partisan sort*. University of Chicago Press.

40. Arceneaux, K., Johnson, M., Lindstadt, R., & Vander Wielen, R. J. (2015). The influence of news media on political elites: Investigating strategic responsiveness in Congress. *American Journal of Political Science, 60*(1), 5–29; also see Clinton, J. D., & Enamorado, T. (2014). The national news media's effect on Congress: How Fox News affected elites in Congress. *Journal of Politics, 76*(4), 928–943.

41. Arceneaux, K., Dunaway, J., Johnson, M., & Vander Wielen, R. J. (2020). Strategic candidate entry and congressional elections in the era of Fox News. *American Journal of Political Science, 64*(2), 398–415.

42. Ladd, J. M. (2013). The era of media distrust and its consequences. In T. N. Ridout (Ed.), *New directions in media and politics*. Routledge.

43. Peterson, E., & Kagalwala, A. (2021). When unfamiliarity breeds contempt: How partisan selective exposure sustains oppositional media hostility. *American Political Science Review, 115*(2), 585–598.

44. Ladd, J. M., & Podkul, A. R. (2020). Sowing distrust of the news media as an electoral strategy. In B. Grofman, L. Suhay, & A. Trechsel (Eds.), *The Oxford handbook of electoral persuasion*. Oxford University Press.

45. Hopkins, D. J. (2018). *The increasingly United States: How and why American political behavior nationalized*. University of Chicago Press.

46. Lelkes, Y., Sood, G., & Iyengar, S. (2017). The hostile audience: The effect of access to broadband internet on partisan affect. *American Journal of Political Science, 61*(1), 5–20.

47. Schaffner, B. F. (2006). Local news coverage and the incumbency advantage in the US House. *Legislative Studies Quarterly, 31*(4), 491–511.

48. Trussler, M. (2020). Get information or get in formation: The effects of high-information environments on legislative elections. *British Journal of Political Science*, 1–21; Trussler, M. (2020). The effects of high-information environments on legislative behavior in the US House of Representatives. *Legislative Studies Quarterly*.

49. Snyder, J. M., Jr., & Strömberg, D. (2010). Press coverage and political accountability. *Journal of Political Economy*, 118(2), 3

50. Padgett, J., Dunaway, J. L., & Darr, J. P. (2019). As seen on TV? How gatekeeping makes the US house seem more extreme. *Journal of Communication*, 69(6), 696–719.

51. Darr, J. P., Hitt, M. P., & Dunaway, J. L. (2018). Newspaper closures polarize voting behavior. *Journal of Communication*, 68(6), 1007–1028; Hopkins, D. J. (2018). *The increasingly United States: How and why American political behavior nationalized*. University of Chicago Press; Trussler, M. (2020). Get information or get in formation: The effects of high-information environments on legislative elections. *British Journal of Political Science*, 1–21; Trussler, M. (2020). The effects of high-information environments on legislative behavior in the US House of Representatives. *Legislative Studies Quarterly*.

52. Darr, J. P., Hitt, M. P., & Dunaway, J. L. (2021). *Home style opinion: How local newspapers can slow polarization*. Cambridge University Press.

53. Martin, G. J., & McCrain, J. (2019). Local news and national politics. *American Political Science Review*, 113(2), 372–384; for a study of the potential for persuasive effects, also see Levendusky, M. S. (2021). How does local TV news change viewers' attitudes? The case of Sinclair Broadcasting. *Political Communication*. https://doi.org/10.1080/10584609.2021.1901807

54. Darr, J. P., Hitt, M. P., & Dunaway, J. L. (2021). *Home style opinion: How local newspapers can slow polarization*. Cambridge University Press; Moskowitz, D. J. (2021). Local news, information, and the nationalization of US Elections. *American Political Science Review*, 115(1), 114–129.

55. This section draws heavily from Dunaway, J. L., & Settle, J. E. (2021). Opinion formation and polarization in the news feed era: Effects from digital, social, and mobile media. In D. Osborne & C. Sibley (Eds.), *The Cambridge handbook of political psychology*. Cambridge University Press.

56. Pariser, E. (2011). *The filter bubble: How the new personalized web is changing what we read and how we think*. Penguin; Sunstein, C. R. (2017). *#Republic: Divided democracy in the age of social media*. Princeton University Press.

57. Arceneaux, K., & Vander Wielen, R. J. (2013). The effects of need for cognition and need for affect on partisan evaluations. *Political Psychology*, 34(1), 23–42; Druckman, J. N., Peterson, E., & Slothuus, R. (2013). How elite

partisan polarization affects public opinion formation. *American Political Science Review*, 107(1), 57–79.

58. Bakshy, E., Messing, S., & Adamic, L. A. (2015). Exposure to ideologically diverse news and opinion on Facebook. *Science*, 348(6239), 1130–1132.

59. Hindman, M. (2018). *The internet trap*. Princeton University Press; Flaxman, S., Goel, S., & Rao, J. M. (2016). Filter bubbles, echo chambers, and online news consumption. *Public Opinion Quarterly*, 80(S1), 298–320.

60. Goel, S., Mason, W., & Watts, D. J (2010). Real and perceived attitude agreement in social networks. *Journal of Personality and Social Psychology*, 99(4), 611; Messing, S., & Westwood, S. J. (2014). Selective exposure in the age of social media: Endorsements trump partisan source affiliation when selecting news online. *Communication Research*, 41(8), 1042–1063; Settle, J. E. (2018). *Frenemies: How social media polarizes America*. Cambridge University Press.

61. Hasell, A. (2020). Shared emotion: The social amplification of partisan news on Twitter. *Digital Journalism*, 1–18.

62. Peterson, E., Goel, S., & Iyengar, S. (2021). Partisan selective exposure in online news consumption: Evidence from the 2016 presidential campaign. *Political Science Research and Methods*, 9(2), 242–258.

63. Guess, A. M., Barberá, P., Munzert, S., & Yang, J. (2021). The consequences of online partisan media. *Proceedings of the National Academy of Sciences*, 118(14).

64. Feezell, J. T., Wagner, J. K., & Conroy, M. (2021). Exploring the effects of algorithm-driven news sources on political behavior and polarization. *Computers in Human Behavior*, 116, 106626.

65. Bail, C. A., Argyle, L. P., Brown, T. W., Bumpus, J. P., Chen, H., Hunzaker, M. F., Lee, J., Mann, M., Merhout, F., & Volfovsky, A. (2018). Exposure to opposing views on social media can increase political polarization. *Proceedings of the National Academy of Sciences*, 115(37), 9216–9221.

66. Stroud, N. J. (2017). Selective exposure theories. In K. Kenski & K. H. Jamieson (Eds.), *The Oxford handbook of political communication*. Oxford University Press.

67. Dunaway, J., Searles, K., Sui, M., & Paul, N. (2018). News attention in a mobile era. *Journal of Computer-Mediated Communication*, 23(2), 107–124; Dunaway, J., & Soroka, S. (2019). Smartphone-size screens constrain cognitive access to video news stories. *Information, Communication & Society*, 1–16; Settle, J. E. (2018). *Frenemies: How social media polarizes America*. Cambridge University Press.

68. Bode, L. (2016). Political news in the news feed: Learning politics from social media. *Mass Communication and Society*, 19(1), 24–48; Feezell, J. T. (2018). Agenda setting through social media: The importance of incidental news

exposure and social filtering in the digital era. *Political Research Quarterly*, 71(2), 482–494.

69. Settle, J. E. (2018). *Frenemies: How social media polarizes America*. Cambridge University Press.

70. Dunaway, J., Searles, K., Sui, M., & Paul, N. (2018). News attention in a mobile era. *Journal of Computer-Mediated Communication*, 23(2), 107–124.

71. Dunaway, J., Searles, K., Sui, M., & Paul, N. (2018). News attention in a mobile era. *Journal of Computer-Mediated Communication*, 23(2), 107–124.

72. Newspapers fact sheet. (2021, June 29). *Pew Research Center*. https://www.journalism.org/fact-sheet/newspapers/

73. Local TV news fact sheet. (2021, July 13). *Pew Research Center*. https://www.journalism.org/fact-sheet/local-tv-news/

74. Mahone, J., Wang, Q., Napoli, P., Weber, M., & McCollough, K. (2019). *Who's producing local journalism? Assessing journalistic output across different outlet types*. Duke University Press.

75. Snyder, J. M., Jr., & Strömberg, D. (2010). Press coverage and political accountability. *Journal of Political Economy*, 118(2), 3.

76. Schulhofer-Wohl, S., & Garrido, M. (2013). Do newspapers matter? Short-run and long-run evidence from the closure of *The Cincinnati Post*. *Journal of Media Economics*, 26(2), 60–81; Rubado, M. E., & Jennings, J. T. (2019). Political consequences of the endangered local watchdog: Newspaper decline and mayoral elections in the United States. *Urban Affairs Review*; but see Gentzkow, M., Shapiro, J. M., & Sinkinson, M. (2011). The effect of newspaper entry and exit on electoral politics. *American Economic Review*, 101(7), 2980–3018.

77. Arnold, R. D. (2004). *Congress, the press, and political accountability*. Princeton University Press; Waldman, S. (2011). Information needs of communities: The changing media landscape in a broadband age. *FCC*. http://www.fcc.gov/infoneedsreport; Napoli, P. M., Stonbely, S., McCollough, K., & Renninger, B. (2017). Local journalism and the information needs of local communities: Toward a scalable assessment approach. *Journalism Practice*, 11(4), 373–395. https://doi.org/10.1080/17512786.2016.1146625

78. Guess, A., Nyhan, B., & Reifler, J. (2018). *All media trust is local? Findings from the 2018 Poynter Media Trust Survey*. http://www-personal.umich.edu/~bnyhan/media-trust-report-2018.pdf; Gramlich, J. (2019). Q&Q: What Pew Research Center's new survey says about local news in the U.S. *Pew Research Center*. https://www.pewresearch.org/fact-tank/2019/03/26/qa-what-pew-research-centers-new-survey-says-about-local-news-in-the-u-s/

79. Prato, L. (1998). In local TV news we trust, but why? *American Journalism Review*, 68; Guess, A., Nyhan, B., & Reifler, J. (2018). *All media trust is local?*

Findings from the 2018 Poynter Media Trust Survey. http://www-personal.umich
.edu/~bnyhan/media-trust-report-2018.pdf; Fowler, E. F. (2020). Strategy
over substance and national in focus? Local television coverage of politics and
policy in the United States. In A. Gulyas & D. Baines (Eds.), *The Routledge
companion to local media and journalism* (pp. 185–192). Routledge.

80. Gentzkow, M., Shapiro, J. M., & Sinkinson, M. (2011). The effect of newspaper
    entry and exit on electoral politics. *American Economic Review, 101*(7), 2980–
    3018; Hayes, D., & Lawless, J. (2015). As local news goes, so goes citizen engage-
    ment: Media, knowledge, and participation in U.S. House elections. *Journal of
    Politics, 77,* 447–462. https://www.journals.uchicago.edu/doi/10.1086/679749;
    Hopkins, D. J. (2018). *The increasingly United States: How and why American politi-
    cal behavior nationalized.* University of Chicago Press.

81. This section draws heavily from Dunaway, J. (2021). Polarisation and misin-
    formation. In H. Tumber & S. Waisbord (Eds.), *The Routledge companion to
    media disinformation and populism* (pp. 131–141). Routledge.

82. Silverman, C. (2015). *Lies, damn lies, and viral content: How news websites spread
    (and debunk) online rumors, unverified claims, and misinformation.* Tow Center
    for Digital Journalism, Columbia University. http://towcenter.org/wp-content/
    uploads/2015/02/LiesDamnLies_Silverman_TowCenter.pdf.

83. Silverman, C. (2015). *Lies, damn lies, and viral content: How news websites spread
    (and debunk) online rumors, unverified claims, and misinformation.* Tow Center
    for Digital Journalism, Columbia University. http://towcenter.org/wp-content/
    uploads/2015/02/LiesDamnLies_Silverman_TowCenter.pdf; also see Nyhan, B., &
    & Reifler, J. (2010). When corrections fail: The persistence of political misper-
    ceptions. *Political Behavior, 32*(2), 303–330; Weeks, B. (2013, August 29–
    September 1). Feeling is believing? The influence of emotions on citizens' false
    political beliefs [Paper presentation]. The American Political Science
    Association, Chicago, Illinois, United States. http://wp.comm.ohio-state.edu/
    misperceptions/wp-content/uploads/2014/05/Weeks-FeelingisBelieving.pdf;
    Lawrence, R. G., & Schafer, M. (2012). Debunking Sarah Palin: Mainstream
    news coverage of "death panels." *Journalism, 13*(6), 766–782; Thorson, E.
    (2016). Belief echoes: The persistent effects of corrected misinformation.
    Political Communication, 33(3), 460–480.

84. Allcott, H., Gentzkow, M., & Yu, C. (2019). Trends in the diffusion of misin-
    formation on social media. *Research & Politics, 6*(2); Vosoughi, S., Roy, D., &
    Aral, S. (2018). The spread of true and false news online. *Science, 359*(6380),
    1146–1151.

85. Petersen, M. B., Osmundsen, M., & Arceneaux, K. (2020). *The "need for chaos"
    and motivations to share hostile political rumors.* https://doi.org/10.31234/osf
    .io/6m4ts; Miller, J. M., Saunders, K. L., & Farhart, C. E. (2016). Conspiracy

endorsement as motivated reasoning: The moderating roles of political knowledge and trust. *American Journal of Political Science*, 60(4), 824–884.

86. Flynn, D. J., Nyhan, B., & Reifler, J. (2017). The nature and origins of misperceptions: Understanding false and unsupported beliefs about politics. *Political Psychology*, 38, 127–150; Weeks, B. E., & Garrett, R. K. (2014). Electoral consequences of political rumors: Motivated reasoning, candidate rumors, and vote choice during the 2008 U.S. presidential election. *International Journal of Public Opinion Research*, 26, 401–422.

87. Kunda Z. (1990). The case for motivated reasoning. *Psychology Bulletin, 108*, 480–98; Lodge, M., & Taber, C. S. (2013). *The rationalizing voter*. Cambridge University Press; Leeper, T. J., & Slothuus, R. (2014). Political parties, motivated reasoning, and public opinion formation. *Political Psychology, 35*, 129–156.

88. Jerit, J., & Zhao, Y. (2020). Political misinformation. *Annual Review of Political Science, 23*; Druckman, J. N., Peterson, E., & Slothuus, R. (2013). How elite partisan polarization affects public opinion formation. *American Political Science Review, 107*(1), 57–79; Lodge, M., & Taber, C. S. (2013). *The rationalizing voter*. Cambridge University Press.

89. Flynn, D. J., Nyhan, B., & Reifler, J. (2017). The nature and origins of misperceptions: Understanding false and unsupported beliefs about politics. *Political Psychology*, 38, 127–150; Jerit, J., & Zhao, Y. (2020). Political misinformation. *Annual Review of Political Science, 23*.

90. Leeper, T. J., & Slothuus, R. (2014). Political parties, motivated reasoning, and public opinion formation. *Political Psychology, 35*, 129–156.

91. Schaffner B. F., & Roche C. (2017). Misinformation and motivated reasoning. *Public Opinion Quarterly, 81*, 86–110.

92. Uscinski, J. E., & Parent, J. M. (2014). *American conspiracy theories*. Oxford University Press; Miller, J. M., Saunders, K. L., & Farhart, C. E. (2016). Conspiracy endorsement as motivated reasoning: The moderating roles of political knowledge and trust. *American Journal of Political Science, 60*(4), 824–884.

93. Thorson E. (2016). Belief echoes: the persistent effects of corrected misinformation. *Political Communication, 33*, 460–480.

94. Nyhan, B., & Reifler, J. (2010). When corrections fail: The persistence of political misperceptions. *Political Behavior, 32*(2), 303–330.

95. Arceneaux, K., Johnson, M., & Cryderman, J. (2013). Communication, persuasion, and the conditioning value of selective exposure: Like minds may unite and divide but they mostly tune out. *Political Communication, 30*(2), 213–231; Bail, C. A., Argyle, L. P., Brown, T. W., Bumpus, J. P., Chen, H.,

Hunzaker, M. F., Lee, J., Mann, M., Merhout, F., & Volfovsky, A. (2018). Exposure to opposing views on social media can increase political polarization. *Proceedings of the National Academy of Sciences, 115*(37), 9216–9221.

96. Scriber, B. (2016, September 8). Who decides what's true in politics? A history of the rise of political fact-checking. *Poynter.* http://www.poynter.org/2016/who-decides-whats-true-in-politics-a-history-of-the-rise-of-political-fact-checking/429326/

97. Nyhan, B., & Reifler, J. (2015). Displacing misinformation about events: An experimental test of causal corrections. *Journal of Experimental Political Science, 2,* 81–93; Nyhan, B., & Reifler, J. (2010). When corrections fail: The persistence of political misperceptions. *Political Behavior, 32*(2), 303–330; Nyhan, B., & Reifler, J. (2012). Misinformation and fact-checking: Research findings from social science. New America Foundation; Nyhan, B., Reifler, J., & Ubel, P. (2013). The hazards of correcting myths about healthcare reform. *Medical Care, 51*(2), 127–132.

98. Huertas, A. (2016, December 22). Despite fact-checking, zombie myths about climate change persist. *Poynter.* https://www.poynter.org/2016/despite-fact-checking-zombie-myths-about-climate-change-persist/443460/.

99. Nyhan, B. (2014, July 5). When beliefs and facts collide. *The New York Times.* https://www.nytimes.com/2014/07/06/upshot/when-beliefs-and-facts-collide.html

100. Nyhan, B. (2016, November 5). Fact-checking can change views? We rate that as mostly true. *The New York Times.* http://www.nytimes.com/2016/11/06/upshot/fact-checking-can-change-views-we-rate-that-as-mostly-true.html

101. Bode L., & Vraga E. K. (2015). In related news, that was wrong: The correction of misinformation through related stories functionality in social media. *Journal of Communication, 65,* 619–638.

102. Kahan, D. M. (2015). Climate-science communication and the measurement problem. *Advances in Political Psychology, 36,* 1–43; Lewandowsky, S., Ecker, U. K. H., Siefert, C. M., Schwarz, N., & Cook, J. (2012). Misinformation and its correction: Continued influence and successful debiasing. *Psychological Science in the Public Interest, 13*(2), 106–131.

103. DiFonzo, N., Beckstead, J. W., Stupak, N., & Walders, K. (2016). Validity judgments of rumors heard multiple times: The shape of the truth effect. *Social Influence, 11*(1), 22–39; Flynn, D. J., Nyhan, B., & Reifler, J. (2017). The nature and origins of misperceptions: Understanding false and unsupported beliefs about politics. *Political Psychology, 38,* 127–150; Pennycook, G., Cannon, T. D., & Rand, D. G. (2018). Prior exposure increases perceived

accuracy of fake news. *Journal of Experimental Psychology: General, 147,* 1865–1880; Thorson, E. A., Shelbe, L., & Southwell, B. G. (2018). An agenda for misinformation research. In B. G. Southwell, E. A. Thorson, & L. Sheble (Eds.), *Misinformation and mass audiences* (pp. 289–293). University of Texas Press; Weaver, K., Garcia, S. M., Schwarz, N., & Miller, D. T. (2007). Inferring the popularity of an opinion from its familiarity: A repetitive voice can sound like a chorus. *Journal of Personality and Social Psychology, 92,* 821–833.

104. Bennett, W. L., & Iyengar, S. (2008). A new era of minimal effects? The changing foundations of political communication. *Journal of Communication, 58,*(4), 707–731; Iyengar, S. (2017). *A typology of media effects.* In K. Kenski & K. H. Jamieson (Eds.), *The Oxford handbook of political communication* (pp. 59–68). Oxford University Press.

105. Gaines, B. J., Kuklinski, J. H., Quirk, P. J., Peyton, B., & Verkuilen, J. (2007). Same facts, different interpretations: Partisan motivation and opinion on Iraq. *Journal of Politics, 69,* 957–974; Garrett, R. K., Weeks, B. E., & Neo, R. L. (2016). Driving a wedge between evidence and beliefs: How online ideological news exposure promotes political misperceptions. *Journal of Computer-Mediated Communication, 21*(5), 331–348; Schaffner, B. F., & Luks, S. (2018). Misinformation or expressive responding? What an inauguration crowd can tell us about the source of political misinformation in surveys. *Public Opinion Quarterly, 82*(1), 135–147; Schaffner, B. F., & Roche, C. (2016). Misinformation and motivated reasoning: Responses to economic news in a politicized environment. *Public Opinion Quarterly, 81*(1), 86–110.

106. Stromer-Galley, J. (2014). *Presidential campaigning in the internet age.* Oxford University Press; Kreiss, D. (2016). *Prototype politics: Technology-intensive campaigning and the data of democracy.* Oxford University Press; Lapowsky, I. (2016, November 15). Here's how Facebook *actually* won the Trump presidency. *Wired.* https://www.wired.com/2016/11/facebook-won-trump-election-not-just-fake-news

107. Hindman, M. (2009). *The myth of digital democracy.* Princeton University Press.

108. Hindman, M. (2009). *The myth of digital democracy.* Princeton University Press; Hindman, M. (2008). What is the online public sphere good for? In J. Turow & L. Tsui (Eds.), *The hyperlinked society.* University of Michigan Press; see also Hindman, M. (2018). *The internet trap: How the digital economy builds monopolies and undermines democracy.* Princeton University Press.

109. Potter, J., & Dunaway, J. (2016). Reinforcing or breaking party systems: Internet communication technologies and party competition in comparative context. *Political Communication, 33,* 392–413.

110. Mossberger, K., Tolbert, C., & Franko, W. W. (2013). *Digital cities: The internet and the geography of opportunity*. Oxford University Press; Lelkes, Y., Sood, G., & Iyengar, S. (2017). The hostile audience: The effect of access to broadband internet on partisan affect. *American Journal of Political Science*, 61(1), 5–20.

111. Internet/broadband fact sheet. (2021, April 7). *Pew Research Center*. http://www.pewinternet.org/fact-sheet/internet-broadband/. Data are from Pew Research Center surveys conducted between 2013 and 2018. Data for each year are based on a pooled analysis of all surveys conducted during that year.

112. Mossberger, K., Tolbert, C., & Franko, W. W. (2013). *Digital cities*. Oxford University Press.

113. Internet/broadband fact sheet. (2021, April 7). *Pew Research Center*. http://www.pewinternet.org/fact-sheet/internet-broadband/. Data are from Pew Research Center surveys conducted between 2013 and 2018. Data for each year are based on a pooled analysis of all surveys conducted during that year.

114. Donner, J. (2015). *After access: Inclusion, development, and a more mobile internet*. MIT Press; Dunaway, J. L., & Searles, K. (forthcoming). *News attention in a mobile era*. Oxford University Press.

115. Napoli, P. M. (2015). Social media and the public interest: Governance of news platforms in the realm of individual and algorithmic gatekeepers. *Telecommunications Policy*, 39, 751–760.

116. Geller, H. (1990). Mass communications policy: Where we are and where we should be going. In J. Lichtenberg (Ed.), *Democracy and the mass media*. Cambridge University Press.

117. *FCC v. Midwest Video Corp.*, 440 U.S. 689 (1979).

118. Cable TV. (1987). *Consumer Reports*, 52(September), 547–554, p. 555.

119. FCC approves sweeping internet regulation plan, Obama accused of meddling. (2016, February 26). *Fox News*. http://www.foxnews.com/politics/2015/02/26/fcc-approves-sweeping-internet-regulation-plan-obama-accused-meddling.html

120. Graber, D. A. (2003). Terrorism, censorship, and the First Amendment. In P. Norris, M. Kern, & M. Just (Eds.), *Framing terrorism: The news media, the government, and the public*. Routledge.

121. Chester, J. (2002). Strict scrutiny: Why journalists should be concerned about new federal and industry deregulation proposals. *Press/Politics*, 7(2), 105–115.

122. FCC approves sweeping internet regulation plan, Obama accused of meddling. (2016, February 26). *Fox News*. http://www.foxnews.com/politics/2015/02/26/fcc-approves-sweeping-internet-regulation-plan-obama-accused-meddling.html; How Trump administration could reshape the

internet. (2016, December 2). *CBS News*. http://www.cbsnews.com/news/trump-administration-could-re-shape-internet-policy-net-neutrality/.

123. Anderson, N. (2009, February 10). The future of the internet is . . . regulation? *Ars Technica*. http://arstechnica.com/tech-policy/news/2009/02/the-future-of-the-internet-is-regulation.ars.

124. Burkart, P. (2014). *Pirate politics: The new information policy contests.* MIT Press; Burkart, P. (2010). *Music and cyberliberties.* Wesleyan University Press.

125. Lasar, M. (2009, May 6). Senator to FCC: Time for black-and-white net neutrality rules. *Ars Technica*. http://arstechnica.com/tech-policy/news/2009/05/senator-pressures-fcc-on-net-neutrality.ars.

126. Balmer, C. (2017, February 12). After a barrage of sexist insults, top Italian official calls on Facebook to do more against hate speech. *Business Insider*. http://www.businessinsider.com/r-top-italian-official-says-facebook-must-do-more-against-hate-speech-2017-2

127. Oltermann, P. (2016, December 17). Germany to force Facebook, Google, and Twitter to act on hate speech. *The Guardian*. https://www.theguardian.com/technology/2016/dec/17/german-officials-say-facebook-is-doing-too-little-to-stop-hate-speech

128. Lomas, N. (2020, June 19). Germany tightens online hate speech rules to make platforms send reports straight to the feds. *TC*. https://techcrunch.com/2020/06/19/germany-tightens-online-hate-speech-rules-to-make-platforms-send-reports-straight-to-the-feds/

129. Gagliardone, I., Gal, D., Alves, T., & Martinez, G. (2015). *Countering online hate speech.* UNESCO. http://unesdoc.unesco.org/images/0023/002332/233231e.pdf.

130. Gagliardone, I., Gal, D., Alves, T., & Martinez, G. (2015). *Countering online hate speech.* UNESCO. http://unesdoc.unesco.org/images/0023/002332/233231e.pdf.

131. Napoli, P. M. (2015). Social media and the public interest: Governance of news platforms in the realm of individual and algorithmic gatekeepers. *Telecommunications Policy, 39,* 751–760.

132. McGregor, S. C., & Kreiss, D. (2017). *From distribution channels to active intermediaries: How technology firms shape political communication* [Working paper].

133. Ford, P. L. (Ed.). (1894). *Writings of Thomas Jefferson* (Vol. 5). Putnam's, p. 253.

Index

Early research on media depictions of women, 360

Early voting and campaign news coverage, 504

echo chambers, 122, 151, 283, 527–28, 549, 573, 575, 577, 595–97, 648, 651

economic competition news media, 537

economic news, 42, 90, 312, 550, 656

economic news coverage, 115

Economic policy and media bias, 543, 589, 644

economic pressures, 89–90, 100, 273, 307, 514, 518, 534, 571, 623

economics of local news, 247

Edgerly, 431–32, 500–501, 598, 600

editorial bias, 530

effect for news stories, 376

effective transmitters of state and local political news, 260

effect of access to broadband internet, 152, 155, 199, 646–47, 649, 657

effects of gatekeeping on foreign affairs coverage, 295

effects of gatekeeping on patterns, 79

effects of high-information environments, 72, 239, 650

effects of high-information environments on legislative behavior, 239, 650

effects of high-information environments on legislative elections, 72, 239, 650

effects of incivility, 520

effects of intersectionality, 363

effects of local newspaper closures, 618

effects of media coverage, 233, 423

effects of media fragmentation and selective exposure, 608

effects of media ownership, 46

effects of mis- and disinformation, 642–43

Effects of newsroom and audience diversity on trait coverage, 392

effects of partisan media, 529

effects of selective exposure, 527

effects of television violence on antisocial behavior, 441

effects on public opinion, 564

Elasmar, 570, 590, 594–95

election and COVID-19, 401

election campaigns, 454, 473, 493, 503
  general, 4, 177, 480, 557
  presidential, 7, 31, 276

election coverage, 174, 411, 472, 474, 479, 482, 485, 489, 505, 515
  current, 485
  general, 4, 458, 484
  local senate, 550

election coverage fatigue, 504

election news, 456–57, 466, 472, 474, 486–87, 490, 504, 506, 546, 550, 562

Election News Sources, 562, 572

election outcomes, 12, 168, 466–67, 470

elections, 8, 31–33, 42–43, 98–99, 168–69, 172–74, 176–77, 276–77, 401, 451–52, 462, 471–73, 476–80, 482–86, 489–94, 496–99, 501–3, 505, 507–8, 606
  changing, 500–501, 600
  legislative, 72, 239, 266, 389, 650
  political, 466

election stories, 472, 490, 493

electoral politics, 72, 92, 136, 287–88, 362, 382, 389, 545, 652–53

electronic media, 7, 66, 83, 260, 265, 304, 382, 419, 436, 438, 583

elite polarization, 608, 613, 615, 627, 630, 649

empowered news audiences, 111, 113, 150

English-language media, 106, 374

entertainment and news media, 358

entertainment media, 357–58, 429, 573

entertainment programs, 21, 23, 60, 70, 253, 355, 395, 402, 409, 425, 479

Entman, 32, 35, 118, 325, 335–36, 386, 392, 434, 438

foreign news, 293–95, 297–98, 300, 304, 310–13, 315, 319–21, 329, 334

Foreign news in American media, 337

foreign policy, 81, 194, 293–94, 311, 321–23, 326–32, 334–38, 385, 592

foreign policy crises, 321, 337

Fowler, 116, 196, 287, 448, 495, 501, 516, 546–47, 600–601, 653

Fox effect, 615

Fox News, 6–7, 121, 173–74, 214, 356, 480, 483–84, 489, 498–99, 527, 539–40, 571–73, 612, 615–16, 649, 657

  selected, 457

fragmentation bias, 523

frames, 14, 17, 26, 89–90, 345, 353, 358, 361–62, 364, 373, 564–65

  viability, 362, 364

frames in coverage, 166, 229, 345

framing effects, 435, 564–65, 570, 594

Frenemies, 150, 430, 651–52

front-runners, 449–51, 458, 462, 488

Full-Time Newsroom Workers, 369

Gainous, 153–54, 440, 593

game frame, 90, 127, 229–30, 504, 550

Gannett, 44, 49, 54, 369–71

Gannett Newsrooms, 367, 369–70, 391

Gannett Newsroom Workers by Race and Gender, 369

GAO (Government Accountability Office), 186

Garrett, 151–52, 654, 656

gatekeeping, 79, 83, 88, 95, 97, 111, 114, 273, 287–88, 319, 329, 332, 545–46

Geer, 200, 499, 502–3, 505, 507, 546

Gender and media, 385, 387

Gender and race in congressional, 389–90

gender differences, 360, 389

gender diversity, 369, 371

gender identities, 339, 348–49, 357, 379–80

gender inclusion, 367

general election, 31, 174, 363, 389–90, 447, 457, 461, 476, 499, 505–6

general election campaign stories, 480

genres, 294, 346, 349–50, 354–55, 378

Gentzkow, 72, 75, 151, 287–88, 551, 590, 596–97, 601, 652–53

Geographic coverage by local television news, 281

Gerbner, 114, 117, 383, 432–33, 569, 594

Germany, 312, 388, 640, 658

Global Media, 333, 348

Global Media Monitoring Project (GMMP), 349, 385

GMMP (Global Media Monitoring Project), 349, 385

Goel, 113, 151, 283, 549, 596–97, 648, 651

Google News, 256, 282

Google News initiative, 368, 372

Google Politics and Elections Blog, 501

government, 19–23, 25, 27–29, 31, 38–40, 63, 79–81, 99, 164–66, 174–76, 199–202, 264–66, 307–8, 341–42, 379, 414–15, 489–90, 520–21, 635–37, 639–41

  democratic, 27, 380, 606

  federal, 40, 64, 69–70, 189, 342, 344

  local, 40, 222, 245–46, 253, 264, 271, 294, 342, 510, 623, 636

  national, 164, 195, 222

Government Accountability Office (GAO), 186

government and politics, 265, 341, 525

Government Control, 3–35, 39, 553, 637, 639, 642

government news, 175

government news management, 318

government officials, 20–21, 27, 99, 102, 164, 171, 188, 190, 195, 273, 326, 333

  sourcing, 319

government ownership, 38, 40

government policies, 38, 40, 99, 322, 325, 378

government pressure, 315

media use, 151, 288, 403, 433, 596, 648
media watchers, 5, 50, 178, 351
Megamedia, 35, 74–75
members of congress, 85, 168, 183, 207, 209–12, 215–21, 235–36, 241, 268, 272, 363
meta-analysis, 361, 389, 440–41, 598
military, 46, 104, 117, 312, 317–19, 335, 396
minorities, 41, 64, 359, 363, 366, 373, 377–78, 383, 386, 389–91, 568
minority candidates, 343, 359, 363–64, 388, 392
minority congresswomen, 389–90
minority women, 363, 388, 390
misinformation, 139, 143, 148, 505, 587, 605–6, 624–30, 641, 645, 653, 655–56
    corrected, 653–54
    political, 641, 654, 656
Misinformation and motivated reasoning, 654, 656
misinformation and political misperceptions, 626
misinformation research, 656
misperceptions, 11, 574, 627–30, 654–55
misrepresentation of groups, 380
misrepresentation of race and crime on local television news, 288, 434
misrepresentations, 275, 345, 349–51, 355, 379–80
mobile and social media, 465
mobile devices, 56, 60, 97–98, 134–36, 147, 149, 400, 403, 417, 421, 465, 577, 580
mobile internet access, 154, 599
mobile media, 399, 494, 549, 553, 587–88, 590, 620, 650
Mobile Media Effects, 574, 577, 579
Mobile Network, 632, 635
mobile news, 134, 141, 587
mobile news consumers, 417, 622
mobile news consumption, 134, 421
mobilization, 148, 154, 447, 465, 553, 582, 584–85, 588

model news consumption, 431–32
modern voter, 438, 548
monopolies, 282–83, 555, 589, 596, 644, 656
motivated reasoning, 123, 529, 574, 627, 630, 654, 656
Muslims, 275, 322, 348, 355, 384
Mutz, 435, 437, 507, 544–45, 547–48, 551, 593, 600

NAACP (National Association for the Advancement of Colored People), 225
NAB (National Association of Broadcasters), 66–67
NAHJ (National Association of Hispanic Journalists), 353, 386
Napoli, 71, 150, 152–54, 280, 283, 384–87, 590, 594–95, 599, 641, 644, 652, 657–58
Narcotizing Effects, 567, 569
    mass media's, 567
National Association for the Advancement of Colored People (NAACP), 225
National Association of Broadcasters (NAB), 66–67
National Association of Hispanic Journalists (NAHJ), 353, 386
national broadcast, 207, 238, 240–41, 269, 618
nationalizing, 213, 245, 248, 267, 271, 279, 617
nationalizing news environment, 212, 214, 247, 271, 617
national media, 168, 219–20, 241, 265–66, 268, 272
national news, 213, 219, 246, 262, 266–68, 270–72, 353, 526, 617–19, 623
National News on Local Media, 267
national newspapers, 56, 267
national political events and issues, 257
national politics, 74, 77, 182, 239, 248, 257, 266, 268–69, 287, 619, 624

National Public Radio. *See* NPR
national television audience, 526, 554
Native Americans, 16, 298, 342, 348,
    350, 355
NBC News, 199, 203, 292
negative news, 322, 328, 519–20, 532
Negative political news content, 490
negativity, 5, 115, 263, 312, 359, 458,
    476, 479, 489, 499, 509–51
  increasing, 515
  rising, 514–15
Negativity and positivity biases in
    economic news coverage, 115
negativity bias, 115, 510, 514, 518,
    521, 545, 547
negativity in campaign news, 489
Negativity in democratic politics, 115,
    544–45, 547–48
negativity in election coverage, 479
negativity in media coverage, 514
negativity in news, 509, 515
negativity in political news,
    517, 520
negativity in politics, 510, 517
negativity in presidential campaigns,
    200, 489, 503, 505,
    507, 517, 546
negativity of election coverage, 489
network coverage, 267, 310
  sparse, 93
network news, 86, 165, 176
  dominant mainstream-television, 9
  national, 353
network news audiences, 125
network news framing, 331
Network News Outlets, 208
networks, 31, 66, 68, 89–90, 131–33,
    147–48, 174, 176, 309–10, 384,
    391, 555, 576, 579, 584–85
network structure of social media, 585
network television news, 6, 53, 96, 116,
    141, 178, 386, 391, 436
Neuman, 119–20, 151–52, 434,
    437–38, 440, 503, 600
New directions in media and politics,
    31, 151, 197, 199, 238–41,
    500–501, 551, 600, 649

new media, 30, 51–52, 54, 128, 151–52,
    166, 182, 201, 276, 324, 328
New Media & Society, 114, 153, 156,
    431–32, 496, 595, 598
new media age, 117, 240, 432
new media campaign activity, 467
new media culture, 153, 505
new media giants, 49, 77
New media news distributors, 53
new media production, 598
New political television, 32
news, 9–10, 12–15, 20–27, 30–35,
    50–54, 70–75, 81–85, 89–100,
    102–4, 107–392, 404–10,
    414–21, 432–39, 507–12,
    526–29, 531–37, 540–51, 573,
    576–81, 589–93
News & World Report, 31, 200
news aggregators, 421, 528, 575
news and political information, 131,
    399, 487, 529, 554, 560, 572,
    574, 577, 611, 633
news and social media, 495, 543,
    589, 644
news articles, 376, 474, 572, 595, 629
news attention, 150, 429, 435, 438,
    589, 597, 599, 644,
    651–52, 657
  national, 206
news attitudes, 330–31
news audience behaviors, 421
news audience demographics, 60
news audiences, 22, 115, 142, 154, 262,
    438, 440, 490, 525, 578, 599
  inflated, 507
  political, 596, 648
  sizeable local, 255
news biases, 74, 532
  partisan, 530, 533
  systematic partisan, 526
news brands, 126
News Briefings, 188
news bureaus, 250, 297, 310
  foreign, 309–10
newscasts, 89, 265, 276, 284, 288,
    309, 416, 563
news channels, 60, 125, 284, 308

origins of misperceptions, 654–55
outlets, 47, 51–52, 62, 64, 91–92, 121,
    186, 256, 268, 315, 356, 456–57,
    571–72, 578, 587
  local, 127, 267, 270–71
  traditional, 126–27
owners, 39–40, 43, 47, 50–51, 82,
    269, 373, 637
ownership, 3, 30, 37–77, 115, 282,
    284–86, 289, 504, 550

PACs (political action committees),
    467, 518
Padgett, 88, 114, 208, 238, 240–41,
    287–89, 505, 545–46, 650
Paletz, 332, 335–37
Parents Television Council, 423, 440
partisan bias, 269, 360, 433, 510,
    526, 528, 530–31, 537, 541,
    550, 596
partisan brands on social media, 621
partisan enclaves, 528, 575, 577
partisan media, 85, 121, 123–24, 176,
    409–10, 525, 529, 612,
    614–16, 648, 651
partisan media polarize America,
    152, 155, 544, 647, 649
partisan news, 12–13, 149, 152, 525,
    528, 531, 537, 542–43, 549,
    573, 611–14, 616, 648–49
  empirical study of, 549–50
  reemergence of, 526–27
  social amplification of, 545, 651
partisan perceptual bias, 123, 152
partisan polarization, 432, 448, 527,
    555, 573, 575, 619,
    621, 651, 654
partisan selective exposure, 121–22,
    148, 411, 537, 571, 575, 596,
    614, 616, 620, 648–49
partisanship, 30, 121–22, 171, 409, 531,
    537, 553, 555, 615, 618, 627
  local news deemphasizes, 272
  local newspapers deemphasize, 618
  social group attachments
    strengthen, 646
pattern of political news tone, 514

patterns in coverage, 70, 111, 295,
    301, 315, 329, 352, 360,
    366, 473, 475
patterns of presidential news
    coverage, 166
Patterson, 30–31, 77–78, 113, 115–16,
    174, 483–84, 489, 497, 499,
    505–7, 546–47
PBS (Public Broadcasting Service),
    41–42, 73, 92, 392, 572
Peace Research, 316, 332–33
people process information, 529
people's arms, 191–92
People's exposure, 620
people's minds, 353, 629
people's perceptions, 101, 483
people tame, 432–34, 437, 507
perceptions
  elite attacks influence, 549
  news-finds-me, 597
  rampant, 629
Perceptions and use of social media on
    Capitol Hill, 240
perpetrators, 233, 265, 275,
    346, 351, 407–8
persistence of media effects on
    learning, 398
Persistent media bias, 75, 551
personalization, 91, 215, 445, 494,
    496, 501, 522–23, 601
perspectives
  historical, 109, 520
  media sociology, 544, 550
  social identity, 646
persuasion, 443–507, 529–30,
    542–43, 555, 557–60, 567–68,
    574, 578, 586, 589, 611,
    644, 648
  mass surreptitious, 542
persuasion and attitude change,
    557–58, 586
persuasion by partisan news
    messages, 530
persuasive effects, 149, 529, 558–59,
    588, 612, 630, 648, 650
Peterson, 72, 75, 77, 112, 153, 239,
    281, 286, 335–36, 649–51, 654

political opinions, 13, 572
political organizations, 579, 587
political orientations, 104, 117,
    303, 432, 572, 642
political participation, 154, 157, 399,
    426, 432, 490, 567, 573,
    583–84, 588, 598–600
political parties, 80, 145, 430,
    449, 495, 632, 654
  major, 81, 269
  new, 145, 316
political polarization, 154, 305, 542,
    551, 608, 611–12, 642, 646–47,
    649, 651, 655
political power, 77, 83, 151, 157, 197,
    206, 308, 605, 631
political predispositions, 147, 431,
    533, 560
  existing, 529, 616
political preferences, 38, 113,
    521, 533, 555,
    594, 621
political pressures, 28, 41, 57,
    65, 89, 304–5
  internal, 65
political problems, 102, 179
  major, 70, 488
political process, 22, 83, 145, 167, 309,
    428, 522, 541
political psychology, 385, 430, 432,
    438, 508, 549, 590, 646–47,
    650, 654–55
Political Psychology, 117, 654–55
political public affairs stories, 264
political satire, 455, 511–12
Political Science, 72, 77, 112, 151–55,
    239, 243, 281, 285–86, 383–85,
    431–33, 435, 507, 545–46,
    548–51, 593–96, 646–47,
    649–50, 654
Political Science & Politics,
    240, 499, 503, 505
political significance, 90–91,
    103, 167, 170, 313, 488
political socialization, 18, 35, 395–96,
    402, 428–29, 431, 593
political successes, 13, 181, 235, 563

political symbols, 103, 396
political system, 15, 21, 35, 102, 110,
    226, 235, 396, 398, 403, 406
Political turbulence, 150, 299, 589, 644
political units, 251, 253
political violence, 307, 333–35
politicians, 89–90, 109, 133–34,
    146–48, 162, 201, 267–68,
    278, 359, 361, 511, 513–14, 517,
    527–28, 539, 549–50, 554–55,
    608–9, 628–29
  strategic, 445, 521
politics, 29–35, 72–73, 77–78, 111–16,
    119–57, 237–41, 264–66,
    283–87, 334–37, 339–91,
    429–38, 489–90, 497–501,
    504–7, 509–11, 543–51, 589–90,
    595–600, 642–49, 653–56
  contentious, 511, 601
  election, 481
  elite, 225, 511
  global, 267, 324
  international, 10, 322
  national party, 80, 511
  networked, 499–500
  partisan, 51, 225
  statewide, 275
  subnational, 259, 624
Politics & Gender, 389–90
Politics & Policy, 389–90
politics of groups and identity,
    388, 391
politics of illusion, 31, 114, 116–17,
    543–44, 546–48, 589, 644
politics of persuasion, 543, 589, 644
polls, 3, 8, 216, 449–50, 465, 467, 476,
    480, 492, 494, 508
population, 7, 41–42, 59, 146, 266,
    311, 339–43, 347–48, 354,
    380, 402–3
positive coverage, 4, 169, 260, 363,
    449–50, 476
positive news, 268, 514
Post-broadcast democracy, 439,
    549, 593, 595–96, 648
Postwar press coverage on Capitol Hill,
    546–47